THE UNMAKING OF THE MIDDLE EAST

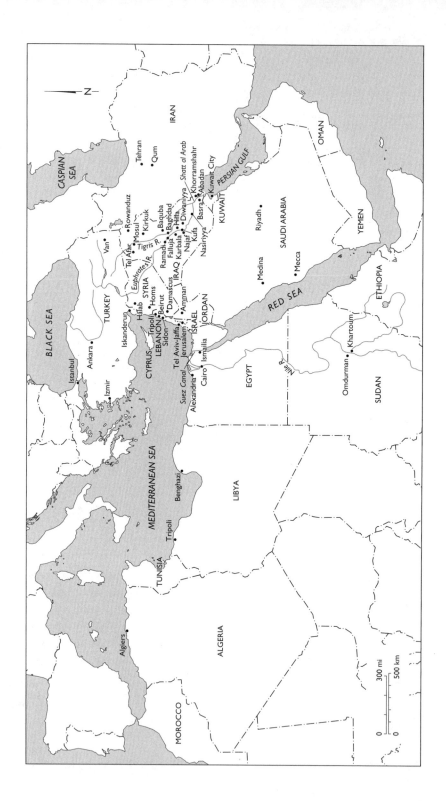

THE UNMAKING OF
THE MIDDLE EAST
A History of Western Disorder in Arab Lands

JEREMY SALT

UNIVERSITY OF CALIFORNIA PRESS
BERKELEY   LOS ANGELES   LONDON

University of California Press, one of the most distinguished university presses in the United States, enriches lives around the world by advancing scholarship in the humanities, social sciences, and natural sciences. Its activities are supported by the UC Press Foundation and by philanthropic contributions from individuals and institutions. For more information, visit www.ucpress.edu.

University of California Press
Berkeley and Los Angeles, California

University of California Press, Ltd.
London, England

Library of Congress Cataloging-in-Publication Data

Salt, Jeremy.
    The unmaking of the Middle East : a history of Western disorder in Arab lands / Jeremy Salt.
        p.   cm.
    Includes bibliographical references and index.
    ISBN: 978-0-520-25551-7 (cloth : alk. paper)
    1. Middle East—Colonization.   2. East and West.   3. Arab-Israeli conflict.   4. Persian Gulf War, 1991.   5. Iraq War, 2003–   6. United States—Politics and government, 2001–   I. Title.

DS44. S315   2008
303.48'25601821—dc22   2007043802

Manufactured in the United States of America

17   16   15   14   13   12   11   10   09   08
10   9   8   7   6   5   4   3   2   1

This book is printed on New Leaf EcoBook 50, a 100% recycled fiber of which 50% is de-inked post-consumer waste, processed chlorine-free. EcoBook 50 is acid-free and meets the minimum requirements of ANSI/ASTM D5634-01 (Permanence of Paper).

The publisher gratefully acknowledges the generous contribution to this book provided by the Humanities Endowment Fund of the University of California Press Foundation.

CONTENTS

INTRODUCTION

The first step on the long road to this book was taken in 1965 when I booked a passage on a Greek ship bound for Beirut. In those days flying was only for the wealthy and I was far from that. I was a young journalist on a Melbourne newspaper, not earning enough money for an air fare or even a return fare on a cut-rate Greek passenger liner. I traveled with my best friend of the time. We had decided to get out of Australia a year earlier. We knew where we didn't want to go—London because that was the destination of most young Australians leaving their native shores for the first time—but we couldn't work out where we did want to go. Some adventurous Australians a generation ahead of us, notably the writers Charmian Clift and George Johnston, had gone to Greece. So Greece was a possibility and Alexandria a temptation because we had read Lawrence Durrell's exotic novels (on which basis we might as well have gone to Prague because of Kafka or Oran because of Camus), but in the end Lebanon was the name that came up. It was my friend's idea. I think the connection might have been a childhood Lebanese friend. I never met him but I do remember the name, Fatty Jabour, surely Fathi before he ended up on the playground of an Australian school. I asked a few basic questions. Was Lebanon very sandy? He thought it was quite green. What else could he tell me? Not much. Somehow I got the impression that Lebanon was an island, but wherever and whatever it was, Lebanon wasn't London, and that was good enough. The paper's shipping correspondent arranged a discounted fare, and a year later we sailed away from Station Pier on the *Patris*. We stayed in Athens for a few weeks before doubling back to Beirut on another ship, disembarking with a few pounds in our pockets, no friends, no contacts, no work arranged, and no way of getting out if things went bad, but that possibility didn't even cross our minds. My friend was twenty and I was twenty-two. The world was no older than we were. What could there possibly be to worry about? Beirut rose up in the early morning from the sea, gleaming white against the dramatic background of the mountains. We lugged our sea trunk into the western center of the city and found accommodation with a widow and her daughter in an apartment off Rue Hamra. Without difficulty we also found work as reporters and desk editors with the English-language *Daily Star*, whose publisher, Kamil Mroweh, was to be killed within a year by an assassin sent from Cairo by the Egyptian secret service. Somewhere in a box I still have the front page of the paper as it appeared the following day, nothing on it but a stark black-edged photograph of the dead publisher.

Our colleagues in the editorial room included a transplanted American who wrote mostly about Beiruti society (always a lot to write about) and a Palestinian who spent a lot of time monitoring radio broadcasts from other Arab countries. A year earlier, while were planning our departure from Australia, the Palestine Liberation Organization had been established under the aegis of the Arab League. In January 1965, a few months before our arrival in Lebanon, Yasser Arafat's Fatah guerrillas had launched their first attack inside Israel, but even in Beirut little was known about Fatah or Arafat at that time. When I got to know Tawfiq he told me he was from Jaffa and had been forced to leave Palestine with the rest of the family in 1948. He did not make a big deal of it. There was no resentment or anger. He just told me where he was from and what the family had left behind (only because I asked him) before going back to monitoring the radio broadcasts. It was probably the first time I had ever heard the word *Palestine* spoken, and I cannot have seen it very often in print. I had read the Leon Uris bestseller *Exodus* and I had seen the film of the same name, but that had been a story about a people returning from exile, not a people being driven into exile, and not about the Palestinians at all but about "Arabs" trying to prevent a desperate people from living in peace in a homeland they had built up out of nothing.

My curiosity was piqued, but I was too young and too entranced with Beirut to notice much of anything outside it. The city was a tableau vivant of which we were now a very small part. The girls were surely the prettiest anywhere. We were living among people who spoke three or four languages as a matter of course. The terrace of the Café Negresco was filled every morning with spies and political exiles (as I imagined them to be and some of them probably were) reading French and Arabic newspapers in the shade of the hibiscus dropping pink petals onto the tables. I took to walking along the seafront with the collar of my trench coat turned up, smoking Disque

Bleu and casting melancholy, brooding looks across the Mediterranean from time to time. If there were police and tax inspectors we weren't aware of them. This was a city where anything was possible. The freedom was exhilarating but at the same time as fragile as the hibiscus petals gathering around the tables at the Negresco. That was the part we didn't see.

After a few months in Beirut we moved to a village in the mountains. I spent a lot of my time hanging out with the *mukhtar*. I still feel privileged to have known this kind and generous man. There is no precise English translation of the word, but "mayor" or head of a town council probably comes closest. He was not an old man. He was probably only in his late thirties when I knew him, but his mustache curled up at the ends in the old Ottoman style and he dressed in a formal Old World fashion. He always wore a three-piece striped suit and tie, but I imagine that was what a *mukhtar* was expected to wear. In his small shop I would sit around the oil stove with the Druze elders who had wandered up from their villages down the hill and eat green plums dipped in salt with them and have a tipple of brandy or arak with the *mukhtar* when they had left. One day he took me by the hand for a walk up the mountainside and showed me the walls of buildings that had been spattered and gouged with bullets during the civil war of 1958, only seven years before. Many years later, after another civil war that almost tore the heart out of the country, I went back to the village hoping to find the *mukhtar*. The mist still crept down the mountainside as before, and the shop where he had thrown back the shutters so I could get a full view of the country he loved was still there, but he and the brother who had run the gas station across the street were dead. The chateau where we had been given a home in the servants' quarters stood on a ridge outside the village like a stone skeleton, the windows blasted out by gunfire, the stairwell and every room strewn with debris, and the iron-girded wall of the balcony where we used to sit watching those magnificent silver, rose, and lemon Mediterranean sunsets smashed and crumpled in a dozen places. It was because it had been such a wonderful place to be, with a view over the mountains all the way down to the city and the sea, that the village had become a contested vantage point between warring factions in the 1980s. By then the Beirut we knew had gone so completely that the postcards of the time we were there don't seem real but more like stills from a film set.

In 1967 I was in London when Israel launched a lightning military strike against Egypt and Syria. A vindictive sense of glee permeated the newspapers. By pulling Nasser—the "Arab dictator"—off his pedestal, Israel had succeeded where Britain had failed eleven years before. Israeli soldiers were photographed weeping as they prayed at the Wailing Wall and waving as they reached the Suez Canal. The other dominant images of this war were the tanks still smoldering in the Sinai desert, the blackened remains of planes destroyed on the tarmac before they had time to take off, and the hundreds of thousands of West Bank Palestinians, many of them refugees from the war of 1948, stumbling across the wreckage of the Allenby Bridge into Jordan. Nasser made a memorable resignation speech but withdrew it amid tumultuous emotional street scenes that were matched only by the outpouring of public grief when he died three years later. No Arab leader before or since has touched the emotions as he did, and in life or death most Arab leaders have not touched the emotions of their people at all.

The 1967 war was followed by the "war of attrition" along the Suez Canal, by Israel's commando raid on Beirut International Airport in 1968, by the failed attempt to regulate the Palestinian presence in Lebanon through the Cairo Agreement of 1969, by airliner hijackings and the civil war they triggered in Jordan, by the attack on Munich's Olympic village in 1972 and the shocking denouement on the tarmac a few hours later as German sharpshooters opened fire on the minibuses taking the Palestinians and their hostages to the plane that would have flown them to safety in Algiers, by the Israeli air strikes against Lebanon and Syria that followed, and by the next big war between the Arabs and Israel in October 1973. I was back in Beirut in April that year when Israeli commandos paddled ashore on Ramlet al Baida (White Sands) beach, teamed up with special forces already positioned in the city, and stormed into an upper-middle-class residential area—not the crumbling dockside building shown in the Steven Spielberg film *Munich*—killing three leading Palestinians and anyone else who got in the way. They included a wife trying to shield her husband and an elderly Italian woman who opened her door to see what the noise was all about. I did not go back for a long time, but I was there in 2002 when Eli Hobeika, the Falangist militia commander during Israel's invasion of Lebanon in 1982, was blown to pieces by a car bomb a few days after threatening to reveal what he personally knew of Ariel Sharon's complicity in the massacre of Palestinians at Sabra and Shatila.

These are some of the milestones leading up to the decision to write this book. Its central theme is the consequences in the Middle East of decisions taken in the centers of world power over the past two centuries. The techniques of domination and control employed by distant governments, ranging from invasion and occupation to a more discreet exercise of power, through treaties and more latterly through the dependence created by large amounts of foreign aid, are not quite an exact template for what has happened everywhere but are reasonably representative of the range. Like the lion on the back of the wildebeest, these governments are only doing what powerful governments have always done, but frightened, suborned, and co-opted Arab leaders have certainly made the killing much easier. There is a book waiting to be written about their responsibility for what the Middle East has become, but this one is mostly concerned with how the West pushed at an open door in 1798 and has kept pushing ever since. The similarities across the centuries, including the rhetorical justification for intervention (civilization and order in the nineteenth century; civilization, freedom, and democracy in the twentieth) and the theatrical double acts characteristic of each epoch (from Muhammad Ali and Lord Palmerston in the 1830s down to Anthony Eden and Nasser in the 1950s and George W. Bush and Saddam Hussein in 2003), indicate that a certain pathology is at work here, resting on a cultural substructure of who they are and who we are, what we are entitled to do, and how they must respond if they are to avoid punishment.

The Unmaking of the Middle East was written most urgently for the general reader who feels the need to know more about the Middle East than the mainstream media are able or willing to tell. The book is the product not just of several years' research and writing but of everything I have learned about the Middle East since stepping ashore in Beirut back in 1965. It is infused by my understanding and my experiences as well as the thousands of documents and hundreds of books and articles that I read as part of the process of putting it together. I am naturally glad that the University of California Press decided to publish the book pretty much at the length I wrote it because the events of September 11, 2001 have justifiably raised the level of concern among ordinary people (i.e., not politicians or government spokespeople) about what is going on in the Middle East, why their governments are so deeply involved, and why the lives of their soldiers are being put at risk. The dangers are increasing rather than diminishing. One country in the region has nuclear weapons and another is continuing to develop nuclear energy even at the risk of coming under military attack to stop it. Chemical weapons have already been used against soldiers and civilians alike. Peace plans and road maps put forward as a solution to the "Palestine problem" have turned out to be no more than scraps of paper whirling in the wind along with other plans and solutions long since forgotten. Thousands of American soldiers have died in Iraq along with hundreds of thousands of Iraqis who have been killed or who have died as the indirect result of war and occupation. At the time of writing there was no end in sight to any of these problems. The standing of the

United States and the West across the region has never been lower. Is there a central reason for all of this, something basically wrong with the way the West has dealt with the Middle East ever since the beginning of the nineteenth century? The telling of the story might suggest the answer by the time the end is reached.

The book covers familiar ground as well as terrain that might not be so familiar to readers (the Balkan War of 1912–13 and the Greek invasion of western Anatolia in 1919), but in the writing of every chapter I have looked for the documentary material that adds to our store of knowledge even as it changes our understanding. A case in point is the Arab-Israeli war of 1967. Recently declassified documents demonstrate beyond any reasonable doubt that the Israeli attack on Egypt and Syria in June that year was not "preemptive" at all but eagerly sought by the Israeli military command and ultimately allowed by President Lyndon Baines Johnson. If this is to be accepted as a truth, Israel's justification for occupying Arab lands ever since—that it had no option but to go to war—clearly lies in tatters. The documents also shed light on the struggle taking place behind the scenes during the Johnson administration as senior policy makers tried to use the supply of weaponry (mostly tanks and planes) to compel Israel to sign the Nuclear Non-proliferation Treaty (NPT) and maintain the Middle East as a nuclear-free zone. Ultimately the Americans failed not because of Israeli obstruction but because of President Johnson's intervention to make sure that Israel got the weapons it wanted without having to commit itself to the NPT and international safeguards. The president's perceptions of the power of the Israeli lobby add historical depth to the paper produced in 2006 by Stephen Walt and John Mearsheimer on the contradictions they see between the U.S. national interest and the interests of Israel and those who campaign for those interests in Washington.

The book is divided into four parts. Part I sets the scene by looking at the origin of "civilization" and the formation of what Samuel Huntington calls "Islam's bloody borders."[1] While borders were certainly imposed by Muslims during the period of Arab and Ottoman ascendancy, in the period of decline the borders were imposed on them, and from the French invasion of Egypt in 1798 onwards it was their blood that was shed most copiously in the process. The narrative moves from a second French invasion (of Algeria in 1830) to the British invasion of Egypt in 1882 and the machine-gun slaughter sixteen years later of protonational Sudanese tribal warriors in the battle of Omdurman—Winston Churchill's "signal triumph" of science over barbarism. Part II begins with the breakdown of the Ottoman Empire but takes as its starting point the Balkan War of 1912–13, when Bulgaria, Serbia,

Greece, and Montenegro took advantage of turbulence in Istanbul to launch a combined attack on what was left of the Ottoman domain in southeastern Europe. Hundreds of thousands of Muslims died or were stampeded from southeastern Europe into the empire's Anatolian heartland.[2] This first epic tragedy of the twentieth century was followed within a year by more civilian suffering on a Tolstoyan scale as the "Young Turk" triumvirate plunged the empire into the First World War alongside the Central Powers. A key episode in the wartime Western narrative is the fate of the empire's Armenian Christian population. In this book their suffering is juxtaposed against the fate of Muslims in the territories conquered by the Russians and held by them or the Armenians (after the Bolshevik revolution ended Russia's participation in the war) until the Ottomans were able to return in 1918.

The big war of 1914–18 was followed by smaller wars as the victorious powers chopped up Ottoman lands and sought to impose their terms on Arabs and Turks to the advantage of their protégés. The consequences tended to be disastrous, not just for the Arabs or the Muslims of Anatolia, but for those whom Western governments sponsored on the grounds of racial or religious superiority. It is common to talk of Arab betrayal by the West, but with the singular exception of the Zionists, and to a lesser extent the Maronites of Lebanon, the Christian protégés of the British and French governments, especially the Armenians and Assyrians, were to fare no better. The British government sponsored a Greek invasion of western Anatolia in 1919; though David Lloyd George believed in the superiority of the Greeks over the decadent Turks, the Greek army was driven back to the sea three years later and the Greeks of the emerging Turkish state and the Turkish Muslims of Greece subsequently were uprooted from the lands on which they and their forebears had lived and farmed for generations and sent to the other side of the Aegean in a population "exchange."

"Small Wars in Iraq" is built around critical episodes in the history of the country from the great revolt of 1920 (a similar revolt against the French was to erupt in Syria five years later) to the revolution of 1958. "Double Colonialism in Palestine" deals with the implantation of Zionism at the geographical heart of the Middle East from the 1920s onwards. "Civil War along the Potomac" (Dean Acheson's phrase) describes the conflict that developed between different branches of the U.S. administration over policy on Palestine in 1948. Similar tensions were to emerge when President Johnson consolidated the "special relationship" with Israel in the 1960s. This key period in U.S.-Israeli relations is discussed in Part III, which follows U.S. involvement in the Middle East from the Eisenhower years to the commitment of Marines to Lebanon in the 1980s. Other presidents have their place in the narrative. Jimmy Carter, whose presidency came down with the helicopters in the failed mission to snatch back hostages held in Tehran and who has since been traduced for daring to compare Israel's occupation policies with apartheid;[3] Ronald Reagan, who sanctioned Israel's invasion of Lebanon in 1982, only for the United States to be sucked into the quagmire along with everyone else; and of course, the two Bushes, organizing the father-and-son wars on Iraq that are discussed in Part IV. The final chapter in the final section of the narrative ("The Long Campaign") returns to Iraq and Palestine before summing up the effects of two centuries of Western involvement in the Middle East. There are numerous issues I have not been able to deal with because even a big book has its limits, but it seems to me that the geographical and political terrain I have covered is where the future of the region is going to be decided.

A few words on sources and names. The research material includes many volumes of declassified documents culled from the British and American archives, as well as declassified material available electronically (in George Washington University's excellent National Security Archive collection, for example), supplemented by an extensive range of secondary material—books, articles, diaries, first-person accounts, memoirs, and newspaper articles from the nineteenth century until the present. As much documentary evidence as possible has been built into the text to allow the reader to form an opinion not just on the basis of the author's mediated reading but on what the politicians, statesmen, and diplomats were quietly saying to each other at the time. A word also about personal and place names. The standard Westernized forms have been used throughout. These include the print media adaptations (i.e., Nasser instead of Nasir, and Bin Laden rather than Ladin, but Usama rather than Osama), and the auto-Westernized names of politicians (Chamoun for Sham'un and Gemayel instead of Jumayyil) who regard themselves as heirs to the Western heritage around the eastern Mediterranean and, for this reason, either reject or remain ambivalent about their status as Arabs. One final issue that had to be resolved was how to refer to "the West." The debate over its existence as a self-contained civilizational, cultural, and political entity is something I only touch upon, but there is no doubt of its instrumental use to justify or mask the real intention of policies that have far more to do with the strategic and commercial interests of particular governments than something as amorphous as "the West" or "Western values." The questions that had to be settled related to the use of the quotation marks and the capital W. My preference was for a lower case "west," but as this would have resulted in an untidy litter of single quotation marks throughout the manuscript, we—

the editors and myself—eventually agreed on the removal of the quotes and the insertion of the capital W. However, the dictates of good editorial housekeeping should not be taken to imply a change of heart on my part. I have the same reservations about the West with or without the capital or quotation marks, and wherever the phrase or its variations occur in the manuscript, invariably in the context of something a politician has said, my ascription of instrumental use should be assumed.

I would like to thank a number of colleagues and friends who have given support and understanding during the writing of this book, including the chairman of the Department of Political Science at Bilkent University and dean of the Faculty of Economics and Administrative and Social Sciences, Professor Metin Heper, who approved my application for research leave in Australia; Professor Brian Galligan, head at the time of the Department of Political Science at the University of Melbourne, who helped to arrange the Senior Research Fellowship that gave me access to the university's Baillieu Library; Dr. Adam Tarock, of Melbourne, and Professor Norman Stone, of Bilkent University, both of whom read an early draft of the manuscript; the late and greatly missed Professor Stanford J. Shaw, also of Bilkent, for guiding me through the intricacies of late Ottoman history; and Marlene D. Elwell, who helped me dig up research material when she was a graduate student in the Department of Political Science at Bilkent. Dr. Töre Fougner, Dr. Ayça Kurtoğlu, and Afaf Shaʿasha, all of Ankara, helped through steady friendship and good advice. I would like to single Töre out for special thanks. He gave me articles he had used in his own research and helped me over certain obstacles as the manuscript was being hammered into shape. Havva Alkiş and Burcu Atay, of the Bilkent Library, tracked down an elusive volume of documents for me; Betil Gürün, the information resources coordinator at the U.S. embassy in Ankara, arranged my use of the embassy's library, directing me to another volume of documents I had trouble finding, and many thanks are due to her, Havva, and Burcu for their assistance. Walter Struve, of the State Library in Melbourne, and Humphrey McQueen of Canberra helped to track down a number of references. I would also like to thank the anonymous prepublication readers of the manuscript for their constructive criticisms and for picking up a number of careless mistakes. At the University of California Press, Niels Hooper, Rachel Lockman, Kate Warne, and Elisabeth Magnus looked after the manuscript on the long path to publication; no author could wish for better editors. Sebastian, Miranda, and Maslyn Salt cheered me on throughout; what father would not count himself privileged to be part of their lives. I would also like to pay tribute to two dear departed friends, first the late Dr. Kemal Özudoğru, professor of engineering at Istanbul Technical University, my first and oldest friend in Istanbul, a man of the utmost integrity and honesty, who would have read the book before delivering his verdict over a glass of *rakı* and *mezze* in our *meyhane* of choice in Istanbul, Imroz; and second, Dr. Nasseh Ahmad Mirza, my first professor of Arabic and Middle Eastern studies at the University of Melbourne, "Uncle Nasseh" to my children, an outstanding scholar of Ismailism and the most humane and gentle of men. Finally, I take the usual responsibility for mistakes made and views expressed: furthermore, the help I have been given does not imply that anyone whom I have thanked shares my views.

PART I. "WHY DO THEY HATE US?"

I. CIVILIZATION AND ITS CONTRADICTIONS

In the Western mainstream media the contemporary debate on the relationship between "Islam" and "the West" often begins with a rhetorical question: "What went wrong?" "Is Islam a threat to the West?" "Why do they hate us?" Or, "Who is the enemy?" An article entitled "Can Any Good Come of Radical Islam?" begins with still more questions: "What is going on in the Muslim world? Why does it produce suicide hijackers on the one hand and, on the other, lethargic and haphazardly capitalist societies that have delivered neither economic development nor democracy?" Even Samuel Huntington's article in *Foreign Affairs* comes with a question mark: "The Clash of Civilizations?"[1]

All these questions lead to different answers and other questions. How are Islam and the West to be defined? What do the commentators mean when they talk about "us" and "them"? Are "we" really all on one side and "they" all on the other? Are George Galloway and Tony Blair or Noam Chomsky and George Bush on the same planet, let alone on the same side?

WEST OF EDEN

Throughout history, like the colors coming through a prism that change as the crystal is turned, the West has been fabled, historical, imagined, civilizational, religious, sentimental, secular, imperial, and political. Europe was the provincial Western seed from which sprouted the tendrils of a global West. Parson Samuel Purchas concluded that God had withheld knowledge of navigation from "the Persian, the Mogoll, the Abassine, the Chinois, the Tartarian, the Turke" so that the "Sunne of righteousness might arise out of our West to Illuminate the East."[2] For Christians stepping ashore in the new world, the West was not so much the antithesis of the East as its divine successor. History dawns in the East but matures in the "evening lands" of the West. Eastern decay is followed by Western renewal: for the peoples of the West, God's providence is manifest in fertile plains, broad rivers, lush valleys, thick forests, and majestic mountains stretching out before them.

The idea of the West in world history was amplified by a geography that served a European and then West-centric view. Geographical Europe was a small part of a vast land mass reaching halfway around the world.[3] There was no separate continent of Europe, indeed no abrupt point of separation at all, but rather a slow merging of topographies and cultures, their borrowings from each other illustrated by the mythological origin even of the name given to the western extreme of the Eurasian land mass. (Europa was the Phoenician princess abducted by Zeus and carried off to Crete.) Arnold Toynbee described the antithesis between "Europe" and "Asia" (his quotation marks) as false and the two "so-called" continents as fictions, "with no relation to the real geographical entities."[4] The distorting world map drawn by Gerardus Mercator in 1569 enlarged the West at the expense of the East and the North at the expense of the South. Mercator was a scientist applying innovative mathematical means to cartography, but a map that seemed to put Europe at the center of the world was certainly not out of place in an age of expansion. The geographical and cultural sorting of the world that followed the great "discoveries" (bestowing sole right of possession on the king who had paid for the discoverer's ships) was essential to imperialism: without a "them" there could not be an "us," and without barbarians and savages there would be no need to enter distant lands in the name of civilization.

The genesis of the term *civilization* lies in the Latin *civis* (citizen) or *civilis* (of the citizen). By the fourteenth century *civil* had entered the English language. In both English and French *civil* related to legal or political rights and *civility* to manners. In the sixteenth century the Anglican theologian Richard Hooker used the expression *civil society* to describe a system of government established with the consent of the people and implying a political, legal, social, and religious relationship between ruler and ruled. The Latin root was then turned into a verb *(to civilize)*, and *civilized* became the description of a well-mannered person. Somewhere around the middle of the eighteenth century the noun *civilization* emerged as a description of a large social unit subsuming cultures bound together by a common level of morality and development.[5] Boswell tells us that Dr. Johnson did not like this French neologism at all: "He would not admit *civilization* but only *civility*. With great deference to him, I thought *civilization*, from to *civilize*, better in the sense opposed to *barbarity*, than *civility*."[6]

The development of *civilization* from *civis* took place as Portuguese, Dutch, Spanish, French, and British mariners and explorers were discovering new lands and peoples. Some could be called civilized, some were barbarians whom it might be possible to civilize, and others were savages who scarcely seemed human. Rational thinkers of the Enlightenment did not—could not—believe in innate differences between any human beings. Guizot put his faith in "one universal civilization" and a common human destiny. The "families of people" sitting in the shade of the tree of civilization were all destined eventually to be covered by its foliage.[7] From this point we move onward to the view that the globalization of the late twentieth century cemented a global civilization.[8] The alternative is the view of a world of many civilizations (Western, Confucian, Japanese, Islamic, Hindu, Slavic-Orthodox, Latin American, "and possibly" African in Samuel Huntington's typology)[9] that are at risk of "clashing" because of their innate differences.

By their historians, civilizations are generally regarded as organic in nature, proceeding from birth to inevitable death but being reborn in different incarnations. The ancient and numerous civilizations of what was known as the "Levant" or the "Near East" until Alfred Thayer Mahan, the high-imperialist U.S. naval geographer and expert on the strategic use of sea power, began referring to the region as the Middle East early in the twentieth century, arise anew as Arab civilization, Islamic civilization, or Arabo-Islamic civilization. There is no consensus on how many civilizations there have been, let alone how many there are. Classifications are obviously fraught with difficulties because of the substantial cultural and linguistic differences between many of the subgroups pushed into the supergroup. Ottoman, Turkic, and Arab cultures might be entitled to their own civilizational rankings, but for Huntington and others the similarities outweigh the differences. The fact that cultures are often not confined within the same geographical space or national boundaries has propelled the search over the last two centuries for a mystical something else that defines civilization, perhaps a soul, a mentality, a character, a sense of itself, a personality—in short, an essence.

"Western civilization" reached high points of achievement at different stages of its development. The Renaissance was obviously one of them, the Enlightenment another, and the set of technical advances that gave rise to the Industrial Revolution still another, but in the nineteenth century, when slavery was still sanctioned, when children of seven or eight worked in textile mills and down mines, when all women and most men had no electoral rights, when Jews were kept out of the professions and felons were executed in public places, the civilizing process even in the West obviously still had a long way to go. In distant parts of the world, "civilized" Western man was still giving proof of how savage he could be: by the twentieth century the most destructive conflicts ever fought in world history were to show that the dark Janus face of Western civilization was not an aberration but a pathological condition.

The 1914–18 war blew a gaping hole in the notion of a unified Western civilization. It was all of a sudden no longer clear who was "us" and who was "them." The Germans who had made massive philosophical, scientific, and musical contributions to civilization now had to be turned into its deadliest enemies. This was done by reverting to the barbarian past and investing them with the nasty characteristics of an Oriental Turkic people who had swept into the European continent from the east centuries before and sullied civilization. One could not hate a people who produced Mozart and Beethoven, but through the repetition of crude propaganda one could be taught to loathe a crop-headed, bull-necked Hun wearing a funny helmet. The civilizational aspect of the war was indeed confused. The Hunnified Germans were fighting their Saxon cousins and royal relatives alongside a contemporary Oriental people (the now Germanized Turks), while the British and French had entered into an alliance with the half-Asiatic (and therefore half-barbarian) Russians. Dusky Orientals and even darker Africans helped fight their war for them, the various ethno-religious groups of the Indian subcontinent for the British and the North African Arabs and West African Senegalese for the French. Now that civilization was divided, Allied propaganda represented the war as a struggle between its higher and lower forms.[10] Great were the sacrifices justified in the name of a "higher form of civilization," the phrase used by Field Marshal Sir Douglas Haig, architect of the military operations that ended in the slaughter of British soldiers on the battlefields of Belgium and France.[11]

The coming trends of Western civilization were foreshadowed well before 1914. Huxley and Orwell's soulless new worlds were antedated by the Futurists, who glorified speed, the machine, and the power that the machine created or symbolized; the army, the arsenal, railway stations, factories, bridges, "deep-chested" locomotives (from Marinetti's first manifesto of 1909), sleek aircraft, and the man behind the wheel were the new icons. Governments began to grow into the bureaucratic manifestation of the machine, embodying management, discipline, order, organization, efficiency, and output. Transit systems, elevators, skyscrapers, subways, and department stores replicated the need to simultaneously control and serve the needs of rapidly growing urban masses.

At the dark far end of the production line stood the death camp. Mass destruction and genocide were as much the product of "Western civilization" as the works of the greatest writers and composers. Goya could see it centuries before. As Richard Rubinstein has remarked: "The world of death camps and the society it engenders reveals the progressively intensifying night side of Judeo-Christian civilization. Civilization means slavery, wars, exploitation and death camps. It also means medical hygiene, elevated religious ideas, beautiful art and exquisite music. It is an error to imagine that civilization and savage cruelties are antitheses. . . . Both creation and destruction are inseparable parts of what we call civilization."[12] The ideologies of fascism, national socialism, and communism were all based on the repudiation of Western liberal values. As Ian Buruma has observed, "The idea of the West as a malign force is not some Eastern or Middle Eastern idea, but has deep roots in European soil."[13]

The 1939–45 war represented another great split in the ranks of the "civilized" nations. By the late 1930s Germany and Italy had defected from the Western world in favor of a three-way axis with Oriental Japan. Half-barbarian Russia—now communist into the bargain—fought alongside the "liberal" democracies. This hot war for civilization and civilized values was followed straightaway by a cold war fought between the "West" and the "East," this time not Near, Middle, or Far but the Soviet Union and the satellite or "captive" communist states stretching from eastern Europe into the eastern region of Germany. This new struggle in the name of civilization, democracy, and freedom marked the real beginning of the birth of the West as a political idea, but with the collapse of the Soviet Union in 1989 older tensions and submerged differences within and between Europe and the United States quickly resurfaced.

Long before the September 11 attacks on New York and Washington, the United States had broken away from the global pack on such critical questions as arms control, environmental protection, and economic development. This was followed by the adoption of a radically conservative foreign policy that overturned the seventeenth-century Westphalian principles o mutual respect for the sovereign rights of states. Henceforth, the Unite States would not hesitate to launch "preemptive" or "anticipatory" strik against states it regarded as threats to its security. It would pursue this p icy whatever the UN or its partners in the Western alliance thought: w' France and Germany refused to go along with the attack on Iraq in 2 U.S. Defense Secretary Donald Rumsfeld jeered at them for exempli' the "old" Europe as compared to the "new" (central and eastern)

insults tailed off as the United States struck unexpected difficulties in Iraq, forcing it to return to the UN and seek the cooperation of those governments it had only recently been abusing. In short, the concepts of "West" and "East" are political constructions whose content has varied over time according to changing governmental agendas.

CIVILIZATIONS ON THE FRONT LINE

"The sword of Mahomet, and the Coran, are the most stubborn enemies of Civilisation, Liberty and Truth which the world has yet known." So wrote the nineteenth-century Scottish Orientalist Sir William Muir in his study of the life of the Prophet Muhammad.[14] The line was taken up by clerics, politicians, and pamphleteers fighting for the rights of Christian minorities exposed to the evils of "Muhammadan government" in the Ottoman Empire. They welcomed this scholarly reinforcement of their view that Islam itself was the cause of their problems and not mundane quarrels over cattle or land or sectarian tensions ignited by meddling outside powers. Muir expanded on this theme in a second work, on the caliphate: "As regards the spiritual, social and dogmatic aspect of Islam, there has been neither progress nor material change since the third century of the Hegira. Such as we found it to have been then, such is it also at the present day. The nations may advance in civilisation and morality, in philosophy, science and the arts; but Islam stands still. And thus stationary, so far as the lessons of this history avail, it will remain."[15]

Muir's depiction of an inert, unchanging religion blocking progress was generous compared to the invective heaped on Islam by others. In the nineteenth century success on the battlefield seemed to confirm the Christian view of where God's religious preference lay. Notions of religious, racial, and civilizational superiority were still held by the politicians who took their countries into the First World War. The discourse of race continues in politics today, though often in a more muted and coded form; in addition, religion has been re-embedded in the public life of many countries and civilization brought back to the center of political debate as pundits, scholars, and commentators search far and wide for explanations of tensions between "Islam" and "the West."

Although Samuel P. Huntington has taken the lion's share of the attention, Bernard Lewis (born in 1916) was writing on the themes of civilizational difference and conflict decades earlier. At the height of imperial domination of the Middle East in 1950, he claimed that the Arabs would have to resolve their "problems of readjustment" in the modern world by

submitting to "one or [an]other of the contending versions of modern civilization that are offered to them, merging their own culture and identity in a larger and dominating whole."[16] A decade later Professor Lewis turns the crisis *of* a civilization faced with this "offer" into a clash *between* civilizations: "When civilizations clash there is one that prevails and one that is shattered. Idealists and ideologues may talk glibly of 'a marriage of the best elements' from both sides, but the usual result of such an encounter is a cohabitation of the worst."[17] Thus, he argues, a civilization thrown into crisis is finally reacting "against the impact of alien forces that have dominated, dislocated and transformed it": "We shall be better able to understand this situation if we view the present discontents of the Middle East not as a conflict between states or nations but as a clash between civilizations."[18]

The phrase is out. Three decades later, returning to his theme, Professor Lewis writes that "we" are now facing "a mood and a movement far transcending the level of issues and policies and the governments that pursue them. This is no less than a clash of civilizations—that perhaps irrational but surely historic reaction of an ancient rival against our Judeo-Christian heritage, our secular present and the worldwide expansion of both."[19] In Lewis's view, Muslim rage at Western domination has finally metastasized into a "profound, pervasive and passionate hatred of the West and all it represents, as a world power, as an ideology, as a way of life, and that hatred is extended to embrace a wide range of local Westernizers and modernizers. It is a hatred so deep that it has led those who feel it to rally to any plausible enemy of the West."[20] The roots of this hatred "must be sought in the millennial history of relations between Islam and Christendom."[21] In a sense "they've been hating us for centuries and it's very natural that they should. You have this millennial rivalry between two world religions and now from their point of view the wrong one seems to be winning."[22] If a significant number of Muslims "are hostile and dangerous" to the West, it is not because "we" need an enemy "but because they do."[23]

"THWARTED" SOCIETIES

Samuel Huntington describes a primordial world in which humans live in a state of actual or incipient conflict not because of their animal nature (as Hobbes argued) but because of civilizational difference. Even the fact that the most destructive conflicts in world history have been the national, imperial, and global wars launched by European governments in the nineteenth and twentieth centuries does not deter him from asserting that "the most prolonged and the most violent conflicts" over the centuries have been generated by civilizational difference.[24] The severe conflicts that have broken out over centuries *within* "Western civilization" are rationalized as being "Western civil wars."[25] Huntington makes his most provocative claims about Islam and the West. In *The Clash of Civilizations and the Remaking of World Order*, he argues under the heading "Islam's Bloody Borders" that the greatest number of "fault line" conflicts have been occurring "along the boundary looping across Eurasia and Africa that sep-arates Muslims from non-Muslims. While at the macro or global level of world politics the primary clash of civilizations is between the West and the rest, at the micro or local level it is between Islam and the others."[26]

Muslims, according to Huntington, are "far more involved in inter-group violence than the people of any other civilization," and they seem to have a "propensity" for violent conflict.[27] In the wake of 9/11, when his "clash of civilizations" argument apparently scored a technical knockout over Francis Fukuyama's "end of history" theory, Huntington returned to his main theme even more forcefully: "Contemporary global politics is the age of Muslim wars. Muslims fight each other and fight non-Muslims far more often than do peoples of other civilizations. Muslim wars have replaced the cold war as the principal form of international conflict. These wars include wars of terrorism, guerrilla wars, civil wars and interstate conflicts. These instances of Muslim violence could congeal into one major clash of civilizations between Islam and the West or between Islam and the Rest. That, however, is not inevitable and it is more likely that violence involving Muslims will remain dispersed, varied and frequent."[28]

Up to Muir's time the Christian polemicists described Islam as a religion of sex, power, and violence; paradoxically, in Huntington's and Lewis's modern variations on this old theme, Muslim powerlessness now drives the violence. Both authors deemphasize the "impact of the West" as a valid reason for Muslim anger. "The West" is presented as a good uncle landing on the doorstep of a distant relative with a bagful of gifts—rather like a successful Lebanese emigrant returning to the mountain village from Sierra Leone or São Paulo. The good uncle disburses his gifts to all and sundry: democracy, parliaments, the printing press, roads, bridges, factories, railways, and elec-tricity, all wrapped up in a parcel called "modernity," but to his consternation he discovers that the recipients resent his wealth and take out their frustra-tions on him. The homecoming ends in disaster. The whole modernization process comes crashing down and the party is over. Dear old Uncle West is bewildered and hurt. "I was only trying to help." The complaint of every par-ent! He should have known better, but it is too late for regrets. The damage has been done. Democracy has been installed by "autocratic decree," creating a new game of politics that is "ignored or watched with baffled incomprehension by the great mass of the people."[29] Pulled into the modern world whether they are ready or not, wrenched out of the "comfortable torpor of decay" and "illusions of superiority and self-sufficiency," Muslim peoples move from "ignorant complacency" to "anxious emulation" and "envious rancor" before ending up toward the end of the twentieth century in a curdled mess of humiliation, resentment, and rage.[30] Only this line of thinking can possibly explain their state of mind. Certainly Uncle West has made a few mistakes along the way but nothing bad enough to account for this—it's "their" behavior that needs skilled counseling and not "ours." Palestine as a central cause of Arab and Muslim hostility can be brushed aside: it is merely, in the words of Professor Lewis, the "licensed grievance."[31]

The civilizational argument has bred numerous elaborations. Francis Fukuyama contrasts Western success with Muslim failure.[32] For Fukuyama the immediate issue is not terrorism per se but "the Islamo-fascist sea within which the terrorists swim," and which constitutes "an ideological challenge that is in some ways more basic than the one posed by communism." The "Islamo-fascists" reject everything the West stands for, especially its tolerance and plurality, which Muslim societies in general find hard to accept because of "the often-noted lack of a tradition of secular politics" in their own histories.[33] For Fouad Ajami, the "men in the shadows" attacking American targets feed off "a free-floating anti-Americanism that blows at will and knows no bounds among Islamists and secularists alike."[34] When the passenger jets were flown into the twin towers on September 11, 2001, there was satisfaction in "thwarted, resentful societies" that "the American bull run and the triumphalism that had awed the world had been battered [and] that there was soot and ruin in New York's streets."[35] The bombing of the twin towers has led to a search for justice in Afghanistan and Iraq, where U.S. soldiers are standing by to help with "rifle in one hand" and "wrench in the other."[36] The streets of Falluja and Najaf are mentioned, not as the corridors of death they had been turned into under the impact of U.S. air and ground fire, but as places "where the early American hopes of a culture that would be grateful for its liberty and eager to create a new political order" seem to have taken a battering notwithstanding the "nobility" of the war effort.

EUROPE'S MUSLIMS

These dark forebodings of threat from an alien civilization have been fortified by what people read in the newspapers or watch on the television

every day. Suicide bombings in the Middle East, security swoops on suspected terrorists, the increasing number of Muslims (bearded men and
veiled women) filling the streets of European cities, and the sight of
mosques where once there were only churches (or the occasional synagogue) feed prejudice and ignorance. The bombings in London and
Madrid, the murder of the Dutch filmmaker Theo van Gogh, and the controversy over the publication in Denmark and then other countries of cartoons lampooning the Prophet Muhammad have precipitated an upsurge
of Islamophobia. After the bombing of Madrid's Atocha railway station in
March 2004, the Spanish government insisted that the Basque separatist
organization ETA was responsible, even though from an early stage it was
receiving evidence that Muslim terrorists were behind the attack; the
deceit and the connection between the bombing and participation in a war
that the Spanish people had not wanted from the start was enough to put
the conservative government of Jose Maria Aznar out of office. In video-
tapes released after the event, the four suicide bombers who had killed
fifty-two commuters in attacks on the London transit system on July 7,
2005, gave as their motive retaliation for British participation in the inva-
sions of Afghanistan and Iraq and the deaths of thousands of Muslims that
had followed; in September 2005, responsibility for the attack was claimed
by al Qaʿida. The bombings in both cities were regarded with revulsion by
Muslims and non-Muslims alike and were condemned as anti-Islamic by
Muslim organizations in Europe and around the world.

The murder of van Gogh in November 2004 by a Dutch-born Muslim
"of Moroccan origin" (as he was generally described) was followed by
dozens of arson attacks on Islamic schools and mosques in the Netherlands
and by the proposal of parliamentary legislation to ban Muslim women
from covering their faces in public places. In the immediate aftermath, the
owner of a Web site of condolences had to remove more than five thousand
anti-Muslim and anti-Moroccan statements.[37] Like the anti-Muslim immigration politician Pim Fortuyn, who had been murdered the year before
(by a non-Muslim young Dutchman who believed Fortuyn was exploiting
a vulnerable minority for political gain), van Gogh believed that multiculturalism had been a disaster for the Netherlands. His rhetorical style was
confrontational and frequently abusive. He struck back at "political correctness" in his writings and in the short film he made on forced marriages
and the mistreatment of women, *Submission*.[38] Ayaan Hirsi Ali, the
Somali-born member of the Dutch parliament who had renounced Islam
and cooperated with him in making the film, which shows verses of the
Quʾran inscribed on the body of a naked woman, received death threats

and left the Netherlands after van Gogh's murder to take up a position as a Resident Fellow at the American Enterprise Institute in Washington. She was herself a controversial figure, whom Professor Halleh Ghorashi, of Vrijne University, Amsterdam, admired as a pioneer for the emancipation of Muslim women until, in Ghorashi's view, she turned out to hold "dogmatic views that left little room for nuances. I soon realized that Ayaan had become part of the 'rightist' discourse on Islam in the Netherlands that pictures Islamic migrants as problems and enemies of the nation."[39]

The publication of cartoons mocking the Prophet Muhammad scandalized Muslims no less than did the inscription of verses of the Qu'ran on the body of a naked woman. The mockery only aggravated the offense: in the eyes of Muslims everywhere, pictorial representation of the prophet constitutes blasphemy. Flemming Rose, the cultural editor of *Jyllands-Posten*, which published the cartoons in September 2005, intended them as a response to "several incidents of self-censorship in Europe caused by widening fears and feelings of intimidation in dealing with issues related to Islam."[40] If others could accept mockery, scorn, and ridicule, why not Muslims?[41] His declared goal was "to push back self-imposed limits on expression that seemed to be closing in tighter," but as time went by it became clear that more was involved than just free speech. Invited to explain his position in the international media, Rose expanded on his dislike of political correctness, moral relativism, the welfare state model that allowed Muslim immigrants to go straight on the dole, and the "utopian state of multicultural bliss" in which he had lived as a younger man.[42] The language could be taken from any neoconservative publication coming out of Washington:[43] the picture of someone who has finally seen the light after years of being deluded by utopian multiculturalism is filled out by "The Threat from Islam," Rose's empathetic account of his interview in Pennsylvania with Daniel Pipes in 2004.[44] But irrespective of the political perspective that influenced Rose's decision to publish the cartoons that incensed Muslims around the world, the arguments for free speech, tolerance, and acceptance obviously cut both ways. Rose conceded that *Jyllands-Posten* imposes its own restrictions (no pornographic material, no dead bodies, and swear words only rarely).[45] The cartoons were "different," but in publishing them it was surely not the toleration of the white middle-class readers of his newspaper that he wanted to test. They were more likely to be amused by the cartoons than provoked. If provocation of the paper's mainstream readership was the purpose, more obvious means were at hand: perhaps the Danish royal family, swear words not usually uttered in polite company, or graphic images of the bodies of children dismembered by bombs in Iraq.

There was certainly a point to be made here about the way the media hide the central product of war. The paper could also have published the cartoons lightly satirizing the resurrection of Christ that it had been offered two years before, but in an e-mail to the cartoonist the paper's Sunday editor replied that it could not. "I don't think *Jyllands-Posten's* readers will enjoy the drawings. As a matter of fact I think they will provoke an outcry. Therefore I will not use them."[46] Instead of the majority, a marginalized Muslim minority, about 5 percent of the Danish population, had to be provoked in the name of expanding the limits of freedom of expression.

While governments and nongovernmental organizations across Europe got on with the job of damping down the fires lit in Denmark and the Netherlands, right-wing politicians and anti-Muslim commentators lost no time in taking advantage of the moment. Their talk was of surrender, of "dhimmitude" (the alleged servitude of Christians and Jews living under Muslim rule), and of a continent invaded through migration and sinking under the burden of supporting rapidly proliferating Muslim families.[47] What could previously only be whispered was finally spoken openly when the Italian author Oriana Fallaci, resorting to a metaphor previously used by the Nazis against the Jews, remarked that "the sons of Allah breed like rats."[48] There was a lot more. Muslims had tried to conquer Europe before and were now trying again, but this time with "children and boats" rather than "troops and cannons"; if Spain was more tolerant of Muslim immigrants, it was because "too many Spaniards still have the Koran in the blood."[49] These statements opened her up to accusations of crude racism, yet Fallaci, who died in September 2006, had numerous admirers (her 2002 book *The Rage and the Pride* sold off the shelves in Italy), to whom she remained brave, refreshingly outspoken, fearsome, iconoclastic, incisive, and so on, right to the end. The issues at the heart of Fallaci's diatribes were "muddle-headed multiculturalism" and not so much Islamic "extremism" as Islam itself.[50] "Europe is no longer Europe," she remarked in 2005. "It is 'Eurabia,' a colony of Islam, where the Islamic invasion does not proceed only in a physical sense but also in a mental and cultural sense. Servility to the invaders has poisoned democracy, with obvious consequences for the freedom of thought and for the concept of liberty itself."[51]

"THE THIRD WAVE OF ATTACK ON EUROPE"

These are the themes taken up recently by Bernard Lewis. In January 2007 he told an interviewer from the *Jerusalem Post* that Muslims seemed to be on the point of taking over Europe. Europeans were losing their loyalties and self-confidence and, in a mood of self-abasement, political correctness, and multiculturalism, had "surrendered" to Islam on every level.[52] Delivering the Irving Kristol Lecture at the American Enterprise Institute in March 2007, Professor Lewis observed that the Muslims had made two attempts to conquer Europe, the first by the Arabs and the second by the Turks. Now, "in the eyes of a fanatical and resolute minority of Muslims, the third wave of attack on Europe has clearly begun. We should not delude ourselves as to what it is and what it means. This time it is taking different forms and two in particular—terror and migration." Unlike a disorganized and effete West trapped by its own political correctness, "they" (the Muslims) know what they are doing: "They have certain clear advantages. They have fervor and conviction which in most Western countries are either weak or lacking. They are self-assured of the rightness of their cause whereas we spend most of our time in self-denigration and self-abasement. They have loyalty and discipline and perhaps most important of all they have demography, the combination of natural increase and migration-producing major population changes which could lead within the foreseeable future to significant majorities in at least some European cities or even countries."[53] Muslims regarding themselves deficient in fervor and conviction, and lacking the advantages enjoyed by others (employment, reasonable housing, sports facilities, opportunities for their children, representation in parliament, a sympathetic ear in government), might smile at this, and even Professor Lewis referred to the presence in his audience of Vice President Dick Cheney, a man not generally regarded as lacking fervor, conviction, and assurance in the righteousness of his cause.

Population statistics indicate that even with a higher birth rate (assuming that it remains static and is not brought down by urbanization, acceptance, and greater education and prosperity) Muslim Europeans have some way to go if they are to vindicate Lewis's dire prognostications. As of January 1, 2006, the population of the twenty-seven European Union countries was close to 493 million,[54] of which number about 25,000,000 were Muslims (about 5 percent of the total).[55] The Muslim population (as of 2005) of each EU country amounts to no more than a few percent: for example, Austria, 4.1 percent; Belgium, 4.0 percent; Denmark, 5 percent; Germany, 3.6 percent; Italy, 1.4 percent; the Netherlands, 5.8 percent; Spain, 2.3 percent; the United Kingdom, 2.8 percent, and France, the country with the largest number of Muslims, less than 10 percent.[56] In any case, the Muslim citizens of European countries are far too diverse to warrant use of the monolithic and phobic "they." They speak different languages, they come from different countries and different ethnic or tribal backgrounds, and—like all other Europeans—they vary in their political, philosophical, and religious perspectives even if comparatively greater numbers go to mosque than other Europeans go to church. What the majority do have in common apart from their religion is their social and economic marginalization. Many live under the official EU poverty line (currently fixed at an income of 770 euros a month) and would seem to be far too preoccupied with the daily struggle to keep their heads above water to think of taking Europe over just yet. In the words of a research report, "Migrants, including those from predominantly Muslim countries, generally appear to suffer higher levels of homelessness, poorer quality housing conditions, poorer residential neighborhoods and comparatively greater vulnerability and insecurity in their housing status. Very serious housing problems include lack of access to basic facilities such as drinking water and toilets, significantly higher levels of overcrowding than for other households and exploitation through higher rents and purchase price."[57]

The subversion of the "dialogue of civilizations" between Muslims, Christians, and Jews in European countries and between European and Muslim governments across the Mediterranean is built into in all these statements that decry multiculturalism, political correctness, moral relativism, and the dangers arising from Muslim immigration. The Algerian grocer living in one of the suburbs of northern Paris, the Muslim schoolgirl who dreams of becoming a doctor, the teenage Muslim boy who likes techno music and has no idea what he is going to do with his life are all compressed into the threatening "they." Feeling their exclusion, Muslim teenagers cooped up in the poor outer suburbs of Paris take out their anger by burning cars and throwing bricks through shop windows in rioting that police are hard-pressed to stop. Are they rioting as Muslims or as marginalized young people who live in poverty and see no future for themselves? By the time the sociologists get around to looking at the causes, however, the images have appeared in the media and multiculturalism has taken another blow. The evidence suggests that these young people want nothing more than to get out of the ghetto and be accepted within the broader society.[58] Marginalization would appear to strengthen religious sentiment. According to the Pew Forum on Religion and Social Life, "Surveys show that many Muslims in Europe, especially the young, now identify with Islam more than either the country of their heritage or the country of their birth. Not feeling entirely accepted in either place, they look to Islam to help define themselves."[59] Catholic immigrants arriving in the United States a century ago reacted to negative attitudes to their religion in the same way,[60] but they eventually merged into the mainstream. European

Muslims are less inclined than non-Muslims to believe there is an inconsistency in being a devout Muslim and being modern.[61] A poll taken in 2004 showed that 68 percent of French Muslims regarded the separation of religion and state as "important" and 93 percent supported republican values.[62] They are Muslims living in Europe and therefore the West, yet their religion and ethnic backgrounds are still barriers that must be overcome. "How am I supposed to feel French when people always describe me as a Frenchman of Algerian origin? I was born here. I am French. How many generations does it take to stop mentioning my origin?"[63]

BLACK ATHENA

When Parson Purchas concluded that God had withheld the secrets of navigation from the Mongols, the Abbasids, the Turks, the Chinese, and the Tartars so that Christians could reach the New World first, he could not have known that many of the instruments they used to get there, including the astrolabe, the compass, and the lateen sail, were in fact invented, developed, or refined by the Chinese, the Arabs, and the Persians.[64] How Parson Purchas would have reacted had he known that God gave his favors to the heathen Chinese and the fanatical Muhammadan first we cannot say, but we do know how sensitively some people react now to the suggestion that the sources of Western civilization are not purely Western at all but a mixture of knowledge borrowed, infused, or (more provocatively) stolen from Eastern civilizations.

In 1987, Martin Bernal published the first volume of a two-volume study, *Black Athena,* in which he argued that the ultimate source of much ancient Greek knowledge, and thus of classical civilization, was not Greek at all but Egyptian and therefore African.[65] According to Bernal, the Greek debt to Egypt and the Near East remained an "unbroken part of the European historiographical tradition" down to the establishment of the classics as an academic discipline in the eighteenth and nineteenth centuries.[66] At that point, under the influence of Indo-European linguistics, "but mainly due to extrinsic European social and intellectual forces," the "ancient model" of Greek civilization was supplanted by an "Aryan model" that rejected Semitic and Egyptian influences entirely.[67] This model has since been modified to the extent that Semitic influences on the classical tradition are allowed but the Egyptian influence is still rejected. The implications are clear: in a century shot through with notions of race and racial superiority based on color, manifest destiny, and social Darwinism, any idea that the Afro-Nilotic Egyptians could have played a role in the development of Greek and therefore Western civilization had to be summarily rejected. The hand that rocked the cradle of Western civilization could not possibly be black.

It is only common sense to think that some of the tremendous knowledge accumulated during Pharaonic civilization must have seeped across the Mediterranean, and some readers of Bernal might be comforted by the reaffirmation of common humanity implicit in the idea of a sharing or a borrowing of knowledge, but others clearly were not. The outrage directed against Bernal from within the classics "establishment" was distilled in the 1996 publication *Black Athena Revisited.*[68] The object of the ire of the professors who contributed chapters to the book was denied the right to answer back in a chapter of his own. Further, Bernal was subjected not just to criticism of his scholarship, reasonable or otherwise, but to attacks on his personality and motives (e.g., the comment that the "entire enterprise" of *Black Athena* was a "massive, fundamentally misguided projection upon the second millennium B.C.E. of Martin Bernal's personal struggle to establish an identity during the later twentieth century").[69]

The suggestion that Western civilization is not self-contained is deeply subversive of a tradition that has been used for centuries to justify assumptions of Western exceptionalism and superiority. There is a political element in all of this. Bernal has been accused of bringing his political convictions (apparently left-liberal) into his scholarship by people who seem to be doing the same thing themselves; he has fired back by drawing attention to the right-wing connections of one of his chief detractors and by claiming that he is the target of organizations and journals that want "to turn back what their members and contributors view as the tides of liberalism and multiculturalism that have engulfed not only society but also education and the highbrow media."[70] Even for many of those who disagree with Bernal but are civilized enough to disagree politely, his book opens up new ways of thinking about the past; others, however, regard it as an outrageous challenge to the historical postulates on which the ideas of classical civilization, Western civilization, and the West have been built.

CONNECTED CIVILIZATIONS

Not all Western scholars of the Middle East and Islam have depicted insular civilizations and an Islam intrinsically hostile to the West and civilizationally separate from it. Hamilton Gibb dominated Middle Eastern and Islamic studies in British and American universities in the first half of the twentieth century much as Bernard Lewis did in the second. In an essay first published in 1951, about the time Lewis was coming up with his ideas about a "clash of civilizations," Gibb challenged the artificial distinction between Western and Islamic or Arab civilizations: "On this point there can be no doubt—that the civilization of the Middle East and that of the so-called 'Western' world are closely related; both before and after the rise of Islam there had been inter-penetration between them."[71]

Greece, Gibb argued, borrowed from Oriental sources and later returned what it had borrowed. Medieval Christianity and medieval Islam, "thanks to their common heritage and their common problems, were linked by bonds of both spiritual and intellectual affinity," and the Arab world was "an integral part of the Western world in the broad sense of that term."[72] As for the imposition of Western forms of government on a bewildered Middle East, "it was not Westerners who advocated the adoption of legal codes, parliamentary institutions, compulsory education and freedom of the press; all these institutions were demanded by the peoples of the East themselves."[73]

According to Gibb, it is untrue that the Middle East entered modern history without a secularized tradition, for the Muslim ruling classes practiced over centuries a morality "based on values drawn from the ancient imperial tradition of Western Asia and far removed from the Islamic values."[74] The distinguished Arab historian Philip K. Hitti amplified this by observing that Muslim societies have a secularized tradition of government going back almost to the beginning of Islam.[75] Indeed, in the life of all the major "Islamic" states, dogma invariably took second place to dynastic interest and statecraft, with jurists and scholars in the religious establishment invariably called on to find religious justification for whatever the ruler had already decided he wanted to do. The scholar who stuck his neck out and said something the ruler did not want to hear might find it soon separated from his head.

WHOSE "BLOODY BORDERS"?

> In the most thrilling match of the season so far, Islam raced away to a commanding lead by halftime. Süleyman booted a truly magnificent goal from left field. Islam was running all over the field, positioning itself beautifully and passing with superb accuracy. West just wasn't in it; the game was almost painful to watch. But the transformation when the players ran back on to the field after the break was almost unbelievable. Now it was Islam caught flat-footed down the center and in front of goal, unable to block the relentless drive of West as it surged in the direction of the net time and time again. It was hard to believe this was the same

Islam we had seen in the first half. They seemed to have run out of
steam, and West romped home to an unexpectedly comfortable victory.

If the putative struggle between "Islam and the West" could be reduced
to a game of soccer, perhaps this is how the day's game would be reported.
The speed of the Muslims in moving outside the Arabian peninsula in the
seventh century certainly caught all opposing teams in the major league by
surprise, and with Turkish substitutes brought onto the field from the
benches they seemed unstoppable. The turquoise-tiled domes and minarets
surrounding the tomb of the great Sufi mystic Jalal al Din Rumi in Konya
and the double minaret of the central mosque at Erzurum are among the
architectural reminders of the achievements of the Seljuq Turks, but it was
the Ottomans who were to leave the greater stamp on world history. In
their first imperial century (following the conquest of Constantinople in
1453) they swept into the vulnerable territories around them. In 1514 they
crushed the Persians at Chaldiran. Iraq, Syria, western Arabia, and North
Africa right across to the Atlantic were all incorporated within the sultan's
domains. In 1526 they defeated the Hungarian king at Mohacs. Three years
later they laid siege to Vienna and suffered one of their first setbacks: hampered on the way by bad weather and the loss of thousands of transport
camels whose legs broke in the rough terrain, they then came up against a
defense they could not break and had to retreat. In 1683 the Ottomans
reached Vienna again but were driven off by a combined Christian army.
They had reached the plateau of their power. Their dramatic rise was now
to be followed by slow decline.

No Muslims aroused as much wrath among Christian polemicists as the
Turks. The Islam was the Islam of old—an abomination—but the Turks
were not the mild "Saracens" of old. Perhaps if they had disappeared into
history the Christian tractarians would have been kinder to them too, but
they remained very much in the present. Out of their battlefield victories
came lurid tales of massacre, impalement, forced conversion, and women
choosing death before dishonor at the hands of Muslims by jumping off
cliffs. In the Christian reckoning Islam was a religion of power above all
(not of justice, as the Muslims would see it), and in the Turks it had found
the ideal conduit for the expression of its worst characteristics. These
themes were pounded into the Christian consciousness generation after
generation. Islam itself or the evils of a "Muhammadan government" in
the hands of the Turks were regularly invoked as the causes of all problems
arising in the Ottoman Empire that involved Christians. The reality of
Christians living at peace with Muslims between these episodes of disorder

prompted few to put aside the all-purpose transhistorical explanations and look for other causes. The Turks were simply where they should not be; many were the prayers uttered that the day would come when Constantinople would return to Christian hands and the great disks bearing the names of Muhammad and the first four caliphs could be ripped from the walls of Aya Sofia, the great cathedral-become-mosque (now a museum) standing outside the sultan's palace.

By the nineteenth century that moment seemed to be fast approaching. In wars with Russia the Ottoman Empire had lost great swaths of territory around the Black Sea and in the Caucasus, and now it was the Balkans where most of the bleeding continued. In 1821 the Greeks of the Morea launched a general attack not just on the symbols of the authority of the Ottoman government (tax collectors and other officials) but on the entire Muslim population of the region. In the space of a month perhaps fifteen thousand Muslim villagers were killed and thousands of homes destroyed. At the sultan's request an Egyptian army led by the redoubtable Ibrahim Pasha crossed the Mediterranean to suppress the revolt. He undoubtedly would have succeeded but for the military intervention of Britain, France, and Russia. Their warships destroyed the Ottoman-Egyptian fleet at Navarino (October 20, 1827) and forced the sultan to give the rebels independence, sending a clear signal to other Christians that if they rebelled the European governments might intervene to secure their independence as well.

When the Christians of Bosnia-Herzegovina rebelled in 1875 and the Bulgarians followed suit the next year, William Ewart Gladstone, the British politician and long-standing campaigner for the rights of Christians in the "Sclavonic provinces" of the Ottoman Empire, stirred up popular hatred of the Turks with his outrage. "They are not the mild Mahometans of India nor the chivalrous Saladins of Syria nor the cultured Moors of Spain," he wrote in his atrocity tract *Bulgarian Horrors and the Question of the East* (1876). "They were, upon the whole, from the first black day when they entered Europe, the one great anti-human specimen of humanity. Wherever they went, a broad line of blood marked the path behind them; and as far as their dominion reached, civilization disappeared from view. They represented everywhere government by force as opposed to government by law. For the guide of this life they had a relentless fatalism; for its reward hereafter, a sensual paradise."[76] The London newspapers were filled with accounts of villagers massacred by Ottoman irregulars—many of them Pomaks (Bulgarian Christian converts to Islam) or Muslim Circassians driven out of Transcaucasia by the Russians and resettled in the Balkan domains of the sultan—and of bodies stacked up in villages like cordwood.

Gladstone did not appear to notice the Muslims (about a thousand of them) who had been slaughtered by Bulgarian rebels before the Ottomans intervened. In the ferocious suppression that followed, between three thousand and twelve thousand Christians lost their lives,[77] but even greater horrors than the "Bulgarian horrors" were about to be inflicted on the Muslims. When Russian soldiers were sent to war against the Ottomans in the name of persecuted Christianity in April 1877, they and the Bulgarian volunteers who moved in the train of the Russian army slaughtered Muslim civilians out of hand. Village after village was pillaged and destroyed. Columns of Muslim refugees were attacked by predatory Bulgarian bands even as they streamed out of the conquered territories. The victims of this frenzy of killing, rape, and plunder included Jews (fully protected under Ottoman Muslim rule). More than 260,000 Muslims were killed or died from war-related causes, and more than a half million were driven out of Bulgaria, representing a total Muslim population loss of about 55 percent.[78] Gladstone had nothing to say about this either. There were no tracts, no atrocity propaganda, and no town hall meetings at which he spoke up for the Muslims plundered, robbed, and killed by Christians. The Muslim population of the remaining Ottoman territories was to be purged again in the Balkan War of 1912–13 (to be described later in this book). The war came to a diplomatic end at the Congress of Berlin in 1878; the treaty that ensued was like an ax blow directed against the roots of the Ottoman Empire. Encouraged by what the Bulgarians had achieved with European support, Macedonians and Armenians now launched their own insurrections.

This historical sketch shows the untruth of the phrase "Islam's bloody borders." In the give and take between "Islam" and "the West," borders have swayed back and forth over the centuries depending on military strength and diplomatic prowess, but no side has been favored all the time. From early in the nineteenth century the imperial West was deciding the borders and mostly Muslims, in Central Asia, the Caucasus, the Balkans, and Africa, were dying in the process. The Ottoman sultan was hard pressed to hold on to what he had, let alone impose borders on anyone, as the following chapters, which examine what happened when British and French armies entered the Muslim lands of the Near East, will show.

2. SCIENCE AND BARBARISM

At the very end of the eighteenth century the European powers began their assault on the Arab flanks of the Ottoman Empire. On July 2, 1798, Napoleon entered Alexandria at the head of a triumphant French army and began preparing for battle with the Mamluks.[1] In the Battle of the Pyramids on July 21, the Mamluk cavalry was shattered in the face of concentrated fire from the disciplined French squares. Egypt was a first step that would allow Napoleon to move overland toward British India, but the French ships had scarcely arrived before a British squadron under the command of Rear Admiral Horatio Nelson was hunting them down. The Battle of the Nile, fought on August 1 off Abu Qir (now a popular summer resort near Alexandria), ended in a crushing British victory. In Palestine, the assault on Akka by the Armée d'Orient collapsed when the British captured its siege cannon. Frustrated by the traditional enemy, Napoleon returned to France, but two more years of conflict followed between the French and a combination of British, Ottoman, and Mamluk forces before the occupation was finally ended in 1801.

Into the gap created by the defeat of the Mamluks and the departure of the French stepped a common Albanian soldier sent to Egypt as part of the Ottoman force. Mehmet Ali (in Arabic, Muhammad Ali, the father of Ibrahim and several other sons) demonstrated his capacity by crushing the remnants of the Mamluks, uniting the notables under his leadership, and persuading the sultan to invest him as his viceroy, but a strong Muslim ruler in Egypt was scarcely more acceptable to the British than Napoleon had been. In March 1807 an expeditionary force was dispatched under the command of General Mackenzie Fraser to block the rise of Egypt's new master, but in heavy fighting inland with Egyptian infantry and Albanian cavalry the British were forced to retreat to Alexandria, having lost nearly nine hundred men killed or wounded in the campaign. Hundreds of British prisoners were paraded through Cairo between the impaled heads of their fallen comrades. In September the British fleet sailed away, having failed to bring down a ruler who would repeatedly challenge their strategies in the Near East.[2]

In 1830 France launched its second great military assault on the Muslim lands of North Africa. The trigger three years earlier had been a celebration gone badly wrong. On April 29, 1827, the French consul-general in Algiers (Pierre Deval) had visited Hussein Dey, the local ruler, to pay his respects on the occasion of *'id al fitr* (the breaking of the fast after Ramadan). In conversation, the dey asked him why the French king had not responded to his inquiries about millions of francs owing to two Jewish finance houses for the shipment of grain for the French army. He wanted an answer because the finance houses owed him money and could not pay because of the unpaid French debt. M. Deval responded loftily with words to the effect that it was beneath his august majesty's dignity to deal with someone as lowly as the dey, at which point he was rapped sharply across the forearm with a peacock feather fly whisk and told to get out. Apologies demanded (by France) were not given, leading to a naval blockade and the dispatch from Toulon of an armada of more than three hundred ships loaded with thirty-five thousand soldiers and seamen. The fleet arrived on June 13. Within a month Algiers was in French hands.

It was not the first time that a dey had aroused the wrath of a distant government. All along the North African coast—the "Barbary Coast"—the finances of local rulers depended on the pirate raids and slave taking carried out across the Mediterranean by the "corsairs." The presence of Ottoman garrisons implied the sultan's tacit acceptance of the piratical means by which local rulers raised the revenue needed to pay the annual tribute to Istanbul, as well as maintain themselves in the style to which they were accustomed. These raiders were a menace to all ships traversing the Mediterranean as well as the residents of towns and villages on the other side of the water.

In 1804, after the capture of the U.S.S. *Philadelphia* and its three hundred men, U.S. navy lieutenant Stephen Decatur led his own party of raiders into Tripoli harbor and destroyed the ship as it lay at anchor. Eleven years later Decatur—by now a commodore—was sent to Algiers to bomb the town and the dey into submission. A treaty was signed but ignored almost as soon as the Americans left. In 1816 the British and Dutch made their own attempt to suppress this lair of piracy, sending a joint fleet that inflicted heavy damage on the town in a daylong bombardment, forcing its ruler to sign yet another treaty promising to bring piracy and the seizure of

Christians as hostages or slaves to an end. Again the treaty was ignored as soon as the ships sailed away.

French ships were also being harassed by the corsairs. The dey's behavior was such an affront to Christianity and maritime law that nothing was left but to remove him. The annoyed rap with the fly whisk was merely the final straw. Other reasons for sending the fleet across the Mediterranean could be advanced. One was Anglo-French rivalry (strategic, commercial, and colonial) and France's desire to capture Algiers before the British did. Yet another was the French king's wish to use a brilliant naval expedition abroad to outmaneuver a rebellious assembly at home and establish himself as an absolute monarch.[3] If this was the strategy it did not work, but by the time it was played out in Paris Algiers had been conquered, the dey had fled to Naples, and the army had begun moving into the interior. The assault on the city was ferocious. Civilians were cut down, property was plundered, and the sanctity of mosques was violated: it was an appropriate beginning for what was to become one of the worst Muslim experiences at the hands of an invading European power.

Occupation was followed by colonization. Tens of thousands of Frenchmen and women were shipped across the Mediterranean in the coming decade to turn Algeria into a North African extension of the homeland. Vast areas of land were seized and parceled out to the settlers, quarries were dug and vineyards planted. Ruedy estimates that the settlers took possession of more than 2,700,000 hectares of some of the richest cultivable land in the occupied territory.[4] By 1847 Algeria had a settler population of 109,380; by 1954 the number had increased to 984,000.[5] A two-tier law system was established, one for the settlers and another for the natives, with disputes between them being settled according to French law.

The occupation was exceptionally brutal. At the height of resistance in the 1840s, the French army resorted to the cruelest of measures in "pacifying" the Algerians. In one instance Pélissier, a future governor-general and marshal of France, caused the death by burning or asphyxiation of several hundred men, women, and children (the figures vary between five hundred and eight hundred) when he had fires lit at the entrance to the caves in which they were hiding. Abun-Nasr reports four occasions between 1844 and 1847 when French officers ordered the burning of Muslims in their caves "even after they offered to surrender."[6] Mosques were turned into churches. In one episode described by B. G. Martin, a French administrator in Algiers, the Duc de Rovigo, had a road built through two Muslim cemeteries, "scattering the skulls and bones of former beys, deys and notables in every direction."[7]

The Sufi brotherhoods were the principal network for mobilizing a proto-national resistance movement. Numerous pietistic charismatic figures also rose against the French out of the rural Muslim population, among them the female mystic-saint Lalla Zaynab and the "goat man" Bou Maza, who proclaimed himself Mahdi and vowed to drive the Europeans into the sea. Then there was another Mahdi, Bou Ziyan. In October 1849, his home village of Zaᶜatsha was besieged by eight thousand troops and its date palms were cut down. The French were armed with field artillery and bolt-loading rifles against Bou Ziyan's muskets and homemade bullets—"date pits covered with a thin layer of lead since this precious war material was in short supply."[8] The result was inevitable: "By December, 1849, the village was totally demolished, its inhabitants put to the sword and the region devastated; thousands fled from the ensuing repression; many more succumbed to the cholera epidemic unleashed by the confrontation. Lest others be tempted the French commander had Bu Ziyan's severed head exhibited on a pole at the entrance to Zaᶜatsha's ruins as a warning to future troublemakers."[9]

While suppressing revolts in North Africa, the French continued to consolidate their position around the Atlantic shoulder of the continent. Once West Africa was safely established as a French preserve, they could look farther afield. In late July 1896, an expedition led by Major Jean-Baptiste Marchand plunged into the heart of the continent from Loango. Thus began the "race for Fashoda"—in fact a race for the Upper Nile—as the French, the Belgians, and the British closed in on the southern Sudan from the west, the north, and the southwest in what David Levering Lewis has described as "one of the great galvanic moments of the last century."[10] The Belgian expedition was brought to a digestive end when the Congolese soldiers revolted against their brutal officers and ate them, but the French managed to get there, planting the flag on the banks of the Nile at the old slaving outpost of Fashoda on July 10, 1898. The British had just crushed the Mahdiyya at Omdurman when news reached them that they had been trumped upstream by one of their great imperial rivals. On September 19 a gunboat was sent to Fashoda to deal with the problem. The British set up a rival camp, and for a brief period the confrontation threatened to end in an imperial war before the French backed down and instructed Marchand to leave.

"EGYPT FOR THE EGYPTIANS"

In Egypt the khedives had slowly sunk into a morass of debt. Mehmet Ali, understanding full well where economic dependence leads, had refused to accept money from foreign lenders. His descendants had to learn the lesson the hard way. They borrowed heavily on European markets to finance various projects. Indebtedness had compelled the Khedive Ismail to sell Egypt's share of the Suez Canal company to Britain for the paltry sum of £4 million, but this only temporarily slowed an accelerating slide into bankruptcy. In April 1876, Ismail was forced to suspend the payment of interest on treasury bonds. He signed his private estates over to the government, dismissed army officers, and delayed the payment of retirement benefits, but these measures only staved off the day of reckoning. The country's finances and public works were placed under the dual control of the British and the French, but by 1879 the situation was such a mess that the two powers had succeeded in securing the sultan's assent to Ismail's deposition in favor of his son Tawfiq.

By this time the nationalists had adopted a slogan that was to be repeated until Egypt finally won independence through the revolution of 1952: "Egypt for the Egyptians." Their leader was Urabi Pasha, an army colonel. Patriotic and a man of the people, whereas the khedive was an alien in all ways, he had risen through the ranks, capturing the imagination of the people and compelling the khedive (whom he regarded as no more than an instrument of foreign domination) to bring him into the government. By late spring 1882 popular support for Urabi had forced the khedive to accept him as war minister. The establishment of a defiant patriotic government ended foreign supervision of Egypt's finances. The controllers left the country. Momentarily impotent, Britain and France demanded that the khedive dismiss the government and send Urabi and his troublemaking colleagues into the country. No sooner had he bowed to their demands than the Alexandria garrison mutinied, forcing Tawfiq to reappoint the ministry as quickly as he had brought about its downfall.

A torrent of propaganda was now directed against Urabi from afar. Egypt had "fallen into the hands of a clique of obscure officers, most of whose names had never been heard of in Egypt twelve months before."[11] Gladstone, using language strikingly reminiscent of Sir Anthony Eden's attacks on President Gamal abd Al Nasser in 1956, called Urabi a "usurper and dictator."[12] British and French warships were sent to Alexandria in the name of being on hand to protect the lives of Europeans should the "rabble" turn on them. They took up their positions in the late spring and lay waiting, as motionless at anchor as couched animals on a hot day. The British fleet consisted of nine warships (*Alexandra*—the flagship—*Inflexible, Superb, Téméraire, Sultan, Condor, Monarch, Invincible,* and *Penelope*) and five gunboats *(Bittern, Cygnet, Beacon, Helicon,* and *Decoy)* fitted with "torpedo apparatus" as well as the Gatling guns and Nordenfeld cannon with

which the ironclads were also equipped. They were later joined by the warship *Achilles*. This display of naval power must have filled the inhabitants of
the city with rising apprehension as the days went by without the warships
moving.

Alexandria's population of about 230,000 included 70,000 "Europeans,"
a category that included Maltese, Armenians, Greeks, and Jews as well as
the nationals of European states (including about 4,500 Britons). The
provocative, ominous presence of the warships inevitably ended in disturbances. On June 11, a fight in the Rue des Soeurs between two donkey
boys—one a Maltese Christian and the other a Muslim—triggered rioting
in which about 300 people died. The estimated 150 European dead included
the chief engineer of the *Superb* and two other Englishmen, Mr. Ribton
and Mr. Pibworth, who were "literally done to death" in the street.[13]
Many of the victims were Maltese; others were Muslims cut down with
rifles distributed beforehand to local Christians by the British consul (Mr.
Cookson, who was seriously injured in the rioting) with the help and planning of the commander of the British fleet and the "implicit backing" of
the Foreign Office and the Admiralty.[14]

News of the rioting caused panic in Cairo. Thousands of European and
local Christians fled to Alexandria to book passages on ships out of the
country. About fourteen thousand had left by June 17, and a further eight
thousand were waiting to leave. The departure of so many trained personnel threatened to disrupt government services, including railways, posts,
telegraphs, and the provision of water to Alexandria.[15] The khedive was
urged to move government offices to the port city, where the British fleet
riding at anchor would be close at hand in case of further trouble.

A conference that was convened in Constantinople to resolve the crisis
ended without a solution being found. On July 3, the commander of the
British flotilla (Sir Beauchamp Seymour) warned the Egyptian government to stop strengthening coastal fortifications at Alexandria or face the
consequences, and on July 9 Gladstone gave his approval for an attack two
days later. Having stationed their warships off the coast of another country and triggered serious disorders by their presence, the British now
claimed the right to attack as "a measure of self defence."[16]

"MATURED SCIENCE AND MODERN SKILL"

Alexandria was about to be turned into a testing ground for the latest
advances in British military technology, including hydraulics, swiveling
gun platforms, and compound armor. The standard British guns were supe-

rior to the Egyptian in every respect. They had a larger bore, faster muzzle velocity (the speed at which the shell leaves the barrel), and much more effective target penetration at a far greater range. The guns were mounted on rotating platforms on the *Téméraire* and within rotating turrets on the *Inflexible*, allowing both ships to fire in different directions without having to change position; they could also fire from a distance of up to five thousand yards, putting them well outside the range of the shore guns. The *Inflexible* was the first warship in the Royal Navy to be fitted with compound armor and underwater torpedo tubes. Each of its four "monster guns," as they were described in the London newspapers, now about to be fired for the first time in action, weighed eighty-one tons, had a barrel length of 26 feet, 9 inches, and could fire a 1,700-pound projectile (propelled by a charge of 370 pounds of powder and traveling a third of a mile a second) capable of penetrating twenty-two inches of iron plate at a thousand yards. Every shell fired from one of these guns cost the British taxpayer £25 10s.[17] The destructive power of the *Téméraire*'s four twenty-five-ton guns and four eighteen-ton guns was also very great. Against this massed naval might, the Egyptian shore guns were almost completely ineffective; Sir Beauchamp had no reason not to sleep well on the night of July 10.[18]

At 5:15 A.M. the Egyptian government sent a steamer to the *Alexandra* with a message accepting the British demands to stop work on the shore forts, only to receive a message from Sir Beauchamp that "the time for negotiations was past."[19] The ships took up battle stations ranging from 1,000 to 3,700 yards offshore and opened up at 7:00 A.M., when the *Alexandra* fired the first shell at the Adda fort. The shelling continued until 5:00 P.M. "All that matured science and modern skill could add to the inhuman science of death, mutilation and dire destruction was at work now," one commentator wrote.[20] Another thought the spectacle as exciting as watching a rugby match between Eton and Harrow.[21] The effect on the Egyptian defenders as the coastal forts were pulverized by these giant shells was understandably demoralizing.[22]

Mansions on the shoreline were shattered. Even the royal palace at Ras al Tin was set on fire, starting in the harem and burning through the day. In the European quarter of the city, hotels, consulates, and shops were destroyed by the shelling or set on fire and pillaged as outraged Muslims struck back. As the bombardment continued, the French, Portuguese, and British consulates burnt to the ground. The Anglican church was damaged by a shell. The central market lay in ruins, the main square looked as if it had been swept by a hurricane, and some streets were so choked with debris that they could be traversed only in single file. The destruction was so great that a British correspondent who had lived in the city for seventeen years could no longer recognize the street where he lived even when he was standing in it. The European quarter was still burning days later. Perhaps two thousand Egyptian soldiers and an unknown number of civilians lay dead in the ruins of the forts or in the bombarded and burned center of the city. Admiral Seymour, the British government, and the London newspapers blamed bedouin, convicts, Egyptian soldiers, and incendiaries for the damage when most of the destruction had clearly been caused by the naval shelling. The British finally restored the order they had just destroyed by clearing the streets with Gatling guns, shooting arsonists, and hanging or flogging looters in what was left of the main square, but by this time most of Alexandria had been turned into "rubble and ash."[23] In this welter of death and destruction British military casualties amounted to five killed and twenty-seven wounded.

After the event it was argued that "the bombardment of this magnificent city, so long the emporium of Oriental commerce, produced dire consequences which had not been foreseen and to preclude which no measures had been taken."[24] European residents of the town were shocked that they had not been warned. "Had Admiral Seymour given even forty-eight hours notice of his intentions to bombard, he and his government would have been spared the frightful responsibility which now weighs upon them of causing the horrible death of European men, women and children who perished miserably in the interior and the deaths of hundreds of Egyptian women and children who perished in the bombardment and in the panic flight from the hastily bombarded town."[25] In the wake of the shelling, reports started to come in from Zagazig, Tantah, Damanhour, Mahalla al Kabir, and other towns of the gruesome killings of Europeans (including an entire family dragged out of their train and laid across the line in front of the engine).

Having established themselves in Alexandria, the British were now reinforced by a land army of more than forty thousand, many of them Indian Army veterans of the campaigns in Afghanistan. The pursuit of Urabi inland involved all the paraphernalia of a great imperial army on the move, from field hospitals, a postal department, and a wagon with a printing press (a wartime propaganda first) to pontoons, war balloons, heliographic equipment, and an armored siege train.[26] A "specially ingenious arrangement" enabled a forty-pounder or a Gatling gun to be fired from the carriages without the train being damaged from the recoil.[27]

Urabi made his final stand at Tal al Kabir on September 12. The British force of thirteen thousand launched a night attack on a force at least twice the size and routed it. "Enemy ran away in thousands, throwing away their arms when overtaken by our cavalry," telegrammed the British commander, Sir Garnet Wolseley. "Their loss is very great."[28] The bodies of thousands of slain Egyptians "lay in heaps of thirty and fifty" across the battlefield. Many were headless, while others had been disemboweled or "literally cut in two."[29] The British losses were almost trivial: nine officers and forty-eight NCOs and men killed, twenty-seven officers and 353 NCOs wounded, and twenty-two men missing. Urabi was captured and exiled to Ceylon for eighteen years after a sham trial. In the meantime, "Mr Gladstone went out of his way to contend that the landing of British troops in Egypt was not an act of war."[30] Apparently the bombardment, invasion, and battlefield butchery were all acts of something else.

THE MAHDIYYA

Upon occupying Egypt, the British moved quickly to extend their reach down the Nile. In September 1883 an expeditionary force left Khartum under the command of General William Hicks to bring order to regions from which reports had come of a religious uprising. Hicks had ten thousand men at his disposal, including seven thousand infantry, five hundred cavalry, four hundred mounted irregulars, and one hundred cuirassiers "dressed in medieval coats of mail," along with twenty field guns, five thousand camels, and five hundred horses.[31] Waiting to meet him were tens of thousands of warriors of the Mahdiyya, another protonational movement, this time centering on the religious teachings and charismatic power of one Muhammad Ahmad. The British called his followers "dervishes"; they called themselves *ansar* (helpers), a word linking Muhammad Ahmad's army to the sympathizers who had given the Prophet Muhammad sanctuary in Medina when he had to flee Mecca.

The size of the Hicks force was more impressive than the quality of the fighting men. The officers were British, but the infantry were Egyptian and trained so poorly in these early years of the occupation that the first parade in Khartum turned into a fiasco. Hicks himself was a retired Indian Army officer with "little experience of commanding troops in the field."[32] Months of preparation and squabbling over money preceded the expedition's departure for the province of Kordofan. Twelve days after leaving Khartum it reached al Dueim, 130 miles away. After a final decision had been taken on the route to be followed farther south, the army set out again on September 27, a "great crawling mass in the formation of a vast square, with all the camels, baggage and stores in the centre" presenting a target that "no marksman, however erratic, could miss."[33]

What followed was a catastrophe unfolding stage by stage. Short of water, marching through thorn bush in barren country stippled by dry watercourses and continually harassed by guerrilla attacks, the force steadily disintegrated. On November 5, Hicks broke the army down into three squares, forming the points of a triangle and separated by hundreds of yards, perhaps to present smaller targets rather than one big one (as Theobald writes), but at the risk of exposing the whole force to piecemeal destruction. The same day the Mahdi mustered his forces for prayer and then ordered the final attack. Square by square the invading army was wiped out. Hicks and his officers died as their men were "butchered all around them."[34] Few prisoners were taken and few escaped.[35] When the news reached Cairo the shock was profound: as Neillands puts it, "the British were not accustomed to having their generals slaughtered."[36] Further disasters were in store, beginning with the destruction in February 1884 of the expedition sent inland from the Red Sea under the command of General Valentine Baker. This was not a proper army but an Egyptian force cobbled together, according to Edward Dicey, from police constables, fellahin, young men dragooned in their villages, and "the refuse of the state prisons."[37] Of the force of 4,000 men, 2,500 were killed. The destruction of the Baker force was followed by the killing of the shotgun-toting adventurer Fred Burnaby at Abu Tulaih and finally the recapture of Khartum in 1885 and the killing of General Gordon.

Shortly after the death of Gordon the Mahdi died of typhus. To the British he was a "Muhammadan fanatic." The view from the Muslim side is well summed up by Neillands: "Few leaders of any nation have achieved as much as the Mahdi in such a short space of time. In four years he had freed his country from the Egyptians and defeated the British. He had returned his people to what he saw to be the true path of the Muslim religion and demonstrated how effective and inspiring this doctrine could be. After seventy years of foreign domination the Sudan was free. The Mahdi was, and remains today, a hundred years after his death, a hero to his people and his creation, the Mahdiya, is still remembered as a golden age."[38] Muslims elsewhere were inspired by his victories.

ERASING THE "BARBARIANS"

In the final great collision with the British at Omdurman on September 2, 1898, the warriors assembled under the leadership of the Khalifa Abdullah (the Mahdi's successor) could have had only the faintest understanding of the killing machine facing them on the other side of the battlefield.

They were brave, but they were equipped with weapons—swords, lances, muskets, and a few modern rifles—that were virtually useless against the artillery, concentrated rifle fire, and the Maxim gun (invented in 1883). The Maxim was a most versatile killing machine. It could be stood on legs, wheeled onto the battlefield, bolted to the deck of a ship, or towed by a team of six horses. This version was known as the "galloping Maxim."[39] General Kitchener had positioned twenty Maxims on the battlefield near Omdurman alongside forty-four field guns (including howitzers and twelve-pounders) and sundry other artillery pieces bolted to the decks of Nile steamers converted into gunboats.

The Khalifa had already been weakened by severe losses at the hands of the British. In the Battle of Atbara (on April 8), twelve thousand British or British-commanded Egyptian troops had collided with an *ansar* army of sixteen thousand consisting of Baggara tribal cavalry and *jihadiyya* (holy war) infantry. "The results gained could not be overstated," wrote the correspondent G. W. Steevens. "Mahmud's army was as if it had never been. These two short hours of shell and bullet and bayonet had erased it from the face of the earth."[40] Yet the Khalifa was still able to send fifty to sixty thousand warriors to confront the British at Omdurman.

The battle began on a plain six miles from the town at 5:30 A.M. when a wall of men and cavalry began sweeping toward the British lines along a front of three to four miles. They were carrying tribal battle standards and the black standard of the Khalifa. The British waited until the running warriors were eight hundred yards away before shattering them with Maxim and rifle fire from serried ranks of soldiers. Thousands of men were cut down in this first blinding storm of metal poured in their direction. "The torrent swept into them and hurled them down in whole companies," wrote Steevens.[41] The survivors threw themselves to the ground and began "emptying their poor, rotten home-made cartridges dauntlessly."[42] Some managed to kill the enemy, but British losses were not to be compared to "the awful slaughter of the Dervishes. If they still came on, our men needed only time and ammunition and strength to point a rifle to kill them off to the very last man."[43]

By 11:30 the battle was over. Strewn across the killing field were the bodies of an estimated 9,700 Sudanese dead and another 10,000 to 16,000 wounded, many of whom must have died for want of treatment. Of the 8,200 British soldiers and 17,600 Egyptians who went into battle, 3 officers and 25 men from the British division and 2 officers and 18 men from the Egyptian division were killed. The casualties were "so small as to be ridiculous."[44] "Talk of fun! Where will you beat this?" So wrote

Winston Churchill, attached to the Twenty-first Lancers as a supernumerary lieutenant and reporting on the battle for the *Morning Post*.[45] The weapons, the methods, and the fanaticism of the Middle Ages had again collided with the organization and inventions of the nineteenth century. "Thus ended the battle of Omdurman—the most signal triumph ever gained by the arms of science over barbarians."[46]

After victory the British advanced into the town, "this huge fungoid growth of barbarism and immorality of every description."[47] Stopping by the shattered dome of the Mahdi's tomb, they made the local people pull out his remains. These were burned in the furnace of one of the steamers and the ashes "thrown into the Nile."[48] Only the skull was retained. Churchill later condemned the "barbarous manner" in which the Mahdi's skull had been carried away in a kerosene tin, the same means by which General Gordon's head had been taken to the Mahdi in 1885.[49] No medical aid was delivered to the wounded Sudanese, for which Kitchener was criticized at home.

Omdurman was a shambles. Sections of the town were in ruins. Mud walls could scarcely stand against the impact of lyddite shells. The outskirts were devastated, but "the scenes inside the city were more terrible than in the suburbs. The effects of the bombardment were evident on every side. Women and children lay frightfully mangled in the roadway. At one place a whole family had been crushed by a projectile. Dead Dervishes, already in the heat beginning to decompose, dotted the ground. The houses were crowded with wounded. Hundreds of decaying carcasses of animals filled the air with a sickening smell."[50] The day after the victory a memorial service was held for Gordon where he had been cut down in 1885. British and Egyptian bands played selections from Handel before turning to "Abide with Me" (Gordon's favorite). Civilization had triumphed over barbarism only if the two could be distinguished so neatly. "The English gentleman is half barbarian, too. That is the value of him," Steevens reflected.[51] The Khalifa was finally trapped and killed in November 1899, marking the end of the Mahdiyya, but resistance continued wherever Muslim lands were occupied.

Around the horn of Africa the "Mad Mullah of Somaliland" evaded British capture for two decades. As Martin has observed, the "Mad Mullah" (Sayyid Muhammad bin Abdullah Hasan) was "neither insane nor a mullah (in this context an Anglo-Indian term reserved for Muslim clerics) but an important Somali intellectual and religious leader."[52] The British sent expeditions after him in 1901, 1902, 1903, 1904, and 1910–11 but met with little success. After the First World War they began using De Havilland DH 9 bombers in combination with infantry and camel-mounted troops. They "counted on the factors of surprise and fright as well as on the ability of the pilots to pursue the dervishes from the air, bombing and machine-gunning with little fear of retaliation."[53] The Sayyid fought on from the Ogaden but died in December 1920 at the age of fifty-six. "Somalis, arise from sleep!" began one of his last poems. If "Muslims" is substituted for "Somalis," it is an injunction that still echoes around the Muslim world.

By the time British planes were chasing the "Mad Mullah," the "powers"—Britain, France, and Russia—were within reach of grasping the richest prize of all: the vast central lands of the Ottoman Empire, stretching from southeastern Europe to the Persian Gulf and bounded by the fertile coastlines of three seas (the Aegean, the Black Sea, and the Mediterranean). These contained great rivers and natural resources, probably including more of the oil that had just been discovered at Masjid al Sulaiman in Persia (1908), and were ruled from one of the greatest cities of all—Istanbul.

PART II. SACRED TRUSTS

3. OTTOMAN BREAKDOWN

In the 1880s the Ottoman sultan, Abdülhamit II, recalled his first encounter with a British ambassador:

> When a young boy of eight years I happened to be in the society of my father, of blessed memory, when the British ambassador, then Lord Stratford Canning, was announced and at once admitted. My father, being intimately connected with this great man and sincere friend of Turkey, they embraced each other and the ambassador kissed me. In those days we were not accustomed to mix up so freely with Christians, fanaticism was much stronger than today and as it was for the first time that the lips of a Christian had touched my lips an intense shudder and horror overcame me and I began to cry. Thereupon my father approached me and said: "You must not be shocked at being kissed by this man for he represents a nation which is full of sincere friendship for our country and which treats the Turks like brothers." Of course I was astonished to hear to hear this. I raised my eyes to Lord Stratford and from this very moment the idea of Anglo-Turkish friendship grew with me.[1]

The point of the story was how things had changed. In 1878 the Ottoman Empire's good friend had joined other diplomats in divesting it of a mass of territory at Berlin. It occupied Egypt in 1882. In the 1890s it was still trying to push the sultan into accepting "reforms" for the Armenians, no matter how many times he told them they were unworkable and dangerous. This same good friend had persuaded the sultan to hand over Cyprus and had then turned a blind eye when Armenian revolutionaries smuggled arms from the island to the Anatolian coast.[2] Abdülhamit felt that the British were treating him with a lack of respect, for his opinions and for his position as sultan-caliph, and like anyone who feels let down he was receptive to approaches from those who promised to be more reliable.

He was interested in the United States because it was new, but it was also far away. Outside the old European imperial circle only Germany fitted the bill. It had no known designs on Ottoman territory. It did not poke its nose into what the sultan regarded as his business. It was industrious and productive. Its Krupp factories made the best cannon in the world, and its navy and merchant marine were beginning to challenge British domination of the high seas, so there were all sorts of reasons for the sultan to give the Kaiser an especially warm welcome when he visited Istanbul in 1898. In this period—the last two decades of the nineteenth century—the foundations of the German-Ottoman alliance of 1914–18 were built over the ruins of the Anglo-Ottoman friendship of earlier years.

BALKAN BREAKDOWN

The Young Turks' revolution (July 1908) and the restoration of the constitution (declared in 1876 and suspended in 1877) were greeted with general euphoria, but over the next four years the transition to a parliamentary regime was repeatedly blown off course by counterrevolution and by ethno-religious violence. In 1909, agitated by "greatly exaggerated" stories of the activities of Armenian revolutionaries, Muslims turned on Armenians living in and around Adana.[3] Perhaps eighteen thousand Armenians and two thousand Muslims died in this rekindling of the hatred and fanaticism that had torn the eastern provinces apart in 1894–96. The turmoil in Istanbul—excitement mixed with uncertainty—was quickly exploited by Balkan governments. On October 5, 1908, the autonomous principality of Bulgaria declared its independence of the Ottoman Empire and installed Prince Ferdinand as tsar. On October 7 Greece annexed Crete. The same day the Austro-Hungarian government breached the 1878 Treaty of Berlin by annexing Bosnia and Herzegovina, which had nominally remained within the Ottoman Empire. Russia, Germany, England, France, and Italy all reacted with alarm to this threat to their alliances and their interests in the Balkans. The crisis lasted for six months and threatened to bring on a general European war six years before it finally broke out.[4]

In 1910 it was the turn of the Albanians to rise up against the Ottoman authorities in the name of freedom and independence. In 1911 Italy jumped into this fast-developing free-for-all, launching a propaganda campaign centering on the "mistreatment" of Italians in the two Libyan provinces of Tripolitania and Cyrenaica before declaring war on September 29, 1911. Once the Italians had suppressed the Ottoman garrisons on the coast they began spreading out into the interior, where they were resisted by Sanusi tribal warriors, fighting in the name of jihad, alongside Ottoman troops sent from Istanbul under the command of Enver Paşa and Mustafa Kemal (later Atatürk). A proposal by the chief of the general staff in June 1912 that Italy should declare total war on the empire was not followed through, but Italy did occupy islands in the eastern Mediterranean and launch naval attacks on the straits leading into the Sea of Marmara.

While the diplomats were negotiating an end to the war in North Africa, Montenegro, Bulgaria, Serbia, and Greece were preparing to drive the Turks out of Europe once and for all. Montenegro opened the campaign by declaring war on October 8, 1912, the very day Ottoman and Italian diplomats ended the war in Africa with a treaty signed in the romantic setting of the Lake Geneva port town of Ouchy. Declarations of war on the Ottoman Empire by the other three members of the "Anti-Ottoman League" followed ten days later.

EXTIRPATION OF THE MUSLIMS

As much as the Balkan Christians fought and intrigued among themselves, the extirpation of the Muslims was a central unifying element in their history. The unraveling of Muslim power through the piecemeal partition of the Ottoman Empire in the nineteenth century allowed Balkan Christians to express their animosity and their intentions more openly. Bishop Petar Njegoš's 1857 novel *The Mountain Wreath* centers on the extermination of the Muslims of Montenegro by the Serbs in the eighteenth century. The bishops and notables decide "to honor the feast day of Pentecost by cleansing the nation of non-Christians," and the book culminates with "a graphic depiction of the Christmas-day slaughter of these Slavic Muslims of Montenegro—men, women and children—and the annihilation of their homes, mosques and other monuments."[5] In 1877–78, the Russian-Ottoman War had opened a vent for the release of these hatreds, and in 1912 the turmoil in Istanbul created the opportunity for another round of religiously driven massacre and dispossession of Balkan Muslims.

The assault by the Balkan states on the Ottoman Empire in 1912 was manifestly a religious war—a crusade—in which aged ecclesiastics stood alongside military commanders and Balkan kings and queens in cathedrals overhung with crucifixes and packed with the faithful as the priests exhorted them to join the struggle against the Muslim Turks in the name of an oppressed Christianity. One by one the Balkan monarchs—Ferdinand of Bulgaria, George of Greece, Nikola of Montenegro (father-in-law of King Victor Emmanuel of Italy), and Petar of Serbia—joined the anti-Ottoman pact, and on September 30 their four governments mobilized simultaneously. The Bulgarian and Serbian armies—the strongest of the four in the "defensive alliance"—were equipped with the latest in European weaponry, their stocks including Mannlicher and Mauser carbines, howitzers, Krupp and Schneider-Creusot mountain batteries, and large-bore siege artillery. Facing the combined Christian forces of 912,000 men and the Bulgarian and Serbian terrorist *komitadjis* who would move into conquered territories as the Muslims were driven out were 580,000 Ottoman soldiers.[6] But for many of these soldiers there were not enough arms to go around. Some were sent to the front only to be sent back because there were no weapons.

King Nikola declared war on October 8. Bulgaria and Serbia followed suit on October 17 and Greece on October 19. King Ferdinand made his announcement in the cathedral of Starazagora, the forward headquarters of the army command: "In this struggle of the Cross against the Crescent, of liberty against tyranny we shall have the sympathy of all those who love justice and progress."[7] As soon as the troops began to move, the Greek prime minister, Eleutherios Venizelos, sent a message to his friend James Bourchier, the *Times* correspondent and "unattached diplomatist" who had "broken up the Turkish Empire in Europe."[8] Bourchier had been traveling between Balkan capitals with the message that the only way the Christians could get the Turks out of southeastern Europe would be to join forces and drive them out. Wrote Venizelos: "I thank you and I clasp your hand as one of the principal artisans of this magnificent work of cementing the union of the Christian peoples of the Peninsula."

The "ninth crusade" had begun.[9] The Greeks moved north toward the Macedonian city of Salonica: when they captured it on November 8 (just ahead of the Bulgarians), Athens rejoiced with church bells and cannon fire. For the first time since the surrender of Granada in 1492, a "great Christian city" had been "rescued from the infidel and brought once more under the standard of the Cross."[10] King George arrived in triumph on November 11, taking part in the celebratory mass in the cathedral before formally entering the city behind a squadron of cavalry the next day.[11] In the meantime the Bulgarians were advancing rapidly toward Istanbul, capturing Kirkkilise, besieging Edirne (Adrianople), and inflicting crushing defeats on the Turks at Lüleburgaz (an important junction town) and Çorlu. By the first week of November they had reached the outskirts of the Ottoman capital. The artillery bombardment along the front at Çatalca (twenty-five miles away) was so intense it could be heard in the city. People gathered in the streets and on rooftops to listen. A state of siege and a 10:00 P.M. curfew had been declared on October 30, and now sailors were landed from European warships anchored in the Sea of Marmara in case popular anger at reports of Bulgarian atrocities degenerated into an attack on foreign European residents.

By the middle of November "the Turkish rule at Constantinople seemed to be doomed."[12] A truce signed on December 4 allowed peace talks to begin in London on December 16. Immense pressure was applied to the Ottoman delegation to surrender Edirne. On January 22, the news that the city had been conceded to Bulgaria brought about the overthrow of the government in Istanbul and the rejection of the proposed settlement. The Bulgarians resumed their bombardment of Edirne on February 3, and on March 26 the city surrendered. Between fifty thousand and sixty thousand civilians had died during the siege; the remaining Muslim population was subjected to a wave of terror as the Bulgarians took over. By now the Ottoman presence in Europe had been virtually ended, with the sole exception of the great city straddling the Bosporus, but a reprieve was unexpectedly at hand: in attacking the Ottomans the Balkan states had "set in motion rivalries among themselves which they could not control."[13]

The problem was Macedonia. The Internal Macedonian Revolutionary Movement (IMRO) had launched a series of uprisings against Ottoman authority during the previous two decades, but the territory the Macedonian nationalists wanted for their independent state was also the object of desire of Greece, Bulgaria, and Serbia. In November 1912 the Albanians had declared their independence, and when this was ratified by the powers, Serbia and Montenegro were obliged to withdraw from the Albanian territory they had captured from the Ottomans. Serbia sought compensation in Macedonia; the Greeks, who had been engaged in skirmishes with the Bulgarians in and around Salonica ever since capturing the city, supported the Serbs against Bulgarian claims to the same territory. When peace talks broke down in June 1913, Bulgaria attacked Serb and Greek positions in Macedonia. Montenegro and Rumania (which came into the war in July) joined in on the Serbian side, and the Bulgarians—now also under attack by the Ottomans—were quickly defeated and forced to surrender most of their wartime gains. The slaughter by the Christians of each other in this second Balkan war, and especially the atrocities committed against the Bulgarian peasant population by the Greek and Serb armies, was every bit as vicious as their slaughter of the Muslims.

Taking advantage of this collapse of Christian unity, the Ottomans managed to recapture Edirne (July 22) and eastern Trakya (Thrace), but by the time the last of the peace agreements had been signed with the belligerent states, just before the outbreak of the First World War, they had lost more than 80 percent of their remaining territory on the European side of the Bosporus. Coming less than half a century after the eviscerating partition of Ottoman lands effected through the Treaty of Berlin, the attack by the Balkan states was another mighty ax blow delivered to the roots of the empire. The European powers that had given away great tracts of Ottoman territory at Berlin while guaranteeing the sanctity of what remained looked the other way as the remains of the treaty were torn up on the battlefield. The outcome (ratified in the August 1913 Treaty of Bucharest) satisfied no one, not the governments and not the hundreds of thousands of people driven from their homes during the war. The settlement was "not one of justice but force," wrote Viscount Grey,[14] and the "peace" no more than a temporary accommodation. Within a year, all Europe was swept into what Grey described as "the cataract of war" rising from its headwaters in the Balkans when a Serbian nationalist assassinated the heir to the Austro-Hungarian throne and his wife in Sarajevo on June 28, 1914.[15]

DEATH AND DEPOPULATION

The military losses on all sides during 1912–13 were very great compared to those of previous wars if not those of wars yet to come. The Ottomans alone lost about 250,000 men dead or wounded. The First and Second Armies were broken; the military was still being reorganized and reconstituted when the First World War broke out, partly accounting for the crushing defeats the Ottomans suffered in the early stages of the war. The breakup of the Balkan coalition flooded Sofia and other cities with Christian refugees. Atrocities were committed against Christian villagers, but it was primarily the suffering of the Muslims that turned the Balkan War into the first great European human tragedy of the twentieth century. In the territories taken from the Ottoman Empire in 1912–13, Muslims had constituted an overall majority of the population before the war began, but by the time it ended they had been reduced to a minority. McCarthy has calculated that of the 2,315,293 Muslims living in the territories taken from the Ottoman Empire during the Balkan War, 1,445,179 (62 percent of the Muslim population) were gone by the time it ended. Of this number, 812,771 survived as refugees, but 632,404 (27 percent of the Muslim population) were dead.[16] It will be remembered that this followed the massive purging of Muslims in the Ottoman-Russian War of 1877–78.

The situation in Istanbul and along the Aegean coast was chaotic as tens of thousands of Muslims fled in panic before the advance of the Balkan armies. Behind them lay hundreds of abandoned villages. There was good reason for the panic that drove them onwards. Reports of massacres and numerous other atrocities—including the burning of villagers alive in barns and mosques, the destruction of villages, rape, pillage, and the theft of crops and animals—were coming in from all directions and from numerous sources. The British vice-consul at Kavalla reported that the track of the Bulgarian army was marked by "80 miles of ruined villages."[17] The destruction of mosques and forced conversion of Muslims to Christianity were further indications that "the obvious intention of those who murdered Muslims and forced their exodus was to 'de-Turkify' the Balkans."[18] The roads to the Ottoman capital were clogged with long straggling lines of men, women, and children and wounded soldiers trying to make their way to some kind of safety on foot or in the back of carts. Eastern Trakya (Thrace) was left "an unpeopled waste."[19]

Before long a new force joined the struggle, "invisible and deadlier than the Bulgarians." "Men stiffened, stumbled forwards, lay on the ground arching themselves backwards as they retched up a poison that had come from Asia. In a few hours they were dead and their bodies turned blue."[20] This enemy striking indiscriminately at whomever it encountered was cholera. Global pandemics were common up to the twentieth century. Epidemics had swept across the Ottoman Empire in 1910 and 1911. In the most recent war (with Greece in 1897), outbreaks of typhus, dysentery, malaria, and cholera had taken the lives of thirty thousand Ottoman soldiers alone.[21] Cholera was an old enemy and now it "traveled the country with the rapidity of the Black Death, infected the army and threatened to devastate all Turkey."[22]

Between Istanbul and the Ottoman front line at Çatalca corpses lay in ditches or in heaps by the road; in the desperation of their thirst, refugees and soldiers had drunk from puddles and streams tainted by the bodies of dead horses and then died themselves. The dead and the dying were brought in from the surrounding district to the nearby village of Hadımköy. This was where the general staff had established its frontline headquarters, but it was no more immune from the rapidly traveling disease than anywhere else. "I saw pictures of misery that were never recorded before," wrote one correspondent.[23] The dead were thrown onto a "grisly pile" before being pulled into a trench with hooks, the terrible smell attracting wolves from the Belgrade Forest, near the meeting point of the Bosporus and the Black Sea.[24] Cholera took the lives of an estimated forty thousand Ottoman soldiers along the Çatalca defense line in 1912 alone.[25]

Many of the sick were dead by the time the trains carrying them to Istanbul reached Yeşilköy (Green Village) or the last stop at Sirkeci station.

At Yeşilköy they were carried to tents or laid on the ground because there were not enough tents to go around. An estimated twenty thousand cholera victims were taken to Yeşilköy alone during the course of the war.[26] From Sirkeci the ill were moved on to a lazaretto at Beykoz, on the Asian side of the Bosporus, or carried to hastily improvised hospitals in police stations, military barracks, mosques (including Aya Sofia), and government buildings, where Red Cross and Red Crescent Society doctors, nurses, and volunteers (Ottoman and Indian) tried to look after them. "The scenes in these crowded buildings were beyond all description," a correspondent for the London *Daily Chronicle* wrote on November 21. "It was impossible to attend to more than a tithe of the sufferers, many of whom were carried into the mosques only to be soon carried out dead without having received any attention in the interval."[27] Others were carried into parks and gardens because there was nowhere else to put them. Below Topkapi palace, "the open ground at Seraglio Point was strewn with dying soldiers who had been carried there from the railway station and left to die unattended."[28] Some of the refugees given shelter in mosques were still camping in the courtyards when Arnold Toynbee visited the Near East in 1921.[29]

THE LAST OTTOMAN WAR

For Europe the Great War began in 1914 and ended in 1918. For the Turks the Great War began in 1912 and ended in 1923, the First World War being preceded by conflict in the Balkans and followed by more conflict in western Anatolia, southeastern Anatolia, and the Caucasus until the final peace settlement of 1923. By spring 1915 Ottoman armies were fighting the British and their allies at Gallipoli, the Russians in northeastern Anatolia and the Caucasus, and the British in Mesopotamia, with a military footnote soon to be added through the "Arab revolt" on the Arabian peninsula. While battlefield losses on all fronts were heavy, the greatest suffering by far was experienced by the civilian population. The emphasis on military campaigns (especially at Gallipoli) in Western histories of the First World War has not yet been balanced by studies on the effects of the war on the civilian population of the Ottoman Empire. There is no reliable figure for the number of deaths from all causes, but there is a tremendous discrepancy between Ottoman military and civilian losses and those of the entente powers. French battlefield deaths were 1,375,800; British, 703,000; Ottoman, between 550,000 and 600,000 (a further 891,000 soldiers were disabled).[30] French civilian losses were about forty thousand and British more than thirty thousand, but the Ottoman figure was probably somewhere between three and four million. No other country—not even Russia with its 1.7 million battlefield and two million civilian dead—suffered so greatly.

Starvation and disease spread across Ottoman lands and into the Caucasus as the effects of the war began to bite. Food was soon in short supply, and the conscription of all able-bodied young men meant that only old men, women, and children were available to sow and harvest the crops. In Istanbul the price of food soon exceeded people's capacity to buy it. The price of rice and beans shot up six- or sevenfold. Coal was four times its usual price, its production and transport having all but ceased,[31] and after a series of fires that raged through the city's wooden houses, thousands did not even have a roof over their heads.

The allied naval blockade in the eastern Mediterranean disrupted local cash economies. In Syria there were no longer any buyers for the silk grown on Mt. Lebanon. In Beirut and other towns women and children rummaged through garbage for food or pulled up weeds to eat.[32] The sick and the famished died in the streets. On Mt. Lebanon entire villages began to perish, with men walking away to die out of the sight of their women and children and people pulling down roof tiles to sell for bread. In one village a visitor found "whole families writhing in agony on the bare floor of their miserable hut."[33] A correspondent talks in 1916 of the

> black misery that prevails at Outilias [Antilias], Jedide, Junie and Burj and the neighborhood. The people are pale, thin and too feeble to stand upright. To look at them you would say they were living ghosts. The famine has hit hardest the middle class and the poor. On the 24th of June 14 persons died of hunger in Junie [Jounieh]. During this morning (the 25th) five others have succumbed. In Kesrouan the famine has depopulated entire villages. Most of the sick I have visited have their bodies swollen up, especially the feet, through eating weeds out of the field. At Beyrout poverty is seen everywhere, 40 to 50 persons dying daily from insufficient nourishment, not counting those who die as a result of fever.[34]

In Beirut the supply of flour dropped from sixty or seventy tons a day to fifteen or twenty. On some days not a single sack of flour entered warehouses. Merchants worsened the situation by hoarding stocks of food at the bottom of wells and in cemeteries. There was no grain to be found in Beirut or Damascus, where famine was "raging" and twenty to twenty-five people were dying every day.[35]

In Palestine nothing could come in from the sea. "Manchester goods, leather, coal, iron nails, matches, tea, cocoa, chocolate, sugar, lubricating oils, drugs etc. etc. are entirely exhausted, people of wealth even wear rags."

The naval blockade of the coast had created an "awful state of things."[36] All exports of oranges, wine, cereals, and almonds had been stopped; without income, orchards could not be maintained and people were "starving" for bread. Because there was no fuel for irrigation pumps, citrus trees died for lack of water, but there was no one to tend them anyway. All able-bodied men were in the army, leaving only "old men and children" to drive the plow. Animals were either dead or requisitioned. The land was left "bare."[37] Adding to the tribulations of the local people was the locust plague of 1915, a stream of insects several kilometers long that stripped all vegetation in its path, including "the branches in the orange groves, eaten away down to the white wood" and stretching into the distance "like skeletons in the air."[38] Antonius estimated that at least 350,000 died from starvation or disease across Syria and that the total death toll was "not far short" of half a million out of a total population of four million.[39]

In eastern Anatolia, close to one million people fled west and south ahead of the invading Russian army. The cities bulged with refugees. By October 1916, 659,100 refugees from the eastern Black Sea coast and the provinces of Erzurum, Van, and Bitlis were living on relief provided by the Ministry of Interior. By the end of the war the official number of refugees had increased to 868,962.[40] The combination of the sequestration of animals and crops by the government or their theft by an invading army, the conscription of all young men of fighting age, and the collapse of authority and destruction of villages in the war zone left those who did not flee without shelter or means of sustenance and defenseless against attack by armed bands.

SECONDARY WARS

Over almost a century the long Ottoman peace had been ruptured by ethno-religious nationalist uprisings, often backed by outside powers and often ending in war. In the two decades before 1914, Greece and the Ottoman state had gone to war over Crete (1897–98), where Muslims and Christians had massacred each other; in 1894–96 the Armenians were the chief victims of a complete breakdown of order across the eastern provinces of the empire and in Istanbul itself as the volatile "Armenian question" finally burst into flames; finally, in 1912–13, the attack on the Ottoman state by the four Christian Balkan states injected further toxins into the relationship between Christians and Muslims, just ahead of a great war in which battlefield defeats, uprisings, and the suspicion of disloyalty would lead to the dislocation of millions of people. Many were Muslims, fleeing or driven out of conquered territory, or in some cases moved away from the war zone (along with Jews) by the government for their own safety; a large number were Christians (Greeks and Armenians) "relocated" after acts of treachery and sabotage behind the lines. The overriding aim of most Christian civilians was probably to keep out of harm's way, but uprisings and rebellions by a minority threw a pall of suspicion over all. Of the numerous Armenian groups that took up arms against the state, the Tiflis-based Federation of Armenian Revolutionaries (the Dashnaks) was the best organized and most dangerous from an Ottoman point of view. Founded in 1890, the Dashnaks advocated extreme violence (against Armenian "traitors" as well as Turks and Kurds) with the aim of establishing an Armenian state that would stretch from the Caucasus into the eastern Ottoman lands. Despite their ideological differences and differing long-term objectives, the Committee of Union and Progress (the "Young Turks") and the Dashnaks had reached an understanding with regard to the sultan. He was the common enemy. One of their objectives was reached in 1908 when the sultan was compelled to restore the suspended constitution of 1876 and another when he was forced off the throne in 1909 and packed off to exile in Salonica. When the Ottoman Empire entered the war alongside the central powers at the end of October 1914, the Dashnaks and other Armenian political organizations were still operating freely in Istanbul and across the eastern provinces, but armed uprisings from behind the lines made their suppression in 1915 inevitable. Many young Armenians who had been drafted into the military deserted, joining insurgent bands engaged in general acts of sabotage or crossing a porous eastern border to join forces with Caucasian Armenians fighting in the Russian army or in the volunteer units formed alongside it for the specific purpose of "liberating" the "Armenian provinces" of the Ottoman Empire in the name of a common Christianity. Uprisings, desertions, and reports of Armenian collusion with the Russians prompted the military command to issue orders in February 1915 that Armenian conscripts should be removed from the ranks of the military and paramilitary forces and formed into labor battalions instead.

By early 1915, the Ottoman military position in the east was already critical. In December 1914 the Ottoman minister of war, Enver Paşa, launched an attack on Russian positions across the northeastern Anatolian border. The outcome of the fighting that took place around the town of Sarıkamış in January was the decimation of the Ottoman Third Army. Of the ninety-five thousand troops sent into action in this mountainous terrain, about seventy-five thousand died, most because the simple precaution had not been taken of providing them with winter clothing or wood for heating. They arrived at the front wearing not boots but sandals,[41] and they froze to death as heavy snowfalls turned into a blizzard. Only the remnants of the army (about eighteen thousand men) were left to stem the Russian advance westward in the direction of Erzurum (captured in February 1916) and south toward Bitlis.

In the first half of 1915 the Armenian insurrection across the eastern provinces intensified. By April Van, Bitlis, Erzurum, and Sivas provinces were sliding into complete chaos, confirmed daily in reports coming in from the military command and provincial authorities of pitched battles, attacks on *jandarma* (gendarmerie) posts, the ambush of supply convoys and convoys of wounded soldiers, and the cutting of telegraph lines. What was happening could no longer be described as disparate uprisings; it was rather a general rebellion, orchestrated principally by the Dashnaks and encouraged by Russia. The victims included not just soldiers or *jandarma* or officials but the Muslim and Christian villagers who were the victims of massacre and countermassacre.

On the battlefront an Anglo-Indian force had captured Basra in November 1914, and by the middle of April it was ready to move up the Euphrates toward Baghdad. On April 25 a combined French and British empire force (including Australians, New Zealanders, and Indians) landed at Gallipoli: meanwhile, across the eastern Ottoman border in northwestern Persia, garrisoned by the Russians since the Anglo-Russian agreement of 1907 had divided Persia into foreign "spheres of interest," an Ottoman army was moving into position to fight a combined Russian and Armenian volunteer force in the Dilman region. At this critical juncture, between April 13 and 20, thousands of Armenians inside the walled city of Van rose up against the governor and the small number of regular and irregular forces garrisoned in the city.[42] The extent to which the rebellion was coordinated with the Russians remains an open question, to which the answer must lie buried somewhere in the Russian state archives, but the effect was to weaken the Ottoman campaign in eastern Anatolia and Persia. Troops had to be withdrawn from the front and sent to Van, but the relief force could not reach the city ahead of approaching Russian troops.

The weapons in the hands of the rebels, including the latest machine pistols, rifles, bombs, and large stocks of ammunition, plus the digging of tunnels between houses, were the proof that preparations for conflict had been made over a long period of time and that the uprising was not simply a spontaneous defensive response to Ottoman "repression" (through the murder of two Dashnak leaders as the result of the governor's "brutal and illegal" policy)[43] or harassment of Armenian women, as claimed by the missionaries. Indeed, the Armenian charge of Ottoman repression and the Ottoman charge of Armenian rebellion (treachery, as the Ottoman government regarded it) were equally true. The government, the Armenian committees, and Muslim and Christian civilians sucked into the conflict as active participants or as innocent victims were now all fully caught up in a Darwinian struggle for the survival of a stricken empire on one hand and the birth of an Armenian state stretching from the Caucasus into eastern Anatolia on the other.

The fighting in Van continued until the middle of May. Scarcely able to defend the city and certainly unable to offer any help to the Muslims of the province, the besieged governor (Cevdet Bey) sought and received permission from Istanbul to authorize their flight. Thus began the *büyük kaçgın* (great flight) as an estimated eighty thousand Muslim civilians fled to the west and south.[44] The defeat of the Ottoman army at Dilman, the approach of a Russian force from the Caucasus, and the inability of an Ottoman relief column to reach the city in time sealed Van's fate. The tribulations of the civilians in the path of the approaching Russians (Cossacks and Armenians among them) and the local Armenian bands that had joined them have been described by Justin McCarthy:

> The Muslim villagers on the Russian and Armenian line of march naturally suffered the losses expected when villages are invaded by an enemy army—rape, theft, expropriation of animals and feed and death for those who resisted the conquerors. The suffering reported by the villagers on the line of march, however, went far beyond what might ordinarily be expected in war. The attacks on villages and refugees were not military confrontations. They were simply slaughtered. Refugees were particularly defenseless. Most of the men were at the front. The refugee columns were largely made up of old men, women and children. All were attacked. Children were not spared.[45]

Survivors identified Armenians and Cossacks as the principal killers. On May 16, with the Russians not far away, the governor of Van and the remaining Ottoman officials and military forces withdrew. Much of the old city had already been destroyed in the fighting, and now the Muslim quarter was subjected to an orgy of pillage, arson, and murder that continued for several days:

> From May 16 to 18 the Armenians looted and burned all that was left of the Muslim houses and government buildings in the city. Except for some of the very old and very young, Muslim males and a large number of females who had remained in the city were killed. Survivors, almost all of them women, recorded details of the massacres, usually

listing the murders of those they had known and of religious and public officials. Their reports all relate the same series of events: adult males (except some of the very old) and teenaged boys were separated from the women and girls. The males were killed in various ways, many of them horrible. Some women and young children were killed at the same time as the men, some were raped and others were simply released to wander among the rubble. From very limited evidence it also seems that some were assisted by Armenians.[46]

The killing extended to Muslim villages around the shore of the nearby lake. In the northeast, Russian forces had crossed the border in the direction of Çaldiran (where in 1514 a Persian army had suffered a crushing defeat at the hands of the Ottomans). Villagers fleeing their advance made their way to south to Van, only to find that many of the Muslims in the region had fled. They were now caught between the advancing Russian forces in the north and the Armenians in the south. In the hope of escaping by ship across the lake the refugees went to the village of Zeve, where the local people put them up in their homes and in tents and barns. Their arrival swelled the population from 500 to about 2,500. Armenian bands consisting of local Armenians and armed Armenian "volunteers" from across the eastern borders were by now moving from one village to the next, slaughtering and destroying.[47] The men of Zeve took up defensive positions to prevent the village from being overrun but after a morning of fighting were overwhelmed. A general massacre followed. Almost all the Muslims—men, women, and children—were killed. The only survivors were six women and a boy of eleven who was saved by the intervention of an Armenian friend of his father's.[48] As an old man, Haci Osman Gemicioğlu ("son of the ship operator"), an Armenian convert to Islam, described what he saw when he and other children went out to fetch an empty beehive and came across the scene of the massacre. "When we arrived at Zeve the village couldn't be passed through because of the stench. It was as if the bones in our noses would fall off. . . . There were bodies everywhere." Haci Osman heard that Armenian bands had also done "the same thing" to the Muslims on Çarpanak island, but "I did not see it for myself."[49] No records were kept, but the evidence of survivors indicates that in all the villages attacked by the Armenians "the slaughter was nearly complete."[50]

The Ottomans managed to recapture Van in early August before being forced to retreat at the end of the month. Retribution and revenge killings followed, but this time the Armenians were the victims as their Russian protectors retreated. Tens of thousands of Russian and Armenian soldiers and Armenian civilians streaming out of the province in the direction of the Persian border were harassed by Kurdish tribes as they struggled over mountain passes. Thousands were killed. By the time Ottoman forces recaptured Van for good in April 1918, it was filled with the ruins of mosques, hamams, public buildings, and the houses of those who had been killed or driven out or had fled in the preceding three years. In 1919 Emory Niles and Arthur Sutherland were sent to eastern Anatolia by the U.S. government for the purpose of assessing relief needs. They painted a picture of overwhelming destruction and desolation. In Van, only three of the 3,400 houses of Muslims were still standing; in Bitlis, all of the 6,500 Muslim houses had been destroyed. By comparison, 1,170 of the 3,100 Armenian houses in Van and 1,000 of the 1,500 Armenian houses in Bitlis were still intact.[51]

The uprising in Van precipitated a series of decisions taken by the government in Istanbul. The first was put into effect on April 24, when the offices of the Armenian political committees in the capital were closed down, documents were seized, and more than 230 Armenians were arrested. The second decision developed in stages. On May 2, as fighting continued in and around the city of Van, Enver Paşa proposed that "this nest of rebellion be broken up" by "relocating" the Armenian population across the border into the Caucasus (from which large numbers of Muslims had fled or had been driven out) or into other parts of Anatolia.[52] On May 26 the military high command informed the Ministry of the Interior that it had started to remove Armenians from Van, Bitlis, and Erzurum and a number of villages and towns in the southeast. They were to be resettled south of Diyarbakir, but only up to the point where they would constitute no more than 10 percent of the local population. The same day Talat Paşa, the minister of the interior, informed the grand vizier of the decision to move the Armenian population from the Van, Bitlis, and Erzurum *vilayet*s (provinces) and from areas in the southeast corner of Anatolia around the cities of Maraş, Mersin, Adana, Iskanderun, and Antakya. This was being done

> because some of the Armenians who are living near the war zones have obstructed the activities of the Imperial Ottoman Army, which has been entrusted with defending the frontiers against the country's enemies; because they impede the movement of provisions and troops; because they have made common cause with the enemy; and especially because they have attacked the military forces within the country, the innocent population, and the Ottoman cities and towns, killing and plundering; and because they have even dared to supply the enemy navy with provisions and to reveal the location of our fortified places to them.[53]

The Armenians were to be "resettled" in the Mosul *vilayet* (but not where it bordered on the *vilayet* of Van), around Urfa (but not in the city itself), and in the eastern region of Syria around Deir al Zor. The following day the cabinet adopted a Provisional Law Concerning the Measures to be Taken by the Military Authorities Against Those Who Oppose the Operations of the Government during Wartime. This law, ratified by the parliament when it reconvened on September 15, authorized the military to arrest Armenians suspected of treachery and to move populations. On May 30 the government issued a series of regulations dealing with the practicalities of the "resettlement." It was to be organized by local authorities; the Armenians could take movable property and animals with them; they were to be protected en route and provided with food and medical care; on arrival they were to be housed in villages built with proper concern for local conditions but at a distance of at least twenty-five kilometers from railway lines, and only up to the point where they constituted no more than 10 percent of the local population. It soon proved impossible to move the Armenians in accordance with these instructions. The army had first claim on food, medicine, and all means of transport; it is doubtful whether the government would have been organizationally and administratively capable of shifting so many people in any circumstances, let alone at such short notice; and the Armenians would be passing through regions where Kurdish tribes and other ethno-religious groups badly affected by the war would not hesitate to take surrogate revenge for the crimes committed against Muslims. On the grounds of military necessity, however, a directive had come from the military command that the bulk of the Armenian population had to be moved. What could not be done had to be done. The outcome was calamitous. In the coming months hundreds of thousands of Armenian men, women, and children were wrenched from their homes, from the Black Sea region and the western provinces as well as the eastern, and moved southwards toward Syria.[54] Thousands died before they reached their destination, dropping dead by the roadside, succumbing to starvation, exposure, and disease (typhoid and dysentery being two of the chief killers), or massacred in attacks on their convoys; the desperate scenes in and around the transit camps, of starving and dying people, of filth and stench, were described by American, German, and Austrian officials.

The survivors of the relocation reached the Arab provinces in a state of complete distress. They were resettled in various parts of Syria. Large numbers were moved to camps set up near Ras al Ain, to the northeast of Aleppo, or along the Euphrates River valley to the southeast. The famine that killed hundreds of thousands of Syrians during the war was at its height when they arrived. By the summer of 1916, between fifty-five thousand and sixty thousand people were said (by a German consul and an American oil company employee distributing relief) to have been buried around the camp at Meskene after being "carried off by hunger, by privations of all sorts, by intestinal diseases and typhus which is the result."[55] Thousands more were massacred. How many it is not possible to say with any precision: even if the estimates of foreign aid workers, consuls, missionaries, survivors, and local people were not blown up for propaganda purposes, they are not reliable enough for historians to be able to arrive at anything like firm figures. Many were reported killed by Circassians or Kurdish *jandarma* at the Ras al Ain camp, in the desert northeast of Aleppo, in the spring of 1916. A German missionary visiting the region the following year thought the motive was greed.[56]

In 1916 a large number of Armenians who were being moved onward to Mosul from Deir al Zor because they had reached the 10 percent limit of the local population set by the central government died from heat and exposure or were murdered near the River Khabur. Survivors said the killers were Kurdish *jandarma*, Circassians, Chechens, and Arabs.[57] Whether the local governor was complicit in these killings or whether the Circassians and Chechens living along the Khabur River, who had a reputation for religious intolerance and no doubt had bitter memories of Christian mistreatment of Muslims in the Caucasus, had acted "on their initiative" is something that has never been resolved.[58] At Ras al Ain, the possessions of the Armenians were found crammed into the huts of the Circassians, while at Deir al Zor the clothing and possessions of those killed near the Khabur River were recognized "in the possession of these brigands and others to whom they were sold."[59]

More than one hundred thousand other Armenians were moved southwards through central Syria to Damascus and points farther south in the Hawran region. Many settled in the towns. Some (even at Meskene) found work as agricultural laborers or artisans or with the railway. At Raqqa (along the Euphrates) thousands of Armenians were living in houses "which the kindness of the governor has procured for the most poor," while others squatted in a camp on the opposite bank of the river. Within months the situation had worsened because of lack of food and the outbreak of a typhus epidemic.[60] In Damascus, under an aid program headed by an enlightened former governor, a hospital was established and work was found in a knitting factory for widows and orphans,[61] but lack of funds and hostility to the Armenians among local officials and villagers severely weakened the effect of these good intentions. The personal factor was obviously important. Some high officials were praised for doing their best to relieve the distress of the Armenians, but others were criticized for not doing enough or for taking decisions that exposed them to greater dangers. No place had enough food or enough hospitals to take in the ill. Of the numbers of Armenians who were moved southwards through central Syria, an estimated 20,000 out of 132,000 still died, but there were no massacres. Overall, it is impossible to separate the numbers of Armenians who were massacred from those who died of other causes, but on the accumulated evidence of foreign consuls and aid workers there is no doubt that the death toll from starvation and disease was enormous. Given that the Armenians were in a much worse situation than the large number of Syrians who were already dying from the famine gripping the entire region, this was inevitable.

As news reached Istanbul that Armenians were being massacred on the way south, the government ordered the provincial authorities to catch and punish those responsible, "but the fact that these orders were repeated on numerous occasions would seem to indicate that they had little effect on the killing."[62] On September 28, 1915, continuing reports of attacks on the convoys by Kurdish tribesmen, along with shortages of medicine and food and transport problems, compelled Talat Paşa to seek a full government inquiry. The following day the Council of Ministers set up a special investigative council, involving the Ministries of the Interior, Justice, and War, which it directed to work together in investigating the crimes that had been committed. The Finance Ministry was ordered to fund their work.[63] Hearings were held across the eastern provinces, followed by court-martials, at which more than one thousand civilian officials or military personnel were found guilty "of organizing or failing to prevent the attacks" on the Armenians or of stealing their property.[64] Muslims were also put on trial for crimes against Muslims. The sentences included imprisonment and some executions.[65]

Estimates of the numbers of Armenians who were "relocated" between May 1915 and February 1916 range from just under half a million (the figure counted from Ottoman archival statistics) to just over seven hundred thousand.[66] Estimates of the number who died during the entire war (not just in 1915–16) that were made when it was over, even by sources hostile to the Turks and the Ottoman government, ranged from six hundred thousand to eight hundred thousand. In recent decades, Armenian writers have based their arguments on figures of one million or 1.5 million dead. The differences in estimates illustrate a general problem with statistics dating back to the late nineteenth century, when the number of Armenians who lived in the Ottoman Empire (or who died there) were often exaggerated for political purposes. Muslims were undercounted for the same reason. Only the Ottoman government actually counted the population, but even its figures stand in need of adjustment. Justin McCarthy, a specialist in Ottoman demographics, has put the Armenian population of the whole empire in 1912 at 1,698,301, of which number 1,465,000 lived in Anatolia. Hundreds of thousands of Armenians survived the war. Herbert Hoover's estimate of 450,000 to 500,000 Armenians fleeing from "Turkish Armenia" into "Russian Armenia" is consistent with other figures. Many settled in Syria, and others managed to leave the region altogether, emigrating to the United States and many other countries. Taking all of these factors into account, McCarthy has arrived at a total wartime Ottoman Armenian death toll from all causes of 584,000, or 41 percent of the Ottoman Armenian population. If the Armenian patriarchate population estimate of about two million is to be accepted over the official census figures, the number of dead would be increased by about 250,000, on McCarthy's calculations, bringing the total Ottoman Armenian death toll from all causes for the entire war to a maximum of slightly more than 800,000. It will be noted that these figures are in line with the estimates made at the end of the war.[67] Other computations put the number of Armenian dead at no more than 300,000,[68] but the fluctuations remain enormous, even between historians who share the same basic point of view about what happened.[69]

These figures have to be situated within the overall Ottoman civilian death toll of between three and four million. The Ottoman armies returned to the shells of cities, villages, and towns, still littered with corpses, in which the signs and symbols of the Ottoman Muslim presence—mosques, schools, tombs, Sufi lodges, markets, and government buildings—had been destroyed. In a region in which the Muslim population was predominantly Kurdish, it follows that most of the Muslim victims of the war in the eastern and southeastern provinces were Kurdish, a point that underlines the neglected Kurdish aspect of the "Armenian question." Captain C. L. Woolley, a British officer traveling through "Kurdistan" after the war, was told by tribal leaders that four hundred thousand Kurds had been massacred by Armenians in the Van-Bitlis region alone.[70] Two volumes of recently published Ottoman documents—mostly the reports of refugees, police, *jandarma*, and provincial officials—covering the period from 1914 to 1921 indicate that this Kurdish estimate of Kurdish dead through massacre by the Russians and/or their Armenian protégées is probably fairly accurate. Counted on a village-by-village or town-by-town basis, with the names of the killers often being given, the number of Muslims who were massacred across the region is put at 518,105.[71] Hundreds of thousands of others died from the same starvation, disease, and exposure that were killing the Armenians. The killing of civilians began well before the "relocation" was ordered and clearly had a powerful influence on the decisions that were taken by the government in Istanbul. In November 1914, Armenian bands operating in the Saray and Başkale regions near the Persian border raped, slaughtered, and plundered and in at least one village drove the villagers into a mosque and burnt them alive.[72] This individual episode is fully consistent with the documentary evidence of atrocities committed by Armenians over a period of years and recorded in gruesome detail in the documents coming out of the Ottoman archives. Even allowing for the possibility of lies or exaggeration, the evidence is both consistent and overwhelming. There is too much of it, coming from too many places over too long a period of time, to be credibly denied. Guenter Lewy is correct in drawing attention to the "special" nature of the calamity that overwhelmed the Armenians. They lost not only their lives on a huge scale "but also their existence as an organized ethnic community."[73] What the history of the war underlines most strongly (as do the histories of all wars) is humanity's common capacity for inhumanity. The suffering of the Muslims was "special" in its own terrible way: there certainly was a holocaust in the eastern Ottoman lands, but it devoured Muslim Kurds and Turks just as greedily and cruelly as Christian Armenians.

The Muslims suffered tremendous loss of life (the Muslim population of Van province fell by 62 percent, of Bitlis by 42 percent, and Erzurum by 31 percent) but could survive the ravages of war because they were an overwhelming majority (more than 80 percent overall) in the territory that the Armenian national committees wanted to incorporate into an independent Armenian state. The Ottoman Armenians were a small minority and could not survive losses of such magnitude. The wartime suffering of the Muslims in this region, against the historical background of Russian expulsion of Muslims from the Caucasus since early in the nineteenth century, suggests that had Russia stayed in the war their future would have been bleak in the extreme. The entire region and its civilian population were devastated by the big war and the secondary ethno-religious conflicts fought out across the length and breadth of eastern Anatolia, from the Black Sea down to the Mediterranean, spilling over into northwest Persia and the Caucasus across to Baku and continuing for years after 1918. The Bolshevik revolution ended centuries of Russian interference in Ottoman affairs in the name of defending the rights of Ottoman Christians. The withdrawal of Russia from the war and the renunciation by the Bolsheviks of all territorial claims abruptly ended Armenian hopes for a state that would include the eastern lands of the Ottoman Empire. The Dashnak gamble on a Tsarist victory had failed. The withdrawal of Russian troops and the return of the Ottomans precipitated the flight of thousands of Armenians into the Caucasus, where fighting between Turks and Armenians was to continue for two more years. By the end of the war the ancient Armenian presence in eastern Ottoman lands had virtually come to an end.[74]

The numbers of Armenians who died during and after the relocation, the causes of death, the identity of those who killed them (bandit gangs, tribal Kurds or Circassian refugees out for revenge, and the *jandarma* or soldiers who were supposed to be protecting them) or plundered the convoys as they moved south into Syria and Mosul, the culpability of senior officials, the role of the special operations force known as Teşkilat i-Mahsusa,[75] and the intentions of the Ottoman government remain subjects of acrimonious debate to this day.[76] A few months before the end of the war, and his flight to Berlin, where in 1921 he was assassinated by a young Armenian, Talat admitted to a friend that the relocation had turned into a complete disaster. Given that he remains at the center of continuing accusations by Armenian historians and propagandists and those who support their case that the Ottoman government met at some point in 1915 and decided not just to relocate the Armenians but to wipe them out, his voice should perhaps be given a posthumous hearing:

> Rauf Bey, what happened is over. Whatever is said about it in the future will have no effect. We entered the war with the expectation of saving the homeland from the decay into which it had fallen. There are many who now both approve and disapprove of what we did. There is the Armenian deportation problem about which not only our enemies but even our friends now violently criticize us. But whoever might have been in our place would have had to do the same thing for the safety of our country. Think a bit. At a time when our armies were in a life or death struggle with enemies who were vastly superior in both numbers and equipment the Armenians, who were our fellow countrymen, had armed themselves and revolted all over the country and were cooperating with the enemy for the purpose of striking us in the rear. What other choice was there but to remove this race away from the war zones? There was absolutely no other solution. This was not at all an easy task. For that reason, therefore, while this policy was being carried out, some instances of bad management and evil deeds took place. But one cannot blame members of the government like myself for such instances which took place in far away provinces and of which we had no knowledge. It grieves me that we were unable to save some Armenians who had no connection with the revolt, among whom were two of

my very closest colleagues. One can accuse us of lack of experience, incapacity and ignorance. But no-one can say that we were thieves. I still to the present day feel great pain and distress that I was unable to prevent the atrocities that were carried out against people who were outside the area of the revolt and had absolutely nothing to do with it.[77]

Relief workers sent to the east once the armistice was declared in 1918 were overwhelmed by the distress and desolation they encountered across a vast mass of territory stretching from the Ottoman lands into Persia and up into the Caucasus. The Russian advance into northern Persia and what is now northeastern Iraq had stripped the country bare of food and livestock. Driving from Khanaqin to Hamadan in April 1918, the British high official put in charge of Mesopotamia, Arnold Wilson, saw a sight "I hope I may never again witness—a whole people perishing for want of food." At Hamadan, two hundred people were dying every day at one stage, the survivors being reduced to such desperation "that children were slain for food." Such food stores as did exist in northwest Persia and elsewhere were often in the hands of wealthy landowners and grain dealers who "combined to keep the price up."[78] Istanbul itself was under Allied occupation, with the British Allied high commissioner (Admiral Calthorpe) making it plain in his public statements that the Turks would now have to suffer for their sins.

"EQUITABLE" SHARES

Long before the war ended, the Allies had planned the division of the spoils. In the Constantinople Agreement (1915) Russia was allocated Istanbul and the Straits; the Treaty of London (1915) promised Italy an "equitable share" of the Mediterranean coast around Adalia (Antalya), as well as islands in the Aegean (the Dodecanese); in the Husain-McMahon correspondence (1915–16), Britain pledged support for Arab independence in return for an uprising against the Ottomans; the Sykes-Picot treaty (May 1916) divided Iraq, Syria, and south-central Anatolia between British and French zones of direct control and spheres of influence; St. Jean de Maurienne (April 1917) added Izmir and Konya to Italy's share; in June 1917, the Allies brought Greece into the war by holding out the promise of expansion into western Anatolia once it was won; in the Balfour Declaration (November 1917) Britain opened up Palestine to Zionist settlement in the name of establishing a "national home" for the Jewish people.

Russia's entitlements naturally lapsed after the Bolshevik revolution. Among the victorious powers, relative strength on the ground once the fighting stopped basically decided who would get what, irrespective of what governments had promised each other during the war. Britain was in the box seat. It held all occupied territory in the Near East. France, in no position to insist on anything, agreed in December 1918 to surrender its claim to Mosul in return for a share of oil from the region; the amount was clarified in 1920 when Britain agreed to give France 25 percent of the net output of Mesopotamian oil fields at prevailing market rates or a 25 percent share in any private company formed for oil development. It would also receive up to 25 percent of Persian oil pumped by the British-owned Anglo-Persian Oil Company through pipelines laid across French-mandated territory to the Mediterranean.

France also yielded on Palestine, which under Sykes-Picot was to have been placed under international control, but it was determined to retain the rest of Syria and as much as it could take of the Anatolian territory it had been allotted under Sykes-Picot. Its area of direct control included most of the Syrian coast (stopping just north of Haifa) and a large chunk of Anatolian territory extending northward to Sivas (to the west of Lake Van). Its "sphere of influence" centered on the Syrian hinterland. In southeastern Anatolia the commercial and strategic draws for the French were the cotton wealth of the Çukurova (Cilician) plain and the strategic ports around the rim of the eastern Mediterranean. As soon as the war ended, France hastened to make good on its claims, moving a mixture of French, colonial (Senegalese and Algerian), and Armenian forces into the region and opening up the region to the resettlement of tens of thousands of displaced Armenians still stuck in Syria. Britain watched these developments with great suspicion. Because of its own commitments and the rapid demobilization of the British army, it had to accommodate French demands, but at the same time it was determined to prevent France from building a base from which it could threaten Britain's "possessions" in the East. In the British view, Anatolia would have to be separated from Syria and a buffer state established in Palestine to limit French ambitions in that direction.

In modern Middle Eastern studies the emphasis on the partition of Arab lands has overshadowed the savage conflict that broke out in southeastern Anatolia in 1918 between nationalist Turks on one side and French and Armenian forces on the other. France had hoped to be given a mandate over the Armenians, but the Armenians wanted independence and made it plain that if there had to be a mandate they would prefer it to be in the hands of the United States. The resettlement of the Armenians and their recruitment into a special Armenian Legion sent into southeastern Anatolia with French troops were designed to strengthen France's claims to the region. Difficulties arising from conflicting long-term aims were compounded on the

French side by growing disgust at the indiscipline and excesses of Armenian soldiers and the realization that sooner or later France would have to deal with the Turkish nationalists. Well ahead of Britain, France realized that they were too strong a force to subdue and were indeed the coming power in the region. While fighting the Kemalists in the southeast the French were quietly negotiating with them and, with the aim of keeping the British off balance in and around Istanbul, were even providing them with arms and ammunition smuggled along the Black Sea coast.[79] Cutting its losses, France decided on September 20, 1920, to withdraw from Çukurova and concentrate on Syria.

Diplomacy continued while armies tried to create faits accomplis on the ground. The partition of the central Arab lands of the Ottoman Empire was ratified during the postwar "peace" conferences convened in Paris (from January 1919 to January 1920) and San Remo (April 19–26, 1920). The French occupation of Syria and the British occupation of Iraq and Palestine were both sanctioned by Article 22 of the covenant of the League of Nations. Their "mandate" over these territories was to be held until such time as the peoples living under the authority of the mandatory power were able to determine their own future. The terms of the Balfour Declaration were written into the mandate for Palestine. The die was cast for a conflict that has continued to the present day.

The future of "Turkey" (a state not yet created) was settled—so the victors thought—in a treaty signed in the Paris suburb of Sèvres (August 10, 1920). The main business was disarmament, the partition of the eastern provinces of the Ottoman Empire into an Armenian state and perhaps a Kurdish state—if the Kurds could show within a year that they were ready for independence—and the incorporation of western Anatolia along the Aegean coast into a greater Greece. In fact, an Armenian republic had been proclaimed in the Caucasus on May 28, 1918, but Bolshevik and nationalist Armenians were fighting over its future, and by the time the diplomats met in Paris its status was about to change. On November 29, 1920, the republic was incorporated into the Soviet Union, which had renounced all territorial claims outside the borders of Tsarist Russia at the time of the revolution. Abandoned by the French in the southeast and the Bolsheviks in the northeast, following their settlement with the Kemalists, the Armenian nationalists now had no hope of incorporating any part of eastern Anatolia into an Armenian state.

The contradictory assurances given to Greece and Italy during the war had already been resolved by ushering a Greek army into Izmir. Under the Sèvres agreement the inhabitants of Izmir would remain Turkish nationals, but sovereign powers were transferred to Greece, which would administer the city, would set up a parliament, and would be able to base troops there. It was also given the right to incorporate Izmir into the Greek state within five years if it could be shown that this was what the people wanted. Elsewhere, Sèvres required "Turkey" to recognize the British annexation of Cyprus (proclaimed on November 5, 1914) and the Italian occupation of fourteen islands in the Aegean and to cede to Greece the northern Aegean islands of Imbros and Tenedos (which eventually reverted to Turkey as Gökceada and Bozcaada).

Already evident in this narrative but perhaps in need of summing up is the great power manipulation of Near Eastern minorities from the nineteenth century through to the postwar period and indeed to the present. Anatolia was to be bounded by an expanded Greek state at one end and an expanded Armenian state at the other, with the Kurds given the right to a state if they could organize themselves. The Greeks were British clients, while the Armenians were cultivated by the French, who were also playing on the cupidity of the Maronites of Mt. Lebanon. There was no susceptible minority in Palestine, so Britain created one by fostering Zionist settlement. As the absorption of eastern and western Anatolia into Armenian and Greek states could have been effected only by driving out the Muslim majority, the fate of the Palestinians in 1948 would almost certainly have been the fate of the Muslims in both regions, had not a strong Turkish national movement arisen to block the partition of Anatolia.

In Article 22 of the League of Nations the mandates given to the victorious powers were described as a "sacred trust of civilization." The wishes of all communities were to be "a principal consideration in the selection of the Mandatory." In fact, when consulted, the wishes of those who did not want foreign occupation of their lands were shrugged off. In private, beyond the rhetorical veneer, the architects of the new world order were utterly cynical, as this account of a meeting between senior British delegates (including Prime Minister David Lloyd George and Foreign Secretary Arthur James Balfour) and Italian delegates (Prime Minister Vittorio Orlando and Foreign Minister Sidney Sonnino) makes clear: "Finally they [Orlando and Sonnino] appear ready to accept a mandate over the Adalia region but it is not quite clear whether in return for this they will abandon Fiume and Rhodes. We get out the League Covenant regarding Mandates. We observe (I think it was Milner who observed) that the article provides for 'the consent and wishes of the people concerned.' They find that phrase very amusing. How they all laugh! Orlando's white cheeks wobble with laughter and his puffy eyes fill with tears of mirth."[80]

The grubby postwar dealings of the European powers—and the smaller states angling for their share of the spoils—were what President Woodrow Wilson summed up once as "the whole disgusting scramble" for the Middle East. He was determined that the disposition of conquered territories should not develop into a "game of grab," but that was how it turned out. The League of Nations, he wrote, seemed to be composed of "intriguers and robbers."[81] Under the top hats and behind the frock coats of the diplomats and statesmen, the European powers were divided in their ambitions by what they all had in common—hypocrisy, greed, suspicion, self-interest, and prejudice. They rooted around in the ruins of the Ottoman Empire like pigs after truffles. High rhetoric was matched by low reality. Liberation for some spelled oppression for others. Moral concern for Christian minorities was matched by moral indifference to the interests of the Muslim majority. A vast land mass lay prostrate as this banquet of thieves began. The Ottoman Empire did not "collapse." That is far too passive a term. It was ripped apart as a chicken might be disjointed; not even Germany had to suffer dismemberment and evisceration.

AN AEGEAN ADVENTURE

After the war an immediate priority was the reconciliation of overlapping Italian and Greek territorial claims. The crucial protagonist for the Greeks was Lloyd George, a Welsh nonconformist who had described General Allenby's conquest of Palestine, culminating in his triumphant entry into Jerusalem, as the "last and greatest of the Crusades."[82] The pro-Zionist Lloyd George was also a "romantic philhellene"[83] who "hated the Turks as much if not more than Gladstone had loathed them fifty years earlier" and regarded them as a "decadent race" compared to the Greeks.[84] It was for strategic rather than romantic reasons, however, that he wanted Greece in the war. King Constantine (married to the Kaiser's sister and pro-German for numerous other reasons) managed to stay on the sidelines for two years but was forced to abdicate in June 1917; the removal of the king, the installation of a government in Athens headed by Eleutherios Venizelos, and the "private offer" of a large area of western Anatolia finally brought Greece into the war on the Allied side.[85]

The size of Anatolian territory granted to Italy in the St. Jean de Maurienne treaty was so great as to indicate that at least two of the three negotiating parties (Britain, France, and Italy) must have had a "bad conscience."[86] In any case, Italy's ambitions in the Balkans, the Adriatic (centering on the port of Fiume), the Aegean, and Africa (Libya, Somalia, and Abyssinia) were too dangerous to French and British interests for it to be allowed to have Izmir after all. In the expectation that wartime pledges would be fulfilled, Italian troops were landed at Marmaris on the Aegean coast and Adalia (Antalya) on the Mediterranean coast in March 1919. They began moving in the direction of Konya and Izmir. The powers were not so much concerned about Konya—what would the Italians do with it when they got there?—but they could not be allowed to reach Izmir. Swift preemptive action had to be taken. On May 6, 1919, Venizelos was "invited" by the Supreme Council to occupy Izmir and environs in the name of maintaining an order that was not then being disturbed. Italy was kept in the dark until May 12 and then told that a Greek presence was necessary in Izmir to prevent massacres. The Greek army—flagged as an Allied army—crossed the Aegean from Salonica and disembarked under the protection of British, French, Italian, and American warships. The Allied commission responsible for the occupation of Istanbul was not told of the landing until the Greek force of thirteen thousand men was about to step ashore just before 8:00 A.M. on May 15. The high commissioners (British, French, Italian, and Greek) were meeting on May 14 when Wyndham Deedes brought them the news that the Greeks were approaching Izmir. "Count Sforza, the Italian High Commissioner for whom Deedes had a warm personal regard, dared not trust himself to speak but got up and rushed from the room, banging the door behind him."[87]

In the first few days of the Greek occupation, perhaps two thousand people, soldiers and civilians, men (including Christian Smyrniots mistakenly identified as Turks because they were wearing the fez), women, and children, were killed in Izmir and nearby villages. Shops and homes were ransacked. Having brought Izmir under their control, the Greeks began moving deeper into western Anatolia, well beyond the limits of the zone they were supposed to be occupying in the name of preventing massacres. In fact, their advance was itself marked by massacre, pillage, and rape on a scale that Allied observers found difficult to credit; after all, was not this the terrain where "the oxygen of the West begins to diffuse the crushing and abstract logic of the Egyptian and Mesopotamian deserts,"[88] as a later writer expressed an old sentiment? Yet here they were behaving just like the so-called barbarous races of the East.

The belated attempts of the Greek government to punish those found guilty of atrocities scarcely expiated the scale of the crimes committed. Arnold Toynbee, visiting western Anatolia from June to August 1921, spoke of a Greek "war of extermination" for which Western statesmen were ultimately responsible.[89] Writing of the destruction in territories occupied by the Greeks up to July 10, 1921, he listed sixteen villages in the Akhisar district whose inhabitants had been massacred along with two east of Akhisar; twenty-five to thirty in the Soğandere (Onion Place) district and fourteen in the Aydin region. He also listed villages that had been merely pillaged, although it seems unlikely that their inhabitants escaped the torment inflicted on others: eighty-two between Akhisar and Manisa; sixty in the Tire-Bayindir-Ödemiş districts; and fifteen in the Yalova region.[90] During the offensive launched by the Greeks after July 10, fifty more villages in the Aydin district were destroyed, 145 out of 150 houses burned at Kizilca, southeast of Izmir, along with the "systematic devastations" inflicted during the retreat from the Sakarya River to Eskişehir. Many of the massacres of the Muslims were the work of the *chettés*, the terrorist bands moving through the conquered territory with the Greek army, the equivalent of the Bulgarian and Serbian *komitadjis* of the Balkan War.

Some of the detail of the invasion is given by Stanford Shaw: "In the Izmit peninsula the towns of Kartal, Şile, and Pendik were almost completely destroyed by Greek bands accompanied by local Greek and Armenian civilians. Children were torn apart. Turkish girls were kidnapped, raped, and killed. Men and boys were beheaded."[91] Farther south an Inter-Allied Committee of Inquiry appointed by the Supreme Council found in its report of October 1919 that "in the part of the *kaza* [provincial subdistrict] of Yalova and Guemlek occupied by the Greek army there is a systematic plan of destruction of the Turkish villages and extinction of the Moslem population. This plan is being carried out by Greek and Armenian bands which appear to operate under Greek instructions and sometimes even with the assistance of detachments of regular troops." Far from carrying out a civilizing mission, the invasion had immediately taken on the aspect of a "conquest and crusade."[92] The chief representative of the International Red Cross supported these findings. M. Gehri, who traveled through the region with the Committee of Inquiry and the Ottoman Red Crescent, wrote that in the past two months elements of the Greek army "have been employed in the extermination of the Moslem population of the [Yalova-Gemlik] peninsula. The facts established—burnings of villages, massacres, terror of the inhabitants, coincidence of place and date—leave no room for doubt in regard to this."[93]

The committee also accused "Kemalist bands" or regular soldiers of committing "acts of violence and barbarism as well as massacre on a large scale" outside the Greek zone of occupation.[94] Indeed, armed Turkish civilian bands did commit atrocities: with Greece about to launch further offensives inland, Muslims and Pontic (Black Sea) Greeks engaged in their own miniwar. Large numbers of people were displaced. When Greek troops were forced to retreat from Ismit (June 1921), the Greek civilians of the town and the surrounding area went with them, but not before a last bout of looting, killing, and attempting to burn Muslim and Jewish quarters of the town. Trapped cattle were burned alive: mosques were looted and defiled, with slaughtered pigs being dragged inside one. A cross chalked over buildings owned by Christians saved them from destruction.[95]

To the King-Crane Commission of Inquiry (officially designated as the American Section of the International Commission on Mandates in Turkey), sent to the Near East in 1919 under the authority of both the League of Nations and President Wilson,

> the question has already been answered as to whether the Balkan State of modern Greece has reached such a degree of civilization that it can be entrusted with mandatory rule over a people of different faith and hostile feeling. The Greek army and all authority of the Greek government ought to be withdrawn from an area where better order was kept by twelve British officers than can be maintained by one hundred thousand Greek troops. There can be no settled peace until either a Greek conquest has swept far to the interior, with great destruction of property and life, or until the Greek power is wholly removed.[96]

The commission recommended against a separate Greek area being created in western Anatolia even if the Greeks did triumph, because within the borders of any territory that might be marked out for this purpose the Greeks would be outnumbered by Turks by a ratio of about 3:1.

In August 1921 the Greeks suffered a major defeat at the battle of Sakarya. A year later, a second defeat (in the battle of Dumlupinar) broke the Greek army. The troops pulled back toward Izmir, abandoning their heavy weaponry and leaving a spiteful trail of tremendous destruction. Cities, towns, and villages were pillaged and put to the torch along with crops, and thousands of civilians were killed. Mosques were destroyed and in some cases—according to British accounts—set on fire with Turks inside them.[97] Turkish accounts of atrocities and destruction were confirmed by foreign observers. "All cities except Menem practically destroyed by burning," wrote a U.S. naval intelligence officer. "There are many stories of robbing, looting, rapine and pillaging by the retreating Greek army. Saw many wounded and dead Moslems passing through this country. Country absolutely desolate and all shelter and food has been destroyed. Magnesia was 80 percent destroyed, Casaba 90 percent, Alasehir 90 percent, Salihli 60 percent. . . . Mosques were particular objects of destruction. Harvested crops were destroyed by fire. . . . The fields are filled with thousands of people searching for food."[98] In Manisa another

U.S. naval intelligence officer was met by a delegation of notables who produced a list of the destruction in the city: it included 10,700 homes, thirteen mosques, two hamams, 2,728 shops, nineteen hotels, three flour mills, five farms, and 3,500 people who had died in fires deliberately lit by "organised bands of incendiaries" spraying houses with oil and then setting them on fire. Traveling around the city, they reported, "It is hard to conceive of such complete destruction as we saw."[99]

The scenes in Izmir were chaotic as the Turkish forces approached in early September. Greek civilians milled around in desperation as the invading and now defeated Greek army waited south of the city for ships to come and take them away. The panic along the waterfront played out against the molten background of a great mercantile city on fire; the cause remains unknown, but if the fire was not accidentally started (as the great fire that devastated Salonica in 1917 had been), those leaving Izmir had far greater reason to burn it down than those arriving. Even at this desperate stage Greek politicians were still talking of establishing an Ionian Republic on the other side of the Aegean, but the situation was irretrievable unless the Western powers that had sponsored the invasion were prepared to intervene again. British forces concentrated around the Dardanelles (the narrow stretch of water dividing the European land mass from Anatolia) were now confronted by a successful and highly motivated Turkish national army determined to recapture all lost territory. Churchill and Lloyd George were ready for someone else to take them on and appealed to the governments of South Africa, Canada, Australia, and New Zealand to send troops. New Zealand was willing to send a battalion; Australia and Canada said they were not interested in getting caught up in a new war; Jan Smuts of South Africa "did not even bother to reply."[100] Back home in Britain there was no appetite at all for more fighting, and in these circumstances Churchill and Lloyd George were eventually compelled to back down. In the culminating act of this drama, more than a million Greeks and half a million Turks had to leave their ancestral homes in western Anatolia and Thrace in a compulsory population exchange. The boundaries of the Turkish republic were established through revision of the Treaty of Sèvres at Lausanne in 1923. After an epic conflict with invading and occupying forces, independence had finally been attained; to the south, however, the Arab struggle against British and French occupation was just beginning.

4. EXIT THE SHARIF

The Sharif Husain of Mecca, the custodian of the holy places in that city and in Madina, placed great trust in the British. "He knows that they are just and highly civilized and he likes them."[1] He had a "profound belief" in their integrity.[2] They were friends of Islam and "the defender and sincere friend of all the Arabs."[3] Initially the British were delighted with him too. "Mild and generous character . . . exceptional ability in religious matters and Mohammedan literature,"[4] "captivating sincerity," and "noble simplicity"[5] were some of the early descriptions of this scion of the Hashimite branch of the Prophet's family. This peerless avatar of the Muslims as he emerges from the pages of official dispatches was at the time raising an Arab revolt against the Ottomans in return for British pledges of support for Arab independence once the war was over. In acknowledgment of the unshakable friendship between the Hijaz and Britain, the sharif was honored with a Grand Commandership of the Bath and his sons Ali and Abdullah with a Grand Commandership of the Order of the British Empire.

The insulting references to the old man began to appear in diplomatic dispatches when the war had been won and his services were no longer required. The sharif was no longer the living embodiment of Muslim virtue but ruthless and weak; childish, foolish, pigheaded, tactless; discourteous, conceited, greedy, and stupid; a megalomaniac who demonstrated "the defects of character and ignorance of systems common to oriental potentates"; a financial incompetent whose methods were "comic opera"; a barbarian; an old despot hated by his neighbors and dreaded by his subjects; a king who "becomes more shameless and less dignified as time goes by" and was at times even "monstrous"; a ruler who "for years has been exploiting our loyalty."[6] When the sharif began looking for a new home after being driven out of the Hijaz by the Suʿudis in 1924, the thought crossed the official mind that he might want to come to London. That could not be allowed. "He would be a great bore here."[7] Coupled with the abuse was a lot of sniggering: reports from the British agent in Jidda would be "packed with material for official laughter, to be circulated more widely than usual in Whitehall of account of their comic value."[8] But even when the sharif was being flattered because he was needed, the British government never accepted his grandiose claims. When he had himself installed as "king of the Arab lands" (on October 29, 1916), Sir Henry McMahon, the British agent in Egypt, wrote that the step he had taken was "ill advised and premature."[9] Britain recognized him only as the king of the Hijaz. The sharif had an even more illustrious title in mind. He was greatly flattered when addressed as caliph, eventually assuming the title two days after the Turkish nationalist government in Ankara abolished the institution (on March 3, 1924).

What the sharif regarded as Britain's betrayal of himself and the Arabs is a pivotal point in modern Middle Eastern history. Not until the Bolsheviks disclosed the text of the secret Sykes-Picot agreement (signed in May 1916) did he realize that Britain and France had divided between themselves the territory he thought had been promised to him. Arab accusations of bad faith center on the letters passed between the sharif and Sir Henry McMahon, the British agent in Egypt, between July 14, 1915, and January 30, 1916. Whatever might have been promised in private, Britain never actually made any formal written commitment to the establishment of one Arab state, let alone one headed by the sharif or his sons. The real dispute centers on the extent of the territory in which Britain was prepared to recognize Arab independence. The boundaries submitted to Britain by the sharif included Syria (including Palestine), Iraq, and much of the Arabian peninsula. McMahon's critical letter of October 24, 1915, was largely about what Britain wanted him to exclude: "The two districts of Mersina and Alexandretta [today's Mersin and Iskanderun] and portions of Syria lying to the west of the districts of Damascus, Homs, Hama and Aleppo cannot be said be said to be purely Arab and should be excluded from the limits demanded." Apart from these exceptions, he wrote, and without prejudice to existing treaties signed with Arab chiefs, "we accept those limits."[10]

The loss of coastal territory was unacceptable to the sharif. On that point he and McMahon agreed to disagree—the sharif did agree to a temporary British presence at Basra—but as the high commissioner made no other specific exceptions, the sharif was entitled to assume that Arab independence would be acknowledged in the rest of the territory he had defined. This was still subject to a caveat. Britain would "recognise and support the independence of the Arabs in all the [other] regions within the limits demanded by the Sharif of Mecca" only insofar as it remained free to act "without detriment to the interest of her ally France."[11] This gave the British government the clause it might need to justify the exclusion of Mosul and Palestine. Mosul went to Iraq, but by retaining sole control of Palestine after France had surrendered its claim, Britain clearly breached the commitment made in the McMahon correspondence. It insisted that it had agreed to support Arab independence only on the basis of reservations "which have always been held by His Majesty's Government to exclude Palestine and West Syria from the scope of the undertaking."[12] But Palestine was not mentioned in McMahon's exemptions, and by no stretch of the imagination can a territory lying to the southwest of Damascus be described as lying to the west of Damascus and the towns of northern Syria. McMahon was an experienced imperial administrator who had drawn borders before (between India and Tibet), and to suggest that misunderstandings arose because he was careless or that the letters were poorly drafted is to sidestep the obvious. Deliberate ambiguity is standard diplomatic practice when governments do not want to reveal their hand. The high commissioner took the trouble to mention territories west of the four northern Syrian towns that the sharif must be prepared to concede. Why not those to the southwest as well? In that direction lay Palestine and its crowning glory, the mosque compound in Jerusalem from which the Prophet Muhammad had ascended into the heavens on his miraculous night journey. Jerusalem was the third holiest city in Islam. Why specifically exclude Homs, a one-horse town, or Hama and not Jerusalem? The answer is surely clear. The British government knew that no Jerusalem for the sharif would have meant no Arab revolt for Britain.

After the war, Britain and the sharif continued to irritate each other, Britain by cutting back its subsidies and the sharif by sending arms to help the Syrian nationalists, thereby challenging the territorial settlement Britain had finally reached with France. In 1923 negotiations over an Anglo-Hijazi treaty stalled largely because of the sharif's insistence that the people of Palestine be given independence without delay,[13] but by this time the old man was losing power even in the kingdom Britain had recognized as being his own (the Hijaz) and for the future of which it had acknowledged its moral responsibility. Suʿudi incursions into the Hijaz from central Arabia ended in full-scale invasion by the *ikhwan* (the zealous Islamic frontline Suʿudi forces), the capture of Taif, and finally the capture of Medina and Mecca. The sharif abdicated on October 4, 1924. Ten days later he and his retinue left Jidda by steamer, followed by a separate ship carrying cars and horses. Three days later they arrived at Aqaba, the very town that the sharif's bedouin warriors, with T. E. Lawrence riding at their head, had captured from the Turks in 1916 to great acclaim in London. The sharif had intended to move on to Amman to be with his son Abdullah, but on arrival he was met by Alec Kirkbride, the senior British resident in Transjordan, and told that the British government did not want him to move anywhere until a decision had been reached on his future place of residence.[14]

So the sharif stayed put. By May 1925 he and his staff (including a doctor) were still living in tents on the shore at the end of a pier, but his presence even there was a complication Britain did not want. Technically it regarded Maʿan and Aqaba as falling within the boundaries of mandatory Palestine, but in practice the two districts had been allowed to remain under the administration of the government of the Hijaz until final borders could be drawn. The conquest of the Hijaz by the Suʿudis and the threat by Abd al Aziz ibn Suʿud to send a force to Aqaba to dislodge the sharif compelled Britain to take a clearer position. Ibn Suʿud was warned that any encroachment on Maʿan and Aqaba would be regarded as an attack on territory for which Britain was responsible.[15] At the same time, the sharif could not be allowed to continue funding resistance to the Suʿudis from Transjordan. On May 27, 1925, he was asked to leave. Ibn Suʿud was informed that his enemy had been invited to "proceed elsewhere."

Husain did not want to move. "If His Majesty sends a warship here to kill me and my family that will be the shortest and best way of delivering me from my problems," he told his former ally.[16] There was still some sympathy for "this aged man whose action during war rendered considerable service to the Allies,"[17] but he could not allowed to settle anywhere that his presence might be an embarrassment, and basically that meant removing him from the Arab world. Basra, Baghdad, ʿAkka, Haifa, or perhaps some town in southern Palestine "where accommodation was available" were all considered as possible next ports of call and rejected.[18] On June 1 Britain succeeded in inducing the sharif to take up residence on board a British warship. He agreed to his removal from Aqaba by June 18. On June 14 he was offered asylum in Cyprus, but as late as June 17 he was still pleading to be allowed to go to Jaffa or Haifa instead. He was told this was not possible, and the next day H.M.S. *Delhi* moved him on Cyprus.

From Nicosia the sharif continued to air his grievances in messages to King George V and Prime Minister Stanley Baldwin. In late November 1929, now eighty-three and gravely ill after a stroke, he was allowed to return to Amman so he could spend his last days with his son Abdullah. He still spoke scathingly of that "acrobat and fox" "Luweed George."[19]

Antonius visited him: "I can never forget him as he sat there, ill at ease, in an arm-chair far too large for his small frame, shrunken with paralysis, his eyes suddenly glowing from the vacancy of resignation to flashes of controlled passion."[20] On June 5, 1931, the sharif died. Antonius criticizes his numerous failings, including his tactlessness and his inability to rule the Hijaz fairly, but he balances this with commendation of his strength of purpose in refusing to budge from his convictions whatever the personal cost. Arab nationalists everywhere looked on the postwar scene with despair, but the last word should perhaps be left to the sharif. In an open letter to the "noble British nation" he summed up the damage done to himself and the Arabs: "Their unity has been torn to pieces—their countries disintegrated and occupied. . . . I know of no sin they did commit deserving such a fate except their absolute trust and loyalty to Great Britain—if this is really a sin. . . . No-one but God knows where their despair will lead them."[21]

YAWM MAYSALUN

By the standards of the colonial encounters already mentioned in this narrative, the battle between invading French troops and Syria's protonational army at Maysalun on July 24, 1920, was a mere skirmish, but as a symbol of nationalist defiance of overwhelming odds Yawm Maysalun (the Day of Maysalun) retains deep symbolic meaning. The Syrians had quickly tried to make good on the independence they thought had been promised to them. In 1919 they held a congress in Damascus and chose a king (the sharif's son Faisal) without being fully aware of the extent to which their rights were being bargained away in London and Paris. In 1920 France partitioned Syria by establishing an enlarged Lebanon and giving it a constitutional arrangement that privileged Christians against Muslims. When negotiations with the Syrian government failed, it sent an army across the Lebanese mountains to bring Damascus to heel. The French forces met stubborn resistance all the way, punishing "rebellious" villages by bombing them from the air or putting them to the torch. At the base of the anti-Lebanon mountains thousands of Syrian nationalists took up defensive positions around the pass at Khan Maysalun. The pitched battle that ensued dragged on for several hours; by the time the nationalists were routed, 150 were dead (including their commander Yusuf al ʿAzma) and another 1,500 wounded. French losses were 42 dead and 152 wounded. Faisal fled before the French entered Damascus and began taking over public buildings.

Over the years the French used the full range of colonial devices to control Syria. The strategic need to anchor the French presence at both ends of the Mediterranean meant not just consolidating a military presence on land and at sea but blocking the growth of religious and national sentiment. Accordingly, the French "did not conceal their preference for Christians above Muslims and for the mountain minorities (Maronites, Alawites, Druzes and Turcomans) above the majority Sunni Arabs of the coast, desert and cities."[22] Separate states—effectively colonial protectorates—were established around Damascus and Aleppo; within the state of Aleppo, the coastal *sanjak* (subprovince) of Alexandretta (Iskanderun) was excluded and given its own autonomous administration before France completely debauched its "sacred trust" responsibility under the mandate by handing the region over to Turkey in 1939 (the very region it had insisted in 1918 was part of *la Syrie intégrale*); the coastal region of Latakia was given statehood, and in the south the Jabal Druze was given autonomy with its own governor and an elected council. These arrangements were modified over the years, but French interests always had to predominate. Each state or autonomous region functioned under the control of French *delegués* and departmental advisers; parliaments (in Lebanon as well as Syria) could be prorogued at the high commissioner's discretion and constitutions suspended indefinitely.

From beginning to end the platform on which this colonial structure was built was force. More than six thousand French soldiers (most of them colonial troops from North or West Africa) had already died suppressing "rebels" and "brigands" since 1920 when the Sultan al Atrash, angered at the arrest of Druze sheikhs, routed a French column in late July 1925 and besieged the occupied Druze town of Suwayda. When a second column sent to punish the sheikh for the destruction of the first was also scattered, a wave of uprisings spread across the whole of Syria with the speed of a grass fire. The "great Arab revolt" had begun, and the French moved swiftly to crush it. In October an uprising in Hama led by Fawzi al Qawuqji—later to make his name fighting the British in Iraq and the Zionists in Palestine—was met with aerial bombardment of the market area and ground action by the hated Senegalese levies that left more than three hundred dead. Outside the town "rebels" set fire to railway stations and pulled up the lines; in the south, eight villages and the town of Majd al Shams in the Golan were left in ruins after French attacks that left tens of thousands of people homeless; attacks on the Druze in one part of Syria led to Druze uprisings elsewhere, with the town of Hasbeyya (in Grand Liban) being recaptured only after an assault by more than three battalions of Algerian infantry backed by cavalry, tanks, field artillery, and air support.

Inevitably, Damascus had to bear the brunt of French imperial anger. The main point of resistance was the orchard area on the outskirts of the city known as the Ghuta. Already by October 15 about a hundred "brigands" had been killed in "clearing operations." Twenty-four of the bodies were carried into the city by French soldiers and put on public display in the central square, a touch of barbarity that only further inflamed public feeling. On October 17, Druze horsemen arrived at the Ghuta, and the nationalists began moving toward the center of Damascus, bypassing the barricades set up to keep them out. The next evening the French began bombarding the southern quarters of the town before turning their attention to the center the following morning, "this time with high explosive shells striking in all quarters from the central bazaars down to the middle of the Maydan."[23] In two days, 1,416 people (including 336 women and children) were killed and much of the central city was ruined by tank and artillery fire and air attack.[24] The Suq Midhat Pasha and the Suq al Hamidiyya markets near the Umayyad mosque were destroyed. Shop fronts were riddled with machine-gun fire. In the biblical "street called straight" (running alongside the Umayyad mosque), whole buildings collapsed into piles of rubble. The palatial mansions of the urban notables were shattered. The French high commissioner (General Sarrail) had made part of the ʿAzm Palace his quarters, and that was quickly besieged by "rebels." The general's rooms were pillaged, and the *selamlik* (where official guests were received) was destroyed. "Very serious damage" was done to the library, "where valuable and irreplaceable prints and books dealing with Arabic art have either been absolutely destroyed or injured beyond repair."[25] Tapestries and carpets were looted both from the ʿAzm Palace and the mosques of the Maydan quarter by persons unknown, but the nationalists accused French troops of taking them before setting the mosques on fire.

There were no apologies from the French government, only outrage at the killing of French troops and the destruction of property by "brigands." A collective fine (of about £35 per person) was imposed on Damascus, and the city was subjected to a house-by-house search for weapons. In the country, villages "where brigands are reported to have been harbored and victualled" were torched,[26] yet the resistance continued. More than 200 Druze fighters were killed and more than 200 wounded in fighting with the French around Majd al Shams in April 1926. Suwayda was retaken by the French the same month after a large-scale battle between 12,000

French troops and a Druze force of 4,000 to 5,000, of which number about 600 men were killed and another 800 wounded for perhaps 120 deaths on the French side.[27]

With resistance slowly being broken in the north and the south, the French were able to concentrate on the center. In February they had made another attempt to crush resistance in Damascus, and on May 7 they struck again:

> In less than 12 hours the French army struck with more intensity than it had either in October [1925] or February. The number of houses and shops destroyed during the aerial bombardment or as a result of incendiaries was estimated at well over 1,000. The death toll was equally staggering, between 600 and 1,000. The vast majority were unarmed civilians, including a large number of women and children: only 50 rebels were reported killed in the attack. Afterwards the troops indulged in pillaging and looting and then paraded their spoils through the streets in the city centre. . . . The French assault made a formerly busy quarter of 30,000 a virtually deserted ruin.[28]

On July 8, a further six days of fighting began when the French military command sent 5,000 troops, backed up by tanks, field artillery, and aircraft, into the Ghuta. Another 1,500 people (an estimate because, like most occupying armies, the French had no interest in counting the people they were killing) died (only a few hundred of them "rebels") at the cost of about 200 "French" (mainly colonial troops) lives.[29] Druze and other nationalist leaders fled into Transjordan; France was to retain its hold on Syria and Lebanon until 1946, when, weakened by the war and disgraced by a final bombardment of Damascus in which hundreds of people were killed, it was compelled to withdraw under British pressure and transfer the authority given to it by the League of Nations to nationalist governments.

EGYPT FOR THE ENGLISH

There is an obvious paradox in Albert Hourani's concept of a "liberal age" in the Arab world. Hourani introduced his seminal work on the subject as "a study of that stream of political and social thought which began when in the first half of the nineteenth century, educated men in the Arabic-speaking countries became aware of the ideas and institutions of modern Europe and, in the second, started to feel its powers."[30] But although a cultural "liberal age" might flourish among Arabs under British rule, a political "liberal age" could not serve interests that were so diametrically opposed. Under British occupation, nationalists and Muslim activists in Egypt were given considerable latitude as long as they did not incite open rebellion, but once the country was given a form of independence in 1922 it was inevitable that the "liberal age" would have to be constitutional and political as well as cultural. All the trappings of such an order were in fact enshrined in the constitution, giving the Egyptians a parliament, elections, and freedom of speech and movement.

For the duration of the war Egypt had the political status of a "veiled protectorate," but the moment it was over the nationalists renewed their clamor for independence. The arrest of Saʿad Zaglul and other leading figures on March 8, 1919, triggered a countrywide revolt that lasted throughout the year. Rail and postal workers went on strike in the cities, while in the delta railway lines were pulled up and buildings sacked. British soldiers were murdered, and an attempt was made to assassinate Prime Minister Said Pasha in Alexandria by throwing a bomb hidden in a basket of grapes at his car. Trains returning to Cairo from Upper Egypt were stoned; in one especially savage episode two British officers and seven men traveling from Luxor were done to death with knives, stones, and sticks when villagers broke into their first-class compartment. Two were killed at one station and the rest at the next. The train continued on with the bludgeoned and stripped bodies stuffed into the luggage van and crowds gathering to cheer at every station.[31] "Order" was restored in the provinces through the dispatch of punitive columns, air attacks, and the imposition of heavy collective fines. Town "riff-raff," "Bolsheviks," and students (especially religious students from Al Azhar University), along with "some out-of-work lawyers and effendis," were blamed for stirring up the trouble.[32] In 1922, Britain finally had to yield, granting Egypt a restricted independence in the form of a constitutional monarchy.

Egypt now had all the stability of a square table with three legs. The first was the politicians, generally at each other's throats; the second was a king installed as an instrument of imperial control; and the third was a British ambassador determined to work on susceptible politicians and an insecure monarch to ensure that Egypt remained within the imperial fold. Sir Miles Lampson's relationship with King Faruq imitated Lord Cromer's earlier relationship with the khedive Abbas Hilmi II,[33] right down to Lampson's patronizing use of *boy* when referring to the king. Abbas Hilmi was only seventeen when he succeeded to the throne in 1892. Faruq was sixteen on his succession in 1937; a regency council took on the royal responsibilities until he was eighteen, but whatever maturity he acquired over the years, he was a youthful lightweight in the continuing struggle for advantage with sly politicians and a domineering British ambassador.

In early February 1942 the government resigned after being criticized by the king for breaking relations with Vichy France without notifying him first. Faruq had public feeling on his side: pro-German and Italian feeling across the Middle East was strong because of the continuing British and French occupation of Arab lands or domination of them from behind the scenes. When news leaked out that Faruq was planning to appoint his friend Ali Mahir as prime minister, Lampson told the king that he wanted Nahas Pasha (the Wafd leader) to form the government. On February 4 he issued an ultimatum. If Nahas was not appointed prime minister by 6:00 P.M., "His Majesty King Farouk must accept the consequences."[34] When six o'clock came and went without Faruq responding, Lampson drove to Abdin Palace in a convoy of armored cars. A British officer drew a gun and shot the lock off the gates. Lampson barged into the king's presence and harangued him for his irresponsibility before brandishing a document of abdication in Faruq's face. If the king did not sign, Lampson threatened, he would meet with something "more unpleasant."[35]

The contest could not have been more uneven. It was Cromer and Abbas Hilmi all over again. Lampson was sixty and physically, at six foot five inches tall, an ox of a man, given to wearing plus fours and hunting with a shotgun. He was sick of having to "frighten the boy" at periodic intervals and wanted him out of the way for good, remarking shortly before the drive to the palace that "it doesn't often come one's way to be pushing a monarch off the throne."[36] Looking at this imperial bully waving a piece of paper in his face was a king who was still slender and a week short of his twenty-second birthday. Lampson thought he had gotten what he wanted until the king looked up and asked for "one more chance" before agreeing to appoint Nahas.[37] Lampson was jubilant but regretted that he had not gone further because "we are still faced with the fact that we have a rotter on the Throne."[38] The humiliation of the king is a plausible turning point in the process of mental and physical degeneration that transformed the debonair young man who took the throne in 1936 into the obese hulk who was tipped off it in 1952. Faruq still intrigued, sometimes with the British and sometimes against them, but his pleasures steadily became more carnal than political, and the end was more pathetic than tragic: sent into exile in 1952, he spent his last years in Italy, a caricatured figure who was still only forty-five when he died.

The entanglement of politicians and the king with a wily imperial power was ruinous to the "liberal" order. There could be no long-term happy cohabitation between British interests and Egyptian aspirations—between an "independence" disciplined and manipulated by an outside power and real independence—and like Siamese twins bonded from birth but surgically separable, one had to die so that the other could live even for a short time. The "liberal age" in Egypt did not succumb to some mysterious virus floating through the colonial window. If Britain was to remain a powerful, dominant imperial state, it had no option but to undermine the very system it had established. Egyptian cynicism and distrust, as the end approached, was born not from a lack of interest in liberalism but from disillusionment and shattered hopes.

AN "INCIDENT"

Faruq's humiliation was hidden from the Egyptian people until the war was over, but much of the political drama was played out before their eyes, and what they could not see they could imagine. In the army, aggrieved middle-ranking officers disgusted by the twin evils of foreign domination and corruption of the political order conspired to take power from the incompetent hands of the misruling elite as soon as the right moment came. By the late 1940s, under the weight of public revelations of political corruption, scandals connected with the disastrous outcome of the war in Palestine, political assassinations, and nationalist opposition to Anglo-French control of the Suez Canal and the massive British military presence in the Canal Zone, this moment seemed to be rapidly approaching. In October 1947 Egypt's unilateral abrogation of the Anglo-Egyptian treaty of 1936 was taken in London as a challenge that could not be ignored. Britain could not just wait in the hope that the Egyptian government would fall of its own volition. In line with this thinking, a plan was cooked up for a provocation, an "incident" in the Canal Zone, perhaps "a major battle with Egyptian terrorists" already attacking British troops as "liberation battalions," or "the imposition of further drastic measures of control" that would bring on a showdown Britain could turn to its advantage.[39]

On January 25, 1952, the Ismailiyya police station was besieged on the grounds that it was being used as a base for attacks on British soldiers. The British commander demanded the surrender of weapons and the expulsion of the police from the Canal Zone. When the Egyptian government ordered them to stand firm, the British troops opened fire, killing more than fifty of the police and wounding many others. In Cairo the next day, a demonstration outside Abdin Palace developed into general anti-European rioting and arson attacks on the upper-class symbols of the colonial presence. Hapless Britons (many of them elderly long-term British residents of Cairo) and other foreigners were seized and murdered. Shepheards Hotel was burnt to the ground, Groppi's café was ransacked, the Turf Club and Barclay's Bank were torched, and fashionable department stores were looted. Abdel Nasser writes that the operation "was planned by the British to the minutest detail, down to its timing and its expected outcomes at every level."[40] It is hard to believe that the British government could have been so totally cynical, but it must have known that the attack at Ismailiyya would put the lives of its own citizens—and other foreigners—in jeopardy. The shelling of Alexandria in 1882 and the suppression of the nationalist movement in 1919 had been answered with terrible reprisals against vulnerable Europeans, so it could hardly be argued that there were no precedents. In the short term the provocation worked. Faruq declared martial law and a curfew and strengthened the guard around Abdin Palace and the British and U.S. embassies. The Wafd government was dismissed and Ali Mahir was appointed prime minister, but the short term turned out to be very short indeed. On July 23 the "Free Officers" came out of the barracks and swept away the remnants of the nationalist generation that had come out in the streets against British occupation in 1919.[41] The age of Arab revolution had finally started. In Iraq, young officers modeling themselves on the Egyptian Free Officers were now inspired to make a final push to end nearly four decades of subjugation, first through invasion and occupation and then through the manipulation of "independent" governments.

5. SMALL WARS IN IRAQ

Flexibility marked all the imperial arrangements in the Arab world: constitutional monarchies for Egypt and Iraq, a mandate for Palestine, a king for Jordan, subsidized sheikhdoms the length and breadth of the Gulf, and support for a dictator in Iran who would look after Britain's oil interests (while furthering his own vaulting ambitions). Profits from the Anglo-Persian Oil Company (later Anglo-Iranian) monopoly in Iran were augmented by returns from the Iraq Petroleum Company, in which it was a 23.75 percent shareholder: the remainder was parceled out to Royal Dutch Shell and the Compagnie Françaises des Petroles (23.75 percent each, slightly less than the 25 percent originally promised to the French), Standard Oil of New Jersey and Socony Vacuum Oil (now Mobil) (11.875 percent each), and Calouste Gulbenkian (5 percent).

In Mesopotamia, an entirely new state had to be created. Divided into Ottoman provinces since the conquest of Baghdad in the sixteenth century, the territory turned into Iraq was an unwieldy agglomeration of tribes, religions, ethnicities, and regions that made no sense without the binding logic of oil. The first wells were successfully drilled in the Kirkuk region north of Baghdad in 1927 (the oil transported by pipeline to terminals in Palestine and Syria), with production later extended to fields around Mosul and Basra. The human population living atop these massive fossil fuel reserves in northern Mesopotamia was an ethno-religious-tribal mix of Sunni Muslim Kurds (the majority), Arabs, Turkmen, an assortment of Christians of various sects, Jews, Yezidis, and some Kurdish Shiʿa. The Kurds regarded Mosul as "an Arab rampart projecting into territory they considered their own" and Kirkuk as an integral part of the historical Kurdish homeland, to be incorporated one day into the independent Kurdish state dangled before their eyes in 1919.[1] Their claim was vigorously rejected by the city's other ethno-religious groups, among whom the Turkmen benefited from the sympathy and support (cemented through ethnic and family ties) of Turks across the border. With a substantial Kurdish population of its own, the government in Ankara regarded the claims of the Iraqi Kurds as a potential threat to Turkey's stability. Britain's intermittent support for Kurdish autonomy alarmed the Arabs as well: in the view of Iraq's first king (Faisal), the concessions it was making (the adoption of Kurdish as an official language and the appointment of Kurdish officials in Kurdish areas) would "not for long satisfy the Kurds whose demands would increase after each concession made to them until they in the end embarked on a struggle for union and independence which would possibly involve Iraq in war with Persia and Turkey."[2]

In the western provinces toward the Syrian border the population was predominantly Sunni Arab, but south between the Tigris and the Euphrates, from Karbala all the way down to Basra, it was overwhelmingly Shiʿa. As was the case elsewhere, tribal loyalties formed a dominant strand of identity along with religion. Baghdad itself was a polyglot city with a substantial Jewish population.

In March 1917, General Maude entered the "fabled city" of Baghdad at the head of the triumphant British expeditionary force.[3] In a proclamation to the people, Maude set out what Britain wanted for them. It was the wish of his king and country that "you should prosper even as in the past when your lands were fertile, when your ancestors gave the world literature, science and art and when Baghdad city was one of the wonders of the world." Britain had no desire to impose an alien civilization on them. Instead it hoped that "the Arab race may rise once more to greatness and renown among the peoples of the earth."[4] On November 7, 1918, the British and French governments repeated these good intentions in a joint declaration on the future of the "liberated territories" in the East. Now that the Turks had been defeated, their aim in Syria and Mesopotamia was "the complete and definite enfranchisement of the peoples so long oppressed by the Turks and the establishment of national governments and administrations, deriving their authority from the initiative and free choice of the indigenous population."[5]

These statements raised hopes that were soon dashed. Britain's formal acceptance of the League of Nations mandate on May 3, 1920, provoked uprisings across the occupied territory as Kurdish ağa, Sunni sheikhs, and Shiʿi *mujtahid* defended tribal, religious, and ethnic interests. Secret societies were formed and jihad was declared. By August 1920 the scale of resistance had forced the British government to declare that "a state of war exists in Mesopotamia."[6]

The dominant symbols of foreign occupation were the army, the air force, the Assyrian levies, and the isolated British political officers stationed in various parts of Mesopotamia. In February 1918 Captain W. M. Marshall, canceling home leave to marry after he received his orders, was sent into the Shiʿi holy city of Najaf. His murder there in March by intruders who overwhelmed his small Punjabi guard was followed by a spate of similar killings: Captain A. C. Pearson, an assistant political officer, killed by Goyan Kurdish tribesmen near Zakho in April 1919; Captain R. H. D. Willey, a political officer, killed at Amadiya in July, along with Captain H. Macdonald and Sapper R. Troup and the levies guarding them; Mr. J. H. H. Bill, an experienced imperial administrator put in charge of Mosul, ambushed and killed by Kurds near Aqra in November along with Captain K. R. Scott; Captain Stuart, an Arab levy officer, shot dead at Tal Afar in June 1920, with his guards, sergeants Lawler and Walker, being killed by a bomb; Captain J. E. Barlow, shot dead after escaping from captivity near Mosul the same month; Lieutenant Colonel G. E. Leachman, a political officer, the "second Lawrence" and recipient of the Royal Geographic Society's Gill Medal for his journey through northeastern Arabia in 1910, murdered in August 1920, having been shot and then finished off with a sword by a tribal leader (Sheikh Dhari) during a meeting at Khan Nuqta between Baghdad and Falluja; Captain W. T. Wrigley, an assistant political officer, Captain Bradfield, commanding a contingent of Arab levies, two British Arab levy instructors, and Captain E. L. Buchanan, an officer with the irrigation department, also murdered in August during an uprising in Shahraban, twenty-seven miles north of Baghdad; Captain G. H. Salmon, killed in late August while held prisoner at Kifri, between Baghdad and Kirkuk. Many of these men were highly decorated First World War officers: more were to die in the years ahead, ambushed or killed in action fighting Kurds and Arabs.

The murder of Marshall was regarded as a "critical moment" by the occupying authorities in Baghdad, and the harsh collective punishment meted out to Najaf was intended as a warning to "fanatical elements" elsewhere in Mesopotamia.[7] "Fatuous" appeals for clemency and proposals for arbitration by Najaf's "Shiʿite divines" were turned down.[8] The town was surrounded by troops and denied supplies of food and water while its notables considered the demands being made. Ten weeks later they agreed to hand over the "ringleaders." Only two men had murdered Marshall, but twelve were hanged in public at Kufa on May 30 after being tried before a three-man military tribunal: others were imprisoned, a hundred "suspects" were deported to India as prisoners of war, and the entire town was fined fifty thousand rupees.

In May 1919 the Kurdish leader Sheikh Mahmud (head of the Barzan tribe) declared himself the ruler of all Kurdistan after imprisoning British officers in Suleimaniyya. A British column sent from Kirkuk was repulsed, suffering severe casualties and losing four armored cars and nineteen Ford vans (used to transport infantry) before the Kurds were overwhelmed in heavy hand-to-hand fighting in a mountain defile near Chamchamal in June.[9] Sheikh Mahmud and his brother were both captured. The Barzan leader was brought before a military tribunal that he argued had no competence to try him: when visited by Arnold Wilson while in hospital, he recited President Wilson's twelfth point (on the right of autonomy for the subject peoples of the former Ottoman Empire) and quoted from the Anglo-French Declaration of 1918, "a translation of which in Kurdish, written on the fly leaves of a Qurʾan, was strapped like a talisman to his arm."[10] In the meantime, "punitive operations" continued in all the Kurdish regions where political or military officers had been killed. Ağas implicated in their murders were captured and executed and villages burned. In three months of campaigning, 137 British officers and men died; most were Indian troops, a mixture of the various ethno-religious groups that had fallen under British occupation and were now being used to enforce British occupation elsewhere. Kurdish casualties can safely be assumed to have been far heavier.

"MACHINE-GUNNED WITH EFFECT"

By 1920, uprisings across the country had crystallized into a general revolt involving Kurds, Turkmen, and Shiʿi and Sunni Arab Muslims. "Sir Percy [Cox], I think rightly, decided that the tribes must be made to submit to force," wrote Gertrude Bell. "In no other way was it possible to make them surrender their arms or teach them that you mustn't lightly engage in revolution even when your holy men tell you to do so. . . . Nevertheless, it's difficult to be burning villages at one end of the country by means of a British Army and assuring people at the other end that we have really handed over responsibility to native Ministers."[11]

The scale of the resistance dictated the decisions taken at the Cairo conference of 1921, convened by Winston Churchill, secretary of state for the colonies, to consider the whole question of British policy in the Near East. Out of the conference came the decision to evacuate most British and colonial troops from Iraq as soon as practicable. They were to be replaced by local troops commanded by British officers and supported by air power. It was calculated that this combination would substantially reduce the annual

£50 million cost of the occupation. Fitting aircraft with machine guns was one of the technological advances of the war, and their effectiveness against "rebels" in isolated regions had already been proven by the time the decision was take to make air power the central element in the war for Iraq. Arnold Wilson had witnessed the effects: "I had taken part in bombing certain Kurdish villages whose occupants had murdered political officers and in machine-gunning Sheikh Mahmud's insurgents, and had thus learnt something of the possibilities latent in this new arm."[12] The airplane was also a psychological weapon of war: just the sound of an approaching aircraft was enough to terrify villagers.

Without the Royal Air Force, Britain might well have lost control of Iraq almost before creating it. "It is undeniable," wrote Wilson, "that the decision to control Iraq by means of the Royal Air Force made it possible to retain the Mandate; under any other system the cost of the garrison, however reduced in numbers, would have been prohibitive and its efforts ineffectual owing to the great length of communications involved."[13] Churchill wanted another weapon used as well. "I am strongly in favor of using poisoned gas against uncivilized tribes," he wrote in a departmental minute to the War Office. "The moral effect should be so good that the loss of life should be reduced to a minimum. It is not necessary to use only the most deadly gasses: gasses can be used which cause great inconvenience and would spread a lively terror and yet would leave no serious permanent effects on most of those affected."[14] Accordingly, the RAF in Iraq was "urged" to use experimental mustard gas bombs that would "inflict punishment upon recalcitrant natives without grave injury to them."[15] They were apparently never used. Conventional weapons proved adequate: bombed and "machine-gunned with effect" by planes sent into action with ground forces, consisting of infantry, cavalry, armored cars, mountain guns, and Lewis guns mounted in Ford vans, the "rebels" were steadily worn down.[16] Air power enabled Britain not only to cut costs but to redeploy troops to Persia to be sent into the struggle with the Bolsheviks for control of the Caucasus.

The combination of air and ground action slowed but did not stop the resistance. The destruction of villages and crops and the arrest of tribal and religious leaders most probably made matters worse. By the summer of 1920, all the names that the global viewing and reading audience became familiar with after the Anglo-American invasion of Iraq in 2003 were sites of resistance and suppression: Mosul, Falluja, Ramadi, Nasiriyya, Hillah, Najaf, Kufa, Baquba, and Tal Afar, plus towns and villages in the Kurdish north. Blockhouses had to be hurriedly built to keep tribal fighters from cutting lines of communication (railways and telegraph wires) and to prevent Baghdad from being reduced to a small island in a sea of rebellion. Some of the heaviest fighting took place in the south. The garrisons at Samawa, Rumaitha, and Kufa were besieged and relieved only after heavy losses among British and colonial troops: by the time a column of troops and artillery reached Rumaitha, a third of the force had been killed or wounded. Without the RAF dropping bundles of ammunition and food and bombing besieging tribesmen, the outcome would have been much worse. The siege of Kufa lasted for three months. Toward the end, the British troops were reduced to eating their own horses to survive. Gunboats on the Euphrates were seized and destroyed; tribal fighters derailed an armored train by pulling up the rails and then killed the British officers and Indian troops trying to protect themselves in the carriages.

The setback that caused the greatest shock in London was the destruction of an entire military column by tribal fighters who should have been no match for well-trained and armed regular forces in what was close to being a set-piece battle. After "rebels" in the Hilla district (south of Baghdad on the Euphrates) besieged Kufa and seized the town of Kifl, a military force consisting of three companies of the Third Manchester Regiment along with a Sikh company, two squadrons of the Thirty-fifth Sind Horse, and field artillery was dispatched to drive them out. The troops, struggling to pull field guns and drive wheeled transport over rough terrain, were badly heat affected, and five miles from Kifl the operation was called off. On July 24 the retreating column was attacked by a large number of tribesmen fighting from well-entrenched positions and broken. British losses were 180 killed, 60 wounded, and 160 taken prisoner.[17] Captured weaponry included a field gun, seven ammunition wagons, twelve Lewis guns, and eighty-nine transport trucks.

By the spring of 1921, 876 British army soldiers (officers but mostly enlisted) had been killed in Iraq and 1,228 wounded; the casualties on the other side were put at 8,450 killed or wounded, excluding civilians. This was not a war between two armies, even though some of the "rebels" fought with the benefit of military experience gained during service in the Ottoman army: this was a guerrilla war of resistance, a war of tribal partisans, as civilians took up arms to defend family, home, village, town, tribe, and religion against an occupying army.

In Britain, public opinion was shocked at the magnitude of the setbacks in Iraq. Questions were being asked about the whole point of the British presence. "We accepted a mandate in order to promote the better welfare of these people and not to fight them," the *Times* commented in an editorial on August 4. Bolshevism and Turkish or sharifian intrigues were no longer adequate explanations for Arab hostility: "When a relieving column runs up against three lines of trenches manned with machine-guns, rifles and bombs as happened near Rumeitha, something more than a merely sporadic 'rising' confronts us. When our beneficial railways are cut, our engines and trucks seized and our telegraph wires torn down it is time for us to drop the pose of liberators." Two weeks later the paper was driven to make even more forceful criticism (echoed in and perhaps prompted by letters to the editor from such respected old Middle Eastern hands as T. E. Lawrence and Valentine Chirol): "Is it accurate to call the tribes engaged in the Mesopotamia rising 'rebels'? Against what authority are they 'rebelling'? Mesopotamia does not form part of the British Empire."[18]

The 1921 Cairo conference was the formal acknowledgment by the British government that even with the advantage of air power the strategy in Iraq was not working. Changes had to be made. It was essential to establish a government that would have the international standing and legal authority to assert Iraq's claim to Mosul (and its oil) against the Kemalist attempt to secure the province for Turkey. Consequently, the decision was taken to establish a constitutional monarchy in Iraq and hold out the promise of independence in the near rather than the distant future.

PLEBISCITE WITHOUT THE PLEBS

Faisal was installed as the first king of Iraq on August 23, 1921. He had been driven out of Syria by the French and reigned from Baghdad with one eye still on Damascus; Hashimite scheming for the unity of the "Fertile Crescent" (Iraq, Syria, and Transjordan) under their rule was to develop into a recurring theme in Arab politics over the coming three decades. Faisal was a decent man but had no hope of winning over the Iraqi people. He was the occupier's choice and he was an outsider. He was from the Hijaz. He was a Sunni Muslim in a country whose southern region was predominantly Shiʿa. He had no tribal affiliations to fall back on, and he was foisted on the country through a one-question plebiscite—yes to Faisal as king or no—that was "more or less a farce."[19] The voting was arranged by local committees established in cooperation with the British; those entitled to vote were not the whole people but notables and other "men of substance" in the districts where the committees were established. The result was 96 percent for Faisal and 4 percent against (about the same percentage of Iraqis who voted for Saddam Hussein as president in the 1980s), the small number of negative votes principally coming from Turkmen in the Kirkuk region. Among the Kurds, who had suffered heavy losses in British ground and air attacks, the plebiscite was largely ignored.

This lack of a popular base made it difficult for Faisal to act in his own interests, let alone Britain's, but at the start he at least tried to be his own man. Within a year the king's refusal to endorse any treaty that validated the mandate had forced the resignation of Iraq's first government. Churchill was extremely annoyed, writing on the very day that the king was receiving guests in Baghdad to celebrate his accession to the throne a year earlier (August 23, 1922) that Faisal was playing "a very low and treacherous game with us." Questions of deposition "and/or" evacuation would have to be considered, but "I think there is no doubt Cox can keep order in Baghdad."[20] The king's guests at his celebration included leaders of what the British regarded as "extreme" national parties. They were still clustered on a balcony of the royal apartments in Serai Square when Sir Percy Cox, the British high commissioner, mounted the steps to pay his own respects. One of them called to the crowd below that Iraq needed a government free of British influence. From the crowd came the reply: "Down with the mandate."

Such a challenge was not to be tolerated in the high commissioner's very presence. On August 27 Sir Percy told Faisal (as he wrote in a telegram to his government) that "we appeared to me to have reached [a] parting of [the] ways." The king had become "personally identified with and [was] responsible for Anti-British vapourings of the extreme nationalist party. . . . He must now in my opinion either publicly disassociate himself from these agitators and definitely come in with us or take consequences which as far as we could see might be end of his Kingship." When Faisal refused to order the arrest of the "ringleaders" of nationalist agitation, Sir Percy went ahead on his own. Four of the "ringleaders" were "bagged" that day and sent to military custody in Basra, but another four "went to earth and have not yet been dug out."[21]

In a public proclamation, Sir Percy explained to the Iraqi people that as there was no functioning cabinet, the government having resigned and the king having "suddenly been incapacitated by serious illness," he had been forced to take steps to maintain stability and had "decided upon the following steps etcetera." The imperial "etcetera" included the arrest and removal from Baghdad of leading nationalists, the temporary closure of two nationalist political parties, the suppression of two nationalist newspapers and the arrest of their editors, the arrest of a tribal leader, and the "voluntary" departure for Persia "at my recommendation" of two leading Shi'i religious dignitaries. Sir Percy felt confident that "these measures would suffice but I warned the public that I would not hesitate to take drastic steps against any persons who should continue to emulate the seditious vagaries of those who had been placed under arrest." Faisal's illness (his appendix had been removed on the 25th) had obliged his British medical advisers "to impose strict orders that His Majesty should not attend to business of any kind."[22] In fact, Faisal was strong enough two days after his operation to refuse to go along with Sir Percy's demands. It was his stubbornness and not his appendix that seemed to be the problem.

"SUBTLE SCHEMER"

The British now had to make the best of a king whom they had put on the throne but no longer trusted. There are more than echoes here of the way Faisal's father, the Sharif Husain, had been treated when he fell out of favor. In a "secret and personal" annex, Sir Percy Cox dwelt on Faisal's personal deficiencies:

> He has charm of manner in ordinary human intercourse and is a kind and unaffected host, but apart from that he does not appear to me to possess any necessary qualities to make a good king. He is morally weak and unstable: he readily gives his word and as readily evades fulfillment of it. He is a subtle and accomplished schemer and a very bad judge of men. . . . In Baghdad he is regarded with profound mistrust by the Naqib [senior representative of descendants of the Prophet] and Sassoon and others of that caliber while in the country he is looked upon with contempt and resentment by all solid and moderate men and in my intercourse with the latter I now continually feel ashamed when asked why we inflicted on them such a paltry character as King. He has certainly not made good and very much doubt whether he ever will.[23]

This was the king of a country that was costing Britain millions of pounds a year to maintain. On September 1 Churchill wrote that Faisal and the Constituent Assembly should be told that unless "they beg us to stay on our own terms," Britain should evacuate Iraq before the end of the financial year: "I would put this issue in the most brutal way, and if they are not prepared to urge us to stay and to cooperate in every manner I would actually clear out."[24]

On October 10, 1922, the king and the government of Iraq were finally persuaded to sign a twenty-year treaty of alliance with Britain. This was represented by both sides as an important step on the road to independence. Faisal issued "a moving proclamation to his people, written by his own hand and testifying to his deep satisfaction at the conclusion of the alliance with Great Britain." The treaty signaled that the mandate would lapse the moment Iraq was admitted to the League of Nations, but for the time being Faisal was obliged to accept the guidance of the high commissioner "on all matters affecting the international and financial obligations and interests of His Britannic Majesty"—a phrase that did not seem to leave much out. In the subsidiary Officials Agreement, the government was obliged to seed the bureaucracy with British "advisers," from the Ministries of the Interior, Finance, Justice, and Defense down to public works and irrigation, police, posts and telegraph, health, education, accounts, and the judiciary, and to pay half their salaries. Under the Military Agreement, the king was required to declare martial law at the request of the high commissioner and to place the wireless station at his disposal. Britain was given the right to maintain a garrison and recruit local forces for its own use. If the Iraqi government failed to heed the advice of the high commissioner regarding the movement and disposition of the Iraqi army, it would be denied British military assistance. Any joint action by British and Iraqi forces would have to be commanded by a British officer.[25]

While purporting to act in the best interests of the Iraqi people, Britain continued to negotiate with the Kurds in a manner that aroused the suspicions of other sectors of the population. In December, Britain and Iraq issued a declaration recognizing the rights of the Kurds to set up their own government and inviting them to send delegates to Baghdad to discuss boundaries and political and economic relations.[26] These arrangements were vehemently opposed by the leaders of Sunni and Shiʿi Arab opinion and broke down only because of British suspicions centering on the activities of Sheikh Mahmud. Since being allowed to return to Suleimaniyya earlier in 1922 he had assumed the title of ruler *(hukumdar)* of all Kurdistan. By November he was signing correspondence as its king, but the British suspected him of negotiating with the Kemalists at the same time that he was enjoying their favors. When he refused to come to Baghdad to clarify the situation, Suleimaniyya was attacked from the air and Sheikh Mahmud driven into the mountains.

IRAQ'S "PERPLEXING PREDICAMENT"

Hostility to the treaty delayed elections to the Constituent Assembly. They were finally held in March 1924, but the treaty still had to be ratified by the assembly and endorsed by the king. After eighteen months of protracted discussions in which only one significant concession was made (the reduction of the life of the treaty from twenty years to four), Britain decided to force the issue. The new high commissioner (Sir Henry Dobbs) announced that if agreement were not reached by June 10 the treaty would be regarded as having been rejected and the League of Nations would be asked to reaffirm the mandate. Only on that day did the Constituent Assembly finally and very reluctantly accept the treaty. It was ratified by the two governments in November and was revised in 1926 after the League of Nations awarded the Mosul *vilayet* to Iraq (December 26, 1925), but at a price to the Iraqis: as part of the package, the duration of the treaty between Iraq and Britain, reduced to four years only three years earlier, was extended to twenty-five.

In February 1929, Sir Gilbert Clayton replaced Sir Henry Dobbs as high commissioner. Clayton hoped to see Iraq in the League of Nations before his term of office ended and acknowledged the "perplexing predicament" of a country that was effectively being run by two governments and had been granted national sovereignty while remaining bound to a mandate.[27] A high commissioner who was sympathetic to Iraqi aspirations for independence was now working in tandem with an Iraqi prime minister (Sir Abdul Muhsin Bey) who had agreed to form a new government only on condition that Britain soften its "unyielding" position on such critical matters as defense, railways, and control of Basra. This promising combination was brought to an end when Clayton died within a few months of his appointment and Sir Abdul Muhsin committed suicide by shooting himself in the heart at his home on November 13. In a note to his son he wrote that "the nation expects service but the English do not agree," expressing at the same time his disappointment in the Iraqi people, who "have been unable to appreciate advice given them by men of honor like myself. They have thought me a traitor to my country and a servant of the British."[28] Sir Abdul Muhsin's tragedy was the ancient dilemma of the man called on to serve two masters only to find that he can satisfy neither. He was succeeded as prime minister by someone who knew how to serve only one. Nuri al Said, an Ottoman army officer taken prisoner by the British in Mesopotamia, would become the staunchest defender in the Middle East of British and "Western" interests. Rashid Ali al Gailani, his political foe, described him as "English from the top of his head to the soles of his feet" and as the servant of imperialism.[29] Few Iraqis or Arabs anywhere would have disagreed with him.

On July 1, 1930, Nuri and the British ambassador signed yet another revised treaty. It gave Britain the right to maintain two bases in Iraq and to station troops there "on the understanding that the presence of these forces shall not constitute in any manner an occupation and will in no way prejudice the sovereign rights of Iraq." In their dealings with other governments, both parties were bound not to adopt an attitude "inconsistent with the alliance" and to come to each other's aid in the event of war. In such circumstances Iraq would be obliged to provide Britain with "all facilities and assistance in [its] power, including the use of railways, rivers, ports, aerodromes and means of communication."[30] There is no reason to think that Faisal was any happier with this treaty than any of its predecessors, but it was the treaty Britain would need before allowing Iraq to take the final step to independence. On May 20, 1933, an equestrian statue of the king created by an Italian sculptor was unveiled on the west bank of the Tigris near the Maude Bridge to mark the king's birthday. An electrical fault marred the ceremony. An angry gush of smoke and flame shot out of the horse's nostrils as the canvas screen around the statue was being pulled back. There was laughter at the mishap, but surely someone in the crowd saw it as a bad omen and remembered it when Faisal died from a heart attack less than four months later. He was in Berne for medical treatment; he seemed well when he left his hotel for a drive to Interlaken but died of a heart attack shortly after returning.

BAKR SIDQI

In October 1932 Iraq was admitted to the League of Nations. In both Egypt and Iraq frustration at the reality of British domination behind the facade of independence fed the rise of a politicized and increasingly impatient officer class. In the Iraqi army of the 1930s the most influential figure was General Bakr Sidqi, the military commander of northern Iraq and the architect of the first military coup in the modern Arab world. In the outside world his name was associated with the repression of the Assyrians in 1933 (see below), but he put down with the same ruthless vigor the tribes who rebelled in the middle Euphrates valley in 1935. "Not endowed with much political wisdom" was one way of describing him.[31] When promoted to chief of the General Staff he attracted more attention. His dyed hair was noted. So was his artistic side: "Dabbles in water colours though he has no technique." His hands were described: "very small, incredibly soft and well kept." He was said to be a good raconteur and host. He was fond of dogs and apparently fond of other men's wives. Officers turned into his bitter enemies because of his interference with their womenfolk. Politically he was a patriot with autocratic tendencies, apparently seeing himself as the iron man his country needed, an Atatürk, a Reza Shah, or a Mussolini.[32]

On October 29, 1936, accusing Prime Minister Yasin al Hashimi's government of incompetence and corruption, Bakr Sidqi overthrew it. The most infamous act of the day was the murder outside Baghdad of the minister of defense, General Ja'far al Askari, as he was carrying a message to Bakr Sidqi from the king. The family and ethno-religious complexities were Byzantine. Bakr Sidqi's chief of staff was the brother of the prime minister he had overthrown; the murdered man's brother-in-law was the overthrown foreign minister, Nuri al Said; Bakr Sidqi was of Kurdish origin, and the two leading politicians who worked with him behind the scenes, Hikmat Sulayman and Abu Timman, were Turkmen and Shi'a respectively; the deposed prime minister was Arab Sunni Muslim. As the coup took hold, ahead of the installation of a government headed by Hikmat Sulayman, Nuri packed a small bag, "slipped across the river in a rowboat," and entered the British ambassador's residence by a water gate. The ambassador was giving a dinner at the time and had to engage in "some play acting to be able to deal with Nuri and my dinner party at the same time." On the verge of collapse, Nuri was given a bed for the night and then waited nervously next day while arrangements were made to fly him to Egypt.[33]

In the view of one observer Bakr Sidqi was a wolf surrounded "by a pack of hyenas still more dangerous and desperate than himself. Hikmat [Sulayman] and his cabinet were only in office on sufferance. When the time came, Bakr Sidqi would cast him aside, and then in his turn Bakr Sidqi would be torn to piece by the hyenas."[34] It was a prediction partly to be fulfilled when Bakr Sidqi and the commander of the air force, Major Muhammad Ali al Jawad, were assassinated on the lawn of the officers' mess at the Mosul airfield on August 11, 1937. At first it was thought that the murders were connected with the massacre of Assyrian Christians in the village of Simel in 1933. It transpired that the assassin was actually taking revenge for the killing in January of Yasin al Hashimi's former cabinet secretary, but regardless of motive Bakr Sidqi was dead, and that was good enough for some. News of the assassination soon reached the widow of Ja'afar al Askari: "The night after the murder a house on the outskirts of Baghdad, usually dark and silent, was gaily illuminated; streams of people came in and out and there were sounds of revelry and song. Madame Ja'far was celebrating the death of her husband's murderer."[35]

GHAZI AND HIS SISTER

One question being asked around Baghdad was whether the king had been involved in Bakr Sidqi's coup even if only by knowing that it was coming but doing nothing. Ghazi had succeeded to the throne after the death of Faisal at the height of the Assyrian crisis in 1933. He never became the

king Britain wanted. He was pro-Italian; he regarded Kuwait as Iraq's by
right, and he had been broadcasting what the British regarded as strident
nationalist propaganda from the palace wireless station. British diplomatic
correspondence of the 1930s is strewn with unflattering references to the
young monarch. He had the usual Hashimite fascination with fast-moving
objects (cars or planes) and was regarded as "idle and lazy and generally
inclined to drift into bad company," though (on the positive side) he was
said to be a keen and courageous horseman.[36] The king's "unsavory" private
life increased his political vulnerability. An anonymous letter was circulated
denouncing him as "a worthless creature by reason of alleged drunkenness,
sexual excess and gambling." The British ambassador wrote that his mode
of life "had long been a cause for whispered scandal and had served to make
the Iraqis hold him in aversion"; the talk whispered around the coffee shops
was of such a kind as to bring the king into contempt.[37] These allusions were
spelled out when a Hijazi palace servant was killed after being persuaded to
join Nuri's son Sabah in a stunt flight in February 1936. The plane's gyra-
tions made the servant sick. Perhaps because Sabah was looking over his
shoulder to see what was going on instead of where he was going, the aircraft crashed. Sabah himself was badly injured, and the "half servant half
catamite" servant was killed through the fracture of his spine.[38]

Four months later, the government was shaken by another Hashimite
family scandal. Holidaying on the island of Rhodes the previous year,
Ghazi's sister, Azzah, had fallen in love with an employee of the Hotel des
Roses. The man, Anastasis Haralambis, Greek but an Italian national, is
variously described in sources as a porter, bar assistant, and waiter and, in a
holiday hotel, may well have been a combination of all three. In May 1936,
Azzah and her sister Rajihah returned to Greece and were staying in
Athens when Azzah disappeared from her hotel room one morning, met
Haralambis, converted to Orthodox Christianity, and married him. They
then returned to the Hotel des Roses, where a cheering crowd showered
them with flowers.

It could have been written for Hollywood, but in Baghdad the government was overcome with rage and shame. The princess, a daughter of the
house of the Prophet, had dishonored her religion, her country, and her
dynasty by marrying a Christian. That he was low class made it even
worse. The prime minister (Yasin al Hashimi) told the British ambassador
(Sir Archibald Clark Kerr) that public feeling was running so high that "it
might be difficult for King Ghazi to hold his own unless his honor was
speedily retrieved": "It was His Majesty's first and obvious duty to kill his
sister with his own hand. His lost honor could not properly be regained by

means of a hired assassin. If King Ghazi killed the princess promptly he could hold up his head again and look people in the face. Otherwise, as time went on, his position might become so shaken as to be beyond saving."[39]

When asked by Clark Kerr what would be done if the princess were brought back to Iraq, the prime minister replied that "she would be declared to be insane and shut up. When I asked if her life would be safe, he admitted that he could by no means guarantee that. He could, in fact, make, no promise that she would not be murdered." Nuri took the same line. The princess had to be killed, preferably by the king—not that it mattered who killed her "as long as she died." At a joint session with the ambassador, both men expressed their view even more vehemently: "To my astonishment Yasin clenched his fist and hammering out his words with blows on the arm of the chair said: 'So long as Nuri and I and every other Iraqi who has felt this disgrace have breath in our bodies, we shall continue to wish for the death of that miserable girl.'"[40]

When the ambassador saw the king, the suggestion that his sister should be murdered struck Ghazi as being rather "odious." On other matters that were causing distress, the king said "he had only just learned that his way of life had become a public scandal. Until now nobody had had the friendliness to come to him to give him any warning. I must not believe everything that was told me. All he had perhaps been guilty of was some harmless little indiscretions with servants to whom he was attached and he certainly would not repeat them." Subsequently the government purged the royal household of "undesirable elements," including the palace master of ceremonies and military aides-de-camp, while making a "clean sweep" of the servants below stairs.[41] Controls were also imposed on the king's movements; Azzah was punished by being stripped of all her assets through retroactive legislation applying to members of the royal household. If she took her sister Rajihah's jewelry with her when she disappeared from her hotel in Athens, as she was reported to have done, it was probably just as well.[42]

When he was overthrown five months later, Yasin al Hashimi accused Ghazi of instigating the coup. He was speaking in Damascus to the British consul. "It will be recalled that as a consequence of the scandal of his sister's marriage," the consul wrote, "King Ghazi was brought severely to heel by Yasin Pasha earlier in the year, and we had already heard that this arbitrary check imposed upon his unpleasant habits of life had given him a grudge against Yasin."[43] Scandal and whispers continued to surround life at the palace. In 1938 a personal attendant of the king was found shot dead, and talk of removing Ghazi continued until he drove his American open sports car into an electric light pole on April 3, 1939. He fractured his skull and died an hour later. His two passengers were injured but not fatally. The car was left at the scene as evidence of death by accident, but rumors quickly swept the city that Britain and the government of Nuri al Said had conspired to have Ghazi killed. When the British consul at Mosul (Mr. G. E. A. C. Monck-Mason) left his office to face demonstrators who had broken into the consulate, he was brained with a pickax handle before the building was burned to the ground. Because the heir to the throne (Faisal II) was still only three, his maternal uncle Abdulillah was installed as regent. Abdulillah, himself only twenty-six, had been educated at Victoria College in Alexandria and had grown into a foppish Middle Eastern carica-ture of an upper-class Englishman. He maintained a stable of racehorses and a pack of hounds and bred pheasants and spaniels. Kermit Roosevelt wrote of "an amiable, smooth, slight young man with a thin mustache and a superior British accent" who was the faithful servant of Britain's inter-ests: "What the British want done is done without instructions by eager guesses on the part of the ministers and the regent."[44]

THE ASSYRIAN LEVIES

The fate of the Nestorian Assyrians living in the southeastern corner of the Ottoman Empire was another calamity arising out of the 1914–18 war. The Nestorian and Jacobite Assyrians were a small minority living among the Kurdish population of the mountainous Hakkari region.[45] The Ottoman government had asked the Assyrians (as well as the Armenians) to remain neutral in the war, but in May 1915, with the Russians advancing into northeastern Anatolia, Nestorian tribal and church leaders committed their people to war on the Russian side. Upon the collapse of the Russian war effort in 1917, the Nestorians of Hakkari and Mosul streamed eastward into northwestern Persia, joining the Assyrians living around Lake Urmia, only for all of them to be overwhelmed by one disaster after another. The first blow was the treacherous murder on March 16, 1918, of the patriarch Benyamin d'Mar Shimun by Ismail Ağa, the Kurdish tribal leader known as Simko (the "little man"). In revenge attacks, hundreds of Kurdish villagers were killed and Simko—the "Kurdish Zapata"—was forced to take flight.

With the collapse of the Russian war effort, the whole of the Caucasus opened up to a struggle for mastery between the Entente Powers and the Bolsheviks. In the British view the Caucasus had to be kept out of Bolshe-vik hands and then sealed off from adjacent territories to prevent "the spread of an anti-British Turanian-Moslem movement working in German interests from Turkey into the heart of Central Asia."[46] In 1918 British emissaries to Urmia encouraged the Assyrians to stand firm against the Turks, assuring them that they would receive the protection due to a "small and oppressed" people but apparently without holding out the specific promise of an independent state (a claim contested by the Assyrians).[47] They also promised arms. The Assyrians had weapons left behind by the Russians but needed more. Toward the end of July more than a thousand men set out from Urmia to take delivery of arms and ammunition, only to find when they reached the rendezvous point that the British had left.

In the meantime, Ottoman forces had closed in on Urmia. A huge refugee column headed south. According to Arnold Wilson: "Several thousands, mostly women and children, perished from exhaustion and disease on their way to Mesopotamia, a distance of some 500 miles, though every effort was made by the military authorities at Hamadan and Kirmanshah to provide food and shelter."[48] By the time the column reached Hamadan, 20,000 of the 50,000 Assyrians who had left Urmia were thought to have died. In August the refugees were taken by lorry to a camp at Baquba, northeast of Baghdad. Many were already too ill to survive. Between September 1918 and September 1919, 5,089 Assyrians or Armenians (out of a camp population of about 50,000) died from typhus or other diseases.[49]

Assyrian hopes and British contemplation of an Assyrian buffer state that could be established across Ottoman, Persian, and Iraqi borders came to nothing. Some Assyrians returned to Hakkari in 1924 but were driven back across the border after an attempt was made to assassinate the Turkish governor of the province. Seeing that the Assyrians could not return to their Turkish homeland, Britain sought to bring their homeland to them by asking the League of Nations to attach Hakkari to Iraq. But in 1925 the league's council awarded Hakkari to Turkey and Mosul to Iraq, on the understanding that homes for the Assyrians would be found somewhere in the Mosul region. Assyrian hopes of being given a "separate and homogeneous existence" had now been dealt a lethal blow: in the view of British officials it would be impossible to find territory for their settlement as a "compact and organized community" in Iraq.[50] Proposals were put forward to resettle the Assyrians in Albania, Brazil, Argentina, Mexico, British Guiana, and Australia, whose government was prepared to relax its "white Australia" immigration policy because the Assyrians were Christians and not much different from the Italians in the color of their skin.[51] None of these schemes came to anything either: the one thing the Assyrians did want they could never get, and that was the autonomy they thought they had been promised to entice them into the war.

The problems involved in resettling the Assyrians were vastly complicated by Britain's creation of separate ethno-religious military units.
Arabs and Kurds recruited for this purpose had to put up with public abuse
and ostracism. They were assaulted with "all sorts of propaganda. For
instance, they were openly called infidels in the bazaars and streets, tea and
coffee would not be served to them in the coffee shops, in several cafes
stone water pots from which they had drunk were broken. Their female
relatives would crowd around the barracks calling on their sons etc. by
name to come and protect them. Those from the tribes realized that to stay
with the Levies meant definitely cutting off relations with their tribes."
Eventually the Arab and Kurdish levies were integrated into the regular
army, but the Assyrian levies, several thousand strong, were retained as a
separate unit and sent into action alongside regular British forces against
Arab and Kurdish "rebels."[52] They were hard to discipline when their
blood was up, but their bravery and their Christianity made them ideal
candidates to fight under British command. The photographs show
smartly dressed soldiers in Australian bush hats, obviously proud of their
new status as embassy and airfield guards and fighting men in the field,
but their use against their putative fellow countrymen gave rise to fierce
resentment. The Kurds, in particular, suffered heavy losses as the result of
operations involving Assyrian ground forces and the RAF. The policy of
moving Kurdish villagers in the Mosul region to make way for Assyrian
settlers (regarded as a form of punishment for the murder of British officers by Kurds) only deepened the antagonism between the two groups.[53]

In August 1923 the presence of armed Assyrians in the town of Mosul
provoked a confrontation with the local people. On May 4, 1924, an alter-
cation between the levies and Muslim shopkeepers in Kirkuk ended in a
massacre of Muslims. The Assyrians opened up with their machine guns.
According to a British account: "In spite of the efforts of their British officers and native non-commissioned officers to restrain them, the Assyrians
ran amok through the town, firing at all Moslems, of whom a number
were killed, and looting shops and houses."[54] It was later estimated that the
Assyrians had killed more than three hundred people.[55] Only the arrival of
British troops and armored cars prevented a wave of revenge bloodletting
directed against Christians. Eight Assyrians were eventually found guilty
of murder; the court was satisfied that they had opened fire on the townspeople with their Lewis guns, "but as it could not be proved that they had
actually killed anyone, the sentence of death was commuted to imprisonment for life."[56] The massacre in Kirkuk and Muslim resentment (Kurdish
as well as Sunni and Shiʿi Arab) at the use of the Assyrians as an instru-

ment of imperial control built up to the tragedy the Assyrians suffered in 1933 after a collision between their fighting men and an Iraqi force led by a commander of Kurdish origin—Bakr Sidqi.

CONFRONTATION AND MASSACRE

The pressure for a separate Assyrian homeland had been maintained by the patriarch Mar Shimun, born in 1908 and invested as patriarch in 1920 in accordance with the tradition of succession from uncle to nephew. In 1931 and again in 1932 he had petitioned the League of Nations to give his people the compact home they wanted. The Assyrians were desperate for their status to be resolved before the mandate ended. It was a struggle against all odds. The Assyrians had powerful Christian supporters in Britain (up to the archbishop of Canterbury), but the Iraqi government had no intention of granting autonomy to any ethno-religious minority. The British government was sympathetic to the cause of a gallant wartime ally and had to take into account public opinion on the domestic front but believed that Assyrian leaders were simply refusing to face "unpalatable facts."[57] Iraq was finally admitted to the League of Nations on October 3, 1932, but without any special provision being made for the Assyrians. On December 5, Mar Shimun addressed the Permanent Mandates Commission, but ten days later the League of Nations council accepted the commission's recommendation that the Assyrians should not be given administrative autonomy. The root of the problem was declared to be land, not identity, and the solution the settlement of landless Assyrians "as far as possible in homogeneous units, it being understood"—here the language was strikingly reminiscent of the Balfour Declaration—"that the rights of the existing population should not be prejudiced."[58] Mar Shimun continued to insist on the recognition of the Assyrians as a "compact national group" and refused to accept the British insistence that his role now must be spiritual and not temporal. On his return to Baghdad the patriarch complained to the king and the minister of the interior, who was prevented from having him arrested only by the intervention of the British ambassador. He was "requested" to stay in Baghdad for the time being; meanwhile, in his absence from Mosul, the movement of bands of armed Assyrians was fast reaching the point of open confrontation with the Iraqi authorities.

On July 22, 1933, news reached the capital that a band of about 1,200 armed Assyrians had crossed the Tigris River in the vicinity of the villages of Feish Khabur and Deir Abun, both of them close to the borders with Turkey and Syria. A number of the Assyrians camping on the Syrian side of the Tigris crossed back into Iraq and were allowed to return to their villages, but on the morning of August 4, Assyrians on both sides of the river opened fire on Iraqi troops.[59] The battle that followed lasted for thirty-six hours before being ended by a combination of Iraqi army machine-gun fire, artillery bombardment, and air strikes: thirty-four Iraqis (three officers and thirty-one soldiers) and at least one hundred Assyrians were killed. According to Bakr Sidqi, the Assyrians had "savagely mutilated the dead: they gouged out their eyes, slit open their stomachs and cut off their noses."[60] As the ferocity of the Assyrians in battle was well known (in 1920 they were reported by Arnold Wilson to have cut off the heads of Kurds who attacked the refugee camp at Baquba), there seems no reason to doubt that they were capable of such acts. According to Brigadier-General Hugo Headlam, acting inspector-general of the Iraqi army,

> The Iraqi Army was attacked at Deirabun by a force of almost equal rifle power, consisting of men who have a great reputation as fighters, the majority of whom had received training in the levies. If these rebels had achieved what they undoubtedly expected to do and had "mopped up" the Iraqi troops at Deirabun, there might have been a disaster of the first magnitude, the far-reaching effects of which might well have proved irretrievable. The government and people of Iraq have good reason to be thankful to Colonel Bekr Sidki and his force for their success on the 4th–5th August.[61]

If by going to the border the intention had been to draw attention to their cause, the Assyrians had succeeded, but in reprisals carried out by troops or tribesmen (the latter according to the king and his prime minister) about forty Assyrian villages were destroyed or severely damaged and looted. In the village of Simel, forty miles north of Mosul, disarmed Assyrians were reported to have been machine-gunned by the same Ibrahim al Tuhallah later to be implicated in the murder of Defense Minister Jaᶜfar al Askari. Although estimates of the number killed ranged from 300 to 3,000, a British official who visited villages in the Simel district counted just 315 bodies.[62] According to British sources, Bakr Sidqi was "known to have" massacred Assyrian prisoners brought to his camp by Kurds.[63] Consul Moneypenny reported that troops returning to Mosul marched under triumphal arches "decorated with water melons steeped in blood with knives embedded in them to represent, so it is stated, the heads of the defeated Assyrians."[64]

If the Assyrian affair was handled badly by the Iraqi government, and brutally by Bakr Sidqi, what is to be said of Britain's role in setting up the Assyrians as an armed force against the people among whom they were supposed to live? In his memoirs, Arnold Wilson wrote of the "exceedingly untoward result of the Eastern Committee's adventure in Persia. It resulted in the creation in Mesopotamia of yet another minority problem which need never have arisen had we not attempted to make a cat's paw of the Christian communities in Persia and the Caucasus."[65]

THE RECKLESS "FAUVE"

By the late 1930s the decisions made by Britain two decades earlier were undermining its strategic interests across the Middle East. No amount of propaganda or name-calling could overcome the damage done by the imposition of mandates, and no wound was uglier than Palestine. The uprising of 1936–39 had been crushed at the cost of increasing hostility to Britain across the Middle East: it could scarcely have done more to antagonize the people whose goodwill it needed to make the region secure for the West. Numerous Palestinians fled to avoid seizure. The mufti of Jerusalem, Haj Amin al Husseini, escaping to Lebanon in 1937 and moving on to Baghdad in October 1939, soon became as much a thorn in the side of Britain in Iraq as he had been in Palestine.

On the outbreak of war in Europe, Nuri al Said, back in office as prime minister, severed relations with Germany without consulting his cabinet and then went a step further by handing German nationals over to the British. Of those figures who sought to block the machinations of Nuri and the British embassy, the most influential were the mufti, the veteran nationalist politician Rashid Ali al Gailani (or Kailani), and the four colonels who constituted the military group known as the Golden Square. By the British they were accused of being Nazi sympathizers, but against the French and British record of partition and occupation of Arab lands they had no reason to support the Allied war effort. One of them, Salah al Din al Sabbagh, described himself in the following terms: "I do not believe in the democracy of the English nor the Nazism of the Germans nor in the Bolshevism of the Russians. I am an Arab Muslim."[66] It was the mufti, the colonels, and Rashid Ali who had public opinion on their side, not Nuri and Britain.

Rashid Ali's nationalist credentials were impressive: joint founder of the Ikha al Watani (Patriotic Brotherhood) Party in 1930, minister of justice in 1924, president of the Chamber of Deputies, chief of the royal *diwan* (council), and prime minister for the first time in 1933. Far too much of a nationalist for British tastes, he was described vituperatively in dispatches sent to London from Baghdad. A British adviser resorted to a French minister's description of him as *un fauve* (a wild animal) who had somehow acquired a patina of civilization. "In times of stress there comes into his eyes a look that is familiar to those of us who have had to deal with untutored tribesmen who have never seen a town or had contact with civilized humanity, a look of combined fear, cunning and savagery."[67]

On March 28, 1940, Nuri resigned after weeks of turmoil caused by the assassination of his finance minister in January. Three days later Rashid Ali formed the new government, retaining Nuri as his foreign minister; as Rashid Ali had repeatedly expressed the desire to maintain good relations with the British, the appointment was a conciliatory signal sent in their direction, but his refusal to break relations with Italy when it entered the war in June was regarded by Britain as a clear breach of Iraq's obligations under the treaty of 1930. Behind his declarations of neutrality and good intentions, the British believed that the prime minister was "actively intriguing" with the Axis powers. "We know for a fact that he has asked Germany and Italy for support in order to enable him to break with us and that he is doing everything he dares to work up feeling against us and intimidate our friends in Iraq."[68]

On November 14, 1940, the British ambassador, Sir Basil Newton, was informed by the Foreign Office that the first opportunity had to be taken to get rid of Rashid Ali "not only as Prime Minister but from the Government altogether."[69] Iraq was squeezed financially. Britain stopped the supply of arms and spare parts, froze the purchase of dates and cotton, and blocked Iraqi access to U.S. dollars. The Foreign Office, covertly but grossly interfering in the internal affairs of the Iraqi government, exhorted Newton to impress on Nuri and the regent the need to take immediate action against the prime minister.[70] The defense minister (General Taha al Hashimi) put forward suggestions for cabinet changes that would eliminate the "extremists," but Newton made it clear to him that "the man we regarded as primarily responsible was Rashid Ali, and that therefore no change would be agreed to which left him in the government."[71]

By the end of January the intrigues set in motion by the Foreign Office through the embassy in Baghdad had culminated in a string of resignations, leaving Rashid Ali with only five ministers in his cabinet. On January 30, he asked the regent to issue a decree dissolving parliament. Abdulillah said he would let him know by 6:00 P.M. and then fled the city before evening for the southern Euphrates town of Diwaniyya without issuing the decree. The following day Rashid Ali resigned, and on February 1 the regent asked General Taha to form a new government. On February 3 he returned to the capital, expressing his determination, now that Rashid Ali had been driven out of office, to see that General Taha remove his enemies in the army. "The struggle may not be over," wrote the British ambassador, "and the danger of military coup, though less menacing, is still present. But the first step has been accomplished and the worst difficulties . . . have probably been overcome."[72]

FLIGHT OF THE REGENT

In the coming month General Taha continued to frustrate the British by refusing to take action against the "Sinister Quadrumvirate"—the four colonels aligned with the mufti and Rashid Ali. Britain still wanted Iraq to sever relations with Italy, and General Taha was not moving on this front either. On March 21 Abdulillah told Newton that he would press the prime minister to deal with the four colonels without further delay. He expected that General Taha would resign if pressed hard enough, in which case Abdulillah would remove himself and the royal family to Basra "and remain there until danger of exposure to military pressure at Baghdad has been removed."[73] There was scarcely any need to mention who would have to remove this danger. General Taha was also under pressure from the Arab Committee, the nationalist opposition group aligned with the four colonels, in which Rashid Ali and the mufti were the dominant figures. He was warned that he should resign before giving way to the British, but on March 26 he finally yielded to pressure by ordering the transfer out of the capital of two of the colonels, Kamil Shabib and Salah al Din al Sabbagh. They simply tore up their orders, whereupon General Taha resigned—just as the regent had predicted he would. On the night of April 1, the four officers went to the palace to ask Abdulillah to accept his resignation and appoint Rashid Ali in his place, only to find that the regent had taken flight, in accordance with the plan of action he had outlined to Newton. (The retreat of Abdulillah before the British intervened to "restore order" was to be duplicated in the withdrawal of the shah from Tehran in 1953 in the penultimate stage of Operation Ajax, the coup launched by the United States and Britain to overthrow the government of Prime Minister Muhammad Musaddiq.)

Kinahan Cornwallis—the ambassador and old Iraq hand appointed to handle the crisis in place of Newton—claimed that the regent had been forced to leave his palace because his liberty "and even his life" were threatened.[74] Whatever the colonels might have had in mind, General Taha's resignation and the regent's flight left Iraq in a constitutional mess. Abdulillah took refuge overnight in an aunt's house. Then he dressed as a woman (presumably in clothes borrowed from his aunt's wardrobe) and made his way by carriage to the American legation, waiting outside until the minister's wife let him in. Soon thereafter the minister (Mr. Knaben-shue) hid him under a rug on the floor of his car and with his wife in the front seat drove across the Tigris to the RAF base at Habbaniyya. "The car slowed down at the bridge and Mr Knabenshue saw a pistol being slightly raised for readiness, the knuckles on the Emir's hand whitening as he gripped it."[75] From Habbaniyya the regent was flown to Basra. When the Iraqi army moved to arrest him he was moved to the safety of a warship before being transferred to Kuwait and then flown to Lydda in Palestine. From there he was driven to the King David Hotel in Jerusalem, where he settled in for the duration with Nuri and other ministers who had fled the country.

"COUP" AND COUNTERCOUP

If the definition of a coup depends on the overthrow of a government, there was no coup in Iraq in 1941. The prime minister had resigned and the regent was about to be asked to act on his constitutional responsibility and appoint a new one. There was no declaration of martial law and no blood-shed. A political crisis had led to a constitutional crisis created by the flight of an unpopular figurehead ruler who had been conspiring with a foreign power against his own government. The country was left with no one to accept the resignation of the old government or appoint a new one. The monarchy was the critical part of a constitutional mechanism set in motion to safeguard Britain's commercial and strategic interests in the country; the regent's flight had left the constitution looking like a clock without a spring, but it was Rashid Ali's "gang of unscrupulous ruffians" whom Britain blamed.[76] In fact, the crisis had been deliberately engineered with the objec-tive of setting Rashid Ali up for the blow that would destroy him. He had too much support within the army and the population at large to be kept out of government for long by constitutional means, but now that there had been a "coup," Britain had a pretext for removing him permanently.

Cornwallis passed on to London a compromise offer from Rashid Ali involving his appointment as prime minister, the return of the regent to Baghdad after a few months, the affirmation of Iraq's commitment to the treaty of 1930 on a wider basis than before, the preparation of public opin-ion for a break in relations with Italy, and greater supervision for British advisers over propaganda and the passports of Palestinians.[77] When this overture was rebuffed, Iraq's interim government accused Abdulillah of treason by deserting his post at a time of national crisis. He was deposed at a joint sitting of the Chamber of Deputies and the Senate and replaced by a more senior Hashimite figure, Sharif al Sharaf, who accepted General Taha's resignation and ratified the appointment of Rashid Ali as prime minister. All this was done calmly, with every sign that the new government had the support of the people.

Now that Rashid Ali was exposed to retaliation, Britain began to arrange the detail of his removal. The immediate problem was that it did not have enough troops in Iraq. In accordance with the 1930 treaty, Britain had only the right to maintain modest forces as guards at Basra and Habbaniyya. Their numbers were decided by mutual arrangement between the two governments but they could not be unilaterally increased: in an emergency Britain could send reinforcements to Basra but only after consultations with the Iraqi government. Extra troops could be landed at Basra (with the Iraqi government's consent) but only in the process of being transferred to a third country.

These restrictions were swept aside. In the second week of April, troop reinforcements were flown into the Shaiba air base near Basra and sent from India by warship and aircraft carrier. Rashid was not told until they were almost there. He accepted the fait accompli with reasonably good grace but insisted that the troops must be moved onward as soon as possible, that his government be given advance warning of the arrival of more troops, and that none should disembark before those already in Basra had been moved on. On April 28 the British embassy informed the government of the impending arrival of three more ships. In the late afternoon Cornwallis saw Rashid Ali and was told that Iraq could not consent to the disembarkation of the troops on board until a corresponding number had been moved on. However widely the relevant article of the treaty was interpreted, Rashid Ali argued, it could not be construed as giving Britain the right to maintain forces in Iraq outside those necessary for guard duties at Basra and Habbaniyya. If the ships berthed before troops already on the ground were moved on, his government could not be held responsible for the consequences. Public opinion was already disturbed, and if more troops were brought in over his objections, "he would broadcast a denunciation of our action to the nation." Cornwallis pushed back. The troops would be landed, and "the consequences of any opposition or obstruction would be serious."[78]

With conflict now imminent, all British women and children in Baghdad were moved to Habbaniyya. On April 30, with more British troops having now been disembarked at Basra, Iraqi forces were deployed around Habbaniyya "as a precaution taken in the face of the several threatening acts of His Majesty's Government including the retention of troops at Basra."[79] When the commander of the Iraqi forces, fearing an attack, warned that any planes trying to leave the base would be shelled, Cornwallis raised the cry that the lives of women and children were being threatened. At 5:00 A.M. on May 2 the air officer in command of Habbaniyya (Air Vice Marshall Smart) ordered an air attack on the Iraqi forces "without giving any warning." Minutes later Cornwallis sent Rashid Ali a note saying the base commander had been "compelled" to take this action by the threatening presence of the Iraqi troops, a deceit compounded by a lie when Churchill declared that Rashid Ali had "attacked the British air cantonment at Habbaniyah."[80]

THE THIRTY-DAY WAR

The Thirty-Day War had begun. From London came a message stressing the political and military importance of "making it clear to the Arab world that we are not fighting Iraq but only the supporters of Rashid Ali."[81] In fact the "supporters" of Rashid Ali—a small clique by implication—constituted the vast bulk of the Iraqi population. Patriotic feelings were expressed in songs, poems, martial music, and parades, leaving no doubt that whatever their political, ethnic, or religious differences, the prime minister had the people behind him. No event since the revolt of 1920 had created such a feeling of national unity: "In Baghdad and other towns the sentiments of Shiʿi and Sunni and Arab and Kurd merged for the moment and while the fighting lasted."[82]

Most of the Iraqi air force was destroyed on day one when the British bombed the landing strip near Baquba where they had been hidden. Air attacks also forced the Iraqi troops outside Habbaniyya to retreat in the direction of Falluja, the western desert city on the Euphrates that had been a focal point of resistance in 1920 (and was to become one again in 2004). On May 5, British planes trapped an Iraqi military convoy of about seventy vehicles on a road softened by floodwaters near the city. Unable to turn around or maneuver, the column was shot up from the front and the rear before the center was obliterated. Ahead of a ground assault on May 21, Falluja came under heavy air attack, with bombs falling on the military hospital and military ambulances bombed or strafed. According to a local resident, "Even the Turks who had a reputation for brutality had never shelled or bombed a town full of women as the British had done Felluja. The inhabitants of Felluja were scattered as refugees all round the neighbouring tribes, many of them being destitute."[83]

Britain responded by accusing six German aircraft (flying from Vichy Syria) of deliberately machine-gunning two British ambulances on May

16. Ramadi was also bombed, while in an air raid on Mosul by Wellington bombers thirty-two people were reported killed and twenty-six wounded, most of them old men, women, and children.[84]

Glubb Pasha's Arab Legion troops entered Iraq from Jordan (after being delayed by a mutiny that resulted in the accompanying Trans-Jordan Frontier Force being sent back to the barracks) along with a military column sent from the "sacred trust" territory of Palestine to take part in the ground assault on Falluja. As the British troops and a company of Assyrians steadily gained control, their commanding officer ordered the city to be cleared of civilians: "A considerable number of Iraqis had remained behind disguised in civilian dress and were engaged in accurate sniping. Accordingly, the next day, some 1500 local Arabs were driven out of the town, which became far more habitable as a result."[85]

By May 30 the war was over. Rashid Ali, the four colonels, and the mufti fled to Iran. The mayor and police chief of Baghdad surrendered the city at four in the morning on May 31. The regent and Nuri had been flown to Habbaniyya from the Mafraq air base in Jordan on May 22 and were now free to return to the capital. A photograph taken on the plane by de Gaury shows the regent, in military uniform with a movie camera on his lap, Nuri looking out of the window at his side, over the caption "A Happy Return."

THE *FARHUD*

For two and a half millennia Baghdad had remained perhaps the most important center of Jewish life, learning, and commerce in the Near East. The city's population in 1908 was still more than 35 percent Jewish.[86] The Jews of Baghdad lived an untroubled life under Ottoman rule, but French and British occupation of Arab lands, the deteriorating situation in Palestine, and Zionist proselytizing in Iraq and other countries brought about a rapid turn for the worse, sowing suspicion where there had been none before. Some Jews were sympathetic to Zionism, but many more took the view that they were Jews in the synagogue but loyal Iraqi citizens outside it. In December 1934 the king and his ministers had assured the British ambassador that "the Government had no prejudice against Jews," but public opinion was a different matter. Feelings were inflamed over Palestine, and the overthrow of a popular government in 1941 was the signal for the mob to take revenge on a helpless surrogate enemy.[87]

In the brief period between the overthrow of the Rashid Ali government and the return of the regent, rioters ran through Baghdad, killing

Jews and destroying their property in what has been known since as the *farhud*.[88] On June 2, Cornwallis reported that "sporadic shooting with murderous assaults on Jews seem to have gone on through the night and from early this morning armed mobs looted principal shopping streets of the town."[89] The destruction, killing, and rape continued until the regent finally gave orders for the troops to be called out, at which point "the soldiers did their work well. There was no more aimless firing into the air: their machine-guns swept the streets clean of people and quickly put a stop to looting and rioting."[90] The official inquiry found that 187 people had been killed, 586 businesses pillaged, and ninety-nine houses burned down. Some Jewish women and children were saved by being taken under the protection of Muslims.[91]

The Thirty-Day War was over. It had taken the lives of 33 Iraqi officers and 464 men of other ranks, with 36 officers and 659 men wounded and another 549 missing; British casualties amount to 150 dead or wounded but mostly wounded.[92] A new government was installed on June 3. Two days later it informed the British ambassador that his government "may station their ground and air forces at such places as may be necessary for the defence of Iraq."[93] On June 8 Iraq broke relations with Italy. In the coming months political refugees from Syria or Palestine were picked up and either repatriated, banished to villages in the Kurdish north, or (in a few cases) sent to exile in southern Rhodesia. Rashid Ali survived to return to Iraq after the coup of 1958, but one by one the four colonels were hunted down with remorseless implacability and brought back to Baghdad for punishment. Two (Fahmi Said and Mahmud Salman) were sentenced to death on January 6, 1942, and hanged on May 5; a third (Kamil Shabib) was captured and hanged on August 17, 1944; the fourth (Salah al Din al Sabbagh), escaped to Iran, moved to Turkey, and was handed over to the British in Syria when the war was over; sent to Baghdad, he was tried and hanged on October 16, 1945, near the gates of the Defense Ministry.

THE LONG-DEFERRED END

The regent and the king were back. By early October Nuri had been recalled from Cairo to form a new government. Life in Baghdad returned to "normal," which meant the rule of an unpopular regent and prime minister and the continuing machinations of the watching British ambassador. "The Hashimites are hated by the Iraqis," Kermit Roosevelt wrote after a visit to Baghdad in 1947. "If it weren't for British protection, which allowed them to build up their own secret police and army, Abdul Ilah and the others would be murdered in two hours." The politicians in Britain's hands were "a sorry, shaky lot, hardly worth owning."[94] The following January the regime was rocked by the mass insurrection known as the *wathbah* (uprising). It was precipitated by the signing of the Portsmouth Treaty, designed to lock Iraq into a regional "defense" arrangement with Britain. The government hanged two communist leaders whom it accused of orchestrating the uprising from prison, but its intensity forced Nuri to repudiate the treaty.

In February 1958, Egypt and Syria formed the United Arab Republic under the presidency of Gamal abd al Nasser. Jordan and Iraq responded by establishing an "Arab Union." In March the British foreign secretary (Selwyn Lloyd) reported from Baghdad that the Iraqi leadership was "in a very jittery state and acting as though they expected to be gone in six months."[95] On May 14 Nuri stepped down as prime minister. On May 19 he was sworn in as prime minister of the Arab Union government and Ahmad Mukhtar Baban as head of the Iraqi government. In June, with Lebanon sliding into civil war and King Hussein under threat in Jordan, the British prime minister, Harold Macmillan, told Eisenhower he believed an "acute crisis" was building up in Iraq.[96]

Early in the morning of July 14 the blow long deferred was finally struck. Nuri and the king were due to fly to Ankara for a meeting of Muslim members of the Baghdad Pact on the crisis in Lebanon but were still in the Iraqi capital when tanks (part of a brigade that was supposed to be on its way to shore up the monarchy in Amman) besieged the Rihab Palace before six in the morning and set it on fire with a shell. Members of the royal family appeared in the gardens waving white handkerchiefs. In Batatu's account they were shot down from behind by an army captain who said later that he was in a "state of frenzy" and had pressed the trigger subconsciously.[97] In another version the royal family was shot down after Abdulillah ordered a palace guard to shoot the commander of the intruding troops; in an even more colorful account, the regent ran around the palace gardens cutting down soldiers with a Sten gun before being shot. However the shooting started, most of the nineteen members of the palace party were killed, including Faisal II, installed as king in 1953 when he reached the age of eighteen; his grandmother, Queen Nafisa; Abdulillah, his sister, and other members of the royal family, including children; and palace guards, maidservants, and cooks. Abdulillah's wife Princess Hiyam was taken to hospital wounded but survived. The regent's body was left for the mob. The hands and feet were hacked off before the rest of the body was taken to the Defense Ministry (outside which Salah al Din al Sabbagh had been executed in 1945) and symbolically hung from a balcony. Elsewhere the equestrian statues of General Maude and King Faisal I were brought crashing down.

Other troops were sent to arrest Nuri. They dynamited steel doors and went from room to room of his house looking for him, but by the time they arrived he had been ferried across the Tigris by fishermen to a friend's house in Kadhimain. In the company of his friend's wife and an elderly female servant, he left the house the following morning wearing women's clothing. When their car had to slow down because of traffic, an air force sergeant somehow recognized Nuri and shot him on the spot. His body was taken outside the city for burial but was unearthed and dragged through the streets by the mob before a car was driven over it, backwards and forwards, until nothing recognizable was left of the man who had been the paramount symbol of Western interests in the Middle East for more than two decades. Three Jordanian cabinet ministers invited to Baghdad to celebrate the establishment of the Arab Union were taken under escort from their hotel to the Ministry of Defense but were snatched from their guard by rioters (or, alternatively, handed over to them by an Iraqi army officer "because you Jordanians killed so many of our people in 1941").[98] Two were killed and the third badly injured. A former governor of Jerusalem, Adnan Husseini, and a junior officer in the Jordanian army were also killed. Three Americans, including the head of the overseas division of the Bechtel Corporation (George Colley Jr.), and a German national were taken from their hotel and killed. Nuri's feckless son Sabah was murdered in the street in the hours after the palace was besieged.

The British embassy was the third main target of the revolution. Tanks rammed the iron gates of the compound before the mob surged in. A British colonel was shot dead and a British woman shot dead a man trying to haul down the British flag. The ambassador, his wife, and the embassy staff were eventually able to leave safely, but the embassy was looted before being set on fire and totally destroyed. Thus was the Iraqi branch of the Hashimite dynasty obliterated; thus were the British driven out of Iraq until the elimination of "weapons of mass destruction" gave them reason to return in 2003. The revolutionary nationalists now looked ahead to the liberation of the occupied Arab Gulf, southern Arabia, Algeria, and, above all, Palestine.

6. DOUBLE COLONIALISM IN PALESTINE

In late March 1925 Arthur James Balfour visited the Middle East. He had been invited to open the Hebrew University of Jerusalem, so it was a good opportunity to see something of a region in which it could not be said his name was unknown. He landed by ship in Alexandria and visited Cairo before moving on to Palestine by land. Protests followed him all the way: in Gaza, Tulkarm, Jerusalem, Haifa, and other towns in Palestine, schools were closed and a general strike was declared. Completely boycotted by the Arabs, his consolation lay in the rapturous reception he was given by the Zionists. An honor guard of young men mounted on horseback met him at Rishon-le-Zion and escorted him to the settlement synagogue. Tel Aviv was bedecked with Zionist and British flags; at a civic reception a choir sang the Hallelujah Chorus. The redeemer had indeed arrived.

In his speeches he described himself as an "old friend" of Baron Edmund de Rothschild (to whom he had addressed his famous declaration of 1917) and "one of the oldest Zionists, whose enthusiasm for Zionism antedated by very many years the Balfour Declaration."[1] On April 1 he declared the Hebrew University open before an audience of distinguished guests who included Sir Herbert Samuel (the high commissioner), Viscount Allenby, and Chaim Weizmann. Then he made the mistake of going to Damascus. As his train rolled northward on the morning of April 8—no stops on this trip—villagers gathered by the side of the line to curse him. Anticipating even greater problems in Damascus, the French mandatory authorities escorted Balfour off the train before it reached the terminal and raced him away in a convoy of cars to the Victoria Hotel. A crowd of men of all ages, waiting at the terminal to greet him, rushed in the direction of the hotel when they learned he had left the train at the Qadam station. They demonstrated for an hour before retreating to the Hamidiyya market around the Umayyad mosque.

The next day thousands of demonstrators marched on the hotel after noon prayers, broke through the police barriers, and almost reached the front door before being scattered. The following day (April 10) there were more demonstrations. Armored cars and tanks were moved into the city and intimidatory runs made by low-flying aircraft. Balfour had still not been outside his hotel, and it was definitely time to move him on. The high commissioner, General Maurice Sarrail, arranged a distraction. Smoke bombs were dropped from aircraft. Balfour and his party were whisked out of a rear door of the Victoria in the confusion. They were driven straight to Beirut, where more trouble awaited. Demonstrations had been organized and a general strike declared, but the convoy veered off the main road and managed to reach the port without incident. Balfour was safely put on board a French ship, which sailed immediately for Alexandria. Perhaps it was an affectation, but he genuinely did not seem to realize how deeply he was loathed across the region. He had visited Syria for pleasure, "and had he the slightest inkling it would cause disturbances he would never have come."[2]

COMMITMENTS "INCOMPATIBLE WITH FACTS"

Balfour seemed to be a man of contradictory impulses. As prime minister in 1905, he had spoken in favor of an Aliens Bill specifically framed to prevent Jews fleeing pogroms in eastern Europe from being able to enter England. By some Jewish observers his remarks were construed as being anti-Semitic.[3] In 1917 he professed to be sufficiently moved by a sense of history to help the Jewish people return to their ancient homeland while remaining coldly indifferent to the history, interests, and aspirations of other Semites—the Arabs. Balfour knew that the contradictory commitments made by his government could never be reconciled. "The literal fulfillment of all our declarations is impossible, partly because they are incompatible with each other and partly because they are incompatible with facts."[4] One important "fact" was that Palestine had only a residual Jewish population, but Balfour had given the Zionists their "great opportunity" and now it was up to them. "My personal hope is that the Jews will make good in Palestine and eventually found a Jewish state," he told Richard Meinertzhagen in 1918.[5] With the writing of the Balfour Declaration into the mandate, Muslim and Christian Palestinians were subjected to a unique form of double colonialism: the occupying British did not settle the land themselves but held the door open so that their protégés could.

Down to the nineteenth century a small number of Jews had continued to live in Palestine. Their lives centered on scholarship and prayer, and they would have been as shocked as the most conservative Muslims by the appearance and behavior of the secularized Zionist Jews who began arriving in Palestine from Poland and Russia in the late nineteenth century. Virtually all of these settlers were "returning" to a land they and their ancestors in living memory had never seen; what united them was the nationalist belief that the Jews constituted a people and should once more have a state of their own in a land where Jewish kingdoms had been established thousands of years before. The very fact that the Eastern origins of the Zionists, such as they might have been (because some were not "Semites" at all but converts to Judaism at some point in the distant past), had been leached out of them, if not sufficiently to save them from pogroms in eastern Europe and an Aliens Bill in London, was what made them such suitable candidates for white European settlement in Palestine. In their own eyes they would return not just as secular state-building Jews but as the standard-bearers of Western civilization in the backward East. It is still greatly to the credit of the early Zionists that they read the British mood so well. The projection of their movement as a conduit for the transmission of civilization "to the primitive people of Asia"[6]—in the very birthplace of Christianity—suited imperialist perceptions perfectly. The Jews might be a people who "remained apart," as Balfour had remarked in 1905, and they were not quite as white as Anglo-Saxons, but they were still white enough and close enough in outlook to be trusted with the mission of protecting imperial interests in the "alien East."[7]

Naturally Zionism benefited greatly from the common Christian-Jewish heritage. Muslim Arabs scarcely figured in the European vision at all except as grubby figures swarming around visitors to the Holy Land demanding baksheesh, postcard desert sheikhs riding camels, or lush naked odalisques reclining on velvet cushions. The Jews were at least familiar even when not liked. Generations of Englishmen and women were still being brought up on Bible stories of a Holy Land stretching from Dan to Beersheba, of Samson tying burning brands to the tails of three hundred foxes and bringing down the temple on the heads of the Philistines at Gaza, and of the cruel Philistines being defeated in battle by the brave Hebrews. The politicians and military commanders who decided the fate of the Near East after 1918 were mostly self-avowed religious men imbued with the history of Israel from Sunday school onwards: the combination of the Bible, racial and religious bias, the strategic interests of European governments, and the sheer geographical and historical ignorance of politicians and statesmen worked against Muslims at every level. The anomaly of Christian Arabs was solved by not regarding them as Arab at all.

For the non-Jewish communities of the "Holy Land"—about 90 percent of the population in 1918—British mandatory rule and the Zionist program were equally unacceptable. The King-Crane Commission sent to the Near East by the U.S. government in 1919 reported that the overwhelming majority of its petitioners (221 out of 260) in Occupied Enemy Territory South (Palestine west of the Jordan River) wanted Palestine to be incorporated into a unitary Syrian state, with most of the rest in favor of autonomy within a Syrian state. More than 85 percent expressed their total opposition to the Zionist program. The commissioners—many of them with a theological background—reported that they had begun their study of Zionism "with minds predisposed in its favor" but that the facts on the ground had led them to revise their opinions. The Zionist claim of a "right" to Palestine based on Jewish occupation of the land two thousand years previously "cannot be taken seriously." For neither Muslims nor Christians could the Jews be considered suitable guardians of sacred sites or the Holy Land as a whole. Indeed, "the places which are most sacred to Christians—those having to do with Jesus—and which are also sacred to Moslems are not only not sacred to Jews but abhorrent to them. It is simply impossible under these circumstances for Moslems and Christians to feel satisfied to have these places in Jewish hands."[8] Moreover, President Wilson had laid down the principle that the settlement of every question arising from the war had to be settled with the consent of the people immediately concerned. The entire non-Jewish population of Palestine was emphatically against Zionism, and "to subject a people so minded to unlimited Jewish immigration and to steady financial and social pressure to surrender the land would be a gross violation of the principle just quoted and of the peoples' rights though it [be] kept within the forms of law." Accordingly, the Zionist program should be greatly reduced, and "the project for making Palestine distinctly a Jewish commonwealth should be given up."[9]

FOUNDATION FICTIONS

The Zionist project as formulated by Theodor Herzl in the late nineteenth century was the opening shot in a long war that is still unfinished. The "land without people for a people without land" was a fiction from the start. Palestine (southern Syria) in the late nineteenth century had a population of about half a million and was far from being the stagnant wilderness depicted by the Zionists and Christians abroad who believed in the return of the Jewish people to the Holy Land. Citrus fruits, wheat, barley, grapes, and olives were all grown in abundance. In the towns and villages were numerous small workshops typical of an agricultural preindustrial society, one that was pervasively Islamic. Some of the patrician families (e.g., the Khalidis) could trace their lineage back to the Islamic conquest in the seventh century, and Jerusalem remained perhaps the best architectural example across the Near East of a medieval Islamic city, one that was stamped with the characteristics of all the Muslim dynasts who had ruled over it.

Herzl's Jewish state was to be founded on the ruins of Muslim and Christian Palestine. The "effendi" property-owning class would see Zionist colonization and investment as being in its best interests; the peasant population would be used for tasks beyond the capacity of the incoming Jewish settlers (e.g., killing snakes and other wild creatures), but in time "we shall try to spirit the penniless population across the border by procuring employment for it in the transit countries while denying it any employment in our own country."[10] Secrecy would be essential. "Both the process of expropriation and the removal of the poor must be carried out discreetly and circumspectly. Let the owners of immoveable property think they are cheating us, selling us things for more than they are worth. But we are not going to sell them anything back." Land would be bought by secret agents; once it was in Jewish hands, "we shall then sell only to Jews and all real estate will be traded only among Jews." Even the Jewish dead were regarded as more suitable tenants; Herzl wrote in his diaries of the possibility of bringing "coffin ships" over from Europe.[11] All these plans had to be hidden from the Arabs. "Who would think of sending them away?" Herzl wrote to Yusif Ziya al Khalidi, the mayor of Jerusalem, of the "non-Jewish population" of Palestine. "It is their well-being, their individual wealth which we increase by bringing in our own."[12]

From the beginning of settlement onwards the image radiated to the outside world by the Zionists was of a hardworking people arriving in a world of sloth, laziness, corruption, and immorality. The abuse of Palestinian culture—morally conservative and bound by tradition at all levels—was intensely racist. "They are slum children in possession of a vast playground where they wallow happily in the dust," a fictional settler writes of the Arabs in a novel by Arthur Koestler.[13] "They are a relic of the middle ages. They have no conception of nationhood and no sense of discipline; they are good rioters and bad fighters, otherwise none of our isolated settlements could have survived. As a political factor they have been negligible since the days of the Kalifs except for their nuisance value. If treated with authority they keep quiet; if encouraged they make an infernal nuisance of themselves." The settlers are a people of boundless health, energy, optimism, talent, and good looks, while the Arabs nearby, down to their decaying teeth, are unhealthy, pockmarked, foul-mouthed, money-hungry, sadistic, and lusting after the "shameless bitches" wandering around the settlements while having to make do with the village slatterns.[14] In his novelistic pseudodocumentary account of the turmoil in Palestine in the late 1940s, Koestler writes that the presence of the Arabs is a "mere accident, like the presence of some forgotten pieces of furniture in a house which has been temporarily let to strangers."[15] He imagines the flight of an old couple after Jewish forces have herded villagers together and dynamited their homes. "The old ones will tie a mattress and brass coffee-pot on the donkey, the old woman will wander ahead, leading the donkey by the rein and the old man will ride on it wrapped in his kefiye and sunk in solemn meditation about the lost opportunity of raping his youngest grandchild."[16]

"COMPLETE DISPOSSESSION"

The severance of the Palestinian people from their land was developed administratively and ideologically. According to the charter of the Jewish National Fund (established in 1901), land once acquired could never be passed back to non-Jewish ownership, and neither could it be worked by non-Jewish hands (a principle hard to enforce in practice because "Arab labor" was cheap and therefore tempting to Jewish employers). As early as January 1917, the Foreign Office was being told that the Zionists "have secured the complete dispossession of the Arabs and established purely Jewish colonies."[17] When the King-Crane Commission visited Palestine in 1919, it concluded that the Zionist colonists had a "radical transformation" of the country in mind. "The fact came out repeatedly in the Commission's conference with Jewish representatives that the Zionists looked forward to a practically complete dispossession of the present non-Jewish inhabitants of Palestine by various forms of purchase."[18] Asked what he understood by the phrase *national home*, the senior Zionist spokesman, Chaim Weizmann, dissembled. The Zionist organization, he remarked, "did not want an autonomous Jewish Government but merely to establish in Palestine under a mandatory power an administration, not necessarily Jewish, which would render it possible to send into Palestine 70 to 80,000 Jews annually. . . . Later on, when the Jews formed the large majority they would be ripe to establish such a Government as would answer to the state of the development of the country and to their ideals."[19]

In fact, Palestine was going to become Jewish, and the British knew it—"our views differ only on the meaning of tempo."[20] The "brutal numbers"—the six hundred thousand Muslims or Christians then living in

Palestine—were not to be compared with "the undeniable fact of our historical right."[21] By no means did all Jews agree. Lucien Wolf, of the Anglo-Jewish Association, told Weizmann that "if the so-called Arabs were really Arabs—that is, natives of Arabia—and if the Jews were really Palestinians—that is, indigenes of Palestine—there might be something to be said for your argument on the crazy basis of Territorial Nationality. . . . But the Arabs are not Arabs. They are only the Moslemized descendants of the indigenous Canaanites and hence they are in their rightful homeland which, however poor and feckless they may be, is their own."[22]

Initially some leaders of Muslim opinion were not hostile to limited Jewish immigration. The Sharif Husain was prepared to accept the Balfour Declaration insofar as it offered a refuge in Palestine for persecuted European Jews, even calling on Muslims to remember their traditions of hospitality and "welcome the Jews to Palestine as brethren and cooperate with them for the common welfare."[23] The sharif's son Faisal negotiated with Weizmann. Leaders of Palestinian opinion also said they were prepared to accept Jewish immigrants as long as it was understood that there could be no question of Palestine losing its Arab identity.

Throughout the 1920s Britain and the Zionists repeatedly assured the indigenous people of Palestine that nothing would be done to harm their interests. Husain's son Abdullah told British officials in 1921 that if they really intended to establish a "Jewish kingdom" west of the Jordan and turn out the non-Jewish population, "it would be better to tell the Arabs at once and not to keep them in suspense." The Allies "appeared to think that men could be cut down and transplanted in the same way as trees."[24] Sir Herbert Samuel continued the arboreal metaphor by saying that "there was no intention either to cut down or transplant but only to plant new ones" and that neither was there any question of establishing a Jewish state or taking land away from the Arabs. Churchill dismissed the Arabs' apprehensions. "They appeared to anticipate that hundreds of thousands of Jews were going to pour into the country in a very short time and dominate the existing population. This was not only not contemplated but quite impossible. There were at present over 500,000 Moslems in Palestine and not more than 80,000 Jews. Jewish immigration would be a very slow process and the rights of the existing non-Jewish population would be strictly preserved."[25] In fact, the whole point of withholding independence from Palestine was that its future had to wait until the demographic imbalance between Palestinian Muslims and Christians on one hand and Zionist settlers on the other had been reversed. Then, if the Jews became the majority in Palestine, "they naturally would take it over"; that was how Churchill really saw the situation unfolding.[26]

In fostering the development of a Jewish national home, the British put Zionists or those sympathetic to their cause into all senior positions in the administration: the first high commissioner (Sir Herbert Samuel), the attorney general (Norman Bentwich), and the director of the immigration office (A. H. Hyamson) were all Jewish and committed to the success of the Zionist project. Weizmann sought to have the "levantine" officials and "subalterns" who filled the offices of the mandatory regime ("our enemies," as he described them) replaced through the "infiltration" of the administration by British Jews.[27] Samuel did his best to oblige him.[28] By 1922 the Zionist Commission's influence over the "political machinery" of Palestine was so great that to Charles Crane it "seems to have more power than the authorised government."[29] The Palestinian Arabs could see what was coming: according to Musa Kazim al Husseini, the leader of a delegation to London, what was being put in motion would mean the extinction of the Arabs sooner or later.[30] The Zionists were coming to "strangle" them.

THE FIRST INTIFADA

In the 1920s the most extreme of the Zionists (Vladimir Jabotinsky's Revisionists) sought to capitalize on the gains already made by staging provocative demonstrations in Jerusalem in the narrow lanes outside the Haram al Sharif. Rioting and killing would inevitably follow. Syrians living under French occupation slipped across the mandatory boundaries to join the bands of fighters forming in the Palestinian countryside. In a manner typical of their class, the urban (and usually urbane) Palestinian notables chose negotiation rather than confrontation, but being polite and having cups of tea with the high commissioner or a district police officer was not going to stop Palestine from being taken over. Some British officials on the spot might be sympathetic, but all the important decisions were being taken in London, and when the Palestinians rebelled it was London that decided they were to be suppressed without mercy.

The Palestine uprising of 1936–39—in effect the first intifada (literally "shaking")—began with a six-month general strike. As it continued the British hanged 112 Palestinians and put thousands more in prisons for interrogation and torture if that was necessary to get information out of them.[31] "The types of torture are varied," the political prisoner Subhi al Khadra wrote of the jail at ʿAkka. "They include beatings with fists and [stomping] with boots . . . as well as using canes for beating and flogging to death. They also included . . . the penetration of the rectums of the victims with canes and then moving the cane left and right and to the front and back." The use of dogs against prisoners and even more depraved practices (sodomy and urination on their faces) are also recorded.[32]

A principal catalyst of the uprising was the killing in 1935 of Sheikh ʿIzz al Din al Qassam, a name now associated with the suicide bombings of Israeli cafes and buses by the ʿIzz al Din al Qassam Martyrs Brigades. Described by the British as a "brigand sheikh" and "outlaw," Sheikh ʿIzz al Din was in fact a man steeped in Islamic learning and culture. After studying at Al Azhar University in Cairo, he returned to Syria and joined the ranks of the resistance to the French; sentenced to death in 1921, he escaped to Haifa, where he established himself as an imam and the marriage registrar of the local shariʿa court. Associated for a time with the Supreme Muslim Council (established by the British in an attempt to control Muslim opinion), Sheikh ʿIzz al Din soon lost patience with the Muslim establishment, regarding direct action as the only effective means of confronting both the British and the Zionist settlers. In 1930 he began mobilizing resistance among the peasant population. His followers launched a number of attacks on British and Zionist targets before the sheikh was trapped in a village near Jenin and killed on November 19, 1935.[33]

The sheikh's death was the trigger for further mobilization of Palestinian resistance. By June 1936, sporadic attacks had crystallized into a broad uprising in which rural religious figures played a dominant mobilizing role. The focus of this guerrilla movement was the mandatory government in all its aspects: troops, police, district officers, and the infrastructural sinews of occupation, primarily roads, railways, and telephone and telegraph lines. Zionist colonies were a secondary target, but when they were attacked the settlers often took the law into their own hands. Under the leadership of the Christian Zionist religious fanatic Orde Wingate—the "Lawrence of the Hebrews," as Koestler described him[34]—special night squads formed in cooperation with the British police and army murdered Arab villagers out of hand. The settlers also began improvising their own weapons, including the inaccurate but destructive Davidka cannon, which could pitch a homemade bomb several hundred meters, and the "barrel bombs"; two such bombs, rolled from the back of lorries into the fruit and vegetable market of Haifa on July 6 and July 25, 1938, killed 74 Arabs and injured another 129.[35] Thousands of active or reserve Jewish "police"—nearly 5,000 by the end of 1937 and 14,411 by 1939—were formed into battalions to guard the settlements, strengthening the nucleus of the military forces that the Zionist leadership would be able to send into action in 1948.[36]

COLLECTIVE PUNISHMENT

Armed Palestinian resistance reached its peak in 1938, when the British recorded 5,708 "acts of violence" (their own violence naturally excluded), among them 986 attacks on police and the military; 651 on Jewish settlements; 331 bombings; 215 abductions; 720 attacks on telegraphic communications; 341 acts of sabotage of railways and roads; 104 ruptures of the oil pipeline; and 430 assassinations or attempted assassinations.[37] Various parts of Palestine (including the old city of Jerusalem) passed from British occupation back into the hands of the people, with the resistance now strengthened by volunteers crossing borders from Transjordan and Syria. The "rebels" even issued their own postage stamps, but they could not hope to withstand the British indefinitely. Perhaps six thousand Palestinians were killed between 1936–39. Thousands more were jailed or interned; many were executed; some prominent figures were exiled to the Seychelles, others managed to escape by sea before capture. In many instances, the villagers were simply cut down by immeasurably superior forces. A British policeman described how at Tulkarm (Tal Karim) "I saw a number of lorry-loads of 'dead Arabs' go by. They had been killed in the nearby hills by troops and police."[38]

To deal with the uprising, troops were brought in from Malta, Egypt, and the home country; concrete blockhouses and a barbed-wire fence (named the "Tegart Wall" after Sir Charles Tegart, summoned to Palestine in 1937 with Sir David Petrie to advise the government on measures against "terrorism") were erected along the northern and northeastern boundaries with French-mandated territories to keep "infiltrators" out of the southern part of their thrice-partitioned homeland. The police were placed under military command in September 1938. Under emergency regulations, villages could be blockaded, raided, and placed under curfew; travel was restricted without a military pass; hundreds of homes in Safad, Nablus, Bethlehem, Hebron (Al Khalil), and numerous other towns and villages were destroyed in the "collective punishment" of "rebels." Collective fines were imposed on 250 villages.[39]

Many of the resistance "ringleaders" were killed in the field or executed after capture. Sheikh Farhan al Saʿadi, the most prominent Muslim figure after Sheikh ʿIzz al Din, was captured on November 22, 1937, tried before a military court two days later on charges of carrying a revolver, and hanged on November 27.[40] He was seventy-five years of age. The military court system had only been established on November 11: under the emergency regulations the death penalty was laid down for any offense involving the carrying of firearms or bombs. "Collective punishment" included the ran-sacking of property by soldiers and police, the "confiscation" of flocks of sheep and goats, and the dynamiting of houses and indeed (according to the testimony of refugees) whole villages.[41] Following the murder of Squadron Leader Alderson in 1938, an eyewitness wrote an account of the "collective punishment" by troops and police of the village of Izgim. Houses were blown up; nine hundred sheep and goats were confiscated and held against the payment of a collective fine; furniture, doors, and mirrors were smashed; sewing machines were "battered to bits"; corn, lentils, and broken crockery were scattered over the floor; jewelry was stolen; and a man who tried to break through the military cordon was bayoneted. Unable to pay the fine, the villagers fled. "I went into houses which showed every sign of hasty flight—an old rush mat on the door, the planks of a divan of which the mattress and cushions had gone, a coat hanging in an otherwise empty cupboard." Sixty houses were damaged or destroyed; later the British picked up a man who told them that the squadron leader's murderer actu-ally came from another village altogether.[42]

"NO ROOM" FOR MORE

Trying to thread their way through the imbroglio created by its own actions, the British government sent one committee or commission of inquiry after another to Palestine: Haycraft (1921), Shaw (March 1930), Hope-Simpson (May 1930), Peel (1937), and Woodhead (1938). All of their reports captured the essence of what angered the Arabs: immigration, land sales, and what Hope-Simpson called the "extra-territorialisation" of land under the "principles" of the Jewish National Fund and other Zionist purchasing bodies. Hope-Simpson, recommending against further immi-gration, found that in the present state of agricultural development there was "no room for a single additional settler if the standard of life of the Arab villager was to remain at its existing level."[43] It was typical of the division and indecision within the British government and its susceptibil-ity to Zionist pressure that his report was watered down in a subsequent "black letter" sent to Weizmann on February 14, 1931.[44] The "immigra-tion certificates" were issued as before, with many of those who could not get them making their way to Palestine anyway and disappearing into the settler population.

In June 1937, the Peel Commission recommended termination of the mandate and partition, allocating the most fertile land and much of the Mediterranean coast to the Jewish immigrant minority, and setting aside a corridor of land stretching from the Mediterranean to Jerusalem (including in it the Arab towns of Jaffa, Lydda, and Ramla) and an enclave around Jerusalem (including Bethlehem and Nazareth) as territories where the mandate would still apply. Given the demographic imbalance this would still leave, the commission also recommended "the compulsory transfer in the last resort of Arabs from the Jewish to the Arab area."[45]

Immigration and land ownership statistics explain the anger of Palestinians at what was being done over their heads. In the 1930s the Jewish population of the mandatory territory exploded. The 1922 census showed a total population of 752,048 (including Muslim 589,177, Christian 71,464, Jewish 83,790); the 1931 census 1,033,314 (Muslim 759,700, Christian 88,907, Jewish 174,606); the December 1944 census 1,739,624 (Muslim 1,061,277, Christian 135,547, Jewish 528,702, with a revised de facto estimate of 553,600).[46] The "natural" increase by the end of 1944 was Muslims, 96 percent; Christians, 71 percent; Jews, 26 percent; the increase of the population through migration was Muslims, 4 percent; Christians, 29 percent; Jews, 74 percent.[47] British figures for Jewish "immigration" show none for 1919, 5,514 for 1920, 12,856 for 1924, 33,801 for 1925, and then a drop until the coming to power of the National Socialist government in Germany, after which the numbers soar—30,327 in 1933, 42,359 in 1934, and 61,854 in 1935—before falling back to 29,727 in 1936. The Arab-Jewish population ratio changed from 91.3/9.7 percent in 1919 to 79.8/20.2 percent in 1933, 70.0/30.0 percent in 1938, and 64.9/35.1 percent in 1946.[48] What the statistical separation of Muslims and Christians tends to obscure is that the Christians were just as strongly opposed to Zionism as the Muslims.

Of the rural settled population, in only one subdistrict (Jaffa) were the Jews in a majority by the end of 1944 (53,000, having increased from 8,948 in 1931, compared to a Muslim population of 36,950 and a Christian population of 660). In Haifa the figures were 31,000 Jews (up from 5,308 in 1931) compared to 48,270 Muslims and 2,050 Christians; in Jerusalem 3,200 Jews (down from 3,559 in 1931) compared to 63,550 Muslims and 4,480 Christians.[49] Outside the towns, the Jewish population mostly lived and worked on settlements. These had increased in number from 5 in 1882 to 110 in 1931 and at least 259 by the end of 1944.[50] The town statistics show similar imbalances, with the striking exceptions of the new city of Tel Aviv, where the Jewish population was 166,000 compared to 410 Muslims and Christians, and Jerusalem, a special magnet for settlers, which had a Jewish population of 97,000 compared to 30,630 Muslims and 29,350 Christians.[51] The population of the Arab port of Jaffa, seized by Zionist militias even before the state of Israel was declared in 1948, consisted of 28,000 Jews compared to a combined Muslim-Christian population of 66,200.

Even as the demographics changed, the bulk of property remained in the hands of the native Palestinians. The Jewish National Fund and the Palestine Jewish Colonization Association had made substantial purchases of land since the 1920s, mainly in Galilee and around Haifa. Many vendors were absentee owners who negotiated through Palestinian middlemen; the deals between them were frequently characterized by evasion of regulations along with the eviction of the fellah land-cultivating population (often done beforehand by the vendor as a condition of purchase). By 1939 land purchased by the Zionists amounted to 5.7 percent of mandatory Palestine; by 1944 the figure had still climbed to only 6.6 percent. The vast bulk of private property and land remained in the hands of Muslim or Christian Palestinians. As Palestine was the collective inheritance of its people, their taxes having paid for its roads, railways, and public buildings, their artisans having built every town and village, and countless generations of their sons having died in the wars fought by the Ottoman Empire, they were entitled to regard the state land as theirs too. Palestinian Muslims or Christians were also the producers of most primary produce. Jewish holdings increased in the 1930s, but of the £P28,237,000 generated by agricultural production in 1944, £P19,500,000 still came from the Arab sector.[52] The division by the mandatory authority into what was "Arab" or "Jewish" included vegetables, fruits, olives, grains, fodder, cattle, sheep, goats, horses, mules, camels, donkeys, and pigs.[53]

As war approached in 1939, Britain, seeking to appease Arab opinion, dropped partition in favor of a binational state. A white paper declared that the government would do "everything in their power to create conditions which will enable the independent Palestinian State to come into being within ten years." Over the coming five years a further seventy-five thousand Jewish settlers would be allowed into Palestine, ten thousand each year, with a further twenty-five thousand being accepted "as a contribution towards the settlement of the Jewish refugee problem." After that, however, "no further Jewish immigration will be permitted unless the Arabs of Palestine are prepared to acquiesce in it." A further blow to the Zionists was delivered with the reiteration of Hope-Simpson's conclusion that if Arab cultivators were to maintain "their existing standard of life," and if a considerable landless Arab population was not soon to be created, land sales would have to be limited. Accordingly, the high commissioner was given general powers "to prohibit and regulate transfers of land."[54]

The Zionists were furious at what they regarded as British betrayal and began looking even more in the direction of the United States. On May 11, 1942, an Extraordinary Conference of American Zionists that was convened at the Biltmore Hotel in New York approved a program rejecting the white paper and urging "that the gates of Palestine be opened; that the Jewish Agency be vested with control of immigration into Palestine and with the necessary authority for upbuilding the country, including the development of its unoccupied and uncultivated lands; and that Palestine be established as a Jewish Commonwealth integrated in the structure of the new democratic world."[55] Few thought to ask how a "Jewish commonweath" was going to be established in a land where the Jews remained in a minority despite more than a decade of intensive immigration and settlement.

THE MENDICANT EMPIRE

Britain's failures in the Middle East between the two world wars drew biting criticism from a young scholar of Lebanese origin, Albert Hourani:

> Her fundamental defect was that she had nothing to offer the world.
> Regions within her Empire and States linked to her could expect nothing more attractive than good order and sanitation. Everywhere she fell under the imputation of maintaining her position by allying with vested interests and so came to be regarded as an obstacle in the way of beneficial change. She carried to its limit this quality of opportunist flexibility which many Englishmen regard as the virtue of their policy though in reality it is a profound weakness. . . . There was no attempt to understand the problems of the Arab World and to think out a coherent policy. . . . There was a profound moral complacency, an assumption that Great Britain had a claim on the "loyalty" of the Arabs no matter how she treated them.[56]

Hourani concluded with the observation that "the Arab attitude to every aspect of Western civilization will be largely determined by the political treatment they receive from the Western powers."[57]

By 1945 Britain was an exhausted imperial power. More than £1,200 billion of capital invested abroad had been liquidated to pay for the war. Even after the United States wiped out the Lend Lease debt of £4.2 billion in August 1945, the government was left with a debt of £26 billion. Export trade had shrunk to 29 percent of the immediate prewar figure. In 1946 the government borrowed $3.75 billion from the United States and a further $1.25 billion from Canada, but by September 1947 all but $400 million of the U.S. loan had gone. Compounding these severe financial problems were shortages across all sectors and an unemployment rate of 15.5 percent.[58]

Simply put, Britain was a mendicant state, heavily and humiliatingly dependent on a former colony for aid. It was a power but no longer a great one, and British policies of this period have to be set in the appropriate emotional context; it must indeed have been painful for men who had grown up in the days of grandeur to acknowledge that behind the imperial façade lay "weakness and bankruptcy."[59] The country could no longer afford its colonial domains. If one hundred thousand more Jews were allowed into Palestine, as recommended by the Anglo-American Committee of Inquiry, the garrisons would have to be reinforced to keep the peace. The costs were unthinkable. Furthermore, Churchill's enthusiasm for Zionism was not shared by the incoming government of Clement Attlee, who regarded the Jewish national home as "a wild experiment that was bound to cause trouble."[60] Truman's announcement that the United States was ready to take "technical and financial responsibility" for transporting one hundred thousand Jews to Palestine but was not prepared to commit troops to help keep the peace only inflamed British irritation at American interference. In these circumstances, Attlee made it plain, he was "determined to liquidate Palestine as an economic and military liability."[61]

TERROR AND DIPLOMACY

From Balfour onwards Zionist colonization had taken root under British protection, but now that Britain had nothing more it could or would deliver, the Zionists turned on the mandatory power with remorseless ferocity. Soldiers, policemen, and civilians were killed and workshops, railway lines, trains, and bridges sabotaged in wave after wave of well-coordinated assaults. On August 8, 1944, terrorists tried to kill the high commissioner (Sir Harold MacMichael), and on November 6 the Stern Gang succeeded in assassinating the British minister in Cairo, Lord Moyne. On July 22, 1946, senior British administrators were among the ninety-one people killed when Irgun terrorists detonated milk churns packed with explosives in the basement of the King David Hotel in Jerusalem and "chipped off" a wing.[62] Letter bombs were posted by the Stern Gang to senior figures in the British government and opposition; in October the British embassy in Rome was bombed. The hand that had fed was being savagely bitten.

The British sought to reassert their authority through police and judicial suppression. Jews convicted of terrorist offenses were hanged or imprisoned and senior figures in the Jewish Agency were arrested, but clearly a diplomatic solution would have to be found to the mess that Palestine had become. In February 1947 Whitehall prepared a plan for a five-year trusteeship on a cantonal basis as a preliminary to independence; when this was rejected by both Zionists and Arabs, it decided to pass the problem on to the United Nations, asking the secretary-general on April 2 to place the question of Palestine on the agenda of the General Assembly at its next regular annual session. On April 28 a special session was called, and on May 4 the assembly set up the Special Committee on Palestine (UNSCOP). The committee took evidence in the Middle East and Europe (from displaced-persons camps) before adopting a "majority" plan at the end of August recommending the partition of Palestine into Arab and Jewish states, with Jerusalem set aside as a *corpus separatum* under international administration. The three segments were to be joined economically, with the Arab and Jewish states to be given independence after a two-year period of transition (beginning September 1, 1947), during which time a UN supervisory commission would steer them into the new framework. The minority plan (adopted by five members against eight for partition) called for the establishment of a federal state after a transitional period of three years.

In November the General Assembly began moving toward a vote. On November 24, delegates convening as an ad hoc committee voted 29–12 against an Arab proposal for the establishment of one Palestinian state. A proposal by Arab members that the fate of Palestine be submitted to the International Court of Justice was lost by one vote, and on November 25 the ad hoc committee adopted the UNSCOP majority plan recommendation, amended at the insistence of the United States to include the Naqab (Negev) region in the Jewish state after last-minute intervention by Weizmann at the White House.

However, support for partition still fell one vote short of the two-thirds majority necessary for its passage through the plenary session of the General Assembly. Weizmann again turned to Truman for support. "I am aware of how much abstaining delegations would be swayed by your counsel and the influence of your government. I refer to China, Honduras, Colombia, Mexico, Liberia, Ethiopia, Greece. I beg and pray for your decisive intervention at this decisive hour."[63] A push was needed to get partition over the line, and the White House gave it. "We went for it," Clark Clifford, Truman's special counsel, said later. "It was because the White House was for it that it went through. I kept the ramrod up the State Department's butt."[64] Liberia, France, the Philippines, and Latin American states, including Cuba and Haiti (poor but with a vote just as valuable as anyone else's), all had the whip cracked across their back by the president's friends or business acquaintances.

All the cajolery, intimidation, and bribes eventually paid off. When the vote—postponed twice while delegates and governments were still being worked on—was finally taken in plenary session of the assembly on November 29, it passed 33–13 with ten abstentions: of the seventeen countries that had abstained on November 25, seven had buckled to pressure and voted "yes." Truman's role had clearly been critical. Herschel Johnson, the State Department's deputy head of mission at the UN, burst into tears while talking to Loy Henderson: "Loy, forgive me for breaking down like this but Dave Niles called us here a couple of days ago and said that the President had instructed him to tell us that, by God, he wanted us to get busy and get all the votes that we possibly could; that there would be hell if the voting went the other way."[65]

"PREVENTIVE DEFENSE"

The Zionists had been mobilizing and planning for this moment for years. The Palestinians called a three-day general strike beginning on December 2, but in the field it was soon clear that they were no match for the Zionist forces. Zionist militias soon began moving deep into the territory set aside for an Arab state. In early February 1948 the U.S. consul-general in Jerusalem wrote that

> in the field of offense, which the Jewish Agency prefers to term "preventive defense" we have seen all three Jewish armed groups in action, Haganah, Irgun and the Stern Gang. Their offensives generally consist of demolitions of Arab strong points and forays into Arab villages which they believe to have been used as bases for Arab guerillas. The blowing up of the Old Serail in Jaffa (by the Stern Gang), the same type of action against the Semiramis Hotel in Jerusalem (by the Haganah) and the shooting of Arabs in Tireh village (by the Irgun) are all examples of Jewish offensives. Such activities are designed, according to the Jews, to force the Arabs into a passive state.[66]

In the two months since the passage of the partition resolution, one thousand people had been killed.[67]

In these last few months of the mandate, when the British were still nominally in charge, the Zionists began clearing Palestine of its indigenous population. By early May up to two hundred thousand Palestinians had fled or had been deliberately driven from their homes; according to the Haganah's own military intelligence, "hostile acts" committed by the Haganah, Irgun, and the Stern Gang had caused the flight of 70 percent of the four hundred thousand people who had left their homeland by June 1.[68] The Zionist militias were well trained and armed, were operating according to clearly defined military plans, and were united in their determination to see a Jewish state come into existence. The Arabs in Palestine and beyond were too disorganized to meet a challenge of this nature. On the eve of the end of the mandate, U.S. Secretary of State George C. Marshall drew attention to the internal weaknesses that made Arab success in Palestine unlikely:

> Whole government structure of Iraq is endangered by political and economic disorders and Iraq Govt cannot at this moment afford to send more than a handful of [the] troops it has already dispatched. Egypt has suffered recently from strikes and disorders. The army has insufficient equipment because of the refusal of Brit aid and what it has is needed for police duty at home. Syria has neither arms nor army worthy of name and has not been able to organize one since French left three years ago. Lebanon has no real army while Saudi Arabia has small army which is barely sufficient to keep tribes in order. Jealousies between Saudi Arabs and Syrians on one hand and Hashemite govts of Transjordan and Iraq prevent Arabs from making even best use of existing forces.[69]

In July 1948 the CIA made a secret estimate of Israeli forces compared to Arab forces "in or near Palestine." The estimate for the Israelis was 97,800 compared to an Arab total of 46,800, about 20,000 of them troops who were "near" rather than "in" Palestine.[70] Syria had 1,000 troops actually in Palestine, Iraq 9,000, and Egypt an estimated 5,000. Saudi Arabia had a notional 3,000 never seen in any fighting. The 6,000 troops from Transjordan—the Arab Legion—were deployed to defend the territory that would fall to King Abdullah in line with his secret dealings with the Zionists.

These figures are close to the estimates given by Walid Khalidi. Until May 1948 Arab Palestine was being defended by less than 6,000 men, most of them volunteers in the Arab Liberation Army recruited and trained in Damascus and mostly armed only with rifles. After May 15, 1948, a total of 13,876 Arab soldiers from five countries (Syria, Iraq, Transjordan, Egypt, and Lebanon) moved into Palestine, backed by light tanks, armored cars, a range of field artillery, and ten Spitfires (from the Egyptian air force). The Zionist forces of about 100,000, consisting of frontline troops, reserves, garrison troops, settlement police, the home guard, and irregular forces (Irgun and the Stern Gang), were armed with rifles, thousands of machine guns, mortars, antitank rifles and antitank mines, several field guns, armored cars, half-tracks, and a rudimentary air force consisting of several Messerschmitt ME-109s and transport planes.[71] On these figures the combined Arab forces amounted to about one-fifth of the fighting men or women the Zionists could summon into action. The image of massive Arab armies descending on Palestine from all directions was a lie, and as the fighting continued the balance swung even more heavily in favor of the new state. This was largely because of the arms the Israelis were getting from outside (principally from Czechoslovakia) and the arms being denied by Britain— the sole supplier of weapons of all descriptions—to Egypt, Iraq, and Trans-jordan. By November 1948 its arms embargo had "reduced the Arab forces and the Arab Legion to a state of almost complete impotence."[72]

Much of the fighting in 1948 was done by forces operating under the command of Abd al Qadir al Husseini,[73] the Arab Liberation Army led by Fawzi al Qawuqji, or lightly armed villagers trying to defend their homes as they came under attack. They had no military training, whereas many of the Jews had fought with the British army or had received paramilitary training as settlement police. Writes Nafez Abdullah Nazzal of the fighting in northern Palestine: "As of May 1948 the total rifle strength of the Arab forces in Western Galilee was estimated at about 140 rifles, with the rural forces commanded by Abu Mahmoud Saffari and about 30 rifles in the city garrison of Acre. The Jewish strength consisted of the Carmeli brigade com-manded by Moshe Carmel which comprised 1667 men as of April 1, 1948, and was intended to be 2,750 by the beginning of May although this total was never reached."[74] The eastern Galilee hamlet of al Tabigha (population about 330) had three hunting rifles when an Israeli column arrived in early May. The people fled to the neighboring village of al Samakiyya, whose inhabitants had five rifles between them; both villages were "cleared" and destroyed in accordance with Haganah operational instructions. In his memoirs, Qawuqji details shortages of gasoline, money, food, and clothes as well as arms and ammunition.[75] Possessing superior weaponry, the Israelis also "greatly benefited" from the civilian infrastructure and mili-tary bases abandoned by the British, including Sarafand, Bayt Nabala in the Ramla district, and "various encampments in the south."[76]

"BETWEEN STATEHOOD AND EXTERMINATION"

Commenting on the refusal of the Jewish Agency to take part in on-the-spot negotiations in Palestine, Dean Rusk commented that it "clearly reveals the intentions of the Jews to go steadily ahead with the Jewish sep-arate state by force of arms." If they did, he wrote, "we shall find ourselves in the UN confronted by a very anomalous situation": "The Jews will be the actual aggressors against the Arabs. However, the Jews will claim they are merely defending the boundaries of a state which were traced by the UN and approved, at least in principle, by two-thirds of the UN membership. The question which will confront the SC in scarcely ten days time will be whether Jewish armed attack on Arab communities in Palestine is legitimate or whether it constitutes such a threat to international peace and security as to call for coercive measures by the Security Council."[77] In the event of an armed attack by Arab armies from outside, "the Jews will come running to the Security Council with the claim that their state is the object of armed aggression and will use every means to obscure the fact that it is their own armed aggression against the Arabs inside Palestine which is the cause of Arab counter-attack."[78]

In a letter to Truman dated April 9, 1948—the same day as the Deir Yassin massacre—Weizmann melodramatically declared that the choice ahead of the Jews was "between statehood and extermination."[79] What he and others said in remarks not intended for public consumption was rather different. In the summer of 1947, before the partition decision was even taken, the mayor of Tel Aviv, Israel Rokach, told Kermit Roosevelt that the Zionists had nothing to fear from the Arab states. "They are disorganised and infirm of purpose. We can handle them easily. The only army they have worth anything is Transjordan's Arab Legion and . . . we have assurances that the king is well disposed towards us. He is a sensible man."[80] In conversation with members of the U.S. delegation at the UN, Weizmann dismissed the Arabs as a threat of any kind, saying that

> [he] had tried very hard but did not understand the reasons for the "switch" in the US position [i.e., the decision to move from partition to trusteeship]. Was it fear of the Arabs? Was it oil? Or was it fear of Russia? He said there was no reason whatever to fear the Arabs. They were woefully weak. The Arabs could do nothing with their oil except sell it to the US. Did we [the United States] fear they would sell it to Russia? If so, what would the Arabs do with Russian rubles? Were we afraid that the Jewish state would be dominated by Russia? There was no possible occasion for such fears. . . . In response to our questions and comments he said the Jews had absolutely no fear of the Arabs and he elaborated on this by indicating that the Arab states were so disorganized and weak as to constitute almost the military factor of zero.[81]

In fact, nothing could have been more dangerous to the Zionists than a peaceful transfer of power under the administration of a UN commission. An orderly partition would have left the Muslim and Christian population in place, owning the vast bulk of the land and constituting half the population in the Jewish state as well as virtually the entire population of their own. This had been the crux of the problem from the start, and by 1948 it had still not been resolved: How could there be a Jewish state when, even after two decades of a massive intake of colonists, Jews were still outnumbered more than two to one by the Arab population and nearly all the land and immovable property was still owned by Balfour's "existing non-Jewish communities"?

The figures tell the story. Within the boundaries laid down in the 1947 partition plan, the Jewish state would have had a Jewish population of 498,000 compared to 495,000 Arabs (including 90,000 bedouin), but the seizure of nearly 3,500 square kilometers of land in 1948–49 in addition to the territory allocated to Israel by the UN would have increased the number of Arabs in Israeli-held territory to 892,000 (had they all been able to stay) compared to 655,000 Jews.[82] As the Zionists had no intention of handing back conquered land, the "Jewish state" would have come into existence with a substantial non-Jewish majority. This contradiction could be resolved only by "clearing" the land, and this could be done only in the chaos and disorder brought on by war. "The war will give us the land," Ben-Gurion believed. "Concepts of 'ours' and 'not ours' are peacetime concepts only and they lose their meaning during war."[83] The objective remained the conquest of all Palestine. In his memoirs the Palmach strike force commander Yigal Allon refers to the "mistaken political considerations" that led to the abandonment of operations "to liberate the rest of the country (the Hebron hills, Old Jerusalem and the Triangle)," which could "at this stage of the war have been attained with less effort and greater assurance of success than were the big victories in the big campaigns in the Negev and Sinai."[84] But the opportunity was lost. As a result, Israel had come into existence with more territory than it was given but with "much less than it was within her military capacity to achieve and much less than was necessary for her defence against further threats from the same enemies."

EXODUS OR NUMBERS?

By early 1948 a critical juncture had been reached. The historical desire to remove the Palestinians from their land now intersected with the possibility of actually being able to do it. Initially, when the Zionists were still struggling to establish a foothold in Palestine and were in no position to dislodge the indigenous people, Ben-Gurion professed nothing but honorable intentions,[85] but he had lived through a period of extensive population "transfers" (especially of Greeks and Turks), and the removal of the indigenous population of Palestine remained on his mind as the solution to the demo-graphic problem confronting the Zionists. In the 1930s he discussed possi-bilities for resettling Palestinians in Transjordan; he was encouraged by the Peel Commission report of 1937, even if he did not believe the British would ever follow through on the recommendations of partition and compulsory transfer of part of the Arab population. "Of course they will not do it . . . if we do not will it and if we do not urge them with all our might and main." The Zionists had to prepare themselves. "We must do this transfer *now*—and the *first* and *decisive step* is *preparing ourselves* to implement it."[86] In a letter to his son he wrote that "we must expel Arabs and take their place."[87]

This was not a subject any Zionist leader wanted to talk about openly. The references to "transfer" as the solution to the demographic problem are nearly all to be found in diaries and private papers. Israel Zangwill had summed up the central dilemma in 1905. "We must be prepared either to drive out by the sword the tribes in possession as our forefathers did or to grapple with the problem of a large alien population, mostly Mohammedan, and accustomed for centuries to despise us." Criticizing Weizmann for not speaking more honestly, he remarked that "if you shirk Exodus you are confronted by Numbers."[88] Without removal of the population one way or another, the Zionist project could not succeed. It was left to Joseph Weitz, of the Jewish National Fund's land development division, to sum up what had to be done: "It should be clear to us that there is no room in Palestine for these two peoples," he confided in a diary entry of December 20, 1940. "Not one village, not one tribe should be left. And the form of the transfer needs to be the creation of a refuge for them in Iraq, in Syria and in Trans-jordan. . . . There is no other way out."[89]

"WE DID NOTHING"

The debate over whether there was a "master plan" behind the expulsion of the Palestinians has continued intermittently since 1948. "We did nothing to cause this mass flight," wrote Weizmann. Palestine had been invaded by "hired assassins," and "although the Jews had practically no arms at that time and had to meet tanks with revolvers or rifles they drove them off." This fact so impressed the Arabs that that they began to run, and now "you can travel the length and breadth of the country and meet few Arabs except in the triangle of Jenin-Nablus-Tulkarm."[90] This stock version of history prevailed in Israel until a generation of young historians began digging up an accumulating pile of evidence of deliberate mass expulsions in the 1980s, confirming what the Palestinians themselves had been trying to tell the world for decades. If proof of a "master plan" depends on the discovery of one specific incriminating document, it is never likely to have been written in the first place, but random statements, gestures, and diary entries written in the field, plus the fact that towns and villages were being deliberately emptied from early 1948 and then destroyed in accordance with explicit operational instructions, are all evidence that, within their own ranks, the Zionist leadership had decided to "clear" Palestine of as many of its people as possible before international intervention forced an end to the conflict.

Evidence of Ben-Gurion's intentions as Palestine slid into open conflict lies in his diary entry of early 1948, when he wrote of expelling Arab townspeople "so our people can replace them."[91] He specifically mentioned the need for expulsions during military operations and the "destruction of Arab islands in Jewish population areas."[92] Like Weizmann, he rejoiced at the sight of towns, cities, and rural areas emptied of their non-Jewish inhabitants. Hundreds of Palestinian civilians had already been killed in the onslaught on Lydda in July 1948, when, in accordance with a directive issued by Ben-Gurion, Yitzhak Rabin, the operational military commander, ordered the expulsion of all inhabitants "without attention to age." The same instructions were given to troops occupying the nearby town of Ramla, where there had been no shooting and the town notables had signed a document of surrender.[93] By late May Ben-Gurion was already planning what would come next: "When we break the Arab Legion and bomb Amman, we shall liquidate Jordan and it is then that Syria, too, will fall." Muslim power in Lebanon was artificial and would be "easy to smash. We must create a Christian state whose southern border will stretch along the Litani River. . . . It is then that we will sign a peace treaty with it."[94]

Like many politicians Ben-Gurion was calculating and opportunistic, anxious to be seen in the best possible light even when planning discreditable actions. The statements he made during his life and during the war of 1948, along with his actions, are sufficient evidence that he thought of a Palestine not partitioned but broken down, emptied of its people, and reconstituted as a Jewish state. The "enemy" for the Zionist leadership were not just the armed fighters but all Palestinians. Their very presence challenged the rationale of a Jewish state in a land that was predominantly Muslim, as did their villages, their mosques, their tombs, their monuments, and their cemeteries.

The most compelling evidence of system and method behind the expulsion of Palestinians lies in the military plans drawn up for the conquest of Palestine. Two early postwar plans (Plan A and Plan B) were followed by Plan C (Gimmel) of November 1947, the three of them culminating in Plan

D (Dalet) of March 1948, the aims of which were not just the protection of the borders of the Jewish state but the seizure of territory outside it. Apart from the role of the Palmach strike force, specific regions and tasks were allocated to each of the six brigades (Golani, Carmeli, Alexandroni, Kiryati, Givʾati, and Etzioni); the objectives of the thirteen operations launched under Plan Dalet included the destruction of Arab villages and the expulsion ("cleaning," to use Yigal Allon's word) of the population.

Khalidi does not hesitate to call Plan Dalet the "master plan" for the conquest of Palestine.[95] Benvenisti argues for a distinction between the meaning of military operations undertaken before and after the establishment of the state and casts doubt on Plan D as an instrument of deliberate depopulation despite the very explicit language in the instructions issued to the brigade commanders and the attempts through psychological warfare and acts of terror to panic the Palestinians into taking flight before May 14. In his view it was only after the state was established that the expulsions came "dangerously close to fitting the definition of 'ethnic cleansing,'"[96] but whether before or after the establishment of the state, the wishes and intentions of the Zionist leadership were clear. A wink was as good as a nudge: Ben-Gurion did not have to issue instructions for his commanders to know that if they expelled Palestinians no one high up was going to complain and that the more that fled or could be driven out the better it would be for the new state.

The attempts of truce supervisors to pull the two sides apart proved futile. In the second half of 1948, truce supervision lost "whatever authority and moral force it may have had at one time," wrote the senior U.S. military representative on the UN truce supervision team, Brigadier General William Riley. All parties were obstructing or ignoring truce calls, but "this attitude is most pronounced in the Jews. . . . Wilful and premeditated violations of the truce by the Jews are now routine." Their offensive military capacity was so much greater than all Arab forces combined that if they desired "they could undoubtedly clear Palestine of Arab forces in a relatively short time" (as Allon believed).[97] The Arabs were in such a weak position that the main concern of the military observers was that they should do nothing to give the Israelis the pretext for further attacks.

THE *NAKBA*

Beginning in early 1948 and continuing in waves until truces and then armistices were signed between Israel and Arab governments in 1949, about 750,000 Palestinians fled or were herded out of their homeland in what has since been known as the *nakba* (the catastrophe). They walked in the direction of Syria, Lebanon, and Jordan with whatever possessions they could carry (invariably including the key and title deed to their house). They lived in caves, mosques, and wherever else they could find shelter until the UN established a refugee agency that could provide for them. In numerous parts of Palestine civilians were slaughtered out of hand, terrifying others into taking flight. The massacre at the village of Deir Yassin by Irgun and Stern Gang terrorists on Friday, April 9, followed an attack that would have failed, in the face of a spirited defense by the village men, but for the intervention of a Palmach (Haganah strike force) unit. A survivor described how he saw the bodies of women "lying in houses with their skirts torn up to their waists and their legs wide apart; children with their throats cut open [and] rows of young men shot in the back after being lined at an execution wall." The villagers were butchered with knives, swords, and guns or blown up with hand grenades after the village had been overwhelmed; many of the women were raped before being murdered; two-thirds of the estimated 110 to 140 dead were women, children, and men over 60; stolen property included rings and bracelets ripped from the arms of the women.[98] About twenty-five males (men and boys) who survived the first wave of killing were paraded through Jerusalem in a truck before being taken back to Deir Yassin and murdered in the village quarry.[99] Fifty-five orphaned children dumped from a truck on the streets of Jerusalem near the Mandelbaum Gate were taken in by an extraordinary woman, Hind al Husseini, who turned her grandfather's house into the Dar al Tifl al Arabi (House of the Arab Child) orphanage. The cleanup at Deir Yassin continued during the weekend, the spectacle of mutilated bodies traumatizing members of the burial party and news of the massacre horrifying Jews from the nearby settlement of Givat Shaul, which had lived at peace with Deir Yassin throughout the fighting. Menachem Begin, later Israeli prime minister and winner of the Nobel Peace Prize but in 1948 the leader of the Irgun, congratulated his men for their heroism. Four days after the massacre, on April 13, Palestinians took their revenge by ambushing a convoy traveling to Mt. Scopus and killing more than seventy Jewish medical personnel. Perhaps appropriately, Deir Yassin is now enclosed within the grounds of the Givat Shaul Mental Health Institute.

Arthur Koestler described Deir Yassin as an "isolated episode."[100] It was not. It was not even the worst of numerous massacres committed by regular and irregular Zionist forces: at Duwayima (Dawayma), where several hundred men, women, and children were killed in and around the village, the adults shot in the street, in their homes inside the village mosque, and in a cave where they had taken shelter, the children dispatched by having their skulls broken with sticks; at Safsaf, where about seventy men were blindfolded and shot one by one; at Lydda, where hundreds of civilians were killed, including about eighty machine-gunned to death inside the Dahmash mosque before the town was captured and the population expelled (the expulsion order was signed by Yitzhak Rabin, a future prime minister).[101] Despite the denials, many of these atrocities "were known at the time to ministers, military commanders and even the general public."[102]

By early 1949 the partition plan lay on the diplomatic landscape like an abandoned car gutted of all its usable parts. Israel had seized 24 percent more of Palestine than the 54 percent it had been allocated and had also captured western Jerusalem; repeated assaults to take the Old City as well were held off only by the Arab Legion. The partition plan had been rejected by the Palestinians and Arab governments from the beginning. Now that it had served its purpose, it was thrown aside by Israel too: Ben-Gurion declared on November 11, 1948, that his government no longer considered itself bound by its provisions.

All "abandoned" property—citrus orchards, olive groves and presses, wheat fields, workshops, factories, and not just houses but whole villages and towns—fell into the hands of the new rulers of Palestine. It included even the minutiae of domestic life, "carpets, books, equipment and furniture, even window frames and doorhandles."[103] What the Palestinians left behind was parceled out by Israel's "custodian of absentee property" to incoming Jewish settlers. According to Weizmann, by now Israel's first president, "abandoned" land amounted to

> about five million dunums of land at least which could be taken under plough almost at once, but we have not yet got the people. In the district between Ramleh and Latrun there are about two million dunums of the best land in Palestine, for which, if we had to buy it, we would have to pay at least LP50–60 per dunum and as you know, one could never buy land between Ramleh and Latrun. Now it is all free, overgrown with weeds, and it is very doubtful whether the Arabs will ever come back to work it. Everybody seems to think they have gone for good.

An opportunity was open to Israel "which may not recur for centuries."[104] There is no shame or remorse, only exultation. The U.S. ambassador James G. McDonald recounted that Weizmann "spoke to me emotionally of this 'miraculous simplification of Israel's tasks' and cited the vaster tragedy of six million Jews murdered during World War II. He would ask, 'What did the world do to prevent the genocide? Why now should there be such excitement in the UN and the Western capitals about the plight of the Arab refugees?'"[105]

In the new state, regions with a substantial Arab population were closed and villagers subjected to a night curfew along with a range of other restrictions (including banishment and administrative detention) invoked under the defense emergency regulations inherited from the British. Dozens of collective settlements were established on expropriated Palestinian land. Close to 500 Palestinian villages or hamlets (at least 472 according to Palestinian researchers) were destroyed as part of a topographical assault that continues to the present in the attempt to obliterate what Palestine was. Some ruins still stand, but most of the villages were bulldozed and the land built or planted over with settlements, forests endowed by philanthropists and sympathetic foreign governments, and parks (even theme parks).[106] Mosques were destroyed or converted to other purposes; cemeteries were plowed under to make way for redevelopment or allowed to fall into disrepair so that eventually nothing was left but broken tombstones lying amid the weeds. Every Palestinian village had its cemetery, but of the hundreds that existed in 1948 "vestiges of only about forty are still discernible" half a century later.[107] Countless generations of Palestinian dead remain in a land emptied of most of their living descendants in 1948. Such was the outcome of the Balfour Declaration's assurance in 1917 that in the creation of a homeland for the Jewish people nothing would be done "to prejudice the civil and religious rights of the existing non-Jewish communities in Palestine."

"PRESENT ABSENTEES"

Even Palestinians who had remained within the boundaries of the new state lost homes when their villages were destroyed in the name of "security." Others who had stayed but were not at their usual place of residence during the fighting—"present absentees," as they were officially classified—had their property taken from them in the same way as absent absentees. The armistice agreements signed on Rhodes in 1949 left many Palestinians within sight of their expropriated land: a case in point was the central Palestinian town of Qalqilya, whose extensive orange groves were placed on the other side of the dividing line, allowing Israel to keep the land without the burden of the people.[108] In the first two years of Israel's life as a state, thousands more Palestinians—not "infiltrators" but people who had stayed put during the war—were driven across the armistice lines into Jordan.

The fighting had ended but the war had not. Neither had Israel's thirst for land been slaked. In a memo sent to Truman during the "peace" negotiations of 1949, Undersecretary of State James Webb outlined what the Israelis wanted:

(1) While Israel makes no demands on Lebanon at present it would later like a portion of southeastern part of southern Lebanon considered necessary to Israeli development plans.

(2) Israel desires to acquire from Egypt the Egyptian-occupied Gaza Strip allotted to the Arabs under the partition resolution of November 29, 1947.

(3) Israel makes no demands upon Syria at present but will accept the international frontier with the proviso also to be applied to Lebanon that if either state desires to open negotiations in the future for border rectification this may be done.

(4) Israel will make further demands on Transjordan for territory in Arab Palestine considered necessary for Israeli development plans. Israel has in mind giving Abdullah a few villages in return.

(5) Israel will retain occupied areas such as Western Galilee and Jaffa, Lydda and Ramla, allotted to the Arabs under the partition plan.

(6) Israel will relinquish none of the Negev.[109]

The armistice lines left southern Lebanon, Syria, and Gaza as the focal points of territorial and strategic objectives yet to be satisfied, with the revisionist Zionists still openly claiming territory on the east bank of the Jordan River. To some hopeful souls, however, the conflict between Arab and Jew in Palestine was now over and the armistice lines would eventually turn into permanent borders. In the future, wrote James McDonald, the first U.S. ambassador to the new state, "there is the strongest evidence that Israel will not be an aggressor nor be in the camp of an aggressor." Responsible opinion was firmly in control in Israel "and has accepted the present boundaries of the State as the basis for final settlement with its neighbors."[110] The ambassador expected Israel to have made peace with all its "neighbors," with the possible exceptions of Iraq and Saudi Arabia, within a decade.

7. CIVIL WAR ALONG THE POTOMAC

In the period between the partition resolution of November 1947 and the declaration of the state of Israel in May 1948, the State Department, the Zionist lobby, and the White House fought their own triangular war over Palestine. The Zionists had identified their most dangerous enemy in Washington years earlier. "Our difficulties were not connected with the first rank statesmen," Weizmann wrote in his memoirs. "These had, for by far the greatest part, always understood our aspirations. . . . It was always behind the scenes and on the lower levels that we encountered an obstinate, devious and secretive opposition which set at naught the public declarations of American statesmen."[1]

Already by 1946 the differences within the administration over Palestine were being described by Dean Acheson, then the undersecretary of state, as "civil war along the Potomac."[2] The Zionists concentrated their attention on the White House, whose incumbent was a self-educated man "deeply trained in the moral values of Graeco-Judaic-English thought,"[3] however such values are to be understood in the context of a president who had only recently authorized the nuclear bombing of two Japanese cities. Truman's understanding of the Middle East was practically zero, and his suggestions for solutions to complex problems were naive or disingenuous. His belief that the Balfour Declaration was consistent with "the noble principles of Woodrow Wilson, especially of self-determination," was not shared by senior State Department officials.[4] As the department's director of Near Eastern affairs and African affairs, Loy Henderson, wrote in 1945: "The active support by the Government of the United States of a policy favoring the setting up of a Jewish state in Palestine would be contrary to the policy which the United States has always followed, of respecting the wishes of a large majority of the local inhabitants with respect to their form of government."[5] Two years later Henderson was warning that U.S. support for the creation of a Jewish state "will eventually involve us in international difficulties of so grave a character that the reaction through-out the world as well as in this country will be very strong."[6] The secretary of state (George C. Marshall) was himself not in favor of partition.

The partition resolution called for the transfer of administrative powers from the mandatory government to the UN Commission on Palestine, which would then delegate them to the incoming Jewish and Arab pro-visional governments. However, Britain, arguing that the division of responsibility would only make a bad situation worse, declared that the commission would not be allowed to enter Palestine until two weeks before the end of the mandate; except at a distance, the commission was thus pre-vented from fulfilling the responsibilities that it had been given. But even if it could take over from the British, how could it compel the contending forces to do what it asked?

In February the commission informed the Security Council that it would be unable to establish security in Palestine and maintain law and order "unless military forces in adequate strength are made available to the Com-mission when the responsibility for the administration of Palestine is trans-ferred to it."[7] Britain refused to be involved, arguing that the British public would not tolerate British lives being put at risk in defense of a plan that was unworkable because of the total opposition of the Arabs. The United States balked on the grounds that such a force could be established only to counter a threat to international peace and security, but this was not the real reason. Any emergency Middle East force sanctioned by the Security Council would almost certainly have to include Soviet troops, and Western governments were never going to agree to this. Unable to respond posi-tively to the commission's request but unwilling to respond negatively, the council dithered. On March 29, the permanent members issued a ringing statement urging the council—urging themselves in fact—to "act by all means available to it to bring about an immediate cessation of violence and the restoration of peace and order in Palestine."[8]

To sum up the situation at this stage, the General Assembly had disre-garded the wishes of the majority of the population of Palestine in voting for partition; it had taken this decision without having the means of enforcing it or knowing whether the Security Council was prepared to enforce it; now that the council had shirked the responsibility, Palestine was like a ship stripped of rudder and main sail and abandoned by captain and crew. In such disarray did the UN go about its business, the left hand of the General Assembly not knowing what the right hand of the Security

Council was prepared to do. With the Security Council unwilling to take any action other than issue statements calling for action, the United States government quickly began casting about for alternatives to a partition that could not be effected without bloodshed.

PARTITION TO TRUSTEESHIP

Already by January 19, 1948, the State Department's policy planning staff had recommended that the administration consider a federal state or trusteeship as options to partition.[9] "The Palestine partition plan is manifestly unworkable," Loy Henderson wrote on February 6. "I think that with each passing day our task will be rendered more difficult and that by mid April general chaos will reign in Palestine."[10] The implications of attempting to abide by the partition vote were spelled out in a top-secret departmental report dated February 24: "If . . . we decide that we are obliged by past commitments or any other consideration to take a leading part in the enforcement in Palestine of any arrangement opposed by the great majority of the inhabitants of the Middle Eastern area, we must be prepared to face the implications of this act by revising our general policy in that part of the world."[11] This, the report went on, would entail a review of "our entire military and political policy." Four days later the CIA concluded that as "the failure of partition is already evident," the only way ahead was to have the UN reconsider the whole issue.[12]

The State Department's Office of Near Eastern and African Affairs prepared the first draft of a trusteeship arrangement on February 11 and a second draft the next day, nominating the UN as the supervisory authority. The Security Council was notified in March by the head of the U.S. delegation at the UN, Warren Austin.[13] On March 30, the U.S. delegation submitted two resolutions to the Security Council, one calling for a truce in Palestine and inviting the Arab Higher Committee and the Jewish Agency to confer with the council, and the other seeking a special session of the General Assembly to consider the question of trusteeship. Negotiations with the Jewish Agency and the Arab Higher Committee quickly broke down, but the special session was called into session on April 16, allowing the United States to go into the detail of its plan. Palestine would be placed in the hands of the UN Trusteeship Council for an indefinite period. A governor-general would rule by decree until a legislative body could be elected and a government appointed. Under the trusteeship agreement land sales and immigration would be suspended: the United States would provide a police force if necessary to back up the new administrative structure.

On May 4, John E. Horner, an adviser to the U.S. delegation, declared that trusteeship seemed "virtually to have been abandoned by almost all delegations,"[14] but on May 9 the ambassador himself declared that "our estimate of general situation is that we could pass such a proposal as this by a two-thirds vote."[15] These polarized positions are most probably an indication of the differences of opinion running through the U.S. delegation, whose members included the staunchly pro-Zionist Eleanor Roosevelt (a Truman appointee) as well as the State Department professionals.

The end of the mandate was only a few days away. The switch in U.S. policy had led to cries of betrayal from the Zionists and further approaches to Truman by Weizmann and other leading Zionists. Inside the White House, the sabotage of the trusteeship proposal was coordinated by Clark Clifford and David K. Niles, Truman's administrative assistant and adviser on minority affairs. In the Zionist campaign for partition and then recognition, few played as critical a role as this backroom figure. His relationship with senior administration officials was difficult: a committed Zionist, totally emotional when it came to the question of Israel, Niles was for the Zionist leadership an invaluable asset standing right by the president's side.

"A DEFINITE CLEARANCE"

The danger to the Zionists if trusteeship was pushed through the UN was clear to senior State Department officials: "If the trend in the Security Council continues . . . we shall presently find ourselves involved in a special session of the General Assembly whose probable outcome will be the establishment of a United Nations trusteeship for Palestine. In such event the emphasis will be shifted, so far as the maintenance of international peace and security is concerned, from the threat of Arab aggression to a new threat of Jewish attempts by violence to establish a de facto State in Palestine."[16]

In his memoirs, Truman claimed that that the trusteeship policy was "at odds with my policy and the policy I had laid down."[17] In fact, he had endorsed trusteeship on March 8, giving the State Department discretionary power to introduce it "if and when necessary."[18] The secretary of state himself said at a press conference on March 20 that "I recommended it to the President and he approved my recommendation."[19] In response to Clifford's claim that Truman had never approved Austin's speech, Carlisle Humelsine, director of the Executive Secretariat, informed Marshall that it had been given to Clifford for delivery to Truman on March 6. Wrote Humelsine: "There is absolutely no question but what the President approved it. There was a definite clearance there. I stress it because Clifford told me the President said he did not know anything about it."[20]

However, leaving the timing of the announcement up to the discretion of the State Department was a strategic oversight. Austin was directed to make the speech when he thought the time was right. There were no instructions for Truman to be told in advance.[21] In fact, there was no doubt where the president's preferences lay, but he did not want to go out on a limb. He needed evidence that the Zionists could hold their own, and his espousal of trusteeship in March was an indication that he had yet to be convinced. On May 8, only six days from the end of the mandate, Marshall and Lovett met two representatives of the Jewish Agency, Moshe Shertok and Eliahu Epstein:

> Mr. Shertok had related that the British Minister for Colonial Affairs, Sir Arthur Creech Jones, had told him that Abdullah, the King of Transjordan, might enter the Arab portions of Palestine but there need be no fear that Abdullah's forces, centered upon the British offi-cered and subsidized Arab Legion, would seek to penetrate Jewish areas of Palestine. Furthermore, Mr. Shertok told the Secretary that a mes-sage, a week delayed in transmission, had been received from the Jew-ish Agency in Palestine recounting overtures by a Colonel Goldy [sic] an officer of the Arab Legion, suggesting that a deal could be worked out between Abdullah and the Jewish Agency whereby the King would take over the Arab portion of Palestine and leave the Jews in possession of their state in the remainder of that country.
>
> Mr. Lovett said this intelligence had obviously caused an abrupt shift in the position of the Jewish Agency. Only a week before the Jew-ish Agency had officially communicated to the Security Council its charges that Arab armies were invading Palestine. Likewise, only a week before, Mr. Shertok and other representatives of the Jewish Agency had seemed seriously interested in proposed articles of truce. Now, however, their attitude had shifted and they seemed confident, on the basis of recent military successes and the prospect of a "behind the barn" deal with Abdullah, that they could establish their sovereign state without any necessity for a truce with the Arabs of Palestine.[22]

Zionist confidence seemed to shore up Truman's own. On May 12 Clif-ford argued against U.S. support for the declaration of a truce in Palestine and urged Truman not only to recognize Israel as soon as the state was declared but to announce his intentions in advance the following day.[23] This met with vehement objections from both Marshall and Lovett. The former described Clifford's suggestions as a "transparent dodge" based on domestic political considerations "while the problem which confronted us was international. I said bluntly that if the President were to follow Mr. Clifford's advice and if in the elections I were to vote, I would vote against the President."[24] Lovett argued that premature recognition would be "highly injurious" to the UN as well as the prestige of the president: "It was a very transparent attempt to win the Jewish vote, but in Mr. Lovett's opinion it would lose more votes than it would gain. Finally, to recognize the Jewish state prematurely would be buying a pig in a poke. How did we know what kind of Jewish state would be set up?"[25] Marshall and Lovett wanted to wait until May 15 when "we would take another look at the situation in Palestine in light of the facts as they existed. Clearly the question of recognition would have to be gone into very carefully."[26]

This was the professional State Department view, but the White House was not prepared to wait until May 15. On May 13 Weizmann sent a message to Truman in which he pleaded yet again for recognition of Israel when the provisional government declared its independence at midnight in Palestine the next day. The next afternoon—with the end of the mandate only hours away—Clifford told Lovett that Truman was under "unbearable pressure" to recognize the Jewish state promptly: "At six o'clock on Friday night there would be no government or authority of any kind in Palestine. Title would be lying around for anyone to seize and a number of people had advised the President that this should not be permitted." According to information given to the White House, the new state "proposed to live within the conditions of the November 29 General Assembly resolution and to restrict its claims to the borders therein defined," which of course Zionist forces in Palestine had already totally violated and which the government of Israel was eventually to repudiate. Clifford said the timing of recognition was "of the greatest possible importance to the President from a domestic point of view." Asked if the president could hold off until the General Assembly had come out of session, he "said again that time was terribly important and that he did not feel the President would do this."[27]

FARCE AT THE UN

At 6:00 P.M. Washington time David Ben-Gurion began reading out Israel's "act of independence"; exactly eleven minutes later Truman followed up with a statement of recognition of the provisional government, without informing his own delegation at the UN until the last minute. Dean Rusk's account of the day's events is worth recalling in some detail:

> The General Assembly was in session that day. About 5:45 that afternoon I got a call from Mr. Clark Clifford, Special Counsel to President

Truman, telling me that the State of Israel would be declared at 6:00 pm, that the United States would recognize Israel and that the President wished me to inform our Delegation at the United Nations. I said, "But this cuts across what our Delegation has been trying to accomplish in the General Assembly under instructions, and we already have a large majority for that approach." Mr. Clifford replied "Nevertheless, this is what the President wishes you to do." I thereupon telephoned Ambassador Warren Austin who had to leave the floor of the Assembly to take my call. He made a personal decision not to return to the Assembly or to inform other members of the Delegation—he simply went home. My guess is that he thought that it was better for the General Assembly to know very clearly that this was an act of the President in Washington and that the United States delegation had not been playing a double game with other delegations.[28]

At six o'clock—with Austin back in his suite at the Waldorf Astoria—someone from the delegation phoned Rusk to find out what was going on. From the floor of the assembly, Francis Sayre stepped up to the podium to say he knew nothing of recognition, but news soon reached the delegation that Truman's statement had come through on UN ticker tape. A staff member was sent off to find a copy. The trail led to the office of the UN's secretary-general, Trygvie Lie, where a crumpled-up copy of Truman's statement was found tossed into his wastepaper basket. It was plucked out and taken to the General Assembly, where Austin's deputy, Philip C. Jessup, read it out. In such a manner did tragedy in Palestine descend to repertory farce in New York.

The chamber was thrown into pandemonium. Rusk recalls that one of the U.S. mission staff literally sat on the lap of the Cuban delegate to stop him from going to the podium and pulling Cuba out of the UN. "In any event about 6:15 pm I got a call from Secretary Marshall who said 'Rusk, get up to New York and prevent the US delegation from resigning en masse.' Whether it was necessary or not, I scurried to New York and found that tempers had cooled so that my mission was unnecessary."

PARTITION "MODIFICATIONS"

Truman had waited until the last moment before pulling the rug out from under the feet of his own State Department professionals. Since 1946, he had consistently ignored their advice in favor of the electoral considerations he was hearing from his White House advisers. He had seized the headlines in 1946 when he pulled "the plum out of the pudding" of the Anglo-American Committee of Inquiry by calling on Britain to admit one hundred thousand Jewish refugees to Palestine without delay.[29] When another Anglo-American committee (Grady-Morrison) came up with a plan for federation that made the rate of immigration conditional on Arab approval, Truman consulted his cabinet "and other advisers" before concluding that he could not support such a proposal as part of an Anglo-American plan.[30] Then came the partition vote, which would never have passed without a final push orchestrated from the White House.

Truman's rationale all along was that he was the one who made policy ("the buck stops here") and not second- or third-level professional officers in the State Department, but behind the barrage of tough-guy talk about who was in charge he buckled and yielded to the Zionists on every important occasion. At a meeting of the National Security Council on October 21, 1948, the secretary of defense, James Forrestal, said his government's Palestine policy had been made for "squalid political purposes" and had largely been the work of David Niles and Clark Clifford. Forrestal had no objection to the Jews establishing a homeland in Palestine, "but United States policy should be based on United States national interests and not on domestic political considerations."[31] When Truman finally recognized Israel, "virtually all foreign policy experts of the government were arrayed against the President's policy and were dumbfounded—some still remain so—that a responsible political leader could so flout their considered counsel."[32]

On October 24, 1948, Truman made the astonishing declaration that "modifications" to the partition plan should be made "only if fully acceptable to the state of Israel."[33] Since early 1948, Zionist forces had been creating "facts on the ground" that had "modified" the partition plan beyond all recognition, but with elections coming up, the Democrats and the Republicans were outbidding each other in declarations of support for Israel. Neither party was about to insist that Israel respect the partition plan.

The immediate focus of Israeli hostility was Count Folke Bernadotte, the UN mediator sent to Palestine. In a letter to the American Christian Palestine Committee of New York, Republican candidate Governor Dewey "in effect repudiated Administration's policy with regard to the Bernadotte plan."[34] As president, Truman could not go so far, but his statement the next day (that no modifications to the partition plan should be made that were unacceptable to Israel) indicated his clear desire to distance himself from what Count Bernadotte was proposing. Bernadotte had affirmed that Jerusalem should be placed under UN control and had recommended that if the Israelis were to be allowed to keep the "Negev" (the Arab Naqab) they should be prepared to give up western Galilee in return. He had also recommended that Haifa should be developed as a free port, that a free airport should be established at Lydda, and that the right to decide the final borders between Arab and Jewish states should rest with the UN.

In a top-secret dispatch to Truman on August 16, the secretary of state referred to "inflammatory speeches" by Moshe Shertok on the subject of Jerusalem and the refusal of the Israeli military governor of the city to cooperate with Bernadotte.[35] Israel's plans had been outlined on August 12 by Golda Meir, then the minister-designate to the USSR. Internationalization was dismissed out of hand. The imperious Mrs. Meir said Israel might consent to partition, short of Jerusalem becoming an all-Jewish city, but only on the following lines: "New Jerusalem to be part of Israel. Old city to be considered a museum and given some sort of international status under the United Nations. Allocation of some small area outside of old city to Arabs might be given consideration."[36]

Truman did his best to accommodate the demands of the government of Israel. He instructed Clifford to sent a telegram to Marshall (then in Paris) "completely disavowing the statement made by the Secretary on September 21 in support of the Bernadotte plan." After opposition from senior State Department officials he settled for a cautious public position of accepting the plan, but only as the "basis" for continuing efforts to reach a settlement.[37] By this time Bernadotte was entirely out of the picture: on September 17 he and his military attaché, Colonel Serot, were ambushed and murdered by Stern Gang terrorists as they drove through Jerusalem.

"OURS BY RIGHT"

The Bernadotte plan—the count's attempt to stitch Palestine together from the shredded remains of the partition plan—had been accepted as the basis for a territorial settlement by Britain and the U.S. government. Undersecretary of State Lovett confirmed U.S. policy "as meaning that Israel should not have both Negev under Nov. 29 resolution plus [western] Galilee under Bernadotte plan,"[38] but fortified by Truman's support, the Israelis refused to withdraw from either. On November 2, the Security Council had called on "interested governments" to withdraw their forces back to the positions they held on October 14 (when the council had called for a cease-fire in the Negev as it was called in New York and the Naqab as it was known across the Arab world). At a meeting in Washington on November 10 Lovett told the chief of the Israeli mission in Washington (Eliahu Epstein) and the Israeli representative at the UN (Michael Comay) that if Israel wanted to keep the Negev it would have to give up western

Galilee: "I said that I would hate to see the matter come to sanctions but that the United Nations could not continue to be disregarded."[39]

In the partition plan, the northern part of the Naqab/Negev had been allocated to the Arab state. The southern sector below (but not including) the Arab crossroads town of Beersheba (Bir Saba‹) had been set aside for the Jewish state, even though it had only a miniscule Zionist settler population living among largely sedentarized bedouin tribes. Amplifying their Arab nature, historically, geographically, and politically, the Naqab/Negev and the Gulf of Aqaba were bounded on both sides by Arab states (Egypt, Transjordan, and Saudi Arabia). The narrow stretch of sea between those states was just water, but in the way of political geographers it would be reasonable to call it an Arab sea. To the Israelis, however, the acquisition of the entire region was critical for the future of the state. It represented space for future development and population growth, and it gave Israel a southern coastline, where it planned to build the port of Eilat. There was no such place on the map, but the Israelis spoke as if there was, and so did U.S. officials when referring to Israel's insistence that it "must have" Eilat. They were effectively adopting Israel's language of conquest. On the real map the intended location for Eilat was a Jordanian (and former Ottoman) coastal police outpost called Umm Rashrash. There may have been other reasons for Israel wanting this arid land besides room for development and access to the sea in the south. Weizmann told the U.S. ambassador that it was also "rich in mineral resources."[40] Israel, he said, could not possibly give it up: "I must warn you that the Jews will never surrender the Negev."[41]

On these questions of territorial "concessions" the Israelis refused to budge. Michael Comay said Israel regarded the territory allotted to Israel in the partition resolution "as belonging to Israel by right and considered that the territory militarily occupied outside this area could be a matter for discussion." Moshe Shertok argued that although western Galilee had not been allotted to Israel, "they [the Israelis] had subsequently won it by force of arms" and should be allowed to keep it anyway for reasons of defense and the settlement of Jewish immigrants.[42] In other words, territory set aside for a Jewish state was Israel's by right, and territory taken from the putative Arab state was Israel's through right of conquest.

In the event, Israel retained all the territory it had conquered, whether allotted to it under the partition plan or not. In a lightning run to the Gulf of Aqaba in March 1949, Israeli forces—troops in jeeps and armored cars supported by aircraft—broke through paper-thin Arab Legion lines (consisting of about a hundred men, according to Glubb Pasha)[43] before seizing Umm Rashrash and hoisting the Israeli flag on the coast. The entire

Naqab, including Beersheba, a mustering point for British and Australian forces during the First World War, was now incorporated into the state of Israel as the Negev. Once the port of Eilat was developed, Israel demanded the right of passage through the narrow stretch of water dividing states with which it was in a state of war.

The seizure of the Naqab/Negev cut the Middle East in two. In the partition plan the northern Naqab and an elongated stretch of the coast north of Gaza were linked to the rest of the putative Palestinian state near Latrun. It was a slender link, but it would have ensured territorial contiguity between Egypt, the Arab state of Palestine, Transjordan, and the rest of the eastern Arab world. In Israeli hands the Negev—as it had become— was like "a dagger blade dividing [the] Arab world."[44] Even on the map it has the shape of a flint blade, narrowing to a point on the Gulf of Aqaba.

Now that there was a new state on the map, it needed new names. The switch from Naqab to Negev is only one example of the cartographical transformation of Palestine. Meron Benvenisti has described in some detail the work of the mapping committees created to replace Arabic place-names with Hebrew adaptations. "We are obliged to remove the Arabic names for reasons of state," Ben-Gurion told the Negev Names Committee. "Just as we do not recognize the Arabs' political proprietorship of the land so also we do not recognize their spiritual proprietorship and their names."[45] Renaming involved the application of names to wrong or doubtful sites in a "pseudo-Biblical" process "necessitated by the dearth of Hebrew names in the ancient sources. Only a small number of place-names are to be found in early Jewish sources."[46] Renaming was an important part of the struggle over Palestine: every time diplomats or newspapermen used the Israeli replacement or the Israeli alternative (such as the Temple Mount for the Haram al Sharif) they were effectively accepting Israel's claim of prior right.

"UNREALISTIC AND UNJUST" DEMANDS

Well before the end of 1948, the fighting in Palestine was effectively over. The Galilee was finally "cleared," and its defenders were chased into southern Lebanon, where the Israelis occupied sixteen villages up to the Litani River before withdrawing. An Israeli attack on Egypt (Operation Ten Plagues) ended only when Britain threatened to act on the mutual defense provisions of the Anglo-Egyptian treaty of 1936. It warned of "the gravest possible consequences not only to Anglo-American strategic interests in the Near East but also to American relations with Britain and Western Europe."[47] Shortly after the cease-fire with Egypt was supposed to have come into effect on the Egyptian front (January 7, 1949), the Israelis shot down five British Spitfires flying a reconnaissance mission, drawing attention to the fact that "some Israeli detachments were still beyond the international border."[48]

Having secured all the territory they could get for the time being, the Israelis sat tight. Truman made some halfhearted moves to dislodge them. A top-secret cable sent to Ben-Gurion in the president's name on May 29, 1949, "expressed deep disappointment at the failure of Eytan at Lausanne to make any of the desired concessions on refugees or boundaries." Israel's attitude indicated disregard for the UN resolutions of 1947 and 1948 dealing with borders and refugees and was dangerous to peace. The message carried the implied threat that the United States might have to reconsider its attitude. Ben-Gurion reacted with irritation. The American demands were "unrealistic and unjust."[49] A subsequent attempt to impose sanctions by withholding an Import-Export Bank loan of $100 million collapsed. George C. McGhee, the U.S. coordinator on Palestinian refugee matters, was given the job of informing Israel's ambassador in Washington that $49 million of $100 million in loans from the bank would be withheld unless his government agreed to take back two hundred thousand refugees. He recounted later how the ambassador, Eliahu Elath, "looked me straight in the eye and said, in essence, that I wouldn't get by with this move, that he would stop it. . . . Within an hour of my return to my office I received a message from the White House that the President wished to dissociate himself from any withholding of the Ex-Im Bank loan."[50] In another account, Elath flew back to Washington from Israel when he heard the loan was being blocked and spoke to Truman, who "jotted down a note on a pad"; the loan was announced a few days later.[51]

The battlefield casualties in the "civil war along the Potomac" included Loy Henderson, who was assigned as ambassador to Turkey before it was decided that Ankara was too close to the Middle East and he should go to India instead. Acheson regarded the charges leveled against Henderson by the Zionists, that he had tried to block Truman's policy on Palestine, as being "untrue and grossly unfair."[52] In fact, Henderson and others in the State Department were simply doing what they were supposed to be doing, which was develop policies favorable to U.S. interests in the Middle East. They were blocked at every turn by a president who seemed prepared to give the Zionists virtually everything they wanted in return for campaign contributions and electoral support.[53] Undoubtedly "the boys in GADel" (the General Assembly delegation) fought the good fight step by step "and even though hamstrung, did better than we had reason to hope," as the first secretary at the U.S. embassy in London wrote on December 8, 1948,[54] but although they had gone down fighting, they had still gone down. And that was the critical part. Partition, trusteeship, recognition, western Galilee, Eilat, and the Negev: between 1947 and 1949, against an Israel backed up on every important occasion by the White House, the State Department had lost every important round.

PART III. THE AMERICAN ASCENDANCY

8. THE "TRIPARTITE AGGRESSION"

Humiliation in Palestine was the last straw for nationalists determined to drive the British and French out of the Middle East. Now corrupt Arab regimes would have to go as well—what other solution could there be for a situation that had led to Arab armies being "thrust treacherously into a battle for which we were not ready, our lives the playthings of greed conspiracy and lust."[1] Revelations of corruption, from arms profiteering down to the supply of tainted cooking oil to Syrian soldiers on the front line with Israel, filled the newspapers, and one by one the governments began to fall. Syria went through three military coups in one year (1949); in Egypt young officers prepared to bring a corrupt system crashing down.

Gamal abd al Nasser was a staff major with an Egyptian battalion sent into action against the Israelis in the northern Negev. The strategic importance of the region lay in the roads connecting Gaza to Hebron and the northern Negev to the south. In September Nasser was assigned to the brigade deployed around the villages of Falluja and ʿIraq al Manshiyya, between Gaza and Hebron. By late October the Israelis had encircled the "Falluja pocket," but the Egyptians fought well and managed to hold out until the Israeli-Egyptian armistice agreement was signed in February 1949. In the following two months the population of both Falluja and ʿIraq al Manshiyya were driven out by the victorious Israelis and the two villages subsequently destroyed. Nasser returned to Egypt more than ever convinced of the need for the Arab people to wrench their destiny out of the hands of those conspiring against them, Israel and its Western backers and the Arab governments controlled and manipulated by them.

In Egypt the overthrow of the monarchy in July 1952 was followed by the establishment of a one-party state. Revolutionary Egypt—young and dynamic—was in a hurry to make up for lost time: hospitals, housing estates, schools, and roads were all built, at the cost of the suppression of the right to dissent and challenge, but on balance most Egyptians seemed to accept the trade-off. On questions of regional and foreign policy Nasser spoke strongly on Palestine, Algeria, and the British occupation of southern Arabia, while backing up his rhetoric by removing the symbols of foreign invasion, occupation, and domination at home. In 1954 he negotiated an amicable end to the British military presence in the Canal Zone: all troops were to be withdrawn within two years; technical staff would remain for seven years, sharing the zone with the Egyptians; only if Egypt and Turkey were attacked by any "outside power" (an expression that the signatories explicitly agreed did not include Israel) could the base be reactivated and British troops returned.

While negotiating with Nasser, Britain took measures to contain him. The Baghdad Pact (February 1955) brought Turkey, Iraq, Britain, Pakistan, and Iran into a "defense" arrangement whose primary purpose was to serve as a barrier against the spread of both communism and Arab radicalism across the Middle East. A full-scale incursion by Israel into the Gaza Strip (held by Egypt since the termination of fighting in Palestine) only four days after Iraq and Turkey had set the pact in motion underlined how poorly prepared Egypt was for the possibility that the war of words with its enemies would end in open conflict. Its military situation was desperate. In the event of war Israel could put more troops into battle than all the Arab states combined (250,000 compared to 205,000). It was being supplied with a range of modern weapons by France, including Mystère supersonic jet fighters; in comparison Egypt had "six serviceable military aircraft and enough tank ammunition for a one-hour battle."[2] Nasser approached the United States for help but was told he would have to pay for the weapons he needed in the hard cash the Americans knew he did not have; adding insult to injury, the United States agreed to supply arms to Nasser's Hashimite enemies in Iraq.

At the Bandung conference of nonaligned nations in April 1955, Nasser spoke to Chou En-lai about his difficulties in procuring weapons and was advised to approach the Soviet Union; in fact, the Chinese premier said he would speak to Soviet leaders himself. By July Egypt and the USSR had reached agreement on an arms package consisting of tanks, fighter jets, and bombers, all of which would be paid for over a number of years in shipments of cotton. To lessen the shock for Western governments, it was agreed that the deal would officially be made through the Czech government (ironically, Israel's main arms supplier in the late 1940s). Up to the end Nasser hoped to get his weapons from the United States but was repeatedly rebuffed: "The Egyptians wanted to buy the kind of weapons that we didn't want them to get" was the explanation given by a senior naval figure (Admiral Radford) to a congressional committee.[3] Unable to get arms from the United States, Nasser was then accused of aligning his country with the enemies of the "Free World" when he sought them from the Soviet Union.

In the atmosphere of "containment," the arms deal with the Soviet bloc and the recognition of China in May 1956 were about the greatest crimes Nasser could have committed in American eyes. Initially the Americans were understanding of these young Egyptian army officers, but John Foster Dulles, the U.S. secretary of state and the architect of the policy of containment, was never going to be persuaded to cooperate with a government that was dealing with both the Soviets and the Chinese, even though Nasser had been driven in their direction by the refusal of both Britain and the United States to supply him with weaponry and to listen to him on the question of Israel. Egypt's recognition of China was the last straw: the United States and then Britain pulled out of the project to finance (in conjunction with the World Bank) the construction of a high dam at Aswan, humiliating the Egyptian leader, infuriating him, driving him even deeper into the "Soviet camp," and provoking him into preparing a blow—the nationalization of the Suez Canal—that would completely take the wind out of the sails of his enemies.

"INFILTRATION" AND "REPRISALS"

Violations of the 1949 armistice lines between Israel and the Arab states were inevitable. The presence in Egypt, Syria, Jordan, and Lebanon of hundreds of thousands of angry and embittered Palestinians exposed Israel to small-scale "infiltration" and the Arab states that had been forced to give them shelter to large-scale "reprisals." UN Secretary-General Dag Hammarskjold regarded Israel's policy of retaliation as immoral and inexpedient but was unsuccessful in persuading Ben-Gurion to drop it.[4] These "reprisals" were usually totally out of proportion to whatever outrages Israel alleged had been committed, often resulting in the killing of large numbers of civilians. Israel blamed governments even when it knew that they were doing what they could to maintain calm. Jordan had declared six months' imprisonment for anyone caught crossing into Israel.[5] The Israel Defense Forces (IDF) itself had "repeatedly stated explicitly that the Arab Legion and occasionally the Egyptian army as well were making efforts to curb infiltration."[6]

Many expelled Palestinians crossed back into their homeland for mundane reasons, to search for possessions, relatives, or employment or to harvest crops,[7] but others were bent on revenge. In the worst of these episodes, on March 17, 1954, eleven Israelis were killed when a passenger bus traveling from Eilat to Beersheba was attacked in a narrow pass. Israel's representatives walked out of the Israel-Jordan Mixed Armistice Commission when it refused to condemn Jordan without an investigation; a number of Jordanian civilians were killed when Israel exacted retribution in the Jordanian village of Nahalin. As it turned out, the attack on the bus had been launched not from Jordan but from Sinai; the raiding party were bedouin of the Azazmah tribe taking revenge for being driven off their traditional lands in the demilitarized zone of Al Auja along the Sinai armistice line.[8] Thousands of them had been expelled in 1950, with those who remained subjected to harassment (the burning of their tents) and punitive military operations (strafing from the air) intended to force them into the Sinai. In 1953 the Israelis established the paramilitary "pioneer farming settlement" of Ketzion in the zone.[9] By the end of November 1955, after years of conflict with Egypt and argument with the UN, Israel had succeeded in occupying the whole of Al Auja; the zone was now a gate that could be swung open to a future invasion of Sinai by its ground forces.

All of Ben-Gurion's actions leave no doubt that he was determined to challenge, confront, and confine Nasser. Provocations along the armistice line were combined with covert operations designed to discredit the Egyptian government in the eyes of the West. In 1954, Israeli agents sent to Cairo and Alexandria planted small bombs in a post office, movie theaters, and the U.S. Information Service libraries, with the objective of disrupting both Egypt's relationship with the United States and the negotiations with Britain over the evacuation of the Canal Zone. According to the head of Israeli military intelligence, the aims were to "break the West's confidence in the [existing] Egyptian regime through the creation of public disorder and insecurity. The actions should cause arrests, demonstrations and incidents of vengeance. The Israeli origin should be totally covered while attention should be deviated to any other possible factor. It is necessary to prevent economic and military aid from the West to Egypt."[10] The operation collapsed when one of the bombs (inside a spectacle case) went off in the trouser pocket of the man who was carrying it. All the Israeli agents but one (who managed to get back to Israel) were rounded up; two were subsequently executed and the rest imprisoned.[11]

A POLICY OF CONFRONTATION

Every statement Nasser made as the Arab champion was grist to Israel's propaganda mill, but behind the image of defiance and confrontation the last thing he wanted was war. He was anxious to stop infiltrations that might be used as the pretext for an attack and signaled that he wanted to reduce tension between the two countries, at one stage sending agents to Paris to talk to the Israelis.[12] These conciliatory moves were all ignored by Israel in favor of the policy of confrontation, of which the prime architects were Ben-Gurion and the army commander Moshe Dayan.

Even some of Ben-Gurion's cabinet colleagues realized there was no substance to his accusations of imminent Arab aggression. The following diary entries were made by Moshe Sharett in 1955 when he was prime minister and Ben-Gurion (appointed on February 17) defense minister. The first deals with the possibility of quiet negotiations with the Egyptians:

> (25/1/55) I met with Roger Baldwin, the envoy of the US League of Human Rights, who had just visited Cairo. . . . Nasser talked to him about Israel, saying that he is not among those who could be accused of wanting to throw Israel into the sea. He believes in coexistence with Israel and knows that negotiations will open some day.

> (28/1/55) Cable from Eban: The US is ready to sign an agreement with us whereby in exchange for a commitment on our part not to extend our borders by force it will commit itself to come to our aid if we are attacked.

> (10/2/55) The CIA informs [us] that notwithstanding the Cairo trials, Nasser is as ready to meet us as before. The initiative is now up to Israel.[13]

The following entry was made after discussions with Ben-Gurion and Dayan a little over a fortnight later: "(27/2/55) Ben-Gurion arrived in my office accompanied by the chief of staff [Dayan] whose hands were full of rolled-up maps. I understood at once what was to be the subject of the conversation. He proposed to hit an Egyptian army base at the entrance to the city of Gaza. [He] estimated that the enemy losses will be about ten . . . and that we have to calculate that there will be a few victims on our side."[14]

Another entry refers to remarks made by Dayan during a meeting with Sharett and the Israeli ambassador to Washington several months later:

> (26/5/55) We do not need [Dayan said] a security pact with the US: such a pact will only constitute an obstacle for us. In reality, we face no danger at all from Arab military force. Even if they receive massive

military aid from the West we shall maintain our military superiority for another 8–10 years, thanks to our infinitely greater capacity to assimilate new armaments. On the other hand, the "retaliation" actions are our vital lymph. Above all, they make it possible for us to maintain a high tension among our population and in the army. Without these actions we would have ceased to be a combative people, the settlers would leave the settlements. We must tell these settlers that the US and Britain wish to take the Negev away from us. It is necessary to convince our young people that we are in danger.[15]

To this the prime minister adds his own interpretation:

The conclusions from Dayan's words are clear: this state has no international obligations, no economic problems, the question of peace is non-existent. It must calculate its steps narrow-mindedly and live by the sword. It must see the sword as the main and only instrument with which to keep its morale high. Towards this end it may—no it must—invent non-existent dangers, and to do this it must adopt the method of provocation and retaliation. And above all—let's hope for a new war with the Arab countries so that we may finally acquire our space (B.G. himself—Dayan recalled—said that it would be worthwhile to pay an Arab a million pounds to start a war against us!).[16]

A "NIGHT OF HORROR"

Israel's thunderous attacks across the armistice lines included the assault on the Buraij refugee camp in Gaza on August 28, 1953, when more than seventy civilians were killed or wounded, most of them women and children, and an especially savage raid on the Jordanian village of Qibya (October 14, 1953) in retaliation for the killing of a woman and her two children in an attack by three "infiltrators" on an Israeli settlement. Jordan, which lived in a state of permanent fear of Israel, tried to track them down,[17] but Israel struck back nevertheless, launching a large-scale operation led by Ariel Sharon.

The assault was spearheaded by infantry shooting at anyone who moved. Sappers placed satchels full of explosives in the doorways of houses and blew them up over the heads of their occupants. In evidence subsequently laid before the UN Security Council, "witnesses described their experiences as a night of horror during which Israeli soldiers moved about in their village, blowing up buildings, firing into doorways and windows with automatic weapons and throwing hand grenades." The riddled bodies found in doorways "indicated that the inhabitants had been forced to remain inside until their homes were blown up over them." Sixty-six bodies were dug out of the rubble, two-thirds of them women and children. The destroyed buildings included forty houses, the village school, the police station, and the water-pumping station. One man lost his entire family of eleven. Even cattle were shot and shops were looted before the soldiers left. In November the UN Security Council censured Israel (in Resolution 101, the same number as Unit 101, the unit that had attacked Qibya), but no punitive measures were taken.[18]

Qibya caused revulsion within Israel, as well as condemnation around the world, but in the coming years the cross-border attacks continued. On February 28, 1955, dozens of people were killed when an Israeli armored column stormed into Gaza. The dead included civilians (children among them) and twenty-two soldiers shot or burned to death when their truck was ambushed. Before the Israelis withdrew they destroyed buildings, bridges, and a pumping station that supplied a third of the town's water. Infuriated Palestinians rioted outside UN offices, stoned Egyptian soldiers, and demanded to be given arms. It was this attack that finally pushed Nasser into seeking arms from the Soviet Union.

On August 22, 1955, the Israelis crossed into the Gaza Strip again. Three days later Nasser came back at them by launching the first retaliation attacks by *fidayin* guerillas across the armistice line. In five days they penetrated deep into Israel, killing five soldiers and ten civilians. On August 31 Israeli forces retaliated with a large-scale assault on Gaza. In September Nasser responded by tightening Egypt's formal closure of the Straits of Tiran to Israeli shipping. In fact, since 1948 Egypt had turned a blind eye to Israeli ships bound for Eilat as long as they flew a flag of convenience. They had even been allowed to pass through the Suez Canal: Nutting estimates that at least sixty ships taking cargo to Eilat had been quietly allowed to traverse the canal between 1949 and 1954.[19] Now, however, Nasser brought this tacit understanding to an end. No Israeli ships would be allowed to pass through the straits even quietly, and even other governments would have to seek Egypt's permission before entering or flying over a stretch of water Egypt regarded as its own. Yet all this was said without Egypt taking any practical steps to blockade the gulf; the real point of this maneuver was to reinforce Nasser's image as the Arab champion, but without the means of defending Egypt should Israel decide to test him, he was playing a dangerous game.

On November 2 Ben-Gurion replaced Sharett as prime minister. The same day he warned that while "we have never initiated and shall never initiate war against anybody" and "do not desire a single inch of foreign territory," the combination of *fidayin* action from the Gaza Strip and the blockade of the straits could end in war.[20] Indeed, Ben-Gurion soon presented a plan for attack to his cabinet; the cabinet did not reject it, deciding only that the moment was not propitious and adding, "Israel should act in the place and time that she deemed appropriate."[21]

In the meantime, conflict along the armistice lines continued nonstop: on April 5, 1956, sixty-three civilians, thirty-one of them women or children, were killed when the Israelis mortared Gaza on market day, just ahead of a new peace mission to the Middle East by Dag Hammarskjold. Nine of the women were killed when shells hit a hospital. The *fidayin* retaliated savagely, killing fourteen Israelis in five days, including six children shot as they were saying their prayers in a school near Ramla; both sides engaged in further "reprisals," with the Israelis shooting down four Egyptian planes on April 12. Three days later Ben-Gurion warned that "the hosts of Amalek" were gathering.[22]

The same high level of tension prevailed on the Syrian and Jordanian fronts. Jordan had been colluding with Israel for years, but surreptitious contacts counted for nothing when balanced against its instrumental value as a risk-free target. As planning for an attack on Egypt was cranked up in the autumn of 1956, the assaults on Jordan reached an unprecedented level of intensity. On September 11, the Israelis killed five policemen and ten soldiers in an attack on a police post; two days later, another police post was destroyed and nine policemen and two civilians were killed; on the night of September 25, scores of Jordanian soldiers and civilians were killed in a large-scale assault directed against targets in the Husan area; on October 1, the Israelis attacked Qalqilya (five hundred meters from the armistice line), killing twenty-five Jordanian soldiers; on October 25, the Israelis were back in the Husan area with infantry, armored cars, bazookas, and heavy artillery.

Jordan had no means of ending these attacks and certainly was not going to respond with cross-border retaliation of its own. Indeed, there were never any Arab military incursions into Israel in retaliation for Israeli "reprisals," and at no stage was Israel in danger of being attacked, Ben-Gurion's claims to the contrary. "Today in the Cabinet meeting Ben-Gurion shouted that Nasser is the most dangerous enemy of Israel and is plotting to destroy her," Sharett wrote in his diary on April 24, 1955. "Where does he take all this from? How can he express all this peremptorily and with vehemence, as if it were based on well-grounded facts?"[23] Neither Ben-Gurion nor Dayan was interested in the U.S. offer of security guarantees if they were prepared to accept the armistice lines as final borders: in Dayan's words, such an arrangement would "put handcuffs on our military freedom of action."[24] In 1955, Ben Gurion pushed hard for the seizure of the entire Gaza Strip and the expulsion of the refugees into the Egyptian hinterland; opposed by Sharett, his answer was "full of anger" against "those who demonstrate incapacity to understand that we must not miss an opportunity." To the Israeli leader, the refugees were "a nuisance, but we shall chase them out."[25] For a man who thought in terms of opportunities, the Suez crisis was an opportunity not to be wasted.

NATIONALIZATION AND WAR

On July 26, 1956—a week after the United States and Britain had withdrawn their offer to finance the dam at Aswan—Nasser made the dramatic announcement in Alexandria that his government was taking over the running of the Suez Canal even as he spoke. It was a blow driven into Britain's imperial solar plexus, the equivalent of the action by the Iranian prime minister, Muhammad Musaddiq, taking oil out of the hands of the Anglo-Iranian Oil Company five years earlier.[26] One basic fact about the nationalization of the Suez Canal could not be concealed in spite of British attempts to smother it. The takeover was legally unassailable. Nationalization was a right reserved by all governments. The British prime minister, Sir Anthony Eden, might equivocate by referring to the nationalization of "what is technically an Egyptian company" as a legal quibble,[27] but this view was not shared in Washington. States were entitled to nationalize— had not the British nationalized the steel industry in 1949?

As Eisenhower later wrote: "The inherent right of any sovereign nation to exercise the power of eminent domain within its own territory could scarcely be doubted provided that just compensation were paid to the owners of the property so expropriated. The main issue at stake, therefore, was whether Nasser would and could keep the waterway open for the traffic of all nations in accordance with the Constantinople Convention of 1888. This question could not be answered except through the test."[28] In fact, the Egyptians ran the canal flawlessly, removing operational incompetence as a pretext for the war that Eden had already decided he wanted rather than to see Britain pulled down from the elevated heights of empire to the level of a second-rate country like Portugal or the Netherlands (as he put it). He wanted Nasser destroyed, and nothing less would do.

The crafty Nuri al Said, in on the plot as always, shared his view. He hoped that "we would soon make up our minds to finish Nasser off" and was confident that the Egyptian government would collapse if the Western powers could just keep up the pressure,[29] but not even this arch-schemer, in his ardent desire to see Nasser punched out of the ring, could have imagined that Britain would admit Israel into the conspiracy, thereby exposing its Middle Eastern friends to imminent destruction.

Israel was brought into Anglo-French war planning in the first week of September and reacted with guarded enthusiasm. The collusion between the three countries, directed toward an attack known ever since in the Arab world as the "Tripartite Aggression," was cemented as late summer gave way to autumn; the decision by Britain and France to "take the law into their own hands" was finally taken at a meeting in Paris on October 16.[30] The pact with Israel was sealed on October 24, after two days of negotiations, in the Paris suburb of Sèvres, where in 1920 the punitive and ill-fated treaty destroying the Ottoman Empire had been issued. In a more superstitious age, the court astrologer might have been called in and might have put them off.

The plan of attack called for Israel to invade Sinai on October 29. Britain and France would issue an ultimatum the following day calling on both sides to withdraw ten miles from the banks of the canal. Nasser would refuse, and then Britain and France would send in troops to "restore order" and guarantee safe passage of ships through the canal. In discussions with the United States, Eden and his cabinet colleagues maintained the pretense that it was Jordan that was in danger of an all-out Israeli offensive. At 1:00 P.M. on October 29—the very day Israel launched the first stage of the assault on Egypt—U.S. ambassador Winthrop W. Aldrich sent a telegram to the State Department giving details of a discussion he had just had in London with Selwyn Lloyd. The British foreign secretary was "equally concerned with us over Israeli mobilization," was "inclined to believe Israeli attack more likely to be directed against Jordan than Egypt," was "unwilling to believe Israel would launch a full-scale assault on Egypt despite temptation to do so," and had "no reason to believe French are stimulating such an adventure." It was totally perfidious. Lloyd's feigned concern over Israel's intentions was expressed so convincingly that Aldrich concluded that "any UK complicity in such a move is unlikely."[31]

At no point did the Hashimite regimes seem to realize that they were being used as a decoy to draw attention away from the real target of the coming war. On September 14, Hussein flew to Baghdad to see his cousin Faisal II (at the ages of twenty and twenty-one respectively, both were still little more than boy kings) and discuss the rapidly deteriorating situation in the region with Iraqi political and military leaders. "Nuri tells me," wrote the British ambassador, Sir Michael Wright, "that Hussein was in a frightened and somewhat distracted frame of mind when he arrived. They had gradually calmed him down. . . . He was convinced that Jordan was in danger of a major attack by Israel and he did not know where to turn for help except to Iraq. He had come to ask whether Iraq would now send a division into Jordan to act as a covering reserve to the Jordanian forces."[32] Hussein told Nuri he had asked Britain for additional arms "but had not received an encouraging answer."[33] Iraq offered to help by sending a division of troops, on condition that they were not stationed west of the River Jordan "or at any point on the frontier" for fear of provoking Israel.

On October 10 Israel launched another attack on Qalqilya. A message from the U.S. embassy in Tel Aviv described it as the "heaviest Israel-Jordan military engagement since war of independence": nine Israelis were killed, twelve wounded, and more than one hundred Jordanians killed or wounded.[34] Unconfirmed reports suggested that the assault involved Mystère jet fighters recently supplied by France "despite categorical assurances that planes provided would be used entirely for defensive purposes."[35] What further irritated the Americans was that Israel had far more Mystères (supplied by France with U.S. approval) than the U.S. administration had been led to believe.

Two days later the British ambassador spoke to the Israeli foreign minister, Golda Meir. Israel had driven Jordan into a panic through its attacks, but now that a small contingent of Iraqi troops was about to be sent across the border as nonaggressively as possible, Mrs. Meir expressed alarm and suspicion at this "unfriendly act."[36] Eden talked Nuri out of sending the troops anyway, so Israel did not even have this minor distraction to worry about.

On October 27 Ben-Gurion ordered UN observers out of Al Auja, and in the late afternoon of October 29 several hundred Israeli paratroops were dropped into the Mitla Pass, creating the threat to the canal that would compel Britain and France to intervene according to the script written in Sèvres. Three days later Britain and France issued their "ultimatum." Eden feigned an anxiety to see the fighting ended without delay: Israel could be accused of "technical aggression," he wrote to Eisenhower, and Britain did not wish to support "or even condone" its actions, but "the first thing to do is to take effective and decisive steps to halt the fighting." The Hashimites in Amman and Baghdad and governments across the Middle East were assured that "our immediate action in Suez is merely an emergency and temporary fire brigade operation. Our military reports indicate that unless something is done quickly Israeli forces will inflict crushing defeat on Egypt. Our first aim is to separate the combatants, secure a cease-fire and safeguard the canal."[37] The Foreign Office instructed the ambassador in Baghdad that at the same time "You should be careful to avoid committing us to calling on the Israelis to withdraw to the armistice lines in the immediate future."[38] This made sense: the Israelis could hardly be asked to withdraw from the canal before they had reached it.

DOUBLE-CROSSED

The United States was planning to give assistance to the victims of aggression in the Middle East, but what if the aggressors were not communists or radical nationalists but Israel and America's own close transatlantic allies? What would the United States do then?[39] Eisenhower corresponded with Eden throughout the crisis but on September 2 broke with him on the use of force: "I am afraid, Anthony, that from this point onward our views on the situation diverge. As to the use of force or the threat of force at this juncture I continue to feel as I expressed myself in the letter Foster carried to you some weeks ago. . . . I must tell you, frankly, that American public opinion flatly rejects the thought of using force."[40]

By September 20 the British had three aircraft carriers based in the Mediterranean, along with a light cruiser and a destroyer sent from Malta to Cyprus and another light cruiser in the Red Sea within twenty-four hours' sailing time of the canal. Canada was about to supply Israel with two dozen American-made F-86 fighters: the numbers of advanced Mystère fighters reaching Israel from France seemed to be multiplying like rabbits (in Eisenhower's words). Yet despite all the reports coming in about the buildup of British forces and the supply of planes and battlefield equipment to Israel, the Americans could not quite bring themselves to believe that Britain and France really would attack Egypt. They remained deeply suspicious but mystified: during discussion at the White House on October 21, John Foster Dulles said he was "baffled" by British and French intentions but "perhaps they did not know themselves."[41] After Israel called up reservists and civilian vehicles on October 26, Dulles expressed his "sense of foreboding," sending a message to the embassy in London repeating his suspicion that something was up. As late as October 28 Eisenhower was telling Dulles, "I just cannot believe the British would be dragged into this."[42] The following day the Joint Chiefs of Staff concluded that Israel had gone to war "with at least the tacit approval of the British,"[43] but at that stage the Americans still did not know that Britain and France were the joint architects of the invasion and that the Israeli attack was only the first stage of an unfolding conspiracy.

Britain's refusal to support action against Israel at the UN filled Eisenhower with consternation. The president asked Eden for his help in clearing up "my understanding as to exactly what is happening between us and our European allies, especially between us, the French and yourselves."[44] The U.S. ambassador to the UN had asked his British counterpart (Pierson Dixon) to cooperate in presenting a case to the UN, but "we were astonished to find that he was completely unsympathetic, stating frankly that his government would not agree to any action whatsoever to be taken against Israel."[45] France and Britain issued their ultimatum—regarded by Dulles as "about as crude and brutal as anything he has seen"[46]—and then vetoed a Security Council resolution, tabled by the United States, calling for an unconditional withdrawal by Israel to the other side of the armistice lines. Selwyn Lloyd said Britain would be put in an impossible position if Israel were declared an aggressor. In any case, he argued, Israel was not an aggressor: its actions were "a clear case of self-defense," and the world could rest assured that it had no intention of attacking Jordan.[47] Eden continued to talk of a "police action," but air attacks and the landing of Anglo-French forces were the final proof for the Americans that they had been double-crossed. Eisenhower prepared to impose economic sanctions; when Dulles remarked that the United States could not sit by and let the British go under economically, the president replied caustically that he did not see much value in "an unworthy and unreliable ally and that the necessity to support them might not be as great as they believed."[48]

Israel played its part in the deceit to the end. On October 28, its ambassador in Washington, Abba Eban, tried to convince the Americans that it was the Arab states (including Jordan) that were actually planning an attack. At a time when Israeli mobilization was complete, he said that Israel was calling up "some reserve battalions," dutifully echoing Ben-Gurion's line that only a "few battalions" had been mobilized as a precautionary measure.[49] Israel wanted peace but had been surrounded with a "ring of steel" and was being penetrated by Nasser's "gangs" from Egypt and Lebanon.[50] Eden, feigning concern, wrote to Eisenhower that "when we received news of the Israeli mobilization we instructed our ambassador in Tel Aviv to urge restraint."[51]

Britain and France committed their armed forces to the war on October 31, launching air and sea attacks and landing troops at Port Said and Port Fuad a few days later. Egypt struck back by filling ships with cement and sinking them in the canal (a process helped along when British aircraft bombed and sank ships resting at anchor); in Syria the government sent demolition teams to blow up three pumping stations on the (British-owned) Iraq Petroleum Company's pipeline to the port city of Tripoli, cutting off the flow of oil from Kirkuk for six months. The three invading countries were now practically without friends in the world, except for imperial stalwarts like the Australian prime minister, Sir Robert Menzies, whose mission to Cairo in September had failed because it was an attempt to impose on Nasser what he had just ended—foreign control (through the establishment of an international authority) of the canal. But the appearance of negotiations gave Britain and France the time they needed to complete their preparations for war. In their own country, Eden and Selwyn Lloyd were under furious attack in Parliament, in the press, and in the streets, with police closing off Downing Street to keep the demonstrators away from the prime minister's official London residence.

On the night of November 5, Marshall Bulganin, the Soviet prime minister, sent Eden a message accusing Britain of launching a predatory war against the Arab people: "In what situation would Britain find herself if she were attacked by stronger states possessing all types of weapons of mass destruction? Indeed, such countries, instead of sending to the shores of Britain their naval or air forces, could use other means, for instance rocket equipment. If rocket weapons were used against Britain and France you would certainly call it a barbaric action. Yet what is the difference?"[52] A similar message of warning went to the French prime minister, Guy Mollett, and Ben-Gurion was told that his government was sowing hatred for Israel among "the peoples of the East" that threatened its future and even put its existence in jeopardy.

The Russian rocket threat was alarming, but of more direct consequence in ending the war was British dependence on U.S. financial support. The canal crisis had been followed by a run on the English pound: Britain's dollar reserves fell by $57 million in September and $84 million in October and were estimated to fall by a further $250 million in November (the published figure of $279 million fell far short of the real figure of $401 million).[53] On November 6 the British government asked the United States to approve the massive loan that would enable it to keep buying sterling on the world market and maintain its value relative to the dollar. The United States made its approval conditional on the acceptance of a cease-fire. Britain accepted without demur, and in return the U.S. secretary of the treasury, George Humphrey, authorized the loan of about $1.5 billion in dollar credits.

Suez was no morality play. The outraged Soviets had just invaded Hungary. The angered American president was involved in an Anglo-American–Iraqi plot to overthrow the Syrian government at about the time the Israelis were being parachuted into the Mitla Pass. But for the all-seeing eyes and long arms of Abd al Hamid al Sarraj, the redoubtable head of the Syrian *mukhabarat* (intelligence services), the plot might have succeeded. It is tempting to think that Eisenhower's anger was sharpened by the suspicion that Britain had inveigled the United States into a plot in Syria so that it would be too compromised to react when Egypt was attacked. And were not the CIA-organized coups that brought down the Musaddiq government in Iraq in 1953 and Guatemala's socialist Arbenz government the following year also "crude and brutal"? In the amoral arena of power politics, the British and French governments had simply miscalculated, the cardinal sin in the world of realpolitik. In the face of superior power they turned out to be all appetite and no teeth. Both quickly recalled their invading forces. Eden suffered a nervous collapse and disappeared to the Caribbean to recover; on January 9, 1957, he stepped down as prime minister on the grounds of ill health.

The attack on Egypt had severe repercussions in Jordan and Iraq. The Hashimites wanted Nasser brought down but not like this. They were now the targets of protests and demonstrations that threatened to bring them down instead. The Baghdad Pact and Britain's oil interests in Iraq had been put in jeopardy as a consequence of actions no British ambassador to an Arab country could have welcomed. "Nuri was more deeply discouraged and depressed than I have ever seen him," Sir Michael Wright wrote from Baghdad on November 11.[54] The threat to the stability of the Iraqi government had arisen "because we acted simultaneously with Israel. Since the King, the Crown Prince and Nuri, together with the government as a whole, had based their policy on friendship with us, our action placed in grave, and at one moment, imminent danger their political future and the safety of the regime, and their lives as well. The final outcome of the crisis still depends, more than anything else, on our future attitudes towards Israel."[55]

SHOWDOWN OVER GAZA

France and Britain might have been forced to back off, but their junior partner insisted that it had no intention of leaving the territory it had captured. By November 5, Israel had occupied most of the Sinai Peninsula, the Gaza Strip, the two islands in the Gulf of Aqaba close to the Straits of Tiran (Sanifar and Tiran), and the strategic Egyptian headland position of Sharm al Sheikh. Now that the Israelis were back in Sinai they had no intention of leaving. The General Assembly had decided to establish an emergency force (UN Emergency Force),[56] but on November 7 Ben-Gurion told the Knesset that his government would not allow any UN forces to be stationed in Israel "or areas occupied by Israel." The Israeli-Egyptian armistice line of 1949 was "dead and buried."[57] He read out a triumphant message to the armed forces:

You have brought us back to that exalted and decisive moment in our ancient history . . . and to that place where the Law was given and where our people were commanded to be a chosen people. Once again we see before our eyes the eternal words of our scriptures and of the coming of our forefathers into the desert of Sinai. . . . With a mighty sweep of the combined arms of the Israel Defence Forces you have stretched out your hand to King Solomon. . . . Elath will again be the leading Hebrew port in the south, the straits of Suez will be open to Israeli shipping and Yotvat, hitherto called Tiran, which was an independent Hebrew state until 1400 years ago, will return as an integral part to the Third Israel Commonwealth.[58]

What was Egyptian to everyone else was not Egyptian to Ben-Gurion: "Our forces did not infringe upon the land of Egypt and did not even attempt to do so," he remarked. "Our operations were restricted to the Sinai peninsula alone."[59]

By this time all the scales were falling from Eisenhower's eyes. He had been deceived by America's transatlantic allies and by a state that would not have come into existence but for a push from behind the scenes by a U.S. administration. He fought the election campaign on his own terms,[60] and his landslide election win put him in an even stronger position to deal with governments that had betrayed his trust. In a letter to the Israeli leader on November 7, the president expressed his "deep concern"; at the State Department, the Israeli chargé was told Ben-Gurion's statements "came as a great shock to the US" in view of other statements that Israel had no desire for territorial gain.[61] Israel used every rhetorical weapon in its attempt to retain captured territory. "Speaking as a member of the free world and not only as Prime Minister of Israel," Ben-Gurion drew a picture of a Middle East threatened by the Soviet Union and its stalking horses in the Middle East, Nasser and the Syrian prime minister, Shukri al Quwatli.[62] But under continuing U.S. pressure he backed down. Israeli troops began pulling back from Sinai on December 3, "systematically destroying telephone and telegraph lines and breaking up the railroad and asphalted roads" as they went and destroying military buildings in the town of al Arish and all houses in the villages of al Qusaima and Abu Agheila.[63]

Gaza remained under occupation. The strip was packed with Palestinian refugees, but in Washington Eban argued Israel's right to rule them. Its absorption of Gaza and "the assumption of responsibility for the people living there" could be "a large contribution to an eventual settlement." For the present, however, Israel was content to seek "a non-Egyptian solution for Gaza that would leave open the possibility of eventual Israeli sovereignty over the Strip."[64] Israel set about consolidating its claim by extending its postal, banking, and communications service to the occupied territory.[65] Yet while refusing to withdraw from occupied territory the government insisted that Israel wanted nothing more than to live at peace with the Arabs: Golda Meir told U.S. officials that if peace in the Middle East had depended on Israel, "there could have been peace at any time since 1948."[66]

On February 3, 1957, Eisenhower again asked Israel to withdraw from Gaza. Ben-Gurion said Israel would not do this unless it was given police and administrative powers in the strip and unless the Gulf of Aqaba was opened to Israeli shipping. On February 15 the Israelis again refused to budge. By this time the United States was about to launch the "Eisenhower Doctrine" (finally declared on March 9), designed to shore up pro-Western Arab states against the radicals and, standing behind them with arms and economic aid, the Soviet Union. Dulles felt the scheme was not going to work unless the United States was prepared to take a tough line with Israel over Gaza: it had "reached the limit in efforts to make it easy for the Israelis to withdraw."[67] Eisenhower agreed:

> In considering various possible courses of action I rejected from the outset any more United Nations resolutions designed merely to condemn Israel's conduct. Once more I rejected also any new resolution like that of October 30, 1956, which had called only for a suspension of governmental support of Israel. Indeed, such a suspension against both Israel and Egypt was already in effect by the United States. To prevent an outbreak of hostilities I preferred a resolution which would call on United Nations members to suspend not just governmental but *private* assistance to Israel. Such a move would be no hollow gesture.[68]

Eisenhower had done the math. "Philanthropic" tax-free donations to Israel were running at $40 million a year and the sale of government bonds at between $50 and $60 million—chicken feed by today's standards but a substantial amount of money at the time—and Israel was also seeking loans through the Export-Import Bank. Ben-Gurion—now trying to stir up the American Jewish community over the president's head—complained of "double standards," but at a meeting in the White House with Democrat and Republican congressional leaders, Dulles reiterated the administration's determination to "oppose Israel's refusal to conform to United Nations decisions."[69] Eisenhower sent another warning message before posing the crux of the matter in a radio and television address to the nation: "Should a nation which attacks and occupies foreign territory in the face of United Nations disapproval be allowed to impose conditions on its own withdrawal?" If the UN admitted that international disputes could be settled by the use of force, then the best hope of establishing world order would have been destroyed, so the UN "has no choice but to exert pressure on Israel to comply with the withdrawal resolutions."[70] Ben-Gurion was right—but on this occasion he was not the beneficiary, and that was the problem. Double standards were involved, but while Eisenhower could not do much about the attack on Hungary, because the Soviet Union was too big and dangerous, he didn't have to put up with this behavior from Israel.

Ben-Gurion was enraged. "Every attempt to impose on us perverted justice and a regime of discrimination will encounter unshrinking opposition from the Israeli people," he told the Knesset. "It is well known that the Gaza Strip had never been Egyptian territory. Its life and economy will always be bound to Israel. . . . No matter what may happen, Israel will not submit to the restoration of the status quo in the strip."[71] While the Israeli cabinet went into urgent session to consider the American position, Arab states, along with Afghanistan, Pakistan, and Indonesia, prepared a UN resolution calling for the end of all military, economic, and financial assistance to Israel. Sanctions were coming, with the United States prepared to play the unusual role in the Security Council of being a passive spectator, but before the blow could be delivered Israel buckled: Golda Meir told the General Assembly on March 1 that Israel agreed to a "full and complete withdrawal" of its forces. But it salvaged something worthwhile from the retreat. Egypt was obliged by the United States to open the Straits of Tiran to Israeli shipping. Far from being punished for its role in launching a war that had extinguished the lives of thousands of Egyptian soldiers and civilians, Israel had been rewarded. The question of reparations for lives lost and property destroyed did not even arise.

THE HUMAN COST

The first civilian victims of the war were probably the forty-nine Palestinians massacred by Israeli border guards in or around the village of Kafr Qasim, near Tel Aviv, late in the afternoon of October 29. The villagers did not know that the usual night curfew had been brought forward from 6:00 P.M. to 5:00 P.M. Men, women, and children returning from working in the fields and a quarry in trucks, on bicycles, and on a horse cart were stopped and shot with submachine guns and automatic rifles. The victims included young girls, a pregnant woman, old people, and parents and their children.[72]

The civilian victims also included the hundreds of Palestinians killed in the Gaza Strip when the Israelis went on a house-to-house hunt for arms and *fidayin* and fired into demonstrators at the Rafah refugee camp: at least 111 Palestinians were killed in this one episode.[73] In Egypt hundreds more civilians were killed in the French and British air and sea bombardment of Port Fuad and Port Said or in the ground action that followed. "They arrived in trucks, hearses, ambulances and even a Coca-Cola lorry," a British paratroop wrote of the dead in Port Said. "Loads and loads of bodies of all ages and both sexes. They were buried in roughly bulldozed mass graves."[74] In Sinai civilians caught in the path of the invading Israeli army were summarily executed (murdered as some might say—execution denotes legality); when the Egyptians returned to the Sinai they found the bodies of civilians hanging from telegraph poles. Numerous other atrocities were reported.[75] The total Egyptian civilian death toll came to about one thousand. The military death toll included several thousand Egyptian soldiers, many of whom were captured in Sinai, disarmed, and herded in the direction of the canal; without food or water few would have survived. There were reports of prisoners of war being massacred. Britain lost 16 men killed and 96 wounded; France, 10 killed and 33 wounded; and Israel, a total of 171 dead or wounded.

The canal had been blocked. The oil had been cut off from Iraq. Thousands of people had died. The most senior politicians and "statesmen" in Britain and France had been exposed as liars and dissemblers. Nasser had gained a victory by default, and Israel had gained access to the Gulf of Aqaba, but the adventure had ended in humiliation for its senior partners in this adventure. Their remaining possessions and their protégés in the Middle East were now at further risk. Fury against the West and Israel ran unrestrained across the region from Morocco and Algeria down to the Gulf.[76] Israel, which had established itself in the Middle East as an outpost of "civilization," could hardly have done a better job of confirming the Arab view that it was an agent of imperialism.

9. MY ENEMY'S SPECIAL FRIEND

After the Suez War the emotional flood tide of "Nasserism" flowed into every corner of the Middle East. From Cairo, Sawt al Arab (Voice of the Arabs) urged the masses to stand firm against imperialism and the forces of "Arab reaction." The idols of the age were Nasser and the great Egyptian singer Umm Kulthum. When he spoke and she sang, the whole Arab world stopped to listen. While the euphoria lasted nothing seemed impossible. Revolution in 1952 had been followed by victory at Suez in 1956—a victory by default but still a victory—and by 1958 the time had come for a final push that would cleanse the Middle East of the imperialists and their agents. In this surging sea of passion and expectations that were doomed to wildly exceed any possibility of fulfillment, the friends of the West were like small islands whipped by a typhoon. In Beirut President Camille Chamoun could not have chosen a worse time to decide that he wanted to amend the constitution so that he could stay in power longer. Dissatisfaction with a lopsided constitution and an arrogant president—an ally of the West to boot—determined to change the rules to suit himself finally boiled over. By June Chamoun was besieged in his palace, on the roof of which he was easily identifiable by his yellow sports shirt as he strode around taking pot shots at rebels with his hunting rifle. The United States had no particular feeling for Chamoun one way or the other, but it could not allow a "pro-Western government" to be overthrown. A victory for the "radicals" in Lebanon would be a victory for radicals elsewhere, encouraging attacks on other Western allies and tilting the strategic balance in favor of Nasser and the Soviet Union. The challenge was met by invoking the Eisenhower Doctrine, allowing the United States to intervene militarily on behalf of an embattled friend. Nasser protested his innocence, but in Washington the view expressed by Eisenhower in 1956 that he was an "evil influence" still prevailed.[1]

The United States and Britain—at loggerheads over Palestine in 1948 and Suez in 1956—prepared to land an Anglo-American force on the beaches south of Beirut. French participation was considered but dropped as being too much of a liability because of France's past as the mandatory power. The eruption of two other crises forced the two governments to modify their plans still further. The Iraqi regime was obliterated on July 14, and two days later the Hashimite government of Jordan, fearing that it would be next, appealed to the West to intervene on the grounds that it had uncovered evidence that an Egyptian-inspired coup was imminent. Nothing could be done about Iraq, but emergency measures were already under way to "save" Lebanon and Jordan from Nasser and "Arab radicalism." The United States and Britain decided to split the responsibility. The Sixth Fleet was sent to Lebanon on July 15, and the "first elements" of a brigade of British paratroops were flown to Jordan from Cyprus two days later with instructions to secure Amman and protect the king, the government, and Western interests. One of the "two little chaps" had gone, Harold Macmillan remarked of the murdered king of Iraq, but the necessary steps had been taken to ensure the survival of the other one—Hussein of Jordan.[2]

"GETTING THINGS BACK"

Macmillan wanted the two operations to be extended across the Middle East as part of a general cleanup. In a telephone conversation with Eisenhower on the eve of intervention in Lebanon, he rambled on obliquely about the "things" that now had to be done: "If we do this thing with the Lebanese, it is only really part of a much larger operation because we shall be driven to take the thing as a whole. . . . If this thing is done, which I think is very noble, dear friend, it will set off a lot of things throughout the whole area. I'm all for that as long as we regard it as an operation that has got to be carried through." Eisenhower quickly deduced from all these "things" where Macmillan was heading. "Now just a minute, so that there is no misunderstanding. Are you of the belief that unless we have made up our minds in advance to carry this thing on through to the Persian Gulf that we had better not go in the first place?" Macmillan's answer was "no," when he really seemed to mean "yes": there was no point in sitting in one part of the Middle East only for the rest to go up in flames. "As soon as we start we have to face it—we have probably got to do a lot of things." Eisenhower did not agree: "Well, now, I will tell you of course I would not want to go further. . . . If we are now planning the initiation of a big operation that could run all the way through Syria and Iraq, we are far beyond anything I have the power to do constitutionally."

Macmillan persisted. The three crises spelled ruin for Britain; he talked of "blitzing through" and "getting things back," but the U.S. president had no intention of being drawn into this imperial salvage operation, telling Dulles later that while the British were taking "hard knocks" all over the region, he had tried to tell Macmillan that he "cannot take such a decision as this."[3]

British intervention stabilized the Hashimite regime in Jordan, and by the time U.S. Marines landed on the beaches of Beirut the Lebanese had settled their crisis themselves. Chamoun's presidency was finished, though, the parliament electing General Fuad Chehab as president on July 31. Beirut was able to live on for another decade as the glittering gem of what was left of the old Middle East. It was a city of politics and publishing; a city of spies and agents, of exiles reading their newspapers under the hibiscus trees on the terrace of the Negresco; a city of pleasure, of the Casino du Liban up the coast at Jounieh, of the Kit Kat and Caves du Roy nightclubs, of deck chairs by the pool at the Phoenicia and the St. George; a city of silly cliches, the "Paris of the Middle East," where the traveler could swim in the morning and ski in the afternoon, or presumably the other way around; a city of poets, students, and universities; and a city of poverty and Palestinian refugees, squatting in their camps behind the red earth hillocks on the way to the airport in Beirut, dreaming of *al awda* (the return) and producing their house keys and title deeds as proof of their right.

"WE KNOW YOU'RE IN TROUBLE"

The State Department knew that Nasser's domination of the Arab world was far from absolute; it also knew that he was hostile to communism and that his relationship with the Soviet Union was based on the pragmatic view that it was "a great power with interests and policies in the Middle East which happen at this stage to coincide with his own."[4] If the United States identified with the Arab desire for freedom, independence, and unity and let Israel know that "its continued existence as a sovereign state depends on its willingness to become a finite and accepted part of the Near East nation-state system," Arab suspicions could perhaps be overcome.[5] Hesitation in the United States on the question of relations with Israel was partly the lingering consequences of American resentment at Anglo-French-Israeli deception in 1956, but it also remained difficult for many U.S. policy makers to see how deeper involvement with Israel could do anything but harm to America's strategic interests in the region.

During his short term in the White House, John F. Kennedy tried to balance out these overlapping foreign policy considerations. The new president came into office with a strong Jewish support base: in the 1960 elections a greater percentage of Jews (81 percent) had voted for Kennedy than Catholics (73 percent). Israel's interests would have to be carefully considered on all matters of Middle Eastern policy, and Kennedy was bound to feel the heat from Zionist lobbyists if in any way he seemed to be jeopardizing them. Two figures who did their best to make sure that he remained on the Zionist side were Abe Feinberg, who had raised an estimated $400,000 for Truman in the campaign of 1948, and a newer figure in Washington, Meyer (Mike) Feldman.[6] Feinberg had stayed out of the Democratic campaign of 1960 because of the anti-Semitism of Kennedy's father but was later brought in through his connection with Governor Abraham Ribicoff of Connecticut.

Kennedy is said to have been outraged by the bluntness of the quid pro quo demanded in return for Zionist support. "We know your campaign is in trouble," he is said to have been told at an August 1960 meeting with thirty Jewish leaders in Feinberg's New York apartment. "We're willing to pay your bills if you'll let us have control of your Middle East policy."[7] In public, however, Kennedy declared (at a conference of the Zionist Organization of America) that support for Israel was "not a partisan matter [but] a national commitment."[8] After the election he appointed Feldman as the presidential "point man" on matters involving Jews and Israel, thus putting him in the position occupied by David Niles during the Truman presidency. Feldman was authorized to monitor all State Department and White House cable traffic on the Middle East despite his position as a "de facto Israeli advocate."[9] The appointment caused ructions in the White House; even Kennedy regarded Feldman "as a necessary evil whose highly visible White House position was a political debt that had to be paid."[10]

As a senator Kennedy had called for the repatriation of all Palestinians willing to live at peace with their neighbors (in line with UN General Assembly Resolution 194 of 1948), and when he went into the White House the State Department drew up a plan for peace based on a mix of repatriation, emigration to third countries, and compensation for all Palestinians who chose not to return. In trying to broker a solution, Kennedy decided to deal directly with Egypt's president. "Nasser's got his problems, I've got my problems," he remarked. "I'm not going to persuade him to act against his interests. I won't even try. But it can't hurt down the line if we understand each other a little better."[11] On May 11, 1961, Kennedy sent Nasser a letter setting out the means he had in mind for a settlement, along with the assurance that the United States would help any country that wanted to control its own destiny and was prepared to allow its neighbors "to pursue the same fundamental aims."[12] In reply, Nasser stressed the Arab fear of Israeli expansion and appealed to Kennedy to change a situation in which both American principles and interests seemed to have been set aside.

The overtures to Egypt were followed through with cash loans, rice, cotton, and insecticides, but good intentions were not enough to overcome the domestic, national, regional, and global entanglements standing in the way of a better relationship. At Kennedy's behest, Dr. Joseph E. Johnson, president of the Carnegie Endowment for International Peace, traveled to the Middle East in 1961 and 1962 under the aegis of the UN Palestine Conciliation Commission with details of a pilot plan for peace. It was acceptable to the Arabs but not Israel. In any case, reconciliation with Nasser was not just a question of sorting out the "Palestine problem." Nasser was a leading figure in the nonaligned movement and a fountain of anti-colonial and anti-imperialist Third World rhetoric. He might have been forced into the arms of the Soviet Union by Western policy errors, but the fact was that he was there. He had nettled the United States by holding it responsible (along with Belgium) for the murder of the "African Castro," Patrice Lumumba, in January 1961, and his support for the Yemeni republicans after the overthrow of the imam in September 1962 ended any lingering possibility of Egyptian-U.S. rapprochement. The conflict in Yemen developed into a surrogate war between the "radical" and "conservative" antipodes of the Middle East, Egypt and Saudi Arabia, with the United States standing strongly by the Saudis because of the perceived threat to the stability of the kingdom and Western access to its oil reserves.

THE MYTH OF BALANCE

America's relationship with Egypt began to frost over again just as the relationship with the Israelis was warming up. On the top of the Israeli agenda was the acquisition of U.S. weaponry, especially Hawk surface-to-air "defensive" missiles. Kennedy demurred because he did not want to involve the United States in a Middle East arms race, but by mid-1962 he had concluded that if the arms balance in the Middle East were to be preserved the Israelis should get the missiles they wanted. The United States had given Israel sensitive electronic material before but not arms; in acceding to Israel's request for arms, Kennedy is thought to have been looking for leverage that would induce the Israelis to open up the Dimona nuclear reactor to outside inspections and perhaps wean them off the idea of developing a nuclear "deterrent." In the view of the CIA station chief in Tel Aviv, however, the Israelis took the view that "if we were going to offer them arms to go easy on the bomb, once they had it, we were going to send them a lot more for fear that they would use it."[13] In the end, Israel secured the Hawk missiles without having to given anything in return. "Your administration has done more to satisfy Israeli security preoccupations than any of its predecessors," Robert Komer, a senior staff member attached to the National Security Council, told Kennedy on December 5, 1962. "We have promised the Israelis Hawks, reassured them on the Jordan waters, given a higher level of economic aid (to permit expensive arms) and given various security assurances. In return we have got nothing for our efforts. . . . The score is 4-0."[14]

Indeed, while speaking of the need to maintain balance between Israel and the Arabs, successive U.S. administrations had always deliberately upheld a policy of imbalance. Speaking to Shimon Peres in 1964, Komer referred to three "myths" about U.S. policy:

> First was the myth that the US pursued a strictly "even-handed" or "impartial" policy as between Israel and the Arabs. This was what we often said publicly. But if one looked at actions, not words, it was clear that from 1947 on our policy had basically favored Israel. We had been Israel's strongest backer from the outset, financially and otherwise, and it was our deterrent power (not that of the British, French or anyone else) which really provided Israel its insurance policy. What we did do was to seek an "appearance" of balance in our policy, which would permit us to exercise continued influence in the Arab world. This influence was imperative in Israel's interests as well as ours because it served not only to protect US assets (oil and bases) in the area but to limit Soviet penetration.[15]

The second myth, said Komer, was that the United States had shifted to a "pro-Nasser" policy. This could be disproved just by looking at the countries to which the United States was providing aid to "contain" Nasser's "expansionist ambitions" (a list that included royalist Libya, Sudan, Ethiopia, Saudi Arabia, and Jordan, "in fact every country around the UAR"). The third myth was that the United States could not be relied upon to back Israel "in a pinch."[16]

ISRAEL'S "BEST FRIEND"

The trickle of weapons Kennedy sent to Israel set a precedent for Lyndon Baines Johnson, who had long and strong connections with Israel's lobbyists and—as Senate Democratic leader—had tried to block Eisenhower's drive to get the Israelis out of Gaza in 1956. It was during the Johnson years, after a protracted period of gestation from Truman to Kennedy, that the extraordinary "special relationship" between the United States and Israel was finally born.

A wily politician, thin-skinned and aggressive, bullying and sycophantic, idealistic and ruthlessly practical, regarded by enemies as duplicitous and even by friends as sly, Johnson never lost sight of what the "Jewish lobby" could do for him or to him, and he made sure he befriended many of its leading figures. They included Arthur and Mathilde Krim (who built a house close to Johnson's Texas property so they would have their own place to stay when they came visiting), Supreme Court Justice Abe Fortas (a genuine friend from the days when he and Johnson were both young men in Washington), and Abe Feinberg. Critical positions inside the White House and in the administration were filled with ardent Zionists, including Supreme Court Justice Arthur Goldberg (U.S. ambassador to the UN), Eugene Rostow (undersecretary of state for political affairs), Rostow's brother Walt (special assistant to the president), Ben Wattenberg (Johnson's speechwriter), and Larry Levinson (his adviser on domestic affairs). The close relationship between Johnson and the minister plenipotentiary at the Israeli embassy in Washington, Ephraim Evron, was regarded by some as "unmatched by anything since the days of Teddy Roosevelt and the British diplomat Cecil Spring-Rice."[17]

Was Johnson's partisan support for Israel in the national interest? Many Americans involved in Middle Eastern policy making did not think so. In 1964 Lucius Battle, the U.S. ambassador in Cairo, expressed his frustration at his government's refusal to check Israel's "inexorable drive" not only to gain sovereignty over the demilitarized zones along the armistice lines but to remilitarize them, violating the letter and spirit of the armistice agreements and the UN Charter in the process. Israel had been boycotting the Israel-Syria Mixed Armistice Commission since 1951, it was denouncing the armistice agreement with Egypt, it was still refusing to comply with UN resolutions calling for the repatriation of the Palestinians, it was flouting the express wishes of the U.S. government, yet it was still getting what it wanted. "The above picture is not very pleasant," wrote Battle. "It is compounded by the fact that Israel and its friends in the United States have been able to establish widespread credence in an upside-down world, where Syria is the trigger-happy party in the demilitarized zones, Nasser is dedicated to the destruction of 'peace-loving Israel' and the plight of the Arab refugees is somehow the fault of the Arab governments." In summary, "Israel's interests (as determined by Israel) do not at all times and in all respects coincide with those of the United States."[18]

ARMS NEGOTIATIONS

In terms of weaponry, the number of soldiers it could put into battle at short notice, and the level of their training and equipment, Israel had a clear edge over any combination of Arab armies. Its air force consisted mostly of a formidable combination of French Super Mystère, Vautour, and Mirage fighters and bombers and British Centurion tank brigades. These weapons had all been provided by third parties with the consent of the United States. Previously the Hawk "defensive" missiles had been the only weapons the United States provided through direct agreement, but with a gushingly sympathetic president now in the White House the Israelis began lobbying for more. The acquisition of U.S. Patton tanks was discussed in April 1964, when Myer Feldman and the U.S. ambassador to Israel, Walworth Barbour, sat down for talks with Levi Eshkol.[19] When Eshkol visited Washington in June, Johnson agreed to supply tanks in a surreptitious round-robin scheme. West Germany would buy the more advanced M48-A2 or A3 Patton tanks and supply its older M48-A1s to the Israelis through Italy. The Italians would refit them under German supervision before the tanks were re-exported from Naples.

This clandestine arrangement came unstuck when Arab governments found out and threatened West Germany with an economic boycott. The Germans backed out, increasing the pressure on the United States to drop the third-party mask and supply the remainder of the tanks directly. News of the tank deal also affected America's relationship with Jordan's King Hussein: he was seeking arms too, and the disclosure that the United States was supplying tanks to Israel on the quiet strengthened his own bid for tanks and aircraft.

The Israelis protested. How could the United States even think of arming Jordan? In Washington Feldman's "flank attacks" from inside the White House heightened Johnson's concern at the prospect of a damaging struggle with the Israeli lobby.[20] The very possibility that the United States would provide arms to one of Israel's enemies (as Jordan was represented to be) strengthened the case that Eshkol, Eban, and Meir were all making for the direct supply of U.S. arms.[21] They expressed concern that Hussein might be tempted to place "substantial forces" on the West Bank, compelling them to redeploy troops currently facing Egypt and Syria, and they could not go along with arms sales to Jordan unless additional steps were taken to enhance Israel's security. Komer bought their arguments. If the United States wanted to deter the Arabs, he wrote, emphasizing his words, *"we must become direct arms suppliers to Israel.* Only this way could we deprive Nasser of his psychological victory over Bonn in the short run and convince the Arabs that they could not overpower Israel in the long run."[22] He recommended that the United States begin delivering advanced tanks to Israel to make up for the shortfall created by the collapse of the arrangement with West Germany. Jordan should be helped out but should not be given advanced tanks.

Johnson's only problem in accepting this recommendation was how to persuade Israel that Jordan would also have to be given some weapons. Phoning the White House, Abe Feinberg was asked by the president whether Israel was prepared to live with the possibility that Jordan might turn to the USSR for the weapons it could not get from the United States. Israel had to understand that "we'll furnish both of you" or "we'll furnish nobody." It was up to Eshkol to decide. "I want Eshkol to tell me what he wants me to do." And he wanted help from Eshkol in making the arms package acceptable to "people over here": "What I need is to be able to say privately that the Israeli Government supports what we do, even if it cannot publicly applaud, and to have that Government back up my words. In turn Prime Minister Eshkol needs to be enabled to say that Israel's security needs can be adequately met and that Israel can face the future with confidence in the strong support of its friends."[23]

Johnson attached four conditions to the supply of the tanks to Israel. *"These are an integral part of any program of mutual reassurances; they must be considered as a package and accepted as such.* I do not propose to have Israel take what it likes and then argue about the rest." The first condition required Israel to give "quiet but unmistakable support" to the Jordan arms assistance program; the second required it to keep secret all matters under discussion; the third required Israel to reiterate its commitment to not building nuclear weapons; the fourth stated that "the US cannot accept Israeli pre-emptive action against the Arab [water] diversion works but must instead have Israeli agreement to take this problem to the United Nations." The instructions also reiterated U.S. opposition to what the United States, repeating the Israeli euphemism, called "pre-emptive action" against Jordan. There must be a "meeting of minds" on various points, but if minds could meet, "the US will make selective direct sales on favorable credit terms."[24]

The president issued his approval of direct arms supplies to Israel on February 28, 1965, and by late July the deal had been arranged. Israel would get 110 advanced M48-A2C tanks to replace the tanks that had not been delivered from Germany and 100 M48-A1 "basic" tanks to match the hundred that would be sold to Jordan. Conversion kits would be provided to give the older tanks greater firepower, along with ammunition and spare parts.[25] Jordan was disappointed at being given inferior tanks but was placated with the assurance that deliveries of more advanced models would be considered for 1967–68. As a condition of supply, King Hussein had to agree that his government would not station the tanks on the West Bank. The attention of all three countries now turned to aircraft.

"BLUE SKY" BIDDING

In a memorandum of understanding signed in March, the United States had agreed to provide Israel with a "certain number" of combat aircraft (later set at twenty-four) regarded as having a defensive capacity. It still did not want to provide either Israel or Jordan with sophisticated and "clearly offensive" aircraft because this would spell "an end to our arms policy," which, "though tattered and torn" had been "a major factor in keeping us out of the Near East arms race and protecting the United States from the political damage that would result from a policy of uncontrolled military sales."[26]

In October the commander of the Israeli air force, General Ezer Weizman, made a "blue sky opening bid" for 210 fighter bombers but was told such a number was out of the question. Israel's persistent lobbying on the supply of advanced aircraft irritated Komer and most probably other senior advisers. On January 12, 1966, Komer fired off a caustic dispatch to Johnson about how Feldman hoped to see him in the coming days, "probably to pass on a complaint about how poorly we're treating Israel. . . . Such gambits are part of a standard Israeli effort to put pressure on us for more military and economic help." It was par for the course, "and so is sending in Feldman and Feinberg to harry you. Thus I'd see merit in telling Feldman to pass back word that we naturally bridle when Israel tells us how to run our business and that if Israel expects help from us it must be a two-way street."[27]

The negotiations ended in an agreement by the United States to sell Israel twenty-four Skyhawk A4E "intruder type" aircraft with an option for Israel to buy twenty-four more at a later date. Israel accepted the sale to Jordan of thirty-six of the inferior F-104 or F-105 "secondhand interceptor" aircraft but, in requesting further supplies of advanced weaponry, exposed itself to more questioning of its nuclear intentions. Paul H. Nitze, then deputy secretary of defense, later recalled how he had opposed the sale of planes unless "they come clean on Dimona. Then suddenly this fellow Feinberg comes into my office and says right out 'You can't do that to us.' I said 'I've already done it.' Feinberg said 'I'll see to it that you get over-ruled.' I remember throwing him out of the office." Three days later Nitze got a call from McNamara. "He said he'd been instructed to tell me to change my mind and release the planes. And I did. . . . Feinberg had the power and brought it to bear. I was surprised McNamara did this."[28] The United States succeeded only in extracting a commitment from Israel that it would "not be the first to introduce nuclear weapons into the Arab-Israel area."[29] Israel also agreed to open up the Dimona facility to the U.S. "visits" begun during Kennedy's time: it would not allow "inspections," on the grounds that they would constitute an infringement of its sovereign rights.

The military balance in the Middle East now greatly favored Israel. On May 1, 1967, Undersecretary of State Nicholas Katzenbach confirmed earlier intelligence estimates when he told Johnson that Israel had a "safe margin of superiority over any combination of Arab forces likely to attack it and can be expected to maintain that position for at least the next five years." The Arabs had made little progress in military coordination and were showing no signs of being ready to rush to each other's defense. Furthermore, said Katzenbach, Israel had signed a contract with the French Dassault company for the acquisition of surface-to-surface ballistic missiles, capable of being fitted with nuclear warheads; Egypt's surface-to-surface missile program, on the other hand, "has reached a virtual standstill. Most of the West German scientists who were assisting this effort have departed. Flight testing of the UAR missiles has been suspended and it is estimated that the missile program, at its present level of activity, could not be successfully completed within the next decade."[30]

WATER WARS

At the Paris peace conference in 1919 the Zionist delegation had failed in its attempt to have the water resources of southern Syria included in the mandated territory of Palestine, and water remained one of the most contentious issues between Israel, Lebanon, Syria, and Jordan. What Israel sought to do in the 1950s was build its own water diversion works while preventing the three Arab states from building theirs. In 1953 Eisenhower had appointed a mediator (Eric Johnston) to come up with a plan for joint exploitation of the water flowing from the heights of southern Syria into the River Jordan. This had foundered on the refusal of the Arab states to cooperate with Israel and on the latter's refusal to put development of water resources under international supervision: the Johnston plan would have given Israel 40 percent of the water compared to 45 percent for Jordan and 15 percent for Syria and Lebanon combined, but the Israelis calculated that by building their own plant they could increase their share from an estimated 400 to 490 million cubic meters of water a year to 550 million cubic meters.[31] Any lingering hopes that the Arabs and Israelis could be induced to work together on a common plan were shattered by Israel's ferocious attack on Syria in December 1955; Israel's claim of provocation was dismissed by General E. L. M. Burns, head of the UN's Middle East truce supervision operations, and even Abba Eban remarked that the Syrian "attack" (shots allegedly fired at Israeli fishing boats) had caused slight damage and no casualties.[32] Finally, in 1959, Israel announced that it was going ahead with the development of its Lake Tiberias (the Sea of Galilee) national water carrier plant.

In January 1964, with the Israeli plant soon to be completed, Arab leaders responded with a plan of their own. Water would be channeled from the Hasbani River in southern Lebanon to the Banyas River in Syria before the increased flow was diverted to the Yarmouk River (a tributary of the River Jordan) for its use by Jordan. The sensitivity of the Banyas diversion scheme was complicated by its close proximity to the territory that had been declared a demilitarized zone during the 1949 Syrian-Israeli armistice agreement. The armistice line was not a political border. Ultimate sovereignty over this territory was a matter to be decided sometime in the future, but because the DMZ had been placed on the Israeli side of the pre-1947 border between Syria and Palestine the government of Israel claimed it as theirs and began sending in armored tractors to work the land while simultaneously driving out the Syrian farming population. Armistice line clashes continued throughout the 1960s, but in all these trials of strength (as Patrick Seale has observed), Israel was escalating from a position of strength and Syria from one of weakness.[33] The commander of the UN truce force believed that Israel was setting out deliberately to provoke the Syrians,[34] but censure of Israel by UN observers on the ground was not often followed up by condemnation in the Security Council. The combination of conflict over water, incursions into the demilitarized zone, and the rise in 1966 of a Syrian government committed to armed struggle as the means of liberating Palestine turned the Syrian-Israeli armistice line into the most volatile area along the Arab front.

The pious observation by Lyndon Johnson at a Friends of the Weizmann Institute of Science banquet in 1964 that "water should never be a cause of war; it should always be a force for peace" was clarified later when

Johnson told Eshkol that "we back Israel fully on the Jordan water. We want Israel to have more water. . . . We will help Israel on this as much as possible. We have told the Arab Governments about this. Of course, we will get some backlash from the Arab countries as a result of your visit with me. However, I am not worried by that. It is important to you and to the United States that everybody should know that we are friends."[35]

As a condition of arms sales Johnson had insisted that Israel must not attack Arab water schemes, but State Department officials from the secretary down remained suspicious. Rusk forcefully reiterated the official line in a message to Averell Harriman: "Please be sure that Eshkol understands we cannot accept the idea that we should proceed to assist in the arming of Israel when we are on notice Israel plans to take preemptive military action with respect to Jordan waters. We will not support such preemptive action."[36]

In fact, there was little for Israel to attack because work on the Banyas plant had been crawling along and consisted of little more than cleared land and a collection of bulldozers sitting on site. However, now that Israel had developed its own water diversion project, it was determined to stop the Arabs from completing theirs. Ignoring the American warnings, Israel shelled the Banyas site on May 13, 1965; Eshkol argued that the attack served "the useful purpose of demonstrating Israeli capability of interdicting diversion works by measures short of full-scale war."[37] The attack was clearly intended to warn Lebanon that unless it stopped work on its part of the diversion scheme it could be next.

On July 14, 1966, Israel finally destroyed the Banyas diversion works. Syria complained to the Security Council that Israeli fighters and bombers had "violated Syrian air space, shelled seven Syrian areas situated on the site of the Jordan River Development Scheme, hit mechanical and engineering equipment, destroyed bulldozers with napalm bombs, wounded nine civilians and killed one woman."[38] Israel claimed it had been provoked by a sudden surge of sabotage attacks across the armistice line by Palestinian guerillas in the previous two days. This was enough to get it off the hook at the Security Council: while "deploring" the Israeli attack, the United States, France, and Britain refused to support a resolution condemning Israel when it was put to the vote in August.

INCURSIONS AND REPRISALS

In 1956 the UN Security Council had passed Resolution 111 (January 19) condemning Israeli breaches of the General Armistice Agreement (GAA) with Syria, "whether or not undertaken by way of retaliation."[39] In April

1962 it had condemned Israel for a further "flagrant violation" of the agreement through military attacks on March 16–17, but with Israel's best friend sitting in the White House, such censures were now even fewer and further between, despite the view of UN observers that Israel was deliberately provoking conflict. By 1966 Israeli land incursions, artillery bombardment, and air strikes were forcing Syrian villagers out of their homes on the Golan Heights. Tension had reached a similar level on the Jordanian front. In a "reprisal" attack for what the Israeli government said were Fatah guerrilla strikes, troops struck at two villages several kilometers inside Jordan on April 29–30, 1966, destroying nineteen houses in one village and four in another and killing eleven farmers. On May 1, Jordanian and Israeli troops exchanged fire across the armistice line, and on May 27–28, Israeli troops were sent into action inside Jordan again, during a meeting of Arab prime ministers in Cairo; in Rusk's view, the timing of the attack made the situation "even more explosive."[40]

In August (a month after the destruction of the Banyas water diversion plant), two Syrian planes were shot down in an air battle that broke out after an Israeli patrol boat inexplicably "ran aground" on the Syrian side of Lake Tiberias. On November 7 Nasser entered into a defense agreement with Syria in the apparent hope of restraining the Syrians and deterring the Israelis, while reinforcing his image as a strong leader prepared to stand up for Palestinian and Arab rights. Six days later Israel slapped his face by launching an attack on Jordan described in a CIA memorandum as "the worst single incident since Suez."[41]

The force that crossed the armistice line consisted of an infantry brigade supported by tanks (U.S.-supplied Patton tanks reportedly among them) and heavy artillery. Air cover was provided by Mirage jets. The targets were three villages in the Hebron district, Al Samuᶜ, Al Rafaat, and Al Tawawini, from which Israel claimed guerrilla attacks had recently been launched across the armistice line, killing two soldiers. During the operation fifty Jordanian soldiers or civilians were killed and about 150 buildings were destroyed.[42] Riots broke out on the West Bank and in Amman. In the words of Patrick Seale: "King Hussein's Palestinian subjects demanded a radical change of policy: what was the point of protecting Israel rather than letting loose the guerrillas, when you were punished for it? Why was Jordan at odds with Syria, Egypt and the PLO? Why did it cold-shoulder the Soviet Union?" The turmoil caused by the attack had driven the Arab states "to the very edge of the precipice."[43]

In Israel Abba Eban, Israel's foreign minister, dismissed the operation as something that had simply "got out of hand" and should not be regarded as the prelude to an invasion.[44] Eshkol's office passed on the laconic message to Washington that the original plan was just "to blow 40 houses" but that the operation had turned out to be "unexpectedly violent" because of the arrival of Arab Legion forces. Komer phoned Feinberg to pass on the message to Tel Aviv that Israel had gone too far and had better "lay off."[45]

Frustration with Israel was apparent throughout the administration. Within the past two years the United States had made a major change of policy by agreeing to the direct sale of tanks and aircraft to Israel. It had asked Israel not to attack the Banyas water project, but Israel had gone ahead and destroyed it anyway and the attack transgressed all acceptable limits. Walt Rostow, usually very understanding of Israel's concerns, wrote to Johnson that "this 3000-man raid with tanks and planes was out of all proportion to the provocation and was aimed at the wrong target."[46] The Israelis had undercut Hussein: "We had his tacit agreement to keep his armor off the West Bank of the Jordan and he had made an honest effort to round up terrorists . . . [but] continuing this cooperation will become all but impossible now."[47] In the view of National Security Council staffers, Israel had left the United States with "a tremendous bill on our hands. We'd be entirely justified in suspending all aid to Israel simply to offset that bill."[48]

In the Security Council, the United States further showed its irritation by voting on November 25 with all permanent members for a resolution (Resolution 228) censuring Israel for a "large scale and carefully planned military action" that violated both the UN Charter and the armistice agreement with Jordan.[49] Yet only four days later Israeli fighter aircraft shot down two Egyptian MiG-19s along the Sinai armistice line. Katzenbach wrote to the U.S. embassy in Tel Aviv that while the administration was in no position to accept or reject Israel's version of the air battle, "neither are we certain that Israel's behavior is as 'innocent' as it claims. We have some difficulty understanding how aircraft allegedly destroyed over Israel territory happened to fall in UAR."[50] The Israelis should not be allowed to believe "that they can practice their version of realpolitik with neighboring Arab states at this critical juncture without attracting notice of USG and arousing doubts as to their professed peaceful intentions."

These remarks indicated irritation with a specific action and not a general policy. On all the big questions the United States and Israel saw eye to eye. Their differences lay only in when and how to act. At the beginning of 1966 no country was taking as much of their attention as Syria, where radical Ba‘athist factions were engaged in the last stage of a power struggle that had begun with the collapse of union with Egypt (through the formation of the United Arab Republic) in 1961. No outcome could possibly be satisfactory in Washington or Tel Aviv. The only question was how radical the triumphant faction would be, so when Israel passed on the message to Washington that its patience with Syria had just about run out, the response was sympathetic.[51] The cause of the continually deteriorating situation along the armistice line was the same mix as before. Syrian complaints of the cultivation of the demilitarized zones by Israeli armored tractors, the harassment and expulsion of Arab farmers, and the shelling of Syrian military positions were countered by Israeli accusations of sabotage, mine-laying, and "terrorist" infiltration across the armistice line. As usual the United States chose to support the Israeli position. "We're instructing Ambassador Smythe to tell the Syrians we believe Israel is on the brink of an attack and they can't count on us to hold Israel back," Rostow told Johnson on January 16, 1966.[52]

In February the battle lines hardened with the coup that brought the leftist, neo-Marxist wing of the Ba'ath Party, a client Soviet regime in U.S. eyes, to power in Damascus. Syria had agreed to an emergency meeting of the Israel-Syria Mixed Armistice Commission but wanted it to deal with what it regarded as the basic cause of tension on the border, Israel's "farming" incursions into demilitarized territory, rather than the symptoms as manifested in artillery barrages and air duels. Israel's refusal to cooperate with the commission since 1951 had rendered it dysfunctional, but on this occasion it agreed to take part in an emergency session, while refusing to accept any questioning of its "right" to the land in the demilitarized zone. The commission met three times before the negotiations ended in impasse, without cultivation rights even being discussed, "because both parties had first insisted on bringing up broader issues."[53]

On April 7, 1967, the Middle East was pushed to the very edge of another war when an Israeli armored tractor began plowing land in the DMZ on the shores of Lake Tiberias. The Syrians responded with artillery and mortar fire, and a battle broke out that lasted almost the whole day. An attempt by the Mixed Armistice Commission to put a cease-fire in place failed when Israel refused to commit itself to stop sending armored tractors into the DMZ. The fighting built up to an air battle in which six Syrian MiG-21s were shot down (two over Quneitra and four near Damascus) as they intercepted Israeli aircraft. Syrian villages were bombed as well as military positions, and fourteen civilians were killed in one village before the Israeli planes wound up the action by flying in triumph over the Syrian capital.

NUCLEAR COOPERATION

Central to all the security discussions ahead of the outbreak of war in June 1967 was the nuclear question. Israel began developing a nuclear capacity as soon as the state was established; the uranium-yielding potassium deposits of the Negev were already known and were most probably a strong additional reason that the Zionist leadership lobbied so hard for its inclusion within the borders of the Jewish state in the first place. According to Weizmann, the mineral resources of the Negev included as much as two million tons of iron ore, chrome, potash, oil in unknown quantities, and "possibly uranium."[54] Even then Ben-Gurion was looking for Jewish scientists who could "either increase the capacity to kill masses or cure masses."[55]

Scientists at the Weizmann Institute at Rehovoth began developing a nuclear energy program soon after the state was established, extracting small amounts of uranium from the phosphate deposits of the Negev. In 1952, the Israel Atomic Energy Commission was established under the aegis of the Ministry of Defense. The following year Israel signed an atomic cooperation agreement with France that gave the Israelis access to French knowledge and installations and gave France in return the use of Israeli techniques for the processing of low-grade uranium ore and the production of heavy water.[56] In 1955 the United States signed an agreement with Israel within the framework of Eisenhower's "Atoms for Peace" program, opening up U.S. nuclear facilities to Israeli technicians and allowing the transfer of nuclear information to Israel through the provision of thousands of research reports on nuclear development. In addition, the United States agreed to provide the Israelis with a small reactor and a small quantity of enriched uranium.

The site chosen for this first nuclear plant was Nahal Soreq, close to the Weizmann Institute south of Tel Aviv. Construction began in 1958. The plant was finished in May 1960, but by this time Israel had embarked on a second nuclear venture of which the United States knew nothing. In the wake of the Suez War, France offered to help Israel construct a much larger second nuclear plant on the understanding that it would not be used for the development and construction of nuclear weapons. The offer was accepted, and in 1957 the government decided to go ahead with the construction of the plant near the Negev development town of Dimona ("south" in Hebrew), thirty-six kilometers south of Beersheba.

Construction began in 1958. French engineers and technicians supervised excavation of the site, and Israeli scientists and technicians were admitted to French nuclear institutes to be given the expertise they would need to run their own plant. By 1961 France had supplied Israel with eighty-five tons of yellowcake, with twenty tonnes of heavy water being provided by Britain through Norway.[57] Israeli and French officials explained that what was being built was a desalination plant needed for the greening of the Negev. Israel assured France that it would not build nuclear weapons at Dimona and fobbed off the suspicious Americans by describing Dimona as a textile plant and then as a "metallurgical research laboratory."[58]

Gradually the United States pieced together what was going on. With the evidence rapidly reaching the point where a flat denial would no longer be credible, Ben-Gurion admitted part of the truth in a speech to the Knesset on December 21, 1960. Israel had established at Beersheba "a scientific institute for research in problems of arid zones and desert flora and fauna" and was also engaged "in the construction of a research reactor with a capacity of 24,000 thermal kilowatts, which will serve the needs of industry, agriculture, health and science." It was designed "exclusively for peaceful purposes," and reports that Israel was producing atomic weapons were "deliberate or unwitting untruths."[59]

In 1961, the U.S. Senate Foreign Relations Committee went into secret session to discuss Dimona. "I think the Israelis have lied to us like horse thieves on this thing," one member, Senator Bourke Hickenlooper, concluded. "They have completely distorted, misrepresented and falsified the facts."[60] On May 18, 1961, U.S. scientists were shown through Dimona without being allowed to see anything that might reveal the plant's true purpose. When Ben-Gurion met Kennedy at the Waldorf Hotel in New York twelve days later, he continued to dissemble, claiming now that Dimona was being developed to provide nuclear power for desalinization and that "for the time being the only purposes are for peace."[61]

Kennedy was not taken in. He told a friend that the Israelis were "sons of bitches who lie to me consistently about their nuclear capability."[62] In May 1963, following the decision to supply Israel with the Hawk missiles, he sent Ben-Gurion a stern letter. "This commitment and this support would be seriously jeopardized in the public opinion in this country and the West as a whole if it should be thought that this Government was unable to obtain reliable information on a subject as vital to peace as Israel's efforts in the nuclear field."[63] In reply, Ben-Gurion repeated the assurance he had already given, that Dimona was being developed for peaceful purposes. He agreed to allow "annual visits" to the reactor but not on terms satisfactory to the Americans. A further strong letter from Kennedy was sent on June 15, but Ben-Gurion had resigned before it could be delivered.[64] Dealing with the Americans on the nuclear question then became Levi Eshkol's problem.

Israel continued to stand firm in the face of American pressure to open up its nuclear facilities to International Atomic Energy Agency (IAEA) inspections, but "visits" by U.S. scientists went ahead. However, what the Americans were shown during one such visit to Dimona, according to Seymour Hersh, was nothing less than a nuclear Potemkin village in the northern Negev:[65] "The Israeli scheme, based on plans supplied by the French, was simple: a false control room was constructed at Dimona complete with false control panels and computer-driven measuring devices that seemed to be gauging the thermal output of a twenty-four megawatt reactor (as Israel claimed Dimona to be) in the fake control room."[66] In a concealed area off a false "control room," the Israelis monitored the inspectors and made sure the control panels were functioning at the appropriate level. The Israelis would not allow the Americans into the nuclear core "for safety reasons." According to Abe Feinberg, "It was part of my job to tip them off that Kennedy was insisting on this [an inspection]. So they gave him a scam job."[67]

The CIA told Kennedy that Dimona would probably come on line in late 1963 or early 1964. By April 1964 Feldman and Walworth Barbour had concluded that there was virtually no hope of persuading the Israelis to halt missile development and production, but Kennedy's attempts to put restraints on their nuclear program continued into the final years of the Johnson administration. Calculated "opacity" was the technique the Israelis used to mislead the Americans for as long as possible. In a meeting with Shimon Peres, Komer complained that "the secretive and evasive way" in which Israel responded to U.S. inquiries about missile development and Dimona "inevitably raised suspicions on our part. For the President of the US to have to intervene personally and repeatedly to get the necessary reassurances was frankly counter-productive; it only made us feel that Israel really did have something to hide."[68] The Americans wanted inspections every six months, with sufficient time (a minimum of two days) given to the "visitors" to do their work. A delayed "visit" was finally made on January 30, 1965, but as the American scientists were able to spend only ten hours on site, their findings were inconclusive and did nothing to allay suspicions that the Israelis were secretly developing nuclear weapons.

It was the U.S. president himself who undermined attempts to bind Israel to the IAEA. The State Department was arguing that if Israel wanted U.S. tanks it should be prepared in return to accept international supervision of its nuclear program. The president seemed to go along with this.

"Given the strengthening of Israeli security by the actions we contemplate, we wish a firm reiteration of Israel's intentions not to develop nuclear weapons and that Israel certify this by accepting IAEA safeguards on all of its nuclear facilities." However, "so long as we receive the pledge . . . I do not insist on acceptance of IAEA controls now."[69] So there was nothing Israel had to do but say it would not develop nuclear weapons, which it did in language of such ambiguity that its commitment could not be regarded as a commitment at all. Yet the State Department kept trying. When Harriman went to Tel Aviv in March, Rusk instructed him to emphasize that "the United States cannot support any flirtation with nuclear weapons. On nuclear matters the United States is as old as Methusaleh and utterly cold-blooded in terms of US vital interests. We shall resist with every resource at our command the dissemination of nuclear weapons into the Near East. We shall try to find ways to bring the UAR into IAEA safeguards but there should be no misunderstanding between us and Israel as to our view of Israeli acquisition of such weapons."[70]

In discussions with Harriman, Eshkol repeated previous assurances that Israel was not "flirting with nuclear weapons" while allowing ambiguity to hang in the air by adding the rider that the Israelis "are not willing to commit themselves irrevocably at least until they know Egyptian intentions."[71] The red herring of what Egypt might do—perhaps by building a radiological "garbage bomb"—was dragged across the trail to take attention away from what Israel was actually doing.[72]

MOVING TO PRODUCTION

By this time (early March 1965) the director of the State Department's Office of Near Eastern Affairs (Rodger P. Davies) had reached the conclusion that Israel was developing nuclear weapons. He reported that the science attaché at the embassy in Tel Aviv "has calculated that the target date for acquisition of a nuclear weapons capability by Israel is 1968–9. He has discovered information that Israel has already acquired the know-how for Plutonium metal production. There is no need for sizeable domestic ore production facilities since Argentina has been a ready source."[73] The attaché believed that parts of the Dimona facility had been "purposely mothballed" to mislead American scientists during their recent visit. He and other embassy staff had concluded that Israeli scientists were preparing "all necessary elements for production of a nuclear device, leaving undone only last-minute assembly." Building the weapons without moving the rest of the way toward producing them gave Israel a "flexible basis of choice."[74]

Barbour professed not to be convinced that Israel was developing nuclear weapons and argued against putting pressure on Eshkol for further inspections because of the political problems the issue was already causing him.[75]

A memorandum of understanding signed on March 11 in the context of arms sales set out the formula Israel was to repeat thereafter on the question of nuclear development. "The Government of Israel has reaffirmed that Israel will not be the first to introduce nuclear weapons into the Arab-Israel area."[76] In a memorandum on May 10, Rusk reminded Johnson that Eshkol had subsequently added the qualification that Israel "could not forever foreswear nuclear weapon development" in the absence of binding security guarantees that President Kennedy had decided could not and should not be given. Rusk was clearly disturbed by "the Israeli strategy," telling the president that from the way the United States had been deliberately misled over Dimona "we must assume Israel intends to make its decisions on whether to produce nuclear weapons without consulting us. Lower level Israeli officials speak frankly about Israel's strategy towards the United Arab Republic a) surface-to-surface missiles targeted on the Nile delta and b) a capability to bomb and release the waters behind the Aswan High Dam. Destruction of the Aswan Dam would require a nuclear warhead; bombing with high explosives could not be counted on to do the job. The world recognizes Israel's nuclear capability and the fact that we have compelling leverage on Israel because of our special relationships [sic]. *So long as the Dimona reactor operates without publicly recognized safeguards, the credibility of our worldwide efforts to prevent proliferation is in doubt.*" Dimona was jeopardizing the credibility of the United States on nonproliferation issues. Israel had accepted IAEA safeguards on its smaller reactor and should be expected to accept their application to all its nuclear facilities. "There is great urgency about this matter in view of the disturbing signals we have been getting from Israel. I think, therefore, that this is something we must come to grips with promptly."[77]

In a letter to Eshkol on May 21, Johnson followed through by again asking Israel to place Dimona under IAEA safeguards. Israel could rest secure in the knowledge of its military superiority over the Arabs and "the steadfast assurances of US support against aggression"; the voluntary acceptance of IAEA controls would remove the threat of nuclear war from the Middle East, would encourage others to adopt the same controls, and would ease regional tensions.[78] However, because Eshkol had parliamentary elections coming up in November, Johnson agreed to a postponement of the regular six-monthly "visit" to Dimona due at the end of July. Finally admitted to Israeli nuclear sites between March 31 and April 4 the following year, a three-man team of U.S. nuclear experts gave Israel a clean bill of health.

They found no evidence of production or the intention to produce nuclear weapons material; there was a possibility that they had been deliberately deceived, "but members of the team believe that this is unlikely."[79] This would seem to contradict Avner Cohen's judgment that while the Israelis made sure that the Americans saw no more than was absolutely necessary during their visits, "to suggest that they were fooled into thinking that Dimona was only a peaceful facility would be inaccurate."[80]

On February 23, 1967, Rusk speculated that Israel "could be much closer to nuclear weapons capability than we had supposed."[81] Inside the State Department, intelligence reports were concluding that Israel might be able to assemble a nuclear weapon in six to eight weeks. The attempt was again made to tie economic and military aid to an unequivocal assurance by Israel that it would not develop nuclear weapons and would open up its plants to IAEA inspections. In April, Rostow advised Johnson to delay the current aid package as a means of putting pressure on Israel to sign the NPT (which opened for signature on July 1, 1968):

> By purely foreign policy standards we should be drawing back a little now to signal how seriously we take this issue. I realize this creates a domestic dilemma but I should think the Jewish community itself with its liberal tendencies would be strongly attracted to the NPT. Israel has never leveled with us on its nuclear intent. Our intelligence people have scattered—but as yet unconfirmed—evidence that Israel is quietly but steadily placing itself in a position to produce nuclear weapons on short notice. We also know that Israel is investing large sums in a French built surface-to-surface missile designed to carry a nuclear warhead. I must emphasize that we *do not know* exactly what Israel is doing or what its position on the NPT will be. But we know enough to be seriously concerned.[82]

On May 1, Undersecretary of State Katzenbach told Johnson that Dimona was producing enough plutonium to produce two bombs a year while on the Arab side "no state is anywhere near a nuclear weapons capability." "We [are] disappointed not only in the lack of progress of our arms discussions with the Israelis but in the lack of Israeli candor that has characterized them," wrote Katzenbach. "There is a large area of Israeli activity and planning that is a closed book to us. During the coming year we would like to see arms control results linked more directly to Israel's requests for military and economic aid."[83]

"DON'T BOTHER ME"

Attempts to write Israeli adherence to the NPT into contracts for the supply of weapons (this time Phantom aircraft) continued throughout 1968.

In July George Ball saw Eshkol in Tel Aviv and raised the question of Israel's "delay" in signing the NPT. "All other states in area had signed and GOI's intransigence called into question their basic good faith." The Israeli position was unacceptable. Eshkol made the ritual reference to Israel not being the first to introduce nuclear weapons into the region, but his confusion on the subject left the impression that "his government had been caught with fingers in the cookie jar."[84]

By this time Johnson had called off the bombing of North Vietnam and announced that he would neither seek nor accept nomination for reelection. The supply of planes to Israel now became an election issue. The Republican candidate, Richard Nixon, committed himself to providing them in September. Under section 651 of the Aid Authorization Act, the House of Representatives had urged the administration to provide Israel with supersonic aircraft necessary to offset its losses in the 1967 war (such as they were) and simultaneously to match arms provided to Arab states and prevent "future Arab aggression."[85] There was no doubt Israel would get the Phantoms, but again the occasion created the opportunity to compel Israel to renounce the development of nuclear weapons.

On October 14, Harold Saunders wrote that he believed that both the State and Defense Departments would recommend that the sale be made conditional on Israel's agreement to sign and ratify the NPT, reaffirming assurances already given that it would not be the first to introduce nuclear weapons into the Middle East and that it would go no further in the development of surface-to-surface missiles.[86] Only a week later, however, Johnson told Eban that he would not make adherence to the NPT a formal condition of sale.[87] The knowledge that the president was behind them gave Israeli officials all the confidence they needed to fob off the most senior figures in the administration. When Rusk voiced the suspicion on October 22 that Israel was developing nuclear weapons and missiles "for use with nuclear weapons" and not just high explosives, Eban said he was exaggerating. Israel was far from being in a situation to have operative missiles ready for deployment and would not be the first to introduce nuclear weapons into the region; he even asserted that Israel had not made a decision to become a nuclear power.[88] It was a lie. In the coming weeks Johnson continued to take Israel's side, telling Rusk that he remained "strongly opposed to twisting arms on the nuclear thing in connection with Phantoms. Doesn't want them linked."[89]

On November 2, Undersecretary of Defense Paul Warnke recommended that the United States attach four conditions to the sale of Phantoms. In a meeting with the Israeli ambassador (Yitzhak Rabin) two days later, he explained what they were and why the United States wanted them in the arms contract. The United States was about to become Israel's principal arms supplier, "involving us even more intimately with Israel's security situation and involving more directly the security of the United States."[90] The standard contract for the supply of weapons to other governments permitted the cancellation of deliveries "under unusual and compelling circumstances," which in his view would be created by Israel's acquisition of strategic missiles and nuclear weapons. Therefore the United States needed assurances that Israel would not test or deploy strategic missiles, would not develop or manufacture, or otherwise acquire, strategic missiles or nuclear weapons, and would sign and ratify the NPT.[91] The United States had not sought these assurances before because the development of nuclear weapons did not seem imminent, but present indications indicated that Israel was "on the verge of nuclear weapons and missile capability," a development that would dramatically change the situation in the Middle East and adversely affect the security interests of the United States through the risk of a confrontation with the USSR.

Rabin did not dispute Warnke's assertions at the time,[92] but he came back fighting the next day. "I don't believe Israel is going to accept conditions within a Memorandum of Understanding about selling the Phantoms. We were told more than once that there would be no conditions—at least not these kind of conditions."[93] In a discussion on the evening of November 8, Rabin asked Warnke whether he had changed his mind; when Warnke replied "in the negative," the ambassador began reading from a prepared paper, in which Article 3 in the proposed Memorandum of Understanding on the conditions of sale—Israel's adherence to the NPT—was identified as the most offensive in the eyes of the Israeli government: "We have come here for the purpose of purchasing 50 Phantoms. We have not come here in order to mortgage the sovereignty of the State of Israel, not even for 50 Phantoms. Furthermore, I wish to state that we consider Article 3 to be in the nature of a very major condition precedent to the sale of aircraft and it is therefore not acceptable to us also as a matter of principle."[94]

As for inspections of Dimona, "The word 'visit' means you are a guest in our country—not an inspector," and in any case, "You are only selling arms. How do you feel you have the right to ask all these things?"[95] Warnke was being treated like a door-to-door salesman who won't take no for an answer. In a memorandum prepared later for the record, Rabin was described as having "flatly and rather brutally" refused to give the assurances sought by the United States.[96]

The key to understanding why Rabin felt able to speak to Warnke in such a peremptory manner on November 8 lies in a working lunch given by Johnson at the White House on November 7. The guests were Rusk, Clifford, Rostow, CIA director Richard Helms, and Generals Maxwell Taylor and Earle Wheeler. Clifford and Rusk argued strongly for conditions to be attached to the sale of Phantoms, only to be told by Johnson that "he had promised the F-4s without any conditions and that was his position."[97] Warnke returned from Germany at 5:00 P.M. on November 8 "and was told of the President's position just before the Israelis arrived." When Rabin and his team walked into Warnke's office just after 6:00 P.M., "it was abundantly clear that they had been told of the President's position and of his instructions to the Secretaries of Defense and State."[98] According to Seymour Hersh, Johnson told Clark Clifford in a phone conversation to sell the Israelis "everything they want"; when Clifford asked about nuclear weapons, the president replied, "Don't bother me with this any more" before hanging up.[99]

On the morning of November 9, Warnke and Rabin met again. The session is said to have gone well, but the nuclear question continued to hover over the negotiations. The point at which a nuclear weapon could properly be described as a weapon formed the substance of discussions with Rabin and the commander of the Israeli air force (General Mordechai Hod) on November 12. Warnke, still concerned with the "unusual and compelling circumstances" that might require the United States to cancel an arms contract, observed that

> he could not find in the record any understanding of what Israel meant by the provision "Israel will not be the first to introduce nuclear weapons into the area." Mr. Warnke asked the Ambassador what was meant by this term. Ambassador Rabin said that "it means what we have said, namely, that we would not be the first to introduce nuclear weapons." Mr. Warnke asked what specifically was meant by the word "introduce." Ambassador Rabin said "you are more familiar with these things than we are. What is your definition of nuclear weapons?" Mr. Warnke said there are two aspects to the question: the definition of what is and what is not a nuclear weapon, and what is and what is not introduction into the area. Regarding the first of these, if there are components available that could be assembled to make a nuclear weapon—although part A may be in one room and part B in another room—then that is a nuclear weapon. As for introduction that is your term and you will have to define it. Does it mean no physical presence? Ambassador Rabin said "I suppose so."[100]

General Hod argued that a weapon could be described as "introduced" only after it had been tested. Rabin agreed. Later in the discussion, Warnke took up this point again: "Then in your view an unadvertised, untested nuclear device is not a nuclear weapon." Ambassador Rabin said: "Yes, that is correct." Warnke asked: "What about an advertised but untested nuclear device or weapon. Would that be introduction?" Ambassador Rabin said: "Yes, that would be introduction." Warnke said he would interpret mere physical presence in the area as constituting, in itself, "introduction."[101]

Warnke could make no further headway in his attempt to draw the Israelis out, but with Johnson taking such a strong stand against the imposition of conditions there was no point in pursuing the subject anyway. The United States agreed to sell Israel fifty Phantoms in return for assurances that it would not be the first power in the Middle East to introduce nuclear weapons and that it would not use "any aircraft supplied by the United States" as a nuclear weapons carrier. Warnke stressed the U.S. view that the physical possession and control of nuclear arms would constitute their "introduction," tying this to the "unusual and compelling circumstances" that might arise from inconsistencies that might (by implication) compel the United States to cancel the supply of weapons. There was no mention of Israel's adherence to the NPT in the present or the future.[102]

What many suspected or believed or had concluded but could not confirm was that Israel already had nuclear weapons. In early 1967, the CIA reported that Israel had all the components necessary to assemble a nuclear weapon.[103] By June it had established an "operational nuclear weapons capability," according to Avner Cohen.[104] "Almost all the components of an Israeli nuclear weapon were in place" before Israel went to war against Egypt and Syria. They were quickly assembled so that that by the time the fighting started Israel had two "improvised" nuclear bombs that were ready for delivery.[105]

The question arises as to when Johnson had proof positive that Israel had developed nuclear weapons. In 1978 Carl Duckett, the CIA's deputy director for science and technology a decade earlier, gave evidence before the Nuclear Regulatory Commission that he had taken a National Intelligence Estimate concluding that Israel had nuclear weapons to CIA director Richard Helms and had been instructed by him not to publish it. In an official editorial note prepared for the record, Helms was quoted as telling Duckett that he had taken the matter up with Johnson and had been told by him: "Don't tell anyone else, even Dean Rusk and Robert MacNamara."[106] No date is given for this conversation. MacNamara resigned as defense secretary on November 29, 1967, and left government service on February 29, 1968, to take up his new position as president of the World Bank. According to Seymour Hersh, the CIA informed the president around the time of Eshkol's visit to Washington in January 1968 that Israel had manufactured at least four nuclear weapons. The president ordered Helms to bury the report.[107] So much for the administration's unbending opposition—as "old as Methusaleh" and "utterly cold-blooded," as Rusk had described it—to the introduction of nuclear weapons into the Middle East.

In the coming years Israel acquired krytrons (nuclear triggers) and supercomputers, enabling it to simulate the testing of nuclear weapons, from the United States.[108] The acquisition of other nuclear material involved deceit, theft, and skullduggery on the high seas, yet in the eyes of those who defend Israel's acquisition of nuclear weapons, Ben-Gurion and the prime ministers who followed him would have been less than responsible if they had not proceeded with the development of one of the ultimate weapons of war. "Never again" was the core of the argument. With nuclear weapons "there will be no more Auschwitzes."[109] Now that Israel had these weapons, it was only a question of time before other states in the region sought to develop their nuclear deterrent to Israel's nuclear deterrent, but when Israel's generals decided to attack Egypt and Syria in June 1967 they did so in the certain knowledge that only one state had them.

10. LBJ'S OTHER WAR

In the years leading up to the war of 1967, the Israelis frequently threatened to launch preemptive strikes against Arab targets.[1] Israel was already engaging in disproportionate "reprisals" on all fronts, but *preemptive strike* implied the start of something much bigger. In his memoirs, the Palmach commander Yigal Allon argues that a "pre-emptive offensive" is justified when it is known for certain (through the concentration of an enemy's military forces) that an invasion is imminent. The mere possession of armaments is not sufficient to deter an enemy; it is the knowledge that a state is prepared to use them "that might prevent their having to be used at all."[2] In practice, the preemptive strike has had more to do with propaganda than military strategy. Over the years Israel has been frequently urged not to take preemptive action when it was clear there was nothing to preempt.

The most likely targets of Israeli "preemptive" action were the "radical" Arab nationalist regimes governing Egypt and Syria. When Fatah guerrillas based in Syria launched raids across the armistice line after the Israelis shot down six Syrian aircraft in April 1967, the Israeli media ran stories of plans being made for military action "going further than any previous reprisal raid." On May 12, a military spokesman talked of responses ranging from guerrilla operations to "the invasion and conquest of Damascus."[3] The following day Eshkol warned that Israel "may have to teach Syria a sharper lesson than that of April 7."[4] Rabin joined in, warning that any Israeli action against Syria "will be far different from the reprisals against Jordan in the past."[5] A "highly placed" source warned of military action aimed at overthrowing the Syrian government "even at the risk of Egyptian intervention."[6] By the middle of May the only question that needed answering was not whether Israel was going to strike but when—"everyone knew it was about to happen."[7] Threat and counterthreat followed each other with the predictability of a ticking clock. The absence of heavy armor from Israel's Independence Day parade in Jerusalem on May 15 (held in violation of the armistice arrangements) seemed evidence to the Arabs that it was being marshaled elsewhere for the coming attack. On May 14 Nasser moved more troops into Sinai; on May 16 he sought a partial withdrawal of the United Nations Emergency Force (UNEF) troops stationed along the armistice line. He had been warned by the Soviet Union that Israel was massing troops near the Syrian border,[8] but his response must also be assessed in the context of the Suez War. Israel had struck without warning in 1956. Why wouldn't he believe it was getting ready to do the same thing again, even if ultimately he didn't think the United States would allow it?

The UN forces constituted no more than a symbolic presence. They had neither the authority nor the means to prevent hostilities. In the aftermath of the Suez War, the General Assembly had authorized the deployment of a peacekeeping force on both sides of the armistice line, but Israel had invoked national sovereignty in refusing to allow UN troops on to its soil. Indeed, the acknowledgment of sovereign right was critical to the UNEF operation. The UN troops were based in Sinai with the consent of the Egyptian government and would have to leave if the Egyptians asked them to go. That had been the understanding from the beginning, and accusations by some governments that the UN secretary-general, U Thant, could have delayed and even prevented the outbreak of war struck him as an unfair attempt to lay the blame for their own neglect on his shoulders. For ten years the presence of the UNEF had "to a considerable extent" allowed UN members to ignore "some of the hard realities underlying the conflict."[9] The cause of the current crisis was not the withdrawal of the UNEF force—not completed until a week after the coming war was over—but the unresolved Arab-Israeli conflict.

Nasser did not initially seek the withdrawal of UNEF forces from the most volatile spots along the armistice line, the Gaza Strip and Sharm al Sheikh, but when the Egyptian request was relayed to New York, the answer came back from U Thant that withdrawal had to be all or nothing. The Egyptian leader, his pride, prestige, and standing across the Arab world on the line, deliberated before requesting the withdrawal of all forces, but he still hesitated before moving Egyptian troops forward to Sharm al Sheikh, and he assured U Thant that Egypt would not take offensive action. His proposals for reactivation of the moribund mixed armistice commissions on the Egyptian and Syrian fronts and for full observance of the General Armistice Agreements were incorporated in a draft Egyptian resolution submitted to the Security Council on May 31. Even the United

States stressed the need to revitalize the armistice machinery.[10] U Thant's suggestion that the UNEF force be moved to the Israeli side of the armistice line was rejected by Israel's government despite American pressure. Eban's response when the subject was raised by Ambassador Barbour was "strongly negative."[11]

"WE WILL LEAVE THEM ALONE"

Nasser's statements have to be divided between what he said for public consumption in Egypt and across the Arab world and the messages he passed along to Britain and the United States in private. He told Egyptian trade unionists that if Israel dared to attack Egypt or Syria "the battle will be a general one . . . and our basic objective will be to destroy Israel," but when Christopher Mayhew, the British MP, asked him on June 2, "If they do not attack will you leave them alone?" he replied: "Yes, we will leave them alone—we have no intention of attacking Israel."[12]

On May 22 Nasser, in a speech to air force officers, announced the closure of the Straits of Tiran to Israeli shipping without following through by actually closing it: as late as May 29, U.S. satellite photographs showed no evidence of the five thousand Egyptian troops who were supposed to be ready to defend Sharm al Sheikh.[13] Nasser was still aggrieved that he had been compelled to open the straits to Israeli ships after the "Tripartite Aggression" of 1956—reward instead of the punishment Israel deserved, as he saw it—but also felt Egypt had a strong case in international law over access to the Gulf of Aqaba. India and some other countries agreed with Egypt that the gulf constituted an "inland sea" and that the Straits of Tiran lay within Egyptian territorial waters. The United States supported Israel's right of access on the grounds that the gulf was an international waterway, but it still called for a peaceful settlement in line with Article 33 of the UN Charter, which requires parties to a dispute to seek a solution through negotiation, arbitration, mediation, conciliation, or "other peaceful means of their own choice."

It was most uncharacteristic of Nasser not to leave a door open behind him, Assistant Secretary of State Lucius Battle wrote after the closure of the straits, yet "that is exactly what he appears to have done in this case."[14] He had risen to the bait of provocations along the armistice line with Syria, and Israel's military commanders had no intention of letting him off the hook. As Patrick Seale has written, they could "barely restrain themselves" and wanted to attack at once. "Their great fear was that a leak might reveal how promising the prospects were and so rob them of a unique chance to smash the Egyptians."[15] The Israel Air Forces had drawn up a plan for a "pre-emptive" attack to wipe out Egyptian air power and Israel Defense Forces (IDF) chief of staff Yitzhak Rabin was "confident that it would work."[16]

By May 23, Egypt had increased the number of troops in Sinai from 30,000 to 50,000, establishing them along two defensive lines. Three days later this number remained the same, but by now Israel had mobilized 55 to 65 percent of its ground forces (160,000 soldiers).[17] The war machine was rolling. Israeli operations chief Ezer Weizman sent armor moving toward the Egyptian border on May 24 for a combined air and land "pre-emptive strike" two days later, but the operation was blocked by Eshkol, apparently after intervention by the U.S. ambassador.[18] On May 30 Eban referred to the decision of the cabinet two days earlier "not to go it alone" while diplomatic moves were under way, but at the same time Israel did not want any discussion at the UN Security Council on the rights of passage through the Straits of Tiran because it would only cloud the issue.[19] The next day a badly rattled King Hussein flew to Cairo and signed Jordan into Arab defense arrangements. Iraq joined several days later, and once four Arab countries (Egypt, Syria, Jordan, and Iraq) were linked in the same pact, the war party in Israel had even more evidence to present to a credulous world that Israel was being encircled by yet another ring of steel. In fact, because of their deep mutual suspicions, political rivalries, and personal dislike, Arab governments had a hopeless record of military coordination, as the Americans and the Israelis well knew. The pact was virtually meaningless outside propaganda directed toward Arab audiences and the slim hope that this show of Arab solidarity might deter Israel. All it did was give Israel's military commanders further opportunity to frighten nervous politicians into accepting the need to go to war without delay.

"TERRITORIAL FULFILLMENT"

On June 1 the generals demanded the formation of a war cabinet and got one. Moshe Dayan was appointed defense minister, and Menachem Begin was brought into the government as minister without portfolio, establishing a cabinet that would launch a war to expand the borders of the state in the process of destroying Arab armies. Yigal Allon noted that a central aim of the offensive would be "the territorial fulfillment of the land of Israel."[20] Begin, who believed that not only the rest of Palestine but "the far and wide land eastward across the Jordan River" belonged to Israel as of right,[21] later admitted that the Israelis knew Egypt was not planning to attack. "The Egyptian army concentration in the Sinai approaches did not prove that

Nasser was really about to attack us. We must be honest with ourselves. We decided to attack him."[22] Rabin said much the same thing when remarking in 1968 that he had not thought Nasser wanted war. "The two divisions he sent to Sinai on May 14 would not have been sufficient to launch an offensive against Israel. He knew it and we knew it."[23] Most of the further five divisions sent to Sinai "to lend credibility to Nasser's bluff" were held in reserve one hundred miles back from the armistice line.[24]

From the closure of the Straits of Tiran onwards, Israel's generals worked on Eshkol and his cabinet colleagues to get the war they wanted. "If you do not give the order to go to war, Jewish history will never forgive you," Weizman told Eshkol.[25] Land and air commanders assured him that if Israel took the initiative and attacked right away it would crush the Arabs. Ariel Sharon, the commander of the northern (Syrian) front and the principal architect of provocations along the armistice line, was confident that "we have the power to destroy the Egyptian army."[26] Uzi Narkiss, the commander of the central (Jordanian) front, still regretting that Israel had missed the opportunity to seize the West Bank and the rest of Jerusalem in 1948, scoffed at the notion that Arab armies were a threat. "They're soap bubbles—one pin will burst them."[27] Yitzhak Rabin talked of giving Nasser a "knockout punch" and changing the entire order of the Middle East.[28] Moshe Dayan counseled restraint on both the Syrian and Jordan fronts but only because he wanted to get Egypt out of the way first. "Bite your lip and hold the line," Narkiss was told. "Within a week we'll get to the Canal and to Sharm el Sheikh, then the whole IDF will come here and get you out of trouble."[29] In Yigal Allon's view, expressed on June 2, "There is not the slightest doubt about the outcome of this war and of each of its stages, and we are not forgetting the Jordanian and Syrian fronts either."[30] The pressure worked. On June 3 the CIA concluded that Eshkol had "suffered a setback and must adapt his policy to the views of the tough-minded military whom Dayan represents." Israeli popular support for his appointment— "Go, go Moshe"—indicated a mood in favor of action.[31]

As all these statements show, while Israel's diplomatic representatives abroad were talking of another Holocaust in the making, as part of what Seale has described as "one of the most extensive and remarkable exercises in psychological warfare ever attempted,"[32] directed as much against the Israeli public as the outside world, Israel's generals wanted war and were confident of victory. None of them made any suggestion that Israel should seek a peaceful end to the crisis. By the beginning of June its armed forces were "wound up like a mighty spring," with 275,000 men, 1,100 tanks, and two hundred planes in position to attack.[33] The generals and now the government knew that the pieces of a diplomatic settlement were slowly sliding into place, but they did nothing to allay the fears of their own people and indeed did everything to heighten them. Once the decision to go to war had been taken, the greatest fear was that the crisis would be resolved diplomatically before the spring could be uncoiled.

MIDDLE EAST "DOMINOES"

After Suez, Israel had decided never to go to war again without the approval of its current great power backer. Now that an Israeli government was ready to go to war again, it had to secure American approval first. It began its campaign by painting a picture of an Israel standing on the brink of imminent destruction. In Washington, Eban warned on May 26 that Israel's "very existence" was threatened by an imminent Egyptian-Syrian attack.[34] Ambassador Avraham Harman talked of another Munich and genocide, referring to the "farce" being played out at the Security Council.[35] In a letter to Johnson, Eshkol spoke of Nasser's "proclaimed intention to strike at Israel at the first opportunity with a view to bringing about her destruction."[36] But Nasser, "more inclined to reaction than action" by nature,[37] had never threatened to attack "at the first opportunity" or even to attack at all, only to respond with full force if the Israelis went to war again. The Israelis claimed that Nasser had "crossed his Rubicon."[38] In fact, they had crossed theirs and they were the ones who were about to launch a surprise attack.

Israeli intelligence chief Meir Amit played on the Soviet aspect of the crisis, telling U.S. Defense Secretary Robert McNamara that the closure of the Straits of Tiran was mere window dressing for a "grand design" according to which Egypt—backed by the Soviet Union—"hopes to roll up the whole of the Middle East all the way to the borders of Russia to include Iran under Arab domination."[39] The pieces would fall like dominoes, a metaphor calculated to appeal to McNamara at a time when other dominoes seemed to be falling in Southeast Asia. On June 2, Evron repeated an earlier cabinet commitment to "hold steady"—not to go to war—for about two weeks, which meant that "things might happen in the week after next," beginning on June 11.[40] Later that day Evron and Harman saw Rusk and other officials to ask whether the United States was prepared to force Nasser's hand by sending an international armada (including an Israeli warship) through the Straits of Tiran. At this meeting Rusk disclosed that Egyptian Vice President Zakaria Muhi al Din would be arriving in Washington in a few days for talks on a negotiated settlement;[41] since the

Israelis were bent on war if the United States was not prepared to take the lead in forcing the Straits of Tiran, telling them a few days in advance of the Egyptian vice president's visit was as good as a signal to preempt his visit with a "preemptive" war.

Even the Americans refuted Israeli claims that Nasser had actually gone ahead and blocked the straits. According to their information, at least two ships bound for Eilat had passed through them by June 1.[42] The Egyptian leader continued to send signals to Washington that he was looking for a negotiated settlement. Anthony Nutting, who had known Nasser since 1954, concluded in his account of the crisis: "Certainly Nasser could not have made it clearer that he wanted a settlement and that he preferred not to enforce the right of blockade before there had been a chance to sort things out."[43] In a two-hour meeting with Robert Anderson, the former secretary of the treasury, whom Johnson had sent to the Middle East as his special envoy, Nasser amplified his position. He had moved troops into Sinai because of the reports of Israeli mobilization, and "he did not want repetition of the 1956 affair when he was reluctant to believe that an attack had begun and was slow in moving troops to Sinai, only to be caught between the Israelis in the north and the British at Port Said." He would not start a war "but would wait until the Israelis had moved." If Israel attacked Syria or Jordan, he would have no choice but to go to their defense. Asked whether he was prepared to accept Israel as a matter of fact, he replied that he did not believe a stable and lasting peace could be established "without disposing of the refugee problem."[44]

On June 4 the U.S. administration's Middle East Control Group met to review the latest developments, in particular the pending arrival of the Egyptian vice president. Decisions were taken to send a memorandum to Johnson to prepare him for his talks with the Egyptians, to revise a draft letter by Rusk to Nasser, and to withhold a planned letter to Soviet Premier Alexei Kosygin until the talks with the Egyptians were over. The delegation from Cairo was due to fly in on the evening of June 7, and talks would begin the following day. The Americans knew they had to act quickly if the Israeli "tiger" was to be held back, but at 2:50 A.M. the following day reports reached Washington that hostilities had begun. Rusk's draft letter to Nasser, which he had decided to revise, adding certain "Levantine touches," was found in a file with a note appended. "Sec was changing this when time ran out."[45] The Israeli tiger was off and running.

The outbreak of war immediately raised the issue of U.S. commitments made in the Tripartite Declaration of 1950 (United States, France, and Britain) and in the reiteration by Eisenhower and Kennedy that the United

States would not accept changes to Middle Eastern borders by force. The draft of a letter to be sent to Eshkol by the president in late May specifically stated that the American commitment to stop aggression in the Middle East "definitely includes Israel. I can assure you that it remains firm so far as we are concerned." But these sentences were deleted by Johnson himself before the letter went to Tel Aviv.[46] King Hussein told the U.S. ambassador to Jordan that he had been assured on "countless occasions" that the United States would not permit the Israelis to alter the status quo by force and that if he needed protection he would get it from the Sixth Fleet.[47] But even when it knew who had launched the war, the United States did not invoke the 1950 declaration.

"DEFENSIVE" DEPLOYMENT

By and large the Americans chose to accept the Israeli view that the crisis had arisen as the result of "persistent raids by Palestinian terrorists" into Israel and not the Arab view that infiltration was "only symptomatic of the underlying situation," as King Hussein told the U.S. ambassador, and that in reality Israel was looking for an opportunity to change the status quo in favor of its own long-standing strategic, territorial, and religious ambitions.[48] But by and large the U.S. administration did *not* believe Israeli claims that the state was in danger of attack—let alone destruction. On May 23, the CIA concluded that Israeli ground forces "can maintain internal security, defend successfully against simultaneous Arab attacks on all fronts, launch limited attacks simultaneously on all fronts or hold on any three fronts while mounting successfully a major offensive on the fourth." Air superiority was less clear, but as long as Israel's air facilities were not damaged beyond repair the IAF would probably outfight the Egyptians. Israel had more "operationally assigned fighter aircraft" than Egypt, 256 to 222, and would have more than double the number of Arab troops deployed near the borders if war broke out (280,000 to 117,000). As the Arab states had a total troop strength of 500,000, a long war would slowly tip the balance in their favor. Nevertheless, "We conclude that the Israeli forces have retained an overall superiority."[49]

On May 25 the CIA sent Johnson an appraisal of an Israeli document, "Israeli Estimate of the Israeli-Arab Crisis." The document itself is not published in the official U.S. record, but in an attached note Rostow remarked that the CIA appraisal "throws a great deal of cold water on the Israeli estimate." The CIA did not believe that the Israeli document was a serious estimate "of the sort they would submit to their own high officials.

We think it is probably a gambit intended to influence the US to do one or more of the following (a) provide military supplies (b) make more public commitments to Israel (c) approve Israeli military initiatives and (d) put more pressure on Nasser." The CIA did not agree with the Israelis on the number of Egyptian forces deployed in Sinai, it had no information on the formation of a Second Army Group, it did not know of any Egyptian vessels that had left the Red Sea and entered the Mediterranean, and it did not believe that "the Arabs intend an all-out attack on Israel." Indeed, Egypt's military dispositions in Sinai "are defensive in nature":

> We believe that the UAR is acting in this crisis essentially to put pressure on Israel short of an attack on Israeli soil. Whereas the UAR armed forces have improved in capability in the past decade Nasser still probably estimates that he does not have—even with the support of the other Arabs—the capability to destroy Israel by a military attack. . . . The steps taken thus far by Arab armies do not prove that the Arabs intend an all-out attack on Israel. . . . There have been no coordinating maneuvers by the various Arab states and it would be difficult if not impossible for the various Arab units cited in paragraph 3 of the Israeli estimate to be used in concert. In sum, we feel these are merely gestures which the Arab states feel compelled to make in the interests of the fiction of Arab unity but have little military utility in conflict with Israel.[50]

Rusk repeated the gist of these findings to Eban and Harman the same day. The president wanted Eban to know, Rusk said, that he did not have the authority to give an assurance that "an attack on you is an attack on us" without full congressional backing and had emphasized that "preemptive action" by Israel would cause extreme difficulty for the United States because of the question of who was responsible for starting a war.[51]

"YOU WILL WHIP THEM"

On May 26, military attachés at the embassy at Tel Aviv reported that "Israel is approaching a decision in favor of a preemptive attack."[52] As Israel was at no risk of attack by Egypt or Syria, and the United States knew it, an attack by Israel obviously could not be preemptive, but this was the phrase Johnson and all senior administration figures continued to use. In summing up the situation at a critical meeting with the president in the early afternoon, General Wheeler, chairman of the Joint Chiefs of Staff, said there were no indications that the Egyptians would attack. Trying to absorb all the advice he was getting, Johnson was looking for firm recommendations because "about sundown I have to bell this cat. I need to know what I am going to say." He asked whether Britain had sufficient interests at stake to "stand up with us like men" and join the United States in forcing the straits. Wheeler mentioned oil and said Britain "could not tolerate Nasser as the dominant force in the Middle East." Justice Abe Fortas argued that Eban should be told that the United States would use whatever force was necessary to ensure the passage of an Israeli flagship through the Straits of Tiran, to which Johnson replied that "he did not believe he was in a position now to say that." In Rusk's view, "If Israel strikes first, it will have to forget the US."[53]

In a special report the same day, the Watch Committee reiterated earlier intelligence conclusions when stating that "we do not believe the Israeli claim that Egypt is preparing to launch an attack against Israel."[54] In a separate memorandum the CIA concluded that Israel would establish air superiority over Sinai within twenty-four hours if it attacked first and within two or three days if it were attacked; despite a quantitative disadvantage, it reiterated that the IDF maintained qualitative superiority over Arab armed forces "in almost all aspects of combat operations." The Arabs were hampered by friction between their leaders, and the United Arab Command, "even at the present state of alert, is ineffective either as a command or a coordinating structure."[55] Johnson told Eban that his government believed no attack was imminent but that if Israel were attacked by the Arabs, "our judgment is that the Israelis would lick them," or, as he put it later in the same meeting, "you will whip hell out of them."[56] Presumably if Israel attacked first it would whip even greater hell out of them.

What comes through with great clarity from all the documents is that while Nasser was seeking to avoid open hostilities the Israelis could hardly be held back. They were not interested in a negotiated settlement. They made demands that the U.S. administration could not meet because of constitutional barriers and then used its inability to force Nasser's hand within a time limit they imposed as further justification for launching a "preemptive" strike. Brick by brick, they built up their case for a war the Americans knew Nasser did not want. The constantly reiterated conclusions of intelligence and military specialists that Israel was in no danger and would need no American help in dealing with the Arabs probably only strengthened the feeling in Washington that the leash should be slipped so that the Israelis could do the job Harold Saunders and others felt they should have been allowed to do in the first place. Rusk continued to regard the question of responsibility for initiating hostilities as "a major problem for us," but others were bullish in their support for Israel. General Wheeler felt the United States should back Israel with "all the support it needs for long-term military operations. If we are convinced that the Israelis can hold the Arabs then we should back them down the line, and rely on Arab inefficiency and lack of homogeneity to weaken the Arab cause."[57]

SLIPPING THE LEASH

In the last two weeks of May Johnson was like a man putting the last pieces of a puzzle together. He needed to know whether the United States had the capacity to handle two crises—Vietnam and the Middle East—simultaneously, and his advisers assured him that it could. The only real danger for the United States was not that Israel might be defeated—no one in the American or British intelligence services believed that it could be—but that a regional crisis would somehow be amplified into a Great Powers standoff. If the United States intervened, could the USSR avoid coming in as well? Johnson asked. General Wheeler thought the USSR might "just cut its losses and back out." Helms felt the Soviet Union would relish a propaganda victory as a peacemaker and savior of the Arabs but was not ready to rush in on their behalf. Asked whether Nasser was looking for someone to hold him back, Eugene Rostow, undersecretary of state for political affairs, replied that "he was looking for someone to hold the Israelis back."[58]

In the early evening of May 26, Johnson, McNamara, the two Rostows, White House press secretary George Christian, and Assistant Secretary of State Joseph Sisco met Eban, Harman, and Israeli embassy minister Ephraim Evron. Johnson defended the United States against Israeli insinuations that it was retreating, backing off, or forgetting the commitments it had made in public. He realized that a dangerous situation had been reached, but Eban should tell his cabinet about "our problems": "We have constitutional processes which are basic to any action the US takes in this matter. The Secretary-General has not yet reported to the Security Council and the Council has not yet shown what it can or cannot do. You can assure the Cabinet, the President said, we will pursue vigorously any and all possible measures to keep the Strait open."[59]

Then Johnson did what he had said earlier in the day he had to do before sundown. He belled the cat: "At the same time Israel must not make itself responsible for initiating hostilities. With emphasis and solemnity the President repeated twice, Israel will not be alone unless it decides to go it alone."[60] Johnson repeated the importance of the constitutional process to questions of war and peace, stressing again that "while this process was going on, Israel should not make itself the guilty party by starting a war and that it was inconceivable the Cabinet would take such a fateful decision."

The point was made again in a message to Eshkol on May 27,[61] and the enigmatic phrase "Israel will not be alone unless it decides to go it alone" was repeated as late as June 3.

When the Israelis finally launched the war that the Americans and others had long anticipated at 7:10 A.M. on June 5, the diplomatic processes still had a long way to run. The UN secretary-general still had to report to the Security Council. The Egyptian vice president was due to arrive in Washington two days later, and Johnson was preparing to send "a very senior representative of the President" (Vice President Hubert Humphrey) to Cairo in return.[62] All the signs were positive. Negotiations were going to begin whether the Israelis liked it or not, blocking the last few steps to war. The Israelis had already been talked out of attacking once before. If the moment was not to be lost, it was either strike now or not at all.

GOING IT ALONE?

Since the late 1940s Johnson had strongly identified himself with Israeli interests. He had engineered a fundamental shift in U.S.-Israeli relations in the early years of his presidency, and in the crisis of 1967 he was faced with the greatest test of his "friendship." He knew there was unlikely to be a war unless Israel attacked. Constitutional and congressional problems prevented him from exposing U.S. forces to conflict with the Arab states on Israel's behalf, but from all the advice he was getting he knew that Israel could defeat any combination of Arab states without anyone's help. All along, by warning Israel not to attack and simultaneously appearing to push forward the diplomatic process, he gave the impression of doing his best to stop the outbreak of hostilities. Then toward the end of May came the oracular injunction "You will not be alone unless you decide to go it alone," in which the president effectively surrendered his own power to stop war in favor of giving Israel the liberty to start one.

The phrase was not likely or probably even intended to deter Israel from going on the attack. Its forces were mobilized. It was interested, not in a negotiated settlement, but in a settlement through confrontation. It did not need help. It was ready and willing to "go it alone" and in fact could hardly wait. William Quandt has interpreted the Johnson statement as the president's way of making clear to the Israelis "that he could not do much to help if they got into trouble,"[63] but since their getting into trouble was most unlikely the phrase might be read more accurately as the president's oblique way of telling them that they were finally free to move.

Quandt also contends that while Johnson did not quite give the Israelis a "green light" he removed the veto on their actions. This surely comes very close to saying the same thing. Richard Parker takes the view that while there was no green light, American opposition to an Israeli attack "was not as unequivocal as it could have been."[64] Others talk of the ambiguity, ambivalence, and lethargy of the U.S. effort to maintain the peace. The claim that the "serious effort" made by the United States to restrain all parties failed "because the Arabs were not really interested in restraint" does not stand up at all in the face of documentary evidence of the Arab desire to end the crisis through negotiations.[65] Johnson's statement to Eban was one of tacit encouragement rather than deterrence, of tacit consent and therefore tacit complicity. A president who had done his best throughout his political career to give the Israelis what they wanted was now capping these efforts by giving them a war that they wanted.

Johnson's part in the "serious effort" by the United States to prevent war also has to be assessed on the basis of what he could have done. He could have followed Eisenhower's example and threatened Israel with economic and political sanctions if it dared to go to war before all the diplomatic processes had been exhausted. He could have threatened to remove the tax-free status of "philanthropic" donations. He could have blocked Export-Import bank loans and the supply of arms. The crisis involved U.S. national security, so these were all valid means an American president could have used to prevent war, but Johnson resorted to none of them. At no stage did he involve the power and authority of the world's most powerful country against a government dependent on U.S. aid and presenting a case for war based on obvious untruths and exaggerations. On the contrary, when the Israelis first threatened to strike on May 24, he effectively bought them off by agreeing to supply more war material over the coming two years. Armored cars, tank spare parts, $14 million in military credits at low interest, $27.5 million in food aid at even lower interest rate (2.5 percent compared to 5 percent), $20 million in Export-Bank loans, and the provision of facilities for Hawk missile maintenance were all included in a $75.2 million aid package.[66] On June 1, Harman put in a bid for more weaponry: 100 missiles "to be flown to Israel immediately," 140 M-60 tanks, and 24 A4E Skyhawks "for immediate delivery," along with ground equipment, armaments, and operating parts for five thousand hours of flying time.[67] At least on this occasion the administration dragged its feet: Rusk was advised by Defense that neither the Hawk missiles nor the planes were available and that the tank production line was tight but "we are studying availabilities."[68]

War was just around the corner. Warnings were coming from numerous quarters that the Israelis were about to strike one way or another. On June 2 Rostow passed on to Johnson an Israeli scenario in which the straits would be forced by an Israeli ship, provoking an Egyptian response that Israel would meet by attacking Egyptian installations at Sharm al Sheikh. "The next move would be Nasser's. The Israelis believed he would attack Israel on a wide front and probably other Arab nations would join in the attack."[69] Ambassador Harman was insisting that the right of passage through the straits must be tested in a week.[70] On the same day Johnson received a message from Robert Anderson in Cairo that Nasser "actually seemed quite eager for a negotiated settlement."[71] In a direct message to Johnson, welcoming the planned visit of Vice President Humphrey, Nasser emphasized the importance of returning to the origins of the crisis, "namely the rights of the Palestinians to return to their homeland and the responsibility of the international community in securing them the exercise of this right."[72] Yet Johnson still did nothing to warn the Israelis off. He and Rusk later argued that they thought they had more time to find a peaceful solution, when weeks had already passed without Johnson taking the firm action that might have averted war.

Once the shooting started, and it was clear that Israel was on top of the situation, there was no shock or outrage from on high in the administration. On the contrary, there was unrestrained glee in some quarters—"Gentleman, do not forget that we are neutral in word, thought and deed," Eugene Rostow remarked, mocking an earlier statement by a press spokesman, as news of the Israeli victories came into the State Department war operations room—followed by the determination "to ensure as speedy and total an Israeli victory as possible."[73] The mood turned sour only on the morning of June 8, when news reached Washington that Israeli planes and gunboats had strafed and torpedoed a U.S. communications vessel, the U.S.S. *Liberty*, in international waters off the Egyptian coast. Thirty-four seamen had been killed. U.S. jet fighters were scrambled from carriers in the Sixth Fleet before being recalled when it was realized that the attacking boats and planes were Israeli and that the attack itself was a "mistake," an official Israeli explanation accepted by the U.S. administration but never by the captain and surviving crew.

Wars do not "happen." They do not "break out." These are evasions. Someone starts the actual shooting, and this simple truth has to be kept in mind when assessing the conflict between Israel and the Arab states in 1967. The Israeli attack was not a preemptive strike but a war of opportunity. The territories that came into Israel's possession were not, as Patrick

Seale has written, "acquired in a moment of absent-mindedness nor by the unforeseen fortunes of war."[74] Israel was in no danger of attack or of defeat even if it were attacked. The road to the conquest of the West Bank lay through the military defeat of Egypt and Syria or any other Arab state that dared to stand in Israel's way; the generals who manufactured a regional crisis out of tensions along the Israel-Syrian armistice line in 1967 had created an opportunity that might not come Israel's way again for a long time. From the symbiotic relationship between Israel and Johnson, it is difficult to avoid the conclusion that whatever the president hoped to gain domestically (including the support of the "Jewish lobby" in Congress and the media)[75] or in his foreign policy (a bloody nose for Nasser and humiliation for the USSR), he was as much a piece as a player on the chessboard of Israel's greater designs. If there was miscalculation, it lay in Johnson's ignorance of the extent of Israel's war aims.

AGGRESSIVE WAR, DEFENSIVE LIES

On the morning of June 5 an emergency session of the UN Security Council was convened to discuss the war that had just "broken out." In complaints lodged with the president of the council Egypt and Israel accused each other of starting hostilities. According to Israel Egyptian armored columns "had moved in an offensive thrust against Israel's borders while at the same time Egyptian planes from airfields in Sinai had struck out towards Israel," which had then exercised its right of self-defense under Article 51 of the UN Charter.[76] In other variations an Israeli army spokesman said Egypt had opened "an air and land attack" by sending armored forces "toward" southern Israel. Egyptian aircraft had been picked up on radar "coming towards the country's shores."[77] Egypt's Fourth Armored Division had teamed up with a mobile task force "with the apparent intention" of striking across southern Israel toward Jordan. In Eban's version, Egyptian ground forces had begun the fighting by shelling Israeli border "villages."[78]

As the world was soon to discover, the Israeli accounts constituted a multilayered lie. It was Israeli planes that had "struck out," and not just "toward" or "against" but deep into Egypt, destroying the bulk of its fighter aircraft and bombers as they sat on runways or in hangars and then destroying the runways so that the few planes still intact could not take off anyway. There was little air action by Egypt. In Washington, Rusk told Johnson in an early-morning telephone call that "my instincts tell me that the Israelis probably kicked this off" and that Israel's claim of a tank advance looked "just a little thin on the surface."[79] Eban told Walt Rostow that Israel had been attacked and was counterattacking, but by midday, with reports pouring in that Israel planes were "all over the place," destroying Jordan's limited air capacity as well as the Egyptian air force, Clark Clifford had concluded that Israel had "jumped off on minimum provocation" and had in fact initiated the war.[80] McGeorge Bundy, the National Security Council executive secretary, recalled that a meeting in the White House, attended by Johnson, Rusk, Acheson, McNamara, Clifford, Battle, Rostow, and George Christian, was "mainly concerned with the awful shape we would be in if the Israelis were losing. We didn't really know anything about the situation on the ground. When, in the course of that day, it became apparent that the Israeli Air Force had won, the entire atmosphere of the problem changed. It was in a way reassuring when it became clear that the fighting was the Israelis' idea and that the idea was working. That was a lot better than if it had been the other way around."[81] Later in the afternoon Rostow told Arab ambassadors that the United States would be interested in receiving any documentary evidence that Israel was responsible because "this was an important, if not decisive subject in the context of the rule of law and supremacy of the United Nations."[82] He can hardly have been serious; in any case, with Israel clearly on the winning side, there was not to be much more pious talk of the UN Charter or the rule of law.

There was no attack on Israel. No Egyptian tanks were breaching the armistice line or even heading toward it, nor were any Egyptian planes picked up on radar flying in the direction of the Negev. Except for a handful of Arab planes that managed to scramble, only Israeli planes were in the air. Arab air forces were destroyed piecemeal on the ground as the Israelis extended the air war from Egypt to Syria, Jordan, and Iraq while beginning the ground assault by crossing into Sinai. All the predictions of the U.S. and other military chiefs of staff and the intelligence specialists were confirmed. Israel crushed Arab forces even more spectacularly than they thought it could, and Arab governments fell into disarray just as quickly and predictably. There never had been any real military or political coordination, and now they set about proving it. Like horses pulling in different directions or some shambling mechanical contraption whose parts do not quite fit, they responded to the Israeli attack as though they, alone in the world, had not seen it coming. The destruction from the air was so devastating, the direction from which it had come (north over the Mediterranean) so unexpected, that Egypt concluded that U.S. and British aircraft and ships had to be involved. The same windy braggadocio that gave the Israelis the opportunity to talk up the Arab threat before the war continued after it started, with Arab radio stations broadcasting reports of great victories in the air before the shattering truth could no longer be avoided.

Israel had formally asked King Hussein to keep out of the war when it was obvious that he could not. The king was boxed in by the mutual Arab defense pact and the fury sweeping the Arab world in the wake of the Israeli attack. In a meeting with chiefs of foreign missions in Amman, Hussein said that in view of the Israeli aggression against Egypt "Jordan is now at war. Our forces have been put under UAR command."[83] UN Truce Supervision Organization Chief of Staff General Odd Bull carried a message to Hussein from the Israelis that no action would be taken against Jordan unless it attacked first, "in which case Israel would hit back hard."[84] Yet in making this request Israel knew that Jordan was committed to the general Arab defense and would not be able to keep out of the war. Indeed, by the time the message from Israel was received, Jordanian gunners had already fired a few rounds across the armistice lines. Having been "attacked," Israel now had justification for responding. "These idiots are absolutely determined to make you mayor of a united Jerusalem," General Narkiss told Teddy Kollek, the Israeli mayor of West Jerusalem.[85] The seizure by Jordanian troops of the UNEF headquarters (the former Government House) and the fear that the Mt. Scopus enclave (illegally fortified by the Israelis) would be next prompted the Israeli military command to launch an immediate ground assault on East Jerusalem after destroying Jordan's air force. Within hours Hussein had only one warplane left, and within a day he was telling the Americans that unless the Israelis stopped their attack his regime would be finished. Jordan had no offensive capability, "and its army was in the process of destruction." He could not declare a unilateral cease-fire, obviously for political reasons, and wanted instead a "decrease" in "punitive destructive actions" by both sides.[86] But it was too late for this. Israel was not interested even in a secret cease-fire, was not interested in saving the Jordanian regime, and was not attracted by the minor putative gains of splitting Jordan off from the Arab world.[87] When Jordan sought help from the United States, Rusk urged Israel to comply with a UN Security Council resolution and arrange "at least" a de facto cease-fire with Jordan, but the fighting was to continue until Hussein had lost East Jerusalem and the western Palestinian half of his kingdom.

By the evening of June 8, Egypt had agreed to a cease-fire. Only Syria stood in the way of an overwhelming Israeli victory. From aerial photos the Israelis knew that army camps around the Golan Heights city of Quneitra had been deserted and that Syria's entire military disposition on the heights was "possibly collapsing." They had also intercepted a message from Nasser advising Syria to accept the cease-fire without delay.[88] The effective end of the war on the Egyptian front and the apparent weakness of the Syrian military position persuaded Dayan to launch a ground assault on the Golan Heights in the name of protecting the Israeli settlements below; the attack began at 6:00 A.M. on June 9.

Later in the morning the Security Council met in urgent session at the request of Syria, which had by now accepted the calls for a cease-fire made in the council's resolutions of June 6 and 7 and was demanding that Israel do the same. The Syrians reported that the Israelis were attacking by aircraft, tank, artillery, and infantry along the whole length of the armistice line. Just after 1:00 P.M. (New York time) the UN Security Council passed a further resolution (Resolution 235) calling for compliance with earlier cease-fire resolutions, but by this time fighting for control of the Golan Heights had intensified and Israel was in no mood to stop. Although the Soviet Union had supported Egypt at all levels and was being humiliated by having to witness the destruction of much of the military material it had provided Arab states, only when the ground attack was ordered on Syria did it issue statements indicating that it was getting ready to intervene. On June 10 it broke off relations with Israel and called for yet another meeting of the Security Council. At the same time, using the emergency "hot line" set up between Moscow and Washington, and insisting that Johnson stand by the machine as the message was sent, the Soviet premier, Alexei Kosygin, warned that in the wake of the failure of the Security Council to secure a cease-fire "a very crucial moment has now arrived which forces us, if military actions are not stopped in the next few hours, to adopt an independent decision. We are ready to do this. However, these actions may bring us into a clash, which will lead to a grave catastrophe." Israel would be warned that if it did not cease fire the Soviet Union would take "necessary actions," including military measures.[89] Johnson replied by saying that a message had been sent to the Israelis the night before calling on them to observe the cease-fire immediately.[90] A second message from Kosygin later informed Johnson that the Israelis were showing no signs of halting hostilities as the president had assured him in his reply but were instead advancing on Damascus "and that action cannot be postponed."[91]

The specter of direct Soviet involvement galvanized the Americans into action, but fortunately for the Israelis the conquest of the Golan was just about complete by this time. Already on June 9 Rusk had warned Eban that there was likely to be broad condemnation of Israel at the Security Council unless it responded to the calls for a cease-fire. At 10:00 A.M. on June 10 Rusk told Harman and Evron "most emphatically" that a cease-fire on the

Syrian front "simply had to be reached without delay" before the diplomatic and political situation deteriorated any further.[92] Israel delayed as long as it could, giving itself the time it needed to reach all its objectives, but finally agreed to cease fire at six in the evening. On June 11 U Thant told the Security Council that as of 3:00 P.M. that day no serious breaches were being reported, but it had been a close call. Wrote Barbour in a telegram: "It seems clear that, driven by military necessity of achieving viable military posture for protection border settlements, Israelis played for time in political maneuvers in Security Council to hair raising proximity to brink, but also evident tonight that they think they have gotten away with it. There is generally relaxed atmosphere in official circles and every indication to hold to ceasefire."[93] As the war wound down, Israel admitted that it had started the shooting but still argued that the Arabs were to blame for the war, surrounding it with such threatening military forces that it had no option but to launch a preemptive strike.

"MUNICIPAL FUSION"

The war brought the Israelis back to Sinai and Gaza, which the Israeli government continued to regard as Israel's by right anyway. Eban told the U.S. ambassador to the UN, Arthur Goldberg, that Israel had no "colonial aspirations."[94] In conversation with Goldberg and Rusk on June 22 he said it was "natural" for Israel to be in Gaza. However, as the addition of Gaza's population of 350,000 to Israel's present Arab population would bring the number of Arabs "in Israel" to about 700,000, Israelis were wondering "whether some could not be settled elsewhere, e.g. northern part of Sinai, 'Central Palestine' or Jordan."[95] In fact, Israel wanted to have Gaza without its people "but did not see how that could come about."[96]

By this time Johnson had been warned by Joseph Sisco that Israel's objectives "may be shifting from original position seeking peace with no territorial gains toward one of territorial expansion."[97] On June 28 the Yugoslav delegation tabled a resolution in the General Assembly calling for Israeli withdrawal from all occupied territory. On June 27 the Knesset had passed legislation extending Israeli laws to East Jerusalem, effectively annexing the rest of the city despite the defense by Harman and Evron that the word *annexation* did not appear in the Knesset bill. They insisted that the measures taken "do not constitute annexation but only municipal fusion."[98] On June 28 the government followed through by dissolving the East Jerusalem municipal council, seizing Jordanian records, and closing Arab banks. The United States had been working on a counter-resolution linking Israel's withdrawal from occupied territory to recognition by the Arabs, but with this unilateral Israeli move weeks of work, in Eugene Rostow's words, had "vanished in smoke."[99] Johnson did not seem perturbed. When a draft statement responding to the Israeli action was discussed on July 14 in the Cabinet Room, at a meeting of the special National Security Panel on the Middle East, he suggested that the word *deplore* be changed to *regret*. "What I want to say is that we regret their unwillingness to budge." At this point there was laughter.[100]

The same day that Johnson and his senior advisers were chuckling in the Cabinet Room, the General Assembly passed Resolution 2254 (ES-V), deploring (not regretting) Israel's failure to observe a July 4 resolution and calling on it to rescind all measures already taken and desist from any further action that would alter the status of Jerusalem.[101] This and other resolutions on the status of the city were simply ignored. The Israelis began reshaping the city by clearing a space along the western wall of the mosque compound known to Muslims as the Haram al Sharif and to Jews as the Temple Mount. This operation involved the demolition of the 135 dwellings that constituted the Magharibah quarter, a *waqf* (religious foundation) founded in the twelfth century by a son of Salah al Din al Ayyubi (Saladin) for pilgrims and scholars arriving from North Africa. The Zionists had long regarded the Magharibah, dismissed by Weizmann as "some doubtful Moghreb community,"[102] as an obstruction to the Wailing Wall that would have to be removed. What Oren calls "hovels,"[103] and what the Jordanian foreign minister described as "priceless architectural gems," were bulldozed into nonexistence in one afternoon.[104] The thousand residents of the quarter were scattered into the streets and lanes "at a few minutes notice."[105] The destruction of the Magharibah was followed by the bulldozing of all but a remnant of the ancient Mamillah cemetery to make way for gardens, a parking lot, and lavatories.[106] The bones of the Companions of the Prophet were among the Muslim remains in Mamillah. The UN secretary-general's special representative in Jerusalem, Ernesto A. Thalmann, recorded the shock of the Muslim population at the desecration of holy sites.[107] Two months after bulldozing the Magharibah quarter, the Israelis demolished the Fakhriyah hospice, the residence of the mufti of the Shafiʿi school of Islamic law.[108] About 5,500 people whom the Israelis called squatters were driven out of what the Israelis called the Jewish quarter.[109] Some were 1948 refugees from other parts of Palestine, but most were "old Jerusalem families who had lived there from generation to generation."[110] In fact, though Jerusalem was a natural magnet for Jews arriving in Palestine, so that from the nineteenth century the majority of the city's population was Jewish, by

1948 only 18 percent of its land area was Jewish owned. On the eastern side of the city, Jews owned less than 1 percent of the land; even the small "Jewish quarter" was only 20 percent Jewish owned.[111] Israeli claims—brazenly exaggerated, in Hirst's view—of vandalism of Jewish sites under Jordanian rule were surely no defense for the destruction of these historical Arab and Muslim areas. Blowing his shofar (a ram's horn) on the Haram al Sharif, the chief rabbi of the IDF, Shlomo Goren, wanted the army to go even further and demolish the two mosques within the compound.[112]

In a report issued on September 12, Ernesto Thalmann found that by extending its laws to East Jerusalem the Israeli government had expanded the municipal area of West Jerusalem by more than sixty square kilometers to more than one hundred square kilometers. A postoccupation census had shown a population of seventy thousand in East Jerusalem (81 percent Muslim) and about two hundred thousand in the western part of the city. Israeli leaders had made it clear that Israel "was taking every step to place under its sovereignty those parts of the city not controlled before June 1967" and had stated unequivocally that the process of integration was "irreversible and not negotiable."[113] Eban claimed that "where there had been hostile separation there was now harmonious civic union" and where there had been violence now there was peace.[114] If the Israelis rejected the word *annexation*, it was because they regarded Jerusalem as theirs by right—and what was theirs by right did not have to be "annexed." What they set out to do now was obliterate the city's Arab and Muslim character through a rolling process of pseudolegal, administrative, and topographical change.

LOOTING AND FLIGHT

The conquest of Arab territory was accompanied by the flight of its population. On July 4 the UN Relief and Works Agency (UNRWA) commissioner-general estimated that 80,000 civilians had fled occupied Syrian territory and at least 150,000 from the West Bank, perhaps 80,000 to 100,000 of whom were already UNRWA-registered refugees. A "second wave" had begun on June 20, and in the preceding ten days about 36,000 people had crossed the Jordan,[115] bringing to close to 300,000 the number of people who had left the territory during or after the war. In an address to the General Assembly, King Hussein accused the Israelis of using napalm and fragmentation bombs, of destroying Arab towns and villages, and of worsening the flight of the civilian population through vandalism and terror. Photographs show Israeli soldiers standing by as refugees stream into Jordan across the wreckage of the Allenby Bridge.

On July 6, the secretary-general appointed Nils Göran Gussing as his special representative in the Israeli-occupied territories. On the basis of information provided by Gussing, the secretary-general issued a report in September which found that in the occupied Syrian territory the bulk of the population had left.[116] Gussing found it hard to determine the line between physical and psychological pressure on the movement of people from occupied Syrian territory; however, "certain actions allowed by local commanders" had been an important cause of flight, and "he had never been informed of any action taken by the Israeli authorities to reassure the population."[117] The special representative held Israeli forces largely responsible for the extensive looting in the Syrian city of Quneitra. In fact, in the less circumspect language of Patrick Seale, Israel "sacked" Quneitra and "over the next six months forcibly drove some 90,000 people, stripped of everything they owned, off the Golan to join in open fields and tented encampments some 30,000 others who had fled during the fighting."[118] The refugees included 17,000 Palestinians who had fled to the Golan in 1948.

On the West Bank, 850 of 2,000 dwellings were destroyed in the town of Qalqilya, 80 to 85 percent of them after the fighting had stopped, according to the town's mayor; the population had been advised to leave by the Israeli commander but were allowed to return three weeks later.[119] In the Latrun area, however, three villages (Beit Nuba, Imwas, and Yalu) were destroyed on the grounds of "security" and the villagers driven out and not allowed to return. A further two villages in the Hebron area were destroyed for the same reason. Expulsions from the West Bank in the months after the occupation began included the former Jordanian mayor of East Jerusalem (Rouhi al Khatib) and 294 members of the Nuwaseirat tribe, forced to cross to the East Bank after their traditional land was declared a restricted area in the name of "security" (a technique used since 1948 to dislodge both the sedentary and nomadic population from their land). Gussing also referred to what seems to have been an attempt by Israel to thin out the dense population of Gaza in line with the thinking revealed by Eban. The Israelis had made arrangements for the people to "visit relatives" on the West Bank; six buses were said to be leaving daily, but the special representative was unable to say "whether six busloads of people also returned every day."[120]

REJECTING DEFEAT

In the CIA's estimate of battlefield losses the focus is on hardware rather than humans. Syria had lost most of its 85 fighter aircraft and about 100 of its 425 tanks; Jordan's air force had been completely destroyed along with two-thirds of its 200 tanks; Egypt had lost two-thirds of its 365 fighter air-craft, 55 of its 69 bombers, and about half of its 1,000 tanks; the war had "eliminated" from its order of battle two of its four infantry divisions, one of its two armored divisions, and fifteen of twenty-three of its independent brigades. By contrast, Israel had lost less than 100 of its 1,100 tanks and only 48 of its 256 aircraft. Combined Arab combat deaths amounted to "more than 7000" compared to 700 Israelis killed.[121] This figure for Arab battlefield losses was a serious underestimate. Egypt alone seems to have lost at least 10,000 men and 1,500 officers.[122] In a reprise of 1956, many cap-tured Egyptians died of thirst after being forced to take their boots off and herded in the direction of the canal.[123] The evidence supports the accusation of Egypt's delegate at the General Assembly that the Israelis had bom-barded hospitals in Sinai and Gaza, "killing and wounding young men, looting storehouses and leaving wounded stranded in the desert without food or water, stripped of their clothes, to travel on foot some 250 miles."[124] Thousands more Syrian soldiers died in the defense of the Golan Heights. Civilian casualties included UNEF troops still positioned near the armistice line on the Egyptian front. Three Indians were killed when Israeli aircraft strafed a UNEF convoy on the road between Gaza and Rafah; three more were killed by Israel artillery fire in Gaza. In the next few years hundreds of Palestinians would be killed in the Gaza Strip as the Israelis imposed the iron law of occupation under the command of Ariel Sharon.

The crushing defeat they had suffered did not force the Arabs, unstable and irrational by nature according to Warnke, to see reason and accept Israel on terms dictated by Israel.[125] On the contrary, it generated more defiance and fed the conclusion that what had been taken by force would one day have to be taken back by force. Nasser survived after resigning and then agreeing to stay on after the most extraordinary mass demonstration in Egypt's modern history. Having lost the war, the Egyptians could not afford to lose Nasser too. At the Khartum conference in August 1967 he told Arab heads of state that Egypt could wait until military preparations were completed. "We will then be able to carry out the only action that Israel understands well, and that is the liberation of land by force."[126]

The conference voted against peace, negotiations, and recognition, but what was seen across the Arab world as resolution and steadfastness was regarded in Washington as the stubborn refusal to accept reality. On November 22 the UN Security Council passed Resolution 242, emphasiz-ing the inadmissibility of the acquisition of territory by war and calling for an Israeli withdrawal from "territories occupied in the recent conflict" (in the French version, "the" territories; the omission of the definite article from the English text was a loophole through which the Israelis could clamber in arguing against withdrawal from "all" territories).[127] In the months since the war ended, shooting had never stopped. Two armies faced each other across the canal, and both repeatedly broke the cease-fire. The Egyptians fired on Israeli patrol boats sent into the canal, and the Israelis shelled Egyptian shore positions from warships in the Gulf of Suez. On October 21 the Egyptians fired Soviet-supplied Komar missiles to sink the Israeli destroyer *Eilat,* which had been operating close to or in Egyptian territorial waters for months and in July had sunk two Egyptian vessels. In retaliation, the Israelis shelled Suez city, destroying oil refineries, fertilizer plants, and harbor installations and killing numerous civilians.

Nasser always spoke in two languages, one for his domestic and regional Arab audience and one in the private conservations out of the hearing of the Arab public that were a more accurate measure of what he wanted. In November 1968 he seemed to Robert Anderson "more anxious than ever to have some kind of peace because he thinks that if war should come again there would be vast destruction on both sides,"[128] but in the coming months he seemed to give up any hope that Israel could be persuaded to abandon conquered territory in return for a nonbelligerency pact if not an open formal peace.

In July 1969, Nasser referred to the "war of attrition" Egypt was now fighting against Israel. Egypt had been rearmed, and thousands of Soviet advisers had arrived to build a missile defense system along the west bank of the canal, greatly increasing the risk of a U.S.-Soviet confrontation. Artillery exchanges and air action across the canal and Israeli attacks along the Egyptian front line included the killing of one hundred soldiers in a raid by commandos wearing Egyptian uniforms (in breach of the Hague convention on the conduct of war) and using Soviet tanks and APCs captured in the 1967 war. Civilian casualties were heavy. In February 1970, eighty Egyptian workers were killed when Israeli planes bombed a factory at Abu Zaꜥabal; in April forty-six children were killed when their school bus was hit during an Israeli air attack on the town of Bahr al Baqr. These actions were never investigated by the same Western governments that had repeatedly and earnestly proclaimed their desire to bring peace with justice to the Middle East. The civilian casualties included more than one hundred passengers on board a Libyan airliner shot down by Israeli Phantoms in February 1973 when it strayed off course and flew over the occupied Sinai.

By now Nasser was talking of the third stage of liberation, "of which the final stage must be the crossing of the Canal from the West to the East Bank."[129] Planning for the cross-canal operation eventually launched by

Anwar Sadat in 1973 was well advanced when Nasser had a heart attack and died in September 1970. The United States continued to talk of peace, but without showing any determination to push the Israelis out of occupied territories in accordance with UN Security Council Resolution 242 and numerous other more forceful General Assembly resolutions. Indeed, as Golda Meir, appointed prime minister following the death of Levi Eshkol, remarked more than two years after the 1967 war had ended, Israel had been under "no pressure whatsoever" from the United States to pull back to the prewar borders.[130]

In 1969, in accordance with orders issued by Ariel Sharon, the newly appointed commander of the army's southern command, Israeli forces prepared the way for the building of Yamit and other settlements in Sinai by dynamiting houses, pulling down tents, destroying crops, filling wells, and driving an estimated ten thousand farmers and bedouin families out of the occupied territory.[131] Rusk had pointed out that the "transfer" of civilians to occupied territories, "whether or not in settlements under military control," constituted a breach of Article 49 of the Geneva Convention Relative to the Protection of Civilian Persons in Time of War (August 12, 1949), but the movement of Israeli civilians into occupied Arab lands continued without any outside intervention to stop it.[132] When the United States complained about settlements being established on the Golan Heights, Rabin said that in his view "the Arabs would be more eager to negotiate the more they saw a danger that they would not get their territories back."[133]

On April 12, 1968, forty ultraorthodox Jewish families moved into the Park Hotel in Hebron under the leadership of Rabbi Moshe Levinger. The government refused to dislodge them, and by 1970 Levinger's followers had established the settlement of Kiryat Arba on hills overlooking the town. Levinger had been encouraged by Ben-Gurion, who told him that "Hebron is still awaiting redemption and there is no redemption without extensive Jewish settlements." The injunction was *halachic* (enjoined by religious law) as well as political. According to the settler movement's senior religious authority, Rabbi Kook: "There are no conquests here and we are not occupying foreign lands. We are returning home to the inheritance of our ancestors. There is no Arab land here, only the inheritance of our God, and the more the world gets used to this thought, the better it will be for them and for all of us."[134]

THE "SHOUTING HILL"

Following the disengagement agreement signed with Syria in 1974, the Israelis withdrew from 30 percent of the occupied Golan, but not before bulldozing and dynamiting the city of Quneitra until not one building, including churches, mosques, and hospitals, was left intact. In 1977 Eduard Gruner, a Swiss national appointed by the UN Special Committee to Investigate Israeli Practices Affecting the Human Rights of the Population of the Occupied Territories, estimated the damage to furniture, stocks, and sacred goods alone at 226,044,395 Syrian pounds ($57,590,928 at the prevailing official exchange rate).[135] In Resolution 32/91 of December 13, 1977, the General Assembly condemned the "massive damage and deliberate destruction" of Quneitra perpetrated during the occupation.[136] In a 1999 report, the Special Committee listed matters to which its attention had been drawn in Syria.[137] Of the 130,000 people living in the occupied Golan before the 1967 war, 123,500 had been expelled and 244 "residential sites," including villages, hamlets, and the cities of Quneitra and Fit, had been destroyed.[138] Movable property had been looted and herds of sheep, cattle, and goats seized; the value of destroyed homes was put at about $1 billion. The twenty-three thousand people who now lived under Israeli occupation were concentrated in five villages (Majdal Shams, Buqata, Ain Qunya, Masada, and al Ghajar); from the "shouting hill" facing Majdal Shams, they communicated with relatives by calling through a megaphone. In the place of destroyed villages, the Israelis had built about forty settlements, some of which had been given "full or abbreviated Old Testament names or names of supposedly ancient settlements which are Hebrew distortions of Arab place names, thereby exposing the attempts to bestow a Hebrew identity on the area and Israel's intention to continue occupying it."[139] The charges against the Israelis included the excavation and looting of archeological artifacts, the expropriation of the land of remaining Syrian citizens, the marginalization of the Arabic language, the presentation of Arabs in school textbooks as "shepherds or invaders," and the exploitation of water for settlers along with its denial to the occupied population for all but the most basic needs.[140] Having destroyed the Arab diversion works shortly before the 1967 war, Israel now dominated the water resources of southern Syria.

The defeat of Arab armies in 1967 strengthened the appeal of "radical" groups within the Palestine Liberation Organization (founded in 1964 under the aegis of the Arab League), principally George Habash's Marxist Democratic Front for the Liberation of Palestine (DFLP) and Nayef Hawatmeh's Democratic Popular Front for the Liberation of Palestine (DPFLP). In March 1968, Palestinian guerrillas fighting with the backing of Jordanian armor inflicted heavy casualties on an Israeli column around the town of Karameh. The transformation of Jordan into the main center of Palestinian operations against Israel precipitated the civil war of 1970. Palestinian fighters were crushed by the Jordanian army and their leaders were told to find another home.

Only one city offered both proximity to the occupied homeland and the freedom needed to organize: Beirut. Israel had already issued countless warnings to the Lebanese government of what was in store unless it controlled the activities of the Palestinians. In late December 1968, Israeli commandos had destroyed thirteen passenger airliners, most of them owned by the national Lebanese carrier, Middle East Airlines, as they sat on the tarmac at Beirut's international airport. The following year, through the mediation of the Arab League, the Lebanese government and the PLO reached agreement on the limits of Palestinian resistance to Israel from the south of the country, but a shaky accord between a government and a movement that were equally powerless to impose their will ensured Lebanon's rapid descent toward the bottom of the vortex. In April 1973 Israeli commandos landed on West Beirut's Ramlet al Baidah (White Sands) beach, stormed into an apartment block on Rue Verdun, in an upper-middle-class residential area, and killed three senior Palestinian resistance figures, including the poet Kamal Nasser. The dead included the wife of one man killed as she tried to shield her husband and an elderly Italian woman who was shot when she opened the door of her apartment to see what was going on.

By this time another regional war was not far off. Since succeeding Nasser as Egyptian's president, Anwar al Sadat had proclaimed that every year would be the "year of decision," but in 1973 he meant it. The treaty that resulted from the war launched in October took Egypt out of the "Arab camp," enabling Israel to consolidate its hold on the West Bank and the Golan Heights and plan for the destruction of the Palestinian political and guerrilla presence in Lebanon. This sliver of a country running down the Mediterranean coast, a "confessional democracy" ripe for the manipulation of its political and ethno-religious divisions, a country without an army, navy, or air force to speak of, now become the main furnace of war.

11. DISABLING LEBANON

In the war between Egypt and Israel in 1973, Egyptian military commanders pulled off one of the most difficult of military operations, the crossing
of a stretch of water defended on the other side by a well-entrenched
enemy. As Egyptian troops carrying rocket-propelled grenade launchers or
Sagger antitank missiles in backpacks poured over pontoon bridges to the
east bank of the Suez Canal at 2:00 P.M. on October 6, high-pressure water
hoses were used to blow breaches in the sand barriers of the Bar Lev line.
The fortresses that were the pillars of the Israeli defensive position were
then stormed and taken one by one. In the first twenty-four hours, one
hundred thousand troops, more than a thousand tanks, and 13,500 other
vehicles were shifted across the canal in what was "the largest water obstacle first day crossing in history."[1] The operation was coordinated with an
attack on the eastern front, where Syrian troops attacking Israeli positions
on the occupied Golan Heights inflicted heavy losses as well. So many
Israeli planes were shot down by missile fire in the few days of the war that
the Israel Air Force was temporarily prevented from launching a credible
counterattack. For the first week of the war Israel trembled on the brink of
its first military defeat by Arab armies, prompting the Meir government
to declare a nuclear alert, "partly in the knowledge that it would be
detected by the US and the Soviet Union. The Soviets, Israel assumed,
would restrain their Arab allies while the Americans would speed up
resupply efforts. While the USSR did inform Egypt that Israel had armed
three nuclear weapons, the extent to which Israel's nuclear alert affected
the timing of Washington's subsequent decision to rearm Israel is not
clear."[2] In an emergency around-the-clock operation, Israel's depleted
arsenal was rapidly restocked with thousands of tons of U.S. war materiel,
including tanks, planes, ammunition, artillery, and missiles.

238

"Operational pauses" on both the Egyptian and Syrian fronts, along with military supplies airlifted directly into the Sinai desert by American aircraft, ultimately enabled the Israelis to turn the war around. The Egyptians were holding positions fifteen kilometers inside Sinai but moved forward again on October 14 following heavy losses on the Syrian front. What followed has frequently been described as one of the biggest tank confrontations in the history of modern warfare (although involving only about two thousand tanks compared to the six thousand or more deployed by the Russians and Germans in the Battle of Kursk in 1943). The Egyptians suffered a crushing defeat. The following day Ariel Sharon led the Israeli force that crossed the canal to the west side. Within a few days this bridgehead had been consolidated and expanded. Cairo was threatened, and now it was Egyptian forces that were cut off from home base on the east bank of the canal.

Egypt accepted a cease-fire on October 22. Syria reluctantly followed suit the next day. Hafiz al Assad had pleaded with Sadat to continue the war, arguing that the situation was by no means lost on either front, but for Sadat the intervention of the United States, through the replenishment of lost Israeli tanks and planes, meant that he was no longer fighting just Israel. He could not fight the United States as well as Israel, nor could he "accept the responsibility before history for the destruction of our armed forces for the second time."[3] It is true that the United States would never have allowed Israel to go down. It is also true that the massive resupply of weaponry helped Israel to turn the war around, but the failure of the Egyptian military command to take Israel's cross-canal operation seriously until it was too late, and Sadat's refusal to allow the army to capitalize on its initial success by moving deeper into Sinai and seizing the strategic Gidi, Mitla, and Bir Gafgafa passes, were equally responsible for the reversal of Egypt's fortunes. The army had been told to dig in when it should have been moving forward. Israel was given time to bounce back—but Sadat had still achieved more than any other Arab leader on the battlefield. The Arab world rallied to his support. On October 17 members of the Organization of Arab Petroleum Exporting Countries (OAPEC) announced a boycott of oil supplies to the United States and Europe. The "energy crisis" that followed refocused European and American attention on Arab concerns and especially the Palestinian question, embedded in the tortured body politic of the Arab world as firmly as a flint arrowhead, in a way that no appeal to justice or the principles of international law had ever succeeded in doing. The war was a step Sadat had to take. By dismantling the Nasserite one-party system in the "corrective" movement of 1971 and sending thousands of Soviet military advisers home the following year, he had already sent clear signals to the United States about where his political preferences lay. The Israeli occupation of Sinai stood in the way of better relations with the West and the foreign aid Sadat needed to "liberalize" Egypt's economy. The "no war, no peace" stalemate now brought to an end, the United States hastened to bring about disengagement on both the Sinai and Syrian fronts through the "shuttle diplomacy" of Henry Kissinger.

In 1974 Sadat followed up his military and political initiatives with the declaration of an economic "opening" *(infitah)* to the West. Three years later (November 9, 1977) he built on this by announcing in the Egyptian parliament that he was ready to go to the end of the world—"even to the Knesset"—for the sake of peace. Sadat had been assured in secret discussions beforehand that the Israeli government of Menachem Begin was prepared to return all Sinai in return for a peace treaty.[4] Begin invited him to come, and ten days later he was in Jerusalem. The sight of him shaking Begin's hand was enough to brand him as a traitor in many Arab eyes, and the spectacle of him addressing the Knesset and praying in the Aqsa mosque on the Haram al Sharif caused even greater outrage. Egypt was boycotted and the Arab League headquarters removed to Tunis. In his defense, Sadat argued that in delivering this second shock the aim was to secure a settlement for all Arabs, for Syrians and Palestinians as well as Egyptians.

The Begin government had been voted into office only in May. The Labor establishment had run the country since its foundation, but it was not just the end of its long run that caused such shock when the results were announced. The incoming government represented the triumph of an old political tendency—revisionist Zionism—and was led by a man regarded even within Israel as an extremist. In 1948 a number of distinguished Jewish public figures, including Sidney Hook, Hannah Arendt, and Albert Einstein, had written a letter to the *New York Times* (published on December 4) comparing revisionist Zionism to Nazism and Italian fascism. Begin had been secretary to Vladimir Jabotinsky, the theoretician and founder of the revisionist tendency, and had been building his idol's "iron wall" against the Palestinians ever since,[5] taking decisions, as the leader of the Irgun underground, that led to two of the worst atrocities of the immediate postwar period, the bombing of the King David Hotel and the massacre at Deir Yasin. Ben-Gurion and the Labor Zionists had applied their own iron laws against the Palestinians, but even they regarded Begin as a shrill fanatic. No one in the political mainstream could have conceived that the day would come when Israelis would elect this man as their prime minister, but the arrival in Israel of Jews from Arab countries, complaining of discrimination by the Labor government, along with the settlement of the territories conquered in 1967 by religious extremists, created new issues and new constituencies that Begin was able to exploit. On the question of settlement of occupied land, he could argue with complete justification that what he was doing was no different from what all Labor leaders had sanctioned before him. A Labor government had tacitly endorsed the colonization of the territory taken in 1967, and Labor governments continued it after Begin was out of office. Yitzhak Rabin once remarked that Labor did not disagree with the Likud on the "right" of settlement but only on how and when it was to be effected.[6] There was a great deal of hypocrisy in the Labor Party's attitude toward Begin.

Begin never saw the Palestinians as a people, let alone as a people with rights; instead, he saw them as a menace, through their violence and their transgressive presence on the land he regarded as the right of the Jews by divine promise. When Palestinians struck back against settlers occupying their land, he reacted with rage, describing them as " beasts walking on two legs."[7] What belonged to the Jewish people could not possibly be "occupied" by them. His indifference to the slaughter of Palestinians in Lebanon in 1982 was noted during the hearings of the Kahan Commission of Inquiry. In the two days after being told that the Falangists had entered the Sabra and Shatila camps he showed "absolutely no interest" in their actions, even though the military command had known since the first night that hundreds of camp dwellers were being slaughtered.[8] In the remorseless cruelty that marked his life, Begin bore the imprint of what Christopher Sykes has described as "the effect, from the policy of the Endlösung, of Nazi evil on human character."[9] Yet it was this man, the final product of the Final Solution, into whose hands questions of war and peace in the Middle East were placed in the late 1970s.

RABIN AND CARTER

The peace between Egypt and Israel—a cold and sour peace, as it was to turn out—was enshrined in the treaty signed in 1979. It was not the comprehensive peace Sadat had said he was looking for. It certainly meant that Israel had to withdraw from occupied Egyptian territory, if this is reckoned as the price it had to pay, but this was more than counterbalanced by an immense strategic gain—the removal of Egypt from frontline states and the "Arab camp" in general. It can be argued that the signing of the treaty untied Israel's hands for actions elsewhere, but it can also be argued equally persuasively that Israel's attacks on Lebanon even as the treaty was being negotiated indicate that nothing would have stopped Begin once he had made up his mind. The focal point of his wrath was Lebanon. Yasser Arafat had his offices in West Beirut. Palestinian guerrillas had their bases near the armistice line with Israel in the south. In 1976, Syria—Israel's archenemy among the Arab states—had sent an Arab "deterrent force" into the country in an attempt to end the civil war that had been raging unchecked since the previous year. What Israel wanted in a Lebanon cleansed of the Palestinian presence was what it accused Syria of trying to establish—a puppet government, but one manipulated from Jerusalem rather than Damascus. The destruction of the PLO that would have to precede its installation would have a spillover effect for the Palestinians of the territories occupied in 1967. Their cup of despair would be overflowing: What choice would now be left to them but to accept whatever deal the occupier was disposed to offer? It was in Lebanon and not Palestine that the next decisive stage of Israel's struggle with the Palestinians would be fought.

It is most unlikely that Jimmy Carter, idealistic and well-meaning, could imagine the frustration that lay ahead of him when he joined hands with Anwar al Sadat and Menachem Begin to bring peace to the Middle East. He was a southern Baptist for whom the moral strictures of the Bible were a living guide to all aspects of his life. He sympathized with the Jewish attachment to Palestine, but in his view the past deprivation of Jewish rights was no reason to deprive the Palestinians of theirs in the present. In Israel this was interpreted as hostility. In March 1977 Carter had what he later called an "unpleasant surprise" when he sat down for talks with the Israeli prime minister, the unbending Yitzhak Rabin, who regarded the U.S. president as "a dangerously inexperienced outsider who looked like giving Israel a lot of trouble before he learned 'political maturity.'"[10] Three months later Carter went to Geneva for talks with Hafiz al Assad. The two men got on well. Either privately or in public, Carter made it clear that he regarded the creation of a Palestinian "homeland" (the Palestinians thought they already had one) and the retreat by Israel from land taken in 1967 as the critical components of any peace settlement. In May, Rabin lost the prime ministership to Begin. The stage was now set for Carter's confrontation with a man whose political position was anchored in the determination to retain every inch of land he regarded as belonging to Israel by right.

Carter's encounters with the Israeli prime minister were among the most bruising he was ever to have. He had watched him being interviewed on the *Issues and Answers* television program and found him "frightening" in his inflexibility on all the questions that would have to be resolved if there were to be peace in the Middle East.[11] Begin talked of the West Bank as having been "liberated" and of the need to reduce the Arab majority to a minority living alongside a Jewish majority. "I could not believe what I was hearing," Carter wrote in his diary.[12] However, on meeting Begin in July 1977, he was sufficiently disarmed by his congenial manner to feel optimistic. In November Sadat made his dramatic journey to Jerusalem, but by February 1978 he was so disillusioned with Begin's mean-spirited response that he was ready to break off both military disengagement and political contacts with Israel. Carter told the Israeli leader that his December 1977 proposal for "autonomy" for the West Bank Palestinians but not for the land on which they lived was so inadequate that it was likely to lead to Sadat's downfall.[13]

Even as Begin talked peace with Carter in 1977 he was preparing for war on the Palestinians in Lebanon. In the south of the country Israel and its Christian mercenaries, commanded by the renegade Lebanese army "major" Saad Haddad, were continuing to disrupt attempts by the government to end the civil war triggered after years of tension on April 13, 1975, when Palestinian gunmen had fired on a car taking leaders of the Falangist Party away from a Maronite church in the Beirut suburb of Ain Rumaneh.[14] Four were killed. Hours later, twenty-seven Palestinians were killed by way of retaliation when Falangist gunmen shot up a bus also traveling through Ain Rumaneh. The deeper cause of the conflict was the structural weakness of the Lebanese state, creaking and now breaking under the weight of the continuing chain reaction of Palestinian guerrilla raids and Israeli "reprisals." The intervention of Syrian troops was intended to prevent the looming defeat of Maronite militias by a loose alliance of Palestinian and Lebanese leftist forces and thus forestall the direct military intervention of Israel. Through the three-stage Shtaura accord of July 1977, the PLO had agreed to surrender heavy arms stored in the Beirut refugee camps, set up checkpoints at the entrance to the camps, remove Palestinian forces from a six-mile belt of territory adjacent to the border with Israel, and halt cross-border operations. The first two stages of the accord had been fulfilled, and the PLO had just announced that it was ready to implement the third, when in early September the Haddadist militia launched a major offensive, forcing the Lebanese government to abandon plans to send its own troops into the region. On November 9, sixty-five civilians were killed and sixty-eight wounded when Israeli planes blitzed the village of ʿIzziyya. The Begin government's sabotage of the Shtaura agreement and the escalation of violence were both linked to reports that it was preparing to invade Lebanon and was deterred only by U.S. pressure.[15]

When Israel finally launched a large-scale invasion on March 15, 1978, following a Palestinian attack in Israel that left thirty-seven dead, the sense that the Middle East was plunging toward a new regional crisis rather than moving toward peace was inescapable. Lebanon south of Tyre (Sur) was subjected to heavy bombardment day after day from air, land, and sea. Perhaps two thousand civilians were killed, while thousands of buildings were destroyed and more than 250,000 mostly Shiʿi villagers were sent fleeing toward Beirut. In addition, "much of the infrastructure was destroyed; bridges, electricity and telephone networks, hospitals, schools, clinics, water reservoirs."[16] The operation was marked by atrocities committed by the Haddadists (and occasionally Israeli soldiers themselves), but these were far eclipsed by the savagery of the military operation.[17] On March 19 the UN Security Council passed Resolution 425, calling on Israel to "withdraw forthwith" from Lebanon and setting up—at the request of the government of Lebanon—the UN Interim Force in Lebanon (UNIFIL).[18]

Begin visited Washington on March 20 and returned in May, irate that the United States had gone ahead with the sale of Airborne Warning and Control System (AWACS) aircraft to Saudi Arabia and completely unmoved (except to anger) by UN, U.S., and global criticism of his government's policies in Lebanon and the territories seized by Israel in 1967. Carter wrote in his diary after the second visit that "my guess is that he will not take the necessary steps to bring peace to Israel,"[19] but the attempt still had to be made. In July, Carter invited Begin and Sadat to take part in negotiations at Camp David. He had little hope of success, but "we could not think of a better alternative."[20]

CAMP DAVID

Beginning on September 5, Carter spent thirteen days with Begin and Sadat at Camp David. The differences in approach between the Egyptian and Israeli negotiating teams were evident at the start. Flamboyantly, and typically, Sadat wanted a "big bang" settlement with everything done at once—the "comprehensive settlement" he had been promising the Arabs. Begin was after an agreement just with Egypt. There was no reason for him to welcome discussions on the future of "Judea and Samaria" (the occupied West Bank) when as far as he was concerned this territory was Israel's by right. Even the suggested procedural framework was too much for him. When the Americans produced a draft agreement declaring that negotiations should be based on the principle of the "inadmissibility of the acquisition of territory by war," in line with the preamble of UN Security Council Resolution 242, Begin argued that the reference was unacceptable because in 1967 Israel "had been attacked by its Arab neighbors and the war was a defensive act by his country." Israel therefore "had the right to occupy the land taken in its defense."[21] The Israeli leader was truculent and imperious throughout. "I must insist . . ." Carter started to say during one negotiating session when Begin cut him off: "You will insist on nothing."[22] Of the thirteen days at Camp David, eight, so Begin later claimed, were spent in arguments on the preamble to Resolution 242. Only when the Americans agreed to eliminate the reference to the preamble in their draft would he agree to proceed.[23]

By day eleven, Sadat was so fed up he prepared to leave, staying on only when Carter fell back on an appeal to their friendship. Begin was still holding out for an agreement that would allow Israel to retain the Sinai settlements, complaining angrily of "political suicide" and an "ultimatum" when Sadat insisted on a commitment to their removal before he would sign any document. Insofar as the West Bank and Gaza were concerned, Carter's notes showed that Begin committed himself to establishing no new settlements after the signing of a "framework of peace." The Israeli leader later claimed that he had made a commitment only to a ninety-day "freeze." His offer of "full autonomy" to the West Bank Palestinians during a five-year transitional period turned out to be meaningless. No "fully self-governing Palestinian authority" ever emerged to take over "all the functions of the Israeli military government and its civilian administration," as Sadat had said it would.[24] The Palestinians were allowed to take part in the further negotiating process only as individual members of the Jordanian or Egyptian government delegations; their delegates were chosen by these governments and were subject to veto by Israel if it did not approve of the selections that had been made.

While disagreeing with Begin over new settlements, Carter accepted the expansion of existing ones after Begin and Dayan "described to me the problems where they had existing tiny settlements that were being built and a father and mother—the example they used—would go there and build one room in a kind of pioneer environment, leave their children with their grandparents in Jerusalem and even commute at night. And their plans were to build two extra bedrooms in a tiny house and bring the children later on. If we put an absolute freeze on all expansion it would mean the families could not be reunited."[25] The actual right of Palestinians driven from the West Bank to return and be reunited with their families was smothered by the Israelis in talk of the need to define the relationship between the Palestinian self-governing institutions yet to be built and the Palestinians cast out of the territories in 1967. Resolutions passed by the General Assembly affirmed the right of return to the territories taken in

1967, underlining the point that only the Palestinians had rights of habitation in the West Bank, Gaza, and East Jerusalem (as did the Syrians ejected from the Golan Heights). The government of Israel had no rights but only the responsibilities of an occupying power, and by supporting the settlement of any of its civilians in the territories Carter was putting the United States in breach of the Geneva Convention Relative to the Protection of Civilian Persons in Time of War (August 12, 1949). The president's compassion for the "plight" of divided settler families living on occupied land was not only misplaced but a signal to Israel that as long as it put a deceptive gloss on settlement growth by "thickening" existing settlements rather than building new ones, the United States would continue to allow it to proceed as before.

Only when he had successfully blocked any meaningful discussions on the future of the West Bank and Gaza did Begin budge on the Sinai settlements. He agreed to allow the Knesset to decide their fate (it voted for their removal), but the negotiations at Camp David were not long over before he was making speeches that indicated he had no intention even of discussing a timetable for withdrawal from the West Bank and Gaza. Visiting Washington in March, Begin seemed more interested in trying to persuade Carter of Israel's value as a strategic asset (so that the United States would agree to supply it with more tanks and planes) than in pushing peace talks forward. When the subject came up he worked through a list of conditions he was not prepared to accept before signing a treaty, "even though some were Israel's own original proposals."[26] A despairing Carter was convinced that the peace effort was at an end. Begin had continually raised his demands, and "we have gone as far as we can in putting forward suggested compromise language, with practically no constructive response from Israel."[27]

A few days later Carter made a last-ditch attempt to save the negotiations by going to Egypt and then Israel. Sadat was ready to sign a treaty, but in Israel Carter "couldn't believe it" when Begin put even more obstacles in the way, saying that he could not sign any agreement, that it would have to go to the cabinet and then the Knesset for extended debate of all the issues involved, including Jerusalem and the definition of *autonomy*. "I asked him if he actually wanted a peace treaty, because my impression was that everything he could do to obstruct it, he did with apparent relish."[28] Two days of frustrating talks followed, with Carter submitting further proposals to satisfy the Israelis, eliminating any language that might compromise their claims to the West Bank, Gaza, East Jerusalem, and the Golan Heights, before he had an agreement he could take back to Sadat. The Egyptian leader, by this time under great domestic pressure, took what he could get, and on March 26 the "framework of peace" was converted into a peace treaty between Egypt and Israel. Sadat had not got his "comprehensive" settlement. Certainly he had succeeded in getting the Israelis out of Sinai, but Israel had succeeded in getting the largest and most populous Arab country out of the "frontline" states. The opacity of the language, the avoidance of any reference to key UN resolutions dealing with the rights of the Palestinians, and the fudging of the settlement issue, giving Israel more time to create more "facts on the ground," were all to be repeated in the Oslo peace process and finally the Camp David negotiations between Clinton, Barak, and Arafat in 2000. Should there be any wonder that these frameworks, treaties, and processes brought not peace but more violence?[29] On October 6, 1981, during a military parade commemorating the war of 1973, Sadat—the "hero of the crossing"—fell victim to violence himself when members of an Islamist cell that had taken root within the army jumped from a truck and ran toward the reviewing stand firing machine guns. Sadat was cut down. "This is inconceivable," he muttered to Vice President Hosni Mubarak before he died.[30] "I have killed the pharaoh!" his assassin, Lieutenant Khalid al Islambouli, called out in triumph.

OCCUPATION AND "WITHDRAWAL"

With Egypt sidelined, Begin pushed ahead with the colonization of all occupied territories (on the Golan Heights and in the Palestinian territories taken in 1967) while consolidating Israel's grip on southern Lebanon through the operations of its quisling militia. In the plain language of the UN, the Haddadists were "financed, trained, armed, uniformed" and controlled by Israel.[31] They ruled through terror and atrocity.[32] Their brutality, including the torture and murder of Lebanese and Palestinians held inside the notorious prison at Khiyam, was not incidental, accidental, or regrettable but an essential tool of occupation.

Begin treated the UN as it was represented in Lebanon with the same contempt and disregard his government treated it in New York. Following the passage on March 19, 1978, of UN Security Council Resolution 425, establishing UNIFIL "for the purpose of confirming the withdrawal of Israeli forces, restoring international peace and security and assisting the Government of Lebanon in ensuring the return of its effective authority in the area," national contingents began to arrive in Lebanon to join the force.[33] Within a few weeks, more than six thousand UN troops had been placed on the ground in the south under the command of General Emmanuel Erskine. Resolution 425 called on Israel to end military action

248 / The American Ascendancy

and withdraw forthwith all its forces from Lebanon; what was finally agreed after negotiations between the chief coordinator of the UN peace-keeping mission in the Middle East (General Ensio Siilasvuo) and the Israeli military command was a withdrawal in two stages provided that a third followed.

By April 30 Israel had redeployed its forces in two separate enclaves south of the Litani River but was refusing to pull back any farther. Under pressure at the UN, the Begin government announced that withdrawal would be completed on June 13. Indeed, on that day General Erskine announced that the Israeli army had withdrawn from southern Lebanon, but this was not true. The Israelis were to remain in the region until driven out of most of it by Hizbullah in 2000;[34] what they had done was formally turn over the territory from which they had redeployed to Haddad, "on the grounds that the IDF [Israel Defense Forces] considered him a legiti-mate representative of the Lebanese government."[35] On this basis Israel claimed to have complied with Resolution 425.

Mainly through the operations of the Haddadists, Israel blocked both the efforts of UNIFIL to consolidate its presence in the south and the attempts of the Lebanese government to restore its authority over the region. On July 31, 1978, a seven-hundred-man Lebanese army contingent was met at the fringe of the Haddadist enclave with artillery and mortar fire; Israel had refused to help secure the restitution of government authority on the grounds that what happened between the Lebanese was none of its busi-ness. In April 1979—the month that Haddad proclaimed a "State of Free Lebanon" to go with his "Army of Free Lebanon"—the Haddadists shelled the UNIFIL headquarters at Naqoura after a Lebanese army battalion of five hundred men had been deployed in the south under UNIFIL command. UNIFIL could not even fly over the occupied territory without each flight being cleared by Haddad (i.e., by Israel); its access to checkpoints was fre-quently blocked when the Haddadists closed roads to UN personnel; Shiʿi villages that cooperated with UNIFIL were threatened and occasionally shelled. Now and again the Haddadists would raid areas under UNIFIL con-trol to kidnap "pro-PLO" villagers and blow up their homes; they also set up their own positions overlooking important roads inside UNIFIL areas. When the UN secretary-general sought Israel's cooperation in having them removed, he was told that "Israel considered these positions important for its security and would not intervene to have them removed."[36]

Far from withdrawing its forces, Israel continually strengthened its posi-tions, laying land mines, fencing in strips of land, bringing in supplies, rein-forcing the number of troops, establishing new checkpoints and artillery positions, and conducting military exercises near UN observation posts.[37] The Israelis infiltrated UNIFIL zones in pursuit of Palestinian guerrillas and violated Lebanese airspace and territorial waters at will: in November 1980 alone, UNIFIL reported 312 violations of airspace and eighty-nine Israeli intrusions into Lebanon's coastal waters. Begin was thumbing his nose at the UN Security Council, and not even the murder of two Irish UN soldiers (in the presence of an Israeli Shin Bet intelligence officer, according to Robert Fisk) was sufficient to force an end to Israel's unsavory alliance with the Haddadists and bring about a real Israeli withdrawal.[38]

"WHAT KIND OF TALK IS THIS?"

In June 1981, Israeli aircraft had destroyed Iraq's French-built nuclear reactor. The Iraqi Baʿathist regime was undoubtedly unpleasant, but a state that had nuclear weapons and that refused to sign the NPT or allow International Atomic Energy Agency (IAEA) inspections had attacked a state that did not have nuclear weapons and had signed the NPT. The UN Commission on Human Rights condemned the attack as "a violation of the rights of states to scientific and technological progress for social and economic development." Both the commission and the General Assembly called on member states to "cease any moral, material or human assistance which would enable Israel to pursue its policies of aggression, expansion and human rights violations."[39]

In Washington, Carter had gone (voted out of office in the 1980 elections), and Israel again had a good friend in the White House. President Reagan criticized Begin for not informing the United States of the attack on the Iraqi reactor ahead of time because "we could have done something to remove the threat." Nevertheless, "we are not turning on Israel. That would be an invitation for the Arabs to attack."[40] Reagan was just as understanding of Israel's need to use fourteen U.S.-supplied F-15 and F-16 fighter aircraft in the attack. Israel had violated U.S. arms export control laws, but for Reagan the Israeli prime minister should be given the benefit of some doubt that the president managed to see.[41] In spite of the continuing violence in Lebanon, the occupation and settlement of Arab land seized in 1967, and now the attack on Iraq, Reagan found it difficult to imagine how any of Israel's "neighbors" could see it as a threat.[42] A month after the attack on Iraq the "neighbors" complained again when, in the name of destroying PLO offices, Begin authorized a devastating air attack on West Beirut that killed more than 120 people (Lebanese or Palestinian civilians) and wounded 600.

In December, Begin announced Israel's annexation of the Golan Heights. This time even the United States reacted, voting for the UN Security Council resolution censuring Israel, describing the decision as "illegal," and threatening to take its own punitive action unless it was rescinded. After the Reagan administration delivered its own mild punishment, suspending the memorandum of understanding on strategic cooperation that had been signed with Israel only two weeks before, the U.S. ambassador in Israel, Samuel Lewis, was subjected to a harangue that was vintage Begin. "What kind of talk is this?" he demanded to know. "Are we a state or [are we] vassals of yours? Are we a banana republic? . . . You have no right to penalize Israel. . . . The people of Israel lived without the memorandum of understanding for 3700 years and will continue to live without it for another 3700 years."[43] The U.S. secretary of state, Alexander Haig, was hectored in similar fashion by Begin's defense minister, Ariel Sharon, who pounded on the table between them so hard that the dishes jumped.[44] Far from being treated like a vassal, Israel was treating the United States as if it were one.

PROVOCATIONS

On April 25, 1982, amid hysterical scenes played out before the cameras by the uprooted settlers, many of them the followers of the racist New York rabbi Meir Kahane, the coastal Sinai settlement of Yamit was finally abandoned. By now it was evident that Israel was on the brink of launching another large-scale attack on Lebanon, but instead of using the arms and the diplomatic and economic support on which Israel depended as leverage to warn Begin off, the Reagan administration gave Israel a further $350 million in aid.

Alexander Haig's claim that Israel had been "goaded" for more than a year before the 1982 invasion was not just fallacious but the very opposite of the truth.[45] A truce reached between the PLO and Israel through the mediation of Philip Habib, a former U.S. undersecretary of state, had held for a whole year despite thousands of Israeli violations of Lebanon's airspace and territorial waters. It was Israel that was goading the Palestinians, and the declarations by Reagan and Haig that the United States would support an attack on Lebanon only if Israel were the victim of a provocation "of such magnitude that the world would easily understand its right to retaliate" was as good as encouraging Begin to try even harder.[46]

On April 21 Israeli planes had launched heavy attacks close to Beirut and around Sidon (the Palestinian refugee camp of Ain al Helweh was on its outskirts) without the Palestinians responding. The following day, within an hour of Begin's announcement that the withdrawal from Sinai would be completed in three days, Israeli jets bombed the Lebanese coastal town of Damour after an Israeli soldier stepped on an antipersonnel mine in the occupied south. Again the Palestinians did not respond. On May 9 Israeli planes were sent into action again, the government this time claiming the provocation of explosive devices found on a bus in Jerusalem and a high school in Ashkelon. Eleven people were killed and thirty-seven wounded, and on this occasion the Palestinians did retaliate, firing more than one hundred artillery shells or Katyusha rockets in the direction of Israeli settlements without hitting one. They were not incompetent but were sending a warning that if the air attacks continued they had the capacity to cause turmoil among Israel's own civilian population. It was the first time since July 1981 that Palestinian guerrillas had returned fire across the border. No one was hurt, and their response fell far short of the major "provocation" Begin was seeking, but on June 3 a gunman from the renegade Abu Nidal Palestinian faction finally obliged him by trying to kill Israel's ambassador to the United Kingdom.

The Israeli cabinet met the following morning, and in the afternoon Israeli aircraft bombed West Beirut in what it called retaliation for an assassination attempt that had nothing to do with Arafat or the PLO or Lebanon.[47] The targets of the nine air strikes included the Sabra and Shatila camps, where at least 35 people were killed and 150 seriously wounded. Nabatiyeh in the south was also shelled.[48] The Palestinians responded with artillery fire early the next morning (June 5). Arafat, in Saudi Arabia, phoned through an order to halt the shelling, but by this time Begin was metamorphosing into the iron man of destiny preparing to come to grips with the Palestinian Hitler—Arafat—in his bunker. At a cabinet meeting later that day, Sharon sought approval for a punitive "incursion" that he said would last no more than twenty-four hours and would take Israeli troops and armor no deeper into Lebanon than forty kilometers over the armistice line. The ministers were told that the goal would be to put Palestinian artillery beyond the range of Israeli settlements. Beirut itself was "outside the picture,"[49] and on this basis the cabinet authorized a land invasion to begin the following morning. The lightly armed soldiers of various national contingents tried to block the Israeli tanks rolling through UNIFIL areas; the Nepalese contingent guarding the bridge at Khardala stood its ground for two days before Israeli forces partially destroyed their position and crossed over. Other UNIFIL checkpoints were overrun or bypassed.[50]

Only later did it become clear that what Sharon had in mind was not a small operation at all but an attack that would obliterate the "terrorists" and smash their political leadership. Syria would have to be given a bloody nose in the process even though Sharon denied that it was a target. Destroying the "terrorists" would involve purging the refugee camps in West Beirut, Bourg al Barajneh, Sabra, and Shatila, as well as those in the south; the invasion would end with the installation of a Lebanese government ready to sign a peace treaty. Israel was now being run by the most bellicose political-military combination in its history, Begin and Foreign Minister Yitzhak Shamir on the political side and Ariel Sharon and Chief of Staff Rafael Eitan on the military side. Begin sat back and allowed Sharon to set the pace, allowing a question mark to hover over the depth of his own complicity, although from everything he had ever said or done, Sharon's plan to destroy the PLO at the source matched his own thinking perfectly.

GOD AND GOG, REAGAN AND BEGIN

For Jimmy Carter the Bible was morality. For Reagan it was prophecy. Israel was not just a small country forced to live in a perpetual state of war by unpleasant "neighbors." Its redemption was the critical element in God's divine plan. Long before he entered the White House, Reagan had bought into elements of the premillennarian "dispensationalist" Christian package, unfolding from Genesis through to the Rapture, when a trumpet will sound and all true believers will float upwards into the heavens, leaving their clothes and other items behind as reminders of their earthly presence. The Rapture will be followed by the seven-year period of Tribulation, when those whose Christian beliefs were not quite true enough to warrant elevation in the first round will have to suffer; then Armageddon, when good will defeat evil; and finally the thousand years of the heavenly kingdom on earth before the destruction of all things ushers in some kind of fresh start. In 1971, when he was still governor of California, Reagan startled guests at a banquet by reading Armageddon into contemporary political developments:

> Biblical scholars have been saying for generations that Gog must be Russia. What other powerful nation is to the north of Israel? None. But it didn't seem to make sense before the Russian revolution when Russia was a Christian country. Now it does, now that Russia has become communistic and atheistic, now that Russia has set itself against God. Now it fits the description of Gog perfectly.... Everything is falling into place. It can't be long now. Ezekiel says that fire and brimstone will be rained upon the enemies of God's people. That must mean they'll be destroyed by nuclear weapons.[51]

The evangelical court of the incoming president a decade later included the 1950s Christian crooner Pat Boone ("Love Letters in the Sand"), Jerry Falwell (of the Moral Majority), Jim Bakker, Hal Lindsey, and numerous other fundamentalist luminaries lured to Babylon on the Potomac by the presence of one of their own inside the White House. The committed Christians around Reagan included Attorney General Ed Meese, Defense Secretary Casper Weinberger, and Secretary of the Interior James Watt. Religious feeling was stimulated through prayer breakfasts, and doors were opened wide for the evangelicals to take the gospel truth to military and political doubting Thomases and, in return, for military commanders to brief them on their strategic concerns. In a 1982 fundraising letter, Texas televangelist Mike Evans wrote of how Reagan had invited him to "challenge 58 generals and admirals with the truth of God in the middle of a White House meeting."[52] The rapid growth of evangelical Christianity in the United States opened up a new line of support for Israel. Begin welcomed the evangelicals to the Holy Land with a broad smile and open arms despite their perverse doctrines, rooted as they were in the belief that in the "last of days" the Chosen People would see the error of their ways and convert to Christianity. Falwell was awarded the Jabotinsky Prize for his services to Israel, and the evangelicals were allowed to run a gospel radio station from occupied southern Lebanon. These Christian prolifers had no problems with the killing of thousands of civilians during Israel's invasion of 1982. In the words of televangelist Pat Robertson, speaking on his CBN program *700 Club*, the confrontation with Israel's enemies was no less than a "modern Joshua event."[53]

Reagan often used evangelical television programs or conferences to explain his religious and political views. He chose the Jim Bakker PTL television network to tell an interviewer in 1980 that "we may be the generation that sees Armageddon." Only a few weeks into the presidency he remarked in an aside to Falwell that "Jerry, we are heading very fast for Armageddon now." In 1983 he told Thomas Dine, the executive director of the American-Israel Public Affairs Committee, that "I turn back to your prophets in the Old Testament and the signs foretelling Armageddon and I find myself wondering if we are the generation that is going to see that come about. I don't know if you have noted any of those prophecies lately, but believe me, they describe the times we are going through."[54] Possibly Dine had not noticed. He was the sort of man, as Israel Zangwill might have remarked, likely to be more interested in Numbers than Prophets.

Speaking at the annual convention of the National Association of Evangelicals on March 8, 1983, Reagan connected evil on earth with the "evil empire" of the Soviet Union. "There is sin and evil in the world and we're enjoined by the Scriptures and the Lord Jesus to oppose it." That meant standing up to the Soviet Union even at the risk of nuclear war.[55] In the Middle East the "evil empire" was spreading discord through its regional satrapies, Libya, Syria, and the PLO. In a spot "where Armageddon could come," the president had told Jewish leaders during the 1980 election campaign, Israel was "the only stable democracy we can rely on" and a formidable force any invader of the region would have to reckon with.[56]

Reagan's twinning of prophecy and evil in his understanding of the temporal world was clearly shared by the millions of "born again" Christian evangelicals who voted for him; it was not just the "evil empire" of the Soviet Union that had to be challenged but the evil within—abortion, gays in the military, and homosexual marriages. In the context of world politics, the impact of the president's religious views cannot be dismissed as meaningless or irrelevant unless everything he said was born of a total cynicism, and this does not appear to have been the case. Reagan does not appear to have known much about the politics of the Middle East, apart from what he learned on the job, but his outlook was strongly shaped by what the Bible told him had happened and would happen—and inevitably that was going to work in favor of the Israelis and not the Palestinians.

MIXED SIGNALS?

In September 1981 Begin visited Washington and argued that as Israel had gone "more than halfway to meet the Arabs on the road to peace" at Camp David it was now owed everything the United States could do to preserve its security.[57] Miffed at Reagan's refusal to block the sale of AWAC early-warning reconnaissance aircraft to Saudi Arabia, he went behind the president's back in time-honored Israeli fashion and lobbied against him on Capitol Hill. In December, the relationship between "Ron" and "Menachem" was further shaken by Israel's annexation of the Golan Heights. The president was also receiving reports that Begin and Sharon were preparing another invasion of Lebanon. As the president remembered his discussions with the two men: "We tried very hard to persuade Begin and Sharon that these radical Palestinian elements were trying to goad, manipulate and provoke them into war. They listened but they did not hear."[58] It does not seem to have occurred to Reagan that they did not want to hear.

Haig's recollections of the period are set down in a chapter of his memoirs entitled "Mixed Signals Bedevil Our Diplomacy." In fact, as usual, only the signals passing between various branches of the U.S. administration (especially between the White House and the State Department) were mixed. The signals Israel was sending Haig were perfectly clear. As early as October 1981, after the funeral for Anwar Sadat, Begin, speaking in his usual contradictory fashion about how he was ready to move quickly on the "peace process" as long as he was not expected to stop building settlements in occupied territories, informed Haig he was contemplating a "move" into Lebanon and was "warned" in return that "if you move, you move alone."[59]

On May 28, 1982, Haig wrote that he and Reagan "sincerely hoped" Israel would refrain from taking any military action against Lebanon. Begin responded by saying that "the man has not been born who will ever obtain from me consent to let Jews be killed by a bloodthirsty enemy," leading Haig to conclude that the United States "would probably not be able to stop Israel from attacking."[60] Again paraphrasing Lyndon Johnson's injunction of 1967, Haig told Begin that "you will not be alone unless you decide to go alone." The parallels between 1967 and 1982 were indeed striking. Johnson urged restraint and so did Reagan; both knew Israel was on the verge of launching a major war but still approved a multimillion-dollar aid package; Johnson made no attempt to use American aid as practical leverage to stop the Israelis and neither did Reagan, even though Israeli dependence on U.S. arms and economic support had taken a quantum leap since Johnson's time. Both claimed afterwards that they had done their best to stop the war.

There is one important difference. Well before June, the Reagan administration knew the full extent of the invasion Begin and Sharon had in mind. In February 1982, Yehoshua Saguy, the director of Israeli military intelligence, was sent to Washington to put the administration on notice that if there were further violations of the cease-fire Israel would send an army "from the Israeli border to the southern suburbs of Beirut."[61] In fact, as indicated previously, there had been no Palestinian violations of the cease-fire since the previous July. The same month that Saguy was in Washington, the UN secretary-general told the Security Council that the cease-fire had continued to hold since the adoption of the December 1981 resolution reaffirming the UNIFIL mandate until June 19, 1982.[62] When Haig warned Begin that such an operation would have "far reaching consequences," the Israeli leader agreed to hold off only on condition that no attack was made on Israeli citizens "or territory or any border or sector."[63] Again, on this point, he needed only what could be passed off as a "major provocation" to satisfy the Americans.

In March 1982 the Falangist leader Bashir Gemayel told a Beirut newspaper: "Don't be surprised if you stick your head out of the office windows and see Israeli tanks in the streets."[64] On April 8, NBC commentator John Chancellor exposed Israeli war plans in detail, including the decision to take the war to Beirut, and what he knew "was surely known in far greater detail within the Pentagon and the State Department."[65] A "remarkably detailed" account of the plan was also published by the *New York Times.*[66] The Israelis were making no attempt to hide their intentions. On the contrary, they were hanging them out for all to see. The coming invasion was "no longer much of a secret," wrote Haig, "nor was it a any secret that time was running out."[67] Visiting Washington in May, Ariel Sharon "shocked a roomful of State Department bureaucrats by sketching out two possible military campaigns: one that would pacify southern Lebanon and a second that would rewrite the political map of Beirut in favor of the Christian Phalange. It was clear that Sharon was putting the United States on notice: one more provocation by the Palestinians and Israel would deliver a knockout blow to the PLO."[68]

Haig took Sharon to one side and again told him that the United States would support no military action against Lebanon that had not been preceded by an "internationally recognized provocation" and that even then the response had to be proportionate. Sharon reacted in his usual bellicose fashion: "No one has the right to tell Israel what decision it should take in defense of its own people."[69] Reagan received the same message: "Mind your own business."[70]

When the Israelis finally invaded, Leonid Brezhnev accused the United States of complicity. "The facts indicate that the Israeli invasion is a previously planned operation whose preparations the US must have known about." Reagan protested: the Soviet accusation was "totally without foundation."[71] But against all the evidence, the president's denial of prior knowledge was a lie. The pious appeals for restraint coming out of Washington were the propaganda screen for a war that Haig in particular—Reagan seems to have been led along—was tacitly encouraging because it would strike a blow at the Soviet Union through third parties. The lure of seeing Soviet clients—"rogue state" Syria and the "terrorist" PLO—being given a bloody nose must have been very seductive. When the Israelis shot down dozens of Syrian planes, Haig's glee was unrestrained. The inferiority of the Soviet MiGs had been demonstrated "once again"; they had been "swept from the skies by American-Israeli technology and Israeli manpower while the whole world (and especially the Arab world) watched."[72] Haig's signals were certainly not confusing to the Israelis or to Jimmy Carter, who remarked that "the word I got from very knowledgeable people in Israel is that 'we have a green light from Washington.'"[73]

After the Israelis attacked, Haig blocked every effort to haul them off. Tipped off on June 8 by national security adviser Judge William P. Clark that the United States was likely to vote for a UN Security Council resolution condemning Israel for the invasion and invoking sanctions, Haig saw Reagan straightaway and advised him that the United States must veto the resolution, "not only because it placed the entire blame for hostilities on Israel but also because sanctions were implied." As soon as he had persuaded Reagan to change his mind, he phoned Jeanne Kirkpatrick at the UN to tell her to veto the resolution "regardless of any other instructions she may have received."[74] When Reagan wanted to send Begin a letter calling for an unconditional withdrawal, Haig talked him out of it. Begin was refusing to accept a cease-fire "until Israeli objectives had been achieved,"[75] and Haig backed him up. Against the death and destruction being meted out to Lebanon, his defense of an Israeli "solution" that basically consisted of bombing the Lebanese and Palestinian civilian population senseless eventually became untenable even within his own capital; on June 25 Reagan announced Haig's resignation and the appointment of George P. Shultz as his replacement.

BREAKING BEIRUT

On July 4, the invading Israeli army cut water and electricity supplies to West Beirut. Clearly Sharon wanted to submit the city to such pain that it could find relief only by driving out the Palestinians. Then the remaining "terrorists" in the refugee camps could be "mopped up." In accordance with this strategy Sharon escalated the air, land, and sea assault up and down the Lebanese coast. Inevitably unarmed civilians took the brunt of the punishment. Cars and buses full of passengers were obliterated on the open road. Whole apartment buildings were destroyed. In West Beirut an orphanage, a home for the disabled, and a mental home were all bombed. The children's hospital at the Sabra camp was hit and patients were killed; the Gaza hospital at the Bourg al Barajneh camp was bombed, and so were the ʿAkka Palestinian hospital, the American hospital near the American University of Beirut, and a hospital in the foothills town of Aley. In one day seventeen hospitals were hit. The scenes inside these hospitals—further scenes from Goya or the *Inferno*—were complete pandemonium as the bodies of the dead and wounded were brought in. Administrators and doctors protested that their hospitals were clearly marked with Red Cross or Red Crescent signs. According to the Lebanese Red Cross, the Israelis also attacked its ambulances, cars, and volunteers, preventing them from evacuating the wounded and bringing in food and medical supplies. The Begin government, ignoring UN calls for a cease-fire and refusing to accept the stationing of a UN peacekeeping force in the city to supervise the withdrawal of the Palestinians (as proposed by Reagan's special envoy Philip Habib), sought to justify the attacks by claiming that Palestinians gunners were deliberately placing their guns alongside these institutions.

The onslaught on the city reached a terrifying crescendo in August. During fourteen hours of nonstop bombardment on August 1, Israeli planes bombed a seven-story building in an aerial attempt to assassinate Arafat. He had left only "minutes before,"[76] but more than two hundred other people inside were killed or wounded. The building itself "collapsed in a pile no more than four feet high, leaving surrounding structures virtually intact. More than forty West Beirut buildings were destroyed by such Israeli bombs."[77] On August 12, the ferocity of Sharon's attack reached its apogee: dozens of Israeli planes streaked over Beirut, killing hundreds of civilians on this one day alone. In the two months and six days since the invasion was launched, more than eleven thousand people had now been killed. Standing on the steps of the presidential palace at Baʿabda, in the foothills overlooking the city, Prime Minister Shafiq Wazzan shouted: "If the Israelis want to kill us all let them do it and let's get it over and done with."[78]

By now negotiations for the supervised withdrawal of the PLO were well advanced. On August 21, units of the multinational force (American, French, and Italian) assigned to Lebanon to supervise the departure of the Palestinians, at the request of the Lebanese government and with the consent of the Israeli government, arrived in Beirut. The first contingent of Palestinians—more than eight thousand of them along with several thousand Syrians—left the city that day by sea or land. Arafat sailed away on August 30, and within two more days the Palestinian armed and political presence in the city was at an end.

On September 1, Reagan made a belated attempt at damage control by unveiling a peace plan based on Israeli withdrawal from Gaza and "most of the West Bank," but even though it was short on specifics and long on generalities and made no mention of a Palestinian state, it was too much for Begin.[79] He was irate that Reagan had shown his plan to Saudi Arabia and Jordan and not him, irate that Reagan had decided to go public before consulting him first, and hurt that "in your speech to the American people you did not, Mr. President, even mention the bravery of the Israeli fighters nor the great sacrifices of the Israeli army and people." Israel had gone into Lebanon only to destroy "armed bands" and smash "terrorists." It had lost 340 men killed and 2,200 wounded, "100 of them severely." As for the West Bank, "millennia ago, there was a Jewish kingdom of Judea and Samaria where our kings knelt to God, where our prophets brought forth a vision of eternal peace." In short, Camp David or no Camp David, Reagan or no Reagan, Begin had no intention of giving up the occupied territories. In the Knesset he built on parliamentary opposition to the U.S. president's plan to announce a five-year plan for the settlement expansion in the West Bank, the Golan Heights, and Gaza. The timing was impeccably but typically offensive. "We have no reason to get down on our knees," he declared. "No one will determine for us the borders of the Land of Israel."[80] He shrugged off the Fez plan, put forward by Arab governments nine days after Reagan's initiative and very similar to it, with the same contemptuous indifference.

Having supervised the withdrawal of the Palestinians, the multinational force departed. Habib had secured an assurance from Begin that Israeli forces would not enter West Beirut. The Palestinian leadership had sought guarantees from the Americans before departing out of fear for the safety of the Palestinian civilian population left behind. In fact, Israeli soldiers were already in West Beirut. They watched the Palestinians leave the port from a few hundred meters away and entered residential districts to begin the search for remaining "terrorists."

"CLEANING" THE CAMPS

The essence of the alliance forged between Bashir Gemayel and Sharon was that the IDF would clean out the Palestinians up to the municipal boundaries of Beirut and then Falangists would take over. But when the Israeli army reached Beirut and Sharon was driven to Jounieh for a meeting with Bashir, he was disturbed by what he saw. "On my way here I thought I would see people digging trenches and filling sandbags. I expected to see long lines outside your recruiting offices. Instead your people are sitting in cafes and the only lines I see are outside the movie theatres."[81] He clearly did not know Lebanon. In fact, having gotten Israel to do his dirty work for him, the swaggering Gemayel, elected president on August 23 when sufficient deputies were coerced, persuaded, or bullied into attending a session of parliament convened in a military barracks in East Beirut, had no intention of carrying out his part of the bargain. Almost certainly the Falangists would have been defeated by the Palestinians and their allies in street-to-street fighting, and Gemayel knew that as president he could rule only through dialogue and consultation with the *zaims*, Lebanon's sectarian leaders. He could not be the puppet Israel wanted and remain president, especially when the country's Christians were in an even smaller minority than generally realized (only 30 percent according to the Falangists' own figures).[82]

Neither were they any kind of cohesive minority. The Christians included Greek Orthodox, Greek Catholic, Armenian Apostolic, Armenian Orthodox, Assyrian Nestorians, and Protestants. While the Maronite parties were closely identified with the church, the most influential political party among the Greek Orthodox, the Syrian Social Nationalist Party, maintained a strong secular position and regarded Lebanon's ethno-religious divides as the fundamental source of the country's problems. Lebanese and Palestinians who were nominally Greek Orthodox had also played a significant role in Arab nationalist and Palestinian politics. Neither did the Maronites speak with one voice. After an initial show of unity in the 1970s, when they formed the Lebanese Front (LF) against the Lebanese National Movement (LNM), a loose coalition of Druze, Sunni Muslim Arab nationalists, independent Nasserites, communists, Ba'athists, and Palestinian factions, they impaled themselves on the lethal spears of their internecine rivalries.[83] Some of the most vicious attacks of the civil war were directed by Bashir Gemayel against other Maronite factions. These included the July 7, 1980, assault on the headquarters of the Lebanese "Tigers" (the National Liberal Party militia established by former president Camille Chamoun), in which more than eighty people were killed. Their leader, Dany Chamoun, escaped, only to be assassinated in 1991 with his wife and two young sons. In June 1978 Bashir had ordered an assault on the home of Tony Frangieh, the son of former president Suleiman Frangieh and the head of the personal militia (the Marada or "Giants") he had founded. Tony Frangieh, his wife, their young daughter, and their domestic staff were all killed. The following year, by way of revenge, Bashir's daughter and bodyguard were killed by a car bomb. The destruction of rivals established Bashir as the undisputed strongman among the Maronites but at the cost of destroying any hope that they could reassemble. Even among themselves, the Falangists often found it hard to contain their differences of opinion without resorting to violence.[84]

Sharon had outlined his intentions on July 11 during discussions in his office at the Defense Ministry in Tel Aviv. The camps in southern Lebanon had been destroyed. Now the southern part of West Beirut, where other camps had been established following the flight from Palestine in 1948, had to be "cleaned out" and "utterly destroyed":

> We don't touch the Lebanese population. We're dealing with the terrorist camps. The camps must be in our hands so that the terrorists

can't build a new infrastructure there, so that they don't start restoring them. . . . You should know that the Prime Minister has issued a directive not to have anything to do with the reconstruction of the camps in the south, just as we won't have any interest in doing so in Beirut. It's in our interest to have [the Palestinians] move on elsewhere. The Lebanese will take care of that but we have to lay the groundwork.[85]

The southern part of West Beirut had to be "razed to the ground. We won't touch the city, just the terrorists." The plan of attack was code-named Operation Iron Brain. The destruction of the camps in Beirut was the logical sequence to the destruction of the camps in the south, which Begin had described as an "inadvertent but welcome achievement of the war." In fact, it is clear that one of the objectives Begin had in mind when deciding to attack Lebanon was the "transfer" of the Palestinians living in the south. This was the word he used during a session of the Knesset Foreign Affairs and Defense Committee.[86]

Sharon had come all the way to Beirut. With American support he had succeeded in ejecting the Palestinian leadership and thousands of Palestinian fighters from Beirut. He had punished the Syrians. These were all considerable victories, but the last ripe fruits of his plan were still dangling tantalizingly out of his reach. Gemayel had boasted and bragged and promised much as militia leader, but as president he was stalling on the question of a treaty and beginning to talk of reconciliation. Sharon must have had his doubts about whether his government could be relied upon to purge the camps of the "terrorists" he purported to believe were still there. Now, because of the agreement the United States had reached with his own government, that Israeli forces would not enter West Beirut, he was facing the galling prospect of having to leave the city while the "terrorists" stayed.

In these circumstances, the assassination of Gemayel on September 14 was extremely fortuitous. Bashir had just begun addressing a seminar of adoring female members in the party's Ashrafiyya headquarters when a bomb planted on the third floor by a member of the Syrian Social Nationalist Party brought the building down over his head. Within hours, Begin had broken the Habib agreement and authorized Sharon to lead the army into West Beirut in the name of countering designs "aimed at plunging the area into renewed violence as a smokescreen to enable PLO remnants to regain their lost positions in Beirut and to fan out from there."[87] Israel claimed that more than two thousand "terrorists" armed with light and heavy weapons had stayed behind in the city. Sharon had wanted to lead the IDF into Beirut from the start, and now that Begin had slipped his own leash, Operation Iron Brain was about to be invoked so the "terrorists" could be cleaned out.

IRON BRAIN'S IRON GUARD

The White House and the State Department immediately called for a withdrawal of the Israeli forces. At the UN the United States voted for a Security Council resolution condemning Israel and calling for withdrawal from West Beirut within twenty-four hours or at least an agreement to withdraw. The U.S. statements and the UN resolution had no effect on Begin or Sharon. Their main targets now were the Sabra and Shatila refugee camps. These were sealed off. Checkpoints and observation camps were established while about 1,500 militiamen (Falangists along with some Haddadists) who had been assembled near Beirut International Airport were brought in by Israeli army jeep to purge the camps of the "terrorists" Sharon said were lurking there.[88] Iron Brain now had its iron guard. Ushered into Sabra and Shatila at about 6:00 P.M. on September 16, Israel's local mercenaries, armed with guns, axes, and knives, spent the next thirty-six hours killing as many Palestinian men, women, and children as they could. But *killing* is too colorless a word for the way they killed. They disemboweled and eviscerated. No mercy was shown to the very old or the very young or even the camp animals. It was the indiscriminate massacre of all living things—a truly biblical slaughter of the innocents. There was almost no "resistance" by terrorists because none were there, and, because much of the killing was done with knives, the neighbors of the dead often did not know what was going on until their turn came.

Anyone with the most elementary knowledge of recent Lebanese history would have known what was likely to happen once the Falangists (along with the Haddadist militiamen) were let loose inside the camps. The Israeli commission of inquiry into the massacres at Sabra and Shatila referred to the belief of Mossad agents that atrocities and massacres were a "thing of the past" and that Falangist forces had reached "a stage of political and organizational maturity that would ensure that such actions would not repeat themselves." Yet even the commission referred to the various facts that were "not compatible" with the view that the Falangists had changed for the better. "During the meetings that the heads of Mossad held with Bashir Gemayel, they heard things from him that left no doubt that the intention of this Phalangist leader was to eliminate the Palestinian problem in Lebanon when he came to power—even if that meant resorting to aberrant methods against the Palestinians in Lebanon."[89] In the early evening of September 16, as the militiamen were beginning to spread out through Sabra and Shatila, the Israeli chief of staff, Rafael Eitan, told the cabinet that he expected one of two things to happen following the assassination of Bashir. One would be the collapse of the Falangist power structure. The other would be an "eruption of revenge":

> I can imagine how it will begin but I do not know how it will end. It will be between all of them and neither the Americans nor anyone else will be of any help. We can cut it down but today they already killed Druze there. What difference does it make who or what? They have already killed them and one dead Druze is enough, so that tomorrow four Christian children will be killed, just like what happened a month ago; and that is how it will begin, if we are not there—it will be an eruption the likes of which have never been seen. I can already see in their eyes what they are waiting for.[90]

During Bashir's funeral, his brother Amin had uttered the word *revenge*. It was enough that he said it for the "whole establishment" to be sharpening their knives.[91] But it was not the Druze whom the Falangists hated enough to want to massacre. They were an entrenched part of the Lebanese system. The Maronites and the Druze might kill each other (as they had in the past), but eventually they would overcome their differences. In the view of the Maronite hard-liners (and not all were), the differences with the Palestinians could be resolved only by getting rid of them. They were outsiders—cuckoos in the nest that the Falangists were determined to throw out. The Druze could defend themselves. The Palestinians in the camps could not, now that most of the fighting men had departed with Arafat. They were sitting targets for the men sharpening their knives.

Within two hours of the Falangists' entering the camps, an Israeli intelligence officer "received a report" that one of the men inside the camps had asked the Falangist liaison officer (Eli Hobeika) what he should do with forty-five people he was holding. He was told, "Do the will of God" or "words to that effect." Slightly earlier an Arabic-speaking Israeli officer had heard one of the men asking Hobeika what he should do with fifty women and children he was holding. "This is the last time you're going to ask me a question like that," Hobeika was reported to have told him. "You know exactly what to do." Raucous laughter broke out among other Falangists standing with him on the roof of the IDF forward command post. The Israeli officer "understood that what was involved was the murder of the women and children."[92]

By 8:00 P.M., the Israeli command was being told that about three hundred "terrorists" along with civilians had already been "liquidated." The next morning Israeli correspondents were picking up reports from the IDF that there had been a massacre and passed on what they were hearing to the politicians. In spite of these reports the Israeli military command ordered that that the Falangists, who had complained of poor lighting, be supported with "limited illumination." In fact, flares were fired over the camps for such a long time on Thursday and Friday night that they looked like "a sports stadium lit up for a football match."[93] Already on Friday bulldozers were at work digging mass graves or scooping up bodies to be loaded onto trucks outside the camps to be taken away for burial elsewhere. Houses were bulldozed over bodies.[94] Late in the afternoon Eitan ordered the Falangists to "continue action, mopping up the empty camps south of Fakhani until tomorrow at 5am, at which time they must stop their action due to American pressure." They asked for a tractor to demolish "illegal structures"; the chief of staff "saw [this] as a positive action since he had long heard of illegal Palestinian neighborhoods and therefore he approved their request for tractors."[95]

The killings continued into Saturday morning, with hundreds of Palestinians being led out of the camps. Some were killed on the spot. The rest were taken away by trucks and have never been seen since.[96] The killers moved out of the camps at about 10:00 A.M., and the next day the Lebanese army took control. Asked how many Palestinians had died, a Falangist militiaman replied, "You'll find out if they ever build a subway in Beirut."[97] The death toll could never be firmly established but has been put at between 3,000 and 3,500 people.[98] Hundreds of thousands of horrified Israelis demonstrated as the news spread. Begin was also outraged, but only because the good name of the army was being besmirched. "On the New Year (Rosh Hashana), a blood libel was leveled against the Jewish State and its Government, and against the Israel Defence Forces," reads a statement issued by the cabinet on September 19. "In a place where there was no position of the Israel army, a Lebanese unit entered a refugee centre where terrorists were hiding, in order to apprehend them. This unit caused many casualties to innocent civilians. We state this fact with deep grief and regret." After the Israelis put an end to the slaughter by "forcing" the Falangist "unit" to withdraw, the civilian population of the camps "gave clear expression to its gratitude for the act of salvation by the Israel Defence Forces."[99] The accusations against the Israeli military were "entirely baseless" and rejected by the government "with the contempt they deserve."

The Israeli commission of inquiry (the Kahan Commission) held Sharon personally responsible but only criticized Begin, whom it could not accept was "absolutely unaware" of the likelihood of a massacre if Christian militiamen were sent into the camps. No one spent even an hour in prison for the war crime that had been committed. The "penalty" Sharon paid was to be removed from his post as defense minister.[100] Eitan was criticized for "ignoring" the dangers posed to the camp dwellers but was allowed to remain in the army until retirement and then receive full super-annuation rights. An independent commission of inquiry was established under the chairmanship of Sean McBride, but a proper international investigation of what happened inside Sabra and Shatila and who was responsible was never held.[101]

Between June 4 and August 31—in other words, from the eve of the invasion to the withdrawal of the Palestinians from Beirut—more than nineteen thousand people, almost all Lebanese or Palestinian civilians (mostly Lebanese) had been killed and more than thirty thousand wounded in Israeli military attacks on mostly civilian targets.[102] To this number must be added the number of Palestinians who had been massacred in Sabra and Shatila. A range of proscribed weapons had been used during the invasion, including cluster bombs and phosphorus bombs; besides, all of Israel's U.S.-supplied weaponry was supposed to be used only for defensive purposes. The evidence of what the Israelis were doing was appearing nightly on television screens around the world, producing cognitive dissonance among viewers who had regarded Israel as a beacon of light in a surging sea of Arab and Muslim fanaticism. In the aftermath of Sabra and Shatila, Begin authorized the withdrawal of the IDF from Beirut and the Shuf mountains above the city but refused to pull the army out of Lebanon altogether, as both the General Assembly and the Security Council were demanding in resolution after resolution.

UN CENSURES

Throughout the year a paper storm of Security Council and General Assembly resolutions rained down on Israel's head over the situation in Lebanon and the West Bank and Gaza. The United States played a protective role. On June 8 it vetoed a Spanish UN Security Council draft resolution condemning Israel for its failure to comply with council resolutions calling for a cease-fire and withdrawal from Lebanon, saying that the resolution was "unbalanced" and that the United States would continue its own efforts to end the violence. On June 26, a French draft resolution calling for withdrawal of the Israelis to the periphery of Beirut and of the Palestinians back to the camps and calling for the interposition of UN observers to supervise a cease-fire and disengagement lost 14-1 on the negative vote of the United States. The resolution had the support of the Lebanese government but was blocked by the United States on the grounds that it did not call for the elimination from Beirut "and elsewhere" of armed Palestinian elements "which did not respect the government's authority."

On July 29, the United States abstained from voting on a successful resolution calling on Israel to lift the blockade of Beirut and allow the delivery of essential supplies. On August 4 it voted for a resolution criticizing the entry of the IDF into Beirut only after it had been watered down to remove a reference to atrocities committed by the Israeli forces and to replace the word *condemnation* with *censure*. On September 19 it voted for a resolution that managed to condemn the massacres at Sabra and Shatila without once mentioning Israel. Five days later it voted with Israel against a blunter and stronger General Assembly resolution. On December 10 the General Assembly passed by an overwhelming majority vote twelve resolutions dealing with Israel's occupation of the territories seized in 1967.[103] Inter alia, the resolutions called for an immediate and unconditional Israeli withdrawal from all of the territories and for UN supervision of the territories for a transitional period. Legislative and administrative measures taken with the intention of altering the character of the Golan Heights were declared to be null and void. Israeli breaches of the 1949 Geneva convention (dealing with the protection of civilians in time of war) were described as war crimes. The "systematic Israeli campaign of repression" of Palestinian universities was described as including the closure of universities and the subjection of course material, the admission of students, and the appointment of faculty members to the supervision of the occupation authorities, "in clear contravention of the Geneva Convention." The United States voted against seven of these resolutions and abstained on five, its delegates describing the language of one as "harsh" and "unacceptable" and of another as "severely biased and polemical."[104] On December 16 the United States voted against or abstained from voting on a further series of resolutions dealing with the occupied territories and the recent events in Lebanon.[105] The following day it voted against a resolution reaffirming the illegality of Israel's exploitation of the natural resources of the occupied territories.[106] On December 20 it voted against a resolution expressing alarm at the deterioration of Palestinian living conditions and calling on Israel to give UN experts access to the territories.[107] Time and again the pattern was the same. The mountain of evidence supporting the accusations against Israeli practices in the occupied territories, the fact of an occupation already fifteen years old, and the bombardment of an Arab capital and the killing of thousands of people—none of it was sufficient to persuade the United States to restrain or discipline Israel. And now the United States itself was about to be stung: already awakened by the Muslim liberation theology of such eminent scholar-activists as the Imam Musa Sadr and Sayyid Husain Fadlallah, the Lebanese Shiʾa were mobilizing against Israel and the government that had provided it with understanding, sympathy, diplomatic protection, and the arms used to kill or drive them from their homes.

"THE SOLDIERS OF GOD"

On September 20, 1982, a second multinational force (American, French, Italian, and a small British contingent) had been summoned to Beirut at the request of the Lebanese government. Its mission was to stay until the withdrawal of all foreign forces; as there was no sign that Syria and Israel were prepared to withdraw in the foreseeable future, the multinational troops were likely to be stuck in Beirut for a long time. In Beirut, Shiʿi militiamen defended their turf against all comers and then fought for control among themselves. In the Shuf mountains the withdrawal of the Israelis in early September 1983 was followed by ferocious fighting between the Druze and Falangists. The Shuf was primarily Druze, and the Falangists were being driven out of village after village when the Lebanese army intervened to "restore order" and force adherence to the agreement signed on May 17, 1983, by the United States, the Gemayel government, and Israel. The agreement would have given Israel a "security zone" in the south jointly patrolled by Israeli soldiers and Haddadist militiamen, would have given Israel two "Security Arrangements Supervision Centers" (prisons?) inside Lebanon, and would have obliged Lebanon to remove from its territory forces hostile to Israel.[108] The agreement was opposed by Syria and all the major Lebanese confessional factions but the Maronites, and even they were divided. Signed without regard for the traditional consensus by which stability had been maintained in Lebanon for countless generations, it had no hope of sticking.

On April 18, 1983, the U.S. embassy on the corniche road near the shells of the Phoenicia Hotel and the Hotel St. George was destroyed by a new weapon of asymmetrical warfare. A suicide bomber drove into the embassy forecourt and blew the building up. Bodies were left hanging out of the shattered remains; of the sixty-three people killed, a number were senior CIA regional staff who were meeting at the time. The attack exposed both the vulnerability of the U.S. presence in Lebanon and the depth of hostility created by American support for Israel. In the months ahead gunmen positioned in the foothills of the mountains above Beirut peppered the U.S. Marine barracks with small arms fire. Several marines had been killed when

Reagan wrote in his diary on September 6 that "the civil war is running wild and could result in the collapse of the Gemayel govt. and then stuff would hit the fan." The next day he confided that "I can't get the idea out of my head that some F14s off the *Eisenhower* coming in at about 200 feet over the Marines and blowing hell out of a couple of artillery emplacements would be a tonic for the Marines and at the same time would deliver a message to these gun happy Middle Eastern terrorists."[109]

A day later the U.S. administration took the fatal step of openly siding with the government of President Amin Gemayel (Bashir's brother) by authorizing the naval shelling of a Druze artillery battery in the hills. Factional fighting was concentrated around the village of Souk el Gharb, an Orthodox village off the main Beirut-Damascus highway near the Druze villages of Aitat and Ainanoop (and close to the old British "school for spies" in the village of Shemlan). Precisely because of its commanding view over Beirut and the hills rippling down to the city, Falangist troops sent into the hills in the name of the government and the Druze had converged on the village, and now on September 8 the U.S. Sixth Fleet intervened by directing fire against Druze positions. The U.S. administration had openly and clearly put itself on one side of what Reagan had admitted was a civil war, and on October 23 Reagan's "stuff" hit the fan in an atrocious way for the marines in the multinational force. Two suicide bombers drove trucks into the compounds of the U.S. and French barracks and destroyed both buildings, killing 241 Americans and 58 French paratroopers. The drivers of the trucks were vaporized, but responsibility for the attacks was quickly claimed by an organization calling itself Islamic Jihad. "We are the soldiers of God and we are fond of death. We are neither Iranians nor Syrians nor Palestinians. We are Lebanese Muslims who follow the principles of the Koran."[110]

Both the Americans and the French responded with air attacks and naval bombardment, but without knowing who had dealt them such a devastating blow they were striking out rather than back and thereby demonstrating their impotence rather than their power. In early February 1984 Reagan finally conceded defeat by announcing the withdrawal of the marines. The multinational force quickly disintegrated. The British left first and the Italians last. Israel's attempts to impose a peace treaty on Lebanon finally collapsed on March 5 when President Gemayel discarded the May 17, 1983, agreement.

The principal architect of Lebanon's near-destruction was Israel. The principal architect of its survival was Syria (subsequent Maronite ingratitude notwithstanding). Syria took a beating in Lebanon. The Israelis destroyed its missile batteries in the Biqaʿa valley and destroyed dozens of its planes, but the Syrians (as represented by the iron will of Hafez al Assad) stood their ground with the determination of a bruised but wily boxer determined to stay in the ring long enough to win on points. Having done this, Assad then steered the Lebanese factions toward the peace agreement that was finally signed at Taif in 1989. It was Syria's strategic ally Hizbullah that finally forced Israel out of Lebanon (except for the Shabaʿa farms area) in 2000. As Iran—Syria's other strategic ally—had established Hizbullah in the first place, the outcome in Lebanon was a success for its regional policies as well. By contrast, America's Arab "friends" in the region—Egypt and the Gulf states—did virtually nothing to help Lebanon.

Israel (with the United States behind it) had certainly succeeded in securing the ejection of the PLO from Beirut, but at the price of arousing a Shiʿi resistance movement in the occupied south far deadlier than the Palestinians had ever been. The Israeli troops sent there bled slowly under the increasingly sophisticated and always highly motivated attacks of Hizbullah guerrillas. Israel destroyed "Fatahland" only for "Hizbullahland" to take its place, right down to the fence marking the armistice line. The photographs of Hizbullah's martyrs and its religious and political leaders are everywhere to be seen. Through the combination of successful resistance to Israel, participation in the Lebanese political system, ecumenical and political dialogue with the leaders of the other confessional groupings, and the continuing mobilization of the Shiʿite population, Hizbullah, a "terrorist organization" according to the U.S. State Department but a national resistance movement in the eyes of most Lebanese (and one supported by many Christians), has developed into the most coherent social and political force in Lebanon today. This was scarcely the kind of outcome Begin and Sharon had in mind when they sent the IDF into Lebanon in 1982.

By the time the civil war in Lebanon had been settled, another war had started and ended on the other side of the Middle East. In 1988 the war between Iraq and Iran finally ground to a halt in the deadlock of exhaustion. Saddam had hoped to deliver a knockout punch, but by the spring of 1982 Iraq was doing so badly on the battlefield that the United States, behind the mask of neutrality, was compelled to help out; at stake was not just the imminent victory of a revolutionary Islamic regime that regarded the United States as the "great Satan" but the oil fields of southern Iraq, which Iran seemed on the point of capturing. This could not be allowed. The lengths to which the United States went to ensure that Iraq was not defeated form the substance of part 4.

PART IV. THE BUSH WARS

12. INTO THE GULF

On January 16, 1979, Shah Muhammad Reza Pahlevi fled Iran for eighteen months of global wandering before dying in Cairo on July 27, 1980. On January 31, Ayatullah Ruhullah Khumayni returned in triumph from exile in Paris to lay the foundations of the Islamic republic. On July 16, Saddam Hussein al Tikriti took over from Ahmad Hassan al Bakr as Iraq's president and began preparing the military for war with Iran. On November 4, students stormed the U.S. embassy in Tehran and held sixty-six people inside the compound hostage. In April 1980, President Carter sanctioned an attempt to rescue them by helicopter, but Operation Eagle Claw had to be abandoned when two of the nine helicopters malfunctioned in a sandstorm, a third crashed on landing, and a fourth collided with a C-130 transport plane after the mission had been aborted. In November Carter lost the presidential elections, partly because of the humiliation of the hostage crisis, compounded by the failed rescue attempt, and on January 20, 1981, Ronald Reagan moved into the White House. Within half an hour the remaining hostages had been released.[1] The combination of these dramatic events over two years propelled the Middle East into even more turbulent waters than before. The overthrow of the shah and elections in the United States brought two sets of doctrinaire ideologues face to face. In Tehran the revolutionaries sought the establishment of an Islamic order not just in Iran but across the Middle East and indeed anywhere where Muslims were struggling against their own backsliding leaders, corruption, oppression, and foreign occupation or domination. To Iran's Islamic revolutionaries, the United States, the shah's sponsor and armorer, was the "Great Satan." To Ronald Reagan and the radical conservatives lining up behind him, Iran's Islamic government was a rogue regime situated on an "axis of evil" stretching around the world. Somewhere between these ideological antipodes stood Iraq and its recently installed president.

Eight days after Hassan al Bakr—Saddam's clan relative from Tikrit—had resigned (officially for reasons of "ill health"), Saddam convened a special session of the Baʿath Party to put his stamp on the presidency without further delay. He puffed on a cigar while a humbled member of the hierarchy made a public confession of his crimes against the party, the state, and the people, and then he took over, slowly reading out the names of twenty-two more "traitors." Some shrieked their innocence and loyalty in Moscow show trial fashion, but all were dragged out and twenty-one later executed. Hundreds of other party members were purged and liquidated at the same time. It was a sign of what was to come as Saddam oversaw the transformation of Baʿathist Iraq from an authoritarian state into a totalitarian one. The notion of one nation united by the party and symbolized by the father figure staring at the people from posters, newspapers, billboards, and television screens was promoted by the legislative abolition of regional cognomens. Saddam Hussein al Tikriti became just Saddam Hussein. If only out of prudence people rushed to join the Baʿath. Its tendrils reached into every crevice of Iraqi society, but while securing the home base Saddam could scarcely ignore the menace to the regime coming from outside Iraq's borders.

The Baʿathists and the revolutionary regime in Tehran traded insults for more than a year before Saddam decided to destroy this newly hatched serpent before it grew any larger. Iran was in turmoil. Revolutionary guards were still delivering their victims to Islamic judges. The military command—army, navy, and air force—had been destroyed. Admirals, generals, and air force commanders were dead or in prison, as were numerous politicians who had made the mistake of staying behind when they could have fled. Almost nothing was left of the old regime, and surely there could never be a better time to strike down the new one. Open warfare was now contingent only on timing, circumstances, and justification.

In April the underground Shiʾa movement, al Daʿwa al Islamiyya (Islamic Call), tried to kill Iraqi Foreign Minister Tariq Aziz. In June, Iraq severed relations with Iran. On September 4, 1980, Iranian forces shelled positions inside Iraq. On September 17 the Baʿathist government withdrew from the Algiers Agreement, signed with the shah in 1975; on September 22, 1980, claiming that Iran had already started a war with the shelling of September 4, and implicating Iran in the attack on Tariq Aziz, it ordered a wave of air attacks on Iran in an attempt to destroy its air power ahead of the coming land assault. Imitating Israel's destruction of

Arab air forces in 1967, Saddam hoped to destroy Iran's F-4 and F-5 jet fighters—supplied to the shah by the "Great Satan" only a few years before and superior to Iraq's MiG fighters—and bombers on the ground. Runways were damaged, but most planes were sitting inside specially reinforced hangars and were soon striking back as Iraqi forces crossed the border. What was intended as a short destructive war turned into a long destructive war that continued until both countries could fight no longer.

"A GAIN FOR OUR SIDE"

Saddam was to survive two more wars (the American-led attack of 1991 and the American-led invasion of 2003) before being pulled out of the underground pit where he was hiding in December 2003. The impending trial of the overthrown and unearthed president raised the question of what revelations might come out of his trial about his dealings with the U.S. administration during the war with Iran and, indeed, with previous administrations going back to the early 1960s if not further. Astonishingly, in view of the secrets Saddam surely could have exposed, nothing came out. He berated the court and the occupation but went to his death without saying a word about his dealings with the Americans. Yet they were an integral part of Iraq's Baʿathist history. What President George W. Bush, in an address to the nation after Saddam's capture, described as this "dark and painful" period in Iraq's history actually began with a push from the United States.[2] The Baʿath was America's bludgeon of choice for the dirty work that had to be done after the revolution of 1958 to destroy the Iraqi Communist Party and prevent Iraq from being drawn any deeper into the orbit of the Soviet Union.

The revolution threatened Western interests in the same way that the Iranian revolution did on an even larger scale just over two decades later. In the first year its leaders, Abd al Salam Arif and Abd al Karim Qasim, closed British military bases, took Iraq out of the Baghdad Pact, broke relations with France over Algeria, and began turning to the USSR for arms and diplomatic support. In 1958 Egypt and Syria had merged in the United Arab Republic. Abd al Salam Arif and many Iraqis (including the Baʿathists) wanted Iraq inside the UAR without delay, creating an Arab union that would cross the Middle East from the borders of Libya to the borders of Iran, but Qasim was not prepared to play second fiddle to Nasser. He intended to keep Iraq out of the UAR (as he told the British ambassador),[3] but at the same time he was not yet in a strong enough position to defend himself against his domestic opponents. He needed a strategic support base, and—in the absence of other options—he cultivated one with the Iraqi Communist Party. On either side this was not a love relationship but a marriage of convenience, marred by the usual consequences of such a relationship, chiefly the attempts on both sides to strengthen their position whenever the opportunity arose. Qasim's feints and maneuvers against the party led some of its leading members to conclude that he would have to be overthrown, but uncertainty over tactics prevailed until the Iraqi leader was eventually overthrown by someone else.

In March 1959, internal frictions spilled over when the Partisans for Peace, a Soviet front organization active across the Middle East and elsewhere, held a national conference in Mosul. The arrival in the city of thousands of communists from all over the country was an opportunity for anticommunist army and intelligence officers already planning an uprising with the covert support of the UAR. A "free for all" developed after they arrested communists and attempted to take control of the city, pitting tribe against tribe, Kurd against Arab, peasants against landlords, Christians against Muslims, the poor against the rich, soldiers against their officers, and communists against Nasserite and Ba'ath nationalists.[4] Ending the turmoil gave Qasim his own opportunity to destroy his enemies. At the height of the Cold War it is not hard to imagine the effect in Washington of the triumph of the Iraqi strongman and his communist allies over the Nasserites and Ba'athists. If Iraq were to be prevented from falling into the hands of the Soviet Union, Qasim would have to go. In the assassination plan orchestrated by the CIA, Egyptian intelligence would provide support, but the deed would be carried out by the Ba'ath. On October 7, 1959, Saddam and five accomplices tried to assassinate Qasim as he drove through Baghdad, but they fired prematurely and missed their mark. Saddam escaped and hid out in the Tikrit region before crossing the border into Syria and being transferred by Egyptian intelligence officers to Beirut. Subsequently he was moved on to Egypt. According to UPI correspondent Richard Sale, reconstructing the history of the period on the basis of interviews with former U.S. and British diplomats and intelligence officers, the CIA paid for Saddam's apartments in Beirut and the upper-middle-class Cairo suburb of Dokki. Nominally Saddam was a college student (and a bad one, as he had always been during his schooling). His real interests and affiliations were revealed in his frequent visits to the U.S. embassy, where his contacts included old CIA hand Miles Copeland and the Cairo station chief Jim Eichelberger.[5]

By the early 1960s, Qasim was even more of a bone in the throat of the West. In 1960 Baghdad was the setting for the first conference of the oil-producing states (Organization of the Petroleum Exporting Countries [OPEC]). The next year, in the first stage of a nationalization process completed in 1971, he slashed the size of the territorial concession granted during the mandate to the Iraq Petroleum Company (originally the Turkish Petroleum Company and eventually British Petroleum). He also announced his intention to annex Kuwait, compelling Britain to send troop reinforcements to prop up the Sabah family. The threat to Western interests across the region was metastasizing. In little over a decade, Britain had lost control of the Suez Canal and the huge reserves of oil in Iran. Now it was losing control of Iraq's oil as well, but short of another round of skullduggery it was hard to see how Qasim could be removed. In the years since the revolution he had entrenched his position within his own country and established a reputation across the region as a strong defender of Arab interests against Western intrigues. His anti-imperialist stance and his domestic policies (agrarian reform, low-cost housing, and expansion of hospitals and schools) had turned him into a smaller Iraqi simulacrum of Nasser. In foreign policy he had continued to tilt Iraq toward the Soviet Union. Clearly, in the thinking of internal and external enemies, the only way to remove him would be to resort to the same means he had employed to remove others.

According to former National Security Council staffer Roger Morris, the CIA fomented rebellion from Kuwait and made one unsuccessful attempt to assassinate Qasim (by sending him the gift of a poisoned handkerchief) before coming in behind the Baʿath when it overthrew him on February 8, 1963.[6] Qasim's murder was followed by a purge in which thousands of communists, indeed leftists of any description, many of them middle-class doctors, lawyers, teachers, and other professionals, were rounded up and killed. The CIA helped out by providing a list of names.[7] Many of the victims were liquidated on the spot. Others were taken away for interrogation, torture, and then execution. In Baghdad the infamous Qasr al Nihayat (the "Palace of the End") was the central bloody clearinghouse and Abu Ghraib the main prison. For the United States, the Baʿath takeover was "almost certainly a gain for our side," as the State Department's Robert Komer remarked.[8] No crocodile tears would be shed in Washington for dead communists in Iraq or anywhere else.

By the end of the year the Baʿath-dominated government was overthrown after being weakened by internal ideological turmoil, but in 1968 they regained power through a second coup. Ahmad Chalabi, who was to come to the fore much later as the leader of the anti-Baʿath exile group the Iraqi National Congress, described the coup as the "second stage" of CIA-Baʿath cooperation.[9] On the evidence of American involvement in the plot against Qasim in 1959, however, it should be regarded as the third. Older and wiser, and now well placed in the upper ranks of the party, Saddam Hussein was only a short distance from the very top.

THE GREAT LEADER

If there was a substantial difference between the two leaders who dominated Syrian and Iraqi life for three decades, it was surely the difference between Machiavellian ruthlessness and pathological brutality. Hafez al Assad took no apparent pleasure in the destruction of those who undoubtedly wanted to destroy him, but with Saddam Hussein violence seemed necessary to satisfy an appetite for power and domination. Saddam linked past glories with present achievements and future acknowledgment of his greatness, when he would be seen standing in the pantheon of Iraq's multimillennial history alongside Hammurabi and Nebuchadnezzar, Salah al Din al Ayyubi (Saladin), Saʿd bin abi Waqqas (the conqueror of the Persians at Qadisiya), al Hajjaj (the fearsome Umayyad governor of Kufa), and the Abbasid caliph al Mansur, the builder of Baghdad. In posters and even on the bricks used to reconstruct the ruins of ancient cities, Saddam, the poor boy from Tikrit, twinned his names with theirs. Like all dictators, Saddam made no separation between himself and the state.

Oil revenue in the 1970s turned Middle East producer countries into the wealthiest in the world. Building on the combination of agricultural wealth and the oil that provided 95 percent of its revenue, the Baʿathists turned Iraq into one of the most modern countries in the Middle East—if "modern" means hospitals, schools, universities, free education, equal rights for women, welfare systems, and labor rights. In Kanan Makiya's words, the Baʿath "transfigured Iraq's physical infrastructure. The regime provided free health and education for everyone and it also revolutionized transport and electrified virtually every village in the country. Iraq today has a proportionately very large middle class; its intelligentsia is one of the best educated in the Arab world."[10]

But Baʿathist modernity in Iraq did not come with the trappings of a liberal political state. Saddam's Iraq was authentically modern but only in the sense that national socialist Germany, fascist Italy, or Stalin's Russia were modern. Under Saddam, surveillance, intimidation, torture, murder, and blackmail were streamlined, coordinated, and centralized, so that whether within the ranks of the party or the military or among the general population, the enemies of the state—Saddam's enemies—could be quickly identified and eliminated. This is not to say that Saddam was a man without vulnerabilities. According to former vice president Taha Yassin Ramadan, "Saddam was weak with family members. He punished them but let them go right back to what they were doing in the first place."[11] This was particularly true of his sons Uday and Qusai, but while they could be as brutal as their father, while they occasionally angered and even embarrassed him, earning his punishment, they never betrayed him. That was the real test. Family members who did betray him were treated as mercilessly as anyone else: when Saddam's two sons-in-law succumbed to his blandishments and returned to Iraq in 1996 after defecting to Jordan, he had them murdered.

When the challenge to his power involved an entire discrete sector of society, Saddam calibrated the scale of the violence accordingly. The regime had been destroying villages in the Kurdish north and removing the population since the late 1960s, but under the pressure of the war with Iran these policies against the Kurds were carried to even greater extremes. In 1980, numbers of Fayli Kurds were massacred and others driven across the border into Iran. Three years later, thousands of Barzan tribesmen were reportedly taken away and killed. The charge of Kurdish treachery and the declaration of Kurdish areas as "prohibited zones" were the prelude to the tremendous assault on the Kurdish civilian population in the multistage Operation Anfal campaign of February through September 1988.[12] Conventional and chemical weapons were used, a large number of villages were destroyed, and their people were taken away. Kanan Makiya estimates that the number of Kurds killed during Operation Anfal was "not less than 100,000" and might be higher than 180,000.[13] Many of those who disappeared are thought to have been massacred and buried in mass graves somewhere near the long border with Saudi Arabia (although since the U.S.-led invasion of 2003 these have not been located if they do exist).[14] The greatest single atrocity through the use of chemical weapons was the killing on March 16 of an estimated five thousand to seven thousand Kurdish civilians in and around the northeastern city of Halabja, a few kilometers from the Iranian border, held at the time by Iranian forces.[15] Although the Baʿathist regime had now added, through the course of the conflict with Iran, war crimes and crimes against humanity to a long list of crimes already committed against its own civilian population, the Arab League, the Organization of the Islamic Conference, the United Nations, and individual Western governments did no more than utter statements of shock and condemnation.[16]

South of Baghdad, in the face of Shiʿi defiance, Saddam targeted the Shiʾa for discipline and destruction. In 1980, he ordered the execution of the prominent Shiʿi cleric Ayatullah Muhammad Baqr al Sadr and his sister. When other Shiʿi figures fled to Iran, he arrested members of their families, effectively holding them hostage in the attempt to silence criticism from Tehran. In the continuing attempt to suppress the underground movement al Daʿwa al Islamiyya, thousands of Shiʿa were eliminated by judicial and nonjudicial means. Discriminatory laws were invoked to take citizenship away from Shiʿi Muslims with a "Persian" background and drive them across the border into Iran. For Saddam, however, an enemy was an enemy, whatever his or her ethnic or religious background; as his cousin, Ali Hasan al Majid, remarked in January 2007 during his trial on charges of war crimes and crimes against humanity for his role in the Anfal campaign, "It is not part of our ideology or policy to be against an ethnic group."[17] Saddam's inner circle of old reliables was formed not on the basis of religion or ethnicity but on the basis of unswerving loyalty to the leader.

"INTOXICATED WITH CONCEIT"

By 1985 the struggle between Iraq and Iran had developed into a war of attrition. It ended in August 1988 after Ayatullah Khumayni reluctantly and grimly accepted a cease-fire. Saddam, on the other hand, in the opinion of Hamid Yusif Hammadi, his former secretary and director of the presidential office, was "intoxicated with conceit" and believed that he was now unbeatable,[18] even though the war had ended with the Iranian regime not only still in place but stronger than before and with no other tangible change in the prewar situation except for massive material destruction and vast loss of life (about a million people on both sides). The southern Iranian city of Khorramshahr looked like Grozny after the Russians had finished with it. Iraq's war losses were so great that Saddam's decision to invade Kuwait two years later seemed an act of madness. And American intervention was so certain that if the decision to invade was not made in a moment of rage—because the Kuwaitis were allegedly "slant drilling" across the Iraqi border, because they were refusing to write off the billions of dollars they had given Iraq to fight Iran, because they were overproducing and bringing oil prices down when Saddam needed them up—Saddam really must have thought he had been given the green light in his discussion with the U.S. ambassador (April Glaspie) on July 25, 1990.

Under instructions from President Bush to seek "better relations" with Iraq, Ms. Glaspie told Saddam that "we have no opinion on the Arab-Arab conflicts, like your disagreement with Kuwait." This is the fulcrum for the argument that Saddam was deliberately lured into Kuwait so he could be destroyed. The conversation with Ms. Glaspie was a mixture of pleasantries and threats. "We know that you can harm us although we do not threaten you," Saddam said. "But we too can harm you. Everyone can cause harm according to their ability and their size. We cannot come all the way to you in the United States but individual Arabs may reach you."[19] The weakness of the entrapment theory is that Saddam was a deeply suspicious man in almost any circumstances and was more likely to see any green light flashed in his direction as a danger signal. He trusted no one outside his inner circle of advisers and probably even had his doubts about some of them. He was certainly under no illusions about the motives of the U.S. administration. After Irangate (the scandal in which the profits from arms sold by the United States to Iran were channeled to the Contras in Nicaragua) he had concluded that the United States "was out to get him personally."[20]

In seeking to justify the invasion of Kuwait, Saddam argued that Kuwait had been attached to the province of Basra in Ottoman times and therefore should have been included in the main Gulf successor state after 1918 rather than being given the status of a British dependency and allowed to move forward to independence. This was the argument advanced by Abd ul Karim Qasim in 1961. Iraq's accusations of British chicanery, beginning in Kuwait's case with the treaty Britain signed with Sheikh Mubarak behind the Ottoman sultan's back in 1899, were well founded. The British partition of the Middle East after 1918 left independent Iraq without access to the sea except through the narrow channel of water known as the Shatt al Arab, giving Britain unimpeded domination of a chain of eventually wealthy but weak protectorates all the way down the Gulf from Kuwait to Oman.

In accusing the West of double standards, Saddam was only expressing a general Arab view. Israel had attacked other countries on a number of occasions. It had occupied the West Bank, Gaza, East Jerusalem, and the Golan Heights for twenty-three years, had indeed occupied territory well beyond the limits of the 1947 partition resolution for more than half a century, and had driven the Palestinians out of their homeland on two occasions (1948 and 1967) without any attempt being made to punish it through sanctions or military force. It was still occupying southern Lebanon. It lived in continuing noncompliance with UN resolutions, yet when the Iraqi army moved into Kuwait the UN Security Council waited for only four days before imposing sanctions (Resolution 661 of August 6). On November 29—coincidentally, the same day that the General Assembly had voted to partition Palestine in 1947—the council passed Resolution 678 authorizing Kuwait's friends to use "all necessary means" to bring about Iraq's compliance with previous resolutions if its occupying army had not been withdrawn by January 15.[21]

In only four months the UN had set up the entire machinery for forcing Saddam out of the territory he had occupied. Never before had the

Security Council acted with such speed and determination, yet when the war was finally launched on January 16, without the United States seeking the second resolution many regarded as necessary for the action to warrant the imprint of the UN, the council did not meet again for twenty-eight days. It seemed in no hurry to intervene. "The Security Council has been used as a kind of glove," remarked the chief Cuban delegate to the UN. "When it so suits us we put it on and use it for certain purposes; when it becomes a bother we simply take it off and throw it away."[22]

From President Bush downward, high officials in the U.S. administration stressed morality, civilized behavior, and the need to uphold international law against the barbarity of Saddam and his government. The commander of the armed forces being assembled to drive the Iraqis from Kuwait, General Norman Schwarzkopf, assured the Iraqi people that he had no quarrel with them. "We have said all along that this is not a war against the Iraqi people."[23] The British ambassador, Sir David Hannay, described the crisis in a session of the Security Council as "a confrontation between collective security as provided for in the Charter of the United Nations and the law of the jungle."[24] However, the confrontation cannot be understood without following the path that led toward it. Did Saddam reach the edge of the precipice unaided? How did Iraq manage to develop its weapons of mass destruction (WMD), and might its possession of them, for reasons of their own, have suited the governments poised to go to war in January 1991?

STOPPING IRAN

The oil boycott that followed the 1973 Arab-Israeli war drove prices and profits up to unprecedented levels, distorting economic and social development in the producer countries. In Iran the importance of the agricultural sector, the need to maintain a diversified economy, and reliance on a stable tax base in a country were all swamped in this avalanche of wealth. With profits from oil and gas accounting for 86 percent of revenue by the end of 1974 (compared to 11 percent in 1954), Iran was turned into a country that no longer needed to rely on the comparatively infinitesimal amounts brought in by direct or indirect taxes. There had never been any genuine representation, but at least there was now not much taxation either.[25] The principal beneficiaries of this bonanza were the shah, for whom oil wealth would be the basis of the transformation of Iran from a developing country into a world power, and the self-serving elites around him. In the equally unrepresentative "rentier states" of the Persian Gulf, economic and social development continued to depend on the largesse of the ruler; the power structures did not change in any essential respect but were simply further corrupted by the opportunities for massive individual wealth created by the colossal profits now pouring into oil revenue accounts. Speculation, clientelism, commission taking, and the insistence by governments that foreign companies trade through a local partner further enriched families within the dominant tribal-political elite. For Iran and the insecure Gulf states, oil wealth enabled profligate spending in the Western arms bazaar.

As another principal beneficiary of the oil boom, Iraq's Baʿathist government had all the money it needed to spend on "defense." It wanted to buy up big, and there was no shortage of sellers. Through the 1970s and into the 1980s the United States, Britain, France, Germany, the Netherlands, Sweden, Spain, Italy, China, the Soviet Union, Chile, Brazil, Japan, Egypt, and numerous other countries supplied the Baʿathist regime with tens of billions of dollars worth of weaponry (including jet fighters, tanks, helicopters, armored personnel carriers, artillery, missiles, and missile launchers) and the second-level material that would enable Iraq to develop its own "defense" industry. Included in this category were computers and computer-guided machine tools, lasers, industrial machinery, missile technology, high-quality steel and aluminium, communications equipment, nuclear components—including detonators and fissionable material for uranium enrichment—and chemical warhead filling equipment, precursors that enabled Iraq to manufacture chemical weapons and the pathogenic cultures needed for the production of biological weapons. Much of this second-level war material was "dual purpose," ostensibly for civilian purposes but easily weaponized or cannibalized for parts needed for weapons development.

France alone sold Iraq an estimated $4 billion worth of weapons and war material between 1977 and 1980 and a further $12 billion between 1981 and 1988.[26] The weapons included Mirage F-1 jet fighters, Roland surface-to-air missiles, self-propelled artillery, antiship missiles (Exocets), and a range of auxiliary electronic equipment. France also helped Iraq to develop nuclear energy. Under the Franco-Iraqi Nuclear Treaty of 1976 it provided the Baʿathist government with the Osirak reactor (constructed near Baghdad), supervised its construction, and trained the cohort of Iraqi nuclear technicians needed to run it. Smaller test reactors provided by Russia and France were built in the same complex. Yellowcake was supplied through an agreement with Brazil in 1979,[27] but before the reactor could be loaded with fuel it was destroyed by Israel (June 1981) in the world's first military attack on a nuclear reactor. France had provided Israel with the Dimona reactor in the 1960s and had extracted from the Israelis the same commitment made by the Ba'athist government, that it would not use the reactor to develop nuclear weapons. However, Dimona was developed secretly and did lead to the production of nuclear weapons, whereas the Osirak reactor was constructed openly, was largely run by French technicians, and was operated within the framework of International Atomic Energy Agency (IAEA) safeguards and inspections.

Iraq's weapons and weapons material suppliers in the 1980s included all five permanent members of the UN Security Council. At least twenty countries were involved in building up Iraq's weapons programs. According to leaked information, the 11,800-page weapons "dossier" submitted by Iraq to the UN Security Council in December 2002 included the names of 150 U.S., British, French, and German companies "that had done business in conventional and non-conventional weapons with Iraq."[28] Copies of the full dossier were retained by the five permanent members of the Security Council, but it was "edited" (stripped of some eight thousand of its pages, according to media reports) before the United States handed copies to the nonpermanent members of the council.[29] The U.S. "hijacking" of the dossier—a "mini coup," in the words of a BBC report[30]—violated the council's requirement that the dossier be handed to the council as a whole. The names in material leaked from the dossier included eighty German companies, seventeen British companies, and twenty-four U.S. corporations involved in the sale to Iraq of component parts or material that could be utilized for the development of missiles and nuclear, chemical, and biological WMD. Other names in the culled document included "some 50 subsidiaries of foreign enterprises [which] conducted their arms business with Iraq from the US." Chinese, Belgian, Dutch, Japanese, Spanish, Swedish, and Soviet concerns were also involved in the sale of weapons material or in the establishment of the dual-use pesticide plants that were used to produce chemical weapons.[31] Pure profit was certainly part of the reason for the sales. "With a shrinking defense base our arms exports became more important to American arms suppliers," a State Department official told a Senate committee hearing,[32] but with Iraq struggling to hold back Iranian human-wave assaults, geostrategic concerns rather than support for the domestic arms industry prompted Washington to give Saddam the material needed to repel what was regarded as the greater threat to U.S. interests.

TILTING THE BALANCE

The tilt from official U.S. neutrality in the conflict toward support for Iraq was under way by early 1981. Iraq had broken diplomatic relations in 1967.

The U.S. Interests Section in Baghdad was headed by William L. Eagleton, who wrote on April 4 that the atmosphere was "excellent" now that the United States had decided not to sell arms to Iran and had given the "go-ahead" on the sale of five Boeing aircraft to Iraq. Increased commerce and the mutual upgrading of diplomatic staff also pointed to what Eagleton saw as "a greater convergence of interests with Iraq than at any time since the revolution of 1958."[33] Undersecretary of State Morris Draper's visit to Baghdad and talks with Foreign Minister Saʿadun Hammadi on April 12 took the two-way channel of communications to a higher level. Regional issues plus "the possibilities for developing and strengthening our economic and trade relations" were discussed.[34] On May 28 Eagleton saw Tariq Aziz, not yet foreign minister but a senior member of the Revolutionary Command Council and chief foreign policy spokesman. It was the highest level of exchange between the Baʿathist government and the U.S. Interests Section since 1967, and one that gave the United States its "first access" to the inner circle of the Iraqi leadership. Regional problems were discussed in general, along with the need for a better understanding between the United States and Iraq before they could tackle such difficult issues as the Arab-Israeli conflict, but Aziz assured Eagleton that "when the time is ripe" Iraq would be ready for more detailed discussions of these matters. Increased commerce and trade would obviously be part of this better understanding. Eagleton said his government would support the participation of U.S. companies in the reconstruction of Iraq's oil facilities as soon as the war was over.[35] Indeed, in the next two years, with the supply of oil through the Gulf under threat, Iraq studied two new pipeline projects involving U.S. companies. One pipeline would carry oil to an existing line in Saudi Arabia, from where it could be taken to a terminal on the Red Sea; the other would carry oil across Jordan to the port of Aqaba. Bechtel was among the multinational corporations discussing the construction of this second pipeline. After the Iraqis raised the likelihood of it being bombed by Israel, an unnamed investor in the project reportedly tried to set up a deal through the U.S. administration that would give Israel $70 million a year to leave the pipeline alone.[36] This person might have been the international financier Bruce Rappaport, a friend of CIA director William Casey and a "central figure" in the planning of the Aqaba pipeline.[37] Ultimately both projects lapsed. Bechtel was an American corporate giant that had been involved in the Middle East for decades. Its executive vice president from 1974 to 1982 was George Shultz, who joined the company's board of directors in 1989 after resigning as secretary of state.

In February 1982, the "dedesignation" of Iraq as a terrorist state cleared the way to U.S. government loans and the authorized supply under the

Export Administration Act of dual-use war materials. The administration would naturally insist on an Iraqi commitment not to adapt items in this category for war purposes, but in practice it was impossible to ensure that this did not happen. Trucks could quickly be converted to military use, and so could the U.S.-manufactured helicopters believed to have been used in chemical weapons attacks on the Kurds in 1988. Forty-five helicopters sold in 1985 on condition that they would be used only for civilian transport were later transferred to the military. Some were based in northern Iraq.[38]

The pressure to help Iraq increased in proportion to the urgency of its military situation. By early June 1982 the Iranians were positioning themselves opposite a gap in the Iraqi defenses that would allow them to break through and cut Baghdad off from Basra. The situation was so bad that the CIA concluded that Iraq had "essentially lost the war with Iran. Baghdad's main concern now is to prevent an Iranian invasion. There is little the Iraqis can do, alone or in combination with other Arabs, to reverse the military situation."[39] The United States had satellite imagery of the gap in the Iraqi defenses and the massing of Iranian troops on the border. At this point President Reagan issued a National Security Decision Directive (NSDD) that the United States would do "whatever was necessary and legal" to prevent Iraq from losing the war. According to National Security Council staffer Howard Teicher, who helped draft the directive, it was so secret that even its identifying number was classified.[40] The United States now rapidly stepped up the support it was providing for Iraq at all levels.

On May 10, 1983, George Shultz met Tariq Aziz (by now Iraq's foreign minister) in Paris and was told much of what he might want to hear by this astute person. Iraq was strongly in favor of the withdrawal of all foreign forces from Lebanon, including Syrian and PLO, and while it would not advocate peace at any price between Israel and the Arabs, it thought the time had come for a change of direction.[41] In December Donald Rumsfeld went to Baghdad as President Reagan's special envoy, holding discussions with Tariq Aziz on December 19 and with Saddam Hussein the next day. Common interests and concerns were stressed: in conversation with Aziz, Rumsfeld raised the Aqaba pipeline project, which, because of its vulnerability to attack, "may be an issue to raise with Israel at the appropriate time."[42]

Between Rumsfeld's two trips to Baghdad (in December 1983 and March 1984), Iraq's military situation deteriorated still further. It checked a massive Iranian assault in the south but only after losing control of the commercially and strategically critical Majnun Island oil fields. On his second visit to the region Rumsfeld went first to Israel, where Prime Minister Yitzhak Shamir asked him to deliver an offer of secret military assistance to

Saddam. Tariq Aziz refused even to accept the Israeli letter on the grounds that "he would be executed on the spot if he did so."[43] While Rumsfeld was in Baghdad, UPI quoted UN experts as reporting that the Iraqis were using mustard gas spiked with a nerve gas against Iranian troops. In fact, the administration was well aware of how Iraq was fighting this war. George Shultz was being served with battlefield information that the Iraqis were making "almost daily use" of chemical weapons on the battlefield,[44] yet the rapprochement continued, reaching a high point in November 1984, when the two countries reestablished full diplomatic relations.

COVERT AID

The U.S. program of support for Iraq was alternatingly open and surreptitious but uniformly multilayered. At one level the United States supported the supply of arms through third parties so that Iraq could neutralize the numbers of soldiers and volunteers Iran was pouring onto the battlefield. Iraq was also provided with dual-use war material through contracts authorized by the Department of Commerce and billions of dollars of credits for the purchase of U.S. agricultural products, authorized under the Departure of Agriculture's Commodity Credit Corporation (CCC). These were guaranteed by the U.S. government, which meant that when Iraq defaulted on payments in the early 1990s the corporation was saddled with more than $2 billion of claims.[45] Further financial support came from Export-Import Bank loans and officially unauthorized loans channeled to Iraq by the small and out-of-the-way Atlanta branch of a Rome bank.

After President Reagan issued his secret directive of June 1982, CIA Director Casey "personally spearheaded" the program to ensure "that Iraq had sufficient military weapons, ammunition and vehicles," not to win the war but to make sure that it didn't lose it.[46] Because the bulk of Iraq's tanks, planes, and artillery were of Soviet make, the CIA ran a "Bear Spares" program to ensure a continuing supply of matching ammunition and spare parts through third countries. With the approval of the United States, Egypt manufactured weapons and ammunition of Soviet design and sold them to the Baʿathist government. The Soviet Union, which had placed an embargo on the supply of weapons to Iraq when it attacked Iran, broke it in November 1982, when Iraq seemed on the verge of defeat, providing it with missiles, tanks, helicopter gunships, and other armaments.

In Chile, the cluster bombs sought by the Baʿathists to stop the Iranian human-wave advances were made in arms factories exported under license from the United States to Industrias Cardoenas as "scrap metal."

The technology—a simple matter because plans could be carried in brief-cases—was also provided by the United States. Howard Teicher had attended meetings at which CIA Director Casey or Deputy Director Robert Gates had noted the need for Iraq to have certain weapons to stave off Iranian human-wave assaults, including anti–armor penetrators and cluster bombs, which Casey regarded as perfect "force multipliers."[47] Casey ran the Chile operation as part of his general brief. "We needed an offshore supplier and the Chileans were very cooperative," remarked a former CIA contractor.[48] The supply of the cluster bombs, which could be dropped from French or Soviet aircraft, the backbone of Iraqi air power, was "a mere extension to the United States policy of assisting Iraq through all legal means in order to avoid an Iranian victory."[49] The first shipment was sent off early in 1984.[50] Throughout the 1980s, Industrias Cardoenas bought dozens of tons of zirconium—a vital ingredient in the production of the bomblets stored inside the cluster bomb shell—from the United States. Labor costs were cheap, and the profitability of the operation against European competition was enhanced by building the plant inside a duty-free zone at Iquique.

Helping Iraq also involved the authorization of $5 billion in credits for the purchase of U.S. primary produce (including chickens, eggs, rice, wheat, cattle, timber, and tobacco) and other farm goods. The legitimate use of these credits (paid from 1983 to 1990) enabled Iraq to spend money on weaponry that would otherwise have been needed for food. A principal conduit for these credits was the Atlanta branch of the Italian Banca Nazionale del Lavoro (BNL); according to evidence given before a congressional committee, the bank made false claims when applying to the Department of Agriculture so that even authorized loans intended for the purchase of chickens and timber were "distributed to Iraqi agents through letters of credit" and used to "finance the Iraqi military."[51] A subsequent Department of Agriculture inquiry revealed that "the CCC had no idea whether the credits it had backed were used to purchase US farm commodities that actually reached Iraq or were resold to third countries for hard currency."[52] Whether these credits were lawfully granted in the first place was another question that would only be asked later. Section 112 of the U.S. government's Agricultural Trade Development and Assistance Act stipulates that a country's human rights record be taken into account when the financing of the sale of U.S. commodities is being considered. Iraq's gross violations of human rights were being recorded every year by human rights organizations and even by the State Department, yet the credits continued to flow without letup until Kuwait was invaded.

In May 1992 Deputy Secretary of State Lawrence S. Eagleburger asserted that investigations by the Department of Agriculture and the Attorney-General's Office had uncovered no evidence of diversions to third countries of commodities sold to Iraq or "Iraqi misuse of the CCC program to purchase military equipment."[53] This did not necessarily mean the evidence was not there. A few days later a senior administration trade official issued a report drawing attention to the difficulties his office had encountered when seeking access to documents relating to BNL Atlanta and the Iraq CCC program. It had been allowed to review only five documents at the Department of Justice. The State Department and the Department of Treasury would not allow any documents to be copied. The U.S. embassy in Rome had refused to grant access to its files, and the CIA had refused to give a briefing. In these circumstances, as many thousands of documents were involved, and at best only notes could be made by hand from those that were made available, it was clear that a proper investigation into the government's trade dealings with Iraq and the role of BNL was not possible.[54]

Billions of dollars of officially unauthorized loans were also paid by the Atlanta branch of BNL into the accounts of Iraq front companies described by the CIA as part of "Iraq's complex procurement network of holding companies in Western Europe to acquire technology for its chemical, biological, nuclear and ballistic missile development programs."[55] These companies included the British subsidiary of the Ohio-based Matrix Churchill company, two of whose employees (including a director) were "sources" for British intelligence.[56] The BNL scandal came to the surface only after an employee discovered that the bank was making large "off-the-book" or "gray" loans and called in the FBI. Prosecutions of several employees followed. Christopher Drogoul, the manager, was charged on 347 counts. In testimony before the House of Representatives Banking Committee on November 10, 1993, Drogoul referred to BNL's relationship with Dr. Henry Kissinger, who was a member of its International Advisory Board, and to the activities of the Kissinger Associates consultancy as a "component" in many of the loans being made. Drogoul referred to himself as an "insignificant figure" in an international drama who was being sacrificed in the interests of major governments. "I was aware at all times that the policy of the BNL was to further the policy concerns of both the US and Italy."

It seemed unlikely that the BNL head office or the U.S., Italian, and British governments did not know of the Atlanta branch's activities. After scrutinizing a range of government documents, Atlanta District Court Judge Marvin Shoob concluded that the indicted Atlanta employees of BNL Atlanta were "mere functionaries" who had benefited the BNL management and the foreign policies of the United States and Italy. They were trivial in relation to the scope of a scheme that he described as "a far larger and wider-ranging sophisticated conspiracy that involved BNL-Rome and possibly large American and foreign corporations and the governments of the United States, England, Italy and Iraq."[57] He referred to a generally reliable source "who believed that BNL-Atlanta could not have operated without the knowledge and acquiescence of the Federal Reserve Board, the Department of Agriculture and the Commodity Credit Corporation." Speaking in the House of Representatives on September 14, 1992, Representative Henry B. Gonzalez said the provision of food to Iraq through the CCC program was only the public aspect of the administration's policy. There was also a secret layer, "and that aspect was to allow Saddam Hussein to operate a clandestine military procurement network in this country."[58]

The Ba'athist regime was also granted millions of dollars in loans through the U.S. Export-Import Bank. The bank suspended loans to Iraq in 1979 but resumed them in 1983 under political pressure from the Reagan administration.[59] It made short-term loans in 1984–85, discontinued them after Iraq defaulted on payment, but resumed them in 1987 under pressure from the administration. Over the next two years Iraq was granted about $235 million in short-term loans for the purchase of U.S. products "at US government subsidized interest rates,"[60] but again Iraq was delinquent in meeting repayments. In November 1989 Congress prohibited Export-Import Bank loans to Iraq but left the door open to their being granted by writing in the possibility of exemption through presidential waiver. The State Department quickly drafted one, and on January 17, 1990, President George H. Bush approved a credit line of $200 million, declaring that its prohibition would not be in the national interest. Through this period the bank was also under pressure from the Washington-based Iraq Business Forum.[61]

Apart from the material purchased through subterfuge, Iraq was able to secure war matériel legitimately from the United States through dual-use export licenses issued by the Department of Commerce. Between 1985 and 1990, the department approved 771 licenses for exports to Iraq, including "at least 220 export licenses for the Iraqi armed forces, major weapons complexes and enterprises identified by the CIA as diverting technology to weapons programs."[62] The department continued to grant these licenses despite the evidence of Iraqi chemical weapons development and use; alarm signals were being sounded within the administration, but the White House remained determined to see that Saddam was financed and armed.

In October 1989, a little over a year after the end of the Iran-Iraq War (in August 1988), President Bush signed National Security Decision Directive 26, in which he proposed to give Iraq economic and political incentives to moderate its behavior. Involvement with Iraq was now dictated by the profits to be made from the rebuilding of the country. The secret directive noted that improved relations with Iraq would open the way to the participation of U.S. companies in the reconstruction of the Iraqi economy, "particularly in the energy sector."[63] On this basis the president authorized a further $1 billion loan through the CCC program. At an interagency meeting in November, when representatives of the Federal Reserve, the Treasury, and the Office of Management and Budget objected on the grounds that the United States was likely to be embarrassed because of Iraq's gross human rights violations, the State Department told them that the abrupt termination of the program would "run counter to the President's intentions."[64] The loan was subsequently approved by Secretary of Agriculture Clayton Yeutter. Eighty percent of the first $500 million tranche of the CCC loan had been paid when Iraqi troops crossed the border into Kuwait on August 2, 1990, and the Department of Agriculture abruptly terminated the program.

As summarized by Howard Teicher, the United States had supported the Iraqi war effort against Iran

> by supplying the Iraqis with billions of dollars of credit, by providing US military intelligence and advice to the Iraqis and by closely monitoring third country arms sales to Iraq to make sure that Iraq had the military weapons required. The United States also provided strategic operational advice to the Iraqis to better use their assets in combat. For example, in 1986 President Reagan sent a secret message to Saddam Hussein telling him that Iraq should step up its air war and bombing of Iran. This message was delivered by Vice President Bush, who communicated it to Egyptian President Mubarak who in turn passed the message to Saddam Hussein. Similar strategic operational advice was passed to Saddam Hussein through various meetings with European and Middle Eastern heads of state. I authorized Bush's talking points for the 1986 meeting with Mubarak and personally attended numerous meetings with European and Middle East heads of state where the strategic operational advice was communicated.[65]

According to Congressman Sam Gejdenson, "virtually every arm" of the U.S. government, not just the intelligence agencies but the State, Commerce, Agriculture, and Justice Departments, had cooperated in a program of aiding and abetting Saddam Hussein.[66] All this was clearly orchestrated from the White House. Simultaneously, in violation of U.S. law, the Reagan administration had sold arms to Iran and channeled the profits to the Nicaraguan Contras in the attempt to destroy the Sandinista government.

CHEMICAL WARFARE

Not just moral but treaty obligations were involved in how other governments responded to Iraq's use of chemical weapons. On April 10, 1972, the U.S. and British governments had signed the International Convention on the Prohibition of the Development, Production and Stockpiling of Bacteriological (Biological) and Toxin Weapons and on Their Destruction. On March 26, 1975, both governments ratified it. In Article I each state party undertakes "never in any circumstances to develop, produce, stockpile or otherwise acquire or retain" microbial agents or toxins, "whatever their origin or methods of production, of types and in quantities that have no justification for prophylactic, protective or other peaceful purposes." In Article III, each state party undertakes "not to transfer to any recipient whatsoever, directly or indirectly, and not in any way to assist, encourage or induce any States, or group of States or international organizations to manufacture or otherwise acquire these agents, toxins, weapons equipment or the means of delivering them."[67]

The provision of battlefield information at a time the United States knew Iraq was using chemical weapons would surely fall into the category of assistance or encouragement. Both CIA and Defense Intelligence Agency (DIA) officials were "desperate" to make sure that Iraq did not lose the war, and "the use of gas on the battlefield by the Iraqis was not a matter of deep strategic concern,"[68] whatever moral problems it caused. The administration routinely stressed its opposition to the use of such weapons whenever the subject came up. Global outrage and independent medical confirmation of Iranian allegations compelled it to take a stronger public position. On March 5, 1984, the State Department strongly condemned Iraq's use of chemical weapons and indeed their use "wherever it occurs."[69] The administration insisted that it was doing what it could. Since the beginning of 1982 it had expressed its concern at the highest levels of the Iraqi government, and it had introduced controls on the export of certain chemicals that could be used in the manufacture of chemical weapons. But at no stage did it attempt to compel Iraq to abandon the use of chemical weapons by cutting back on aid and the provision of war materiel, for the simple reason, it must be concluded, that without the aid and without the chemical weapons, Iraq was certain to be overwhelmed by the Iranians.

Iraq began setting up nuclear, chemical, and biological warfare programs when the Iraqi Chemical Corps was set up in 1964 and army officers were sent abroad for specialized training. The conversion of the chemical warfare programs into the industrial-scale production of chemical weapons began after Saddam failed to bring down the Iranian regime in one quick but devastating campaign in 1980. On June 8, 1981, conscious of Iran's superior strength in depth, population, and resources, the Ministry of Defense launched a program to develop and produce chemical weapons in bulk. Later it was extended to include biological weapons and pesticide research. The program was code-named Project 922, and a site was chosen sixty miles north of Baghdad at Samarra, which for a time, at a high point of Arab-Islamic civilization, had been the capital of the Abbassid Empire. The Muthanna complex at Samarra, built in 1982–83 by West German companies using East German designs, was passed off as a pesticide plant but was in fact the world's most modern chemical warfare facility. It seems safe to assume that much if not all of the $1.5 million worth of pesticides sold to Iraq by Dow Chemicals in 1988 ended up at Muthanna. Many other countries were involved in the development of chemical weapons research laboratories and production lines. In the late 1990s Belgian companies had already joined forces to develop a phosphate mine and the "fertilizer" plant at Al Qaim that was to be transformed into a source of material needed for the production of chemical weapons.[70] Austrian, German, Swedish, Danish, and Swiss subcontractors pitched in with their expertise.

Unable to stop Iranian human-wave attacks—the troops advancing behind lines of *basij* volunteers exploding mines with their bodies—Iraq began using chemical weapons on all battlefronts in the summer of 1983. In August of that year Iraqi forces killed one hundred Kurdish *peshmerga* and Iranian forces by using mustard gas at Hajj Umran. Three thousand Kurds and Iranians were killed by mustard gas during the battle for Penjwin three months later. The combination of chemical weapons—used the "cocktails," as they were inevitably called—changed, and the numbers killed rose steeply as the war ground on. In February–March 1984 an estimated 2,500 Iranians were killed by mustard gas in the battle for the Majnun Islands; in March 1985, 3,000 died in a mustard gas and tabun attack on Iranian positions in the marshlands of southern Iraq; in February 1986, mustard and tabun were again used to kill between 8,000 and 10,000 Iranian troops in the struggle for control of the strategically important Faw peninsula. Faw was captured by the Iranians in a surprise attack launched on February 11, 1987, and was retaken by the Iraqis "with American planning assistance" in April 1988 after a massive offensive that involved the extensive use of chemical weapons.[71]

In line with President Reagan's directive that the United States should do "whatever is necessary" to prevent Iraq from losing the war, the CIA began providing the satellite reconnaissance imagery that helped Iraq plan bombing missions and calibrate chemical weapons attacks on Iranian forces.[72] The provision of this technical help was only one aspect of a much broader program. According to a New York Times report, quoting unnamed senior military officers, "Though senior officials of the Reagan administration publicly condemned Iraq's employment of mustard gas, sarin, VX and other poisonous agents, the American military officers said President Reagan, Vice President George Bush and senior national security aides never withdrew their support for the highly classified program in which more than 60 officers of the Defense Intelligence Agency were secretly providing detailed information on Iranian deployments, tactical planning for battles, plans for airstrikes and bomb-damage assessments for Iraq."[73] The use of chemical weapons was morally repulsive but tactically necessary in the name of blocking Iran; as one official remarked, "If Iraq had gone down it would have had a catastrophic effect on Kuwait and Saudi Arabia and the whole region might have gone down. That was the backdrop of the policy."[74] Or, as a Pentagon source remarked, the use of chemical weapons was "just another way of killing people—whether with a bullet or phosgene didn't make any difference."[75]

NERVE GAS

The Baʿathist government became the first in history to use a nerve gas on the battlefield when it used tabun (developed by the German chemicals conglomerate I. G. Farben) against Iranian positions in 1984.[76] During the war with Iran, Iraq "fired or dropped over 100,000 chemical munitions against Iranian forces and its own Kurdish population" and then used more to put down the Shiʾa rebellion of March 1991.[77] This round figure includes 19,500 chemical bombs, more than 54,000 chemical artillery shells, and 27,000 short-range chemical-fired rockets fired between 1983 and 1988, according to the figures compiled by Richard L. Russell.[78] Into the process of making these weapons went 1,800 tons of mustard gas, 140 tons of tabun, and more than 600 tons of sarin.

The extent of U.S. involvement in Iraq's development of chemical and biological weapons was partially unearthed in hearings of the U.S. Senate Committee on Banking, Housing, and Urban Affairs, which is responsible for monitoring the Export Administration Act. Hearings before the committee on October 27, 1992, revealed that UN arms inspectors in Iraq had identified many U.S.-manufactured items exported under license "that were used to further Iraq's chemical and nuclear weapons development and missile system development program." In August 1993 the committee's chairman, Senator Donald W. Riegle Jr., spearheaded research into possible links between the illnesses suffered by war veterans—"Gulf War syndrome"—and Iraq's development of WMD. In September the committee issued its first staff report; in May 1994 it took witness statements and issued its second staff report; and in October it issued its third staff report. Further specialized research by the committee's chief investigator, James J. Tuite III, focused on the destruction of chemical weapons production plants during the 1991 air campaign and the likelihood that microtoxins were carried south by the wind into areas where U.S. troops were deployed.[79]

During the committee's hearings on May 25, 1994, the undersecretary of defense for personnel and readiness, Edward Dorn, referred to the "important role" played by his department in reviewing export license requests for biological and chemical items controlled by the Australia Group.[80] That could only have been after June 1985, when the Australia Group was established at the suggestion of the Australian government to allow exporting or trans-shipping countries "to minimise the risk of assisting chemical and biological weapons (CBW) proliferation."[81] In any case, the Department of Defense did not review all items being exported. Dr. Mitchell Wallerstein, deputy assistant secretary for counterproliferation policy, told the committee that the department was authorized to review "only the potential for retransfer of items to the Soviet Union or other communist countries."[82] These included China, the Warsaw Pact countries, and other countries proscribed by the Coordinating Committee for Multilateral Security Export Controls (COCOM).[83] Iraq was not on the list because it was not communist and, said another witness, "was not considered a hostile country."[84] The department would have reviewed Iraqi requests for biological material only if they had been referred by the Department of Commerce, "and again, they would not have been referring those cases unless they anticipated the possibility of retransfer." Dr. Wallerstein conceded that he could not say one way or another whether biological material sent to Iraq "ended up in Saddam Hussein's war machine," but he believed Iraq would have been capable of incorporating biological weapons into weapons systems.[85]

Dr. Gordon C. Oehler, director of the CIA's Non-Proliferation Center, told the committee that Germany headed the list of Iraq's preferred suppliers for machinery, technology, and chemical precursors throughout the 1980s. German companies would win contracts to build dual-use facilities, enabling Iraq to claim that chemical precursors were needed for the production of plant pesticides when they were actually being used for the development of chemical weapons. European middlemen used the same argument to broker chemical precursor deals. Dutch firms bought from major chemical companies around the world, supplying the Chemical Importation and Distribution State Enterprise in Baghdad in the 1970s and the State Establishment for Pesticide Production (SEPP) in the 1980s, "both cover names for the CW program." The CIA was particularly concerned about the establishment of six separate chemical weapons production lines at Samarra. What he was "running through here," Dr. Oehler told the committee, was

> what we knew at the time and what we had reported to our customers at the time. We had been quite aware of Iraq's chemical weapons development program from its very early inception.
>
> The Chairman: I take it the CIA must have had a concern about it to have kind of zeroed in on it to that degree.
>
> Dr. Oehler: Very much so. And that was reported to our customers, and our customers attempted to take actions.
>
> The Chairman: It would have been reported also to the President, to the Secretary of Defense, the Secretary of State, I assume, as a matter of course?
>
> Dr. Oehler: Yes, sir. Those are our customers, sir.[86]

Occasionally the CIA's Office of Scientific and Weapons Research distributed "alert memos" to the Departments of Commerce, Treasury, and Justice and the FBI when information indicated that U.S. firms were being targeted "by foreign governments of concern" or were involved in possible violations of U.S. law. Between 1984 and 1990, the office had distributed five such memos following approaches by Iraqis to U.S. firms "that appeared to be related to WMD programs."[87] In March 1986 UN Secretary-General Javier Perez de Cuellar had drawn the world's attention to Iraq's use of mustard gas and nerve gas, primarily tabun. The United States refused to support a UN Security Council resolution condemning Iraq's chemical weapons attacks, but as evidence of Iraq's use of chemical weapons mounted in the mid-1980s, Dr. Oehler told the Riegle Committee, it "began to put into effect unilateral controls on exports of chemical precursors to Iraq and other countries suspected of having chemical warfare programs."

It was a bit late for this. To break its dependence on foreign suppliers for precursors, Iraq had begun to produce its own. In 1985 it began the construction of precursor production plants near Falluja, designated as Falluja I, II, and III. When completed, the Falluja complex was capable of producing one thousand tons of sarin a month as well as VX nerve gas. Asked by Senator Riegle where Iraq had gotten the chemical warheads for its missiles, Dr. Oehler replied: "They made them themselves." (In fact, as the committee would conclude later, chemical warhead packing for the missiles came from the United States.)

The contribution of European companies to Iraq's development of WMD had been known for a decade before the Riegle Committee met. In 1984 the British journalist Andrew Beitch reported that British firms sold "thousands of kilos of the basic ingredients of the nerve gas sarin and mustard gas" to Iraq and Iran in 1983.[88] This material included two thousand kilograms of methyl phosphonyl difluoride and thirty-eight thousand kilograms of dimethyl phosphonate, both constituent elements of sarin. Britain continued to supply Iraq with weapons material through the 1980s, yet when asked in the House of Commons on July 1, 2004, about the origin of foreign technology and technical assistance critical to Iraq's development of WMD, the defense minister, Geoff Hoon, blamed Third World countries: "I have already confirmed that Iraq was holding discussions with North Korea, and Her Majesty's Government 2002 dossier on Iraq's weapons of mass destruction mentions an Indian chemical engineering company."[89] He then invoked a defense and security regulation in refusing to release further information.

Dr. Oehler told the Riegle committee that Iraq had

> exploited businessmen and consortia willing to violate the export laws of their own countries. As has been indicated in the press and television reports, the Consen Group, a consortium of European missile designers, engineers, and businessmen, established a network of front companies to cover its role as project director of an Argentine, Egyptian, Iraqi sponsored Condor II ballistic missile program. Iraqi procurement officers, knowing full well the licensing thresholds, requested items that fell just under them but would still meet their needs. Before Desert Storm, US regulations on the export of these technologies were drafted to meet US technical specifications and standards. Technologies of a lower standard worked just as well, and permitted Iraq to obtain the goods and technology consistent with Commerce Department regulations.

Oehler downplayed the role of the United States in Iraq's WMD programs: the "major players" were European, and there was "little involvement" of U.S. companies. It was possible to make such exculpatory statements in 1994, but as the evidence accumulated it became clear that a large quantity of conventional and nonconventional war materiel continued to flow into Iraq from U.S. suppliers and through U.S.-approved third parties long after the U.S. administration knew that the Baʿathist regime was producing and using chemical weapons. UN arms inspectors sent to Iraq after the

1991 attack reported that U.S. equipment and technology had been used in Iraq's nuclear research program along with material from other countries. They also compiled lists of chemicals, missile equipment, and computers supplied to Iraq by U.S. corporations. The Riegle Committee concluded that dual-use material supplied under license by the U.S. government had helped Iraq to develop chemical, biological, and missile-building systems.[90] The items supplied included chemical warfare agent precursors, chemical warfare agent production facility plans and technical drawings (for a pesticide plant), chemical warhead filling equipment, biological warfare–related materials, missile fabrication equipment, and missile-system guidance equipment.

BIOLOGICAL EXPORTS

The Riegle Committee's second staff report lists the chemical and biological warfare material sent under license to agencies of the government of Iraq between February 1985 and November 1989 by a principal supplier, the American Type Culture Collection (ATCC), of Rockville, Maryland.[91] The committee wanted to know how these exports might have contributed to Iraq's offensive or defensive biological warfare program. The company's records showed that the pathogenic (disease-producing), toxigenic (poisonous), and other biological materials sent to Iraq in dozens of batches were not attenuated or weakened "and were capable of reproduction." These toxic exports included several strains of *Bacillus anthracis* (including bovine anthrax), *Clostridium botulinum*, *Clostridium perfringens* (which causes gas gangrene), *Clostridium tetani*, *Brucella melentensis*, *Brucella abortus*, *Histoplasma capsulatum* (which generates a disease similar to tuberculosis and causes enlargement of the liver and the spleen, among other symptoms), salmonella, staphylococcus, *E. coli*, and the West Nile fever virus. Developed as biological weapons, many of these cultures kill or permanently incapacitate any living creature exposed to them. The government agencies to whom this material was dispatched included the Ministry of Higher Education, the State Company of Drug Industries, the University of Basra, and the Iraq Atomic Energy Commission (IAEC), which took delivery of microorganisms capable of being genetically altered through irradiation. Altogether, ATCC made eleven shipments of toxins and bacteria to the IAEC. Between 1985 and 1989, another U.S. supplier, the Center for Disease Control, supplied various institutions in Iraq with *Botulinum toxoid*, *Yersinia pestis*, dengue virus, and West Nile fever virus. Three deliveries of this virus went to the Salman Pak chemical weapons research and production complex for "medical research."[92] Other "deadly pathogens" came from the Pasteur Institute in Paris and from two German suppliers, Sigma Chemie and Josef Kuhn.[93] These transfers were all made after the Australia Group was established to tighten up export controls so that chemical and biological material would not end up in the wrong hands.

According to UN Special Commission (UNSCOM) inspectors tracking down Iraq's chemical weapons at the end of the Gulf War, Iraq had carried out "pathogen enhancement" and biological warfare stimulant research on material identical to that sent from the United States. Indeed, according to the findings of the Iraq Survey Group, Iraq had disclosed that it had been researching different strains of *B. anthracis* and had settled on the ATCC strain 14578 for exclusive use in the development of a biological weapon. This strain, sent by the ATCC to the Iraqi Ministry of Higher Education on May 2, 1986, was taken from a dead cow in South Oxfordshire, "probably in 1937," and maintained at the British government's Microbiological Research Establishment at Porton Down before being transferred to the United States.[94] Senator Riegle was clearly astounded at the role the United States had played in supplying Iraq with the raw material needed for the development of chemical and biological weapons: "It was really astonishing to find that our Government had licensed a shipment of those very things to Saddam Hussein and many of them going directly to military units. There was no subterfuge, they were going to go right into his war production systems. Then, of course, when we decided the necessity of going to war with Iraq, we had our own troops suddenly facing weapons that we had helped develop by providing critical items for them."[95]

All the evidence confirms the deep involvement of the U.S. administration with the war plans of the Baʿathist regime in Baghdad. Iraq was provided with money, dual-use licensed exports, arms covertly transferred through third parties, cluster bombs manufactured by a nominally independent Chilean producer, and battlefield intelligence at a time when the United States knew Iraq was using chemical weapons against Iranian troops. The complicity in Iraq's war with Iran explains the administration's reaction to the killing of thousands of Iraqi Kurdish civilians in the chemical weapons attacks launched by the Baʿathist regime in the late 1980s. Secretary of State George Shultz issued a strong statement of condemnation but gave way to strong pressure from his own department's area specialists and approved a recommendation that the administration oppose an attempt to impose congressional sanctions. A sanctions bill "died in the House."[96]

"THE LAW OF WAR"

In the forty-three days of the campaign against Iraq in 1991, coalition air-craft (American or British) flew 120,000 sorties, 60 percent of them com-bat missions; 35,000 were in the Kuwait theater of war and 32,000 in Iraq. Over either Iraq or Kuwait they dropped 84,200 tons of ordnance. The grand total included 7,400 "smart" bombs. Night after night, viewing audiences around the world were riveted by grainy black-and-white video clips of smart bombs sliding into their targets. In fact, most of the bombs dropped in the war (93 percent) were not smart bombs at all but the same notoriously inaccurate "dumb" iron bombs that the United States had dropped over various targets ever since the Second World War. The carpet bombing of Iraqi positions by B-52s scarcely rated a mention. Neither did the use of CBU-75 cluster bombs, each scattering 1,800 bomblets filled with slivers that cut bodies to ribbons.

While conceding that civilian casualties were as unavoidable in this war as any other, the U.S. administration and the military command painted a picture of an almost flawless campaign. The "embedding" of reporters with military units and the rigorous censorship of written and visual mate-rial from the battlefield ensured that the human consequences of the real war were kept as far away as possible from the media. Citing numerous international conventions and protocols, General Colin Powell, chairman of the U.S. Joints Chiefs of Staff, concluded his summary of the conduct of the war with the finding that the U.S. operations "were in keeping with the historic US adherence to the precepts of the law of war."[97]

In fact, the saturation bombing of the country's civilian infrastructure exposed both the United States and Britain to charges of repeatedly violat-ing the "precepts of the law of war." The destruction of dozens of bridges of all types (rail, traffic, and pedestrian footbridges), railways, and roads across the country was accomplished with the heavy loss of civilian life. In Falluja an estimated two hundred civilians were killed on February 14, 1991, when a British Tornado dropped its bombing load on a market close to the bridge across the Euphrates that was supposed to be its target. Many of the casualties were women shoppers or stall holders. In Samawa, a town on the Euphrates in the south of the country, another two hundred people were killed when aircraft bombed a floating pedestrian bridge. Some of the bombs exploded on land, killing people in the seventy-five-meter space between the river and the market at a time women were washing clothes and children playing.[98] The bombing of the market at Kifl on February 5 (another 150 dead) was completely inexplicable because it was nowhere near any government offices or possible military targets. Many other civilians were killed in strafing and bombing attacks on cars, buses, and tankers carrying oil to Jordan (exempted from sanctions because Iraqi oil was the country's only energy source).

As the air war proceeded it soon became clear that the overriding strategic aim was not merely the destruction of soldiers, armaments, and weapons production plants but the paralysis of Iraq as a functioning social organism. Fuel storage tanks, electric power stations, water purification plants, and the country's communications systems were all put out of action. Food and seed warehouses, grain storage silos and flour mills, bottling plants, and factories producing dairy products, chlorine, cardboard, plastics, sugar, cement, textiles, phosphate, and infant food were all bombed. Even an underwear factory was hit. The country's only animal vaccine laboratory was destroyed. Buildings destroyed or damaged included government offices, schools, hospitals, clinics, movie theaters, a sports stadium, and, according to UN Undersecretary-General Martti Ahtisaari, nine thousand homes in Baghdad, Basra, and numerous other cities. Bedouin were killed in their tents. Visiting Iraq in March 1991 at the head of a UN mission, Ahtisaari wrote, "Nothing we had seen or read had quite prepared us for the particular form of devastation which has now befallen the country. The recent conflict has wrought near-apocalyptic results upon the economic infrastructure of what had been until January 1991 a rather highly urbanized and mechanized society. Now, most means of modern life have been destroyed or rendered tenuous. Iraq has, for some time, been relegated to a pre-industrial age but with all the disabilities of a post-industrial dependency on an intensive use of energy and technology."[99]

Iraq was left with 4 percent of its prewar electricity generation capacity. The Ahtisaari mission found that all previously viable sources of power apart from a few mobile generators were "essentially defunct." Hospitals, clinics, sewage treatment and pumping plants, and irrigation systems and water purification plants were all affected. In Baghdad untreated sewage was being dumped directly into the Tigris River, the source of the city's water. "All drinking plants there and throughout the rest of the country are using river water with high sewage contamination."[100] Garbage disposal was nonexistent. Supplies of flour, rice, sugar, tea, vegetable oil, pulses, and powdered milk were at critically low levels or had been exhausted. The destruction of potato and vegetable seed warehouses, the collapse of irrigation, and the lack of fertilizers, pesticides, and spare parts threatened the current harvest as well as planting for the coming season. In a separate report, a WHO/UNICEF special mission accompanying a convoy of trucks carrying emergency medical supplies for children and mothers from Iran focused on the threat to young children, especially one- to three-year-olds, from gastric diseases and malnutrition.[101]

"THE ENEMY AS A SYSTEM"

The Americans were well aware of the consequences of bombing energy and water purification plants. Through UN sanctions, Iraq was already blocked from obtaining the specialized equipment and chemicals necessary to maintain supplies of clean water. The DIA acknowledged in a memorandum distributed on January 22, 1991, that there was no solution to Iraq's water purification problems outside exemption of supplies from sanctions.[102] The attempt to circumvent sanctions indicated that any useful stocks of water treatment chemicals in Kuwait had already been looted and used. Much of Iraq's groundwater was brackish or heavily salinated. Its rivers were polluted and "laden with bacteria" liable to cause cholera, hepatitis, and thyroid problems unless purified with chlorine. The failure to secure water treatment supplies would result in a shortage of pure drinking water for the general population, leading to the outbreak of diseases, if not epidemics. In the industrial sector, factories and plants dependent on a continuing supply of pure water, including petrochemicals, fertilizers, petroleum refining, electronics, pharmaceuticals, food processing, textiles, concrete construction, and thermal power plants, would become incapacitated.

The destruction of water purification plants, power stations, food, clothing, and seed factories, schools, and government offices during the saturation bombing of Iraq cannot be regarded as unforeseen and unfortunate consequences of war. It was part of an attempt to impose strategic paralysis on a whole system in line with new thinking on air war.[103] Colonel John A. Warden III, described as having played "a leading role in planning and supporting the air campaign in the 1990–91 Gulf War,"[104] has discussed this new approach to aerial warfare in numerous publications. The organizations of the human body, the state, a drug cartel, an electricity company, and even the solar system are represented as having the same basic characteristics, forming five concentric rings: a leader (brain, eye, and nerves in the body), organic essentials, infrastructure, population, and fighting mechanism (leukocytes in the human body).

In war the enemy must be regarded as a system composed of numerous subsystems, much like a human body. Any system is of its nature integrated, and the malfunction of one part will naturally have effects elsewhere. The more complex a system, "the more precarious its maintenance tends to be and the more likely that injections of energy in the wrong places will speed its natural movement towards disorder and perhaps even to chaos."[105] Accordingly, the strategic and operational paralysis of the whole system and not just the military becomes the target. "If we address the system properly its military forces will be left as a useless appendage, no longer supported by its leadership, organic essentials, infrastructure or population." If the ring at the center of the system (the leadership) cannot be threatened directly or removed, the outer rings have to be weakened. In most states beyond the agrarian stage of development, the destruction of power generation and petrol output (organic essentials) makes life in general next to impossible. The destruction of the transport system (infrastructure) weakens the ability of the whole system to resist the demands of the enemy. The fourth ring (population) is harder to calculate because, while actions can be taken that might induce a people to rise up against its government, human nature is unpredictable, so while an indirect approach to the population is worthwhile, "one should not count on it." However, if the measures taken against the system are generally effective, the military, being a means to an end, will be deprived of the support needed for its own maintenance.

In Colonel Warden's words, technology enables the state to make simultaneous "parallel" attacks across a whole system, making very real "what Clausewitz called the ideal form of war, the striking of blows everywhere at the same time."[106] Naturally the state must have the overwhelming power to launch such attacks in the first place. In this context the exclusive possession by the United States of a "hyper war arsenal" gives it the capacity to achieve "virtually all military objectives without recourse to weapons of mass destruction." This was demonstrated during the 1991 air war when "the coalition struck three times as many targets in Iraq in the first 24 hours as the Eighth Air Force hit in Germany in all of 1943."[107] A "parallel war" so defined—against "organic" essentials and infrastructures as well as purely military targets—"brings so many parts of the enemy system under near-simultaneous attack that the system cannot react to defend or repair itself. It is like the death of a thousand cuts; any individual cut is unlikely to be serious. A hundred, however, start to slow a body considerably, and a thousand are fatal because the body cannot deal with that many assaults on it." The initial overwhelming air attack on Iraq stood as "our best example of parallel war to date,"[108] and as the air campaign continued, the theory was clearly applied right across all the concentric rings of the Iraqi system. Colonel Warden reached the same conclusion as the British in Mesopotamia in 1920, that in "modern" warfare the best means of controlling an enemy was from the air.

"STERILIZING" THE TRENCHES

The single most horrific event of the war involving the killing of civilians was the destruction of the Amiriyya (Ameriyya) underground bomb shelter in Baghdad. The huge shelter covered nearly an entire block. It was added to the "target package" on February 11. Hundreds of people, most of them women and children, since many of the men had elected to stay aboveground for reasons of propriety, were inside the shelter when it was devastated by two two-thousand-pound bombs dropped by two F-117A stealth bombers during the night of February 13. Film taken the morning after showed melted iron beds and the charred bodies of infants. Of the estimated 310 people who were melted and burned along with the beds, at least 130 were children.[109] Husbands lost entire families. The U.S. military command claimed that the shelter (also known as al Firdus) was a military command and control center. Reporters were told that the shelter had a camouflage roof, was surrounded by a barbed wire security fence, and was "one of the alternate command and control facilities that we knew was active."[110] In his final report to Congress on the conduct of the war (April 1992), General Powell continued to argue that Amiriyya was a camouflaged military bunker and that the Iraqi government had allowed selected civilians, "apparently the families of officer personnel," to stay in the "former air raid shelter" at night at one level above the military command center that was the target of the attack.[111]

Yet a journalist who went to the shelter straight after the bombing saw no barbed wire fence or camouflage paint on the roof. Neither was there any evidence of a military command center. The building consisted of four levels, one above ground and three underground, two for sleeping and the storage of food and water and a third "for standby electrical generators and other building equipment."[112] The shelter had apparently been reserved for elite families at the start of the war before being opened up to the general public. It was not a military command center, and it was not a "former air raid shelter" but an active one: the hundreds of bodies being pulled out of the smoking and steaming debris the morning after were the evidence of that. Even if the "former" shelter had been filled with the families of the Baʿathist elite one level above the supposed military command center, would its bombing have been justified? In Colin Powell's view, apparently yes.

Battlefield carnage included an unknown number of Iraqi troops buried alive in their trenches on the first day of the ground war by the First Infantry Division (Mechanized) of the U.S. Army VII Corps. The trenches—in the neutral zone between Iraq and Saudi Arabia—were dug behind mounds of sand (berms) stretching along the line. The First Infantry Division's tactic was simply to push the berms on top of the Iraqi troops with earthmovers, entombing them and "sterilizing" the trenches.[113] In his report on the conduct of the war, General Powell described how the division breached the Iraqi defensive positions with Abrams main battle tanks mounted with plows. The tanks "plowed through the berms and minefields erected by the Iraqis. Many Iraqis surrendered during this phase of the attack and were taken prisoner. The division then assaulted the trenches containing other Iraqi soldiers. Once astride the trench lines, the division turned the plow blades of its tanks and combat earthmovers along the Iraqi defense line and, covered by fire from its M-2/-3 armored infantry fighting vehicles, began to fill in the trench line and its heavily bunkered mutually supporting fighting positions."[114] A "number" of Iraqi soldiers died as their positions were bull-dozed. General Powell justified the entombment of living men by arguing that the use of armored vehicles "to crush or bury enemy soldiers" was entirely consistent with the law of war. It was certainly consistent with his view that when the United States went to war it should use overwhelming force against an enemy.[115]

Others filled out the detail. The attack on the eight thousand Iraqi troops dug in along the line was preceded by a devastating thirty-minute bombardment that by itself was sufficient to slaughter the Iraqis. Then 8,400 U.S. troops swept toward the lines in three thousand Abrams M1A-2 main battle tanks, Humvees, Bradley "fighting vehicles," and numerous armored troop carriers. The tanks straddled the trenches and moved along the line, followed by M-2 Bradleys pouring 7.62-mm machine fire at Iraqi troops trying to fight back. "I came right through after the lead company," one soldier told correspondent Patrick J. Sloyan. "What you saw was a bunch of buried trenches with people's arms and things sticking out of them. For all I know we could have killed thousands." These tactics were continued by the different brigades within the division for two days (February 24–25). About seventy miles of trenches and bunkers were filled in. The tanks were followed by an armored burial brigade and then Armored Combat Earthmovers (ACEs), leveling the ground "and smoothing away projecting Iraqi arms, legs and equipment." The commander of one brigade alone estimated that 650 Iraqis were buried in the trenches his force had attacked, so along the line it is evident that the number of entombed troops possibly ran into the thousands and not Powell's vague "number" or the 150 later given out by the U.S. military.[116] Correspondents admitted into the area late in the second day saw about two thousand Iraqi prisoners bunched together but no signs that a battle had taken place. There were "no bodies, no stench of faeces that hovers on a battlefield, no blood stains, no bits of human beings." "Where the hell are the bodies?" one correspondent asked the army public affairs officer. "What bodies?" he replied.[117]

In the same way General Powell defended the attack on an Iraqi convoy that left Kuwait City for the border crossing at Safwan on the night of February 26–27 (the day before President Bush declared the cessation of hostilities) as being consistent with past military practice. In compliance with UN Security Council Resolution 660, the Iraqi government had announced that it was withdrawing all troops from Kuwait. In the view of General Powell, the column that left Kuwait City on the night of February 26 "invited" attack because of its military nature. Accordingly, once on the open road, it was blocked by barricades of mines front and behind and bombed and strafed from the air. Halfway to the border along the Jahra highway—the "highway of death"—a six-kilometer snarl of military and civilian vehicles was obliterated by U.S. and British aircraft. General Powell asserted that more than two hundred Iraqi tanks were "trapped and destroyed in the ambush," along with "hundreds of other military vehicles and various forms of civilian transportation confiscated or seized by Iraqi troops for the redeployment."[118] Strewn among the wreckage was property "pillaged" from civilians in what General Powell described as "the last step in the Iraqi looting of Kuwait." He justified the destruction by referring to the attack on what was left of Napoleon's Grand Armée as it retreated from Moscow in the nineteenth century and the destruction of the Germany army as it retreated from Moscow in the twentieth: "The law of war permits the attack of enemy combatants and enemy equipment at any time." In any case, he wrote, most Iraqi soldiers in the convoy ran off into the desert when the convoy was blocked.[119]

In fact, there were two "highways of death." British and U.S. aircraft also wiped out a second mixed military-civilian column traveling on the coastal road to Basra. Several hundred people survived the attack on the inland road, but there were no known survivors from the obliteration of this second column of retreating Iraqis and civilians. In fact, the withdrawal from Kuwait City was not a "redeployment" or even an organized retreat of a military force but a "stampede" of civilians as well as "enemy combatants" trying to get away before the Americans arrived and the Kuwaitis returned to take their revenge on those they believed had betrayed them.[120] Many of the civilian vehicles were clearly filled with civilians and had not just been commandeered by Iraqi soldiers, as General Powell had implied. The "column" was completely defenseless. Of the 1,500 vehicles destroyed on the Jahra highway and 400 obliterated on the secondary coastal road, only 2 percent were tanks or armored personnel carriers (i.e., not "more than two hundred" and not even twenty, even in U.S. calculations).[121] The carnage and destruction were so complete that General Powell could not possibly have known how many people ran off into the desert and how many were killed. Most of the civilian dead were probably Egyptians and Palestinians. Bodies were charred and carbonized. Film of the attack on the Jahra highway showed a jumble of gutted cars, buses, vans, trucks, and armored vehicles. Thousands of sorties were flown by U.S. planes, from jet fighters to B-52 bombers, some from ships in the Gulf. British aircraft joined in. "Just about anything with wings and a bomb rack" was called into action,[122] and the pilots just kept wheeling overhead until there were no more fish in a barrel or turkeys left to shoot at. In some squadrons, these final avenging attacks were called "sports sorties."[123]

The war closed with further acts of gratuitous slaughter. On February 27—the day a cease-fire was declared—a Scout platoon of the Twenty-fourth Infantry Division (Mechanized) operating inside Iraq rounded up 382 prisoners who had surrendered, including wounded soldiers in a bus marked with the symbol of the Red Crescent society. They were clustered in rows by the side of the road when a line of Bradley fighting vehicles came into view and opened fire. A tape recorder running as the Bradleys began firing records the reactions of the soldiers who were holding the captured men: "There's no one shooting at them. . . . Why'd they have to shoot. . . . Why are we shooting at these people when they are not shooting at us? . . . They want to surrender. They don't have to blow them apart. . . . It's murder." One soldier present thought all prisoners had been hit. The Bradleys were firing 25-caliber rounds (with a capacity of one thousand rounds a minute) into a concentrated group of men, so few if any can have survived. The killings remained yet another uninvestigated atrocity committed during the war.[124]

On March 3 the Twenty-fourth Infantry Division, its commander claiming that it had come under attack by retreating Iraqi forces, wiped out a line of hundreds of tanks, armored cars, and civilian vehicles in the so-called Battle of Rumaila. On the way into Iraq the division had seen little but dispirited soldiers and civilians trying to get out of the war zone. The tanks in the retreating column encountered by the U.S. forces were being carried on flatbed trucks with their barrels pointing backwards, in compliance with cease-fire conditions imposed by the U.S. military command. The Iraqis were clearly anxious to avoid conflict with the Americans, yet the Twenty-fourth Infantry blocked their retreat near a causeway and then launched a full assault. The Iraqis were boxed in. Some of the tanks tried to fire back, but the whole column was helpless in the face of artillery bombardment and missile strikes from the air. It was torn to pieces. The Iraqis tried to save themselves by getting away from the road. The casualties included a busful of civilians, children among them. In the view of one of the soldiers, the attack was "fucking murder." Estimates of the dead remain unknown because the bodies were buried when the shooting stopped.[125]

Because the U.S. military command counted only its own war casualties—147 killed in battle, 145 killed out of battle, and 467 wounded—the estimates of Iraqi military casualties fluctuated wildly from a low of 20,000 soldiers to a high of about 200,000. Thousands of civilians were killed in air strikes, but the total number of Iraqi dead will never be known. A week after declaring the war at an end President Bush told a joint session of Congress that "we went halfway around the world to do what is moral and just and right."[126] Saddam's military capacity had been crushed and his ability to threaten mass destruction destroyed; Kuwait ("that proud nation") had been liberated, and a new world order was coming into view.

GULF UPSTARTS

From 1980 to 1988 the Gulf states had pumped billions of dollars into Iraq, sharing the U.S. hope that Saddam would bludgeon the Islamic regime in Tehran out of existence and, in the process, weaken himself beyond the possibility of further adventures in the foreseeable future. The war ended with Iraq owing multiple billions of dollars in debt to the Gulf states. By refusing to write off Iraq's war debt and by bringing the price of oil down through overproduction at a time Iraq was desperate for revenue, Kuwait held an economic gun at Saddam's head. That is certainly the way he saw it. Kuwait's refusal to make concessions suggests an understanding with key Western governments on the need to continue controlling both Iraq and Iran in the interests of Gulf "stability." This raised the question of how it was to be done. The White House worked with the Ba'athist regime right up to the invasion of Kuwait. It seemed ready to turn the man President Bush once described as "that lying son of a bitch" back into *our* son of a bitch,[127] but Saddam had to learn to toe the line, and by no means was there unanimity on how he should be handled.

In National Security Directive 26, issued on October 2, 1989, President Bush had asserted that normal relations between the United States and Iraq "would serve our longer-term interests and promote stability in both the Gulf and the Middle East." Iraq should be offered "economic and political incentives" to moderate its behavior. At the same time, "we should pursue and seek to facilitate opportunities for U.S. firms to participate in the reconstruction of the Iraqi economy, particularly in the energy area, where they do not conflict with our non-proliferation and other significant objectives."[128] The United States continued to supply Iraq with "dual-use" technology right down to the invasion of Kuwait, and only a week before Saddam ordered the army across the border April Glaspie was telling him of President Bush's wishes for a better relationship.

The question is again raised of whether Saddam was being led into a trap. If so, he would surely have been the first to see it. His capacity to sniff out plots and conspiracies was fundamental to his survival. He was the last man to be swept off his feet by professions of friendship coming from a government he deeply distrusted. Would such a deeply suspicious person be likely to believe the Americans if they suggested he could help himself to Kuwait and its oil and take a chunk of Gulf coastline next to Saudi Arabia without them interfering?

Saddam's injured sense of self might be the key to understanding his decision to strike out at Kuwait. Its rulers had besmirched his heroic self-image. He had made the long journey from poverty in Tikrit to the opulence of the presidential palace in Baghdad. He had crushed all his internal enemies. He was the leader of a powerful Arab state with thousands of years of civilization behind it. He had fought Iran to a standstill, and now that the war was over he was being defied by these Gulf upstarts whose palaces and oil wells he had protected. The Kuwaitis provoked him for more than a year, and then he decided to show them who was boss. He treated them as he treated anyone who crossed him. He struck them down with a mighty blow appropriate to his self-image and no doubt got great satisfaction out of seeing the amirs of the ruling Sabah family scurry across the border into the safety of Saudi Arabia. Then his head would have cleared. The tough guy of the quarter was risking a beating by someone bigger than he was. He had to find a way out of the corner into which he had backed himself, but even at the risk of his own destruction by his enemy's friends he was not prepared to accept withdrawal if the price was total humiliation in his own country, across the region, and before the world. He would rather bring down the roof down on everyone's head.

Before the expiration of the "goodwill pause" on January 15, during a meeting with Husayn Kamil Hasan al Majid, the director of the Military Industrialization Committee (and the son-in-law he later had murdered), and Saʿb Husan Muhammad al Masiri, the air force commander, Saddam directed that preparations be made for the use of chemical and biological

weapons starting on January 15 and stated, "I consider Riyadh a target."
His commanders should be ready for action to begin at any time:

> I will give them an order stating that at "one moment," if I'm not there
> and you don't hear my voice, you will hear somebody else's voice, so
> you can receive the order from him, and then you can go attack your
> targets. I want the weapons to be distributed to targets; I want Riyadh
> and Jeddah, which are the biggest Saudi cities with all the decision
> makers, and the Saudi rulers live there. This is for the germ and chemi-
> cal weapons.
>   . . . Also, all the Israeli cities, all of them. Of course you should con-
> centrate on Tel Aviv since it is their center.

Told by Husain Kamil that the best way of delivering the weapons was
a plane "like a crop plane" because it was a thousand times more harmful,
Saddam replied: "May God help us do it. We will never lower our heads as
long as we are alive, even if we have to destroy everybody."[129] Warheads
and storage tanks were moved into the battle zone, and from the evidence
gathered by the Riegle Committee it seems that at least some chemical
weapons may have been launched. Why more general use was not made of
them is a question that does not have a clear answer. Perhaps the air war
was so intense and disruptive of battlefield supply lines and formations
that Iraqi chemical weapons units did not have the time to fill and prepare
warheads for firing before the start of the ground war. Perhaps Saddam
was talked out of using them, or his commanders did not share his Götter-
dämmerung philosophy and would not use them. They were not fighting
Iran this time. They would have known that the consequences for Iraq of a
widespread chemical weapons attack on U.S. forces would have been catastrophic.[130]

On February 15, toward the end of the air war, Saddam took the risk of
humiliation anyway by accepting UN Security Council Resolution 660,
which had been passed the day of the invasion and which demanded the
immediate and unconditional withdrawal of Iraqi forces from Kuwait.
President Bush responded by calling the decision a hoax and demanding
the withdrawal of all troops within two days. This would have been technically and logistically difficult if not impossible for the Iraqis. On February 21 Saddam accepted a Soviet plan setting a timetable for withdrawal
within twenty-one days. President Bush responded by again demanding
their removal within forty-eight hours, something that could not even be
attempted without chaos and humiliation. Cornered now, with no possibility of escape, Saddam struck back by ordering Kuwait's oil wells to be set
on fire, and on February 24 the ground war was launched.

TOXIC FALLOUT

A neglected question arising from the destruction of Iraq's chemical and biological warfare research centers and production plants in 1991 was the effect on the environment. The Riegle Committee found that the U.S. military had consulted national laboratories (Lawrence Livermore National Laboratory, Livermore, California; Sandia National Laboratory, Albuquerque, New Mexico; and Los Alamos National Laboratory, New Mexico) about the hazards associated with bombing chemical, biological, and nuclear warfare facilities. What the military was told remains classified information, but because of the danger that Iraq would use chemical weapons the United States decided to bomb the plants even though it had no weapons that could destroy toxins without contaminating the environment. In the initial stage of the air campaign, all centers of chemical warfare research, development, production, and storage—at Mosul, Kirkuk, Samarra, Baghdad, al Nasiriyya, al Shuaybah, Falluja, Habbaniyya, al Qaim, Tikrit, al Diwaniyya, and Karbala—were subjected to saturation bombing. Large stocks of sulfur mustard, tabun, sarin, soman, and cyclosarin—hundreds if not thousands of tons of chemical agents—and tens of thousands of pieces of chemical munitions were "destroyed," but not without the diffusion of microscopic debris carried upward and then southward by the wind.

Satellite observation, weather anomalies, scientific and instrumental observation, and the presence of medical effects, according to the Riegle Committee's principal investigator, "all support the hypothesis outlined in this paper that allied bombings of Iraqi chemical warfare agent facilities pumped chemical weapons agents, their precursor materials and their toxic by-products into the passing weather patterns which carried the toxins into allied-occupied areas before they returned to the earth's surface."[131] Visible and thermal satellite imagery and smoke plume data showed that fallout from the bombing "consistently moved with the weather patterns towards and over positions occupied by coalition forces assembling for the coming counter-invasion of Kuwait and Iraq." Commenting on fallout from the bombing of chemical munitions storage sites, Dr. Oehler (the director of the CIA's Non-Proliferation Center) told the Riegle Committee that "the modeling that has been done on this suggests that nothing is going to go further than maybe 10 miles. So if your American troops, if the coalition troops are much farther than that, they are not going to be exposed to chemical warfare." However, the meteorological and scientific data carefully compiled by the committee's research staff showed that microscopic debris was detected at a height of six to seven kilometers above ground and at a distance of nearly two thousand kilometers from the source.

On February 4, 1991, a spokesman for the French Ministry of Defense told the media that chemical fallout—"probably neurotoxins"—from the bombing of Iraq's chemical and biological warfare research, development, and production plants had been detected in small quantities "a little bit everywhere."[132] In July 1993 the Czech minister of defense disclosed that a Czech decontamination unit sent to Saudi Arabia had detected "life-threatening" concentrations of the chemical blister agent yperite (mustard gas) and the nerve agent sarin several times after the beginning of the air war on January 17. The ministry asserted that contamination could not be connected in any way with the use of chemical weapons because it had been "proven" that they had not been used. "One can conclude that the data measured could have had [their] origins from industrial facilities or even storage facilities of chemical ammunition that were hit by allied bombardment. This is supported by a report of the unit's commander, by my statements and by other direct participants."[133] But U.S. soldiers, including one attached to the Czech unit, claim to have been told by the colonel who commanded it that nerve agent was detected after a SCUD missile attack and that "they did hit us with chemicals."[134]

The Riegle Committee's second staff report concluded that chemical warfare agents had been detected "in conjunction with definable events."[135] Chemical alert alarms had sounded repeatedly; chemicals had been detected after missile attacks or unexplained explosions; Czech, British, and French units had detected chemical/biological agents in the air and in puddles on the ground after SCUD missile attacks, as well as the explosion of artillery shells or chemical mines; U.S. units had detected chemical contamination in the air; direct chemical weapon attacks had been corroborated in multiple eyewitness accounts; U.S. and coalition forces had been exposed to fallout caused by the bombing of Iraq's chemical, biological, and nuclear research and development facilities; Iraq had chemical and biological weapons deployed with frontline units "and was prepared to use them."[136]

The committee concluded that the symptoms suffered by the soldiers were consistent with exposure to a mixed chemical agent attack, although it left open other possibilities, such as contact with contaminated enemy prisoners, the administration of a nerve agent pretreatment drug that acted like a nerve agent, and low-level exposure to contamination through Allied bombing. It noted that large numbers of dead mammals, birds, and insects were found in the area where microscopic airborne chemical toxins came to earth. The Department of Defense argued that epidemic illnesses were the possible cause, but the committee noted that birds and insects were especially vulnerable to toxic air contamination and that mammals were exposed by eating contaminated food. After the war the number of terrible birth defects and cancers in southern Iraq surged. The use of uranium-depleted tank shells is widely regarded as one cause, but if the Riegle Committee's conclusions are right, the toxins scattered into the atmosphere during the bombing campaign of January and February are likely to have had the same long-term effects.

SANCTIONS

The sanctions originally imposed under UN Security Council Resolution 661 of August 6, 1990, were sequentially refined, widened, and modified in the decade before the Second Gulf War. Resolution 687 of April 3, 1991, reaffirmed the prohibition of sales of arms and war-related materials and laid down eight conditions that had to be met if sanctions were to be lifted. Resolutions 706 and 712 (August 15 and September 19, 1991) endorsed an oil-for-food program that allowed Iraq to sell $1.6 billion of oil and oil products; 30 percent of the revenue would be held in a compensation fund, 4 percent would be set aside for UNSCOM and other UN costs, and 66 percent would go for purchasing food. In Resolution 986 of April 14, 1995, the ceiling for oil exports was lifted to $2 billion every 180 days, with the Security Council again emphasizing the civilian need for food, medical supplies, and other essentials. In Resolution 1153 of February 1998 the amount was increased to $5.2 billion every six months, with Iraq now allowed to spend on reconstruction of the energy sector. Resolution 1284 of December 17, 1999, authorized UN member states to import "any volume" of Iraqi petroleum or petroleum products and partially lifted the flight embargo. On May 14, 2002, in Resolution 1409, the Security Council adopted a revised goods list allowing states to sell to Iraq any products or commodities other than those falling under the ban on war or war-related materials. Funds held in the UN escrow account set up for Iraqi oil revenue could be used for these purchases.

The loosening of the Security Council's grip took only a fraction of the pressure off Iraq and its suffering people. For a decade the combination of sanctions, weapons inspections, and the "no-fly zones" unilaterally imposed by the United States and Britain over northern and southern Iraq had immobilized the country politically, economically, and socially. When Peter Hain, the British minister with responsibility for Iraq, asserted in 2000 that British air crews were "risking their lives patrolling southern

Iraq," the former UN humanitarian coordinator for Iraq, Hans von Sponeck, pointed out that they were there without the mandate of the UN and could quickly be withdrawn if the point was to save British lives.[137] UNSCOM moved around Iraq locating and destroying huge stocks of chemical weapons and other war material until being withdrawn ahead of Operation Desert Fox, the four-day U.S. air operation launched on December 16, 1998.[138] UNSCOM was eventually discredited when it was revealed that it had been infiltrated by British and U.S. intelligence agencies and that information had been passed on to Israel. The Iraqi government never allowed it to return. In December 1999 it was replaced by the United Nations Monitoring, Verification and Inspection Commission (UNMOVIC).[139]

The accusation that Iraqi authorities had not cooperated with the arms inspectors, as indeed they had not done on some occasions though they had cooperated fully on many more, was played up by the Australian head of UNSCOM, Richard Butler. In fact, the inspection teams had located and destroyed virtually all stocks of chemical and biological warfare material before their withdrawal. Well before the Second Gulf War was launched in March 2003, the chairman of UNMOVIC, Hans Blix, repeatedly said he did not believe Iraq had been able to redevelop WMD. This was also the view of arms inspector Scott Ritter. The IAEA was confident that Iraq had not moved toward the development of nuclear weapons. On all the best evidence, Iraq had been effectively disarmed. Hans von Sponeck, in an interview in December 2001, said he believed the case against Iraq was being overstated "in order to prepare for another round of attacks."[140]

KEPT "ONLY BARELY ALIVE"

In 1993 the Arab Monetary Fund estimated that the invasion of Kuwait had cost Iraq $256 billion. Industry and the civilian infrastructure were kept in an incapacitated state through a sanctions regime that had no parallel in UN history.[141] The two successive heads of the UN's humanitarian mission in Iraq, Denis Halliday (September 1997–October 1998) and Hans von Sponeck (October 1998–March 2000), resigned in disgust at the UN's role in allowing its authority to be used for an Anglo-American agenda aimed at keeping Iraq on its knees.[142] The contamination of water, the degradation of hospital care through the denial of medical supplies and the spare parts needed to repair power plants, and the provision of just enough food to keep the people alive—"but only barely alive"—were all having a catastrophic effect on the people of Iraq.[143] Nine years after the end of the war, Halliday estimated that five thousand children under age five were still dying every month, with another two thousand to three thousand deaths being recorded among other children, teenagers, and adults. The average birthweight of a child was less than five pounds. The country had been reduced to a state of social collapse, and the oil-for-food program was no more than the "continuation of the genocide that the economic embargo has placed on Iraq. I say genocide because it is an internationally sanctioned program to destroy a culture, a people, a country." UN member states had maintained the embargo "despite their knowledge of the death rate of Iraqi children. That is genocide."[144]

Professor Richard Garfield of Columbia University, an epidemiologist, estimated in 2003 that the sanctions had caused between 343,900 and 529,000 infant and young child fatalities.[145] UNICEF statistics show that the death rate among children under five rose from 50 per 1,000 in 1990 to 125 per 1,000 in 2003.[146] Sanctions and war-related illnesses (including cancers and birth defects caused by the use of uranium-depleted shells and possibly toxic fallout from the 1991 air campaign) took the lives of about one million Iraqis in the twelve years between the wars of 1991 and 2003.

The British and American governments argued that sufficient food and medicine were being released for the needs of the Iraqi people but were being diverted by the Baʿath government for its own purposes. However, in December 2001 Hans von Sponeck estimated that "as of two weeks ago" $US4 billion worth of humanitarian aid for Iraq was being held back by the United States despite the presence in Iraq of hundreds of UN observers inspecting hospitals, warehouses, schools, and electricity companies to ensure that supplies were reaching the right destination.[147] Ninety-eight percent of blocked contracts were being blocked by the United States. Between 1996 and 1998 revenue under the oil-for-food program had provided Iraq with no more than $113 per citizen per year. "Now how can that possibly be adequate?" Even though the oil production ceiling had been lifted, output could not be increased because the United States was standing in the way of the reconstruction of the oil industry.[148] Increased revenue had come from higher prices, not increased production, and had been reduced anyway by the UN Security Council's decision to put thirty cents of every oil dollar into the UN Compensation Commission.

In the two years before Iraq was invaded by a new but severely shrunken "coalition of the willing," it was clear that most of the world accepted the finding of Blix, von Sponeck, Halliday, Scott Ritter, and many others involved in arms inspection and control that the Baʿathist regime had been rendered harmless. Like Denis Halliday and Hans von Sponeck, a rapidly increasing number of governments in the region and around the world could no longer stomach the effects of sanctions on the Iraqi people. Saudi Arabia and Iraq reopened their borders, and Iraq and Iran exchanged refugees. Syria and Iraq patched up their differences. Turkish, Arab, and European businessmen visited Baghdad in search of contracts. Iraq's economic and political isolation in the Middle East was "all but over," and Saddam was almost off the hook. Hans von Sponeck believed he had been "very weakened" and was not "the Saddam Hussein described to us as a danger to the US and Europe. That is nonsense." He was a dictator, "but the US, the UK and the west contributed to creating this monster. We wanted him as a business partner, an ally against Iran. We condoned his use of weapons of mass destruction against Kurds in the interest of other objectives. If we preach democracy, yet cooperate with feudal dictatorships, we are contributing forcefully to the kind of situation we saw develop in Iraq."[149]

On December 17, 2000, in Resolution 1284, the UN Security Council had raised the prospect of suspending sanctions once outstanding disarmament and monitoring issues were resolved. This point was not reached until President George W. Bush urged the UN to lift them after the "end" of the Second Gulf War in 2003, simultaneously assuring the Iraqi people that their lives would now be "better than anything they have known for generations."[150]

13. GEORGE THE SON

The invasion of Iraq in 2003 was preceded by a propaganda campaign monumental in its deceit and dishonesty. Practically nothing that was said by the U.S. and British governments turned out to be true. What was claimed to be evidence of the need to go to war based on "intelligence" and "fact" turned out to be an agglomeration of assertions and suppositions buttressed by forged documents and wild claims that had no basis in intelligence or fact. The fraudulent nature of what the U.S. and British governments were claiming was palpable even before the military campaign was launched, but on both sides of the Atlantic and in other countries that joined the attack and occupation the mainstream media bought the propaganda package. Some newspapers argued later that "we got it wrong," but this was not true. They simply did not do their job, if doing their job is partly to be defined as monitoring the claims of government in defense of the public interest. If defending the claims of governments against the public interest is their job, they did it very well indeed.[1]

In his address to the UN General Assembly on September 12, 2002, President Bush referred back to Iraq's chemical weapons attacks on Iran—which his father's administration had tacitly sanctioned—as justification for U.S. military action. The Baʿathist regime was a "grave and gathering" danger. Saddam "continues to develop weapons of mass destruction." UN inspectors believed, according to the president, that Iraq had produced "two to four times the amount of biological agents it declared and has failed to account for more than three metric tons of material that could be used to produce biological weapons." Saddam had gassed "many Iranians and 40 Iraqi villages." In cells and camps terrorists were plotting further destruction and building new bases for their war against civilization, "and our greatest fear is that terrorists will find a shortcut to their mad ambitions

317

when an outlaw regime supplies them with the technologies to kill on a massive scale." Of course, supplying an "outlaw regime" with the technology it needed to kill on a massive scale was precisely what the U.S. administration and numerous other governments had done in the 1980s. In the face of the threats he had outlined, President Bush declared that the UN faced a "difficult and defining" moment. "Are Security Council resolutions to be honored and enforced or cast aside without consequence?"[2] It was a good question but one that was relevant not just to Iraq. The selective application of Security Council resolutions and the selective use by the permanent members of their veto power (most often by the United States) goes to the heart of criticism of the council as a body that serves the interests of these states and not the general UN interest.

In his follow-up address to the Security Council on February 5, 2003, Colin Powell, secretary of state since January 2001, used Power Point, satellite photos, and artists' impressions to portray a country abounding in weapons of mass destruction (WMD), concealed above- and belowground or shifted around to avoid detection.[3] He wanted to share with his UN and world audience "what the United States knows about Iraq's weapons of mass destruction, as well as Iraq's involvement in terrorism." He spoke of an accumulation of facts. "Every statement I make today is backed up by sources, solid sources. These are not assertions. What we're giving you are facts and conclusions based on solid intelligence." The "facts" included Iraq's attempts to devoid detection by moving rocket launchers and warheads filled with biological warfare agents to western Iraq, where most of them were hidden in "large groves of palm trees"—was the attentive listener really supposed to believe that date palm fronds could protect weaponry from detection by supersophisticated satellites and the high-precision photography of unmanned reconnaissance aircraft?—before being moved on again.

On the question of Iraq's chemical weapons capacity General Powell (dramatically flourishing a vial of white powder) pointed out that "less than a teaspoon" of dry anthrax had been sufficient to close down the U.S. Senate when it was sent in letters (addressed to Democratic senators Tom Daschle and Patrick Leahy). Yet Saddam had 8,500 liters of anthrax and—on the basis of UN Special Commission (UNSCOM) estimates—"could have" produced 25,000 liters from which WMD could be developed. In fact, "Our conservative estimate is that Iraq today has a stockpile of between 100 and 500 tons of chemical weapons agent. That is enough to fill 16,000 battlefield rockets. Even the low end of 100 tons of agent would enable Saddam Hussein to cause mass casualties across more than 100 square miles of territory, an area nearly five times the size of Manhattan." Further, said General Powell,

> We know from Iraq's past admissions that it has successfully weaponized not only anthrax, but also other biological agents including botulinum toxin, aflatoxin and ricin. But Iraq's research efforts did not stop there.
>
> Saddam Hussein has investigated dozens of biological agents causing diseases such as gas gangrene, plague, typhus, tetanus, cholera, camelpox, and hemorrhagic fever. And he also has the wherewithal to develop smallpox.

But this was not recent knowledge. Senator Riegle's committee had unearthed the evidence a decade earlier that precursors Iraq needed for development of chemical and biological weapons, along with technologies needed for the development of other weapons, had come from outside and that the United States was indeed part of a clandestine international supply network. "We know that Iraq has embedded key portions of its illicit chemical weapons infrastructure within its legitimate civilian industry." No surprise there either. The key question was not whether Iraq still had the factories where dual-use material had been weaponized in the past but whether chemical weapons were still being produced. General Powell was doing his best to create the impression that they were.

On the question of Saddam's alleged attempts to reconstitute a nuclear program, General Powell referred to Iraq's importation of dual-use aluminium tubes from eleven countries for the probable purpose of turning them into the rotors needed for the enrichment of uranium and the manufacture of nuclear weapons. He linked Saddam to terrorism through Iraq's support for the families of Palestinian suicide bombers and through the training camp from which General Powell said Abu Mus'ab al Zarqawi was producing the deadly toxin ricin. Powell resorted to another kitchen metaphor when he declared that "less than a pinch—imagine a pinch of salt—less than a pinch of ricin"—in food was enough to cause death. At the close of Powell's presentation, the British foreign secretary, Jack Straw, thanked him for "laying bare the deceit practiced by the regime of Saddam Hussein."[4]

In the coming weeks General Powell maintained his argument that Iraq retained the capacity to manufacture chemical and biological weapons and had multifold ways of delivering them. He was to be proven wrong on almost all counts. The Iraqi government had no WMD or stocks of chemical and biological weapons. There were no chemical warheads tucked away underground or behind palm trees. There were no chemical weapons at all. There were no mobile chemical and biological weapons laboratories being shifted around the country on rails or wheels. There was no active nuclear research program. The aluminium tubes were not being imported for uranium enrichment. None of the "solid" facts General Powell presented to the UN Security Council, including material compiled in the "fine paper" Tony Blair had released shortly before he spoke—the "intelligence" dossier cobbled together from pilfered academic work and general information—turned out to be facts at all.[5] It was impossible for Iraq to launch an attack on Britain within forty-five minutes, as Blair had claimed. It did not have the weapons or the means of delivery.[6]

The same deceitful claims were repeated time after time by George Bush, Dick Cheney, Donald Rumsfeld, Tony Blair, Jack Straw, and Geoff Hoon, as well the lesser actors who had been induced to join the attack. Australia's John Howard committed his country's armed forces to the invasion before he even knew what was involved. It was not Saddam Hussein's tyrannical regime that was deceiving the world—because most of what the Ba'athist government told UN arms inspectors turned out to be true—but the free and democratically elected governments of the United States and Britain and their "allies."

In fact—real fact—Hans Blix and Muhammad al Baradei had not given Iraq an entirely clean bill of health but had indicated that for the most part Iraq was cooperating, that its stocks of chemical and biological warfare material had been destroyed, and that its nuclear program had been neutralized before the arms inspectors withdrew in 1998. Their conclusions were supported by documentary evidence brought out of Iraq by defectors. In August 1995 two of Saddam's son-in-laws, General Hussein Kamil and Colonel Saddam Kamil, fled to Jordan. They were murdered in Baghdad on Saddam's orders after being persuaded to return six months later, but while he was in Amman, General Hussein Kamil, who was in charge of weapons production and stockpiling, provided weapons inspectors with a wealth of information. On August 22 he was interviewed by chief arms inspector Rolf Ekeus and two of his senior colleagues. When one of them said UN inspectors had found no traces of chemical weapons being destroyed, General Kamil replied, "Yes, it was done before you came." This must have been before May–June 1991, when the first UN inspections were made of Iraq's nuclear and chemical weapons development and stockpiling sites. According to General Kamil: "We gave instructions not to produce chemical weapons. I don't remember resumption of chemical weapons production before the Gulf War. Maybe it was only minimal production and filling. . . . All chemical weapons were destroyed. . . . I ordered destruction of all chemical weapons. All weapons—biological, chemical, missile, nuclear—were destroyed."[7]

THE NEOCONSERVATIVE NETWORK

Understanding what happened to Iraq means "first understanding what has happened to America."[8] The invasion was preceded long beforehand by the rise to power in Washington of a political cohort of radical conservatives advocating the aggressive use of military power to change the world in U.S. interests. These "neoconservatives," as they were generally (if somewhat loosely) called, had varying views on traditional conservative issues such as abortion, gay rights, and homosexuality in the armed forces, but one issue separated them from the traditional conservatives and warranted their description as a distinctive unified cohort: their position on foreign policy. Some of the neoconservatives had developed their views out of philosophical inquiry and some from the raw experience of life, but all were zealots. Their energy—what the conservative George Will has described as their "crusading zeal"[9]—was directed toward the aggressive reassertion of U.S. power around the world through what they called "preemptive strikes" and "anticipatory actions" against governments perceived as threatening the United States in one way or another.

The dominant figures in the neoconservative cohort as it had developed by the time the United States went to war in 2003 were all Washington insiders with decades of experience behind them. Donald Rumsfeld and Richard Cheney had worked closely together on the White House staff during the Ford administration in the 1970s. Paul Wolfowitz was recruited to the Arms Control and Disarmament Agency during the Nixon administration before moving upward through the ranks at both the Pentagon and the State Department. During the Ford administration Wolfowitz was appointed to the President's Foreign Policy Advisory Board, established by President Kennedy to continually review and assess the activities of the CIA and other intelligence-gathering organizations. He was assigned to "Team B" (Team A being the CIA), headed by Professor Richard Pipes, whose role was to review the military strength and strategic policies of the Soviet Union. "Team B" was uniformly hard-line (other committee members included the father of the atomic bomb, Edward Teller), and the overblown estimates of both the Soviet Union's military strength and intentions that came out of its deliberations were inevitable and no doubt expected. What was significant in the context of the war launched against Iraq nearly three decades later was the precedent for establishing a group that could challenge and perhaps undermine—depending on who was in the White House and what needed to be done—the findings of the CIA and other professional intelligence agencies that did not suit their purposes.

Under President Reagan, Wolfowitz was appointed head of policy planning in the State Department. His staff there included Frances Fukuyama, Dennis Ross (subsequently President Clinton's chief Middle East "peace" negotiator), and Zalmay Khalilzad (President George Bush's ambassador to Iraq and principal guiding hand behind the constitution issued in 2005). His steady rise culminated in his appointment in 2001 as deputy secretary of defense under Donald Rumsfeld.

Richard Perle began developing his skills as a lobbyist and government infighter in the 1970s as a staffer for the right-wing Democrat Senator "Scoop" Jackson (with whom Wolfowitz had a long and admiring connection) before moving to Senate committees on security and arms control. In 1981 President Reagan appointed Perle as assistant secretary of defense for international security policy, a position he held until 1987. Perle was chairman of the Pentagon's Defense Policy Advisory Board before being forced to step down in March 2004 (while remaining on the board as an ordinary member) by the disclosure of conflict of interest. The Center for Public Integrity later revealed that nine of the board's members were connected to companies that had been given more than $76 billion worth of contracts by the Department of Defense.[10]

Others in the neoconservative cohort included Douglas Feith, formerly a "Scoop" Jackson staffer and ultimately undersecretary of defense for policy until his resignation early in 2005; Kenneth Adelman, who was director of the Arms Control and Disarmament Agency in the Reagan administration and who sat on the Defense Policy Advisory Board alongside Perle and Henry Kissinger; Stephen Cambone, undersecretary of defense for intelligence; I. Lewis Libby and Robert Satloff, both national security advisers; Marc Grossman, undersecretary of state for political affairs; John Bolton, former undersecretary of state for arms control and international security and later the U.S. ambassador to the UN; David Wurmser, former special adviser to Bolton and adviser to Vice President Cheney; and Dov Zakheim, chief financial officer and undersecretary of defense. Other key figures included Elliott Abrams, another Jackson staffer, currently attached to the vice president's office, Reagan's assistant secretary for human rights and assistant secretary for inter-American affairs, under the aegis of which he ran the Contras in Nicaragua; David Frum, former resident fellow at the American Enterprise Institute for Public Policy Research (AEI), and the Bush speechwriter credited with coining the expression "axis of evil"; and Richard Haass, director of the State Department's Policy Planning Staff and advocate of "anticipatory" action around the world in defense of U.S. interests.

Many of the neoconservatives (including Wolfowitz, William Kristol and his father Irving, and Abram Shulsky) were strongly influenced by the teachings of the German-born philosopher Leo Strauss, who criticized liberal democracy on the grounds that its endless relativism leads to nihilism. Strauss himself was strongly influenced by Plato and Nietzsche in his emphasis on the need for a select few to guide the uninformed masses in their own best interests. This may mean concealing the truth. Even a disciple admits that the "Straussian text" is "deliberately written so that the average reader will understand it as saying one ('exoteric') thing but the special few for whom it is written will grasp its real ('esoteric') meaning."[11] In this context, Machiavelli's crime was not to advocate untruth as a tool for the consolidation of political power but merely to speak a hidden truth openly. To an unsympathetic biographer, Strauss's views add up to a belief in "the efficacy and usefulness of lies" in politics[12] —hence the connection that has been drawn between Strauss, the neoconservatives, and the lies that were propagated ahead of the attack on Iraq in 2003. His defenders argue that while a strong critic of liberal democracy, Strauss believed in its precepts if not their practical application in a tough world. His vision of reality was in fact dialectical. "Why some of his most promising students missed this essential feature of his thought and why they turned to the right remains one of the mysteries of his intellectual legacy."[13]

Washington's numerous right-wing foundations, the *Weekly Standard* newspaper (financed by Rupert Murdoch) and other publications, and numerous well-funded think tanks, including the AEI, the Heritage Foundation, the Hudson Institute, the Middle East Forum, the Middle East Media Research Institute (MEMRI), the Washington Institute for Near East Policy, the Jewish Institute for National Security Affairs (JINSA), and the Center for Security Policy, have served all along as an auxiliary forum in which the neoconservatives in and out of government can develop and propagate their ideas. Numerous publications in the media mainstream also give them generous space for the transmission of their views.

"A CLEAN BREAK"

The neoconservatives had their worldview all organized when the destruction of the twin towers on September 11, 2001, seemed to confirm that Samuel Huntington's "clash of civilizations" was beginning. In 1991 the draft of a Defense Policy Guideline (DPG) strategy for the 1990s found its way into the press. Written by Paul Wolfowitz and I. Lewis Libby, it called for preeminence over "Eurasia" through "preemptive" military action against states hostile to U.S. interests and seeking to acquire WMD.[14]

This line of argument was taken further in a discussion paper, "A Clean Break: A New Strategy for Securing the Realm," prepared by a study group convened by the Institute for Advanced Strategic and Political Studies (centered in Jerusalem and Washington) to give advice to Benyamin Netanyahu during the Israeli election campaign of 1996.[15] The group consisted of Richard Perle, its leader, representing the AEI; James Colbert, of JINSA; Charles Fairbanks Jr., of Johns Hopkins University; Douglas Feith, then of the Washington and Israeli law firm Feith and Zell Associates; Robert Loewenberg, president of the host institute; Jonathan Torop, of the Washington Institute for Near Eastern Studies; David Wurmser, representing the host institute; and Meyrav Wurmser, of Johns Hopkins University.

The document called for the overthrow of Saddam Hussein, military attacks on Syria, "hot pursuit" of the Palestinians, and rejection of the land-for-peace formula proclaimed by previous Israeli Labor governments. Its starting point was Israel's economic and ideological paralysis, hence the need for a "clean break" (including an end to Israel's reliance on U.S. aid) that would simultaneously open the way to a new relationship with the United States stressing self-reliance as well as strategic cooperation. The paper reverted to the early-twentieth-century image of a Jewish state aligned with the values of the West and standing firm in defense of joint interests with local allies against the forces of mayhem and disorder.

In the Perle vision of the future, the overthrow of Saddam Hussein would be followed by popular Iraqi support for the return of the Hashimites, who "could use their influence over Najaf to help Israel wean the south Lebanese Shia away from Hizballah [*sic*], Iran and Syria. . . . The Shia venerate foremost the Prophet's family, the direct descendant of which—and in whose veins the blood of the Prophet flows—is King Hussein." The idea that the Shiʿi Muslims of Najaf and Karbala or even Sunni Muslim Arabs and Kurds would put themselves at the disposal of the Hashimites, regarded across the Middle East for decades as agents of the West, was pure fantasy.

In 1996 William Kristol and Robert Kagan, in an article entitled "Toward a Neo-Reaganite Foreign Policy," called for U.S. seizure of the new "unipolar world" as a means of projecting American power into the next century.[16] In 1997 Kristol and Kagan took the lead in establishing the Project for the New American Century (PNAC), whose statement of principles was signed by, among others, Elliott Abrams, Gary Bauer, William J. Bennett (of the Christian evangelical organization Empower America), Florida governor

Jeb Bush, Midge Decter, Richard Cheney, Steve Forbes (of *Forbes* magazine), Aaron Friedberg, Donald Rumsfeld, Paul Wolfowitz, Francis Fukuyama, and Norman Podhoretz. PNAC was formulated under the aegis of the New Citizenship Project, funding for which was provided by the Bradley Foundation and office space for which was found in the offices of the AEI (also funded by the foundation). This combination of right-wing secular and religious forces "cemented the alliance between right-wing Republicans like Dick Cheney and Donald Rumsfeld, Christian and Catholic Rightists such as Gary Bauer and William Bennett and the neoconservatives behind a platform of US global military dominance."[17] In September 2000 PNAC issued its blueprint for the future, "Rebuilding America's Defenses: Strategies, Forces and Resources for a New Century," which foresaw a world in which the United States would be fighting "multiple, simultaneous theater wars" to maintain its global preeminence.[18]

In 2000 Daniel Pipes and Ziad Abdenour, of the Committee for a Free Lebanon, chaired a study group that published a "strategy" document entitled "Ending Syria's Occupation of Lebanon: The U.S. Role."[19] The signatories included Feith, Michael Rubin, Elliott Abrams, Richard Perle, Michael Ledeen, Frank Gaffney, David and Meyrav Wurmser, Jeanne Kirkpatrick, Jesse Helms, and Paula Dobriansky, the U.S. undersecretary of state for global affairs. While the document set out strategies for "reconstructing" the Middle East and confronting all "rogue states" in the region, the neoconservatives made Iraq their first priority, frequently claiming that it possessed WMD despite all evidence to the contrary. Questioned before a Senate Foreign Relations subcommittee in March 2001, Richard Perle responded: "Does Saddam now have weapons of mass destruction? Sure he does. We know he has chemical weapons. . . . We know he has biological weapons. . . . How far he's gone on the nuclear-weapons side I don't think we really know. My guess is that it's further than we think."[20]

Less than a fortnight after the aerial attacks on New York and Washington, PNAC issued an open letter to President Bush, signed by, among others, Richard Perle, Jeanne Kirkpatrick, Francis Fukuyama, William Kristol, Frank Gaffney, and the brothers Kagan, Donald and Robert, calling on him to pursue the war against terror beyond Afghanistan to Iraq and to prepare for action against Syria, Iran, and Hizbullah.[21] A further letter to the president, on April 3, 2002, signed by Perle, Pipes, Podhoretz, Kenneth Adelman, and Robert Kagan, among others, again urged the president to remove Saddam Hussein, to stand firm with Israel against regimes situated along the "axis of evil," and to break with Yasser Arafat and the Palestinian Authority, that "cog in the machine of Middle East terrorism."[22]

By this time it was clear that the United States was preparing to attack Iraq. On September 17, President Bush released a new national security policy position signaling the readiness of the United States to take "preemptive" military action against "rogue states and their terrorist clients" and to act alone if necessary.[23] Henceforth no government could fall back on a long tradition of sovereign rights regulating relations between states. Two months before the war was launched, Richard Haass warned that "states risk forfeiting their sovereignty when they take steps that represent a clear threat to global security. When certain regimes with a history of aggression and support for terrorism pursue weapons of mass destruction, thereby endangering the international community, they jeopardize their sovereign immunity from intervention, including anticipatory action to destroy this developing capability."[24] Three years into the invasion, Condoleeza Rice, secretary of state since January 28, 2005, reaffirmed her faith in the purgative value of force.

> A regional order that produced an ideology so savage as the one we now confront is no longer serving any civilized interest.
>
> For 60 years, we often thought that we could achieve stability without liberty in the Middle East. And ultimately, we got neither. . . .
>
> . . . In a world where evil is still very real, democratic principles must be backed with power in all its forms: political, and economic, and cultural, and moral, and yes, sometimes, military.[25]

PLANNING FOR WAR

President W. George Bush took the oath of office in January 2001. The following day, according to an inside source, the question of an attack on Iraq was raised at the first meeting of his national security team.[26] In the coming year Douglas Feith and Harold Rhode, a Pentagon "specialist" on Islam, began stacking the Department of Defense's Near East South Asia (NESA) directorate with researchers and policy advisers who shared their view of what needed to be done about the Middle East. After the attacks on New York and Washington, the AEI's David Wurmser was called in to organize the nucleus of a new research unit established to test CIA intelligence findings. "While the CIA and other intelligence agencies concentrated on Osama bin Laden's Al Qaeda as the culprit in the 9/11 attacks, Wolfowitz and Feith obsessively focused on Iraq."[27] The ostensible purpose of the so far unnamed Pentagon cell was to "reassess" information already made available by the intelligence agencies and to look out for something they might have missed. The real purpose seems to have been to undermine more sober CIA findings and strengthen the case for war. In October 2002, by which time Wurmser had moved on to Undersecretary of State John Bolton's staff and the Pentagon operation had been broadened and given a name, the Office of Special Plans (OSP), Donald Rumsfeld explained that its primary purpose was to cull "factoids" that could then be weighed against the findings of the CIA and other intelligence agencies.[28]

The Pentagon chain of command ran from Rumsfeld through Wolfowitz, Feith, and Defense Undersecretary William Luti, in charge of NESA, all the way down to OSP director Abram Shulsky and his staffers. Shulsky had moved in the same circles as Perle, Feith, and Wolfowitz for decades and had teamed up with Gary Schmitt (one of the founding figures of PNAC) to write a study of intelligence warfare.[29] Perle described the OSP as "the organization within the policy side of the Defense Department that was responsible for planning with respect to the war. . . . You could have called it the Iraq war-planning group. But it made more sense under the circumstances to call it by an anodyne name."[30]

Part of the OSP's mission was the preparation of "talking points" on Iraq and terrorism. An insider described them as "a mélange crafted from obvious past observations and intelligence bits and pieces of dubious origin." These talking points on the need for military action included the fabricated claim that the Ba'athist government was trying to purchase yellowcake from Niger; the claim was stated "mostly in the present tense" and left out the date of the last known Iraqi attempt to buy fissionable material from Niger—sometime in the late 1980s.[31] This false claim was utilized by President Bush in his 2002 State of the Union address.

Karen Kwiatkowski, an air force lieutenant-colonel serving as a staff officer in the Department of Defense and transferred to NESA in May 2002, regarded the OSP as an "ideologically driven network [that] functioned like a shadow government, much of it off the official payroll and beyond congressional oversight." She later wrote of her experiences as being intense, fascinating, and "frightening": "While the people were very much alive I saw a dead philosophy—Cold War anti-communism and neo-imperialism—walking the corridors of the Pentagon. It wore the clothing of counter-terrorism and spoke the language of a holy war between good and evil. The evil was recognized by the leadership to be resident mainly in the Middle East and articulated by Islamic clerics and radicals. But there were other enemies within, anyone who dared voice any skepticism about their grand plans, including Secretary of State Colin Powell and General Anthony Zinni."[32]

Kwiatkowski saw the "agenda bearers" within the OSP "usurp measured and carefully considered assessments and, through suppression and distortion of intelligence analysis, promulgate what were, in fact, false-hoods to both Congress and the executive office of the President." Expertise on the Middle East "was not only being removed but was also being exchanged for that from various agenda-bearing think tanks, including the Middle East Research Institute, the Washington Institute of Near East Policy and the Jewish Institute of Security Affairs." The findings from the OSP were transmitted to the White House, where I. Lewis Libby, Vice President Cheney's chief of staff, and the peripatetic David Wurmser, having been moved on from John Bolton's office early in 2003 to work for Cheney as an adviser, were waiting to use them to neutralize CIA reports.

According to other sources, the OSP also forged "close ties to a parallel ad hoc intelligence organization inside Ariel Sharon's office in Israel specifically to bypass Mossad and provide the Bush administration with more alarmist reports on Saddam's Iraq than Mossad was prepared to authorize."[33] Other information relayed to the White House was based on information provided by Iraqi defectors and exiles associated with Ahmad Chalabi's Washington-based Iraqi National Congress. Perle regarded Chalabi, who had been sentenced to twenty years' imprisonment in absentia by a Jordanian court on charges of bank fraud, as "quite brilliant. . . . The arguments against Chalabi have always been without substance. He is far and away the most effective individual that we could have hoped would emerge in Iraq. . . . I think he's been very warmly received in Iraq."[34] This seemed to say more about Perle than Chalabi. Chalabi had no standing in the country of his birth, had not been received warmly there at all, and was eventually dropped even by his American sponsors. Virtually all the evidence provided by defectors and the Iraqi National Congress turned out to be bogus or wildly inaccurate.

IRAQ WAR, ROUND TWO

> Our armies do not come into your cities and lands as conquerors
> or enemies but as liberators.
>
> Lieutenant General Sir Stanley Maude, commander-in-chief of
> the Mesopotamia Expeditionary Force, Baghdad, March 1917

Standing before the UN Security Council again on March 7, 2003, after hearing the latest reports from Dr. Blix and Dr. Baradei, General Powell made it clear that whatever Iraq had done to comply with UN Security Council Resolution 1441, passed on November 8, 2002, it remained in material breach of previous resolutions and its recent efforts were not enough for the United States. In Powell's view, the Blix report had shown that Iraq "had and still has the capacity to manufacture not only chemical but biological weapons; and that Iraq had and still has literally tens of thousands of delivery systems, including increasingly capable and dangerous unmanned aerial vehicles." Nobody wanted war, but "the clock continues to tick and the consequences of Saddam Hussein's continued refusal to disarm will be very, very real."[35]

On the evening of March 19, President Bush announced from the White House that U.S.-led coalition forces around Iraq "have begun striking selected targets of military importance to undermine Saddam Hussein's ability to wage war."[36] In the past year numerous Arab leaders had warned the United States that an attack on Iraq would open the "gates of hell."[37] Finally the gates had swung open, but in the opening phase of the war Donald Rumsfeld spoke confidently of the outcome: "What will follow will not be a repeat of any other conflict. It will be of a force and scope and scale that has been [sic] beyond what has been seen before."[38] In the Pentagon's "shock and awe" attack, new weapons were used and new strategies tested,[39] but as Iraq had not been left alone since 1991 the war was not so much a new one as the re-escalation of a long-running campaign in which air attacks had been combined with sanctions and the closure of airspace to Iraqi planes and helicopters. In the second half of 2002 the U.S. and British governments had authorized "spikes of activity" to put pressure on the Ba'athist government and destroy military targets ahead of open warfare.[40] Now that open war had been declared.

The invasion began with an attempt to assassinate Saddam Hussein from the air, itself an extraordinary violation of the rules and conventions of war and international relations as practiced down through the centuries. Civilian targets were bombed from day one. Basra was put under siege by British forces, and its water and power sources were knocked out of commission. In the Euphrates towns of Hilla and Nasiriyya, hundreds of civilians were killed in air strikes. In Hilla, an International Red Cross worker, Roland Huguenin, witnessed the arrival at a hospital of a truck "delivering dozens of totally dismembered bodies of women and children." The deaths and casualties had been caused by "bombs and projectiles." At Hilla "everybody had very serious wounds and many, many of them small kids and women. We had small toddlers of two or three years of age who had lost their legs, their arms."[41]

The weapons used against Iraq included more of the depleted-uranium tank shells that had been fired in the 1991 campaign and cluster bombs, the standard model and a refined new version, the CBU-105, described in the weapons inventories as a "wind-corrected munitions dispenser." Civilians were killed in streets, in marketplaces, at checkpoints, and on the open road as the advance continued up the Euphrates toward Baghdad. Once U.S. troops moved into the capital it was clear they had no idea what to do next. They stormed a mosque where it was thought Saddam Hussein might be hiding and set up guards around the oil and interior ministries but did nothing as dozens of government buildings and hospitals were pillaged and the national museum was stripped bare of the representative treasures of eight millennia of Mesopotamian history—Sumerian, Akkadian, Babylonian, and Parthian as well as Hellenistic, Arab, and Islamic. The looted artifacts included a gold Sumerian harp dating from 3360 BC, a five-thousand-year-old vase, a copper head of a Ninevah ruler from 2250 BC, statues of Apollo, Poseidon, and Eros, hundreds of cuneiform tablets inscribed with some of the earliest texts ever written, manuscripts, and early Qu'rans.[42] Civilization was being ransacked at its very source under the noses of those attacking Iraq in its name. In their haste the looters smashed many artifacts and left the pieces on the floor. The museum's records of archeological excavations dating back to Layard's "discovery" of the ruins of Ninevah in the nineteenth century disappeared along with much else. The national library, a repository of priceless documents preserved for centuries, and the Qu'ranic library at the Ministry of Religious Guidance were both set on fire. According to Donald Rumsfeld, the impression of widespread looting was magnified by the same scenes being shown over and over again. "The images you are seeing on television you are seeing over and over and over, and it's the same picture of some person walking out of some building with a vase, and you see it 20 times, and you think, 'My goodness, were there that many vases?' [Laughter]. 'Is it possible that there were that many vases in the whole country?'" Rumsfeld remarked that "stuff happens" and "freedom's untidy."[43]

Across the Middle East and around the world the war was seen as a war for oil, a war for Israel, a war for world domination, in fact anything but a war for the freedom of the Iraqi people. "An old-fashioned colonial war, built on lies, greed and geopolitical fantasies, it has nothing to do with 'disarming' Iraq or 'liberating' the Iraqi people," wrote the veteran British Middle East correspondent and author Patrick Seale.[44] And it was "not purely an American project":

> Rather it must be seen as the culmination of America's strategic partnership with Israel which began 36 years ago when President Charles de Gaulle told Israel that it would lose French support if it attacked its Arab neighbors. Israel promptly switched to the United States, which it gradually made its main ally and subsidizer. Much of the ideological justification for this war has come from right-wing American Zionists,

many of them Jews, closely allied to Israel's Prime Minister Ariel Sharon and occupying influential positions both inside and outside the Bush administration. It is neither exaggeration nor anti-semitism, as they would have it, to say that this is a Bush-Sharon war against Iraq.[45]

Iraq was quickly established as a foreign protectorate, first under General Jay Garner, flown over from his retirement home in Florida to Kuwait until it was safe for him to be moved on to Baghdad. Disagreements with the administration over how Iraq should be "reconstructed" dictated an early end to his tenure as head of the Coalition Provisional Authority. In May 2003 he was replaced by L. Paul Bremer III ("Jerry"), a former managing director (1989–2000) of Kissinger Associates, the Washington-based international business consultancy, who stood out on public occasions in Iraq by his eccentric habit of wearing boots under the trouser cuffs of a well-tailored suit.

On May 1, speaking from the deck of the U.S.S. *Abraham Lincoln*, riding off the California coast, President Bush declared that the war was over and had been won by the United States and its allies. "Major combat operations in Iraq have ended." It was yet another victory of science over barbarism. The war had demonstrated, said the president, that "with new tactics and precision weapons we can achieve military objectives without directing violence against civilians. . . . It is a great moral advance when the guilty have far more to fear from war than the innocent."[46]

CIVILIZATION AND BARBARISM

In December 2003 Saddam Hussein was captured. "We got him," Bremer announced. "This is a great day in your history. . . . For decades, hundreds of thousands of you suffered at the hands of this cruel man. . . . Those days are over forever."[47] The following April he told graduating Iraqi police that "once again the Land between the Two Rivers is the focal point of the clash between the forces of darkness and the light of civilization." They were "on the line between civilization and barbarism."[48] In the widening search for "unfriendlies" and "bad guys," in the infantile language of the U.S. military command spokesmen, Iraq was pushed deeper by the day into a darkening crevasse of U.S. land assaults and missile strikes; beheadings by "insurgents"; suicide bombings; massacres; the destruction and depopulation of cities; torture, humiliation, and murder at Abu Ghraib; random and indiscriminate killings in houses, at checkpoints, on the open road, and at wedding parties; and finally "sectarian violence" as the country reached the point of implosion.

The degradation of war slowly eroded the spirit of those fighting it and the social foundations of Iraqi society. The sequential removal of each face from the U.S. military command's pack of playing cards of "Most Wanted" men was an occasion for jubilation. Six months before Saddam Hussein was pulled out of the pit where he had been hiding, the U.S. military command had been told by an informer that his sons Uday and Qusai had taken refuge in a suburb of Mosul. On July 22 the district was blocked off and the three-story villa where the two brothers were hiding out was besieged by two hundred soldiers. After an initial attempt to storm the building was repelled, it was decided, in the words of Lieutenant General Ricardo Sanchez, commander of Coalition Joint Task Force 7, to "prep the objective prior to re-entry." The "prepping" included "the use of OH-58D Kiowa Warrior helicopters and their 2.75 inch rockets, Mark 19 grenade launchers, AT-4 rockets and helicopter and Humvee-mounted 50 caliber machine-guns."[49] At 1:00 P.M. the besieging force fired ten "tube-launched optically tracked wire-guided missiles" into the building. These weapons killed "three of the adults" inside, two of them Uday and Qusai and the third Abd al Hamid Mahmud, described as Saddam Hussein's personal secretary. Twenty-one minutes later, troops entered the villa again, took fire as they reached the second floor, and "killed the remaining individual."

Grisly photographs of Uday and Qusai were later distributed by the U.S. Department of Defense on CD-ROM as evidence to the Iraqi people that they had been killed. The release of the photos caused revulsion across the Arab world, but for Bremer the killings were "certainly good news for the Iraqi people." The White House was said to be "pleased." Tony Blair thought it was "a great day for the new Iraq." The deaths of Saddam Hussein's sons were "a very, very important step forward."[50] The day Uday and Qusai were put on trial might have been a better day for the Iraqi people—but what about the scarcely mentioned "remaining individual" who was killed after the death of "three of the adults"? It turned out that he was not an adult at all but Saddam Hussein's grandson and Qusai's son Mustafa Hussein, fourteen years old, appearing from a back room and shot dead by the troops storming the building.

In Najaf, George W. Bush's army and the Mehdi army of Muqtada al Sadr met face to face in the cemetery surrounding the sacred shrines. Cities were purged of their inhabitants. In April 2004 the western Euphrates city of Falluja (population three hundred thousand) was collectively punished in Operation Vigilant Resolve for the killing and mutilation of the bodies of four U.S. "contractors." U.S. forces besieged the city for a month. In the first week hundreds of people, half of them women and children and nearly all of them unarmed civilians, were killed in air strikes and artillery bombardment. Because access to Falluja's main cemetery was cut off by the presence of U.S. forces, many of the dead had to be buried in gardens or under the oval of the Falluja Sporting Club. So little was left of some bodies that grave markers had to be inscribed "hand" or "finger."[51]

In November Falluja was overrun by U.S. troops and pulverized in air strikes and artillery bombardment that lasted the whole month. This was Operation Phantom Fury. Most of the population had fled by the time the Americans attacked, but enough remained for the civilian casualties to be heavy. Sheikh Taghlib al Alousi, the president of Falluja's Majlis al Shura (Consultative Council), put the number of dead at "1800, 2000, maybe 2500. I don't think it will ever be known exactly." Dr. Hafidh al Dulaimi, head of the Falluja Compensation Commission, listed the material damage in the "city of a hundred mosques" as the destruction of thirty-six thousand houses, 8,400 shops, sixty nurseries and schools, sixty-five mosques, and three water purification plants, with substantial damage also done to electricity and water supplies and the sewage system.[52] In November 2005, the Italian state television station RAI reported that the United States had used white phosphorus shells in the attack. These weapons caramelize the flesh around the bones of the people they kill. Phosphorus bursts were not simply used for the purposes of illumination, as claimed by the U.S. military command. In the words of one soldier: "WP proved to be an effective and versatile munition. We used it for screening missions at two breaches and later in the fight, as a potent psychological weapon against the insurgents in trench lines and spider holes when we could not get effects on them with HE [high explosive]. We fired 'shake and bake' missions at the insurgents, using WP to flush them out and HE to take them out."[53] Numerous other towns, including the Turkmen city of Tal Afar, were depopulated as Falluja had been, their people fleeing ahead of time or driven into the desert so that U.S. forces could get at the "insurgents." Ramadi joined the list in 2006 in the campaign launched after the killing of Abu Musʿab al Zarqawi.

In its human rights report for September 1–October 31, 2005, the UN Assistance Mission for Iraq (UNAMI) recorded the "negative impact on human rights" in the Anbar and Ninevah governorates of "ongoing military and security operations" by joint U.S. and Iraqi forces "with the stated aim of restoring law and order."[54] The "significant" number of civilian losses (i.e., killed or wounded) included women and children, with more than ten thousand families being displaced, their access to basic humanitarian services hampered by the arrest and detention of relief workers and doctors and the military occupation of medical facilities. In the words of the report: "The price paid by civilians, including women and children, during military activity currently underway, calls for further reflection on the nature and conduct of the conflict and on the proportionality of the use of force." In addition to the dead and the numbers of Iraqis fleeing the country were the thousands of mostly young men swept up in mass arrests during military operations and subjected to "lengthy internment for reasons of security without adequate judicial oversight." Already by September 2005, 13,514 Iraqis were being held in this legal limbo by U.S. forces and a further 3,916 by the Interior Ministry of the interim government. UNAMI noted that the review mechanism set up in August 2004, authorizing the application of "exceptional procedures" to detail with the "detainees," violated Iraq's own emergency law, criminal law, "and international standards governing the protection of civilians under the law."

The U.S. administration did not count civilian deaths and refused to make any estimates until the end of 2005. In December 2005 President Bush suggested that 30,000 civilians might have been killed,[55] but conservative estimates were already almost double this figure. By August 27, 2007, the civilian death toll was estimated by Iraq Body Count to have reached a minimum figure of 70,749 and a maximum of 77,272,[56] but these numbers were greatly exceeded by the findings of other very credible sources. On October 28, 2004, the Center for International Emergency Disaster and Refugee Studies at the Johns Hopkins Bloomberg School of Health in Baltimore estimated, on the basis of joint field research with Baghdad's Al Mustansiriya University, that 100,000 more Iraqis had died than would have been expected "had the invasion not occurred." Most of the deaths were violent and the consequence of military action by the coalition forces.[57] Two years later the same team estimated that as many as 654,965 more Iraqis may have died than would have been expected under prewar conditions.[58] Even on the basis of the lower estimates, it seems that somewhere around 1.5 million to two million Iraqis had been killed or had died as the result of war and sanctions since 1991. The human cost of the war to the United States by August 2007 was 3,783 dead and 27,004 wounded, many of the wounded soldiers suffering the loss of limbs or severe brain damage caused by the shock waves from improvised explosive devices (IEDs).[59] The total financial cost of the war toward the end of August was more than $405 billion, according to the U.S. National Priorities Project, with the monthly cost close to $8 billion.[60] The gains to arms manufacturers, consultants, contractors, and corrupt Iraqi politicians had been tremendous.[61]

Added to these human and financial costs inside Iraq were those imposed on surrounding countries and international aid organizations. As of October 2006, some ninety thousand Iraqis were registered with UN High Commission for Refugees offices across the Middle East, but this was only a fraction of a massive outflow of people: the organization estimated that between five hundred thousand and seven hundred thousand Iraqi refugees were in Jordan, including some who had fled before 2003; some five hundred thousand to one million in Syria; twenty thousand to one hundred thousand in Egypt; twenty thousand to forty thousand in Lebanon; and "tens of thousands more" in neighboring countries. The UN's high commissioner for refugees, Antonio Guterres, described the flight of Iraqis as the greatest displacement of people in the region since the Palestinian crisis of 1948.[62] Unable to cope, by February 2007 both Syria and Jordan were tightening passport regulations and border controls to prevent the entry of any more people from Iraq.

"INDEPENDENT" IRAQ

For the UN Security Council, the occupation of Iraq ended on June 30, 2004, the day an interim government under the prime ministership of Iyad Allawi replaced the Coalition Provisional Authority. Although even the mild Kofi Annan had described the invasion of Iraq as illegal, so that intrinsically there was no difference between Iraq's invasion of Kuwait in 1990 and the U.S.-led invasion of Iraq in 2003, UN Security Council Resolution 1546 of June 8, 2004, did not demand the end of occupation but merely stated that the council was "looking forward" to its end on the last day of June.[63] Resolution 1546 and the earlier Resolution 1511 of October 16, 2003, miraculously transform invading and occupying forces into a multinational force under unified U.S. command, authorized to take all necessary measures to contribute to what it defines as Iraq's security and stability. Thus, far from dealing with the rupture of international order represented by the invasion, not to speak of the enormous destruction and the killing of civilians by the invading forces, the Security Council lent its authority in these two resolutions to the continuation of occupation behind the facade of a "sovereign and independent" interim government. In a similar manner did the League of Nations Council, dominated by Britain and France, sanction the occupation of large chunks of the Middle East by these same two countries after 1918 in the name of a "sacred trust of civilization."

In tandem with the government it had established, the United States quickly began the process of remodeling and redescribing Iraq. In October 2005 a new constitution was approved in a countrywide referendum that was mostly boycotted by the Arab Sunni Muslims.[64] The document provides for a weak central government and strong regional governments. It replaces the secular constitution of old Iraq with one that establishes Islam as the official religion of the state and Islamic law as a basic source of legislation, thereby creating an uncertain future for women, non-Muslim minorities, and even Muslims, depending on where, how, and by whom this aspect of the constitution is interpreted. These waters are further muddied by Article 2, which simultaneously prohibits the passage of laws contradicting the "established principles" of Islam and the "principles of democracy."

The constitution waters down Iraq's Arab identity by distinguishing between the ethno-religious "components" of the Iraqi polity. Only the Sunni Muslim Arabs are referred to as "Arabs," as if a Christian or a Shiʻi Muslim or anyone else who lives on the same soil as a Sunni Muslim and speaks Arabic as his or her mother tongue cannot be regarded as an Arab. There is no precedent in modern Arab national history for such a distinction. Ethno-religious differences are further widened by the right granted to regional governorates to establish their own security forces (already a fact in the Kurdish north) and by the stipulation that the armed forces should be representative of ethnic and religious divisions. These distinctions and qualifications put Iraq on the road to the same kind of "confessional" system that has caused so much turmoil in Lebanon. The constitution privileges the Kurds in a variety of ways, by establishing Kurdish as an official language alongside Arabic and by declaring (under Article 150) that all laws passed in "Kurdistan" since 1992 shall remain in effect unless voided by decision of the Kurdish regional authority. The constitution placed the contested city of Kirkuk under the authority of President Jalal Talabani (head of the Patriotic Union of Kurdistan) and cabinet until a census scheduled to be held in the city and "other disputed areas" before the end of 2007. If the census shows that the Kurds are in the majority (over Sunni Arab Muslims and Turkmen), the way will be clear for Kirkuk to be incorporated into the Kurdish governorate. The special status given to Kirkuk and three years' advance notice of a census only stimulated ethno-religious tension between Kurds, Turkmen, and Sunni Muslim Arabs in and around the city. The settlement of Kurds in Kirkuk and the expulsion of Arabs settled in the region by the Baʻathist regime were part of the demographic war being waged ahead of the census. The U.S. military command's deployment of Kurdish troops against Sunni Muslims and Shiʿa in Baghdad echoed Britain's use of the Christian Assyrians against the Kurds in the 1920s and Sunni Muslim Arabs in the 1940s.

The constitutional position on the question of oil raised the question asked when the country was invaded—was this war all about oil? L. Paul Bremer's attempt to fully privatize an economy in which oil resources had been fully nationalized was a premature attempt to take hold of the country's energy sector. It failed largely because foreign corporations were not willing to invest their money in a country that was not only occupied, thus raising the risk that their holdings could be confiscated at some point in the future, but so insecure that the safety of their employees could not be guaranteed. In the constitution, oil and gas are described as "the property of all the Iraqi people in all the regions and the provinces." But Article 10 puts oil and gas extracted from "current fields" under the joint custodianship of the regional governments and the federal government, implying a different arrangement for fields yet to be opened up.

The tremendous violence shattering daily life in Iraq tended to overshadow the closeted negotiations over the country's oil future between Iraqi and foreign government figures and the representatives of the oil multinationals. By the beginning of 2007, the outline of the new legislation was clearer. Nationalization laws passed progressively in 1961, 1971, and 1975 would be replaced by "production sharing agreements" (PSAs) between the Iraqi federal and regional governments and multinational oil corporations. In the short term these would enable the corporations to claim up to 75 percent of profits in the name of recouping start-up and drilling costs and 20 percent thereafter in contracts giving them access to Iraqi oil fields for thirty or more years. According to early reports of the legislation, their representatives would sit on a federal oil and gas council that would decide the terms of the contracts and who should get them. In normal circumstances these measures would most probably have led to widespread popular opposition, but Iraq's circumstances were far from normal. Chaos and the daily struggle for survival guaranteed that there would be no coherent public response to the new oil laws. Disorder has it uses. By 2007, the Iraq put together by the British in the 1920s had been picked apart by the Americans—but could they, did they even want, to stitch it together again?

"DECADES OF EFFORT"

Early in 2005 Douglas Feith resigned as the undersecretary of defense for policy, giving the desire to spend more time with his family as the reason.

That was understandable, but his sudden withdrawal from government could hardly be separated from the scandal enveloping William Luti's NESA section of the Pentagon after the arrest and indictment of one of its desk officers, Lawrence P. Franklin. An Iran specialist who had worked in the DIA before moving to Feith's domain, Franklin was charged with retaining and passing classified information to an Israeli embassy official and two senior AIPAC (American-Israel Public Affairs Committee) staff, Steven Rosen and Keith Weissman. He was accused of having seen a political officer at the embassy on nine occasions between 2002 and 2004. Rosen and Weissman were also charged with conspiring to obtain classified information and then releasing it to the media, to a senior fellow at the Washington Institute for Near East Policy, and to three unnamed foreign government employees. One of them was believed to be Naor Gillon, a political officer and specialist on Iran's nuclear development, who was transferred back to Israel as the FBI began to ask awkward questions about the role of embassy staff. The scandal revived memories of the 1980s theft of classified information from the Department of the Navy and its transmission to Israel by Jonathan Pollard, who is still serving a term of life imprisonment in spite of Israeli pressure for his release.

There were further casualties in the neoconservative ranks. In October 2005 White House staffer I. Lewis Libby and Bush's senior political adviser Karl Rove were revealed as the sources of leaked information on the identity of a CIA agent. Libby resigned just ahead of being indicted on five offenses by a federal grand jury prosecutor. Rove escaped indictment. Other neoconservatives were redeployed or moved on. In March 2005 John Bolton was nominated as U.S. ambassador to the UN, a position he was able to take up only six months later when President Bush finally overrode congressional opposition to the appointment. Paul Wolfowitz took over the presidency of the World Bank. Europeans were astounded. "We were led to believe that the neo-conservatives were losing ground. . . . But clearly the revolution is alive and well."[65]

Like U.S. forces engaged in the war they had set in motion, the neoconservatives were taking casualties in Washington, but they remained ready to fight on for "decades of patient effort."[66] In 2005 President Bush claimed that Muslim radicals wanted to "enslave whole nations" and set up an Islamic empire stretching from Spain to Indonesia. The president sometimes spoke of the higher authority guiding his decisions, by which he meant not his father but the Almighty Father above. Remarks he reportedly made to Palestinian officials on Middle Eastern problems were certainly consistent with belief in a God-given mission: "I am driven with a mission from God. God would tell me 'George, go and fight these terror-ists in Afghanistan' and I did. And then God would say 'George, go and end the tyranny in Iraq.' And I did. And now again, I feel God's words coming to me. 'Go and get the Palestinians their state and get the Israelis their security and get peace in the Middle East.' And by God, I'm gonna do it."[67] As the world could see, just as President Bush had said, the tyranny in Iraq had been brought to an end.

14. THE LONG CAMPAIGN

By September 2005 Israel had unilaterally withdrawn 8,000 settlers from the Gaza Strip, destroying all their homes and deconsecrated synagogues and leaving the mess for the Palestinians to clean up, but that left 246,000 Jewish settlers living in the West Bank, a further 200,000 within the enlarged boundaries of occupied East Jerusalem (in international law the whole of the city is occupied), and 20,000 on the annexed Golan Heights. The steady expansion of settlements had been maintained since 1967. Even when agreeing not to build new settlements, every Israeli prime minister, whether Labor, Likud, or Kadima, had continued the expansion of the old. Each was surrounded by sufficient land in the name of "security" to allow the process to continue for years without any need for new settlements to absorb Israelis attracted to the occupied territories for religious reasons or by financial incentives. The "security fence," a massive concrete wall topped with sensors, much of it on the other side of the 1967 green line, snaked across Palestinian land, cutting villages off from their agricultural land and (in the case of Bethlehem) separating a town from an important historical site.[1] The wall had been ruled illegal by the International Court of Justice sitting in the Hague. Indeed, the international illegality of the occupation of all territories taken in 1967 had been underscored in countless UN documents, including the preamble of Resolution 242 of 1967, but occupation and settlement continued relentlessly without any effective intervention from outside.

Just as previous governments had tried to distinguish between new settlements and the expansion of existing ones, so the Sharon government (2001–6) sought to separate the road map freeze on settlement construction from the "outward expansion" of the biggest current West Bank settlement project, Maale Adumin (population thirty-two thousand by the beginning of 2006). A small number of "pioneer" families began work on the site in 1975. In 1979 the Maale Adumin settlement bloc was given the status of a municipality. In 1991 it was recognized as a city by the government of Israel. Its "master plan" gives it a larger municipal area than Tel Aviv (fifty square kilometers or fifty-three thousand dunums compared to Tel Aviv's fifty-one thousand).[2] When completed, Maale Adumin and an adjacent settlement yet to be built in an area six kilometers to the north, currently designated E1, will stand on the map as a wedge dividing the West Bank in two. Cut off from Jerusalem in the west and separated from each other, the northern and southern Palestinian enclaves will also be separated from Jordan in the east by the planned annexation by Israel of the fertile Jordan Valley. Israel's strategic purpose seems clear: to fragment the territories, to enclose and disarm the Palestinians, to stifle their economic and social development, to break them psychologically, and to prevent them from establishing anything that could be realistically called a state. These plans are tacitly condoned by the United States. In April 2004 President Bush said that any "peace" between Israel and the Palestinians would have to reflect "demographic realities": that is, the retention by Israel of "major population centers" in the occupied territories.[3] The unspoken message sent to Israel was to continue creating "facts on the ground" because with U.S. acquiescence they could be turned into the "demographic realities" that would justify Israel's retention of conquered land.

In East Jerusalem, house demolitions, Jewish settlement, and the denial of IDs or habitation rights to Palestinians (including the denial of the right to return to the thousands of Jerusalem residents who happened to be outside the West Bank when it was conquered in 1967) are all part of a demographic war. The goal is the city's "Judaization" through Jewish settlement and the reduction of the Palestinian presence. A leading Jewish figure in the "developing real estate battle" in Jerusalem dwelled on some of the tactics being employed:

> We have four families who live here in a small enclave amongst all these Arabs and Palestinians in East Jerusalem. And I really think this is the forefront of Zionism today, realizing that there is a land war going on. And whoever wins that land war, Jews or Arabs, is going to be able to take control of the eastern side of the city. We're trying to tempt them into letting us buy their real estate. On the ground Palestinians do have a majority in East Jerusalem. If we want to lay claim to these areas not only on the sovereign level but also on the ground we have to have families living in dots through all of East Jerusalem. Dots which we will try to connect later on.[4]

In summer 2005, the Israeli government sealed off the eastern section of the West Bank (an area stretching inland from the Jordan Valley to the foothills of the West Bank mountain range) from the two million Palestinians living in the territories. The reason given was "security." At four checkpoints, entrance is now denied to all Palestinians whose IDs show that they are not residents of the Jordan Valley.[5] The contingent nature of the Palestinian administrative presence in Jericho (Al Rayha) was underscored in March 2006, when the city prison was destroyed by Israeli troops using tanks and bulldozers: they then seized Palestinian prisoners already tried and imprisoned for their part in the assassination in 2001 of Israeli government minister Rehavam Zeevi (killed in retaliation for Israel's assassination a few weeks earlier of the head of the Popular Front for the Liberation of Palestine in the occupied territories). Yet through thick and thin, Palestinian president Mahmoud Abbas (Abu Mazen) was able to continue his dialogue with the Israeli government.

SMILES AND TRUST

In 1988 Yasser Arafat formally committed the PLO to living alongside Israel. Indeed, the PLO had been working toward a two-state solution since the early 1970s, but this public acknowledgment of willingness to live at peace with Israel precipitated the round of backdoor diplomacy initiated by Norway that culminated in the opening of negotiations in Madrid in 1991 aimed at settling the Palestinian conflict once and for all. On September 9, 1993, Arafat sent a letter to Yitzhak Rabin declaring that the PLO "recognizes the right of the state of Israel to exist in peace and security."[6] In a two-line reply the following day Rabin merely acknowledged the PLO as the representative of the Palestinian people and agreed to open negotiations. On September 13 the Declaration of Principles was signed at the White House by Clinton, Yitzhak Rabin, and a smiling Arafat, representing the PLO "team" in the Jordanian-Palestinian delegation to the Middle East peace talks.[7] The declaration provided for the establishment of an interim Palestinian "self-governing authority" within five years of an Israeli withdrawal from Gaza and the Jericho "area" and the election of a council whose jurisdiction would cover "West Bank and Gaza" territory (omitting the critical "all"). It placed no restriction on Israeli settlement activity and shelved all the "core issues"—Jerusalem, settlements, the right of return, and so on—until the final stage of negotiations. Settlement expansion continued as before. Indeed, in October 1995, a month after the signing of the Israeli-Palestinian interim agreement on September 28

(Oslo 2), Rabin issued a reminder that his government had made a commitment to the Knesset "not to uproot any settlement in the framework of the Interim Agreement, nor to freeze construction and natural growth."[8]

The "framework of peace" carefully avoided the framework of basic Palestinian rights. Article 1 of the Declaration of Principles asserts that the aim of the "peace process" is a permanent settlement based on UN Security Council Resolutions 242 (1967) and 338 (1973), both of which are almost irrelevant in the context of Palestinian rights: Resolution 242 does not even refer to the Palestinians by name, asserting merely the need for "a just settlement of the refugee problem,"[9] and Resolution 338 does no more than confirm the content of Resolution 242. Were the international basis of Palestinian rights to have been built into the negotiations, the framework for the process would have included references to UN General Assembly Resolution 194 (III) of December 11, 1948 (setting out the right to repatriation or reparation); UN General Assembly Resolution 303 (IV) of December 9, 1949 (affirming the intention of the 1947 partition plan to establish Jerusalem as a *corpus separatum*); UN Security Council Resolution 237 of June 14, 1967 (calling on Israel to allow the return of Palestinians who had fled the occupied territories during the war a week earlier); UN Security Council Resolution 252 of May 21, 1968 (reaffirming that the acquisition of territory by military force is inadmissible and affirming that "all legislative and administrative measures and actions taken by Israel, including expropriation of land and properties thereon which tend to change the legal status of Jerusalem, are invalid and cannot change that status");[10] and UN General Assembly Resolution 3236 (XXIX) of November 22, 1974 (reaffirming the inalienable right of the Palestinians to return to their homes and property and recognizing their right as a people to regain their rights "by all means" in accordance with the purposes and principles of the UN Charter).[11]

Continuing settlement growth, land expropriation, road construction, house demolitions, and application of myriad restrictions to Palestinian daily life soon indicated that the negotiations were not heading in the direction of a final agreement acceptable to any Palestinian leadership. After the signing of the agreement on the Gaza Strip and the Jericho area of May 4, 1994 (the Cairo Agreement), Arafat returned to the occupied territories but "as collaborator as much as liberator."[12] The Interim Israeli-Palestinian Agreement on the West Bank and the Gaza Strip of September 28, 1995 (Oslo 2) divided the West Bank into Area A (full Palestinian autonomy), Area B (shared civil responsibility under full Israeli "security" control), and Area C (full Israeli civil and military control). By the end of the year Israeli troops had been redeployed away from most major Palestinian towns, but the vast bulk of the West Bank remained under full Israeli control and the towns themselves subject to checkpoints and curfews. The pace of transfer was glacial. By October 20, 1998, 2 percent of West Bank territory had been moved into Area A and 26 percent into Area B, leaving 72 percent under full Israeli control; by March 21, 2000, a total of 17.2 percent of territory had been moved into Area A and 23.8 percent into Area B, leaving Israel in full control of 59 percent of the West Bank.[13] These figures remained frozen thereafter.

In 1996 the newly elected Israeli prime minister, Binyamin Netanyahu, refused to honor the commitment of the previous government to withdraw Israeli troops from Hebron. Bending before the combined pressure of Israel and the U.S. government, Arafat sanctioned the presence of Israeli soldiers and settlers in an occupied city. In the Hebron Protocol of January 15, 1991, Hebron was divided into a large enclave for the bulk of the population (H1) and, right at the center under full Israeli control, a smaller enclave in which several hundred Jewish settlers lived alongside thirty-five thousand Palestinians. The enclave included the Ibrahimi Mosque (Tomb of the Patriarchs), a site holy to Muslims and Jews. The mosque had long since been taken over by the Israelis and divided into separate prayer spaces for Muslims and Jews. The lines of H2 placed the enclave in close proximity to the settlers of Kiryat Arba, many of the most extreme being Americans,[14] whose outbursts of racist thuggery and vandalism in Hebron had continued unchecked by the Israeli government for more than two decades. In the four years between June 1992 and June 1996, the settler population of the occupied land increased from 96,158 to 145,000; by early 2000 the figure had increased to about 400,000,[15] and it has continued to rise.

Netanyahu came to power after an election campaign in which more than one hundred Lebanese were killed when Israeli forces shelled the UN compound at Qana (where, the Lebanese believe, Christ turned water into wine at a wedding). In September Netanyahu authorized excavations near the Aqsa mosque, triggering off disturbances in which Israeli forces killed scores of Palestinians. He also authorized the construction of the Har Homa (Jabal Abu Ghneim) settlement on the outskirts of eastern Jerusalem, further closing off the city from its Palestinian hinterland. The rise of an extreme right-wing government committed to the consolidation of "greater Israel" finally shattered Palestinian hopes that something good would come out of the "peace process" and paved the way for the rise of the suicide bomber: the social and political pendulum began to swing away from Arafat's mainstream Fatah movement toward Hamas and Islamic Jihad.

CAMP DAVID II

In May 1999 Netanyahu was replaced by the Labor leader Ehud Barak. His decision to put the Palestinians on the back burner and give priority to the "Syrian track" ended precipitously in March 2000, when Bill Clinton met Hafez al Assad at Geneva and told him Israel was prepared to withdraw from most but not all of the Syrian territory Israel had occupied in 1967. Assad rejected the offer and was roundly attacked in the U.S. media for blocking the path to peace. Barak then returned to the "Palestinian track." Operating as a team, Clinton and Barak applied relentless pressure to Arafat when negotiations began at Camp David in July 2000. Barak dangled the offer of Israeli withdrawal from 92 to 95 percent of the West Bank, depending on what Arafat was prepared to give in return, including a heavily colonized chunk of the West Bank on the other side of the green line. On July 18, several days into the negotiations, Arafat sat listening while Clinton read Barak's position paper. Israel was prepared to withdraw from 92 percent of the West Bank and would accept the establishment of a demilitarized Palestinian state; the remaining 8 percent, thick with Israeli settlements, would be annexed by Israel; it would withdraw from all Gaza; in East Jerusalem Israel would agree to "the establishment of a Palestinian capital" in which "some Arab neighborhoods" would become sovereign Palestinian territory and others would enjoy "functional autonomy"; Palestinian sovereignty would extend over half the old city (the Muslim and Christian quarters, which in fact had constituted most of the old city until Jewish settlers began moving in); the Palestinians would be given "custodianship" but not sovereignty over the "Temple Mount" (the Haram al Sharif); refugees would be granted the right of return but only to the Palestinian state (to which most could not "return" because they had not come from this part of Palestine in the first place).[16]

Barak's offer could only have filled the Palestinian side with reservations. The territory would not be returned at once: the pace of withdrawal would clearly be dependent on a Palestinian renunciation of violence, an argument that had already been used to justify nonwithdrawal from the territories. Even if Barak's proposals had been accepted by Arafat, it was most unlikely that they would have been acceptable to the Knesset, given the strength of the settler movement and its advocates in Parliament and popular misgivings about the extent of the "concessions" he had made.[17] The question of what constituted Jerusalem—the city as it existed up to 1967 or the "greater Jerusalem" created by Israel in the thirty years since the seizure of the old city—was not even taken up. The site of a future

Palestinian capital would not be "in" East Jerusalem at all, as it turned out, but in Abu Dis, which was outside even the municipal boundaries of the city as they had been expanded after the 1967 war. Two months before Camp David, Barak's transfer of the town from Area B (Palestinian civic responsibility/Israeli military rule) into area A (Palestinian autonomy) had indicated what he had in mind. "In any future settlement Jerusalem will remain united as Israel's eternal capital. They [the Palestinians] will be in Abu Dis and we will be in united Jerusalem. . . . We are charged with an historic and national responsibility to effect a separation in the Land of Israel, they will be 'there' and we will be 'here.'"[18] This statement encapsulated Barak's true intentions. The "we" would include Jewish settlements he planned to annex to the city, shifting the demographic balance further against the Palestinians. The representation of a "shared" Jerusalem sidestepped the fact that Israel had already taken its "share" by seizing and then annexing the western half of the city in 1948.

In fact, Barak had "repeatedly pledged not to return to the 1967 lines and not to divide Jerusalem."[19] Shibley Telhami recalled that when he asked Arafat what he had been offered on Jerusalem, the Palestinian leader "took out a very small notebook, almost the size of a card. It was his notes from Camp David. He said here is the offer as it came to me delivered by the Americans and the Israelis. You shall be custodian of the holy places; you shall have the right to fly the Palestinian flag under Israeli sovereignty. That was all—under Israeli sovereignty. He said that was absolutely unacceptable."[20]

So Abu Dis would become an ersatz Al Quds while the real Al Quds remained under full Israeli control despite the window dressing of such terms as *autonomy* and the pretense of Palestinian sovereignty. What the Palestinians would be free to do in the name of "functional autonomy" was never spelled out, but then neither was anything else. Had Arafat accepted Barak's package, he would most likely have found himself in the same position as Brer Rabbit, stuck in a briar patch of equivocations and semantic quibbles that would be used to strip back what he thought he was going to get. That had been the fate of the Sharif Husain after 1918, and that had been the story of the "peace process" all along; why Arafat ever thought the negotiations at Camp David would end any differently is the only mystery.

A further issue was Israel's refusal to deal with the Palestinian right of return. The pro forma position of all previous governments reached its apotheosis when Barak refused point blank to give Arafat anything he could take back to his people that might induce them to exchange this right in return for something else. "We cannot even allow one refugee back on the basis of the 'right of return' . . . and we cannot accept historical respon-sibility for the creation of the problem."[21] That was it. In the final gasp of the Camp David negotiations in the Sinai resort town of Taba (January 2000), the views of the Palestinian and Israeli delegations revealed the immensity of the gap that still existed between the two sides on this ques-tion alone, in spite of the claim by Dennis Ross, the chief U.S. negotiator, that they came within an inch of a settlement. They may have moved closer, but with Ariel Sharon about to step into the prime minister's office, the movement was too little and the time too late.

ARAFAT "CORNERED"

On every other page of his memoirs, Dennis Ross demonstrates why he should never have been chosen as chief of the U.S. negotiating team at Camp David unless the purpose was to reassure Israel that the United States would not stray from the positions being set out by Barak. Director of Near Eastern and South Asian Affairs on the National Security Council during the Rea-gan administration and director of the State Department's Policy Planning Department under President George H. W. Bush, Ross had a long associa-tion with the Washington Institute for Near East policy, for which he wrote its first policy paper and to which he returned as counselor and Ziegler Dis-tinguished Fellow after he left government service.[22] He was dismissive of the most basic Palestinian claims, writing in his memoirs that Israel's expul-sion of the Palestinians from their homes in 1948 was just "part of the Pales-tinian narrative" and the right of return a "myth."[23] With such an attitude, Ross was clearly not the person to be dealing with the Palestinians if the objective of the talks really was to produce a peace settlement.

The Palestinian negotiators had already conceded the loss of 78 percent of their homeland when they went to Camp David. Arafat seemed prepared to go along with some of the demands being made of him, but when it came to Jerusalem and the right of return—an individual right that Arafat had no right to surrender anyway—the perennially compliant Palestinian leader finally dug his heels in. According to Shlomo Gazit and Edward Abington: "Essentially Clinton and Barak put Arafat in a corner. They said take it or leave it."[24] Arafat chose to leave it, and when he said "no" after listening to Barak's position paper on July 18 Clinton was enraged.[25]

The stricken "peace process" abruptly skidded to a halt. Vials of wrath were heaped on Arafat's head. The peacemaker instantly metamorphosed back into the terrorist plotting the destruction of the Jewish people. The novelist and erstwhile peace activist Amos Oz, the "desert conscience of

Israel," as he has been romanticized by distant admirers, accused him of
wanting "a full Palestinian justice that claims Palestine for the Palestinians
and claims Israel for the Palestinians, too"; indeed, he wrote, what Arafat
really wanted was the eradication of Israel through "a holy war against the
Jews."[26] Combining forces in one article, Barak and Benny Morris called
on the West's leaders to "treat Arafat and his ilk in the Palestinian camp as
the vicious, untrustworthy, unacceptable reprobates and recidivists that
they are."[27] In another article, Barak described Palestinians as the products
of a culture "in which to tell a lie . . . creates no dissonance. They don't suffer from the problem of telling lies that exists in Judeo-Christian culture.
Truth is seen as an irrelevant category. There is only that which serves
your purpose and that which doesn't. They see themselves as the emissaries of a national movement for whom everything is permissible. There
is no such thing as 'the truth.'"[28]

In fact, behind this barrage of insults and self-justification it was clear
that Arafat had conceded a lot at Camp David:

> He essentially agreed to a demilitarized state, a normalization of rela-
> tions with Israel and some Israeli settlements on the West Bank being
> incorporated into Israel in return for a land swap. He agreed to the con-
> cept of Jewish neighborhoods in East Jerusalem becoming part of Israel.
> And he agreed to the concept that a shared Jerusalem should be the
> capital of Israel and the capital of Palestine. He agreed that the Kotal
> and the Jewish quarter would be under Israeli sovereignty. Arafat
> moved a long way. And on the refugees, he agreed more to the princi-
> ple of return than to actual return. So there was definite flexibility in
> the Palestinian position at Camp David.[29]

Returning to the West Bank, Arafat was eventually trapped, besieged, and
imprisoned in the ruins of his presidential compound in Ramallah. His old
adversary in Beirut, Ariel Sharon, who regretted not having killed him during the invasion of 1982, headed the cabinet that in 2003 decided "in principle" to expel the Palestinian leader from the territories. "Israel will act to
remove this obstacle to peace in the manner, at the time and in the ways that
will be decided on separately."[30] A majority favored plain expulsion, but others (including Defense Minister Shaul Mofaz and Shin Bet head Avi Dichter)
were reported to be in favor of killing the Palestinian leader. This was indeed
the view of the right-wing *Jerusalem Post:* "We must kill Yasser Arafat
because the world leaves us no alternative. . . . When the breaking point
arrives there is no taking half measures. If we are going to be condemned in
any case we might as well do it right."[31] Ehud Olmert, then deputy prime
minister, said killing Arafat was "definitely one of the options."[32]

The threat to assassinate the Palestinian president drew no protests or warnings from the United States, only the insipid comment from Colin Powell that the United States "does not support his elimination."[33] In November 2004 Arafat died in a Paris hospital. The cause of death was not identified despite extensive tests, but the symptoms were consistent with poisoning by an unknown toxin, possibly introduced into food the Palestinian leader had eaten only a few hours before he fell ill. In a previous attempt to murder the Hamas leader Khalid Mish'al, Israel had already shown that it was capable of assassinating by such means.[34] The suspicion—a certainty among Palestinians—remains that Sharon finally ordered the death of the man he had wanted to kill in Beirut two decades earlier.[35]

SHARON'S WAR

In September 2000, even before the elections had been held that would put him in the prime minister's office, Sharon had triggered the second intifada by walking onto the Haram al Sharif compound. The four years that followed were characterized by the worst violence directed against the Palestinians of the territories since the beginning of occupation in 1967. The advent of a "peace process" had prompted Sharon to call on settlers to take over the hills of the West Bank as fast as possible. He was opposed to Oslo from the start. As prime minister he declared that it was "null and void" and that the "peace process" was frozen because Israel had no partner for peace.[36] While paying lip service to the various plans floated out of Washington, Sharon repeatedly set the army and air force loose in the name of combating terrorism. Refugee camps were pulverized in land assaults,[37] and much of the physical infrastructure of the Palestinian Authority was destroyed from the air. In Ramallah Arafat's presidential compound was bombarded and the Palestinian leader imprisoned in the ruins until helicptered out in the first stage of his journey to a Paris hospital. Hamas and Islamic Jihad leaders were obliterated in a string of state-sanctioned murders called "targeted assassinations." On March 22, 2004, the semiparalyzed spiritual leader of Hamas, Sheikh Ahmad Yassin, born as the Palestinians launched their revolt against the British in 1936, was killed by a missile in Gaza as he left a mosque in his wheelchair.

The sequential waves of violence directed against the Palestinians by Ariel Sharon included the massive assault on the Jenin refugee camp from April 3 to 18, 2002. Showing signs of having learned from the public relations disaster of Sabra and Shatila in 1982, the Sharon government sealed the camp off and blocked attempts by international organizations to investigate the extent of human rights violations and war crimes that had been committed. The remains of bodies were still being retrieved from the camp months later; the number of dead remains unknown, but they included women, children, and the mentally and physically disabled, killed by missile strikes, tank fire, and ground troops or crushed when their homes were bulldozed. Many bodies were ground to pieces under tanks and bulldozers, grossly and gruesomely complicating the task of estimating how many people were killed.

According to the Jenin Inquiry, "Homes were not only bombed from [the] air by Apache and Cobra helicopters but were shelled and fired upon by tanks and ground troops. Military bulldozers made by the US company Caterpillar and employed as a weapon of 'urban war' also bulldozed them."[38] Eyewitness accounts that many of the dead were removed from the camp in refrigerated trucks or by tanks and bulldozer were never investigated. Evidence gathered by the inquiry indicated that the Israelis methodically "cleaned" the camp of bodies and kept witnesses out of sections that had yet to be "cleaned." The center of the camp, a densely populated area of about seventeen acres, was bulldozed. Hundreds of buildings were completely destroyed, and hundreds of others needed significant repairs short of demolition. An estimated four thousand people (30 percent of the camp's population) were left homeless. Damage to buildings and infrastructure (roads, communications, water, electricity, and sewage) was put at $43.7 million by UNRWA and $27 million in the UN report.[39] A number of Palestinians were used as human shields as the Israelis broke into buildings. In buildings that were not destroyed homes were vandalized and looted:

> Of the homes we entered those that had not suffered significant damage were the exception. Backs of overstuffed chairs and couches were cut open, pictures were slashed with knives, food, dishes, glasses and all kitchen items were thrown on to the floor, smashing everything into small pieces and wasting the little food the people had. It was common for members of the Jenin Inquiry to walk into a kitchen and never touch the floor but to walk on piles of rice and sugar and broken glass. Dressers of clothing and other household items were broken into and tipped over, often breaking the doors and handles or completely ruining the dresser. Books were thrown around and in at least one case an entire family library was tipped over and left in a huge pile on the floor.[40]

Property reported looted included money, jewelry, televisions, computers, sound systems, and mobile phones. In homes that were taken over for the duration of the invasion, soldiers "urinated or defecated on furniture, in kitchen pots and pans and on tile or carpeted floors." (In Gaza and the West Bank this was a common calling card left by Israeli soldiers when leaving homes they had occupied or offices they had vandalized.) A camp mosque was vandalized, with copies of the Qu'ran thrown to the floor after being torn apart or pierced by bullets. The walls and even the interior of houses were spray-painted with the Star of David and anti-Arab graffiti. Thousands of young men were taken away from the camp, "blindfolded, hands tied behind their back and stripped to their underwear," for interrogation before being released or transferred to other prisons. Reports of mistreatment (of being beaten with rifle butts, kicked, denied food and water and access to lavatories, and forced to remain in a kneeling position for days at a time) were common.[41] The violence and brutality had a clear strategic aim, to inflict such overwhelming punishment on the Palestinians that they would return to negotiations with their heads bowed, in a suitable frame of mind to accept what Israel was prepared to offer them.[42] Allegations that the Israelis had used human shields, had demolished homes over the heads of their owners, had carried out summary executions, and had even subjected disabled Palestinians, including three blind youths left handcuffed in the street for two and a half days, to "various acts of aggression" were recorded by a UN special committee.[43]

Between September 29, 2000, and July 31, 2006, 4,142 Palestinians were killed by the Israeli military in the West Bank and the Gaza Strip. Of this number 845 were minors (under the age of eighteen). Another 41 were killed by Israeli civilians.[44] To this number must be added the 1,378 Palestinians killed by the Israeli military (with an additional 113 being killed by Israeli civilians) during the first intifada (December 1987–September 2000).[45] Many thousands of Palestinians have been permanently disabled as the result of actions taken by the Israeli military or settlers in the occupied territories, about 15,000 in the first intifada (1987–94) and about 5,300 in the first two years of the Sharon government (2000–2002).[46] Palestinian suicide bombers, unable to damage planes, helicopters, and tanks or get near heavily armed Israeli troops or long-distance snipers, struck back at "soft targets" in Israeli towns and cities, blowing themselves up with as many Israelis as they could kill in cafes, in hotels, in a billiards club, in the Dolphinarium discotheque, on buses, in marketplaces, and outside government offices. According to the Israeli Center for Special Studies, 527 people were killed by suicide bombings in 147 such attacks between September 2000 and December 2005, 28 percent of them children under thirteen (including a number under three), teenagers, and men or women over the age of sixty-six.[47]

Nowhere on the West Bank have Israeli policies had more devastating consequences than the city of Hebron, where by September 2005 only ten thousand of the thirty-five thousand Palestinians who had been living within the area designated as H2 when it was placed under Israeli control in 1997 were still there. The rest had been harassed and humiliated into leaving by fanatical settlers fully protected by the Israeli military. The results of a regime "intentionally and openly based on the 'separation' principle" have been summed up by the Israeli human rights organization B'Tselem. By December 2006, 1,829 Palestinian businesses in the enclave (76.6 percent of the total) were no longer open, at least 440 of them having been closed by military orders and others closing because of prohibitions on the movement of traffic and pedestrians. Nearly 42 percent of houses or apartments around the shops had been emptied. In the first three years of the intifada the Israeli army had imposed a twenty-four-hour curfew on Palestinians living in the city center for more than 377 days, including one consecutive period of 182 days "with short breaks to obtain provisions." The assaults on Palestinians by Jewish settlers during the second intifada have included "beatings, at times with clubs, stone-throwing and hurling of refuse, sand, water, chlorine and empty bottles." The settlers have "destroyed shops and doors, committed thefts and chopped down fruit trees. Settlers have also been in involved in gunfire, attempts to run people over, poisoning of a water well, breaking into homes, spilling of hot liquid on the face of a Palestinian and the killing of a young Palestinian girl."[48] According to the Israeli journalist Gideon Levy,

> those who have not visited the city in recent years would not believe their eyes. In the territory under Israeli control—H2 or Israeli territory according to the Hebron accord—they will discover a ghost town. Hundreds of abandoned homes, like after a war, dozens of destroyed stores, burned or shuttered, their gates welded closed by the settlers and all-pervasive deadly silence. According to unofficial estimates no more than 10,000 residents remain in this place. . . . Every day the settlers torment their neighbors here. Every walk to school for a Palestinian child has become a journey of harassment and fear. Every shopping outing by a housewife is a journey of humiliation. Settler children kicking old women carrying baskets, settlers siccing their dogs on the elderly, garbage and feces thrown from the settlers' balconies into the courtyards of Palestinian homes, junk metal blocking the entrances of their houses, rocks thrown at any Palestinian passerby—this is the routine of life in the city. Hundreds of soldiers, riot policemen and cops witness these actions and stand by idly. They occasionally exchange jokes with the rioters and almost never stand in their way.[49]

In the Tell Rumeida district, "the residents walk hunched over in their back yards, keeping close to the walls, whispering for fear of being heard. Children sprint home in a mad dash and neighbors move from house to house on rickety ladders." Along with the stones, the broken windows, the rotting food thrown at Palestinian homes, and the abuse of children comes the call of "Death to the Arabs" and a sign hung up near the Qurtuba school: "Gas the Arabs." The last Palestinian family living in one street in Tal Rumeida had been forced to protect the front of the house with steel mesh and could not leave the building uninhabited for fear that the settlers would take it over.[50] The word used by Levy to describe this situation is *pogrom*.[51] On the road to the fulfillment of *eretz Israel*, a more grotesque inversion of history could scarcely be imagined. In Hebron and elsewhere, in the shattered towns of the Gaza Strip and the refugee camps of Lebanon, Syria, and Jordan, the Star of David has been turned into a symbol of oppression.

AID AND THE ISRAEL LOBBY

The central role of the United States in maintaining this matrix of misery cannot be overstated. The United States arms Israel, gives it tax breaks, protects it from even more censure at the UN, and provides it with the massive amounts of money needed to maintain its grip on occupied territory. From 1949 to 2005 Israel received nearly $105 billion in direct aid (mostly military and economic grants) from successive U.S. administrations.[52] Other estimates are higher,[53] but even they fall well short of what is likely to be the true figure because of the payment of additional amounts for special purposes (i.e., $3 billion for the development of weapons such as the Lavi fighter aircraft) and extra costs incurred as the result of the conflict between Israel and the Arabs. One-third of all U.S. foreign aid goes to Israel, and on preferred-client conditions. Unlike other countries, which receive aid in quarterly installments, economic aid for Israel is paid in a lump sum at the start of the fiscal year so that it can benefit from the accruing interest. Neither is the Israeli government required to account for how it spends its aid: the money goes into general revenue and therefore is part of the funding for military operations and the settlement of occupied territories. Settlement is also funded by the large amounts of money paid to Israel every year in the form of tax-free private philanthropic donations.

Without U.S. financial support Israel could not have overcome the near-collapse of its economy in the 1980s, could not have invaded and occupied, and could not have continued to settle occupied lands but would have been forced to make a real peace with the Palestinians and (through them) with all Arab states long ago. The need for the United States to reassess its national interests and develop policies that will serve these interests more effectively was brought out in the working paper "The Israel Lobby," written by two distinguished academics with impeccably conservative credentials, Stephen Walt and John Mearsheimer, and emphasized by former president Jimmy Carter's comparison made between Israeli state policies and apartheid.[54] The vituperative abuse of Walt and Mearsheimer that followed the publication of their paper underlined the difficulty of speaking openly and freely on the Middle East in the United States. Similarly vilified after publication of his book, Carter remarked that it was "almost politically suicidal" for a member of Congress seeking reelection to take a position that might be interpreted as critical of the policies of the government of Israel, "which is equated as I've seen it myself with anti-Semitism."[55]

An adjustment of U.S. policies that would compel Israel to withdraw from the territories it is now settling would be welcomed by many Jewish Israelis who are standing alongside the Palestinians in a variety of ways and who believe their state has been put on a permanent collision course with the people in whose midst and at whose expense it was established. Palestinian Israelis have made their own position clear. They are naturally sympathetic to the struggle of West Bank and Gaza Palestinians and to the plight of the refugees scattered across the Middle East, yet somehow they have to make their own way in a state where they have the status of second-class citizens. In January 2007 the National Committee of the Heads of the Arab Local Authorities in Israel issued a statement, "The Future Vision of the Arabs in Israel," calling for a "consensual democratic system that enables us to be fully active in the decision-making process and guarantees our individual and collective civil, historic and national rights." The document calls for full citizenship and "institutional self-rule in the fields of education, culture and religion that is in fact part of fulfilling their rights as citizens and as part of the Israeli state." The document says that the definition of Israel as a Jewish state "excludes us" and asks for the recognition of the "historic oppression" in a homeland that is "the unifying element between all even though this homeland is occupied." Publication of the document triggered off a wave of condemnation on the Israeli right wing of "the enemy within." Even within the center-left it was regarded as an attempt to delegitimize the state; challenging the contradictions inherent in the notion of a democratic Jewish state that has a substantial non-Jewish minority, the document also tested alliances with the Palestinians on the Israeli left.[56]

Whether internally or in the occupied territories or across the region, Israel is confronted with problems that it is clearly unable or unwilling as a state to address. In the past decades the Arab states have repeatedly offered full recognition and incorporation into the Middle East state system if Israel withdraws from the territories seized in 1967 and takes the Palestinian right of return seriously. Yet Israel has failed to respond constructively to all of these offers, putting itself in three equally contradictory and untenable positions: first, it holds and settles occupied land but claims that it is committed to peace; second, it occupies and settles the land of other people but claims that it is a democracy; and third, it stresses the Jewish and democratic nature of the state but withholds full and equal rights from the large number of citizens who are not Jewish. Yet neither is Israel willing to consider the radical older alternative to this tangle—one state with equal rights for all between the Mediterranean and the Jordan River—because that would mean the end of what is usually called "the Zionist dream." Unable to deal with the existential problems that are the inevitable product of trying to live this dream, defending what most of the world regards as indefensible, Israel is left only with its power to destroy those who dare to rise up against it.

The failure of a "peace process" that was structurally doomed from the start has led not to a "peace of the brave" (as it was packaged in 1993) but toward an Israeli-dug "peace of the grave" in which Palestinian historical rights are destined to be interred if the Sharon-Olmert tendency has its way. In 2000 Edward Said wrote that the function of the Oslo process was "to cage Palestinians in a remnant of their own lands like inmates in an asylum or a prison."[57] The incremental creep of settlements in the territories seized in 1967, the separation from Jerusalem, the closure of the Jordan River Valley, the wall, the checkpoints, the closure of roads, the curfews, and the operations of the military and death squads in West Bank towns all point to a future in which Palestinian "independence" will be so bleak that it will amount to no future at all. For Olmert and the outright racists he had to bring into his cabinet to keep his government afloat, that seemed to be the whole point.[58] Yet U.S., British, and other "world leaders" continued to talk of their commitment to a "viable peace." Their pledges and their commitments are part of a long history of Western rhetoric, of promise but no fulfillment, to paraphrase Arthur Koestler.

NEED AND GREED

In the neoconservative triad of Middle Eastern rogue states—Iraq, Iran, and Syria, the quartet having been reduced by the defection of a contrite Libya—Iran was slotted to follow Iraq for regime change. The issue developed to justify sanctions or military attack was Iran's development of nuclear energy. Senior Israeli government ministers and intelligence officials declared repeatedly that Israel could not live alongside a nuclear Iran. Threats from Washington and Jerusalem that all options were on the table were met by "defiance" in Tehran: if Israel dares to fire one missile against Iran's Natanz reactor, a revolutionary guards commander warned in August 2004, "then it has to forget forever" the Dimona reactor.[59] As Israel had done nearly half a century earlier, Iran declared that it had no intention of developing nuclear weapons; indeed, the supreme religious leader, Ayatullah Khamenei, even issued a *fatwa* against the production, stockpiling, and use of nuclear weapons.[60] This would seem to be worth an army of IAEA inspectors, but for Israeli officials Iran represented the greatest threat to Israel since 1948.[61] Evidence of its intentions seem to be confirmed in President Ahmedinajad's reported remark that Israel should be "wiped off the map." (This was not what he actually said. After referring to other regimes that had collapsed recently—in Iran, the Soviet Union, and Iraq—Ahmedinajad referred to a statement by Ayatullah Khumayni that "the regime occupying Jerusalem should vanish from the page of time.")[62]

In February 2005 President Bush indicated that the United States would stand by Israel if it attempted to destroy Iran's nuclear capacity. "Clearly, if I was the leader of Israel and I'd heard some of the statements by the Iranian ayatollahs that regarded the security of my country I'd be concerned about Iran having a nuclear weapon as well. And in that Israel is our ally and in that we've made a very strong commitment to support Israel we will support Israel if there's a—if their security is threatened."[63] Despite the threat of sanctions and warnings of military attack, Iran refused to back down. For many Iranians the nuclear question symbolizes national independence, just as oil symbolized it more than a half a century earlier. Iran regards itself as having the same right as all other countries to develop nuclear energy (including the enrichment of uranium) within the safeguards of the IAEA; unlike Israel, it has signed the NPT and allowed inspections of all its plants. In 2006 and 2007 the government declared that it would not retreat before neoimperialist threats and intimidation and warned that the United States was just as susceptible to pain and damage if it dared to take military action. A new cycle of violence seemed about to begin in the Middle East even before the old one had played itself out.

Born of strategic need and commercial greed, the impact of the West has been felt across the Middle East and North Africa in invasion, occupation, collective punishment, incursions, subversion, overthrow, bullying and intimidation, economic exploitation, the support of tyrants, and the manipulation of bribed and suborned kings and prime ministers. What the West has made it has frequently unmade. Over the past two centuries, on occasions and in places too numerous to count, civilization, Western values, and democracy have been the mask and brute force the true face. Not once in these last two centuries of "Islam's bloody borders" have any of the cities, towns, and villages of the West come under attack by Arab or Muslim armies. No Arab or Muslim state was involved in Usama bin Laden's great act of terrorism. The aggression has been entirely one-way, notwithstanding Samuel Huntington's claim that it is the Muslims who have a propensity for violence and that the "bloody borders" belong to Islam. Inevitably, because there has been no period of Islamic history when invasion has not been resisted in the name of Islam, an Arab Muslim nemesis had to arise in the twentieth century. If the aerial attacks of 9/11 caused such shock, it was surely partly because they were such an inversion of a natural order, built on a series of racist assumptions arising out of imperial history: we attack and you are attacked, we invade and you are invaded, we occupy and you are occupied, we threaten and you are intimidated, we lecture and you listen, we kill and you are killed, we are wise and you are defiant. With the exception of the first attack on the World Trade Center (the attempt to bring down the north tower in 1993 by exploding a massive bomb in the underground car park), September 11, 2001, fell outside the whole Western experience of the Middle East. That is surely part of its meaning as a turning point in history. All of a sudden the impact of the West was being felt on the wrong side: in one horrifying instant it had ricocheted and the innocent civilians were not Beirut or Baghdad residents, not worthy of being counted, but Americans killed on their own soil and counted down to the last man, woman, and child. The parallel does not diminish the tragedy but underscores the need to understand why these things are happening and to prevent the causes of violence from being smothered in alarmist rhetoric about "them" and "us."[64] The "clash of civilizations" is a convenient distraction that enables specific governments to avoid dealing with the consequences of their policies and their actions. It is those governments, and not "the West," that must be held responsible for the damage done and justified in the name of civilization, liberation, freedom, and (most recently) democracy.

The failure of Arab governments to define common principles and stand up for them allowed Usama bin Laden to claim—not without many precedents in Muslim history—the responsibility of defending the faith in the name of a harsh and punitive Islam. The world has a Muslim population of about 1.3 billion. In this vast sea the number of Muslims—mostly young—who are prepared to go the whole distance with Usama bin Laden is infinitesimal, but Muslims everywhere can identify with the truth of what he or Ayman al Zawahiri are saying when they talk of Western aggression and Western double standards. In the speech he made on October 29, 2004, Bin Laden said it was Palestine and the Israeli invasion of Lebanon in 1982 that put him on the road to September 11, 2001. "I couldn't forget those moving scenes, blood and severed limbs, women and children sprawled everywhere. Houses destroyed along with their occupants, high rises demolished over their residents, rockets raiding down on our home without mercy."[65] His message was that if you leave us alone we will leave you alone.

The United States does not have to slacken in its pursuit of Usama bin Laden to quietly acknowledge that he has a point and begin reassessing policies that have blackened its name across the Middle East and caused harm to millions of people. The administration of George W. Bush, however, the incarnation of Western power in the present age, has shown no more signs of really listening to Arab world grievances and then acting on them than the West did half a century ago. "This country must go on the offense and stay on the offense," the president told a press conference in April 2004.[66] The strategies formulated by the U.S. government in the 1990s were directed toward maintaining U.S. global domination into the twenty-first century. By the beginning of 2007, however, in Iraq and Afghanistan and even Lebanon, where the United States held the door open in 2006 for an Israeli onslaught that ended inconclusively, the doctrine was already collapsing, raising four final questions at the end of a narrative that began with questions. Will the events of 9/11 be seen one day as the tocsin that sounded the end of the new American century almost before it began? In fact, are we nearing the end of an epoch? Is more than half a millennium of Western domination of the rest of the world finally coming to an end? Would this be bad for the West or good for the rest—or good for all of us?

NOTES

The following abbreviations are used throughout the Notes:

AB   *The Arab Bulletin: Bulletin of the Arab Bureau in Cairo,*
        1916–1919. Including Indexes for 1916, 1917, and 1918 and the
        Supplementary Notes on the Middle East. 4 vols. Oxford:
        Archive Editions, 1986.

ADM   *Arab Dissident Movements, 1905–1955.* 4 vols. Edited by
        A. L. P. Burdett. Slough, UK: Archive Editions, 1996.

FRUS   U.S. Department of State, Foreign Relations of the United
        States (series).

IAR   *Iraq Administration Reports, 1914–1932.* 10 vols. Edited by
        Robert L. Jarman. Slough, UK: Archive Editions, 1992.

PB   *Palestine Boundaries, 1833–1947.* Edited by Patricia Toye.
        Durham, UK: Archive Editions, 1989.

RHD   *Records of the Hashimite Dynasties.* 15 vols. Edited by Alan
        Rush. London: Archive Editions, 1995.

RI   *Records of Iraq, 1914–1966.* 15 vols. Edited by Alan Rush. Lon-
        don: Archive Editions, 2001.

INTRODUCTION

1. Samuel P. Huntington, *The Clash of Civilizations and the Remaking of
World Order* (New York: Simon and Schuster, 1996).

2. Justin McCarthy, *The Ottoman Peoples and the End of Empire* (London:
Arnold, 2001), 91–92.

3. Jimmy Carter, *Palestine: Peace Not Apartheid* (New York: Simon and
Schuster, 2006).

1. CIVILIZATION AND ITS CONTRADICTIONS

1. Bernard Lewis, "What Went Wrong?" *Atlantic Monthly*, January 2002, 43–45, and *The Crisis of Islam: Holy War and Unholy Terror* (London: Phoenix, 2004), 23; Fareed Zakaria, "The Politics of Rage: Why Do They Hate Us?" *Newsweek*, October 15, 2001; Daniel Pipes, "Who Is the Enemy?" *Commentary*, January 2002, www.danielpipes.org/article/103; Francis Fukuyama and Nadav Samin, "Can Any Good Come of Radical Islam? A Modernizing Force? Maybe," *Opinion Journal*, reprinted from the *Wall Street Journal*, September 12, 2002, www.opinionjournal.com/extra/?id=110002251; Samuel P. Huntington, "The Clash of Civilizations?" *Foreign Affairs* 72 (Summer 1993): 22–49.

2. Loren Baritz, "The Idea of the West," *American Historical Review* 66 (April 1961): 635. Many thanks to Töre Fougner for providing this and other references dealing with the origins of "the West."

3. A point amplified by the geographer H. J. Mackinder in "The Geographical Pivot of History," *Geographical Journal* 23 (1904): 421–44.

4. Arnold Toynbee, *The Western Question in Greece and Turkey: A Study in the Contact of Civilisations* (London: Constable, 1922), 332–33.

5. First usage is uncertain but is attributed by some to Mirabeau. Lucien Febvre dates its first use in French to 1766. See Peter Burke, ed., *A New Kind of History: From the Writings of Febvre* (London: Routledge and Kegan Paul, 1973), 221.

6. Quoted in Raymond Williams, *Keywords: A Vocabulary of Culture and Society* (London: Fontana Press, 1988), 57.

7. Burke, *New Kind of History*, 241.

8. See Szymon Chodak, "The Rise of the Global Civilization," *Dialogue and Humanism* 1, no. 1 (1991): 17–36.

9. Huntington, "Clash of Civilizations?"

10. See David Lloyd George's speech "The Great Pinnacle of Sacrifice," September 21, 1914, reprinted in *The Penguin Book of Twentieth-Century Speeches*, ed. Brian MacArthur (London: Penguin, 1993), 31–36.

11. Modris Eksteins, *Rites of Spring: The Great War and the Birth of the Modern Age* (London: Black Swan, 1989), 261. To the Germans *kultur* was of prime importance and *zivilisation* useful "but nevertheless a value only of the second rank." See Norbert Elias, *The Civilizing Process*, 2 vols., trans. Edmund Jephcott (London: Blackwell, 1982), 1:4.

12. Richard L. Rubinstein, *The Cunning of History* (New York: Harper and Row, 1978), 91–95.

13. Ian Buruma, "The Origins of Occidentalism," *Chronicle of Higher Education* 50 (February 6, 2004): B10, http://chronicle.com/weekly/v50/i22/22b01001.htm.

14. Sir William Muir, *The Life of Mahomet: From Original Sources* (London: Smith, Elder, 1878), 535.

15. Sir William Muir, *Annals of the Early Caliphate: From Original Sources* (London: Smith, Elder, 1883), 459. In his later abridgement of the

Annals, Muir uses the same phrase but inserts "Christian" before "nations" and adds "freedom" to "civilization and morality," and this time the book was published by Christian tractarians. See Sir William Muir, *The Caliphate: Its Rise, Decline and Fall* (London: Religious Tract Society, 1891).

16. Bernard Lewis, *The Arabs in History* (London: Hutchinson's University Library, 1950), 178.

17. Bernard Lewis, *The Middle East and the West* (London: Weidenfeld and Nicolson, 1964), 43.

18. Ibid., 46 and 137.

19. Bernard Lewis, "The Roots of Muslim Rage," *Atlantic Monthly,* September 1990, 47–60.

20. Bernard Lewis, *Islam in History: Ideas, People and Events in the Middle East* (Chicago: Open Court Press, 1993), 410.

21. Ibid.

22. Quoted by Ian Buruma in his review essay of Lewis's book *From Babel to Dragomans,* "Lost in Translation: The Two Minds of Bernard Lewis," *New Yorker,* June 14–21, 2004, www.newyorker.com.

23. Lewis, *Crisis of Islam,* 24.

24. Huntington, "Clash of Civilizations?" 25.

25. Ibid., 30. Here he adopts William Lind's phrase.

26. Huntington, *Clash of Civilizations,* 255.

27. Ibid., 256–57.

28. Samuel P. Huntington, "The Age of Muslim Wars," *Newsweek,* December 17, 2001.

29. Lewis, *Middle East,* 59.

30. Ibid., 45.

31. Bernard Lewis, "Islam's Interpreter," interview by Elizabeth Wasserman, *Atlantic,* April 29, 2004, www.theatlantic.com./doc/prem/200404u/int2004-04-29. Lewis used the same phrase in discussion with CBC *Newsworld* interviewer Brian Stewart. See "The Crisis in Islam and the End of Saddam Hussein's Iraq," August 30, 2003, www.cbc.ca/worldview/wvarchives/20030830.html.

32. Francis Fukuyama, "The West Has Won," *Guardian,* October 11, 2001.

33. Francis Fukuyama, "Has History Started Again?" *Policy* 18 (Winter 2002): 3–7. See also Fukuyama and Samin, "Can Any Good Come of Radical Islam?"

34. Fouad Ajami, "America and the Arabs," *Foreign Affairs* 80, no. 6 (2001): 9.

35. Ibid., 16.

36. Fouad Ajami, "Best Intentions: Why We Went, What We've Found," *New Republic,* June 28, 2004, www.tnr.com/doc.mhtml?i=20040628&s=ajami062804.

37. European Monitoring Centre on Racism and Xenophobia, *Muslims in the European Union: Discrimination and Islamophobia* (Vienna: Manz Crossmedia, 2006), 78. In March 2007 the center, an EU body, became the European Agency for Fundamental Rights.

38. For references to van Gogh's writings, see Ronald Rovers, "The Silencing of Theo van Gogh," *Salon*, November 24, 2004, http://dir.salon.com/story/news/feature/2004/11/24/vangogh/index.html.

39. Halleh Ghorashi, "Why Ayaan Hirsi Ali Is Wrong," *Signand sight.com*, March 14, 2007, www.signandsight.com/features/1250.html. This site is an excellent reference point for the fierce debate on Islam, migration, and multiculturalism taking place across Europe.

40. Flemming Rose, "Why I Published Those Cartoons," *Washington Post*, February 19, 2006.

41. In the 1990s *Piss Christ*, a photograph of a crucifix sunk in a bottle of urine, outraged Catholics everywhere, to whom it was not art but abuse. More recently (in March 2007), a statue of Christ carved out of milk chocolate and entitled *My Sweet Lord* infuriated Catholics when it was unveiled in a Manhattan art gallery. The protests forced the exhibition's closure.

42. Flemming Rose, "Europe's Politics of Victimology," *Blueprint*, May 17, 2006, www.dlc.org/ndol_ci.cfm?contentid=253879&kaid=127&subid=177.

43. See, for example, Michael Ledeen, "The Killers: The Dutch Hit Crisis Point," *National Review Online*, November 10, 2004, and the references in the article to political correctness, moral relativism, the Muslim birth rate, the "nanny" state, and the multicultural utopian dream.

44. Daniel Pipes, "The Threat of Islamism," interview by Flemming Rose, anonymously translated from the Danish and originally published in *Jyllands-Posten* on October 29, 2004, as "Truslen fra islamismen," www.danielpipes.org/article/3362.

45. Rose, "Europe's Politics of Victimology."

46. Gary Younge, "On the Offensive," *Guardian*, April 10, 2007.

47. On dhimmitude, see Bat Ye'or, "Eurabia: The Road to Munich," *National Review*, October 9, 2002, www.nationalreview.com/comment/comment-yeor100902.asp. In Islam, the "People of the Book" (Jews and Christians) are known as the *dhimma* (Arabic root meaning protection or care).

48. See Christopher Hitchens, "Oriana Fallaci and the Art of the Interview," *Vanity Fair*, December 2006, http://vanityfair.com/politics/features/2006/12/hitchens200612.htm.

49. See Margaret Talbot, "The Agitator: Oriana Fallaci Directs Her Fury towards Islam," *New Yorker*, June 5, 2006.

50. Ibid.

51. Ian Fisher, "Oriana Fallaci, Incisive Italian Journalist, Is Dead at 77," *New York Times*, September 16, 2006.

52. Bernard Lewis, "Muslims 'About to Take Over Europe,'" interview by David Machlis and Tovah Lazaroff, *Jerusalem Post*, January 29, 2007.

53. Bernard Lewis, "The 2007 Irving Kristol Lecture," American Enterprise Institute, Washington, DC, March 20, 2007, http://aei.org/publications/filter.all,pubID.25815/pub_detail.asp.

54. See Eurostat, "Population and Social Conditions," http://epp.eurostat.ec.europa.eu (accessed July 9, 2007).

55. The collation of precise figures is complicated by the reluctance of some governments (e.g., France) to base statistics on ethnicity or religion. In official EU statistics, religion is not included as a component in the breakdown of population figures. See Statistical Office of the European Communities, *Population Statistics* (Luxembourg: Office for Official Publications of the European Communities, 2006).

56. These figures are taken from "Muslims in Europe: Country Guide," BBC News, December 23, 2005, http://news.bbc.co.uk/2/hi/europe/4385768.stm.

57. European Monitoring Centre, *Muslims in the European Union*, 13.

58. See Henri Astier, "Ghettos Shackle French Muslims," BBC News, October 31, 2005, http://news.bbc.co.uk/2/hi/europe/4375910.stm.

59. Daniel Masci, "An Uncertain Road: Muslims and the Future of Europe," October 2005, Pew Forum on Religion and Public Life, www.pewforum.org/docs/index.php?DocID=60.

60. Ibid.

61. See Pew Global Attitudes Project, "The Great Divide: How Westerners and Muslims View Each Other," June 22, 2006, http://pewglobal.org/reports/display.php?ReportID=253, a thirteen-country survey. The title of the paper underlines the ambiguous status of Muslims who are the citizens of European countries and therefore Westerners—or are they not?

62. Astier, "Ghettos Shackle French Muslims."

63. Ibid.

64. See John M. Hobson, *The Eastern Origins of Western Civilization* (Cambridge: Cambridge University Press, 2004), 121–26.

65. Martin Bernal, *Black Athena: The Afroasiatic Roots of Classical Civilization*, vol. 1, *The Fabrication of Ancient Greece, 1785–1985* (New Brunswick: Rutgers University Press, 1987), and vol. 2, *The Archeological and Documentary Evidence* (New Brunswick: Rutgers University Press, 1991).

66. Molly Myerowitz Levine, "The Marginalization of Martin Bernal," review of *Black Athena Revisited*, ed. Mary R. Lefkowitz and Guy MacLean Rogers, *Classical Philology* 93 (October 1998): 345–63.

67. Ibid.

68. Mary R. Lefkowitz and Guy MacLean Rogers, eds., *Black Athena Revisited* (Chapel Hill: University of North Carolina Press, 1996)

69. Levine, "Marginalization of Martin Bernal," 354.

70. See Martin Bernal, review of *Not Out of Africa: How Afrocentrism Became an Excuse to Teach Myth as History*, by Mary Lefkowitz, *Bryn Mawr Classical Review* 7 (April 5, 1996), http://ccat.sas.upenn.edu/bmcr/1996/96.04.05.html.

71. H. A. R. Gibb, *Studies on the Civilisation of Islam*, ed. Stanford J. Shaw and William R. Polk (London: Routledge and Kegan Paul, 1962), 324.

72. Ibid.

73. Ibid., 328.

74. Ibid.

75. See Philip K. Hitti, *A History of the Arabs,* 10th ed. (London: Palgrave Macmillan, 2005 [first ed. published 1937]), 441, for his remarks on the government of the seventh-century caliph Al Muʿawiya.

76. W. E. Gladstone, *Bulgarian Horrors and the Question of the East* (London: John Murray, 1876), 9.

77. McCarthy, *Ottoman Peoples,* 46.

78. Ibid., 48. See also Justin McCarthy, *Death and Exile: The Ethnic Cleansing of Ottoman Muslims, 1821–1922* (Princeton, NJ: Darwin Press, 1995), 91.

2. SCIENCE AND BARBARISM

1. A dynasty of former slaves, nominally loyal to the Ottoman sultan, who distinguished themselves in the thirteenth century by defeating the Mongols.

2. In 1839 the problems the sultan and the British were both having with the pasha came to a head when an Egyptian army defeated an Ottoman army in northern Syria. The ensuing crisis, at once Ottoman and European, was resolved when Mehmet Ali agreed to surrender Syria in return for being invested as the hereditary ruler of Egypt with the title of khedive.

3. J. E. Swain, "The Occupation of Algiers in 1830: A Study in Anglo-French Diplomacy," *Political Science Quarterly* 48 (1933): 359–66.

4. John Ruedy, *Modern Algeria: The Origins and Development of a Nation* (Bloomington: Indiana University Press, 1992), 69.

5. Jamil M. Abun-Nasr, *A History of the Maghrib* (Cambridge: Cambridge University Press, 1971), 247; Ruedy, *Modern Algeria,* 119.

6. Abun-Nasr, *History of the Maghrib,* 246.

7. B. G. Martin, *Muslim Brotherhoods in Nineteenth-Century Africa* (Cambridge: Cambridge University Press, 1976), 50.

8. Julia A. Clancy-Smith, *Rebel and Saint: Muslim Notables, Populist Protest, Colonial Encounters (Algeria and Tunisia, 1800–1904)* (Berkeley: University of California Press, 1994), 108.

9. Ibid., 92.

10. David Levering Lewis, *The Race to Fashoda: Colonialism and African Resistance* (New York: Henry Holt, 1987), xi.

11. Edward Dicey, *The Story of the Khedivate* (London: Rivington's, 1902), 271.

12. Robert T. Harrison, *Gladstone's Imperialism in Egypt: Techniques of Domination* (Westport, CT: Greenwood Press, 1995), 91.

13. Dicey, *Story of the Khedivate,* 3.

14. Harrison, *Gladstone's Imperialism,* 93.

15. Sir Edward Malet, *Egypt, 1879–1883* (London: John Murray, 1909), 418–22.

16. James Grant, *Cassell's History of the War in the Soudan,* 6 vols. (London: Cassells, [1885–86?]), 1:42.

17. Ibid., 1:38.

18. For details of the firepower, see "The Naval Operation before Alexandria," *Times*, July 13, 1882, 6.

19. Grant, *Cassell's History*, 34.

20. Ibid., 35.

21. "The Crisis in Egypt: Bombardment of the Forts at Alexandria," *Times*, July 21, 1882, 5.

22. Lieut. Col. Herrman Vogt, *The Egyptian War of 1882* (1883; repr., Nashville, TN: Battery Press, 1992), 281.

23. Timothy Mitchell, *Colonising Egypt* (Cambridge: Cambridge University Press, 1988), 128.

24. Grant, *Cassell's History*, 46.

25. Harrison, *Gladstone's Imperialism*, 19.

26. Designed by John Fisher, commander of the *Inflexible* and later First Sea Lord.

27. Grant, *Cassell's History*, 67, taking his description from Vogt, *Egyptian War*.

28. Vogt, *Egyptian War*, 188.

29. Grant, *Cassell's History*, 171.

30. Dicey, *Story of the Khedivate*, 293.

31. A. B. Theobald, *The Mahdiya: A History of the Anglo-Egyptian Sudan, 1881–1899* (New York: Longmans, Green, 1951), 54.

32. Ibid., 51.

33. Ibid., 55.

34. Robin Neillands, *The Dervish Wars: Gordon and Kitchener in the Sudan, 1880–1898* (London: John Murray, 1996), 72.

35. A "handful of camel riders" are said to have got away. Ibid., 72.

36. Ibid., 73.

37. Dicey, *Story of the Khedivate*, 348.

38. Neillands, *Dervish Wars*, 152.

39. Doug Johnson, "The Egyptian Army, 1880–1900," *Savage and Soldier* 8, no. 1 (1976), www.savageandsoldier.com/sudan/Egyptian_Army.html.

40. G. W. Steevens, *With Kitchener to Khartum* (London: Thomas Nelson and Sons, n.d.), 195.

41. Ibid., 315.

42. As described in Steevens, *With Kitchener to Khartum*, quoted in Earl of Cromer [Evelyn Baring], *Modern Egypt*, vol. 2 (London: Macmillan, 1908), 104.

43. Steevens, *With Kitchener to Khartum*, 317.

44. Ibid., 338. The figures given here are taken from Winston S. Churchill, *The River War: An Account of the Reconquest of the Sudan* (1899; repr., London: Eyre and Spottiswood, 1949), 310–11.

45. Winston S. Churchill, *My Early Life: A Roving Commission* (1930; repr., London: Odhams Press, 1947), 182.

46. Churchill, *River War*, 300.

47. "The Battle of Omdurman," *Times*, September 5, 1898, 5.

48. Mohamed Omer Beshir, *Revolution and Nationalism in the Sudan* (London: Rex Collings, 1974), 18.

49. Churchill, *My Early Life*, 225.

50. Churchill, *River War*, 305.

51. Steevens, *With Kitchener to Khartum*, 207.

52. Martin, *Muslim Brotherhoods*, 179.

53. Ibid., 193.

3. OTTOMAN BREAKDOWN

1. As related to Arminius Vambery. Quoted in Jeremy Salt, *Imperialism, Evangelism and the Ottoman Armenians, 1878–1896* (London: Frank Cass, 1993), 147.

2. Ibid., 77.

3. McCarthy, *Death and Exile,* 120.

4. For a detailed account, see Bernadotte Schmitt, *The Annexation of Bosnia, 1908–1909* (New York: Howard Fertig, 1970).

5. Michael A. Sells, "Christ Killer, Kremlin, Contagion," in *The New Crusades: Constructing the Muslim Enemy,* ed. Emran Qureshi and Michael A. Sells (New York: Columbia University Press, 2003), 355.

6. For numbers, see Andrew Mango, *Ataturk* (London: John Murray, 1999), 113, and Lieutenant-Colonel Reginald Rankin, *The Inner History of the Balkan War* (London: Constable, 1914), 551–59.

7. Rankin, *Inner History,* 151.

8. Ibid., 1.

9. F. Yeats-Brown, *Golden Horn: Plot and Counterplot in Turkey, 1908–1918* (London: Victor Gollancz, 1932), 75, 77.

10. Rankin, *Inner History,* 346.

11. Just over four months later, on March 17, King George was assassinated.

12. Rankin, *Inner History,* 310.

13. Viscount Grey of Fallodon, *Twenty-five Years, 1892–1916,* 2 vols. (London: Hodder and Stoughton, 1926), 1:260.

14. Ibid., 1:263.

15. Ibid., 1:277.

16. McCarthy, *Death and Exile,* 164. Slightly different figures are given in *Ottoman Peoples,* 92.

17. McCarthy, *Death and Exile,* 148.

18. Ibid.

19. Rankin, *Inner History,* 303.

20. Yeats-Brown, *Golden Horn,* 88.

21. Hikmet Özdemir, *Salgın Hastalıklardan ölümler, 1914–18* [Deaths from Epidemics, 1914–18] (Ankara: Türk Tarih Kurumu, 2005), 57.

22. John Presland, *Deedes Bey: A Study of Sir Wyndham Deedes, 1883–1923* (London: Macmillan, 1942), 93.

23. Quoted in Rankin, *Inner History,* 308.

24. Presland, *Deedes Bey*, 94; Rankin, *Inner History*, 309.

25. Özdemir, *Salgın Hastalıklardan ölümler*, 60.

26. Ibid., 65.

27. Quoted in Rankin, *Inner History*, 314.

28. Presland, *Deedes Bey*, 94.

29. Toynbee, *Western Question*, 138.

30. Özdemir, *Salgın Hastalıklardan ölümler*, 136.

31. Lewis Einstein, *Inside Constantinople* (London: John Murray, 1917), 128.

32. George Antonius, *The Arab Awakening* (1938; repr., London: Hamish Hamilton, 1961), 203–4.

33. Ibid., 241.

34. *AB*, vol. 1, *1916*, bulletin no. 10, July 14, 1916, 3–4.

35. Ibid.

36. *AB*, vol. 2, *1917*, bulletin no. 48, April 21, 1917, 181.

37. Ibid.

38. Alex Bein, ed., *Arthur Ruppin: Memoirs, Diaries, Letters* (London: Weidenfeld and Nicolson, 1971), 156.

39. Antonius, *Arab Awakening*, 240–41.

40. McCarthy, *Death and Exile*, 223.

41. Justin McCarthy et al., *The Armenian Rebellion at Van* (Salt Lake City: University of Utah Press, 2006), 179.

42. McCarthy writes that revolutionaries launched their attempt to seize the city "during the night of April 13." Other sources give the slightly later starting point. See McCarthy, *Ottoman Peoples*, 107.

43. McCarthy et al., *Armenian Rebellion at Van*, 200.

44. The province of Van also had a small Jewish community that suffered and was dislocated in the turmoil. Ibid., 239–40.

45. Ibid., 236.

46. Ibid., 237.

47. At least nineteen villages were overrun. Ibid., 239.

48. Ibrahim Sargin, the boy who was saved, was among twenty eyewitnesses interviewed by Hüseyin Çelik between 1978–81. See Hüseyin Çelik, "The 1915 Armenian Revolt in Van: Eyewitness Testimony," in *The Armenians in the Late Ottoman Period*, ed. Türkayya Ataöv (Ankara: Turkish Historical Society, 2001), 87–108.

49. Ibid., 104.

50. McCarthy et al., *Armenian Rebellion at Van*, 239.

51. McCarthy, *Death and Exile*, 226.

52. Guenter Lewy, *The Armenian Massacres in Ottoman Turkey: A Disputed Genocide* (Salt Lake City: University of Utah Press, 2005), 152.

53. Ibid., 152.

54. In the same name of military necessity, large numbers of Greeks were moved from the Aegean coast into the interior of Anatolia. Some Muslims and Jews were also removed from the Çanakkale region after the allied landing at

Gallipoli. See Stanford J. Shaw, *From Empire to Republic: The Turkish War of National Liberation, 1918–1923. A Documentary Study*, 6 vols. (Ankara: Turkish Historical Society, 2000), 1:59–60.

55. Lewy, *Armenian Massacres*, 214.

56. Ibid., 210.

57. Ibid., 217. "Local people" spoke of twelve thousand people being killed.

58. Ibid.

59. Ibid., quoting a U.S. consul's report.

60. Ibid., 214–15.

61. Ibid., 218–19.

62. Shaw, *From Empire to Republic*, 1:58.

63. Ibid., 1:58 n. 12.

64. Ibid., 1:58–59. Kamuran Gürün gives a precise figure of 1,397. For a regional breakdown of the court-martials, see Kamuran Gürün, *The Armenian File: The Myth of Innocence Exposed* (London: Weidenfeld and Nicolson, 1985), 213.

65. Shaw, *From Empire to Republic*, 1:58–59, 58 n. 12.

66. See Yusuf Halaçoğlu, *Facts on the Relocation of the Armenians, 1914–1918* (Ankara: Turkish Historical Society, 2002), 101–4 (438,758 Armenians moved from thirty-three locations) and Gürün, *Armenian File*, 214, for a figure of "about 702,900." The difference is partly explained by the difference in time when the numbers were counted. Halaçoğlu's figures are apparently based on a count up to the end of 1915, whereas Gürün is quoting from a Ministry of Interior report drawn up in December 1916. On the Armenian question, no book should ever be published with *fact* in the title.

67. See Justin McCarthy, "The Population of the Ottoman Armenians," in Ataöv, *Armenians in the Late Ottoman Period*, 65–86. See also Herbert Hoover, *The Ordeal of Woodrow Wilson*, with a new introduction by Senator Mark Hatfield (Washington, DC: Woodrow Wilson Center Press, 1992), 142.

68. See Gürün, *Armenian File*, 217–19.

69. See Lewy, *Armenian Massacres*, 240, for a sample of the range.

70. *AB*, vol. 4, no. 113, July 17, 1919, 122–23.

71. See Republic of Turkey, Prime Ministry, *Ermenilar Tarafindan Yapilan Katliam Belgeleri* [Documents on Massacres Perpetrated by Armenians], vol. 1, *1914–1919*, and vol. 2, *1919–1921* (Ankara: State Archives General Directorate, 2001).

72. McCarthy et al., *Armenian Rebellion in Van*, 233–34.

73. Lewy, *Armenian Massacres*, 241.

74. On a smaller scale this was also the fate of the Nestorian Christians of the southeastern Hakkari region, whose tribal and religious leaders also decided to throw in their lot with the Russians and were left out on a limb when the Bolsheviks pulled Russia out of the war. For percentage estimates of Muslim population losses, see McCarthy, "Population of the Ottoman Armenians," 78.

75. Edward J. Erickson, one of the few foreign scholars to have researched in the Turkish military archives, has challenged allegations that the organiza-

tion was an instrument of organized mass murder of civilians. Its primary job was "to foment insurrection in enemy territory, fight guerillas and insurgents in friendly territory, conduct espionage and counter-espionage and perform other tasks unsuited to conventional military forces." It also took part in regular military operations. Further research on this question would require the scrutiny not just of government documents but of the vast amount of material in the military archives. The official military record of the war alone runs to twenty-seven volumes. For all of the above, see Edward J. Erickson, "Armenian Massacres: New Records Undercut Old Blame," *Middle East Quarterly* 13 (Summer 2006), www.meforum.org/article/991, reprinted in *Insight Turkey* 8 (July–September 2006): 44–53, from which the above quotations are taken.

76. See also McCarthy et al., *Armenian Rebellion at Van;* Lewy, *Armenian Massacres;* Taner Akçam, *A Shameful Act: The Armenian Genocide and the Question of Turkish Responsibility* (New York: Metropolitan Books, 2006); and Donald Bloxham, *The Great Game of Genocide: Imperialism, Nationalism and the Destruction of the Ottoman Armenians* (New York: Oxford University Press, 2005). Two older books giving contrary points are Gürün, *Armenian File,* and Vahakn N. Dadrian, *The History of the Armenian Genocide: Ethnic Conflict from the Balkans to Anatolia to the Caucasus,* 2nd rev. ed. (Oxford: Berghahn Books, Oxford, 1997). Both Dadrian and Akçam allege that the Ottoman government, or the Committee of Union and Progress, met at some point and decided to wipe out the Armenians. Dadrian's source for his claim (*History of the Armenian Genocide,* 219, n. 226) that a decision was taken at a "top secret" meeting of Ottoman leaders is an unnamed Armenian member of a German society in Izmir (the Deutscher Verein). Although Akçam also refers repeatedly to a "decision," when he finally gets to the point he is only able to say that it was "very likely" there was a meeting at which such a decision was taken (*Shameful Act,* 152–53). Akçam claims that Mustafa Kemal (Atatürk) "condemned the genocide" (346), that members of the Turkish parliament engaged in "sharp debate over genocide" (257), and that people were detained "for crimes relating to the genocide" (289). Yet clearly neither Atatürk nor any Turkish member of parliament could have used the word, which was coined by Raphael Lemkin in 1943, five years after Atatürk's death. A fuller discussion of what Atatürk actually said is not possible within the scope of this work. The accusation that the Turks decided to cleanse Anatolia of Armenians for racial and ideological reasons requires its proponents to minimize the scale and intensity of the Armenian rebellion and its effect on the military high command. For Bloxham, Ottoman documents "show that some Armenians were coerced into action and also that Armenian communities condemned the reckless behavior of a few of their number" (*Great Gameof Genocide,* 91). Akçam takes a similar position and even claims that some of the attacks on Kurds were actually carried out by Kurds (the Hamidiye cavalry). Since the Hamidiye were recruited locally from among the Kurdish population, this charge is certainly interesting but needs a better source than a footnote saying merely that "this subject was talked about in

some novels as well" (199, 430 n. 314). The controversy over the fate of the Armenians will continue, but after examining all the evidence, including "documents" of dubious provenance (most notoriously the "Andonian Papers" of 1920) and the accusation that Talat Paşa used a secret channel to order the destruction of the Armenians, a scholar who holds neither a Turkish nor an Armenian position, Guenter Lewy, has concluded that "no authentic documentary evidence exists to prove the culpability of the central government of Turkey for the massacres of 1915–16" (*Armenian Massacres,* 250). This is separate from the issue of whether the "relocation" was necessary on military grounds, but the argument that it was not might be easier to make in hindsight than in the heat of war.

77. Shaw, *From Empire to Republic,* 1:61–62.

78. Sir Arnold T. Wilson, *Loyalties: Mesopotamia. A Personal and Historical Record,* vol. 2, *1917–1920* (London: Oxford University Press, 1931), 32–33. Cannibalism was also reported among Armenian refugees in the southern Caucasus.

79. Fully described in Robert F. Zeidner's *The Tricolor over the Taurus, 1918–1922* (Ankara: Turkish Historical Society, 2005).

80. Shaw, *From Empire to Republic,* 2:496, quoting Harold Nicolson.

81. Quoted in Elizabeth Monroe, *Britain's Moment in the Middle East, 1914–1956* (Baltimore: Johns Hopkins University Press, 1963), 66; Hoover, *Ordeal of Woodrow Wilson,* 195; Lloyd E. Ambrosius, *Wilsonian Statecraft: Theory and Practice of Liberal Internationalism during World War I* (Wilmington, DE: Scholarly Resources Books, 1991), 135.

82. Wilson, *Loyalties,* 300.

83. Robert D. Kaplan, *Balkan Ghosts: A Journey through History* (New York: Vintage, 1994), 246.

84. Roger Adelson, *London and the Invention of the Middle East: Money, Power and War, 1902–1922* (New Haven: Yale University Press, 1995), 172, 183.

85. On the offer of part of Anatolia, see Toynbee, *Western Question,* 64.

86. Ibid., 52.

87. Presland, *Deedes Bey,* 308.

88. Kaplan, *Balkan Ghosts,* 241.

89. Toynbee, *Western Question,* 259.

90. Ibid., 311, 318–19.

91. Shaw, *From Empire to Republic,* 2:519.

92. Ibid., 525.

93. Toynbee, *Western Question,* 285. See Shaw, *From Empire to Republic,* 2:521–40, for a fuller account of the committee's findings.

94. Toynbee, *Western Question,* 275.

95. Ibid., 298.

96. American Section of the International Commission on Mandates in Turkey (King-Crane Commission), "The King-Crane Commission," August 28, 1919, in FRUS, *The Paris Peace Conference, 1919* (Washington, DC: Government Printing Office, 1947), 12:838.

97. Shaw, *From Empire to Republic,* 4:1700.

98. Ibid., 4:1710.

99. Ibid., 4:1711.

100. Ibid., 4:1754.

4. EXIT THE SHARIF

1. "Secret Report on the Sherif of Mecca (Hussein) with Covering Notes by Captain G. S. Symes," Enkowit, July 19, 1915 (FO 882/12), RHD, 2:3–10.

2. Antonius, *Arab Awakening,* 174.

3. "King Hussein and Khurma," May 24, 1919, *AB,* vol. 4, no. 111, 59.

4. Appraisal by Ronald Storrs, November 22, 1915, *RHD,* 2:5.

5. Storrs describing meetings with the sharif, *AB,* vol. 1, no. 36, 552–56.

6. "Note on the Grand Sharif's Present Methods of Government and His Relations with Arab Chiefs, Syrians Etc., Lieut. Colonel Wilson," Jeddah, July 10, 1917, *RHD,* 2:153–61; "Hejaz Postwar Finance," January 30, 1920, *RHD,* 2:653; "Extracts from Political Report by Colonel C. E. Vickery," Jeddah, June 1, 1920–June 13, 1920, *RHD,* 2:684–98; R. W. Bullard, British agent, Jeddah, to Foreign Office, October 19, 1923, enc. 1, *RHD,* 3:535–41; for T. E. Lawrence's views, see Lawrence to "Prodrome," London, August 2, 4, and 7 and September 22, 1921, *RHD,* 3:323–26.

7. Telegram from Senior Naval Office, Red Sea, to Admiralty, June 3, 1925, *RHD,* 3:124. In the margin someone has written "certainly not," but whether this refers to the possibility of the sharif moving to London or the possibility that he would be a "great bore" is not clear.

8. Antonius, *Arab Awakening,* 336.

9. Telegram from McMahon to Foreign Office, Cairo, October 31, 1916, *RHD,* 2:43.

10. For the text of this letter, see "Documents on Palestine," in *The Middle East and North Africa 2004* (London: Europa Publications, 2004), 49; for an analysis of the McMahon-Husain correspondence, see Antonius, *Arab Awakening,* 164–83. See also C. H. Dodd and M. E. Sales, *Israel and the Arab World* (London: Routledge and Kegan Paul, 1970), 55–59.

11. Telegram from McMahon to Foreign Office, Cairo, October 31, 1916, *RHD,* 2:43.

12. Foreign Office to Emir Abdullah, January 11, 1923, relating to commitments made by Sir Henry McMahon on October 24, 1915, *RHD,* 3:453–54.

13. "King Hussein's Continuing Negotiations with British Government over Terms of Treaties Requiring His Signature," November 22–January 1924, *RHD,* 3:451–510.

14. "Question of Ex-King Hussein's Future Place of Residence, Report of Proceedings for the Period Ending October 15, 1924," *RHD,* 4:27–32.

15. "Operations of Ex-King Hussein and Emir ʿAbdallah Based on Aqaba and the Vilayet of Maan, Memo on General Question of Akaba [*sic*]," May 22, 1925, *RHD,* 147.

16. Copy of telegram from HMS *Cornflower,* May 29, 1925, transmitting a message from the sharif to the Foreign Office, May 29, 1925, *RHD,* 4:161.

17. High commissioner in Jerusalem to British agent, Jeddah, May 29, 1925, *RHD,* 4:160.

18. Ibid.

19. Antonius, *Arab Awakening,* 183.

20. Ibid., 182.

21. "To the Noble British Nation," November 24, 1923, *RHD,* 3:500–501.

22. Philip S. Khoury, *Syria and the French Mandate: The Politics of Arab Nationalism, 1920–1945* (London: I. B. Tauris, 1987), 53.

23. Ibid., 177.

24. Ibid., 177–79.

25. "More Unrest in Syria," *Times,* November 2, 1925, 14.

26. Ibid.

27. Consul Vaughan-Russell to Sir Austen Chamberlain, Damascus, April 27, 1926, *ADM,* 2:877–78.

28. Khoury, *Syria and the French Mandate,* 196.

29. Ibid., 201.

30. Albert Hourani, *Arabic Thought in the Liberal Age, 1798–1939* (New York: Oxford University Press, 1962), vii.

31. "Order Returning to Egypt," *Times,* April 7, 1919, 11.

32. "False Calm in Egypt," *Times,* April 22, 1919, 9.

33. In the view of a British official, Abbas Hilmi, educated in Paris and Vienna and speaking German, French, and English in addition to Turkish and Arabic, had abandoned "the most useful of virtues, including docility," becoming in the process "too civilized for his position." See Jacques Berque, *Egypt: Imperialism and Revolution,* trans. Jean Stewart (New York: Praeger, 1972), 165.

34. William Stadiem, *Too Rich: The High Life and Tragic Death of King Farouk* (New York: Carroll and Graf, 1991), 201.

35. Ibid., 204.

36. Ibid., 199, 202.

37. Ibid., 204.

38. Ibid., 205.

39. Hoda Gamal Abdel Nasser, *Britain and the Egyptian National Movement, 1936–1952* (Reading, UK: Ithaca Press, 1994), 232.

40. Ibid., 236.

41. For a useful account of the turmoil in Egypt before the revolution, see Charles Tripp, "Egypt, 1945–1952: The Uses of Disorder," in *Demise of the British Empire in the Middle East: Britain's Response to Nationalist Movements, 1943–55,* ed. Michael J. Cohen and Martin Kolinsky (London: Frank Cass, 1998), 112–41.

5. SMALL WARS IN IRAQ

1. For quote, see Hanna Batatu, *The Old Social Classes and the Revolutionary Movements of Iraq* (Princeton: Princeton University Press, 1978), 869.

2. Notes of conversation between the high commissioner for Iraq and King Faisal on May 20, 1930, *RI*, 5:304–5.

3. Edmund Candler, *The Long Road to Baghdad*, 2 vols. (London: Cassell, 1919), 2:97.

4. For full text, see Sir Maude Stanley, "The Proclamation of Baghdad," Harper's, May 2003, http://harpers.org/archive/2003/05/0079593. See also Sir George Buchanan, *The Tragedy of Mesopotamia* (Edinburgh: William Blackwood and Sons, 1938), 169–72.

5. *Middle East and North Africa 2004*, 49.

6. Adelson, *London*, 185.

7. Wilson, *Loyalties*, 74.

8. On appeals for clemency, see ibid., 74–75.

9. Ibid., 138.

10. Ibid., 139.

11. *The Letters of Gertrude Bell*, ed. Lady Bell, 2 vols. (London: Ernest Benn, 1928), 2:575.

12. Wilson, *Loyalties*, 238.

13. Ibid., 239.

14. Departmental minute to War Office, May 12, 1919. See the collection of documentary excerpts headed "Winston Churchill's Secret Poison Gas Memo," July 29, 2004, Centre for Research on Globalisation, www.globalresearch.ca/articles/CHU407A.html.

15. Adelson, *London*, 196–97.

16. Ibid., 185.

17. Wilson, *Loyalties*, 278–79.

18. Editorial, *Times*, August 19, 1921, 11.

19. An official American view. "Subject: Political Situation in Turkey," Alexander K. Sloan to secretary of state, Baghdad, February 3, 1932, *RHD*, 11:572–74.

20. Churchill to prime minister, August 23, 1922, *RHD*, 11:35–36.

21. High commissioner to the secretary of state for the colonies, August 27, 1922, *RHD*, 11:43.

22. Ibid.

23. Ibid., 11:44–46.

24. Churchill to prime minister, September 1, 1922, *RIID*, 11:47 49.

25. For details, see Elizabeth P. MacCallum, "Iraq and the British Treaties," *Foreign Policy Association Information Service* 16 (August 20, 1930): 233–37.

26. *IAR*, 7:356.

27. MacCallum, "Iraq and the British Treaties," 241.

28. Press report and high commissioner's dispatch, November 20, 1929, *RI*, 5:167, 168–72.

29. Interview given by Rashid Ali to the newspaper *Al Tahrir*, February 21, 1956, *RI*, 11:379–81.

30. For full text, see MacCallum, "Iraq and the British Treaties," 244–46.

31. Majid Khadduri, *Independent Iraq, 1932–1958* (New York: Oxford University Press, 1960), 108.

32. Sir A. Clark Kerr, British embassy, Baghdad, to G. W. Rendel, Foreign Office, enclosing notes on new chief of the general staff, November 26, 1936, *RI*, 8:19–23.

33. Sir A. Clark Kerr to Mr. Eden, Baghdad, November 2, 1936, *RI*, 7:508–11.

34. Minute by the ambassador, Baghdad, November 13, 1936, *RI*, 7:519.

35. Oswald Scott to Eden, August 18, 1937, *RI*, 8:111–17.

36. "Position of King Ghazi in Iraq," very confidential, marked with handwritten instruction "not to go outside the FO," October 10, 1936 (FO 371/20017), *RI*, 7:292.

37. Sir A. Clark Kerr to Mr. Eden, June 19, 1936, marked "confidential," *RI*, 7:281.

38. "a.c.k." [Archibald Clark Kerr] to G. W. Rendel, "confidential," February 13, 1936, *RI*, 7:278–80.

39. "Elopement of Princess ʿAzzah and Its Political Effects; Likelihood of King Ghazi's Abdication or Deposition," May–August 1936, *RHD*,12:305–44, passim; for the British ambassador's discussions with the Iraqi prime minister and foreign minister, see Sir A. Clark Kerr to Mr. Eden, July 2, 1936, *RHD*, 12:321–26.

40. Sir A. Clark Kerr to Mr. Eden, July 2, 1936, *RHD*, 12:325.

41. Mr. Bateman to Mr. Eden, June 25, 1936, *RI*, 7:287.

42. The princess eventually returned to the Middle East to live in Jordan.

43. "Flight of Yasin Pasha, Rashid Ali Gilani and Jamil Madfai to Syria," Consul Mackereth to F.O. Damascus, October 31, 1936 (FO 371/20013), *RI*, 7:506–7.

44. Kermit Roosevelt, *Arabs, Oil and History: The Story of the Middle East* (London: Victor Gollancz, 1949), 101–3.

45. The Nestorian Assyrians belonged to the Holy Apostolic Catholic Assyrian Church of the East and the Jacobite Assyrians to the Syrian Orthodox Church.

46. Salahi R. Sonyel, *The Assyrians of Turkey: Victims of Major Power Policy* (Ankara: Turkish Historical Society, 2001), 122.

47. Ibid., 98–108.

48. Wilson, *Loyalties*, 36.

49. Özdemir, *Salgın Hastalıklardan ölümler*, 355.

50. "Memorandum on the Assyrian Question," August 25, 1934, *RI*, 7:604.

51. Sonyel, *Assyrians of Turkey*, 174–75.

52. "Administration Report on Arab and Kurdish Levies for Year 1920–21," *IAR*, 6:89.

53. Wilson, *Loyalties*, 39–40.

54. "Report on the Administration of Iraq for the Period April, 1923–December, 1924," *IAR*, 7:548.

55. Sir Francis Humphrys to Sir Robert Vansittart, Baghdad, August 24, 1933, *RI*, 7:583.

56. "Report on the Administration of Iraq for the Period April, 1923–December, 1924," *IAR*, 7:548.

57. "Memorandum on the Assyrian Question," 604.

58. Ibid., 605.

59. There is agreement in the British diplomatic correspondence that it was the Assyrians who fired first. For an Assyrian view, see Fred Aprim, "Dairaboun (Deir Abun): The Strategic Assyrian Village," *Zinda*, February 1, 2006, www.zindamagazine.com/html/archives/2006/02.01.06/index_wed.php.

60. Sir F. Humphrys to Sir John Simon, September 14, 1933, enclosing a report on "the part taken by the Iraqi army in the repression of the Assyrian rebellion in July and August 1933," *RI*, 7:585–89.

61. Humphrys to Simon, September 14, 1933, *RI*, 7:588–89.

62. "Assyrians in Iraq; Prisoners Shot Untried," *Times*, August 17, 10.

63. "Assyrian Crisis. Sir Francis Humphrys' Return," G. W. Rendel, Foreign Office, August 13, 1933, *RI*, 7:564.

64. Mr. Ogilvie Forbes to Sir John Simon, Baghdad, August 22, 1933, enclosure from Consul Moneypenny, Mosul, *RI*, 7:580–81.

65. Wilson, *Loyalties*, 38.

66. Reeva Simon, *Iraq between the Two World Wars: The Creation and Implementation of a Nationalist Ideology* (New York: Columbia University Press, 1986), 133.

67. Sir B. Newton to Mr. Eden, Baghdad, February 27, 1941, enc. from Mr. Edmonds, adviser to the Iraqi Ministry of the Interior, dated February 15, 1941, *RHD*, 13:161.

68. Telegram from Foreign Office to Mr. Stonehewer Bird, Jeddah, January 10, 1941 (FO/371/27061), *RHD*, 13:134. Rashid Ali was indeed sounding out Germany and Italy. Both refused to make any more than the most equivocal commitments to supporting Arab independence after the war.

69. *RHD*, 13:105.

70. *RHD*, 13:107.

71. Telegram, January 7, 1941, *RHD*, 13:131.

72. *RHD*, 13:157–78.

73. *RHD*, 13: 172–73.

74. Cornwallis to Eden, April 6, 1941, *RHD*, 13:205.

75. Gerald du Gaury, *Arabian Journey and Other Desert Travels* (London: George G. Harrap, 1950), 134.

76. Cornwallis to Foreign Office, April 9, 1941, *RHD*, 13:217.

77. Cornwallis to Foreign Office, April 7, 1941, *RHD*, 13:213.

78. Sir K. Cornwallis to Foreign Office, Baghdad, April 29, 1941, *RI*, 8:460–61.

79. Summary by the ambassador, June 6, 1941, *RHD*, 13:289–303.

80. See Hansard excerpt from House of Commons debate, n.d., *RHD*, 13:261.

81. Foreign Office, London, to Sir Alexander Hardinge, Foreign Office, May 21, 1941 (FO 371/27072), *RI*, 8:476.

82. Batatu, *Old Social Classes*, 30.

83. Colonial Office, London, to Sir Anthony Eden, August 7, 1941, enc. report by Major Glubb Pasha, Arab Legion headquarters, Amman, on role of Arab Legion, dated June 10, 1941, *RI*, 8:511–50; for quoted passage, see 520–21.

84. For details, see ambassador's summary, June 6, 1941, *RHD*, 13:289–303.

85. "Report on Role of Iraq Levies by Lt. A. Graham," n.d., *RI*, 8:529.

86. Batatu, *Old Social Classes*, 215.

87. For a summary of the situation of Iraqi Jews, and the effect of Zionism on popular feeling among Iraqis, see "The Jews of Iraq, 1934–36," passim, *RI*, 7:629–45; for discussions with king and ministers, see Sir F. Humphrys to Sir John Simon, Baghdad, December 27, 1934, *RI*, 7:638–39.

88. An obscure Arabic word meaning "destruction" or "dispossession."

89. *RI*, 8:483.

90. *RHD*, 13:318.

91. Batatu, *Old Social Classes*, 258.

92. Simon, *Iraq*, 160.

93. Sir Kinahan Cornwallis to Mr. Eden, Baghdad, July 11, 1941, *RI*, 8:501.

94. Roosevelt, *Arabs, Oil and History*, 103.

95. Herter to Department of State, March 11, 1958, *FRUS*, 12:294.

96. Ibid., 301.

97. Batatu, *Old Social Classes*, 801.

98. C. H. Johnston, Amman, to Foreign Office, July 28, 1958 (FO371/134201), *RI*, 12:293.

6. DOUBLE COLONIALISM IN PALESTINE

1. "Lord Balfour in Palestine," *Times*, March 27, 1925, 14.

2. Ibid., 10. For a full account of his visit, see Labib Yunan Rizk, "A Balfour Curse: A Diwan of Contemporary Life (361)," *Al Ahram Weekly*, October 26–November 1, 2000, www.weekly.ahram.org.eg/2000/505/chrncls.htm.

3. For Balfour's remarks during the committee stage discussion of the Aliens Bill in the Commons, see Oskar K. Rabinowicz, "The Aliens Bill and Jewish Immigration to Britain, 1902–1905," in *From Haven to Conquest: Readings in Zionism and the Palestine Problem until 1948*, ed. Walid Khalidi (Washington, DC: Institute for Palestine Studies, 1987), 111–12.

4. Mr. Balfour to Earl Curzon, Paris, September 19, 1919, enc. memo by Mr. Balfour respecting Syria, Palestine, and Mesopotamia, dated August 11, 1919, *PB*, 2:295.

5. Richard Meinertzhagen, *Middle East Diary* (London: Cresset Press, 1959), 9.

6. Moses Hess, *Rome and Jerusalem*, quoted in Stephen Halbrook, "The Class Origins of Zionist Ideology," *Journal of Palestine Studies* 2 (Autumn 1972): 89.

7. Herbert Sidebotham, *England and Palestine* (London: Constable, 1918), 107.

8. American Section of the International Commission on Mandates in Turkey, "The King-Crane Commission," FRUS, *Paris Peace Conference, 1919*, 12:794.

9. Ibid., 12:795.

10. Desmond Stewart, *Theodor Herzl: Artist and Politician* (London: Quartet Books, 1981), 191.

11. Theodor Herzl, *The Diaries of Theodor Herzl*, trans. Marvin Lowenthal (New York: Dial Press, 1956), 43.

12. Chaim Simons, *International Proposals to Transfer Arabs from Palestine, 1895–1947: A Historical Survey* (Hoboken, NJ: KTAV, 1988), 8.

13. Arthur Koestler, *Thieves in the Night: Chronicle of an Experiment* (London: Macmillan, 1946), 160.

14. Ibid., 24.

15. Arthur Koestler, *Promise and Fulfilment, 1917–1949* (London: Macmillan, 1949), 34.

16. Ibid., 199–200. The two best-selling Middle Eastern novels of Leon Uris, *Exodus* and especially *The Hajj*, are outstanding, in a crowded field, for their abuse of "the Arabs."

17. *AB*, vol. 2, bulletin no. 39, January 19, 1917, 32.

18. Great Britain, Foreign Office, *The Political History of Palestine under British Administration: Memorandum by His Majesty's Britannic Government presented in July 1947 to the United Nations Special Commission on Palestine* (Jerusalem: Government Printing Office, 1947), 3.

19. Ibid., 3.

20. Chaim Weizmann, *The Letters and Papers of Chaim Weizmann, Series A: Letters*, 23 vols., gen. ed. Meyer W. Weisgal (vols. 1–11) and Barnet Litvinoff (vols. 12–23) (New Brunswick, NJ: Transaction Books and Rutgers University Press, 1968–80), vol. 9, *October 1918–July 1920*, ed. Jehuda Reinharz, 101.

21. Ibid., 105.

22. Simons, *International Proposals*, 41.

23. Antonius, *Arab Awakening*, 269.

24. First conversation on Transjordania, held at Government House, Jerusalem, March 28, 1921, *PB*, 3:702–6; for Abdullah's remarks, see 704.

25. Ibid.

26. Adelson, *London*, 202.

27. Weizmann, *Letters and Papers*, 9:248 and 323.

28. Ibid., 9:358.

29. Crane was speaking to the Times on June 3, 1922. Quoted in memorandum of Palestinian delegation to London, June 17, 1922, *PB*, 3:767.

30. Ibid., 3:772.

31. See Basheer M. Nafiᶜ, *Arabism, Islamism and the Palestine Question, 1908–1941: A Political History* (Reading, UK: Ithaca Press, 1998), 198, for a British reference to the "concentration camp" confinement of Palestinians.

32. Joseph Massad, "Imperial Mementos," *Al Ahram Weekly*, May 20–26, 2004, http://weekly.ahram.org.eg/2004/691/op2.htm.

33. For a succinct account of Sheikh ʿIzz al Din's life and death, see Beverley Milton-Edwards, *Islamic Politics in Palestine* (London: I. B. Tauris, 1996).

34. Koestler, *Promise and Fulfilment*, 74 n.

35. Government of Palestine, *A Survey of Palestine: Prepared in December 1945 and January 1946 for the Information of the Anglo-American Committee of Inquiry*, 2 vols. (1946; repr., Washington, DC: Institute of Palestine Studies, 1991), 1:45.

36. For number of Jewish police in 1937, see ibid., 1:43; for number in 1939, see David Ben-Gurion, "Britain's Contribution to Arming the Hagana," in Khalidi, *From Haven to Conquest*, 371–74.

37. Government of Palestine, *Survey of Palestine*, 46.

38. Roger Courtney, *Palestine Policeman* (London: Herbert Jenkins, 1939), 19.

39. Nafiʿ, *Arabism, Islamism*, 198.

40. Milton-Edwards, *Islamic Politics in Palestine*, 23.

41. Rosemary Sayigh, *Palestinians: From Peasants to Revolutionaries* (London: Zed Press, 1979), 43.

42. Frances E. Newton, "Searchlight on Palestine, 1936–1938," in Khalidi, *From Haven to Conquest*, 357–66.

43. Government of Palestine, *Survey of Palestine*, 27.

44. Ibid., 29.

45. Ibid., 44.

46. Ibid., 141.

47. Ibid.,142.

48. Khalidi, *From Haven to Conquest*, Appendix 1, "Population, Immigration and Land Statistics, 1919–1946," 841–43.

49. Government of Palestine, *Survey of Palestine*, 150.

50. Ibid., 372.

51. Ibid., 151.

52. S. G. Thicknesse, *Arab Refugees: A Survey of Resettlement Possibilities* (London: Royal Institute of International Affairs, 1949), 20. Slightly different figure for the 1944–45 season are given in Government of Palestine, *Survey of Palestine* (327), but they are based only on the "main crops."

53. Government of Palestine, *Survey of Palestine*, 331.

54. Quoted in ibid., 52–56.

55. "The Zionist (Biltmore) Program, May 11, 1942," in Khalidi, *From Haven to Conquest*, 495–97.

56. Albert H. Hourani, *Great Britain and the Arab World* (London: John Murray, 1945), 25–26.

57. Ibid., 42.

58. The statistics are taken from Jacob Abadi, *Britain's Withdrawal from the Middle East, 1947–1971: The Economic and Strategic Imperatives* (Princeton, NJ: Kingston Press, 1982), 1–29.

59. Ibid., 23.

60. Margaret Arakie, *The Broken Sword of Justice: America, Israel and the Palestine Tragedy* (London: Quartet Books, 1973), 45.

61. William Roger Louis, *The British Empire in the Middle East, 1945–1951* (Oxford: Clarendon Press, 1984), 474.

62. Koestler, *Promise and Fulfilment*, 241.

63. Weizmann, *Letters and Papers*, vol. 23, *August 1947–June 1952*, ed. Aaron Klieman, 39.

64. Michael J. Cohen, *Truman and Israel* (Berkeley: University of California Press, 1990), 169.

65. Ibid., 168.

66. Consul-General Macatee, East Jerusalem, February 9, 1948, in FRUS, *1948*, vol. 5, *The Near East, South Asia, and Africa*, pt. 2 (Washington, DC: Government Printing Office, 1976), 607.

67. Other estimates of the dead are considerably higher.

68. Kapeliouk, "New Light on the Israeli-Arab Conflict and the Refugee Problem and Its Origins," *Journal of Palestine Studies* 16 (Spring 1987): 21.

69. U.S. Secretary of State George C. Marshall on the "Arab situation," May 13, 1948, FRUS, *1948*, vol. 5, pt. 2, 983.

70. U.S. Central Intelligence Agency, secret report, enclosure B, July 27, FRUS, *1948*, vol. 5, pt. 2, 1240–48.

71. Khalidi, *From Haven to Conquest*, Appendix 8, "Note on Arab Strength in Palestine, January–May 15, 1948," 858–60, and "Arab Expeditionary Force to Palestine, May 15, 1948," 867–71.

72. Top secret, Ambassador Douglas in London to Acting Secretary of State, November 1, 1948, FRUS, *1948*, vol. 5, pt. 2, 1536–38.

73. Killed in early April.

74. Nafez Abdullah Nazzal, "The Zionist Occupation of Western Galilee, 1948," *Journal of Palestine Studies* 3 (Spring 1974): 60.

75. Fawzi al Qawuqji, "Memoirs, 1948: Part II," *Journal of Palestine Studies* 2 (Autumn 1972): 3–33.

76. Netanel Lorch, *The Edge of the Sword: Israel's War of Independence* (Jerusalem: Massada Press, 1968), 484.

77. Draft memo by Dean Rusk to Undersecretary of State Lovett, May 4, 1948, FRUS, *1948*, vol. 5, pt. 2, 894–95.

78. Ibid., 895.

79. Weizmann to Truman, April 9, 1948, FRUS, *1948*, vol. 5, pt. 2, 807–9.

80. Roosevelt, *Arabs, Oil and History*, 124.

81. Austin to Rusk, April 15, 1948, FRUS, *1948*, vol. 5, pt. 2, 823.

82. John H. Davis, *The Evasive Peace: A Study of the Zionist-Arab Problem* (London: John Murray, 1970), 57.

83. Quoted in Meron Benvenisti, *Sacred Landscapes: The Buried History of the Holy Land since 1948* (Berkeley: University of California Press, 2000), 120.

84. Yigal Allon, *The Making of Israel's Army* (London: Sphere Books, 1970), 53.

85. Simons, *International Proposals*, 16.

86. Ibid., 14.

87. Ibid., 14–15.

88. Ibid., 46.

89. Ibid., 83.

90. Weizmann, *Letters and Papers*, 23:231.

91. Quoted in Kapeliouk, "New Light," 17.

92. Quoted in Simha Flapan, "The Palestinian Exodus of 1948," *Journal of Palestine Studies* 16 (Summer 1987): 13.

93. Benny Morris, *1948 and After: Israel and the Palestinians* (Oxford: Clarendon Press, 1990), 1–4. Also see Benny Morris, "Operation Dani and the Palestinian Exodus from Lydda and Ramle in 1948," *Middle East Journal* 40 (Winter 1986): 82–109, and Michael Palumbo, *The Palestinian Catastrophe: The 1948 Expulsion of a People from Their Homeland* (London: Quartet Books, 1987), 126–38.

94. Quoted in Kapeliouk, "New Light," 19.

95. Walid Khalidi, "Plan Dalet: Master Plan for the Conquest of Palestine," *Journal of Palestine Studies* 18 (Autumn 1988): 3–70.

96. Benvenisti, *Sacred Landscapes*, 145–46.

97. Editorial note from Riley to Ralph Bunche, November 3, 1948, FRUS, *1948*, vol. 5, pt. 2, 1541.

98. Amira Howeidy, "It's Difficult to Count," *Al Ahram Weekly*, April 9–15, 1998, http://weekly.ahram.org.eg/1998/1948/372_yass.htm, in a special supplement on the massacre. The initial figure of 254 dead was subsequently reduced on the basis of further research. For an effective short account of the attack and the massacre, see Matthew Hogan, "Deir Yassin Remembered," undated home page of Deir Yassin Remembered's Web site, www.deiryassin.org (accessed July 19, 2007).

99. Harry Levin, *Jerusalem Embattled* (London: Victor Gollancz, 1950), 57.

100. Koestler, *Promise and Fulfilment*, 160.

101. Morris, *1948 and After*, 2. On Duwayma massacre, see Ilan Pappér, *The Ethnic Cleansing of Palestine* (Oxford: Oneworld, 2007), 195–98.

102. Benvenisti, *Sacred Landscapes*, 153.

103. Thicknesse, *Arab Refugees*, 127.

104. Weizmann to James de Rothschild, December 1, 1948, in Weizmann, *Letters and Papers*, 23:234.

105. James G. McDonald, *My Mission in Israel, 1948–1951* (London: Victor Gollancz, 1951), 161.

106. For an extensive topographical survey of the destruction of Palestine, see Walid Khalidi, ed., *All That Remains: The Palestinian Villages Occupied and Depopulated by Israel in 1948* (Washington, DC: Institute for Palestine Studies, 1992).

107. Benvenisti, *Sacred Landscapes*, 296.

108. Sami Hadawi, *Bitter Harvest: Palestine, 1914–1967* (New York: New World Press, 1967), 230.

109. Donald Neff, *Fallen Pillars: U.S. Policy towards Palestine and Israel since 1945* (Washington, DC: Institute of Palestine Studies, 1995), 94–95.

110. McDonald, *My Mission in Israel,* 256.

7. CIVIL WAR ALONG THE POTOMAC

1. Richard P. Stephens, *American Zionism and U.S. Foreign Policy, 1942–1947* (Washington, DC: Institute of Palestine Studies, 1970), 69–70. See Chaim Weizmann, *Trial and Error* (New York: Harper, 1949), 431–32.

2. Dean Acheson, *Present at the Creation: My Years in the State Department* (New York: W. W. Norton, 1969), 175.

3. Ibid., 732.

4. Harry S. Truman, *The Memoirs of Harry S. Truman,* vol. 2, *Years of Trial and Hope, 1946–1953* (London: Hodder and Stoughton, 1956), 142.

5. Louis, *British Empire,* 422.

6. Ibid., 481.

7. See UN Palestine Commission, First Special Report to the Security Council," A/AC.21/9, February 16, 1948, http://domino.un.org/UNISPAL .NSF/361eea1cc08301c485256cf600606959/fdf734eb76c39d6385256c4c004cd ba7!OpenDocument.

8. For a concise summary of the debate at the UN at this stage, see Evan Luard, *A History of the United Nations,* vol. 1, *The Years of Western Domination, 1945–1955* (London: Macmillan, 1982), 174–78.

9. Top-secret report by the Policy Planning Staff of the U.S. with respect to Palestine, January 19, 1948, FRUS, *1948,* vol. 5, pt. 2, 546 ff.

10. FRUS, *1948,* vol. 5, pt. 2, 601.

11. FRUS, *1948,* vol. 5, pt. 2, 657.

12. "Possible Developments in Palestine," report by the CIA, February 28, 1948, FRUS, *1948,* vol. 5, pt. 2, 666–75.

13. Instructions from Marshall to Austin, March 5, 1948, FRUS, *1948,* vol. 5, pt. 2, 679–81; statement made by Austin before Security Council, March 19, 1948, FRUS, *1948,* vol. 5, pt. 2, 742–44.

14. FRUS, *1948,* vol. 5, pt. 2, 898.

15. FRUS, *1948,* vol. 5, pt. 2, 952.

16. Robert M. McClintock to Lovett, Washington, March 8, 1948, top secret, FRUS, *1948,* vol. 5, pt. 2, 697.

17. Truman, *Memoirs,* 2:173.

18. Louis, *British Empire,* 507.

19. FRUS, *1948,* vol. 5, pt. 2, 748–49.

20. Memo by Humelsine to Marshall, March 22, 1948, emphasis in original, FRUS, *1948,* vol. 5, pt. 2, 749–50.

21. Clifford's notes dated May 4, 1948, FRUS, *1948,* vol. 5, pt. 2, 746.

22. Memo of conversation by secretary of state, May 12, 1948, FRUS, *1948,* vol. 5, pt. 2, 972–76. "Colonel Goldy" was Colonel Hugh Desmond Barré Goldie, commander of the First Brigade of the Arab Legion.

23. Ibid., 974.

24. Ibid., 975.

25. Ibid., 974–75.

26. Ibid., 975.

27. Memo by Lovett, May 17, 1948, top secret, FRUS, *1948*, vol. 5, pt. 2, 1005–7.

28. Editorial note, letter from Dean Rusk, June 13, 1974, FRUS, *1948*, vol. 5, pt. 2, 993. Rusk was then the State Department's director of UN affairs.

29. Acheson, *Present at the Creation*, 173.

30. Truman, *Memoirs*, 2:162.

31. Diary entry for October 21, 1948, by Secretary of Defense Forrestal, National Security Council (Forrestal Papers), FRUS, *1948*, vol. 5, pt. 2, 1501.

32. Peter Grose, "The President versus the Diplomats," in *The End of the Palestine Mandate*, ed. William Roger Louis and Robert W. Stookey (London: I. B. Tauris, 1986), 32.

33. Acting secretary of state to secretary of state, at Paris, October 24, 1948, FRUS, *1948*, vol. 5, pt. 2, 1512–13.

34. Lovett to Marshall, October 23, 1848, FRUS, *1948*, vol. 5, pt. 2, 1507.

35. FRUS, *1948*, vol. 5, pt. 2, 1313–14.

36. Consul general at Jerusalem (Macdonald) to secretary of state, August 12, 1948, FRUS, *1948*, vol. 5, pt. 2, 1307.

37. Telegram from Clifford to Marshall, FRUS, *1948*, vol. 5, pt. 2, 1432; "memo by files" by Robert McClintock, September 30, 1948, top secret, FRUS, *1948*, vol. 5, pt. 2, 1437.

38. Acting secretary of state to U.S. delegation at Paris, Washington, DC, November 18, 1948, top secret, FRUS, *1948*, vol. 5, pt. 2, 1608.

39. Memo of conversation, November 10, 1948, FRUS, *1948*, vol. 5, pt. 2, 1562–63.

40. McDonald, *My Mission in Israel*, 116, recounting a conversation with Weizmann on January 10, 1949.

41. Ibid., 233.

42. Memo of conversation, by secretary of state, Paris, October 5, 1948, FRUS, *1948*, vol. 5, pt. 2, 1453.

43. Sir John Bagot Glubb, *Soldier with the Arabs* (London: Hodder and Stoughton, 1957), 230.

44. Ambassador in UK (Douglas) to secretary of state, at Paris, London, November 18, 1948, top secret, FRUS, *1948*, vol. 5, pt. 2, 1610–12.

45. Benvenisti, *Sacred Landscapes*, 14.

46. Ibid., 20.

47. Annex to memo by acting secretary of state, December 30, 1948, FRUS, *1948*, vol. 5, pt. 2, 1703. Similar treaty complications were raised by Israeli attacks on Transjordan.

48. Lorch, *Edge of the Sword*, 526.

49. McDonald, *My Mission in Israel*, 166.

50. Neff, *Fallen Pillars*, 77.

51. McDonald, *My Mission in Israel,* 171.

52. Acheson, *Present at the Creation,* 173.

53. Truman won the elections of 1948 but failed in New York, "thus earning the dubious distinction of being the first president to be elected without taking that state since Wilson in 1916." M. Cohen, *Truman and Israel,* 259. The president had clearly miscalculated the effect his support of Israel at every turn would have on Jewish voters.

54. Jones to Satterthwaite, FRUS, *1948,* vol. 5, pt. 2, 1650–51.

8. THE "TRIPARTITE AGGRESSION"

1. Anthony Nutting, *Nasser* (London: Constable, 1972), 29.

2. Ibid., 98.

3. Ibid., 104.

4. Hammarsjkold in conversation with John Foster Dulles, August 10, 1956, FRUS, *1955–57,* vol. 16, *Suez Crisis, July 26–December 31, 1956* (Washington, DC: Government Printing Office, 1990), 182.

5. Glubb, *Soldier with the Arabs,* 286.

6. Benny Morris and Ian Black, *Israel's Secret Wars* (London: Warner Books, 1992), 121.

7. Glubb, *Soldier with the Arabs,* 249.

8. Ibid., 318–20. In the first five years of the armistice agreements more than seven thousand bedouin were forced out of Israel or territory it had occupied.

9. Kennett Love, *Suez: The Twice Fought War* (New York: McGraw-Hill, 1969), 12.

10. See Livia Rokach, "Israeli State Terrorism: An Analysis of the Sharett Diaries," *Journal of Palestine Studies* 9 (Spring 1980): 15.

11. Ibid.

12. Dan Kurzman, *Ben-Gurion: Prophet of Fire* (New York: Simon and Schuster, 1983), 371.

13. Rokach, "Israeli State Terrorism," 18.

14. Ibid., 19.

15. Ibid., 20.

16. Ibid., 21.

17. Glubb, *Soldier with the Arabs,* 313.

18. For a summary of the attack and evidence laid before the UN Security Council, see Issa Nakleh, *Encyclopedia of the Palestine Problem,* 2 vols. (New York: Intercontinental Books, 1991), 1:272–76.

19. Nutting, *Nasser,* 93.

20. Robert Stephens, *Nasser: A Political Biography* (London: Penguin Books, 1973), 166–67.

21. Ibid., 167.

22. Love, *Suez,* 121.

23. Rokach, "Israeli State Terrorism," 25.

24. Ibid., 20.

25. Ibid., 23–24, Sharett's diary entries for March 27 and 29, 1955.

26. In August 1953, Musaddiq was overthrown in a coup—code-named Operation Ajax—designed and carried out by the CIA and the British SIS. The destruction by the West of the moderate liberal but strongly nationalist Musaddiq government opened the way to more than two decades of authoritarian secular rule under a shah determined to rule and not just reign before he was overthrown in the Islamic revolution of 1979.

27. Message from Eden to Eisenhower, July 27, 1956, FRUS, *1955–57*, 16:9–11.

28. Dwight D. Eisenhower, *Waging Peace, 1959–1961* (New York: Doubleday, 1965), 39.

29. Foreign Office minute by A. D. M. Ross, June 21, 1956, *RI*, 11:718.

30. Memo by secretary of state's special assistant for intelligence on "evidence of UK-French-Israeli collusion and deception," Washington, DC, December 5, 1956, FRUS, *1955–57*, 16:1249–69.

31. FRUS, *1955–57*, 16:818.

32. Sir Michael Wright to Foreign Office, September 15, 1956, secret, *RI*, 11:740.

33. *RI*, 11:741.

34. Memorandum of a conversation, October 15, 1956, FRUS, *1955–57*, 16:722 n. 2.

35. FRUS, *1955–57*, 16:723.

36. Telegram from Mr. Westlake to FO, October 12, 1956, Tel Aviv, *RI*, 11:745–47.

37. For Eden's message to Eisenhower, October 30, 1956, see FRUS, *1955–57*, 16:871–72.

38. Foreign Office to Baghdad, cipher telegram, October 31, 1956, *RI*, 11:754.

39. Memorandum of discussion at National Security Council meeting, August 9, 1956, FRUS, *1955–57*, 16:165–76; see observations by Dulles, 170.

40. September 2, 1956, FRUS, *1955–57*, 16:355–58.

41. Memorandum of conversation among the president, the secretary of state, and the undersecretary of state (Hoover), White House, October 21, 1956," FRUS, *1955–57*, 16:764–65.

42. FRUS, *1955–57*, 16:807.

43. FRUS, *1955–57*, 16:845.

44. Message sent on October 30, 1956, FRUS, *1955–57*, 16:849.

45. FRUS, *1955–57*, 16:849.

46. Memorandum of phone conversation between the president and the secretary of state, October 30, 1956, FRUS, *1955–57*, 16:863.

47. Telegram from U.S. embassy in London, October 30, 1956, FRUS, *1955–57*, 16:846–47.

48. Memorandum of conversation with president, October 30, 1956, FRUS, *1955–57*, 16:851–55; for Eisenhower's remarks, see 854.

49. Eban, speaking to State Department officials, October 28, 1956, FRUS, *1955–57*, 16:808–11; Ben Gurion, quoted in telegram from U.S. embassy, October 28–29, 16:811–13.

50. Message from Ben-Gurion to Eisenhower, October 29, 1956, FRUS, *1955–57*, 16:822, 843–44.

51. October 30, 1956, FRUS, *1955–57*, 16:856–57.

52. Quoted in Love, *Suez*, 610.

53. Ibid., 624–25. Also see Keith Kyle, *Suez* (New York: St. Martin's Press, 1991), 501.

54. Sir Michael Wright, Baghdad to Foreign Office, November 12, 1956, secret, *RI*, 12:455–56.

55. Sir Michael Wright, from Baghdad to Foreign Office, December 22, 1956, secret, *RI*, 12:100.

56. In Resolution 1000 (ES-1) of November 4, elaborated in Resolution 1001 (ES-I) of November 7. See *United Nations Resolutions on Palestine and the Arab-Israeli Conflict*, vol. 1, *1947–1974*, ed. George J. Tomeh (Washington, DC: Institute of Palestine Studies, 1975), 32–34.

57. FRUS, *1955–57*, 16:1038 n.

58. Michael Ionides, *Divide and Lose: The Arab Revolt of 1956–1958* (London: Geoffrey Bles, 1960), 179; also Love, *Suez*, 589.

59. Love, *Suez*, 637.

60. "I gave strict orders to the State Department that they should inform Israel that we would handle our affairs exactly as though we didn't have a Jew in America." Eisenhower to his friend "Swede" (Everett) Hazlett, November 2, 1956, FRUS, *1955–57*, 16:944.

61. Eisenhower to Ben-Gurion, November 7, 1956, FRUS, *1955–57*, 16:1063–64; memorandum of conversation, November 7, 1956, 16:1065–67.

62. Telegram from embassy in Israel, quoting Ben-Gurion, November 11, 1956, FRUS, *1955–57*, 16:1107–10.

63. Love, *Suez*, 662.

64. Memorandum of conversation, Department of State, November 26, 1956, FRUS, *1955–57*, 16:1198–99.

65. Love, *Suez*, 661.

66. Memorandum of conversation, Department of State, December 28, 1956, FRUS, *1955–57*, 16:1341–44.

67. Quoted in Love, *Suez*, 665.

68. Eisenhower, *Waging Peace*, 185.

69. Ibid., 186.

70. Love, *Suez*, 666.

71. Ibid., 666–67.

72. Those involved in the massacre defended themselves by arguing that they were only obeying orders. They were prosecuted and sentenced to terms of imprisonment ranging from eight to seventeen years. By 1960, following appeals and remissions, all were free; in September of that year the municipality of Ramla appointed Gabriel Dahan, convicted of the murder of forty-three of the villagers of Kafr Qasim, as its Arab affairs officer.

73. Love, *Suez*, 553.

74. Ibid., 620.

75. Ibid., 636.

76. On October 22 the French secret service had hijacked a plane carrying Ahmad Ben Bella and four other leading Algerian nationalists to a conference in Tunis on North African union. The violation of international law was compounded by the personal insult involved in seizing a plane chartered by the king of Morocco.

9. MY ENEMY'S SPECIAL FRIEND

1. Eisenhower to Dulles, December 12, 1956, FRUS, *1955–57*, 16:1297; telegram from embassy in Lebanon to Department of State, June 14, 1958, FRUS, 1958–60, vol. 11, *Lebanon and Jordan* (Washington, DC: Government Printing Office, 1992), 119–20.

2. Macmillan to Eisenhower, July 14, 1958, FRUS, *1958–60*, 11:233.

3. Memo of phone conversation between Washington and London, July 14, 1958, FRUS, *1958–60*, 11:231–34.

4. Special Intelligence Estimate, "Arab Nationalism as a Factor in the Middle East Situation," Washington, DC, August 12, 1958, FRUS, *1958–60*, vol. 12, *Near East Region: Iraq; Iran; Arabian Peninsula* (Washington, DC: Government Printing Office, 1993), 138–42.

5. National Security Council, "Statement of US Policy towards the Near East," draft, Washington, DC, July 19, 1960, FRUS, *1958–60*, 12:262–73.

6. On Feinberg's support for Truman, see Seymour Hersh, *The Samson Option* (London: Faber and Faber, 1991), 94.

7. Ibid., 97.

8. Steven L. Spiegel, *The Other Arab-Israeli Conflict: Making America's Middle East Policy from Truman to Reagan* (Chicago: University of Chicago Press, 1985), 96.

9. Warren Bass, *Support Any Friend: Kennedy's Middle East and the Making of the U.S.-Israel Alliance* (New York: Oxford University Press, 2003), 93.

10. Hersh, *Samson Option*, 98.

11. Douglas Little, *American Orientalism: The United States and the Middle East since 1945* (Chapel Hill: University of North Carolina Press, 2002), 183.

12. Stephens, *Nasser*, 446.

13. Andrew Cockburn and Leslie Cockburn, *Dangerous Liaison: The Inside Story of the US-Israeli Covert Relationship* (New York: Harper Collins, 1991), 91.

14. Bass, *Support Any Friend*, 177.

15. Memo for record, n.d. (but the two men were apparently speaking on June 5, 1964), FRUS, *1964–68*, vol. 18, *Arab-Israeli Dispute, 1964–1967* (Washington, DC: Government Printing Office, 2000), 164–65.

16. Ibid., 18:165.

17. Warren I. Cohen, "Balancing American Interests in the Middle East: Lyndon Baines Johnson vs. Gamal Abdul Nasser," in *Lyndon Johnson Confronts the World: American Foreign Policy, 1963–1968,* ed. Warren I. Cohen and Nancy Bernkopf Tucker (Cambridge: Cambridge University Press, 1994), 282.

18. Lucius Battle, dispatch from Cairo, October 27, 1964, FRUS, *1964–68*, 18:231.

19. Telegram from embassy in Israel to Department of State, April 7, 1964, FRUS, *1964–68*, 18:84–88.

20. Memo from Robert W. Komer of the National Security Council to McGeorge Bundy, Johnson's special assistant for national security affairs, Washington, DC, February 7, 1965, FRUS, *1964–68*, 18:313.

21. Komer to Department of State, Tel Aviv, February 15, 1965, FRUS, *1964–68*, 18:330.

22. Robert Komer to Lyndon Johnson, Washington, DC, February 16, 1965, FRUS, *1964–68*, 18:334–36. All emphases are in the original documents.

23. Editorial note of Johnson-Feinberg conversation on February 20, 1965, FRUS, *1964–68*, 18:341–42.

24. Memo from Lyndon Johnson, February 21, 1965, FRUS, *1964–68*, 18:343–46. Emphasis in the original.

25. In separate arrangements Israel was also taking delivery of hundreds of British Centurion tanks.

26. Action memo from William J. Handley, Deputy Assistant Secretary of State for Near Eastern and South Asian Affairs, to Dean Rusk, Washington, DC, September 8, 1965, FRUS, *1964–68*, 18:492–93.

27. Komer to Johnson, January 12, 1966, FRUS, *1964–68*, 18:533.

28. Hersh, *Samson Option*, 108–9.

29. Memorandum of conversation, February 9, 1966, FRUS, *1964–68*, 18:549–50.

30. Katzenbach to Johnson, Washington, DC, May 1, 1967, FRUS, *1964–68*, 18:814–17.

31. Stephens, *Nasser*, 444.

32. Love, *Suez*, 114.

33. Patrick Seale, *Asad of Syria: The Struggle for the Middle East* (London: I. B. Tauris, 1988), 125.

34. Ibid., 119.

35. The banquet at which the president was speaking was held in New York on February 6, 1964. For text of speech, see "Remarks in New York City at the Dinner of the Weizmann Institute of Science," www.presidency.ucsb.edu/ws/index.php?Pid=26060. For Johnson's comment to Eshkol, see memo of conversation, Washington, DC, June 1, 1964, FRUS, *1964–68*, 18:152–59.

36. Dean Rusk to Averell Harriman, U.S. embassy, Tel Aviv, March 1, 1965, FRUS, *1964–68*, 18:366–69.

37. Telegram from U.S. embassy in Israel, May 25, 1966, FRUS, *1964–68*, 18:465–66.

38. *Yearbook of the United Nations, 1966* (New York: Office of Public Information, 1968), 168.

39. U.N. Security Council, S/RES/111, January 19, 1956, http://domino.un.org/UNISPAL.NSF/314a25bea7f2d8ef0525672700579634/58c97a3d38b43299852560c20071c481!OpenDocument.

40. Circular telegram from Department of State to certain posts, Washington, DC, May 28, 1965, FRUS, *1964–68*, 18:466–67.

41. CIA memo, November 18, 1966, FRUS, *1964–68*, 18:666–68.

42. CIA estimates, November 18, 1966, FRUS, *1964–68*, 18:666–68.

43. Seale, *Asad*, 127.

44. Telegram from embassy in Israel to State, November 22, 1966, FRUS, *1964–68*, 18:682.

45. Memo from Komer to Johnson, November 16, 1966, FRUS, *1964–68*, 18:663–64.

46. In Michael B. Oren, *Six Days of War: June 1967 and the Making of the Modern Middle East* (New York: Oxford University Press, 2002), 33, the number of Israeli troops is put at four hundred.

47. Rostow to Johnson, November 15, 1966, FRUS, *1964–68*, 18:658–60.

48. Memo from W. Howard Wriggins and Harold B. Saunders, of the National Security Council, to Rostow, the president's special assistant, on November 16, 1966, FRUS, *1964–68*, 18:664–66.

49. UN Security Council, S/RES/228, November 25, 1966, www.jewish virtuallibrary.org/jsource/UN/unres228.html.

50. Katzenbach to U.S. embassy, Tel Aviv, November 30, FRUS, *1964–68*, 18:693–94.

51. Rostow's memo to Johnson, January 16, 1967, based on an informal message from Eshkol, FRUS, *1964–68*, 18:742.

52. Rostow to Johnson, January 16, 1966, FRUS, *1964–68*, 18:742–43.

53. *Yearbook of the United Nations, 1967* (New York: Office of Public Information, New York, 1969), 158, 164.

54. McDonald, *My Mission in Israel*, 116.

55. Avner Cohen, *Israel and the Bomb* (New York: Columbia University Press, 1998), 11.

56. Fuad Jabber, *Israel and Nuclear Weapons: Present Options and Future Strategies* (London: Chatto and Windus, 1971), 22.

57. See "UK Covered up Israeli Nuke Deal," BBC News Online, December 10, 2005.

58. A. Cohen, *Israel and the Bomb*, 74, 85.

59. Ibid., 91.

60. Neff, *Fallen Pillars*, 171.

61. A. Cohen, *Israel and the Bomb*, 110.

62. Hersh, *Samson Option*, 117.

63. Bass, *Support Any Friend*, 216.

64. Ibid., 220.

65. *Potemkin village* is the name given to the false villages reportedly constructed to impress the Empress Catherine during her visit to the Crimea in 1787. They were the inspiration of Grigory Potemkin, one of Catherine's most able ministers.

66. Hersh, *Samson Option*, 111.

67. Ibid.

68. Memo for the record, Washington, DC, n.d. but early June 1964, FRUS, *1964–68*, 18:164–67.

69. Johnson to Harriman and Komer, Washington, DC, February 21, 1965, FRUS, *1964–68*, 18:343–46.

70. Rusk to Harriman, March 1, 1965, FRUS, *1964–68*, 18:368.

71. Telegram from U.S. embassy in Israel to Department of State, March 1, 1965, FRUS, *1964–68*, 18:369.

72. Memo from Director of Office of Near Eastern Affairs (Davies) to assistant secretary of state for Near Eastern and South Asian affairs (Talbot), March 5, 1965, FRUS, *1964–68*, 18:382.

73. Ibid., 18:382.

74. For reference to more detailed discussion of the status of the Dimona reactor, see FRUS, *1964–68*, 18:383 n.

75. After his retirement Barbour became a director of Israel's Bank Leumi.

76. Embassy in Israel to State, March 11, 1965, FRUS, *1964–68*, 18:398–99.

77. Memo from Rusk to Johnson, May 1, 1965, FRUS, *1964–68*, 18:454–56. Emphases in original.

78. Johnson to Eshkol, May 21, 1965, FRUS, *1964–68*, 18:463–64.

79. Memo from Director of Defense Intelligence Agency to Secretary of Defense, May 4, 1966, FRUS, *1964–68*, 18:582–83.

80. A. Cohen, *Israel and the Bomb*, 190.

81. Telegram to embassy in Israel, FRUS, *1964–68*, 18:766.

82. Rostow to Johnson, April 20, 1967, FRUS, *1964–68*, 18:796–97.

83. Katzenbach to Johnson, May 1, 1967, FRUS, *1964–68*, 18:814–17.

84. Embassy in Israel to State, July 17, 1968, FRUS, *1964–68*, vol. 20, *Arab-Israeli Dispute, 1967–1968* (Washington, DC: Government Printing Office, 2001), 421–22.

85. FRUS, *1964–68*, 20:548.

86. Harold Saunders, memo to Rostow, October 14, 1968, FRUS, *1964–68*, 20:555–56.

87. Memo of conversation between Johnson and Eban, October 21, 1968, FRUS, *1964–68*, 20:563.

88. Telegram from State to embassy in Israel, October 24, 1968, FRUS, *1964–68*, 20:567–70.

89. Memo of a telephone conversation between Rusk and Clifford, November 1, 1968, FRUS, *1964–68*, 20:585–86.

90. Memorandum of conversation, Washington, DC, November 4, 1968, FRUS, *1964–68*, 20:605.

91. In Warnke's memo of November 2, 1968, to Clifford (secretary of defense since March), on the assurances that should be required of Israel, "semi-annual inspection of specified sites" was laid down as a fourth condition of sale. FRUS, *1964–68*, 20:586–90.

92. Memo of conversation, November 4, 1968, FRUS, *1964–68*, 20:604–7.

93. Memo of conversation (including Rabin; Maj. Gen. Hod, IAF commander; Warnke; and Deputy Assistant Secretary of State Harry H. Schwartz),

November 5, 1968, FRUS, *1964–68*, 20:611–13. Israel was also seeking one hundred Skyhawks plus other military equipment.

94. Memo of conversation, November 8, 1968, FRUS, *1964–68*, 20:613–16.

95. Ibid., 20:616.

96. Draft memo for the record (drafted by Harry Schwartz), November 9, 1968, FRUS, *1964–68*, 20:618.

97. Ibid.

98. Ibid.

99. Hersh, *Samson Option*, 191

100. Memo of conversation, November 12, 1968, FRUS, *1964–68*, 20:627–30.

101. FRUS, *1964–68*, 20:630.

102. FRUS, *1964–68*, 20:661–62.

103. A. Cohen, *Israel and the Bomb*, 298.

104. Ibid., 341.

105. See Warner D. Farr, "The Third Temple Holy of Holies: Israel's Nuclear Weapons," Counterproliferation Papers Future Warfare Series No. 2, U.S. Air Force Counterproliferation Center, Air War College, Air University, Maxwell Air Force Base, AL, September 1999, http://rense.com/general35/isrnuk.htm.

106. Editorial note, n.d., FRUS, *1964–68*, 20:257–58.

107. Hersh, *Samson Option*, 186.

108. Ibid., 214.

109. Ibid., 179.

10. LBJ'S OTHER WAR

1. See Rusk's remarks, memo to Johnson, February 1, 1965, FRUS, *1964–68*, 18:285.

2. Allon, *Making of Israel's Army*, 63.

3. Seale, *Asad*, 129.

4. Stephens, *Nasser*, 468.

5. Seale, *Asad*, 129.

6. Stephens, *Nasser*, 468.

7. Richard B. Parker, *The Politics of Miscalculation in the Middle East* (Bloomington: Indiana University Press, 1993), 16.

8. Israel denied this.

9. *Yearbook of the United Nations, 1967* (New York: Office of Public Information, 1969), 165, report to Security Council, May 19.

10. Ibid., 169.

11. Johnson to Eshkol, May 2, 1967, FRUS, *1964–68*, vol. 19, *Arab-Israeli Crisis and War, 1967* (Washington, DC: Government Printing Office, 2004), n. 47.

12. Stephens, *Nasser*, 480.

13. Draft briefing by CIA director Helms for the president's Foreign Intelligence Advisory Board, Washington, DC, June 14, 1967, FRUS, *1964–68*, 19:494–99.

14. Lucius Battle, memo for the record of National Security Council meeting, May 24, 1967, FRUS, *1964–68*, 19:87–91.

15. Seale, *Asad*, 136.

16. Oren, *Six Days of War*, 80.

17. Memo for the record, May 26, 1967, FRUS, *1964–68*, 19:127–36.

18. Oren, *Six Days of War*, 91–92; for Eban's reference to Barbour's intervention, see Rusk to Johnson, May 26, 1967, FRUS, *1964–68*, 19:123.

19. Telegram from embassy, Tel Aviv, May 30, 1967, FRUS, *1964–68*, 19:180–81.

20. Norman G. Finkelstein, *Image and Reality of the Israel-Palestine Conflict* (London: Verso, 1995), 143.

21. Ilan Peleg, *Begin's Foreign Policy, 1977–1983: Israel's Move to the Right* (New York: Greenwood Press, 1987), 35.

22. Michael Jansen, *Dissonance in Zion* (London: Zed Books, 1987), 67; see also Noam Chomsky, *The Fateful Triangle: The United States, Israel and the Palestinians* (London: Pluto Press, 1983), 100.

23. Nutting, *Nasser*, 410; also Finkelstein, *Image and Reality*, 134.

24. Nutting, *Nasser*, 410.

25. Seale, *Asad*, 136, an account borne out by Oren, *Six Days of War*, 135, in a slightly different version.

26. Oren, *Six Days of War*, 134.

27. Ibid., 155, 133.

28. Ibid., 151.

29. Ibid., 155.

30. Stephens, *Nasser*, 486.

31. CIA memo, June 3, 1967, FRUS, *1964–68*, 19:270–72.

32. Seale, *Asad*, 137.

33. Oren, *Six Days of War*, quoting Rabin on 167; see 168 for numbers.

34. Memo of conversation between senior U.S. and Israeli officials, May 26, 1967, FRUS, *1964–68*, 19:118–22.

35. Memo of conversation, June 2, 1967, FRUS, *1964–68*, 19:247–51.

36. Eshkol to Johnson, May 30, 1967, FRUS, *1964–68*, 19:187.

37. Nutting, *Nasser*, 412.

38. Telegram from embassy in Israel to Department of State, May 27, 1967, FRUS, *1964–68*, 19:155.

39. Memo for record, June 1, 1967, FRUS, *1964–68*, 19:223–25.

40. Memo, Rostow to Johnson, June 2, 1967, FRUS, *1964–68*, 19:245.

41. Memo of conversation, June 2, 1967, FRUS, *1964–68*, 19:247–51.

42. Telegram from Department of State to embassy in Israel, June 1, 1967, FRUS, *1964–68*, 19:200.

43. Nutting, *Nasser*, 411.

44. Telegram from embassy in Portugal, summarizing Anderson's talks with Nasser, Lisbon, June 2, 1967, FRUS, *1964–68*, 19:233–37.

45. Minutes of the ninth meeting of the Middle East Control Group, 11:00 A.M., June 2, 1967, FRUS, *1964–68*, 19:283–86.

46. Johnson to Eshkol, draft, Washington, DC, May 21, 1967, FRUS, *1964–68*, 19:46–47, 46 n.

47. May 18, 1967, FRUS, *1964–68*, 19:16–18.

48. Telegram from embassy in Jordan, May 18, 1967, FRUS, *1964–68*, 19:16–18.

49. CIA memo, May 23, 1967, FRUS, *1964–68*, 1973–74.

50. CIA, "Israeli Estimate of the Israeli-Arab Crisis," May 25, 1967, FRUS, *1964–68*, 19:103–7.

51. Memo of conversation, May 25, 1967, Washington, DC, FRUS, *1964–68*, 19:109–12.

52. FRUS, *1964–68*, 19:122.

53. H.S. [Harold Saunders], memo for the record, May 26, 1967, FRUS, *1964–68*, 19:127–36.

54. Special report of Watch Committee, May 26, 1967, FRUS, *1964–68*, 19:137.

55. CIA intelligence memo, May 26, 1967, FRUS, *1964–68*, 19:138–39.

56. Memo of conversation, May 26, 1967, FRUS, *1964–68*, 19:140–46.

57. Record of National Security Council meeting, May 24, 1967, FRUS, *1964–68*, 19:87–91.

58. Records of National Security Council meeting, May 24, 1967, FRUS, *1964–68*, 19:87–91.

59. Memo of conversation, 8:40 P.M., May 26, 1967, FRUS, *1964–68*, 19:140–46.

60. Ibid., 143.

61. Telegram from Department of State to embassy in Israel, May 27, 1967, FRUS, *1964–68*, 19:162–64.

62. Telegram from embassy in Cairo, June 2, 1967, FRUS, *1964–68*, 19:252 n. 2.

63. William B. Quandt, *Peace Process: American Diplomacy and the Arab-Israeli Conflict since 1967* (Washington, DC: Brookings Institution, 1993), 50.

64. Parker, *Politics of Miscalculation*, 121.

65. Ibid., 121.

66. Rostow to Johnson, May 23, 1967, FRUS, *1964–68*, 19:72–73; see footnote for details of package.

67. Memo of conversation between Harman and Rostow, June 1, 1967, FRUS, *1964–68*, 19:198–200.

68. Memo from Saunders to Rostow, June 1, 1967, FRUS, *1964–68*, 19:220–21, plus footnote referring to further notes.

69. Memo from Rostow to Johnson on discussions with Evron, June 2, 1967, FRUS, *1964–68*, 19:244–46.

70. Memo of conversation, June 2, 1967, FRUS, *1964–68*, 19:247–51.

71. Little, *American Orientalism*, 302.

72. Telegram from U.S. embassy in Cairo, June 2, 1967, FRUS, *1964–68*, 19:254–57.

73. Dan Tschirgi, *The American Search for Mideast Peace* (New York: Praeger, 1989), 302.

74. Seale, *Asad*, 138.

75. By and large, Jewish Americans greatly disappointed him by coming out strongly against his policies on Vietnam.

76. *Yearbook of the United Nations, 1967*, 175.

77. CIA memo, June 5, 1967, FRUS, *1964–68*, 19:318–19.

78. CIA memo, June 5, 1967, FRUS, *1964–68*, 19:318–19.

79. Undated editorial note, FRUS, *1964–68*, 19:293.

80. Memo for the record, "Walt Rostow's Recollections of June 5 1967," Washington, DC, November 17, 1968, FRUS, *1964–68*, 19:287–92.

81. See note of Bundy's recollections, FRUS, *1964–68*, 19:310–11.

82. Telegram from Department of State to all posts, June 5, 1967, FRUS, *1964–68*, 19:307–9.

83. June 5, 1967, FRUS, *1964–68*, 19:297 n.

84. June 5, 1967, FRUS, *1964–68*, 19:305 n. 2.

85. David Hirst, "Rush to Annexation: Israel in Jerusalem," *Journal of Palestine Studies* 3 (Summer 1974): 3.

86. Telegram from Department of State to embassy in Jordan, June 6, 1967, FRUS, *1964–68*, 19:320 n.

87. State Department to embassy in Jordan, enc. message from Rusk, June 6, 1967, FRUS, *1964–68*, 19:324, 324 nn. 2 and 3.

88. Oren, *Six Days of War*, 279.

89. Kosygin to Johnson, June 10, 1967, 8:48 A.M., FRUS, *1964–68*, 19:409.

90. Johnson to Kosygin, June 10, 1967, FRUS, *1964–68*, 19:414.

91. Memo of conversation, quoting former Llewellyn Thompson, U.S. ambassador to the Soviet Union, June 10, 1967, FRUS, *1964–68*, 19:415, 413.

92. Memo of conversation, FRUS, *1964–68*, 19:417–18.

93. Telegram from embassy in Tel Aviv, July 10, 1967, FRUS, *1964–68*, 19:429–30.

94. Telegram from U.S. mission at UN to Department of State, June 9, 1967, FRUS, *1964–68*, 19:386–88.

95. Telegram from U.S. mission at UN to Department of State, June 22, 1967, FRUS, *1964–68*, 19:532–34.

96. Telegram from U.S. mission at UN to Department of State, September 23, 1967, FRUS, *1964–68*, 19:834–38.

97. Telegram from U.S. mission at UN to Department of State, September 23, 1967, FRUS, *1964–68*, 19:838 n. 4.

98. Account of conversation between Rostow and Harman, June 30, 1967, FRUS, *1964–68*, 19:587–89.

99. Telegram from Department of State to embassy in Israel, June 30, 1967, FRUS, *1964–68*, 19:587–89.

100. Memo from deputy press secretary to Johnson, July 14, 1967, FRUS, *1964–68*, 19:654–56.

101. The voting was 100–0 with 18 abstentions, including the United States.

102. Hirst, *Rush to Annexation*, 8.

103. Oren, *Six Days of War*, 307.

104. *Yearbook of the United Nations, 1967*, 210.

105. Hirst, *Rush to Annexation*, 10.

106. Ibid., 13–14.

107. *Yearbook of the United Nations, 1967*, 244.

108. Ibid., 17.

109. The figure given by the UN secretary-general's special representative in Jerusalem was three thousand. See *Yearbook of the United Nations, 1967*, 244.

110. Hirst, *Rush to Annexation*, 19–22.

111. Ibid., 19.

112. Oren, *Six Days of War*, 246.

113. *Yearbook of the United Nations, 1967*, 243–44.

114. Ibid., 216.

115. Ibid., 212.

116. Ibid., 238–42.

117. Ibid.

118. Seale, *Asad*, 141. Oren (*Six Days of War*, 306) refers to an Israeli military order prohibiting the expulsion of civilians.

119. *Yearbook of the United Nations, 1967*, 240.

120. Ibid.

121. Special National Intelligence Estimate, August 10, 1967, FRUS, *1964–68*, 19:770–74.

122. Stephens, *Nasser*, 503. Nutting, *Nasser*, 418, puts the figure at twenty thousand.

123. Nutting, *Nasser*, 418.

124. *Yearbook of the United Nations, 1967*, 213.

125. Memo, Warnke to Clifford, November 2, 1968, FRUS, *1964–68*, 20:587.

126. Abdel Magid Farid, *Nasser: The Final Years* (Reading, UK: Ithaca Press, 1994), 56.

127. For English-language text, see FRUS, *1964–68*, 20:1062–63.

128. Embassy in Iran to Department of State, November 20, 1968, FRUS, *1964–68*, 20:651.

129. Stephens, *Nasser*, 518.

130. Nutting, *Nasser*, 443.

131. Chomsky, *Fateful Triangle*, 106.

132. Rusk to embassy in Washington, April 8, 1968, FRUS, *1964–68*, 20:268–69.

133. Memo of conversation, "Reports of Israeli Plans for Settlements on Golan Heights," Washington, DC, December 4, 1968, FRUS, *1964–68*, 20:672–73.

134. Robert I. Friedman, *Zealots for Zion: Inside Israel's West Bank Settler Movement* (New Brunswick: Rutgers University Press, 1992), 16, 19.

135. The Gruner Report of June 30, 1977, is attached as "Report on Damage at Quneitra," Annex II of "Report of the Special Committee to Investigate Israeli Practices Affecting the Human Rights of the Population of the Occupied Territories," UN General Assembly Resolution A/32/284, October 27, 1977, http://domino.un.org/UNISPAL.NSF/361eea1cco8301c485256cf600606959/9 85e7582c282f25c05256584006b766f!OpenDocument.

136. *United Nations Resolutions on Palestine and the Arab-Israeli Conflict*, vol. 2, *1975–81*, ed. Regina S. Sharif (Washington, DC: Institute for Palestine Studies, 1988), 52, B.

137. Prevented by Israel from entering the occupied territories, the committee heard evidence in Cairo, Damascus, and Amman.

138. See "Report of the Special Committee to Investigate Israeli Practices Affecting the Human Rights of the Palestinian People and Other Arabs of the Occupied Territories," quoting from a report of the Syrian Ministry for Foreign Affairs, UN General Assembly Resolution A/54/325, September 8, 1999, 54th session, item 89 of the provisional agenda, http://domino.un.org/UNISPAL .NSF/f45643a78fcba719852560f6005987ad/82ac4adf343a9aba05256807004e40 23!OpenDocument.

139. Ibid.

140. Israel's water policies were the same on the occupied West Bank.

11. DISABLING LEBANON

1. Major Michael C. Jordan, "The 1973 Arab-Israeli War: Arab Policies, Strategies and Campaigns," http://globalsecurity.org/military/library/report/ 1997/Jordan.htm.

2. "Weapons of Mass Destruction: Strategic Doctrine," n.d., http://global security.org/wmd/world/israel/doctrine.htm (accessed October 18, 2007).

3. Joseph Finklestone, *Anwar Sadat: Visionary Who Dared* (London: Frank Cass, 1996), 115.

4. See Uri Avnery, "Pussycat," March 31, 2007, http://zope.gush-shalom .org/home/en/channels/avnery/1175376939.

5. Begin described Jabotinsky as "our teacher, master and father." See Peleg, *Begin's Foreign Policy*, 13.

6. Chomsky, *Fateful Triangle*, 112.

7. Amnon Kapeliouk, "Begin and 'the Beasts,'" *New Statesman*, June 25, 1982, quoted in George W. Ball, *Error and Betrayal in Lebanon* (Washington, DC: Foundation for Middle East Peace, 1984).

8. See Israeli Commission of Inquiry into the Events at the Refugee Camps in Beirut, "Final Report of the Israeli Commission of Inquiry into the Events at the Refugee Camps in Beirut," *Journal of Palestine Studies* 12 (Spring 1983): 89–116.

9. Christopher Sykes, *Crossroads to Israel: Palestine from Balfour to Bevin* (London: Nel Mentor, 1967), 256.

10. Jimmy Carter, *Keeping Faith: Memoirs of a President* (Fayetteville: University of Arkansas Press, 1995), 287; Seale, *Asad*, 292.

11. Carter, *Keeping Faith*, 295.

12. Ibid., 295.

13. Ibid., 307.

14. The right-wing Falangist (Kata'ib in Arabic) Party was founded in the 1930s by Pierre Gemayel.

15. Walid Khalidi, *Conflict and Violence in Lebanon: Confrontation in the Middle East* (Cambridge, MA: Center for International Studies, Harvard University, 1983), 127.

16. Ibid., 128.

17. Later the United States confirmed that Israel had used cluster bombs in the invasion, in violation of the 1952 Mutual Defense Assistance Agreement.

18. *United Nations Resolutions*, 2:184–85.

19. Carter, *Keeping Faith*, 321.

20. Ibid., 323.

21. Ibid., 343.

22. Jonathan Randal, *The Tragedy of Lebanon: Christian Warlords, Israeli Adventurers and American Bunglers*, rev. ed. (London: Hogarth Press, 1990), 212.

23. Fayez A. Sayegh, "The Camp David Agreement and the Palestine Problem," *Journal of Palestine Studies* 8 (Winter 1979): 26.

24. Ibid., 6.

25. Ibid., 16, transcript of remarks made by Carter to reporters on September 28.

26. Carter, *Keeping Faith*, 424.

27. Ibid., diary entry for March 2, 1979.

28. Carter, *Keeping Faith*, 430.

29. For a critique of the framework for peace, see Sayegh, "Camp David Agreement," 3–40.

30. Finklestone, *Anwar Sadat*, 275.

31. UN Department of Public Information, *The Blue Helmets: A Review of United Nations Peace-Keeping*, 3rd ed. (New York: UN Department of Public Information, 1996), 93.

32. Israeli soldiers were present when Haddad's militiamen herded dozens of Shi'i villagers into a mosque and slaughtered them. Randal, *Tragedy of Lebanon*, 218.

33. *United Nations Resolutions*, 2:184–85.

34. They remained in the Shaba'a farms area, renaming it Mt. Dov.

35. UN Department of Public Information, *Blue Helmets*, 91.

36. Ibid., 94.

37. Ibid., 94–95.

38. Robert Fisk, *Pity the Nation: Lebanon at War* (New York: Oxford University Press, 1992), 152.

39. *Yearbook of the United Nations, 1982* (New York: UN Department of Public Information, 1985), 425.

40. Ronald Reagan, *An American Life* (New York: Simon and Schuster, 1990), 413.

41. Ibid., 413.

42. Ball, *Error and Betrayal,* 33.

43. Alexander M. Haig Jr., *Caveat: Realism, Reagan and Foreign Policy* (New York: Macmillan, 1984), 329.

44. Ibid.

45. See Haig, *Caveat,* 317.

46. See Reagan, *American Life,* 419.

47. Abu Nidal (Sabri al Banna) had actually been declared a renegade by the PLO and sentenced to death for numerous crimes, including the assassination of two early advocates of the two-state solution, Issam Sartawi and Said Hammami.

48. *Yearbook of the United Nations, 1982,* 433.

49. Ze'ev Schiff and Ehud Ya'ari, *Israel's Lebanon War* (London: George Allen and Unwin, 1986), 105.

50. One Norwegian soldier was killed by shrapnel as they moved forward.

51. The guest of honor at the banquet was Senator James Mills, the new president of the California State Senate. He later described the occasion in an article for the August 1985 edition of *San Diego* magazine. See Andrew Lang, "The Politics of Armageddon: Reagan Links Biblical Prophecy with Nuclear War," *Convergence* [n.d., 1980s], www.prop1.org/inaugur/85reagan/85rrarm.htm.

52. Rev. Don Wagner, "Beyond Armageddon: Challenging Christian Zionism," May 27, 2004, www.christianzionism.org.

53. Ibid.

54. Ronnie Dugger, "Does Reagan Expect a Nuclear Armageddon?" *Washington Post,* April 18, 1984, quoted in Wagner, "Beyond Armageddon."

55. The United States "considered the possibility of a nuclear war with the Soviet Union more seriously during the early Reagan years than at any time since the Cuban missile crisis." James Mann, "The Armageddon Plan," *Atlantic Monthly,* March 2004, www.commondreams.org/views04/0318-14.htm.

56. Quoted in Kathleen Christison, "Blind Spots: Official Myths about the Middle East," *Journal of Palestine Studies* 17 (Winter 1988): 47.

57. Reagan, *American Life,* 414.

58. Ibid., 421.

59. Haig, *Caveat,* 326.

60. Ibid., 330.

61. Ibid., 332.

62. *Yearbook of the United Nations, 1982,* 429.

63. Haig, *Caveat,* 333.

64. Randal, *Tragedy of Lebanon*, 245.

65. Schiff and Yaʾari, *Israel's Lebanon War*, 69.

66. Haig, *Caveat*, 333.

67. Ibid.

68. Haig, *Caveat*, 335.

69. Ibid., 335.

70. Reagan, *American Life*, 419.

71. Ibid., 422.

72. Haig, *Caveat*, 342.

73. Chomsky, *Fateful Triangle*, 215.

74. Haig, *Caveat*, 339.

75. Ball, *Error and Betrayal*, 37.

76. Randal, *Tragedy of Lebanon*, 257.

77. Ibid.

78. Fisk, *Pity the Nation*, 322.

79. For discussion of the plan and Begin's reaction, see Ball, *Error and Betrayal*, 52–54.

80. Ibid., 53.

81. Schiff and Yaʾari, *Israel's Lebanon War*, 196.

82. Ibid., 245.

83. The militia arm of the Lebanese Front was known as the Lebanese Forces.

84. LF militia commander Samir Geaʿgea was implicated with Bashir in the killing of Tony Frangieh and the attack on the headquarters of the National Liberal Party militia. In June 1994 Geaʿgea and eight other LF members were referred to trial for the bombing in February of the Sayyidat al Najat (Lady of Deliverance) Maronite church in Jounieh. In July 1996 Geaʿgea was found not guilty of the church bombing but sentenced to ten years' imprisonment on a charge of maintaining a militia in the form of a political party. He was subsequently sentenced to death for the attempted assassination in 1978 of former defense minister Michel Murr (Greek Orthodox), the assassination in 1987 of former prime minister Rashid Karami (Sunni Muslim), the assassination of Dany Chamoun in 1991, and the assassination in the same year of the LF leader Elias al Zayek. All sentences were commuted to life imprisonment. The Maronite Patriarch, Nasrallah Sfeir, petitioned for his release on the grounds that of all the militia leaders active during the civil war he was the only one charged. On July 18, 2005, the Chamber of Deputies passed an amnesty law and Geaʿgea was released after eleven years in prison. Amnesty International strongly criticized the judicial process and the conditions in which Geaʿgea was held at a Ministry of Defense detention center. See Amnesty International, "Samir Geaʿgea and Jirjis al Khouri: Torture and Unfair Trial," November 23, 2004, MDE 18/003/2004, http://web.amnesty.org/library/index/engmde/180032004.

85. Schiff and Yaʾari, *Israel's Lebanon War*, 211.

86. Ibid., 240.

87. *Yearbook of the United Nations, 1982*, 467.

88. Leila Shahid, "Testimonies. The Sabra and Shatila Massacres: Eye-Witness Reports," *Journal of Palestine Studies* 32 (Autumn 2002): 39.

89. Israeli Commission of Inquiry, "Final Report," 91.

90. Ibid., 97 98.

91. Ibid., 98.

92. Ibid., 95.

93. Shahid, "Testimonies," 40.

94. Ibid., 41.

95. Israeli Commission of Inquiry, "Final Report," 103–4.

96. Shahid, "Testimonies," 41.

97. Ibid., 45.

98. Ibid., 44–45.

99. United Nations, "Report of the Secretary-General in Pursuance of Security Council Resolution 521 (1982)," S/15408, Annex I, September 20, 1982, http://domino.un.org/UNISPAL.NSF/2ee9468747556b2d85256cf60060d2a6/d418389102291a1505256609005b9649!OpenDocument.

100. In January 2002, shortly after disclosing that he intended to tell a Belgian war crimes tribunal all he knew about Sharon's role at Sabra and Shatila, Hobeika was assassinated by a car bomb in Beirut.

101. See Sean MacBride et al., *The Report of the International Commission to Enquire into Reported Violations of International Law by Israel during Its Invasion of Lebanon* (London: Ithaca Press, 1983).

102. *Christian Science Monitor*, Lebanese police tally based on figures provided by hospitals, clinics, and civil defense centers, quoted in Ball, *Error and Betrayal*, 47.

103. *United Nations Resolutions on Palestine and the Arab-Israeli Conflict*, vol. 3, *1982–1986*, ed. Michael Simpson (Washington, DC: Institute of Palestine Studies, 1988), Resolution 37/86 (A, B, C, D, and E) and Resolution 37/88 (A, B, C, D, E, F, and G), 25–35.

104. *Yearbook of the United Nations, 1982*, 526 and 543.

105. *United Nations Resolutions*, 3:36–54, Resolution 37/20 (A, B, C, D, E, F, G, H, I, J, and K); Resolution 37/122; Resolution 37/123 (A, B, C, D, E, and F); Resolution 37/134.

106. Ibid., 3:54, Resolution 37/135.

107. Ibid., 3:55, Resolution 37/222.

108. Fisk, *Pity the Nation*, 482.

109. Reagan, *American Life*, 445.

110. Fisk, *Pity the Nation*, 520.

12. INTO THE GULF

1. Fourteen had been released for medical or other reasons.

2. "President Bush Addresses Nation on the Capture of Saddam Hussein," December 14, 2003, www.whitehouse.gov/news/releases/2003/12/20031214-3.html.

3. Said K. Aburish, *Saddam Hussein: The Politics of Revenge* (London: Bloomsbury, 2000), 42.

4. Ibid., 45.

5. See Richard Sale, "Exclusive: Saddam Key in Early CIA Plot," April 10, 2003, www.upi.com/archive/view.php?archive=1&StoryID=20030410-070214-6557r.

6. Kurt Nimmo, "Saddam Hussein: Taking Out the CIA's Trash," *Dissident Voice*, August 2, 2003, www.dissidentvoice.org/Articles7/Nimmo_Saddam-CIA.htm. For the original article by Roger Morris, see "A Tyrant 40 Years in the Making," *New York Times*, March 14, 2003.

7. Peter Sluglett, *Iraq: Reintegrating the Pariah?* (Bonn: Friedrich Ebert Stiftung, 1999), www.fes.de/fulltext/stabsabteilung/00840.htm.

8. R. Morris, "Tyrant."

9. Aburish, *Saddam Hussein*, 73.

10. Kanan Makiya [Samir al Khalil, pseud.], "Iraq and Its Future," *New York Review of Books*, April 11, 1991, www.nybooks.com.

11. See the Iraq Survey Group, *Comprehensive Report of the Special Adviser to the DCI on Iraq's WMD* (Iraq Survey Group Final Report), 3 vols., ed. Charles Duelfer (Washington, DC: Government Printing Office, 2004), 1:21–22. Charles Duelfer, special adviser to the director of Central Intelligence, attached addenda to the original report in March 2005. For full report, see www.globalsecurity.org/wmd/library/report/2004/isg-final-report/.

12. Along the border with Iran, Patriotic Union of Kurdistan (PUK) *peshmerga* guerrillas were collaborating with Iranian forces against a common enemy. This was the regime's reason and justification for the wholesale assault on the Kurdish civilian population. The word *Anfal* has the meaning of "booty," "plunder," or "loot."

13. Kanan Makiya, *Cruelty and Silence: War, Tyranny, Uprising and the Arab World* (New York: W. W. Norton, 1993), 152.

14. Ibid., 155.

15. Although Iraq was generally held responsible for the attack, a paper issued by the Strategic Studies Institute of the U.S. Army War College rates a mention. It blamed Iran, which it said had responded to an Iraqi mustard gas attack with an infinitely more lethal combination of hydrogen-cyanide shells. See Dr. Stephen Pelletiere and Lieutenant Colonel Douglas Johnson, *Lessons Learned: The Iran-Iraq War*, FMFRP 3–203, U.S. Marine Corps Historical Publication, 2000, www.fas.org/man/dod-101/ops/war/docs/3203. A U.S. Defense Intelligence Agency (DIA) report concluded that most of the casualties had been caused by cyanogen chloride, a blood agent not known to have been used by Iraq before. See Roger Trilling, "Fighting Words: The Administration Builds Up Its Pretext for Attacking Iraq," *Village Voice*, May 1–7, 2002, www.villagevoice.com. Following the invasion of Iraq in 2003, the captured Iraqi foreign minister, Tariq Aziz, insisted that Iran had been responsible for the chemical weapons attack on Halabja.

16. For a detailed account of the Anfal campaign, see Human Rights Watch, *Genocide in Iraq: The Anfal Campaign against the Kurds*, Middle East Watch Report (New York: Human Rights Watch, July 1993), www.hrw.org/rcports/1993/iraqanfal/.

17. "Saddam Cousin Says Actions against Kurds Justified," January 24, 2007, *USA Today*, www.usatoday.com/news/world/iraq/2007-01-24-chemicalali_x.htm.

18. Iraq Survey Group, *Comprehensive Report*, 1:21–22.

19. For a full account of their conversation, see "The Glaspie Transcript: Saddam Meets the U.S. Ambassador," in *The Gulf War Reader: History, Documents, Opinions*, ed. Micah L. Sifry and Christopher Cerf (New York: Times Books, 1991), 122–33.

20. Iraq Survey Group, *Comprehensive Report*, the section "Desire, Dominance and Deterrence through WMD: Saddam's Role in WMD Policy."

21. For text, see www.fas.org/news/UN/iraq/sres/sres0678.htm.

22. "Proceedings of Security Council, February 13, 1991," in *Iraq and Kuwait: The Hostilities and Their Aftermath*, ed. M. Weller, Cambridge International Documents Series (Cambridge: Grotius Publications, 1993), 27.

23. Human Rights Watch, *Needless Deaths in the Gulf War: Civilian Casualties during the Air Campaign and Violations of the Laws of War* (New York: Human Rights Watch, 1991), 77.

24. "Proceedings of Security Council," 39.

25. See Afsaneh Najmabadi, "Depoliticisation of a Rentier State," in *The Rentier State*, vol. 2, ed. Hazem Beblawi and Giacomo Luciani (London: Croom Helm, 1987), 211–27.

26. Kenneth R. Timmerman, *The Death Lobby: How the West Armed Iraq* (New York: Bantam Books, 1992), 122; Richard Hornik, "Middle East with a Little Help from Friends," *Time*, June 11, 1990, www.time.com/time/magazine/article/0,9171,970343,00.html.

27. Timmerman, *Death Lobby*, 93.

28. Irene Gendzier, "Dying to Forget: The US and Iraq's Weapons of Mass Destruction," *Logos* 2 (Winter 2003): 20, http://logosonline.home.igc.org/gendzier_iraq.html.

29. See "U.S. Tore Out 8000 Pages of Iraq Weapons Dossier," Sunday Herald (Glasgow), December 22, 2002, http://findarticles.com/p/articlesmi_qn4156/is_20021222/ai_n12579783.

30. "UN Row Erupts over Iraq Dossier," BBC News, December 10, 2002, http://news.bbc.co.uk/2/hi/middle_east/250617.stm.

31. See Neil Mackay, "British Firms Armed Saddam with His Weapons," *Sunday Herald* (Glasgow), February 23, 2003; also Amnesty International, "Who Armed Iraq?" *Terror Trade Times*, no. 4 (June 2003), AI Index 31/002/2003, http://web.amnesty.org/pages/ttt4-article_7-eng.

32. State Department official William Rope, quoted in Irene Gendzier, "Democracy, Deception and the Arms Trade: The US, Iraq and Weapons of

Mass Destruction," *Middle East Report* 234 (Spring 2005), www.merip.org/
mer/mer234/gendzier.html.

33. Joyce Battle, ed., "Shaking Hands with Saddam Hussein: The US Tilts
towards Iraq, 1980–1984," George Washington University, National Security
Archive, Electronic Briefing Book No. 82, February 25, 2003, Document 4,
www.gwu.edu/%7Ensarchiv/NSAEBB/NSAEBB82/index.htm.

34. Letter from Hammadi, April 15, in Battle, "Shaking Hands," Document 7.

35. Ibid., Document 10.

36. Center for Public Integrity, "Windfalls of War: Bechtel Group Inc."
www.publicintegrity.org/wow/bio.aspx?act=pro&ddlC=6.

37. Battle, "Shaking Hands," Document 34, commentary by Joyce Battle.

38. See Human Rights Watch, "Iraq," in *Human Rights Watch World
Report 1989* (New York: Human Rights Watch, 1989), www.hrw.org/reports/
1989/WR89/Iraq.htm.

39. Jeffrey Richelson, ed., "Saddam's Iron Grip: Intelligence Reports on
Saddam Hussein's Reign," George Washington University, National Secu-
rity Archive, Electronic Briefing Book No. 167, www.gwu.edu/~nsarchiv/
NSAEBB/NSAEBB167/index.htm, Document 3, Director of Central Intelli-
gence, Special National Intelligence Estimate (SNIE) 36.2–82, "Implications of
Iran's Victory over Iraq," June 8, 1982.

40. Howard Teicher, affidavit, U.S. District Court, Southern District of
Florida, July 31, 1995, reproduced in "The Teicher Affidavit: Iraqgate,"
www.webcom.com/~lpease/collections/hidden/teicher.htm.

41. Battle, "Shaking Hands," Document 17.

42. Ibid., Document 34.

43. Teicher, affidavit.

44. Michael Dobbs, "US Had Key Role in Iraq Buildup," *Washington Post,*
December 30, 2002, A01.

45. J. B. Penn, undersecretary of state for farm and foreign agricultural
services, quoted in "Iraq's Grain Production Could Double," *Southwest Farm
Press,* May 15, 2003, http://southwestfarmpress.com.

46. Teicher, affidavit.

47. Ibid.

48. Alan Friedman, *Spider's Web: Bush, Saddam, Thatcher and the Decade
of Deceit* (London: Faber and Faber, 1993), 53.

49. Teicher, affidavit.

50. Friedman, *Spider's Web,* the chapter "The Chilean Connection,"
45–55.

51. Gendzier, "Democracy, Deception."

52. Hornik, "Middle East."

53. See Lawrence S. Eagleburger, "US Policy toward Iraq and the Role of
the CCC Program, 1989–90," statement before the House Committee on
Banking, Finance, and Urban Affairs, May 25, 1992, http://findarticles.com/p/
articles/mi_m1584/is_n21_v3/ai_12511751.

54. See Allan I. Mendelowitz, director, International Trade and Finance Issues, General Government Division, "Agriculture's Export Credit Programs: Delays in Accessing Records Relating to Iraq," testimony before the House Committee on Banking, Finance, and Urban Affairs, T-GGD-92-47, May 29, 1992, http://archive.gao.gov/gov/t2pbat6/146760.pdf.

55. Friedman, *Spider's Web*, 247.

56. As described by Senior Judge Marvin H. Shoob during a hearing in the Atlanta District Court on August 23, 1993. For full transcript, see "Judicial Order in the BNL Case Issued by Judge Marvin Shoob on August 23, 1993," www.pinknoiz.com/covert/shoob2.html.

57. Ibid.

58. For the complete testimony of Henry B. Gonzalez, see "The Banca Nazionale Del Lavoro Scandal: High-Level Politics Try to Hide the Evidence," www.globalsecurity.org/military/library/congress/1992_cr/h920914g.htm.

59. According to a bank official quoted in Human Rights Watch, "Iraq."

60. Ibid.

61. Timmerman, *Death Lobby*, 454–57.

62. Gendzier, "Democracy, Deception."

63. Friedman, *Spider's Web*, censored official text, 320–23.

64. George Lardner Jr., "Gonzalez's Iraq Expose—Hill Chairman Details US Prewar Courtship," *Washington Post*, March 22, 1992.

65. Teicher, affidavit.

66. Gendzier, "Democracy, Deception."

67. See Geoffrey Holland, "United States Exports of Biological Materials to Iraq: Compromising the Credibility of International Law," *Deep Blade Journal*, June 2005, http://deepblade.net/journal/Holland_JUNE2005.pdf.

68. Retired senior defense intelligence officer Col. Walter P. Lang, quoted in Patrick E. Tyler, "Officers Say US Aided Iraq in War Despite Use of Gas," *New York Times*, August 18, 2002.

69. For transcript, see U.S. Department of State, "Chemical Weapons and the Iran-Iraq War," March 5, 1984, http://findarticles.com/p/articles/mi_m1079/is_v84/ai_3200104. For Iraqi reaction, see document 5, "Saddam Hussein: More Secret History," December 18, 2003, National Security Archive, www.gwu.edu/~nsarchiv/NSAEBB/NSABB107.

70. Timmerman, *Death Lobby*, 82–84.

71. Tyler, "Officers Say."

72. Norm Dixon, "The Ties That Blind: How Reagan Armed Saddam with Chemical Weapons," *Counterpunch*, June 17, 2004, quoting a Washington Post report by Bob Woodward, www.counterpunch.org/dixon06172004.html.

73. Tyler, "Officers Say."

74. Ibid.

75. Gendzier, "Dying to Forget," 21, quoting from a *New York Times* article.

76. See Iraq Survey Group, *Comprehensive Report*, the section "Iraq's Chemical Warfare Program."

77. Ibid.

78. Richard Russell, "Iraq's Chemical Weapons Legacy: What Others Might Learn," *Middle East Journal* 59 (Spring 2005): 194.

79. See James J. Tuite III, "Report on the Fallout from the Destruction of the Iraqi Chemical Research, Production and Storage Facilities into Areas Occupied by US Military Personnel during the 1991 Persian Gulf War," 1996, www.chronicillnet.org/PGWS/tuite/science6.html.

80. See U.S. Senate, Committee on Banking, Housing, and Urban Affairs., "United States Dual-Use Exports to Iraq and Their Impact on the Health of the Persian Gulf War Veterans," http://chronicillnet.org/PGWS/tuite/hearings .html, transcript of the meeting of the Banking, Housing and Urban Affairs Committee, Wednesday, May 25, 1994, chaired by Senator Donald W. Riegle Jr. and Ranking Member Alphonse d'Amato. James J. Tuite III was the committee's principal investigator. The report that came out of those hearings was U.S. Senate, Committee on Banking, Housing, and Urban Affairs, *United States Chemical and Biological Warfare–Related Dual-Use Exports to Iraq and the Possible Impact on the Health Consequences of the Persian Gulf War: A Report of Chairman Donald W. Riegle Jr. and Ranking Member Alphonse D'Amato of the Committee on Banking, Housing and Urban Affairs with Respect to Export Administration, United States Senate, 103d Congress, 2nd Session, May 25, 1994 [Riegle Report]*, www.gulfweb.org/ report/riegle1.html.

81. See "The Australia Group: An Introduction," www.australiagroup .net/en/intro.htm.

82. U.S. Senate, "United States Dual-Use Exports."

83. COCOM, a seventeen-member organization of all NATO countries except Iceland, but including Japan and Australia, was used to block strategic material going to the Warsaw Pact countries and China for more than forty years. On November 16, 1993, with the Cold War over, members met in the Hague and decided to abolish it in favor of a new multilateral export control arrangement.

84. U.S. Senate, "United States Dual-Use Exports," testimony given by Dr. John Kriese, chief officer for ground forces at the Defense Intelligence Agency.

85. Ibid.

86. Ibid.

87. Ibid., evidence given by Dr. Oehler.

88. See Amnesty International, "Who Armed Iraq?"

89. Holland, "United States Exports."

90. U.S. Senate, Committee on Banking, Housing, and Urban Affairs, "Second Staff Report on US Chemical and Biological Warfare-Related Dual-Use Exports to Iraq and the Possible Impact on the Health Consequences of the War (May 25 1994)," http://chronicillnet.org/PGWS/tuite/2NDINDEX. HTM; see findings in introduction.

91. Ibid., ch. 1, "Iraqi Chemical and Biological Warfare Capability," the section "U.S. Exports of Biological Materials to Iraq."

92. See Michael Barletta and Christina Ellington, "Foreign Suppliers to Iraq's Biological Weapons Program Obtain Microbial Seed Stock for Standard or Novel Agent," November 1998, Centre for Nonproliferation Studies, http://cns.miis.edu/research/wmdme/flow/iraq/seed.htm.

93. Ibid.

94. Holland, "United States Exports."

95. U.S. Senate, "United States Dual-Use Exports."

96. Human Rights Watch, "Iraq."

97. "Conduct of the Persian Gulf War, Final Report to Congress, April 1992," in Weller, *Iraq and Kuwait*, 306.

98. Human Rights Watch, *Needless Deaths*, 103.

99. "Letter from UN Secretary-General to President of Security Council, March 20, 1991," in Weller, *Iraq and Kuwait*, 598.

100. Ibid., 599.

101. Ibid., 593–97, note by UN secretary-general enclosing report of WHO/UNICEF Special Mission to Iraq, March 4, 1991.

102. Defense Intelligence Agency, "Iraq Water Treatment Vulnerabilities as of 18 Jan 91," www.gulflink.osd.mil/declassdocs/dia/19950901/950901_511rept_91.html.

103. See Colonel John A. Warden III, "The Enemy as a System," *Airpower Journal* 9 (Spring 1995): 40–55, www.airpower.maxwell.af.mil/airchronicles/apj/apj95/spr95_files/warden.htm.

104. See biographical notes in *Battlefield of the Future: Twenty-first Century Warfare Issues*, ed. Barry R. Schneider and Lawrence E. Grinter (Maxwell Air Force Base, AL: Air University Press, 1991), www.airpower.maxwell.af.mil/airchronicles/battle/bftoc.html.

105. Warden, "Enemy as a System."

106. Ibid.

107. Colonel John A. Warden III, "Air Theory for the Twenty-first Century," in Schneider and Grinter, *Battlefield of the Future*, ch. 4.

108. Ibid.

109. The estimate is an official Iraqi figure. Other estimates put the number of dead at 800 and even higher. See the estimate of 1,186 dead, given by a woman who lost nine of her ten children in the bombing, in James Buchan, "Children of the Storm," Iraq Special Report, *Guardian*, September 25, 1999.

110. "Excerpts from Briefing by Lieut. General Thomas Kelly and Captain David Herrington, February 13, 1991," in Weller, *Iraq and Kuwait*, 260.

111. Ibid., 297.

112. Human Rights Watch, *Needless Deaths*, 133.

113. Rick Atkinson, *Crusade: The Untold Story of the Persian Gulf War* (Boston: Houghton Mifflin, 1993), 396–97.

114. "Conduct of the Persian Gulf War," 305.

115. See Colin L. Powell, "U.S Forces: Challenges Ahead," *Foreign Affairs* 71 (Winter 1992–93): 32–45.

116. Atkinson, *Crusade*, 397.

117. See the account by the *Newsweek* reporter Patrick J. Sloyan, "What Bodies?" *APF Reporter* 20, no. 3 (2003), www.aliciapatterson.org/APF2003/Sloyan/Sloyan.html.

118. Weller, *Iraq and Kuwait,* 305.

119. Ibid.

120. Aburish, *Saddam Hussein,* 305.

121. Atkinson, *Crusade,* 451.

122. Ibid., 450.

123. Ibid., 451.

124. Quotes and detail from Seymour Hersh, "Annals of War: Overwhelming Force. What Happened in the Final Days of the Gulf War," *New Yorker,* May 22, 2000.

125. Ibid.

126. President George H. Bush, "Address before a Join Session of the Congress on the Cessation of the Persian Gulf Conflict," March 6, 1991, c-span.org/executive/transcript.asp?cat-current_event&code=Bush_admin&year=0391.

127. Atkinson, *Crusade,* 194.

128. For full text, see http://bushlibrary.tamu.edu/research/directives.html.

129. Iraq Survey Group, *Comprehensive Report,* the section "Desire, Dominance and Deterrence through WMD: Saddam's Role in WMD Policy." Discussion recorded in seized tape.

130. Russell, "Iraq's Chemical Weapons Legacy."

131. See James J. Tuite III, "1991 Persian Gulf War: Direct and Indirect Chemical Warfare Agent and Related Exposures," http://chronicillnet.org/PGWS/tuite/science2.html. Also see Tuite, "Report on the Fallout."

132. U.S. Senate, "Second Staff Report," ch. 2, "Gulf War Syndrome: The Case for Chemical/Biological Agent Exposure."

133. Ibid., ch. 3.

134. Ibid.

135. Ibid., see "Findings."

136. Ibid.

137. See Hans von Sponeck, letter to the *Guardian,* December 17, 2000.

138. Although civilians died in the attack, the U.S. administration tried to get the message out that "our quarrel is not with the Iraqi people," as the secretary of state, Madeleine Albright, told a press briefing in Edinburgh on November 14, 1997. "Transcript: Albright, Cook Discuss Increasing Pressure on Iraq," November 14, 1997, www.fas.org/news/iraq/1997/11/97111402_npo.html.

139. Established under UN Security Council Resolution 1284.

140. Larry Everest, "Hans von Sponeck: The Inside Story of US Sanctions on Iraq," *Revolutionary Worker,* December 23, 2001, http://rwor.org/a/v23/1130-39/1132/sponeck_iraq.htm.

141. Remarks by the Cuban delegate, Alarcon de Quesada, during debate in the Security Council on February 13, 1991, quoted in Weller, *Iraq and Kuwait*, 27.

142. Both of these men had been appointed UN assistant secretary-general.

143. See Dennis Halliday, "Death for Oil," interview by Amira Howeidy, *Al Ahram Weekly*, July 13–19, 2000, http://weekly.ahram.org.eg/2000/490/intrvw.htm.

144. Ibid.

145. James Bovard, "Iraqi Sanctions and American Intentions: Blameless Carnage?" *Freedom Daily*, pt. 1, February 9, 2004; pt. 2, February 11, 2004, Future of Freedom Foundation, www.fff.org.freedom/fd0401c.asp and www.fff.org.freedom/fd040c.asp.

146. See "Iraq," www.unicef.org/infobycountry/iraq_statistics.html, for the under-five infant mortality rate in 1990 and "Table 1: Basic Indicators," www.unicef.org/sowc05/english/Table1_E.xls, for the 2003 figure.

147. See Everest, "Hans von Sponeck."

148. Before the war contracts for the reconstruction and redevelopment of the oil industry had been awarded to French, Algerian, Russian, and Chinese concerns.

149. Hans von Sponeck, "Voices on Iraq: Hans von Sponeck," interview by Mark Tran, *Guardian*, March 28, 2004, www.guardian.co.uk/Iraq/voices/story/0,,1164765,00.html.

150. "Bush Urges End to Sanctions," *New York Times*, April 17, 2003.

13. GEORGE THE SON

1. In an editors' note published on May 26, 2004, the *New York Times* admitted that its reporting was "not as rigorous as it should have been." This minor mea culpa was followed up more vigorously a few days later by the newspaper's public editor, Dan Okrent. He referred to flawed reporting, "breathless stories," and unconfirmed links and articles that "pushed Pentagon assertions so aggressively you could almost sense epaulets sprouting on the shoulders of editors." He regarded the failures as institutional, not individual. See Dan Okrent, "The Public Editor: Weapons of Mass Destruction or Mass Distraction," *New York Times*, May 30, 2004, http://query.nytimes.com/gst/fullpage.html?res=9C06E7DC1E3EF933A05756C0A9629C8B63. The paper's own judgment is to be found in "The Times and Iraq," *New York Times*, May 26, 2004, www.nytimes.com/2004/05/26/international/middleeast/26FTE_NOTE.html?ex=1185854.

2. See "President's Remarks at the United Nations General Assembly," September, 12, 2002, www.whitehouse.gov/news/releases/2002/09/20020912-1.html.

3. Colin Powell, "Remarks to the United Nations Security Council," February 5, 2003, www.state.gov/secretary/former/powell/remarks/2003/17300.htm.

4. "British Response," PBS NewsHour, February 5, 2003, www.pbs
.org/newshour/bb/middle_east/iraq/britain_2-5.html.

5. See Prime Minister's Office, "Iraq: Its Infrastructure of Concealment,
Deception and Intimidation," January 30, 2003, ww.number10.gov.uk/output/
page1470.asp.

6. General Powell did not mention the allegation that Iraq had been trying
to buy yellowcake from Niger, but by the time he spoke, the "document" on
which this charge was based had been discredited beyond redemption. Protag-
onists of the war used it against Iraq for months, but when the "evidence" was
finally produced, the IAEA took only a few hours to determine that the letter
on which the claim was based was a forgery, that its provenance was uncertain,
but that apparently it had been fed into the general propaganda mill through
the Italian government's intelligence services.

7. See Seymour M. Hersh, "Annals of National Security: Selective Intelli-
gence. Donald Rumsfeld Has His Own Special Sources. Are They Reliable?"
New Yorker, May 12, 2003, www.newyorker.com. The inspectors were withdrawn from Iraq by the UN before the Desert Fox air strike authorized by
President Clinton in December 1998 and were not allowed to return by the
Iraqi government until November 18, 2002. Iraqi government accusations that
the UN inspections were being used as a cover for spying were denied by the
U.S. administration but substantiated independently by the revelations of
arms inspector Scott Ritter.

8. Jeremy Salt, "Falluja: Slaughter of a City," *Arena*, no. 77 (June–July
2005): 30–32.

9. Quoted in Adam Wolfson, "Conservatives and Neoconservatives," *Public Interest*, no. 154 (Winter 2004), http://finadarticles.com/p/articles/mi
_m0377/is_154/ai_n6062428. The journal closed down, after forty years in
print, with the Spring 2005 issue.

10. See Jihad al Khazen, "Neo-conservative Ascendancy in the George W.
Bush Administration," *Al Hayat*, June 4, 2004, http://dc.indymedia.org/
newswire/display/75151/index.php.

11. Robert Locke, "Leo Strauss, Conservative Mastermind," *Front
PageMagazine.com*, May 31, 2002, http://frontpagemag.com/Articles/Read
Article.asp?ID=1233.

12. Shadia Drury, quoted in Danny Postel, "Noble Lies and Perpetual War:
Leo Strauss, the Neo-Cons and Iraq," *Open Democracy*, October 10, 2003,
http://informationclearinghouse.info/articles5010.htm. Also see Shadia B.
Drury, "Leo Strauss and the Grand Inquisitor," *Free Inquiry* 24 (May 7, 2007),
www.secularhumanism.org/index.php?section=library&page=drury_24_4.

13. Robert Alter, "Neocon or Not?" review of *Reading Leo Strauss*, by
Steven B. Smith, *New York Times*, June 25, 2006, http://nytimes.com/2006/
06/25/books/review/25alter.html.

14. See Jim Lobe and Tom Berry, "The Men Who Stole the Show," *Foreign
Policy in Focus*, October 2002, www.fpif.org/fpiftxt/919.

15. Richard Perle et al., "A Clean Break: A New Strategy for Securing the Realm," Institute for Advanced Strategic and Political Studies, July 2006, www.iasps.org/strat1.htm.

16. William Kristol and Robert Kagan, "Toward a Neo-Reaganite Foreign Policy," *Foreign Affairs* 75 (July/August 1996): 15–32.

17. Khazen, "Neo-conservative Ascendancy."

18. Project for the New American Century, "Rebuilding America's Defenses: Strategies, Forces and Resources for a New Century," September 2000, www.newamericancentury.org/RebuildingAmericasDefenses.pdf.

19. Daniel Pipes and Ziad Abdelnour, "Ending Syria's Occupation of Lebanon: The U.S. Role. Report of the Lebanon Study Group," May 2000, www.meforum.org/research/lsg.php.

20. Hersh, "Annals of National Security: Selective Intelligence."

21. PNAC, letter dated September 20, 2001, www.newamericancentury .org/Bushletter.htm.

22. PNAC, www.newamericancentury.org/Bushletter-04032.htm.

23. For full text, see White House, "The National Security Strategy of the United States of America," September 2002, www.whitehouse.gov/ nsc/nss.pdf; see also Condoleezza Rice, "A Balance of Power That Favors Freedom," Wiston Lecture, October 1, 2002, Manhattan Institute for Policy Research, www.manhattan-institute.org/html/wl2002.htm.

24. Richard Haass, "Sovereignty: Existing Rights, Evolving Responsibilities," address to the School of Foreign Service and the Mortara Center for International Studies at Georgetown University, Washington, DC, January 14, 2003. For text, see http://www.state.gov/s/p/rem/2003/16648.htm.

25. Condoleezza Rice, "Princeton University's Celebration of the 75th Anniversary of the Woodrow Wilson School of Public and International Affairs," September 30, 2005, www.state.gov/secretary/rm/2005/54176 .htm.

26. Richard Dreyfuss and Jason Vest, "The Lie Factory," *Mother Jones*, January–February 2004, http://home.earthlink.net/~imfalse/the_lie_factory .html.

27. Ibid.

28. Ibid.

29. Abram Shulsky and Gary J. Schmitt, *Silent Warfare: Understanding the World of Intelligence* (Washington, DC: Potomac Books, 2002).

30. Richard Perle, "Truth, War and Consequences," interview on *Frontline* PBS, July 10, 2003, www.pbs.org/wgbh/pages/frontline/shows/truth/inter views/perle.html.

31. Karen Kwiatkowski, "The New Pentagon Papers: A High-Ranking Military Officer Reveals How Defense Department Extremists Suppressed Information and Twisted the Truth to Drive the Country to War," *Salon.com*, March 10, 2004, http://dir.salon.com/story/opinion/feature/2004/03/10/osp _moveon/index.html.

32. Ibid.

33. Julian Borger, "The Spies Who Pushed for War," *Guardian,* July 17, 2003.

34. Perle, "Truth, War and Consequences."

35. "Secretary Powell's Remarks at United Nations Security Council Meeting," March 7, 2003, www.whitehouse.gov/news/releases/2003/03/200303307-10.html.

36. "President Bush Addresses the Nation," www.whitehouse.gov/news/releases/2003/03/20030319-17.html.

37. Amr Moussa, Arab League Secretary-General, quoted in Michael Elliott, "Not as Lonely as He Looks," *Time,* September 16, 2002, www.time.com/time/magazine/article/0,9171,1003238,00.html.

38. Department of Defense news briefing, March 20, 2003, www.globalsecurity.org/wmd/library/news/iraq/2003.iraq-030320-dod01.htm.

39. See "Shock and Awe Bombing of Baghdad Begins," CNN breaking news, March 21, 2003, http://transcripts.cnn.com/TRANSCRIPTS/0303/21/bn.02.html.

40. Michael Smith, "The War before the War," *New Statesman,* May 30, 2005.

41. See Dennis Bueckert, "Civilian Casualties Horrifying," April 4, 2003, www.commondreams.org/headlines03/0404-14.htm.

42. David Ebony, "Cultural Calamity in Iraq," *Art in America* 91 (June 2003), http://findarticles.com/p/articles/mi_m1248/is_6_91/ai_102793112.

43. News briefing, April 11, 2003, www.defencelink.mil/transcripts/transcript.aspx?transcriptid=2367.

44. Patrick Seale, "The United States and Britain Are Heading for Disaster," *Mafhoum,* March 28, 2003, www.mafhoum.com/press5/138seale.htm.

45. "War Is the Climax of the American-Israeli Partnership," *Washington Post,* March 21, 2003.

46. For transcript, see http://whitehouse.gov/news/releases/2003/05/20030501-15.html.

47. See "Bremer's Statement in Full," BBC News, December 14, 2003, http://news.bbc.co.uk/2/hi/middle_east/3317861.stm.

48. "Bremer Congratulates Iraq's Newest Police Academy Graduates," April 2, 2004, http://merln.ndu.edu/MERLN/PFIraq/archive/state/2004-April_02-190507.pdf.

49. Kathleen T. Rhem, "Military Commander Details Mission That Killed Hussein's Sons," Armed Forces Press Service, U.S. Department of Defense, July 23, 2003, www.defenselink.mil/news/newsarticle.aspx?id=28686.

50. See "Amb. Bremer Stakeout at the Senate," July 22, 2003, www.defenselink.mil/transcripts/transcript.aspx?transcriptid=2856; "White House Statement on Uday and Qusay Hussein," July 22, 2003, www.whitehouse.gov/news/releases/2003/07/20030722-8.html; "PM: A Great Day for New Iraq," www.number10.gov.uk/output/page4249.asp.

51. Salt, "Falluja."

52. Ibid.

53. George Monbiot, "The US Used Chemical Weapons in Iraq—and Then Lied about It," *Guardian,* November 15, 2005, quoting the March 2005 issue of the U.S. Army magazine *Field Artillery.*

54. UN Assistance Mission for Iraq, "Human Rights Report, 1 September–31 October 2005," www.uniraq.org/documents/HR%20Report%20Sep%20Oct%2005%20EN.PDF.

55. "Bush Says 30,000 Iraqis Killed in War," Agence France Presse (AFP), December 12, 2005, www.globalsecurity.org/org/news/2005/051212-killed-iraqis.htm.

56. See www.iraqbodycount.org/database/.

57. Johns Hopkins School of Public Health, "Iraqi Civilian Deaths Increase Dramatically after Invasion," press release, October 28, 2004, www.jhsph.edu/publichealthnews/press_releases/PR_2004/Burnham_Iraq.html.

58. Johns Hopkins School of Public Health, "Updated Iraq Survey Affirms Earlier Mortality Estimates," press release, October 11, 2006, www.jhsph.edu/publichealthnews/press_releases/2006/burnham_iraq_2006.html.

59. "US Casualties in Iraq," www.globalsecurity.org/military/ops/iraq-casualties.htm.

60. See http://nationalpriorities.org/embed.html. The National Priorities Project maintains a continually increasing running cost of the war.

61. See Ed Harriman, "The Least Accountable Regime in the Middle East," *London Review of Books,* November 2, 2006.

62. UN High Commission on Refugees, "Strategy for the Iraq Situation," revised, January 2007, 3 n., www.unhcr.org/publ/RSDLEGAL/45b6258b4.pdf. See also Noah Merrill, "Top UN Official: Iraqi Displacement Largest in Region since Palestinian Crisis of 1948," February 7, 2007, http://electroniciraq.net/news/aiddevelopment/Top_UN_Official_Iraqi_Displacement_Largest_in_Regi_2895.shtml.

63. For text, see www.globalsecurity.org/security/issues/iraq/document/2004/0608resolution.htm.

64. See "Full Text of Iraqi Constitution," *Washington Post,* October 12, 2005, www.washingtonpost.com/WP-dyn/content/article/2005/10/12/AR2005101201450.html.

65. Michael Cox, Professor of International Relations at London School of Economics, quoted in Keith B. Richburg and Glenn Frankel, "Nomination Shocks, Worries Europeans," *Washington Post,* March 17, 2005.

66. Vice President Cheney, speaking to the Association of the U.S. Army, as reported by Jonathan Beale, "Cheney Warns of 'Decades of War,'" BBC World Service, October 6, 2005.

67. Ewen McAskill, "George Bush: 'God Told Me to End the Tyranny in Iraq,'" *Guardian,* October 7, 2005.

14. THE LONG CAMPAIGN

1. Rachel's Tomb.

412 / Notes to Pages 341–44

2. Graham Usher, "Likud's Death Rattle," *Al Ahram Weekly*, June 3–9, 1997, http://weekly.ahram.org.eg/1999/432/re3.htm.

3. "US Will Accept Israel Settlements," BBC News, March 25, 2005, http://news.bbc.co.uk.

4. Uri Bank, quoted in Matthew Price, "The Changing Face of Jerusalem," BBC News, April 28, 2005, http://news.bbc.co.uk/1/hi/world/middle_east/4490671.stm.

5. Amira Hass, "Israel Cuts off Jordan Rift from Rest of West Bank," *Haaretz*, February 13, 2006, www.haaretz.com/hasen/pages/ShArt.jhtml?itemNo=681938&contrassID=1&subContrassID=5.

6. See "Exchange of Letters between Rabin and Arafat," www.mideastweb.org/osloletters.htm.

7. See "The Oslo Declaration of Principles," www.mideastweb.org/meoslodop.htm.

8. Quoted in Mitchell Bard, "Facts about Settlements," Jewish Virtual Library, http://jewishvirtuallibrary.org/jsource/Peace/settlements.html.

9. For full text, see www.yale.edu/lawweb/avalon/un242.htm.

10. For full text, see www.jewishvirtuallibrary.org/jsource/UN/unres252.html.

11. For full text, see www.mideastweb.org/3236.htm.

12. See David Hirst's obituary, "Yasser Arafat," *Guardian*, November 11, 2004.

13. Geoffrey Aronson, "Recapitulating the Redeployments: The Israel-PLO 'Interim Agreements,'" Information Brief No. 32, Center for Policy Analysis on Palestine, April 27, 2000, www.palestinecenter.org/cpap/pubs/20000427ib.html.

14. In February 1994 one of them, Dr. Baruch Goldstein, burst into the Ibrahimi mosque during Ramadan prayers and murdered twenty-nine Palestinians with a Galil assault rifle. He was beaten to death by the survivors. His tomb in the tourist park at Kiryat Arba, describing him as a "holy hero," has become a shrine for the settlers and those who support them. "Numerous people from all over the world come to pray and honor his memory." "Dr. Baruch Goldstein Gravesite," n.d., www.geocities.com/dr_b_goldstein/kever.htm. The tourist park is named after the racist rabbi Meir Kahane, assassinated in New York in 1990 by an Egyptian American, El Sayyid Nusair, who was later implicated in the first plot to bomb the World Trade Center. In December 2000 Kahane's son and daughter-in-law were murdered by a Palestinian as they drove from Jerusalem to their home in a West Bank settlement. In 1929, more than sixty Jews were murdered in Hebron during riots that swept Palestine following a provocative demonstration outside the walls of the Haram al Sharif in Jerusalem by thousands of supporters of Vladimir Jabotinsky.

15. "Recapitulating the Redeployments." By August 14, 2007, the figures were estimated to have reached 120 Israeli settlements, 120 "illegal" outposts, and 460,000 settlers. See "Israeli Settlements," Palestine Monitor Factsheet, www.palestinemonitor.org./SPIP/IMG/pdf/FS_settlements_14082007_light.pdf.

16. Benny Morris and Ian Black, "Camp David and After: An Exchange. 1. An Interview with Ehud Barak," *New York Review of Books*, June 13, 2002, www.nybooks.com/articles/15501.

17. According to a poll taken by the Palestinian Centre for Policy and Survey Research between July 27 and July 31, 2000, 57.2 percent of Israelis felt that Barak's position on the return of territory taken in 1967 was too much of a compromise, with 55.7 percent believing he had given away too much on Jerusalem. See result of Israeli Public Opinion Poll No. 1, http//pcpsr.org/survey/polls/2000/p1israelipoll.html.

18. "PM Barak's Statement at Cabinet Meeting Regarding Abu-Dis," Jerusalem, May 15, 2000, Israeli Ministry of Foreign Affairs, www.israel-mfa.gov.il/MFA/MFAArchive/2000_2009/2000/5/Barak%20Statement%20to%20Cabinet%20on%20Abu-Dis%20-%20May%2015-%2020.

19. Mustafa Barghouti, "The Moral Courage to Call Us Equals," *Al Ahram Weekly*, February 22–28, 2001, http://weekly.ahram.org.eg/2001/522/op2.htm.

20. Shlomo Gazit and Edward Abington, "The Palestinian-Israeli Conflict," *Middle East Policy Council Journal* 8 (March 2001), www.mepc.org/journal_vol8/0103_gazitandabington.asp.

21. Morris and Black, "Camp David and After."

22. The policy paper was *Acting with Caution: Middle East Policy Planning for the Second Reagan Administration* (Washington, DC: Washington Institute for Near East Policy, 1985).

23. Dennis Ross, *The Missing Peace: The Inside Story of the Fight for Middle East Peace* (New York: Farrar, Straus and Giroux, 2004), 36, 4.

24. Gazit and Abington, "Palestinian-Israeli Conflict."

25. Morris and Black, "Camp David and After."

26. Melvyn Bragg, "The Desert Conscience of Israel," *Guardian*, November 12, 2002, http://books.guardian.co.uk/news/articles/0,,396359,00.html; for Oz quotations, see Amos Oz, "Arafat's Gift to Us: Sharon," *Guardian*, February 8, 2001, and "Why Arafat Must Take the Blame," *Guardian*, October 13, 2000.

27. Benny Morris and Ehud Barak, "Camp David and After—Continued," *New York Review of Books*, June 27, 2002, www.nybooks.com/articles/1554.

28. Barak, quoted in Morris and Black, "Camp David and After."

29. Gazit and Abington, "Palestinian-Israeli Conflict."

30. "Israeli Cabinet Decides in Principle for Arafat Expulsion," *Fox News*, September 12, 2003, www.foxnews.com/story/0,2933,97025,00.html.

31. "Enough," editorial, *Jerusalem Post*, September 10, 2003.

32. David Blair, "Killing Arafat Definitely an Option, Says Israeli Politician," September 15, 2003, www.telegraph.co.uk/news/main/jhtml/?xml=/news/2003/09/15/wmid15.xml.

33. Ibid.

34. In September 1997 two Mossad agents approached Mishʿal on an Amman street and jabbed a syringe with an unknown toxin into his neck.

Only when King Hussein threatened to abrogate Jordan's peace with Israel did the Netanyahu government agree to deliver an antidote.

35. The possibility of Palestinian involvement in Arafat's death has been raised with the publication of a letter said to have been written by Arafat's security chief, Muhammad Dahlan, to Israeli defense minister Shaul Mofaz on July 18, 2003: "Be sure that Yasser Arafat's final days are numbered but allow us to finish him off our way, not yours. . . . And be sure, as well, that the promises I made in front of President Bush I will give my life to keep." The letter was apparently seized after the Fatah-aligned Preventive Security Service force compound in Gaza was stormed by Hamas militiamen in June 2007. See Ali Abunimah, "Overcoming the Conspiracy against Palestine," Electronic Intifada, http://electronicintifada.net/u2/article/7116.shtml.

36. Hirst, "Yasser Arafat."

37. Most notoriously in Jenin.

38. In March 2003 the American peace activist Rachel Corrie was crushed to death by a D-9 Caterpillar in the Gaza Strip. Ms. Corrie was standing in front of the bulldozer as it moved forward to demolish a Palestinian house. The driver drove over her and then reversed over the body. The Corrie family subsequently took legal action against the government of Israel and the Caterpillar Corporation. Quote is from Brian Wood and Rory MacMillan, eds., "A Report by the Jenin Inquiry Regarding the Israeli Invasion of the Jenin Refugee Camp from 3–18 April 2002," Jenin Inquiry, June 24, 2003, www.jenininquiry.org/Jenin%20Inquiry%20Report.pdf. The report was compiled by a group of international human rights workers from the United States, Britain, Ireland, Canada, and Norway. They included the first aid workers to enter the camp, on April 14, before the arrival of the UN and the International Committee of the Red Cross. A full investigation by international organizations, including the UN, was never carried out because of the obstruction by the Israeli government.

39. The authors of the Jenin report were unable to explain this discrepancy.

40. Wood and MacMillan, "Report by the Jenin Inquiry." The similarities with the ransacking of Palestinian homes by the British during the Palestinian revolt of 1936–39 are striking.

41. These allegations were consistent with the behavior of Israeli soldiers in other military operations, for example, during the invasion of Lebanon in 1982.

42. Many of the findings of the Jenin Inquiry have been corroborated by Amnesty International and Human Rights Watch. See Amnesty International, "Shielded from Scrutiny: IDF Violations in Jenin and Nablus," November 2002, http://web.amnesty.org/ library/index/ENGMDE151432002; and Human Rights Watch, "Jenin: IDF Military Operations," May 2002, http://hrw.org/reports/2002/israel3/israel0502.pdf. It should be remembered that an international inquiry was never held on the massacre of Palestinians at Sabra and Shatila in 1982 either—or the killing by Israeli artillery strikes of Lebanese taking shelter in the UN compound at Qana in 1996.

43. See UN General Assembly, *Report of the Special Committee to Investigate Israeli Practices Affecting the Human Rights of the Palestinian People*

and Other Arabs of the Occupied Territories, A/57/207, September 16, 2002, 57th session, item 78 of the provisional agenda.

44. See B'Tselem (Israeli Information Centre for Human Rights in the Occupied Territories), "Fatalities," www.btselem.org/english/statistics/Casualties .asp. The Palestinian National Authority Central Bureau of Statistics, counting from September 29, 2000, to May 31, 2007, gives a total death toll of 4,790 but does not break down this figure into how many Palestinians were killed by the Israeli military and how many by civilians. See www.pcbs.gov.ps/Portals/_pcbs/ intifada/93b5acob-f061-455a-bd93-0337c0f63d43.htm.

45. B'Tselem, "Fatalities in the First Intifada," www.btselem.org/english/ statistics/First_Intifada_Tables.asp.

46. See UN General Assembly, *Report of the Special Committee.*

47. See "Suicide Bombing Terrorism during the Current Israeli-Palestinian Confrontation (September 2000–December 2005)," January 1, 2006, Intelligence and Terrorism Information Center, Center for Special Studies, www.intelligence.org.il/eng/eng_n/pdf/suicide_terrorism_ae.pdf.

48. See B'Tselem, "Hebron City Center," www.btselem.org/English/ Hebron/.

49. Gideon Levy, "The Real Uprooting Is Taking Place in Hebron," *Haaretz,* September 11, 2005, www.haaretz.com/hasen/objects/pages/Print ArticleEn.jhtml?itemNo=623227.

50. Chris McGreal, "Life under Siege in a Divided City," *Guardian,* December 9, 2005.

51. Levy, "Real Uprooting."

52. See Shirl McArthur, "Total Direct Aid to Israel Conservatively Estimated at Almost $105 Billion," *Washington Report on Middle East Affairs,* April 16–17, 2005, www.wrmea.com/archives/April_2005/0504016.html.

53. Writing in March 2006, John J. Mearsheimer and Stephen M. Walt, quoting the U.S. Agency for International Development's "Greenbook," give a total aid figure of $140,142,800 (at the 2003 dollar rate). See "The Israeli Lobby and US Foreign Policy," March 2006, RWP06-01, http://ksgnotes1.har vard.edu/Research/wpaper.nsf/rwp/RWP06-011, a working paper that weighs up the costs and ostensible benefits to the United States of the "special relationship" with Israel. Edited version published as "The Israel Lobby," *London Review of Books,* March 2006, www.lrb.co.uk/v28/no6/mearo1_html

54. Jimmy Carter, *Palestine: Peace Not Apartheid* (New York: Simon and Schuster, 2006).

55. "Balanced Stand on ME Is Political Suicide Says Carter," *Yediot Aharanot,* February 26, 2007.

56. National Committee for the Heads of the Arab Local Authorities in Israel, "The Future Vision of the Palestinian Arabs in Israel," January 12, 2007, www.mossawacenter.org/files/files/File/Reports/2006/Future%20Vision %20(English).pdf. For conflicting perspectives between Israeli and Palestinian "moderates," see Yossi Alpher, "A Profoundly Disturbing Document," and Ghassan Khatib, "A Civilized and Sophisticated Argument," January 27, 2007,

both in *Bitter Lemons,* edition 4, January 29, 2007, www.bitterlemons.org/previous/bl290107ed4.html.

57. Edward Said, "America's Last Taboo," *New Left Review* 6 (November–December 2000), www.newleftreview.net/NLR24002.shtml.

58. Olmert remains the faithful disciple of Menachem Begin and Vladimir Jabotinsky. The name of the governing party, Kadima ("forward" or "eastward"), is rich in symbolism for the Revisionists. See Jacqueline Rose, "The Zionist Imagination," *Nation,* June 26, 2006.

59. "Iran Threatens to Strike Dimona Reactor if Israel Strikes It," *Arabic News,* www.arabicnews.com/ansub/Daily/Day/040819/2004081903.html.

60. See Abbas Edalat, "The US Can Learn from This Example of Mutual Respect," *Guardian,* April 5, 2007, www.guardian.co.uk/commentisfree/story/0,,2050375,00.html.

61. Ross Dunn, "Israel Threatens Strikes on Iranian Nuclear Targets," *Scotsman,* November 23, 2004.

62. See Jonathan Steele, "Lost in Translation," June 14, 2006, www.informationclearinghouse.info/article13641.htm, and for further discussion "Forum: Mail to BBC re Ahmedinajad," www.medialens.org/forum/viewtopic.php?t=15188&sid=0cdfb819ba2a23ee1594e82029d48bd5.

63. Speaking at a White House press conference on February 17, 2005.

64. See Mark LeVine, *Why They Don't Hate Us: Lifting the Veil on the Axis of Evil* (Oxford: Oneworld, 2005), for an effective response to these claims.

65. For transcript, see www.WorldPress.org/Americas/1964.cjm.

66. "President Addresses the Nation in Prime Time Press Conference," April 13, 2004, www.whitehouse.gov/news/releases/2004/04/print/20040413-20.html.

BIBLIOGRAPHY

Abadi, Jacob. *Britain's Withdrawal from the Middle East, 1947–1971: The Economic and Strategic Imperatives.* Princeton, NJ: Kingston Press, 1982.

Abunimah, Ali. "Overcoming the Conspiracy against Palestine." July 18, 2007. Electronic Intifada. http://electronicintifada.net/v2/article/7116.shtml.

Abun-Nasr, Jamil M. *A History of the Maghrib.* Cambridge: Cambridge University Press, 1971.

Aburish, Said K. *Saddam Hussein: The Politics of Revenge.* London: Bloomsbury, 2000.

Acheson, Dean. *Present at the Creation: My Years in the State Department.* New York: W. W. Norton, 1969.

Adas, Michael. *Prophets of Rebellion: Millenarian Protest Movements against the European Colonial Order.* New York: Cambridge University Press, 1987.

Adelson, Roger. *London and the Invention of the Middle East: Money, Power and War, 1902–1922.* New Haven: Yale University Press, 1995.

Ahmad, Eqbal. "The Public Relations of Ethnocide." *Journal of Palestine Studies* 12, no. 3 (1983): 31–40.

Ajami, Fouad. "America and the Arabs." *Foreign Affairs* 80, no. 6 (2001): 2–16.

———. "Best Intentions: Why We Went, What We've Found." *New Republic,* June 28, 2004. www.tnr.com/doc.mhtml?i=20040628&s=ajami062804.

Akçam, Taner. *From Empire to Republic: Turkish Nationalism and the Armenian Genocide.* London: Zed Books, 2004.

———. *A Shameful Act: The Armenian Genocide and the Question of Turkish Responsibility.* New York: Metropolitan Books, 2006.

Allon, Yigal. *The Making of Israel's Army.* London: Sphere Books, 1970.

Alter, Robert. "Neocon or Not?" Review of *Reading Leo Strauss,* by Steven B. Smith. *New York Times,* June 25, 2006. http://nytimes.com/2006/06/25/books/review/25alter.html.

Alterman, Eric. *When Presidents Lie: A History of Official Deception and Its Consequences.* New York: Viking Penguin, 2004.

"Amb. Bremer Stakeout at the Senate." July 22, 2003. www.defenselink
.mil/transcripts/transcript.aspx?transcriptid=2856.

Ambrosius, Lloyd E. *Wilsonian Statecraft: Theory and Practice of Liberal
Internationalism during World War I.* Wilmington, DE: Scholarly Resources
Books, 1991.

American Section of the International Commission on Mandates in Turkey.
"The King-Crane Commission." August 28, 1919. In U.S. Department of
State, Foreign Relations of the United States, *The Paris Peace Conference,
1919,* Foreign Relations of the United States, 12:745–866. Washington, DC:
Government Printing Office, 1947.

Amnesty International. "Who Armed Iraq?" *Terror Trade Times,* no. 4 (June
2003). AI Index 31/002/2003. http://web.amnesty.org/pages/ttt4-article
_7-eng.

Antonius, George. *The Arab Awakening.* 1938. Reprint, London: Hamish
Hamilton, 1961.

Aprim, Fred. "Dairaboun (Deir Abun): The Strategic Assyrian Village." *Zinda*
11, no. 71 (2006). www.zindamagazine.com/html/archives/2006/02.01.06/
index_wedphp.

*The Arab Bulletin: Bulletin of the Arab Bureau in Cairo, 1916–1919. Includ-
ing indexes for 1916, 1917, and 1918 and the Supplementary Notes on the
Middle East.* 4 vols. Oxford: Archive Editions, 1986.

Arakie, Margaret. *The Broken Sword of Justice: America, Israel and the Palestine Tragedy.* London: Quartet Books, 1973.

Aronson, Geoffrey. "Recapitulating the Redeployments: The Israel-PLO
'Interim Agreements.'" April 27, 2000. www.palestinecenter.org/cpap/
pubs/20000427ib.html.

Asad, Muhammad. *The Message of the Qu*ʾ*ran: Translated and Explained by
Muhammad Asad.* Gibraltar: Dar al Andalus, 1993.

Astier, Henri. "Ghettos Shackle French Muslims." BBC News, October 31,
2005. http://news.bbc.co.uk/2/hi/europe/4375910.stm.

Atkinson, Rick. *Crusade: The Untold Story of the Persian Gulf War.* Boston:
Houghton Mifflin, 1993.

Ball, George W. *Error and Betrayal in Lebanon.* Washington, DC: Foundation
for Middle East Peace, 1984.

Ball, George W., and Douglas B. Ball. *The Passionate Attachment: America's
Involvement with Israel, 1947 to the Present.* New York: W. W. Norton,
1992.

Barbour, Nevill. *Nisi Dominus: A Survey of the Palestine Controversy.* London: George G. Harrap, 1946.

Baritz, Loren. "The Idea of the West." *American Historical Review* 66 (April
1961): 618–40.

Bass, Warren. *Support Any Friend: Kennedy's Middle East and the Making of
the U.S.-Israel Alliance.* New York: Oxford University Press, 2003.

Batatu, Hanna. *The Old Social Classes and the Revolutionary Movements of
Iraq.* Princeton: Princeton University Press, 1978.

Battle, Joyce, ed. "Shaking Hands with Saddam Hussein: The US Tilts towards Iraq, 1980–1984." George Washington University, National Security Archive, Electronic Briefing Book No. 82, February 25, 2003. www.gwu .edu/%7Ensarchiv/NSAEBB/NSAEBB82/index.htm.

Begin, Menachem. *The Revolt: The Story of the Irgun.* Translated by Shmuel Katz, Member of Command of Irgun Zvai Leumi. New York: Henry Schuman, 1951.

Bein, Alex, ed. *Arthur Ruppin: Memoirs, Diaries, Letters.* London: Weidenfeld and Nicolson, 1971.

Bell, Gertrude. *The Letters of Gertrude Bell.* Selected and edited by Lady Bell. Vol. 2. London: Ernest Benn, 1928.

Ben-Gurion, David. "Britain's Contribution to Arming the Hagana." In *From Haven to Conquest: Readings in Zionism and the Palestine Problem until 1948,* edited by Walid Khalidi, 371–74. Washington, DC: Institute of Palestine Studies, 1987.

Benvenisti, Meron. *Sacred Landscape: The Buried History of the Holy Land since 1948.* Berkeley: University of California Press, 2000.

Bernal, Martin. Review of *Not Out of Africa: How Afrocentrism Became an Excuse to Teach Myth as History,* by Mary Lefkowitz. *Bryn Mawr Classical Review,* April 5, 1996. http://ccat.sas.upenn.edu/bmcr/1996/96.04.05.html.

Berque, Jacques. *Egypt: Imperialism and Revolution.* Translated by Jean Stewart. New York: Praeger, 1972.

Beshir, Mohamed Omer. *Revolution and Nationalism in the Sudan.* London: Rex Collings, 1974.

Birdwood, Christopher Bromhead. *Nuri as-Said: A Study in Arab Leadership.* London: Cassell, 1959.

Blair, Tony. "PM [Blair]: A Great Day for New Iraq." www.number10.gov .uk/output/page4249.asp.

Bloxham, Donald. *The Great Game of Genocide: Imperialism, Nationalism and the Destruction of the Ottoman Armenians.* New York: Oxford University Press, 2005.

Bovard, James. "Iraqi Sanctions and American Intentions: Blameless Carnage?" *Freedom Daily,* pt. 1, February 9, 2004; pt. 2, February 11, 2004. Future of Freedom Foundation. www.fff.org/freedom/fd0401c.asp and http://www.fff.org/freedom/fd0402c.asp.

Braudel, Fernand. *A History of Civilisations.* London: Allen Lane, 1994.

"Bremer Congratulates Iraq's Newest Police Academy Graduates." April 2, 2004. http://merln.ndu.edu/MERLN/PFIraq/archive/state/2004-April_02-190507.pdf.

"Bremer's Statement in Full." BBC News, December 14, 2003. http://news .bbc.co.uk/2/hi/middle_east/3317861.stm.

Brenner, Lenni. *Zionism in the Age of the Dictators: A Reappraisal.* London: Croom Helm, 1983.

Bryce, James. *The Bryce Report: Report of the Committee on Alleged German Outrages.* London: His Majesty's Government, 1915.

B'Tselem. The Israeli Information Centre for Human Rights in the Occupied Territories. "Fatalities in the First Intifada." www.btselem.org/english/statistics/First_Intifada_Tables.asp.

———. "Hebron City Centre." www.btselem.org/English/Hebron/.

———. "Statistics." September 29, 2000–August 15, 2007. www.btselem.org/english/statistics/Casualties.asp.

Buchan, John. "Children of the Storm." Iraq Special Report. *Guardian*, September 25, 1999.

Buchanan, Sir George. *The Tragedy of Mesopotamia*. Edinburgh: William Blackwood and Sons, 1938.

Bulwer, Henry Lytton. *The Life of Henry John Temple, Viscount Palmerston*. Vol. 2. London: R. Bentley, 1870.

Burdett, A. L. P., ed. *Arab Dissident Movements, 1905–1955*. 4 vols. Slough: Archive Editions, 1996.

Burke, Peter, ed. *A New Kind of History: From the Writings of Febvre*. London: Routledge and Kegan Paul, 1973.

Buruma, Ian. "Lost in Translation. The Two Minds of Bernard Lewis." *New Yorker*, June 14–21, 2004. www.newyorker.com.

———. "The Origins of Occidentalism." *Chronicle of Higher Education* 50 (February 6, 2004): B10. http://chronicle.com/weekly/v50/i22/22b01001.htm.

Bush, George W. "President Bush Addresses Nation on the Capture of Saddam Hussein." December 14, 2003. www.whitehouse.gov/news/releases/2003/12/20031214-3.html.

———. "President Bush Addresses the Nation." March 19, 2003. www.whitehouse.gov/news/releases/2003/3/20030319-17.html.

"Bush Says 30,000 Iraqis Killed in War." Agence France Presse. December 12, 2005. www.globalsecurity.org/org/news/2005/051212-killed-iraqis.htm.

Candler, Edmund. *The Long Road to Baghdad*. 2 vols. London: Cassell, 1919.

Carter, Jimmy. *Keeping Faith: Memoirs of a President*. Fayetteville: University of Arkansas Press, 1995.

———. *Palestine: Peace Not Apartheid*. New York: Simon and Schuster, 2006.

Çelik, Hüseyin. "The 1915 Armenian Revolt in Van: Eyewitness Testimony." In *The Armenians in the Late Ottoman Period*, edited by Türkkaya Ataöv, 87–108. Ankara: Turkish Historical Society, 2001.

Chodak, Szymon. "The Rise of the Global Civilization." *Dialogue and Humanism* 1, no. 1 (1991): 17–36.

Chomsky, Noam. *The Fateful Triangle: The United States, Israel and the Palestinians*. London: Pluto Press, 1983.

Christison, Kathleen. "Blind Spots: Official Myths about the Middle East." *Journal of Palestine Studies* 17 (Winter 1988): 46–61.

———. *Perceptions of Palestine: Their Influence on U.S. Middle East Policy*. Berkeley: University of California Press, 1999.

Churchill, Winston S. *My Early Life: A Roving Commission*. 1930. Reprint, London: Odhams Press, 1947.

———. *The River War: An Account of the Reconquest of the Sudan.* 1899. Reprint, London: Eyre and Spottiswood, 1949.

Clancy-Smith, Julia A. *Rebel and Saint: Muslim Notables, Popular Protest, Colonial Encounters (Algeria and Tunisia, 1800–1904).* Berkeley: University of California Press, 1994.

Clarke, Thurston. *By Blood and Fire: The Attack on the King David Hotel.* London: Hutchinson, 1981.

Cleveland, William L. *Islam against the West: Shakib Arslan and the Campaign for Islamic Nationalism.* London: Al Saqi Books, 1985.

Cockburn, Andrew, and Leslie Cockburn. *Dangerous Liaisons: The Inside Story of the US-Israeli Covert Relationship.* New York: HarperCollins, 1991.

Cohen, Avner. *Israel and the Bomb.* New York: Columbia University Press, 1998.

Cohen, Michael J. *Truman and Israel.* Berkeley: University of California Press, 1990.

Cohen, Michael J., and Martin Kolinsky, eds. *Demise of the British Empire in the Middle East: Britain's Response to Nationalist Movements, 1943–1955.* London: Frank Cass, 1998.

Cohen, Warren I. "Balancing American Interests in the Middle East: Lyndon Baines Johnson vs. Gamal Abdul Nasser." In *Lyndon Johnson Confronts the World: American Foreign Policy, 1963–1968,* edited by Warren I. Cohen and Nancy Bernkopf Tucker. Cambridge: Cambridge University Press, 1994.

Commission of Inquiry into the Events at the Refugee Camps in Beirut. *Report of the Commission of Inquiry into the Events at the Refugee Camps in Beirut (the Kahan Commission).* February 8, 1983. www.jewishvirtual library.org/jsource/History/kahan.html.

Courtney, Roger. *Palestine Policeman.* London: Herbert Jenkins, 1939.

Cromer, Earl of [Evelyn Baring]. *Abbas II.* London: Macmillan, 1915.

Dadrian, Vahakn N. *The History of the Armenian Genocide: Ethnic Conflict from the Balkans to Anatolia to the Caucasus.* 2nd rev. ed. Providence, UK: Berghahn Books, 1997.

Dallek, Robert. *Flawed Giant: Lyndon Johnson and His Times, 1961–1973.* New York: Oxford University Press, 1998.

D'Amato, Anthony. "The Legal Boundaries of Israel in International Law." *Jurist,* April 8, 2002. http://jurist.law.pitt.edu/world/israelborders.php.

Darwish, Adel, and Gregory Alexander. *Unholy Babylon: The Secret History of Saddam's War.* London: Victor Gollancz, 1991.

Davis, John H. *The Evasive Peace: A Study of the Zionist-Arab Problem.* London: John Murray, 1970.

Davis, Uri. *Apartheid Israel: Possibilities for the Struggle Within.* New York: Zed Books, 2003.

De Gaury, Gerald. *Arabian Journey and Other Desert Travels.* London: George G. Harrap, 1950.

Denny, Ludwell. *We Fight for Oil*. New York: Alfred A. Knopf, 1928.

Dicey, Edward. *The Story of the Khedivate*. London: Rivington's, 1902.

Dixon, Norm. "The Ties That Blind: How Reagan Armed Saddam with Chemical Weapons." *Counterpunch*, June 17, 2004. www.counterpunch.org/dixon06172004.html.

Dodd, C. H., and M. E. Sales. *Israel and the Arab World*. London: Routledge and Kegan Paul, 1970.

Dombey, Norman. "Iran and the Bomb," *London Review of Books*, January 25, 2007.

Dreyfuss, Robert, and Jason Vest. "The Lie Factory: A Mother Jones Special Investigation of How the Bush Administration Published Disinformation and Bogus Intelligence and Led the Nation to War." *Mother Jones*, January–February 2004. http://home.earthlink.net/~imfalse/the_lie_factory.html.

Drury, Shadia B. "Leo Strauss and the Grand Inquisitor," *Free Inquiry* 24 (May 7, 2007). Council for Secular Humanism. http://secularhumanism.org/index.php?section=library&page=drury_24_4.

Eagleburger, Lawrence S., Deputy Secretary of State. "US Policy toward Iraq and the Role of the CCC Program, 1989–90." Statement before the House Committee on Banking, Finance, and Urban Affairs, May 25, 1992. http://findarticles.com/p/articles/mi_m1584/is_n21_v3/ai_12511751.

Ebony, David. "Cultural Calamity in Iraq." *Art in America* 91 (June 2003). http://findarticles.com/p/articles/mi_m1248/is_6_91/ai_102793112.

Edalat, Abbas. "The US Can Learn from This Example of Mutual Respect." *Guardian*, April 5, 2007. www.guardian.co.uk/commentisfree/story/0,,2050375,00.html.

Einstein, Lewis. *Inside Constantinople*. London: John Murray, 1917.

Eisenhower, Dwight D. *Waging Peace, 1956–1961*. New York: Doubleday, 1965.

Eksteins, Modris. *Rites of Spring: The Great War and the Birth of the Modern Age*. London: Black Swan, 1990.

Elath, Eliahu. *Israel and Elath: The Political Struggle for the Inclusion of Elath in the Jewish State*. London: Jewish Historical Society of England, 1966.

Elias, Norbert. *The Civilizing Process*. 2 vols. Translated by Edmund Jephcott. London: Blackwell, 1982. Originally published as *Über den Prozess der Zivilisation* (Basel: Haus zum Falken, 1939).

Eppel, Michael. *The Palestine Conflict in the History of Modern Iraq: The Dynamics of Involvement, 1928–1948*. London: Frank Cass, 1994.

Erickson, Edward J. "Armenian Massacres: New Records Undercut Old Blame." *Middle East Quarterly* 13 (Summer 2006). www.meforum.org/article/991. Reprinted in *Insight Turkey* 8 (July–September 2006): 44–53.

———. *Defeat in Detail: The Ottoman Army in the Balkans, 1912–1913*. Westport, CT: Praeger, 2003.

European Monitoring Centre on Racism and Xenophobia. *Muslims in the European Union: Discrimination and Islamophobia*. Vienna: Manz Crossmedia, 2006.

Eveland, Wilbur Crane. *Ropes of Sand: America's Failure in the Middle East.* New York: W. W. Norton, 1980.

Everest, Larry. "Hans von Sponeck: The Inside Story of US Sanctions on Iraq." *Revolutionary Worker,* December 23, 2001. www.rwor.org/a/v23/1130-39/1132/sponeck_iraq.htm.

Fahmy, Khaled. "The Era of Muhammad ʿAli Pasha, 1805–1848." In *The Cambridge History of Egypt,* vol. 2, *Modern Egypt from 1517 to the End of the Twentieth Century,* edited by M. W. Daly, 139–79. New York: Cambridge University Press, 1998.

Farid, Abdel Magid. *Nasser: The Final Years.* Reading, UK: Ithaca Press, 1994.

Farr, Warner D. "The Third Temple's Holy of Holies: Israel's Nuclear Weapons." Counterproliferation Papers Future Warfare Series No. 2. U.S. Air Force Counterproliferation Center, Air War College, Air University, Maxwell Air Force Base, AL, September 1999. http://rense.com/general35/isrnuk.htm.

Fernea, Robert A., and William Roger Louis, eds. *The Iraqi Revolution of 1958: The Old Social Classes Revisited.* New York: I. B. Tauris, 1991.

Ferrell, Robert H. *The Eisenhower Diaries.* New York: W. W. Norton, 1981.

Feurlicht, Roberta Strauss. *The Fate of the Jews.* New York: Quartet Books, 1984.

Finkelstein, Norman. *Image and Reality of the Israel-Palestine Conflict.* London, York: Verso, 1995.

Finklestone, Joseph. *Anwar Sadat: Visionary Who Dared.* London: Frank Cass, 1996.

Fisk, Robert. *Pity the Nation: Lebanon at War.* New York: Oxford University Press, 1992.

Flapan, Simha. "The Palestinian Exodus of 1948." *Journal of Palestine Studies* 16 (Summer 1987): 3–26.

Friedman, Alan. *Spider's Web: Bush, Saddam, Thatcher and the Decade of Deceit.* London: Faber and Faber, 1993.

Friedman, Robert I. *Zealots for Zion: Inside Israel's West Bank Settlement Movement.* New Brunswick: Rutgers University Press, 1992.

Fukuyama, Francis. "Has History Started Again?" *Policy* (Winter 2002): 3–7. www.cis.org.au/policy/winter02/polwin02-1.htm.

———. "The West Has Won." *Guardian,* October 11, 2001.

Fukuyama, Francis, and Nadav Samin. "Can Any Good Come of Radical Islam? A Modernizing Force? Maybe." *Opinion Journal,* September 12, 2002, reprinted from the *Wall Street Journal* editorial page. www.opinionjournal.com/extra/?id=110002251.

Fulbright, Senator J. William. *The Arrogance of Power.* London: Jonathan Cape, 1968.

"Full Text of Iraqi Constitution." *Washington Post,* October 12, 2005. www.washingtonpost.com.

Gamal Abdel Nasser, Hoda. *Britain and the Egyptian National Movement, 1936–1952.* Reading, UK: Ithaca Press, 1994.

Gazit, Shlomo, and Edward Abington. "The Palestinian-Israeli Conflict." *Middle East Policy Council Journal* 8 (March 2001). www.mepc.org/journal _vol8/0103_gazitandabington.asp.

Gendzier, Irene. "Democracy, Deception and the Arms Trade: The US, Iraq and Weapons of Mass Destruction." *Middle East Report* 234 (Spring 2005). www.merip.org/mer/mer234/gendzier.html.

————. "Dying to Forget: The U.S. and Iraq's Weapons of Mass Destruction." *Logos* 2 (Winter 2003). http://logosonline.home.igc.org/gendzier _iraq.html.

Ghazaleh, Pascale. "Industrious Beginnings." *Al Ahram Weekly*, October 13–19, 2005. http://weekly.ahram.org.eg/2005/764/special.htm.

Ghorashi, Halleh. "Why Ayaan Hirsi Ali Is Wrong." *Signandsight.com*, March 22, 2007. www.signandsight.com/features/1250.html.

Gibb, H. A. R. *Studies on the Civilisation of Islam.* Edited by Stanford J. Shaw and William R. Polk. London: Routledge and Kegan Paul, 1962.

Glubb, Sir John Bagot. *A Soldier with the Arabs.* London: Hodder and Stoughton, 1957.

Government of Palestine. *A Survey of Palestine: Prepared in December 1945 and January 1946 for the Information of the Anglo-American Committee of Inquiry.* 2 vols. Jerusalem (?): [Government printer], 1946. Reprinted in 1991 by Institute of Palestine Studies, Washington, DC.

Grant, James. *Cassell's History of the War in the Soudan.* 6 vols. London: Cassell, [1885–86?].

Great Britain. Colonial Office. *Palestine: Termination of the Mandate 15th May. Statement Prepared for Public Information by the Colonial Office and the Foreign Office.* London: His Majesty's Stationery Office, 1948.

Great Britain. Foreign Office. *The Political History of Palestine under British Administration: Memorandum by His Britannic Majesty's Government Presented in July 1947 to the United Nations Special Committee on Palestine.* Jerusalem: Government Printing Office, 1947. A/AC.14/8. UN Information System on the Question of Palestine (UNISPAL). http://domino.un .org/UNISPAL.NSF/eed216406b50bf6485256ce10072f637/16b8c7cc809b7 e5b8525694b0071f3bd!OpenDocument.

Great Britain. General Staff. Geographical Section. *Palestine and Transjordan.* Geographical Handbook Series. B.R. 514. London: Naval Intelligence Division, 1943.

Green, Stephen. *Living by the Sword.* London: Faber and Faber, 1988.

Grey of Fallodon, Viscount [Edward Grey]. *Twenty-five Years, 1892–1916.* 2 vols. London: Hodder and Stoughton, 1926.

Grose, Peter. "The President versus the Diplomats." In *The End of the Palestine Mandate,* edited by William Roger Louis and Robert W. Stookey, 32–60. London: I. B. Tauris, 1986.

Gürün, Kamuran. *The Armenian File: The Myth of Innocence Exposed.* London: Weidenfeld and Nicolson, 1985.

Haass, Richard N. *The Reluctant Sheriff: The United States and the Cold War.* New York: Council on Foreign Relations, 1997.

Hadawi, Sami. *Bitter Harvest: Palestine, 1914–1967*. New York: New World Press, 1967.

Haig, Alexander M., Jr. *Caveat: Realism, Reagan and Foreign Policy*. New York: Macmillan, 1984.

Halaçoğlu, Yusuf. *Facts on the Relocation of the Armenians, 1914–1918*. Ankara: Turkish Historical Society, 2002.

Halbrook, Stephen. "The Class Origins of Zionist Ideology." *Journal of Palestine Studies* 2 (Autumn 1972): 86–110.

Halliday, Dennis. "Death for Oil." Interview by Amira Howeidy. *Al Ahram Weekly*, July 13–19, 2000. http://weekly.ahram.org.eg/2000/490/intrvw.htm.

Hamdi, Walid M. S. *Rashid Ali al Gailani and the Nationalist Movement in Iraq, 1939–1941*. London: Darf, 1987.

Hanson, Brad. "The 'Westoxication' of Iran: Depictions and Reactions of Behrangi, al-e Ahmad and Shariati." *International Journal of Middle Eastern Studies* 15 (February 1983): 1–23.

Harriman, Ed. "The Least Accountable Regime in the Middle East." *London Review of Books*, November 2, 2006.

Harrison, Robert T. *Gladstone's Imperialism in Egypt: Techniques of Domination*. Westport, CT: Greenwood Press, 1995.

Hass, Amira. "Israel Cuts Jordan Rift from Rest of West Bank." *Haaretz*, February 13, 2006. www.haaretz.com/hasen/pages/ShArt.jhtml?itemNo=681938&contrassID=1&subContrassID=5.

Heikal, Mohamed H. *Cutting the Lion's Tail: Suez through Egyptian Eyes*. London: Andre Deutsch, 1986.

Heinrichs, Waldo. "Lyndon B. Johnson: Change and Continuity." In *Lyndon Johnson Confronts the World: American Foreign Policy, 1963–1968*, edited by Warren I. Cohen and Nancy Bernkopf Tucker. New York: Cambridge University Press, 1994.

Hersh, Seymour M. "Annals of National Security: Selective Intelligence. Donald Rumsfeld Has His Own Special Sources. Are They Reliable?" *New Yorker*, May 12, 2003. www.newyorker.com.

———. "Annals of National Security: The Redirection." *New Yorker*, April 5, 2007.

———. "Annals of War: Overwhelming Force. What Happened in the Final Days of the Gulf War?" *New Yorker*, May 22, 2000.

———. *Chain of Command: The Road from 9/11 to Abu Ghraib*. London: Allen Lane, 2004.

———. *The Samson Option: Israel, America and the Bomb*. New York: Faber and Faber, 1991.

Theodor. *The Diaries of Theodor Herzl*. Translated by Marvin Lowen- New York: Dial Press, 1956.

David. "Rush to Annexation: Israel in Jerusalem." *Journal of Palestine* es 3 (Summer 1974): 3–31.

Christopher. "Oriana Fallaci and the Art of the Interview." *Van-* r, December 2006. www.vanityfair.com/politics/features.2006/12 s200612.htm.

Hitti, Philip K. *History of Syria Including Lebanon and Palestine*. New York: Macmillan, 1951.

———. *A History of the Arabs*. 10th ed. London: Palgrave Macmillan, 2005.

Hobson, John M. *The Eastern Origins of Western Civilization*. New York: Cambridge University Press, 2004.

Hodgson, Marshall G. S. *Rethinking World History: Essays on Europe, Islam and World History*. Edited by Edmund Burke III. New York: Cambridge University Press, 1993.

Hogan, Matthew. "Deir Yassin Remembered." Undated home page of Deir Yassin Remembered's Web site, www.deiryassin.org (accessed July 19, 2007).

Hoge, James F., and Fareed Zakaria. *The American Encounter: The United States and the Making of the Modern World. Cuttings from 75 Years of "Foreign Affairs."* New York: Basic Books, 1977.

Holland, Geoffrey. "United States Exports of Biological Materials to Iraq: Compromising the Credibility of International Law." *Deep Blade Journal*, June 2005. http://deepblade.net/journal/Holland_JUNE2005.pdf.

Hoover, Herbert. *The Ordeal of Woodrow Wilson*. With a new introduction by Senator Mark Hatfield. Washington, DC: Woodrow Wilson Center Press, 1992.

Hourani, Albert. *Arabic Thought in the Liberal Age, 1798–1939*. New York: Oxford University Press, 1962.

———. *Great Britain and the Arab World*. London: John Murray, 1945.

Howeidy, Amira. "It's Difficult to Count." Special supplement on Deir Yassin massacre, *Al Ahram Weekly*, April 9–15, 1998. http://weekly.ahram.org .eg/1998/1948/372_yass.htm.

Human Rights Watch. "Iraq." In *Human Rights Watch World Report 1989*. New York: Human Rights Watch, 1999. www.hrw.org/reports/1989/ WR89/Iraq.htm.

———. *Needless Deaths in the Gulf War: Civilian Casualties during the Air Campaign and Violations of the Laws of War*. New York: Human Rights Watch, 1991.

Huntington, Samuel P. "The Age of Muslim Wars." *Newsweek*, December 17, 2001.

———. "The Clash of Civilizations?" *Foreign Affairs* 72 (Summer 1993) 22–49.

———. *The Clash of Civilizations and the Remaking of World Order*. New York: Simon and Schuster, 1996.

———. "The Lonely Superpower." *Foreign Affairs* 78 (March–April 1 35–49.

Ionides, Michael. *Divide and Lose: The Arab Revolt of 1955–1958*. I Geoffrey Bles, 1960.

Iraq Body Count. "Reported Civilian Deaths Resulting from the US-I itary Intervention in Iraq as of August 27, 2007." www.iraqb .org/database/.

Iraq Survey Group. *Comprehensive Report of the Special Adviser to the DCI on Iraq's WMD* [Also known as the Iraq Survey Group Final Report]. 3 vols. Edited by Charles Duelfer. Washington, DC: Government Printing Office, September 30, 2004. www.globalsecurity.org/wmd/library/report/2004/isg-final-report/.

Israeli Commission of Inquiry into the Events at the Refugee Camps in Beirut. "Final Report of the Israeli Commission of Inquiry into the Events at the Refugee Camps in Beirut." *Journal of Palestine Studies* 12 (Spring 1983): 89–116.

Jabber, Fuad. *Israel and Nuclear Weapons: Present Options and Future Strategies.* London: Chatto and Windus, 1971.

Jansen, Michael. *Dissonance in Zion.* London: Zed Books, 1987.

Jarman, Robert L., ed. *Iraq Administration Reports, 1914–1932.* 10 vols. Slough, UK: Archive Editions, 1992.

Jiryis, Sabri. *The Arabs in Israel.* New York: Monthly Review Press, 1976.

Johns Hopkins School of Public Health. "Iraq Civilian Deaths Increase Dramatically after Invasion." Press release, October 28, 2004. www.jhsph.edu/publichealthnews/press-releases/PR_2004/Burnham_Iraq.html.

———. "Updated Iraq Survey Affirms Earlier Mortality Estimates." Press release, October 11, 2006. www.jhsph.edu/publichealthnews/press_releases/2006/burnham_iraq_2006.html.

Johnson, Doug. "The Egyptian Army, 1880–1900." *Savage and Soldier* 8, no. 1 (1976). www.savageandsoldier.com/sudan/Egyptian_Army.html.

Johnson, Lyndon Baines. "Remarks in New York City at the Dinner of the Weizmann Institute of Science." February 6, 1964. www.presidency.ucsb.edu/ws/index.php?pid=26060.

———. *The Vantage Point: Perspectives of the Presidency, 1963–1969.* New York: Holt, Rinehart and Winston, 1971.

Jordan, Major Michael C. "The 1973 Arab-Israeli War: Arab Policies, Strategies and Campaigns." 1997. www.globalsecurity.org/military/library/report/1997/Jordan.htm.

"Judicial Order in the BNL Case Issued by Judge Marvin Shoob on August 23, 1993." www.pinknoiz.com/covert/shoob2.html.

Kapeliouk, Amon. "New Light on the Israeli-Arab Conflict and the Refugee Problem and Its Origins." *Journal of Palestine Studies* 16 (Spring 1987): 16–24.

Kaplan, Robert D. *Balkan Ghosts: A Journey through History.* New York: Vintage, 1994.

Keay, John. *Sowing the Wind: The Mismanagement of the Middle East, 1900–1960.* London: John Murray, 2003.

Kent, Marian, ed. *The Great Powers and the End of the Ottoman Empire.* London: George Allen and Unwin, 1984.

———. *Oil and Empire: British Policy and Mesopotamian Oil.* London: Macmillan, 1976.

Khadduri, Majid. *Independent Iraq, 1932–1958.* New York: Oxford University Press, 1960.

Khalidi, Walid. *All That Remains: The Palestinian Villages Occupied and Depopulated by Israel in 1948.* Washington, DC: Institute of Palestine Studies, 1992.

———. *Conflict and Violence in Lebanon: Confrontation in the Middle East.* Cambridge, MA: Center for International Studies, Harvard University, 1983.

———, ed. *From Haven to Conquest: Readings in Zionism and the Palestine Problem until 1948.* Washington, DC: Institute of Palestine Studies, 1987.

———. "Plan Dalet: Master Plan for the Conquest of Palestine." *Journal of Palestine Studies* 18 (Autumn 1988): 3–70.

Khazen, Jihad al. "Neo-conservative Ascendancy in the George W. Bush Administration." *Al Hayat,* October 10, 2004. http://english.daralhayat.com.

Khoury, Philip S. *Syria and the French Mandate: The Politics of Arab Nationalism, 1920–1945.* London: I. B. Tauris, 1987.

Koestler, Arthur. *Promise and Fulfilment: Palestine, 1917–1949.* London: Macmillan, 1949.

———. *Thieves in the Night: Chronicle of an Experiment.* London: Macmillan, 1946.

Kohn, Hans. *Western Civilisation in the Near East.* London: George Routledge and Sons, 1936.

Kupferschmidt, Uri M. *The Supreme Muslim Council: Islam under the British Mandate in Palestine.* Leiden: E. J. Brill, 1987.

Kurzman, Dan. *Ben-Gurion: Prophet of Fire.* New York: Simon and Schuster, 1983.

Kwiatkowski, Karen. "The New Pentagon Papers: A High-Ranking Military Officer Reveals How Defense Department Extremists Suppressed Information and Twisted the Truth to Drive the Country to War." *Salon,* March 10, 2004. http://dir.salon.com/story/opinion/feature/2004/03/10/osp_moveon/index.html.

Kyle, Keith. *Suez.* New York: St. Martin's Press, 1991.

Lang, Andrew. "The Politics of Armageddon: Reagan Links Biblical Prophecy with Nuclear War." *Convergence,* [1980s]. www.prop1.org/inaugur/85reagan/85rrarm.htm.

Ledeen, Michael. "The Killers: The Dutch Hit Crisis Point." *National Review,* November 10, 2004. www.nationalreview.com/ledeen/ledeen20041110 1620.asp.

Lesch, David W., ed. *The Middle East and the United States: A Historical and Political Assessment.* 2nd ed. Boulder, CO: Westview Press, 1999.

———. *Syria and the United States: Eisenhower's Cold War in the Middle East.* Boulder, CO: Westview Press, 1992.

Levin, Harry. *Jerusalem Embattled.* London: Victor Gollancz, 1950.

LeVine, Mark. *Why They Don't Hate Us: Lifting the Veil on the Axis of Evil.* Oxford: Oneworld, 2005.

Levine, Molly Myerowitz. "The Marginalization of Martin Bernal." Review of *Black Athena Revisited,* edited by Mary R. Lefkowitz and Guy MacLean Rogers. *Classical Philology* 93 (October 1998): 345–63.

Levy, Gideon. "The Real Uprooting Is Taking Place in Hebron." *Haaretz*, September 11, 2005. www.haaretz.com/hasen/objects/pages/PrintArticleEn .jhtml?itemNo=623227.

Lewis, Bernard. *The Arabs in History*. 2nd ed. London: Hutchinson's University Library, 1954.

———. "The Crisis in Islam and the End of Saddam Hussein's Iraq." *CBC Newsworld* discussion between Brian Stewart and Bernard Lewis, August 30, 2003. www.cbc.ca/worldview/wvarchives/20030830.html.

———. *The Crisis of Islam: Holy War and Unholy Terror*. London: Phoenix, 2004.

———. "Did You Say 'American Imperialism'? Power, Weakness and Choices in the Middle East." *National Review*, December 17, 2001.

———. *Islam and the West*. New York: Oxford University Press, 1993.

———. *Islam in History: Ideas, People and Events in the Middle East*. Chicago: Open Court Press, 1993.

———. "Islam's Interpreter." Interview by Elizabeth Wasserman. *Atlantic Monthly*, April 29, 2004. http://www.theatlantic.com/doc/prem/200404u/ int2004-04-29.

———. *The Middle East and the West*. London: Weidenfeld and Nicolson, 1964.

———. "Muslims About to Take Over Europe." *Jerusalem Post*, January 29, 2007. www.jpost.com/serlet/Satellite?pagename=JPost%2FJPArticle%2F ShowFull&cid=1167467834546.

———. "The Roots of Muslim Rage." *Atlantic Monthly*, September 1990, 47–60.

———. "The 2007 Irving Kristol Lecture." American Enterprise Institute, Washington, DC, March 20, 2007. http://aei.org/publications/filter.all,pub ID.25815/pub_detail.asp.

———. "What Went Wrong?" *Atlantic Monthly*, January 2002, 43–45.

———. *What Went Wrong? Western Impact and Western Response*. London: Phoenix, 2002.

Lewis, David Levering. *The Race to Fashoda: Colonialism and African Resistance*. New York: Henry Holt, 1987.

Lewy, Guenter. *The Armenian Massacres in Turkey: A Disputed Genocide*. Salt Lake City: University of Utah Press, 2005.

Little, Douglas. *American Orientalism: The United States and the Middle East since 1945*. Chapel Hill: University of North Carolina Press, 2002.

Lloyd George, David. "The Great Pinnacle of Sacrifice." Speech of September 21, 1914. In *The Penguin Book of Twentieth Century Speeches*, edited by Brian MacArthur, 31–36. London: Penguin, 1993.

Lobe, Jim, and Tom Barry. "The Men Who Stole the Show." *Foreign Policy in Focus*, October 2002. www.fpif.org/fpiftxt/919.

Locke, Robert. "Leo Strauss, Conservative Mastermind." *Front-Pagemagazine.com*, May 31, 2002. http://frontpagemag.com/Articles/ ReadArticle.asp?ID=1233.

Longrigg, Stephen Hemsley. *Syria and Lebanon under French Mandate.* London: Royal Institute of International Affairs, Oxford University Press, 1968.

Lorch, Netanel. *The Edge of the Sword: Israel's War of Independence.* Jerusalem: Massada Press, 1968.

Louis, William Roger. *The British Empire in the Middle East, 1945–1951.* Oxford: Clarendon Press, 1984.

Louis, William Roger, and Robert W. Stookey, eds. *The End of the Palestine Mandate.* London: I. B. Tauris, 1986.

Love, Kennett. *Suez: The Twice Fought War.* New York: McGraw-Hill, 1969.

Luard, Evan. *A History of the United Nations.* 2 vols. 1982. Reprint, London: Macmillan, 1989.

Lutfi al Sayyid Marsot, Afaf. *Egypt and Cromer: A Study in Anglo-Egyptian Relations.* New York: Praeger, 1969.

———. *A Short History of Modern Egypt.* New York: Cambridge University Press, 1985.

MacCallum, Elizabeth P. "Iraq and the British Treaties." *Foreign Policy Association Information Service* 6 (August 20, 1930): 225–46.

Macdonald, A. D. *Euphrates Exile.* London: G. Bell and Sons, 1936.

Mackinder, H. J. "The Geographical Pivot of History." *Geographical Journal* 23 (1904): 421–44.

MacMillan, Margaret. *Peacemakers: Six Months That Changed the World.* London: John Murray, 2001.

Makiya, Kanan [Samir al Khalil, pseud.]. *Cruelty and Silence: War, Tyranny, Uprising and the Arab World.* New York and London: W. W. Norton, 1993.

———. "Iraq and Its Future." *New York Review of Books,* April 11, 1991. www.nybooks.com/.

———. *Republic of Fear: The Politics of Modern Iraq.* Rev. ed. Berkeley: University of California Press, 1998.

Malet, Sir Edward. *Egypt, 1879–1883.* London: John Murray, 1909.

Mandel, Neville J. *The Arabs and Zionism before World War I.* Berkeley: University of California Press, 1980.

Mango, Andrew. *Ataturk.* London: John Murray, 1999.

Mann, James. "The Armageddon Plan." *Atlantic Monthly,* March 2004. www.commondreams.org/views04/0318-14.htm.

Marlowe, John. *A History of Modern Egypt and Anglo-Egyptian Relations, 1800–1953.* New York: Praeger, 1954.

———. *The Seat of Pilate: An Account of the Palestine Mandate.* London: Cresset Press, 1959.

Marr, Phebe. *The Modern History of Iraq.* Boulder, CO: Westview Press, 1985.

Martin, B. G. *Muslim Brotherhoods in Nineteenth-Century Africa.* Cambridge: Cambridge University Press, 1976.

Masci, Daniel. "An Uncertain Road: Muslims and the Future of Europe." October 2005. Pew Forum on Religion and Public Life. www.pewforum.org.

Massad, Joseph. "Imperial Mementos." *Al Ahram Weekly*, May 20–26, 2004. http://weekly.ahram.org.eg/2004/691/op2.htm.

McArthur, Shirl. "Total Direct Aid to Israel Conservatively Estimated at Almost \$105 Billion." *Washington Report on Middle East Affairs*, April 16–17, 2005. www.wrmea.com/archives/April_2005/0504016.html.

McCarthy, Justin. "The Armenian Uprising and the Ottomans." *Review of Armenian Studies* 2, nos. 7–8 (2005): 50–73.

———. *Death and Exile: The Ethnic Cleansing of Ottoman Muslims, 1821–1922*. Princeton, NJ: Darwin Press, 1995.

———. *Muslims and Minorities: The Population of Ottoman Anatolia and the End of Empire*. New York: New York University Press, 1983.

———. *The Ottoman Peoples and the End of Empire*. London: Arnold, 2001.

———. "The Population of the Ottoman Armenians." In *The Armenians in the Late Ottoman Period*, edited by Türkkaya Ataöv, 65–86. Ankara: Turkish Historical Society, 2001.

McCarthy, Justin, and Esat Arslan, Cemalettin Taşkiran, and Ömer Turan. *The Armenian Rebellion at Van*. Salt Lake City: University of Utah Press, 2006.

McDonald, James G. *My Mission in Israel, 1948–1951*. London: Victor Gollancz, 1951.

McGreal, Chris. "Life under Siege in a Divided City." *Guardian*, December 9, 2005.

Mearsheimer, John J., and Stephen M. Walt. The Israel Lobby and U.S. Foreign Policy. New York: Farrar, Straus and Giroux, 2007.

———. "The Israeli Lobby and US Foreign Policy." Working paper, March 2006, RWP06-01. http://ksgnotes1.harvard.edu/Research/wpaper.nsf/rwp/RWP06-011. Edited and revised as "The Israel Lobby," *London Review of Books*, March 23, 2006, www.lrb.co.uk/.

Meinertzhagen, Richard. *Middle East Diary*. London: Cresset Press, 1959.

Mendelowitz, Allan I., Director, International Trade and Finance Issues, General Government Division. "Agriculture's Export Credit Programs: Delays in Accessing Records Relating to Iraq." Testimony before the House Committee on Banking, Finance, and Urban Affairs, May 29, 1992. T-GGD-92-47. http://archive.gao.gov/t2pbat6/146760.pdf.

Mernissi, Fatima. *Beyond the Veil: Male-Female Dynamics in Muslim Society*. London: Al Saqi Books, 1985.

———. *Islam and Democracy: Fear of the Modern World*. New York: Addison-Wesley, 1992.

———. *The Veil and the Male Elite: A Feminist Interpretation of Women's Rights in Islam*. New York: Addison-Wesley, 1991.

Michaelis, Meir. *Mussolini and the Jews: German Italian Relations and the Jewish Question in Italy, 1922–1945*. Oxford: Clarendon Press, 1978.

Middle East and North Africa Yearbook 2004. London: Europa Publications, 2004.

Milton-Edwards, Beverley. *Islamic Politics in Palestine*. London: I. B. Tauris, 1996.

Mitchell, Timothy. *Colonising Egypt.* Cambridge: Cambridge University Press, 1988.

Moorehead, Alan. *The Blue Nile.* London: Hamish Hamilton, 1962.

Morris, Benny. *1948 and After: Israel and the Palestinians.* Oxford: Clarendon Press, 1990.

———. "Operation Dani and the Palestinian Exodus from Lydda and Ramle in 1948." *Middle East Journal* 40 (Winter 1986): 82–109.

Morris, Benny, and Ehud Barak. "Camp David and After—Continued." *New York Review of Books,* June 27, 2002. www.nybooks.com/articles/1554.

Morris, Benny, and Ian Black. "Camp David and After: An Exchange. 1. An Interview with Ehud Barak." *New York Review of Books,* June 13, 2002. www.nybooks.com/articles/15501.

———. *Israel's Secret Wars.* London: Warner Books, 1992.

Mostert, Nöel. *Frontiers: The Epic of South Africa's Creation and the Tragedy of the Xhosa People.* London: Pimlico, 1993.

Muir, Sir William. *Annals of the Early Caliphate: From Original Sources.* London: Smith, Elder, 1883.

———. *The Caliphate: Its Rise, Decline and Fall.* London: Religious Tract Society, 1891.

———. *The Life of Mahomet: From Original Sources.* London: Smith, Elder, 1878.

"Muslims in Europe: Country Guide." BBC News, December 21, 2005. http://news.bbc.co.uk/2/hi/europe/4385768.stm.

Muslin, Hyman C., and Thomas J. Jobe. *Lyndon Johnson: The Tragic Self. A Psychohistorical Portrait.* New York: Insight Books, 1997.

Nafiᶜ, Basheer M. *Arabism, Islamism and the Palestine Question, 1908–1941: A Political History.* Reading, UK: Ithaca Press, 1998.

Najmabadi, Afsaneh. "Depoliticisation of a Rentier State." In *The Rentier State,* vol. 2, edited by Hazem Beblawi and Giacomo Luciani. London: Croom Helm, 1987.

Nakleh, Issa. *Encyclopedia of the Palestine Problem.* 2 vols. New York: Intercontinental Books, 1991.

National Committee for the Heads of the Arab Local Authorities in Israel. "The Future Vision of the Palestinian Arabs in Israel." January 12, 2007. www.mossawacenter.org/files/files/File/Reports/2006/Future%20Vision%20(English).pdf.

Nazzal, Abdullah Nafez. "The Zionist Occupation of Western Galilee, 1948." *Journal of Palestine Studies* 3 (Spring 1974): 58–76.

Neff, Donald. *Fallen Pillars: U.S. Policy towards Palestine and Israel since 1945.* Washington, DC: Institute of Palestine Studies, 1995.

———. *Warriors at Suez.* Brattleboro, VT: Amana Books, 1988.

Neillands, Robin. *The Dervish Wars: Gordon and Kitchener in the Sudan, 1880–1898.* London: John Murray, 1996.

Newton, Frances E. "Searchlight on Palestine, 1936–1938." In *From Haven to Conquest: Readings in Zionism and the Palestine Problem until 1948,* edited by Walid Khalidi, 357–66. Washington, DC: Institute of Palestine Studies, 1987.

Nicolson, Harold. *Sweet Waters: An Istanbul Thriller.* 1921. Reprint, London: Cornucopia, in association with Sickle Moon Books, 2000.

Nicosia, Francis R. *The Third Reich and the Palestine Question.* London: I. B. Tauris, 1985.

Nimmo, Kurt. "Saddam Hussein: Taking Out the CIA's Trash." *Dissident Voice,* August 2, 2003. www.dissidentvoice.org/Articles7/Nimmo_Saddam-CIA.htm.

Nutting, Anthony. *Nasser.* London: Constable, 1972.

———. *No End of a Lesson: The Story of Suez.* London: Constable, 1967.

Olmert, Ehud. "A Country That's Fun to Live In." Interview by Aluf Benn and Yossi Verter. *Haaretz,* March 10, 2006. http://www.almubadara.org/new/edetails.php?id=942.

Oren, Michael B. *Six Days of War: June 1967 and the Making of the Modern Middle East.* New York: Oxford University Press, 2002.

Ovendale, Ritchie. *Britain, the United States and the Transfer of Power in the Middle East, 1945–1962.* New York: Leicester University Press, 1996.

Özdemir, Hikmet. *Salgın Hastalıklardan ölümler, 1914–1918* [Deaths from Epidemics, 1914–1919]. Ankara: Türk Tarih Kurumu, 2005.

Palestine National Authority Central Bureau of Statistics. "Killed Palestinians (Martyrs) in Al Aqsa Uprising." www.pcbs.gov.ps/Portals/_pcbs/intifada/93b5acob-f061-455a-bd93-0337c0f63d43.htm.

Palumbo, Michael. *The Palestinian Catastrophe: The 1948 Expulsion of a People from Their Homeland.* London: Quartet Books, 1989.

Pappé, Ilan. *The Ethnic Cleansing of Palestine.* Oxford: Oneworld, 2007.

———. *The Making of the Arab-Israeli Conflict, 1947–51.* London: I. B. Tauris, 1992.

Parker, Richard B. *The Politics of Miscalculation in the Middle East.* Bloomington: Indiana University Press, 1993.

Pawel, Ernst. *The Labyrinth of Exile: A Life of Theodor Herzl.* New York: Farrar, Straus and Giroux, 1989.

Pearson, Anthony. *Conspiracy of Silence: The Attack on the USS Liberty.* New York: Quartet Books, 1978.

Peleg, Ilan. *Begin's Foreign Policy, 1977–1983: Israel's Move to the Right.* New York: Greenwood Press, 1987.

Peters, Rudolph. *Islam and Colonialism: The Doctrine of Jihad in Modern History.* The Hague: Mouton, 1979.

Pew Global Attitudes Project. "The Great Divide: How Westerners and Muslims See Each Other." June 22, 2006. http://pewglobal.org/reports/display.php?ReportID=253.

Pinter, Harold. "Art, Truth and Politics." Text of statement delivered on receipt of 2005 Nobel Prize for Literature. *Guardian,* December 7, 2005.

Pipes, Daniel. "America's Muslims against America's Jews." *Commentary,* May 1999. www.danielpipes.org/article/308.

———. "Who Is the Enemy?" *Commentary*, January 2002. www.daniel pipes.org/article/103.

Postel, Danny. "Noble Lies and Perpetual War: Leo Strauss, the Neo-Cons and Iraq." *OpenDemocracy*, October 18, 2003. http://informationclearing house.info/article5010.htm.

Presland, John. *Deedes Bey: A Study of Sir Wyndham Deedes, 1883–1923.* London: Macmillan, 1942.

Price, Matthew. "The Changing Face of Jerusalem." BBC News, April 28, 2005. http://news.bbc.co.uk/1/hi/world/middle_east/4490671.stm.

Prime Minister's Office. "Iraq: Its Infrastructure of Concealment, Deception and Intimidation." February 3, 2003. www.number10.gov.uk/output/page1470.asp.

Pry, Peter. *Israel's Nuclear Arsenal.* Boulder, CO: Westview, 1984.

Qawuqji, Fawzi al. "Memoirs, 1948: Part II." *Journal of Palestine Studies* 2 (Autumn 1972): 3–33.

Quandt, William B. *Peace Process: American Diplomacy and the Arab-Israeli Conflict since 1967.* Berkeley: Brookings Institution, University of California Press, 1993.

Rabinowicz, Oskar K. "The Aliens Bill and Jewish Immigration to Britain, 1902–1905." In *From Haven to Conquest: Readings in Zionism and the Palestine Problem until 1948,* edited by Walid Khalidi, 97–114. Washington, DC: Institute of Palestine Studies, 1987.

Randal, Jonathan. *The Tragedy of Lebanon: Christian Warlords, Israeli Adventurers and American Bunglers.* Rev. ed. London: Hogarth Press, 1990.

Rankin, Lieut. Col. Reginald. *The Inner History of the Balkan War.* London: Constable, 1914.

Reagan, Ronald. *An American Life.* New York: Simon and Schuster, 1990.

Republic of Turkey, Prime Ministry. *Ermeniler Tarafindan Yapilan Katliam Belgeleri* [Documents on Massacres perpetrated by Armenians]. Vol. 1. *1914–1919.* Vol. 2. *1919–1921.* Ankara: State Archives General Directorate, 2001.

Rice, Condoleezza. "A Balance of Power That Favors Freedom." Wiston Lecture, Manhattan Institute for Policy Research. October 1, 2002. www.man hattan-institute.org/html/wl2002.htm.

Richelson, Jeffrey, ed. "Saddam's Iron Grip: Intelligence Reports on Saddam Hussein's Reign." George Washington University, National Security Archive, Electronic Briefing Book No. 167. www.gwu.edu/~nsarchiv/NSAEBB/NSAEBB167/index.htm. See Document 3, Director of Central Intelligence, Special National Intelligence Estimate (SNIE) 34/36.2–82, "Implications of Iran's Victory over Iraq," June 8, 1982 (Secret); Document 4, Director of Central Intelligence, SNIE 36.2–83, "Prospects for Iraq," July 19, 1983 (Secret); and Document 7, Central Intelligence Agency, "Iraq: Domestic Impact of the War," January 25, 1991 (Secret).

Rizk, Labib Yunan. "A Balfour Curse: A Diwan of Contemporary Life (361)." *Al Ahram Weekly,* October 26–November 1, 2000. www.weekly.ahram .org.eg/2000/505/chrncls.htm.

———. "Quote Unquote: A Diwan of Contemporary Life (591)." *Al Ahram Weekly,* April 7–13, 2005. www.weekly.ahram.org.eg/2005/737/chrncls .htm.

Robertson, Terence. *Crisis: The Inside Story of the Suez Conspiracy.* London: Hutchinson, 1965.

Rogan, Eugene, and Avi Shlaim, eds. *The War for Palestine: Rewriting the History of 1948.* New York: Cambridge University Press, 2001.

Rokach, Livia. "Israeli State Terrorism: An Analysis of the Sharett Diaries." *Journal of Palestine Studies* 9 (Spring 1980): 3–28.

Roosevelt, Kermit. *Arabs, Oil and History: The Story of the Middle East.* London: Victor Gollancz, 1949.

Rose, Flemming. "Europe's Politics of Victimology." *Blueprint,* May 17, 2006. www.dlc.org/ndol_ci.cfm?contentid=253879&kaid=127&subid=177.

———. "Why I Published Those Cartoons." *Washington Post,* February 19, 2006.

Rose, Norman. *Chaim Weizmann: A Biography.* London: Weidenfeld and Nicolson, 1987.

Ross, Dennis B. *The Missing Peace: The Inside Story of the Fight for Middle East Peace.* New York: Farrar, Straus and Giroux, 2004.

Rovers, Ronald. "The Silencing of Theo van Gogh." *Salon,* November 24, 2004. http://dir.salon.com/story/news/feature/2004/11/24/vangogh/index .html.

Rubinstein, Richard L. *The Cunning of History.* New York: Harper and Row, 1978.

Ruedy, John. *Modern Algeria: The Origins and Development of a Nation.* Bloomington: Indiana University Press, 1992.

Rumsfeld, Donald. "Remarks at News Briefing, March 20, 2003." www.global security.org/word/library/news/iraq/2003/iraq-030320-dod01.htm.

———. "Remarks at News Briefing, April 11, 2003." www.defencelink.mil/ transcripts/transcript.aspx?transcriptid=2367.

Rush, Alan, ed. *Records of Iraq, 1914–1966.* 15 vols. London: Archive Editions, 2001.

———, ed. *Records of the Hashimite Dynasties.* 15 vols. London: Archive Editions, 1995.

Russell, Richard L. "Iraq's Chemical Weapons Legacy: What Others Might Learn." *Middle East Journal* 59 (Spring 2005): 187–208.

"Saddam Hussein: More Secret History." December 18, 2003. Document 5, National Security Archive. www.gwu.edu/ nsarchiv/NSAEBB/NSEBB 107/.

"Saddam's Cousin Says Actions against Kurds Justified." *USA Today,* January 24, 2007. www.usatoday.com/news/world/iraq/2007-01-24-chemicalali_x .htm.

Said, Edward. "America's Last Taboo." *New Left Review* 6 (November– December 2000). www.newleftreview.net/NLR24002.shtml.

———. "A Road Map to Where?" *London Review of Books,* June 19, 2003.

Salem, Elie A. *Violence and Diplomacy in Lebanon: The Troubled Years, 1982–1988.* London: I. B. Tauris, 1995.

Salt, Jeremy. "Falluja: Slaughter of a City." *Arena,* no. 77 (June–July 2005): 30–32.

———. *Imperialism, Evangelism and the Ottoman Armenians, 1878–1896.* London: Frank Cass, 1993.

———. "Inconvenient Facts." *Insight Turkey* 8 (July–September 2006): 54–63.

———. "The Narrative Gap in Ottoman Armenian History." *Middle Eastern Studies* 39 (January 2003): 19–36.

Sayegh, Fayez A. "The Camp David Agreement and the Palestine Problem." *Journal of Palestine Studies* 8 (Winter 1979): 3–40.

Sayigh, Rosemary. *Palestinians: From Peasants to Revolutionaries.* London: Zed Press, 1979.

Scahill, Jeremy. "The Saddam in Rumsfeld's Closet." August 2, 2002. www.commondreams.org/views02/0801-01.htm.

Schiff, Zeʾev, and Ehud Yaʾari. *Israel's Lebanon War.* London: George Allen and Unwin, 1986.

Schmitt, Bernadotte E. *The Annexation of Bosnia, 1908–1909.* New York: Howard Fertig, 1970.

Sciolino, Elaine. *The Outlaw State: Saddam Hussein's Quest for Power and the Gulf Crisis.* New York: John Wiley and Sons, 1991.

Seale, Patrick. *Asad of Syria: The Struggle for the Middle East.* London: I. B. Tauris, 1988.

———. "The United States and Britain Are Heading for Disaster." *Mafhoum,* March 28, 2003. www.mafhoum.com/press5/138seale.htm.

———. "War Is the Climax of the American-Israeli Partnership." *Washington Post,* March 21, 2003.

Sells, Michael A. "Christ Killer, Kremlin, Contagion." In *The New Crusades: Constructing the Muslim Enemy,* edited by Emran Qureshi and Michael A. Sells. New York: Columbia University Press, 2003.

Shahid, Leila. "Testimonies. The Sabra and Shatila Massacres: Eye-Witness Reports." *Journal of Palestine Studies* 32 (Autumn 2002): 36–58.

Shambrook, Peter A. *French Imperialism in Syria, 1927–1936.* Reading, UK: Ithaca Press, 1998.

Shaw, Stanford J. *From Empire to Republic: The Turkish War of National Liberation, 1918–1923. A Documentary Study.* 6 vols. Ankara: Turkish Historical Society, 2000.

Shepherd, William E. "Islam and Ideology: Towards a Typology." *International Journal of Middle Eastern Studies* 19 (August 1987): 307–35.

"Shock and Awe Bombing of Baghdad Begins." CNN, March 21, 2003. http://transcripts.cnn.com/TRANSCRIPTS/0303/21/bn.02.html.

Sidebotham, Herbert. *England and Palestine.* London: Constable, 1918.

Sifry, Micah L., and Christopher Cerf, eds. *The Gulf War Reader: History, Documents, Opinions.* New York: Times Books, 1991.

Simon, Reeva S. *Iraq between the Two World Wars: The Creation and Implementation of a Nationalist Ideology.* New York: Columbia University Press, 1986.

Simons, Chaim. *International Proposals to Transfer Arabs from Palestine, 1895–1947: A Historical Survey.* Hoboken, NJ: KTAV, 1988.

Solh, Rachid el. *Britain's Two Wars with Iraq: 1941, 1991.* Reading, UK: Ithaca Press, 1996.

Sonbol, Amira, trans. and ed. *The Last Khedive of Egypt: Memoirs of Abbas Hilmi II.* Reading, UK: Ithaca Press, 1998.

Sonyel, Salahi Ramsdan. *The Assyrians of Turkey: Victims of Major Power Policy.* Ankara: Turkish Historical Society, 2001.

———. *The Great War and the Tragedy of Anatolia: Turks and Armenians in the Maelstrom of Major Powers.* Ankara: Turkish Historical Society, 2001.

———. *Minorities and the Destruction of the Ottoman Empire.* Ankara: Turkish Historical Society, 1993.

———. *The Ottoman Armenians: Victims of Great Power Diplomacy.* London: K. Rustem and Brother, 1987.

Spiegel, Steven L. *The Other Arab-Israeli Conflict: Making America's Middle East Policy from Truman to Reagan.* Chicago: University of Chicago Press, 1985.

Stadiem, William. *Too Rich: The High Life and Tragic Death of King Farouk.* New York: Carroll and Graf, 1991.

Statistical Office of the European Communities. *Population Statistics.* Luxembourg: Office for Official Publications of the European Communities, 2006.

Steevens, G. W. *With Kitchener to Khartum.* London: Thomas Nelson and Sons, n.d.

Stephens, Richard P. *American Zionism and U.S. Foreign Policy, 1942–1947.* Washington, DC: Institute for Palestine Studies, 1970.

Stephens, Robert. *Nasser: A Political Biography.* London: Penguin Books, 1973.

Stewart, Desmond. *Theodor Herzl: Artist and Politician.* London: Quartet Books, 1981.

Stockholm International Peace Research Institute. "Arms Transfers to Iraq, 1970–2004." www.sipri.org/contents/armstrad/atirq_data.html.

Storrs, Ronald. *Orientations.* London: Ivor Nicholson and Watson, 1937.

Swain, J. E. "The Occupation of Algiers in 1830: A Study in Anglo-French Diplomacy." *Political Science Quarterly* 48 (1933): 359–66.

Sykes, Christopher. *Crossroads to Israel: Palestine from Balfour to Bevin.* London: Nel Mentor, 1967.

Talbot, Margaret. "The Agitator: Oriana Fallaci Directs Her Fury toward Islam." *New Yorker*, June 5, 2006. www.newyorker.com/archive/2006/06/05/060605fa_fact.

Theobald, A. B. *The Mahdiya: A History of the Anglo-Egyptian Sudan, 1881–1899.* New York: Longmans, Green, 1951.

Thicknesse, S. G. *Arab Refugees: A Survey of Resettlement Possibilities.* London: Royal Institute of International Affairs, 1949.

Thomas, Hugh. *Suez.* New York: Harper Colophon, 1967.

Tibawi, A. L. *Anglo-Arab Relations and the Question of Palestine, 1914–1921.* London: Luzac, 1978.

Tignor, Robert L. *Modernization and British Colonial Rule in Egypt, 1882–1914.* Princeton: Princeton University Press, 1966.

Timmerman, Kenneth R. *The Death Lobby: How the World Armed Iraq.* New York: Bantam Books, 1992.

Tivnan, Edward. *The Lobby: Jewish Political Power and American Foreign Policy.* New York: Touchstone, 1987.

Toye, Patricia, ed. *Palestine Boundaries, 1833–1947.* 4 vols. Durham: Archive Editions, 1989

Toynbee, Arnold J. *Armenian Atrocities: The Murder of a Nation. With a Speech Delivered by Lord Bryce in the House of Lords.* London: Hodder and Stoughton, 1915.

———. *A Study of History.* Abridgement of vols. 1–6 by D. C. Somervell. New York: Oxford University Press, 1947.

———. *The Treatment of Armenians in the Ottoman Empire, 1915–1916: Documents Presented to Viscount Grey of Fallodon, Secretary of State for Foreign Affairs, by Viscount Bryce.* London: His Majesty's Stationery Office, 1916.

———. *The Western Question in Greece and Turkey: A Study in the Contact of Civilisations.* London: Constable, 1922.

Trilling, Roger. "Fighting Words: The Administration Builds Up Its Pretext for Attacking Iraq." *Village Voice,* May 1–7, 2002. www.villagevoice.com.

Tripp, Charles. "Egypt, 1945–1952: The Uses of Disorder." In *Demise of the British Empire in the Middle East: Britain's Responses to Nationalist Movements, 1943–1955,* edited by Michael J. Cohen and Martin Kolinsky, 112–41. Portland, OR: Frank Cass, 1998.

Truman, Harry S. *The Memoirs of Harry S. Truman.* Vol. 2. *Years of Trial and Hope, 1946–1953.* London: Hodder and Stoughton, 1956.

Tschirgi, Dan. *The American Search for Mideast Peace.* New York: Praeger, 1989.

Tuite, James J., III. "1991 Persian Gulf War: Direct and Indirect Chemical Warfare Agent and Related Exposures." http://chronicillnet.org/PGWS/tuite/science2.html.

———. "Report on the Fallout from the Destruction of the Iraqi Chemical Research, Production and Storage Facilities into Areas Occupied by US Military Personnel during the 1991 Persian Gulf War." 1996. www.chronicill net.org/PGWS/tuite/science6.html.

Tyler, Patrick E. "Officers Say US Aided Iraq in War Despite Use of Gas." *New York Times,* August 18, 2002.

"UN Row Erupts over Iraq Dossier." BBC News, December 10, 2002. http://news.bbc.co.uk/2/hi/middle_east/2560617.stm.

United Nations. *United Nations Resolutions on Palestine and the Arab-Israeli Conflict* (Institute of Palestine Studies, Washington, DC), 1947–91. Vol. 1,

1947–1974, edited by George J. Tomeh (1975); vol. 2, *1975–1981,* edited by Regina S. Sharif (1988); vol. 3, *1982–1986,* edited by Michael Simpson (1988); vol. 4, *1987–1991,* edited by Jody A. Boudreault (1993).

———. *Yearbook of the United Nations,* 1964–83. New York: Office of Public Information.

United Nations Department of Public Information. *The Blue Helmets: A Review of United Nations Peace-Keeping.* 3rd ed. New York: UN Department of Public Information, 1996.

United Nations General Assembly. *Report of the Special Committee to Investigate Israeli Practices Affecting the Human Rights of the Palestinian People and Other Arabs of the Occupied Territories.* A/54/325. September 8, 1999. Fifty-fourth session, item 89 of the provisional agenda.

———. *Report of the Special Committee to Investigate Israeli Practices Affecting the Human Rights of the Palestinian People and Other Arabs of the Occupied Territories.* A/57/207, September 16, 2002. Fifty-seventh session, item 78 of the provisional agenda.

U.S. Department of State. "Chemical Weapons and the Iran-Iraq War." March 5, 1984. http://findarticles.com/P/articles/mi_m1079/is_v84/ai_3200104.

———. Foreign Relations of the United States. *The Paris Peace Conference, 1919.* Vol. 12. Washington, DC: Government Printing Office, 1947.

———. Foreign Relations of the United States. *1948.* Vol. 5. *The Near East, South Asia, and Africa.* Pt. 2. Washington, DC: Government Printing Office, 1976.

———. Foreign Relations of the United States. *1955–57.* Vol. 16. *Suez Crisis, July 26–December 31, 1956.* Washington, DC: Government Printing Office, 1990.

———. Foreign Relations of the United States. *1958–60.* Vol. 11. *Lebanon and Jordan.* Washington, DC: Government Printing Office, 1992.

———. Foreign Relations of the United States. *1958–60.* Vol. 12. *Near East Region: Iraq; Iran; Arabian Peninsula.* Washington, DC: Government Printing Office, 1993.

———. Foreign Relations of the United States. *1964–68.* Vol. 18. *Arab-Israeli Dispute, 1964–1967.* Washington, DC: Government Printing Office, 2000.

———. Foreign Relations of the United States. *1964–68.* Vol. 19. *Arab-Israeli Crisis and War, 1967.* Washington, DC: Government Printing Office, 2004.

———. Foreign Relations of the United States. *1964–68.* Vol. 20. *Arab-Israeli Dispute, 1967–1968.* Washington, DC: Government Printing Office, 2001.

U.S. Senate. Committee on Banking, Housing, and Urban Affairs. "Second Staff Report on US Chemical and Biological Warfare-Related Dual-Use Exports to Iraq and the Possible Impact on the Health Consequences of the War (May 25, 1994)." http://chronicillnet.org/PGWS/tuite/2NDINDEX.HTM.

———. *United States Chemical and Biological Warfare-Related Dual-Use Exports to Iraq and Their Possible Impact on the Health Consequences of the Persian Gulf War: A Report of Chairman Donald W. Riegle Jr. and Ranking*

Member Alphonse D'Amato of the Committee on Banking, Housing and Urban Affairs with Respect to Export Administration. United States Senate, 103d Congress, 2d Session, May 25, 1994. [Riegle Report]. www.gulfweb .org/report/riegle1.html. The committee had published its first report in 1992 and published a third staff report, "Chemical Warfare Agent Identification, Chemical Injuries and Other Findings," in October 1994.

———. "United States Dual-Use Exports to Iraq and Their Impact on the Health of the Persian Gulf War Veterans." Transcript of the meeting of the Banking, Housing and Urban Affairs Committee, Wednesday, May 25, 1994, chaired by Senator Donald W. Riegle Jr. and Ranking Member Alphonse d'Amato. http://chronicillnet.org/PGWS/tuite/hearings.html.

Uras, Esat. *The Armenians in History and the Armenian Question.* Istanbul: Documentary Publications, 1988.

"US Tore out 8000 Pages of Iraq Weapons Dossier." *Sunday Herald* (Glasgow), December 22, 2002. http://findarticles.com/p/articles.mi_qn4156/ is_20021222/ai_n12579783.

Verrier, Anthony, ed. *Agents of Empire: Anglo-Zionist Intelligence Operations, 1915–1919. Brigadier Walter Gribbon, Aaron Aaronsohn and the Nili Ring.* London: Brassey's, 1995.

Vogt, Lieut. Col. Hermann. *The Egyptian War of 1882.* 1883. Reprint, Nashville, TN: Battery Press, 1992.

Wagner, Don. "Beyond Armageddon: Challenging Christian Zionism." May 27, 2004. www.christianzionism.org.

Warden, Colonel John A., III. "Air Theory for the Twenty-First Century." In *Battlefield of the Future: Twenty-first-Century Warfare Issues,* edited by Barry R. Schneider and Lawrence E. Grinter, ch. 4. Maxwell Air Force Base, AL: Air University Press, 1991. www.airpower.maxwell.af.mil/airchronicles/ battle/bftoc.html.

———. "The Enemy as a System." *Airpower Journal* 9 (Spring 1995): 40–55. www.airpower.maxwell.af.mil/airchronicles/apj/apj95/spr95_files/ warden.htm.

"Weapons of Mass Destruction: Strategic Doctrine." n.d. www.globalsecurity .org/wmd/world/israel/doctrine.htm.

Weizmann, Chaim. *The Letters and Papers of Chaim Weizmann. Series A: Letters.* General editors Meyer W. Weisgal (vols. 1–11) and Barnet Litvinoff (vols. 12–23). 23 vols. New Brunswick, NJ: Transaction Books and Rutgers University Press, 1968–80. Selected volumes: vol. 9, *October 1918– July 1920,* edited by Jehuda Reinharz, and vol. 23, *August 1947–June 1952,* edited by Aaron Klieman.

———. *Trial and Error.* New York: Harper, 1949.

Weller, Marc, ed. *Iraq and Kuwait: The Hostilities and Their Aftermath.* Vol. 3. Research Centre for International Law, Cambridge University. Cambridge International Documents Series. Cambridge: Grotius Publications, 1993.

White House. "The National Security Strategy of the United States of America." September 2002. www.whitehouse.gov/nsc/nss.pdf.

———. "White House Statement on Uday and Qusay Hussein." July 22, 2003. www.whitehouse.gov./news/releases/2003/07/20030722-8.html.

Williams, Raymond. *Keywords: A Vocabulary of Culture and Society*. London: Fontana Press, 1988.

Willis, Michael. *The Islamist Challenge in Algeria: A Political History*. New York: New York University Press, 1996.

Wilson, Sir Arnold T. *Loyalties: Mesopotamia. A Personal and Historical Record*. Vol. 1. *1914–1917*. Vol. 2. *1917–1920*. Oxford: Oxford University Press, 1931.

Wilson, Trevor. "Lord Bryce's Investigation into Alleged German Atrocities in Belgium, 1914–15." *Journal of Contemporary History* 14 (1979): 369–83.

Wood, Brian, and Rory MacMillan, eds. "A Report by the Jenin Inquiry Regarding the Israeli Invasion of the Jenin Refugee Camp from 3–18 April, 2002." Jenin Inquiry, June 24, 2003. www.jenininquiry.org/Jenin%20 Inquiry%20Report.pdf.

Yeats-Brown, F. *Golden Horn: Plot and Counterplot in Turkey, 1908–1918*. London: Victor Gollancz, 1932.

Ye'or, Bat. "Eurabia: The Road to Munich." *National Review*, October 9, 2002. www.nationalreview.com/comment/comment-yeor10092.asp.

Younge, Gary. "On the Offensive." *Guardian*, April 10, 2007.

Zakaria, Fareed. "Cruelty Is All They Have Left." *Newsweek*, March 22, 2004.

———. "The Politics of Rage: Why Do They Hate Us?" *Newsweek*, October 15, 2001.

———. "Time to Take on America's Haters." *Newsweek*, October 21, 2002.

Zeidner, Robert F. *The Tricolor over the Taurus, 1918–1922*. Ankara: Turkish Historical Society, 2005.

Zinn, Howard. "Occupied Zones: Unacceptable Regimes in Iraq and the United States." *Le Monde Diplomatique*, English edition, August 2005.

Zionist Organization. "Statement of the Zionist Organization Regarding Palestine: Presented to the Paris Peace Conference, February 3, 1919." MidEastWeb, www.mideastweb.org/zionistborders.htm.

Zunes, Stephen. "The Influence of the Christian Right on U.S. Middle East Policy." *Foreign Policy in Focus*, June 28, 2004. www.fpif.org/papers/ 0406christian.html.

INDEX

Kollek, Teddy, 227
Komer, Robert, 189, 192, 193, 198, 202, 277
Kook, Rabbi Abraham Isaac, 235
Korea, North, 297
Kosygin, Alexei, 217, 228
Krim, Arthur and Mathilde, 190
Kristol, Irving, 323
Kristol, William, 323, 324
Kufa, 95, 96
Kurdish language, 336
Kurdistan, 336
Kurds, 91–92, 95; Armenian refugees attacked by, 63, 64, 65, 66, 69; Armenian violence against, 59, 67, 369n76; Faisal's plebiscite and, 98; Hashimites and, 324; levies in British forces, 108; Nestorian Assyrians and, 106; resistance to British occupation, 93, 94, 108; Saddam Hussein regime and, 279, 286, 293, 299; spoils of First World War and, 72; U.S. occupation and, 336–37
Kuwait, 104, 277, 294, 302, 308; cost to Iraq of invasion, 314; Gulf War and, 300; Iraqi retreat from, 306–8; oil wells set on fire, 310; Saddam's invasion of, 280–81, 288, 291, 309
Kwiatkowski, Karen, 327

Labor Party, Israeli, 240–41, 324, 340, 345
Lampson, Sir Miles, 87, 88
Lawrence, T. E., 82, 97
Leachman, Lieutenant Colonel G. E., 93
League of Nations, 72, 73–74, 77, 86; Assyrians and, 107, 109; British mandates, 92; Iraq as member, 102; Iraq's prospective membership, 100, 101
Leahy, Patrick, 318
Lebanese Front (LF), 260
Lebanese National Movement (LNM), 260
Lebanon, 1, 138, 148, 241–42; Anglo-American intervention (1958), 185;

Arab–Israeli war (1948) and, 143; civil wars, 3, 119, 242, 243, 268; "cleaning" of Palestinian refugee camps, 259–61; French colonial rule in, 83, 84, 86; Haddadists, 247–49; Hizbullah in, 248, 324; invasion by Israel (1982), 8, 250, 251, 254–67, 358; invasion by Israel (2006), 358; Israeli air strikes on, 4, 243, 250–51; neoconservative strategy and, 325; Palestinian refugees and, 145, 159, 167, 353; prison at Khiyam, 247; "security zone" for Israel in south, 267; UN forces in, 247–49; U.S. Marines in, 7, 267–68; water resources and, 194, 195. *See also* Beirut
Ledeen, Michael, 325
"Levant," 15
Levinger, Rabbi Moshe, 235
Levinson, Larry, 190
Levy, Gideon, 352, 353
Lewis, Bernard, 18–19, 20, 21, 24–25, 28
Lewis, David Levering, 36
Lewis, Samuel, 250
Lewy, Guenter, 68, 370n76
Libby, I. Lewis, 322, 323–24, 328, 338
Liberty, U.S.S., 224
Libya, 50–51, 74, 189, 254, 355
Lie, Trygvie, 155
Likud Party (Israel), 241, 340
Lindsey, Hal, 253
Lloyd, Selwyn, 119, 174, 177
Lloyd George, David, 7, 73, 74
Loewenberg, Robert, 324
London, Treaty of (1915), 70
Lovett, Robert A., 153, 154, 157
Lumumba, Patrice, 188
Luti, William, 327, 338
Lydda massacre, 146

Macdonald, Captain H., 93
Macedonia, 53
Machiavelli, Niccolò, 323
MacMichael Sir Harold, 135
Macmillan, Harold, 119, 185–86

Muhammad, Prophet, 18, 31, 81, 324;
cartoons lampooning, 22, 23–24;
flight from Mecca, 41; Hashimites
and family of, 79
Muhammad Ahmad (the Mahdi),
41–42, 44
Muhammad al Masiri, Saᶜb Husan,
309
Muhammad Reza Pahlevi, Shah, 273
Muhi al Din, Zakaria, 216–17
Muhsin Bey, Sir Abdul, 101
Muir, Sir William, 18, 20, 361n15
multiculturalism, 22, 23, 26, 28
Munich Olympics (1972), 4
Munich (Spielberg film), 4
Murdoch, Rupert, 323
Musaddiq, Muhammad, 113, 173, 179,
384n26
Muslims, 6, 26; Armenian and Cos-
sack massacres of, 61–62, 68; Bin
Laden's message and, 357–58;
"clash of civilizations" and, 19, 20;
of Europe, 21–27; extirpated in
Balkan War, 51–54; Greek invasion
of Anatolia and, 76; in Lebanon, 83;
Palestinian, 126–27, 132, 140;
Slavic, 51; Sufis, 30, 36, 67; Turkish
Muslims of Greece, 7; victims/
refugees of Balkan wars, 7, 31–32,
54–56; world population of, 357

Nahalin, 168
Nahas Pasha, 88
Najaf, 93, 95, 324
nakba (catastrophe), Palestinian,
144–47
Napoleon I, Emperor, 33
Narkiss, Uzi, 215, 227
Nasser, Gamal Abd Al, 5, 8, 90, 177,
190, 275; aftermath of 1967 war
and, 233, 234; Arab–Israeli war
(1967) and, 212, 213, 215, 217, 224,
225; as army officer in actions
against Israel, 165; British relations
with, 166; death of, 235; defense
agreement with Syria, 197; "dictator" label for, 3, 37; as dominant

force in Arab world, 220;
Hashimites as enemies of, 179; as
idol of Arab world, 184, 186; Israeli
policy of confrontation with,
169–70; Kennedy and, 187–88; Suez
(Tripartite) War and, 173; United
Arab Republic and, 119; U.S. policy
toward, 187–88, 189
Nasser, Kamal, 237
Nasserites, 260, 276
National Committee of the Heads
of the Arab Local Authorities in
Israel, 354
nationalists, Arab, 83, 165, 211; in
Egypt, 86–87, 90; in Iraq, 98, 104,
120; in Syria, 83–86
nationalists, Jewish, 123
National Security Archive, 8
National Security Council, U.S., 156,
189, 198, 226, 277, 286
national socialism, 17
Nazis, 24, 111, 240, 241
Nazzal, Nafez Abdullah, 139
Near East, 15, 27, 34, 123; Anglo-
American strategic interests in, 159;
arms race in, 193; King-Crane
Commission and, 124
Near East South Asia (NESA) direc-
torate, 326, 327, 338
Nebuchadnezzar, 278
Negev (Naqab), 148, 156, 161, 170;
Israel's nuclear program and, 200,
201; seized by Israel, 157–59
Neillands, Robin, 42
Nelson, Rear Adm. Horatio, 33
neoconservatives, 321 26, 337 38,
355
Netanyahu, Benyamin, 324, 344, 345
Netherlands, 15, 22–23, 25, 283
"never again" slogan, 210
Newton, Sir Basil, 112, 113
New Zealand, 78
Nicaragua, 281, 291, 322
Nietzsche, Friedrich, 323
Nikola, king of Montenegro, 51, 52
Nile, Battle of the, 33
Niles, David K., 137, 152, 156, 187

wars with Ottoman Empire, 31, 32,
51, 54; Zionist Jews from Russia,
123. *See also* Soviet Union (USSR)

al Saʿadi, Sheikh Farhan, 130
Sabah family, 277, 309
Sabah al Said, 120
al Sabbagh, Col. Salah al Din, 111,
113, 118, 119–20
Sabra and Shatila massacre, 241, 252,
262–65, 414n42; Israeli air strikes
on camps, 251; as public relations
disaster for Israel, 349; Sharon and,
4, 262, 264, 349, 399n100; UN condemnation of, 266
Sadat, Anwar, 235, 237, 255;
Arab–Israeli war (1973) and, 239;
assassination of, 247; Camp David
negotiations and, 244–47; opening
(intifah) to the West, 239–40; peace
with Israel, 241, 242, 243
Sadr, Ayatullah Muhammad Baqr al,
279
Sadr, Imam Musa, 267
al Sadr, Muqtada, 332
Saffari, Abu Mahmoud, 139
Saguy, Yehoshua, 255
Said, Edward, 355
Said, Fahmi, 118
al Said, Nuri, 101, 103, 104, 105; Arab
Union and, 119; death of, 120;
Ghazi's death and, 106; outbreak of
Second World War and, 111;
Rashid Ali and, 112; Suez (Tripar-
tite) War and, 173–74, 179; in
Thirty-Day War, 117
Said Pasha, 87
Sakarya, Battle of, 77
Salah al Din al Ayyubi (Saladin), 230,
278
Sale, Richard, 276
Salman, Mahmud, 118
Salmon, Captain G. H., 93
Samuel, Sir Herbert, 127, 128
Sanchez, Lt. Gen. Ricardo, 332
Sanusi tribe, 51
"Saracens," 30

Sarrail, Gen. Maurice, 85, 122
al Sarraj, Abd al Hamid, 178
Satloff, Robert, 322
Saudi Arabia, 18, 138, 158, 258, 279;
American weapons for, 244, 254;
Gulf War and, 309, 310, 312;
Iran–Iraq War and, 294; Iraq's bor-
der with, 304, 316; Nasser and, 189;
oil pipelines from Iraq, 285; rela-
tions with Israel, 148
Saunders, Harold, 206, 220
Sawt al Arab (Voice of the Arabs), 184
Sayre, Francis, 155
Schmitt, Gary, 327
Schwarzkopf, Gen. Norman, 282
Scott, Captain K. R., 93
Seale, Patrick, 195, 197; on
Arab–Israeli war (1967), 213–14,
224–25, 232; on invocation of Holo-
caust, 215; on Iraq war (from 2003),
330–31
Second World War, 146, 149, 167
September 11, 2001, events ("9/11"),
5, 17, 357, 358; "clash of civiliza-
tions" argument and, 20, 21; neo-
conservatives and, 323. *See also*
terrorism
Serbia, 6–7, 51–53, 54
Serot, Col. Andre, 157
Sèvres, Treaty of (1920), 72–73, 78,
174
Seymour, Sir Beauchamp, 38, 39, 40
Shabib, Col. Kamil, 113, 118
Shamir, Yitzhak, 252, 286–87
Sharaf al Sharaf, 115
Sharett, Moshe, 169, 171, 172, 173
Sharm al Sheikh, 212, 213, 215, 224
Sharon, Ariel: in Arab–Israeli war
(1967), 215, 233; in Arab–Israeli
war (1973), 239; Arafat's death
called for, 348, 349; as Begin's
defense minister, 250, 254; Bush II
administration and, 328; Iraq war
(from 2003) and, 331; Israeli settlements in Sinai and, 235; Jewish settlers and, 349; Lebanon invasion
(1982) and, 251–52, 255, 256, 257,

Text:	10/13 Aldus
Display:	Democratica Bold
Compositor:	BookComp, Inc.
Indexer:	Alexander Trotter
Cartographer:	Bill Nelson
Printer and binder:	Sheridan Books, Inc.